5th EDITION

Entrepreneurship
& NEW VENTURE MANAGEMENT

Van Aardt | Bezuidenhout

Bendeman | Booysen | Clarence | Massyn
Moos | Naidoo | Swanepoel | Van Aardt

OXFORD
UNIVERSITY PRESS
SOUTHERN AFRICA

OXFORD

UNIVERSITY PRESS

Oxford University Press is a department of the University of Oxford.
It furthers the University's objective of excellence in research, scholarship,
and education by publishing worldwide. Oxford is a registered trade mark of
Oxford University Press in the UK and in certain other countries

Published in South Africa by
Oxford University Press Southern Africa (Pty) Limited
Vasco Boulevard, Goodwood, N1 City, Cape Town, South Africa, 7460
P O Box 12119, N1 City, Cape Town, South Africa, 7463

© Oxford University Press Southern Africa (Pty) Ltd 2014

First published 1997 by International Thompson Publishing Southern Africa (Pty) Ltd
Second edition published in 2000
Third edition published in 2008
Fourth edition published in 2011
Fifth edition published in 2014

Entrepreneurship and New Venture Management

Fifth edition

ISBN 978 0 19 905402 2

Typeset in Minion Pro 10pt on 12pt
Printed on 70 gsm woodfree paper

Acknowledgements
Publishing manager: Alida Terblanche
Publisher: Janine Loedolff
Editor: Allison Lamb
Designer: Bongiwe Beja
Cover designer: Cindy Armstrong
Typesetter: Orchard Publishing
Cover image: iStockphoto.com
Printed and bound by ABC Press, Cape Town

121896

Contents in brief

Table of contents

Preface

This book is about entrepreneurship and covers a comprehensive set of aspects and entrepreneurial dilemmas that should be considered when starting a new business venture. This fifth edition takes a new approach to entrepreneurship, it includes not only a theoretical framework and discussion, but also includes successful South African entrepreneurial stories, practical examples and case studies.

The entrepreneurial and business environments are both dynamic and therefore the fifth edition has been updated with the latest changes in legislation, trends and contemporary issues that entrepreneurs face.

The writers of this book come from various backgrounds and experience, including research, general, financial and operations management, entrepreneurship, and consultancy. They are, furthermore, involved in the teaching of entrepreneurship and elements of entrepreneurship on different levels at various academic institutions in South Africa. This has been brought together to add to the practical and academic value of the book.

The first part of the book introduces the reader to the concept of entrepreneurship and the entrepreneurial environment. The second part of the book explores the entrepreneurial process and investigates creativity as a means for opportunity recognition. In the third part of the book the creation of a new venture is discussed. The discussion in this part of the book includes, among others, the information available and needed in the small business environment, entrepreneurial strategy, the start-up process, franchising, business ethics and social responsibilities, the establishment of an entrepreneurial team and the different business functions. Part three further discusses the operational requirements of a venture, finances and the management thereof in order to develop a financial plan. The importance of the elements to consider in the writing of a business plan and the legal aspects are also discussed in this part of the book. The fourth and final part of the book explores the management of the venture by discussing business cycles, aspects surrounding the growth and harvesting within an organisation, corporate entrepreneurship as well as turnaround strategies and the possibility of business failure. The book concludes with a discussion of various contemporary issues.

South Africa is in dire need of entrepreneurs and small business ventures because this is the major source of job creation and the key of sustainability in the country's economy. We hope that we will inspire prospective entrepreneurs to start their businesses and also to keep on studying and growing to become successful entrepreneurs.

We would like to thank the following people for their contribution towards this book:
▸ The contributing authors Hanneli Bendeman, Karen Booysen, Wesley Clarence, Clinton Massyn, Patrick Naidoo, Elana Swanepoel and Carel van Aardt.
▸ Miné Venter, Nicola van Rhyn and Allison Lamb for their efforts in editing and reminding us to keep to our deadlines.

Isa van Aardt and Stefan Bezuidenhout
Centurion

part one

Introduction

CHAPTER 1

Entrepreneurship defined

Karen Booysen

LEARNING OUTCOMES

On completion of this chapter, you will be able to:
▸ Define the concept 'entrepreneurship'
▸ Differentiate between innovation and entrepreneurship
▸ Explain the importance of entrepreneurship in the South African economy
▸ Apply the entrepreneurial process
▸ Evaluate the impact of the environment on entrepreneurship.

OPENING CASE STUDY

The importance of entrepreneurship is continuously reinforced. If the government is not establishing a new support agency for entrepreneurs, economists are talking about the significant impact of entrepreneurship on job creation and growth. However, we also hear a lot of stories about how hard entrepreneurship is in South Africa.

1. What do you think is the most important benefit that South Africa can derive from entrepreneurship?
2. How do you believe entrepreneurship can be promoted in South Africa?

INTRODUCTION

Entrepreneurs, who successfully start their own businesses, are vital to the economic well-being of South Africa. Whether it is for technological progress or economic growth, entrepreneurship is at the root of that development – this is a fact. The question is if entrepreneurship is so important for any economy, why is entrepreneurship so difficult?

And the truth is that there are several possible reasons for this. There is no 'one size fits all' solution to the struggles involved in establishing an entrepreneurial venture. However, what is true for any entrepreneur in any country or industry is that if you are aware of the entrepreneurial process and the intricacies involved in this process as well as the environment in which you will function, your chances of success will increase dramatically.

This chapter is dedicated to a discussion on the concept of entrepreneurship, the entrepreneurial process as well as the environment of entrepreneurship. However, in isolation this chapter cannot provide enough insight to ensure a smooth road to becoming a successful entrepreneur. This textbook was developed as a whole … all the chapters working as parts of a well-oiled machine, each chapter critical to the establishment of a new venture.

In order to better understand how each of the subsequent chapters is linked, a schematic illustration of the textbook is shown in Figure 1.1. This illustration is based on the process of entrepreneurship in order to guide your thinking throughout the process.

This figure illustrates all the chapters of this textbook. At the heart of the entrepreneurial process there are three phases that every entrepreneur should go through. These are Development; Refinement and Implementation. When you consider only these three phases, entrepreneurship sounds very easy. However, there is much more to it than initially meets the eye. In order to complete each of these phases successfully, there are various different steps and aspects to consider.

In order to even consider entrepreneurship as a career option, an individual needs to have an entrepreneurial mindset. An entrepreneurial

Figure 1.1 Schematic overview of the textbook based on the entrepreneurial process

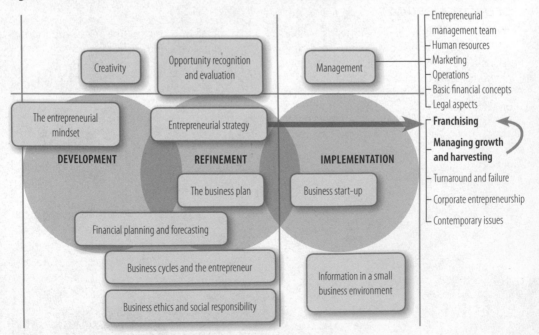

mindset means that you look at a challenge and see an opportunity and of course, in order to achieve this you need to be very creative.

As you end the development phase and move into the refinement phase, you need to ensure that your venture makes sense – business sense. Therefore you will consider your financial affairs through financial planning and forecasting.

The refinement phase entails turning an idea into a viable opportunity. In other words the opportunity that you have recognised must now be evaluated to ensure that it is feasible and sustainable. How do you do that? Well, you draw up a business plan. A business plan forces you to look at each and every corner of your venture and to make sure that all your activities are in order. Part and parcel of the business plan is considering the business cycles and how these will influence your venture through different seasons or market trends.

From here you move to the implementation phase. You will establish and run your venture in the market. A key ability in this phase is the **efficient** management of your venture.

> ### (DEFINITION)
>
> Managers are efficient when they do not waste resources in order to achieve their goals. They understand that any resource, whether it is time, money or knowledge is scarce and limited and they ensure that these resources are applied wisely.

Crucial to the success of running your venture is the ability to recognise and assimilate information from the environment. The environment in which your venture functions will have a huge impact on the success of the venture and it is crucial to identify **opportunities** and **threats** from the environment.

> ### (DEFINITION)
>
> Opportunities and threats are defined in this chapter under Section 1.5 on the impact of the environment on entrepreneurship.

A variety of concepts are included in the term management: You have to establish and manage your management team, as well as all the other employees needed in your venture – in other words, you need to focus on human resource management. Furthermore all the operations – how every aspect of the business will work, what you need and when you need it, must be identified. A marketing campaign that will hit home with your target market is essential to the success of any venture. If people are not aware of your product, it does not matter how great it is, they will not buy it. At the start-up of a new business, the financial resources are extremely limited. Therefore a close eye should be kept on all the finances. The legal aspects should not be overlooked. Entrepreneurs need to ensure that they adhere to all the legal aspects that are applicable to them. Whether it is minimum wages or the legal structures of your venture or laws on waste removal – it will have a devastating effect on your venture if you disregard these legal aspects.

Once your venture has been established successfully in the market you need to ensure that this business will grow and, more importantly, that you have all the needed resources to manage and sustain the growth. Hereafter you have the luxury of franchising your concept and not only obtaining royalties from all of the franchisees, but also to grow your venture even quicker and in various locations. From here corporate entrepreneurship is vital. You need to think of ways in which you can remain innovative within an established venture to ensure that you will continue to be one step ahead of your competitors. Should your venture run into difficulties along the way, you will need to have a strategy in place on how you can turn the business around or at least limit the losses of failure. All of the above-mentioned issues will happen in a rapidly changing environment and therefore the manager must be ever mindful of all the contemporary issues in the environment.

In the next section the concepts of innovation and entrepreneurship will be discussed.

SOUTH AFRICAN SUCCESS STORY

A young entrepreneur from Khayelitsha earns spot in Forbes list
'Doing good for people is good business'. Sizwe Nzima is a young entrepreneur from Khayelitsha whose business has landed him on an illustrious list, *Forbes Magazine's* 30 under-30 Africa's best young entrepreneurs list.

He grew up with his grandparents and used to collect their chronic medication. After school he'd go to the hospitals and wait in the long queues, sometimes in the morning and it would clash with his school time.

He then read an article about how hospitals were struggling to cope with the sheer number of people who collect their medication. Often it meant people would have to lose out on a day's wages, or have to bring their children along because there is nobody to watch them at home. This presents a great challenge to efficiently delivering healthcare service to the community as a whole. However, this challenge presented Sizwe Nzima with an amazing opportunity. He started a bicycle courier business called Iyeza Express, which delivers chronic medication to the residents of Khayelitsha.

Nzima has four men who work for him and they travel around Khayelitsha by bicycle, collecting and delivering chronic medication from the public hospitals and clinics and delivering straight to the door of his clients on the prescribed dates.

As a start-up, Iyeza Express has proven a very useful and effective business model, but still faces many challenges. The financial sustainability and logistics management are primary. Currently Iyeza charges R10 per delivery, but Sizwe admits this cannot cover the operational expenses. 'That is what they are willing to pay', but fortunately Sizwe has a vision for tackling this problem. The Department of Health already allocates a part of its budget for home deliveries through the Chronic Dispensing Unit for deliveries of chronic medication, but there are many challenges that make it a little less efficient than it should be. The Iyeza couriers have a vast knowledge of the cultural and geographical landscape of their communities, and would be an optimal partnership for the Department. Currently they are talking about a pilot scheme, but there are many things to put into place to prove this model is scalable and even replicable. Nzima started off with two clients – his grandparents – but now has more than 250.

Source: Developed from http://leadsa.co.za/?p=13870 and http://asenetwork.org/2013/08/15/social-enterprise-feature-iyeza-express/ [2 March 2014].

1.1 Innovation and entrepreneurship

Innovation and entrepreneurship are often used as synonyms, which is not at all accurate. However, although there is a vast difference between these two concepts, it is very important to note early in your journey to entrepreneurship that innovation and entrepreneurship are two terms that cannot be separated from each other. You cannot have innovation without entrepreneurship or entrepreneurship without innovation.

DEFINITION

Innovation is the specific tool of entrepreneurship by which entrepreneurs exploit change as an opportunity for a different business or service.

In essence, innovation has to address market needs, and requires entrepreneurship if it is to achieve commercial success. It must be stressed that innovation and entrepreneurship are complementary because innovation is the source of entrepreneurship and entrepreneurship allows innovation to flourish and helps to realise its economic value. A combination of the two is vital to organisational success and sustainability in today's dynamic and changing environment (Zhoa, 2005:25–41).

What has become clear, however, is that without the presence of some form of entrepreneurial activity to exploit opportunities as they arise within organisations, innovation remains little more than an aspirational, rather than a tangible destination (von Oetinger 2005:29–36).

Defining the concept entrepreneurship to the extent that everyone is satisfied is much like trying to hammer jelly to a tree. There are many definitions of this term that we use so often – from the economist's perception right through to the psychologist's view.

For the purpose of this book, **entrepreneurship** will be defined as the process of:
▸ Creating something unique and valuable
▸ By committing resources (remember that resources are any input that goes into your organisation. Whether it is time, money, knowledge or machinery),
▸ Thus growing this venture in terms of profit, products and market share
▸ Accepting all the risks involved in the process (whether it is financial risks, family risks or career risks)
▸ In order to generate rewards (rewards may be financial gain, status or self-actualisation).

⌐ DEFINITION ⌐

In order to summarise, entrepreneurship is the process of creating something new through committing resources and enduring risks in order to achieve rewards.

1.2 **Importance of entrepreneurship**

Have you heard of a place called Silicon Valley? Situated in the US just off the shore of San Francisco Bay, it is one of the most well-known areas in terms of innovation. In fact, in the last 50 years, no other place on earth has had so many innovations. However, it is not just the number of innovations that sets Silicon Valley apart, it is also the ability to produce these innovations (Smith, 2010:4).

In other words, the people of Silicon Valley don't just have the ability to think creatively and dream up fantastic ideas, they have the ability to turn these great ideas into tangible products. How they do that you might wonder – the answer is through entrepreneurship!

But what is the relevance of all of this? The importance of changing innovation to entrepreneurship – of changing ideas into products – can be seen in the fact that it builds a **sustainable competitive advantage** for economies, organisations and individuals. Furthermore, these new products do not only lead to profits for individuals and organisations, but also improve the quality of life of all individuals and generate further economic opportunities.

⌐ DEFINITION ⌐

Sustainable competitive advantage refers to an organisation's ability to remain ahead of its competitors. A way of doing business that sets you apart from your competitors and ensures that you stand out in the market.

Through the commercialisation of innovation, the gap between the needs of the market and the inventions which innovators have can be bridged. However, it remains a key challenge to all innovators to take an invention from the idea phase to the market in order to produce economic returns. Ideas or inventions cannot generate economic returns for the innovator.

ENTREPRENEURIAL DILEMMA

	SILICON VALLEY US	SA
Population	3.5–4 million	49.9 million
Unemployment	9.4%	42%
Universities/ Colleges	32	41

Consider the table above. Which of the two, SA or Silicon Valley, do you think is in the best position to innovate? Motivate your answer.

Only when the invention is successfully absorbed into the marketplace can profit be achieved by the inventor and therefore the importance of commercialising inventions is highlighted.

Nieman and Nieuwenhuizen (2009:3) state that 'Economic development can be directly attributed to the level of entrepreneurial activity in a country. Entrepreneurship ensures growth in the economy as entrepreneurs intend to grow their businesses and are responsible for job creation in the economy'.

Nieman et al. (2009:3) furthermore argue that SMMEs play a critical role in the entrepreneurial activities of South Africa as they:

▶ Account for 97.5% of all businesses,
▶ Generate 35% of the gross domestic product,
▶ Contribute 43% of the total of salaries and wages paid and
▶ Employ 55% of all formal private sector employees in South Africa.

Impressive as these statistics are, one might ask 'So what? What exactly is the importance of entrepreneurship?' And the simplest answer lies in the aeroplane, the microwave oven, cellphones and television, to name a few. Without entrepreneurs there would be no progress, no better way of doing things, no new products or means of travel that seemed impossible before. Entrepreneurship doesn't just bring about new products, but also new services that enables organisations to compete efficiently and satisfy customers' needs better.

However, in South Africa the typical innovator struggles to move from **nascent entrepreneurship** to establishing a new business. This is illustrated in Table 1.1. Out of the total population of South Africa, 5.2% of the individuals consider the possibility of starting their own entrepreneurial venture. However, only 4% of these individuals manage to progress to a stage where they physically establish a business. The real reason for concern is actually the low percentage of entrepreneurs who manage to grow their businesses from start-up to an established business, as this rate drops to 2.3%. When just considering the situation in South Africa, the challenges surrounding entrepreneurship may not be clear yet. However, when these statistics are compared to countries similar to South Africa, the reason for concern is clear. Of the 8.4% of individuals

ENTREPRENEURIAL DILEMMA

Where does an entrepreneurial idea come from? What are some of the major product breakthroughs in the 21st century that can be directly linked to entrepreneurial thinking? Perhaps the best way to answer this question is to do an Internet search on Google or YouTube. Just type in the words: 'Entrepreneurial breakthroughs in the 21st century in South Africa' and make a list of the breakthroughs you find.

who consider entrepreneurship as an option from the other countries, 7.2% manage to grow their business to an established business.

DEFINITION

Nascent entrepreneurs are individuals who are thinking about starting their own businesses. They haven't done anything concrete – they are simply playing around with the idea of entrepreneurship as a career option.

1.3 Types of entrepreneurs

Nieman and Nieuwenhuizen (2009) distinguish between different types of entrepreneurs, namely:

▸ *Basic survivalist.* This person operates as an entrepreneur to survive until he or she obtains a formal-sector job or entrepreneurial opportunity.
▸ *Pre-entrepreneur.* This person is involved in welfare-based entrepreneurship where profit maximisation is less important than the collective.

▸ *Subsistence entrepreneur.* This person is involved in independent income-generating activities operating as a small-scale vendor.
▸ *Micro-entrepreneur.* This person is a formal-sector entrepreneur with zero to 10 employees.
▸ *Small-scale entrepreneur.* This person is a formal-sector entrepreneur with 11 to 49 employees.

In addition to this list, the following types of entrepreneurs are often also identified:

▸ *Necessity entrepreneur.* People are starting businesses because they have no other choice. They have been retrenched or have not grown their businesses sufficiently to retire (Phitidis, 2013).
▸ *Lifestyle entrepreneur.* Someone who places a lifestyle above all else in their choice of business – this may be a passion or cause that they support (Phitidis, 2013).
▸ *Tenderpreneur.* As part of South Africa's transformation, tenders issued by government and state-owned enterprises place a strong emphasis on supporting emerging

---

ENTREPRENEURIAL DILEMMA

Bukiwe Ndengezi is a 27-year-old buyer in the fashion industry, who intends to start her own business within the next few years. She is very passionate about her idea, which she believes will close a gap in the market. While she builds up more experience, she is saving money for start-up capital and needs to work out what her business model will be. Discuss what Bukiwe can do to change from an intentional entrepreneur to a start-up or early-stage entrepreneur.

Source: Turtin and Herrington, 2012:31.

TABLE 1.1 The entrepreneurial rates of South Africa versus 23 other efficiency driven economies

	SOUTH AFRICA	AVERAGE OF 23 OTHER EFFICIENCY-DRIVEN ECONOMIES
Nascent entrepreneurship rate	5.2%	8.4%
Rate of new business ownership	4%	5.9%
Established businesses	2.3%	7.2%

Source: Turtin, N. & Herrington, M. 2012. Global Entrepreneurship Monitor 2012, The UCT Centre for Innovation and Entrepreneurship. [Online]. Available: http://www.gsb.uct.ac.za/files/2012GEMSouthAfricaReport.pdf [19 August 2013]. Reprinted by permission of Dr M. Herrington.

entrepreneurs. These entrepreneurs with access to government tenders have an opportunity to use this advantage to grow and build a platform for their businesses to grow (Phitidis, 2013).

▸ *Social entrepreneur.* The social entrepreneur is primarily motivated by a deep desire to improve upon, or fundamentally change, prevailing and detrimental socio-economic, educational, environmental or health conditions. A social entrepreneur has a fierce ambition to alter the present reality of conditions she or he deems unacceptable or inhumane, and stubbornly refuses to accept the norm, or arguments that simply rationalise, if not justify, prevailing circumstances. The key trait of the social entrepreneur is, however, the fact that they are driven to engage in certain activities not by the promise of possible profit, but by an overwhelming sense of social conscience and social responsibility. The goal of this type of entrepreneur is to develop effective models that not only respond to a specific need, but can be propagated and implemented in a variety of settings.

▸ *Serial entrepreneur.* The serial entrepreneur consistently conceptualises and executes business models that she or he intends, ultimately, to sell to shareholders, investors, or other businesses. Serial entrepreneurs can be seen to take on relatively high amounts of risk, display an ability to effectively handle the accompanying stress as they are usually very adaptable to changing conditions, and more often than not display a pattern of success (despite some failures) in the long run. Serial entrepreneurs display a definite propensity to recover both economically as well as in confidence, from business and personal failures.

▸ *Solopreneur.* The 'one man band' – an individual who operates alone in an enterprise and manages all aspects of the business themselves. Increasingly possible and prevalent with the advent of the Internet, email, VOIP, etc. and the consequent ability to perform multiple tasks, coupled with the ease of outsourcing to other freelancers through the ready supply available through websites (Miller, 2014).

ENTREPRENEURIAL DILEMMA

KYA Guards

Mr Lancelot Radebe, managing director of KYA Guards, worked in the security industry for a long time before establishing his own security company in 2001. The company was set up in De Korte Street, Braamfontein, Johannesburg.

Turnover increased by 35% between 2006 and 2007. However, net profit declined from a positive 6% to a negative 3%. The biggest expense was KYA Guards salaries that accounted for 73% of the total expense bill in 2006 and 72% in 2007.

The business faced a number of challenges, including: no documented human resources system, no performance measures (despite employing more than 180 guards placed at different sites), no financial system and increasing numbers of overtime payments, no cost control documented system and an inability to take advantage of their BEE status to tender against bigger companies like ADT and Stallion Security.

To return to profitability, the following measures were implemented: a performance management system, an operations model, a financial management system, a quality management system, a basic business towards training model and tender training for management. Employment levels have grown from 186 to 500 employees. This increase came about because KYA Guards has been able to secure seven additional sites because of the operational plan and tender training that took place. The general attitude of the employees towards work has improved since employee training. The company's ability to assess the viability of new projects has also improved.

Source: ProductivitySA. 2010b. Turnaround Solutions 2009/2010. Midrand, South Africa: Productivity SA.

The entrepreneurial dilemma above tells the story of KYA Guards, a newly established company, and how it managed to survive after setup.

1.4 The entrepreneurial process

In order to bake the perfect cake, you need a complete recipe. More than that, you need to understand the measurements that are indicated and follow the recipe to the letter. All of the ingredients must be readily available and the oven temperature must be perfect.

When baking your entrepreneurial cake, you will need many of the same skills. You will need to understand the entrepreneurial process (What does each step mean and entail? When are the steps successfully completed?), the resources that you will need for this journey must be identified and readily available and the environment in which you will bake your cake must be the right temperature! In other words, the market must also be ready for and accessible to your new venture!

Hisrich, Peters and Shepherd (2005) indicated that the entrepreneur has to follow a certain process to find, evaluate, and develop an opportunity. They referred to this as the entrepreneurial process in which they identified four distinct phases:
▸ Identification and evaluation of the opportunity
▸ Development of the business plan
▸ Determination of the required resources
▸ Management of the resulting enterprise (Hisrich, et al., 2005).

The first phase identified by Hisrich, et al. (2005) is often divided into two separate steps, namely 1) *identification of the opportunity (idea generation)* and 2) *opportunity evaluation*, while a last step is also added, namely *growth and harvest*.

For the purposes of this book the entrepreneurial process consists of the following steps:
▸ Step 1: Idea generation
▸ Step 2: Opportunity evaluation
▸ Step 3: Business plan development (Planning the venture)
▸ Step 4: Determination of required resources
▸ Step 5: Formation and management of business enterprise
▸ Step 6: Growth and harvest

Although it is natural to think of the early steps as occurring sequentially, they are actually proceeding in parallel. Even as you begin your evaluation, you are forming at least a hypothesis of a business strategy. As you test the hypothesis, you are beginning to execute the first steps of your marketing plan (and possibly also your sales plan). We separate these ideas for convenience in description but it is worth keeping in mind that these are ongoing aspects of your management of the business. In the growth phases, you continue to refine you basic idea, re-evaluate the opportunity and revise your plan. We will now briefly discuss the steps in the entrepreneurial process. The details on what should be done during each step will be discussed in the different chapters within this book.

1.4.1 Step 1: Idea generation

Opportunity identification (**idea** generation) is a very difficult task. Most good business opportunities do not suddenly appear, but rather result from an entrepreneur's alertness to possibilities, or in some case, the establishment of mechanisms that identify potential opportunities.

Every new venture begins with an idea. An idea is a concept for a product or service that does not exist or is not currently available in a market niche. It may be a brand-new concept or an improvement of a current product or service. In contrast, an opportunity is an idea for a new product or service with a market that is willing to pay for that product or service so that it can form the basis of a profitable business.

Innovation is the process of making changes to something that adds value to customers.

Often, consumers are the best source of ideas for a new venture. How many times have you heard someone comment, 'If only there was a product that would …' This comment can result in the creation of a new business. One entrepreneur's business resulted from seeing the application of a plastic resin compound in developing and manufacturing a new type of pallet while developing the resin application in another totally unrelated area – casket moldings. Whether the opportunity is identified by using input from consumers, business associates, channel members, or technical people, each opportunity must be carefully screened and evaluated (Hisrich, et al., 2005).

> **DEFINITION**
>
> An idea is a concept for a product or service that does not exist or is not currently available in a market niche.

1.4.2 Step 2: Opportunity evaluation

During this step the entrepreneur should ask whether there is an opportunity worth investing in. Investment is principally capital, whether from individuals in the company or from outside investors, and the time and energy of a set of people. But one should also consider other assets such as intellectual property, personal relationships, physical property, etc. This evaluation of the opportunity is perhaps the most critical element of the entrepreneurial process, as it allows the entrepreneur to assess whether the specific product or service has the returns needed compared to the resources required. This evaluation process involves looking at the length of the opportunity, its real and perceived value, its risks and returns, its fit with the personal skills and goals of the entrepreneur, and its uniqueness or differential advantage in its competitive environment (Hisrich, et al., 2005).

There are five basic questions that you should ask as you evaluate an opportunity:
1. Is there a sufficiently attractive market opportunity?
2. Is your proposed solution feasible, both from a market perspective and a technology perspective?
3. Can we compete (over a sufficiently interesting time horizon): is there sustainable competitive advantage?
4. Do we have a team that can effectively capitalise on this opportunity?
5. What is the risk/reward profile of this opportunity, and does it justify the investment of time and money?

If you can answer all of these questions affirmatively, then you have persuaded yourself that this opportunity is worth investing in. This is the first step toward being able to convince others, whether they be prospective customers, employees, partners or providers of capital.

1.4.3 Step 3: Developing a business plan (planning the venture)

During this step the planning of the venture takes place. This should start with developing the strategy for the venture, the type of business that will be established, the objectives (strategic, operational and tactical plans), who are the competitors in the market and who are the **target customers**, and how you will reach them. These will be discussed in more depth in section two dealing with new venture creation.

> **DEFINITION**
>
> The target customer is the set of potential buyers who are your focus as you design your company's solution.

An element of strategy is the development of the venture's **vision**: how it wants to be known or thought of. A compelling vision is necessary to inspire investors, recruit and motivate employees, and to excite customers and partners. A good business plan must be developed in order to exploit the defined opportunity. This is a very time-consuming phase of the entrepreneurial process. An entrepreneur usually has not prepared a business plan before and does not have the resources available to do a good job. A good business plan is essential for developing the opportunity and determining the resources required, obtaining those resources, and successfully managing the resulting venture.

1.4.4 Step 4: Determine the resources required

The resources needed for addressing the opportunity must also be determined. This process starts with an appraisal of the entrepreneur's present resources. Any resources that are critical need to be differentiated from those that are just helpful. Care must be taken not to underestimate the amount of variety of resources needed. The downside risks associated with insufficient or inappropriate resources should also be assessed.

Acquiring the needed resources in a timely manner, while giving up as little control as possible, is the next step in the entrepreneurial process. An entrepreneur should strive to maintain as large an ownership position as possible, particularly in the start-up stage. As the business develops, more funds will probably be needed to finance the growth of the venture, requiring more ownership to be relinquished. Alternative suppliers of these resources, along with their needs and desires, need to be identified. By understanding resource supplier needs, the entrepreneur can structure a deal that enables the recourses to be acquired at the lowest possible cost and the least loss of control.

1.4.5 Step 5: Formation and management of the business enterprise

After resources are acquired, the entrepreneur must use them to implement the business plan.

The operational problems of the growing enterprise must also be examined. This involves implementing a management style and structure, as well as determining the key variables for success. A control system must be established, so that any problem areas can be quickly identified and resolved. Some entrepreneurs have difficulty managing and growing the venture they created.

1.4.6 Step 6: Growth and harvesting

Before an entrepreneur can pursue a growth strategy, it's essential to make sure that the new business is running efficiently. While they may be spending more time and resources on developing the business, they need to be sure that the core of the business is still performing well. It's vital not to neglect the existing customer base as this will underpin growth and, equally importantly, provide the cash flow needed during this step. Timing is very critical to the success of any growth strategy. It is essential that the present position of the business is evaluated to make sure that consolidation efforts will be as effective as possible.

When planning a harvesting strategy, entrepreneurs generally use profits from mature brands to increase funding for more promising lines of business. For example, a telecommunications company may take profits from its landline business to supplement research and development for its wireless communications business if growth and profits in the wireless business are more likely. Advances in technology and changes in consumer behaviour dictate which brands become cash cows.

1.5 The impact of the environment on the entrepreneur

Regardless of the best efforts of entrepreneurs, they cannot be successful if they are not aware of the impact that the greater environment will have on them.

The best way in which to describe this is in the form of a diagram.

The **micro environment** represents the entrepreneurial venture itself. It is the entrepreneur him/herself, the technology or machinery needed, the team that you will employ and the necessary skills they need to have, all the relevant input materials you need, etc.

DEFINITION

The micro environment refers to the organisation itself. It is everything that is included inside the organisation.

What should be noted about these aspects is that they are under the control of the entrepreneur! Supplier not delivering the raw materials on time? It is within your power to look for a new supplier. Do you have an excellent entrepreneurial team? It is your responsibility to build on their capabilities and send them on training courses to develop their potential fully. Therefore, all the aspects in the micro environment are considered to be strengths and weaknesses.

Strengths and weaknesses are under the control of the entrepreneur. The entrepreneur should reduce the weaknesses in the venture – otherwise your competitors will exploit them – and the entrepreneur should continuously build on the strengths already available in the venture – in order to nullify the impact of competitors.

DEFINITION

Strengths are the aspects in your organisation that you are very good at. Every strength that you have in your venture will help build the competitive advantage of your venture. Strengths include aspects such as excellent technical knowledge, motivated staff and access to scarce resources.

The important link between the micro environment and the market and macro environment is the fact that when an opportunity arises, you must be in a position where you have the necessary strengths to take advantage of the opportunity. The unfortunate part about this is that if a weakness in the venture causes you to lose out on a good opportunity (e.g. you do not have the needed technological skills in your venture to successfully compete in your industry), you only have yourself to blame.

The impact of some threats can be reduced significantly if an entrepreneur has the relevant strengths to handle the situation. If a new trend in the market emerges, but you are mindful of the relevant information in your industry and therefore knowledgeable, you would anticipate certain changes and completely nullify the impact of the threat.

However, if your weaknesses and threats ever meet, be prepared to have your venture fail. This underlines the importance of taking control of the strengths and weaknesses in your venture.

Opportunities and threats arise from the market and macro environments. First we will discuss each of these environments separately.

The market environment encompasses the specific industry in which your venture will

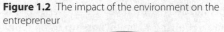

Figure 1.2 The impact of the environment on the entrepreneur

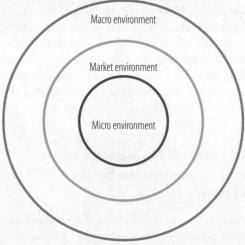

function. In other words, if you are the owner of a Kentucky Fried Chicken (KFC) outlet you will operate, and be influenced by, the fast food industry. However, if you own a hardware store, your market environment will differ significantly from the market environment of the fast food industry.

The market environment consists of the following factors:

▶ Customers
  ▪ Customers are the most important factor to your organisation. If no one buys the products you sell, your venture will never be successful.
▶ Competitors
  ▪ These include direct competitors as well as indirect competitors. A direct competitor for Kentucky Fried Chicken (KFC), for example, is Nando's. Indirect competitors are anything from healthy foods right through to groceries with which you'll prepare a hearty home cooked meal. Why? Because at the core of it, all of these options fulfill the same underlying need, i.e. hunger.
▶ Suppliers
  ▪ Suppliers supply the organisation with input resources. The suppliers of KFC will include the bakery who supplies the buns for the hamburgers, the chicken farm who supplies the high quality chickens, the fresh produce venture who supplies them with fresh tomatoes and lettuce, etc.
▶ Distributors
  ▪ The distributors of Coca-Cola have the responsibility to ensure that every KFC outlet (and many other stores, garages, etc.) have sufficient supplies of their cold drinks. The right amount of cold drinks must be delivered at the right time to ensure that the needs of the customers can be satisfied.
▶ Labour force
  ▪ The labour force of any organisation has a significant impact on the success of the organisation. Capable, helpful, friendly staff are one of the greatest assets any organisation can have. If you do not have access to skilled employees or you employ unmotivated employees, the efficiency of your organisation will decrease dramatically.

Each of these factors has a direct influence on the micro environment. In other words, if something changes in this environment, your venture will have to adapt to these changes – or at the very least be aware of these changes.

The macro environment on the other hand encompasses South Africa as a whole. In other words, regardless of the industry in which you operate or what you sell, we conform to the same laws and economic situation. To better understand this, let's have a look at the factors that the macro environment consists of.

Factors in the macro environment:

▶ Economic factors
  ▪ These factors refer to anything that will influence the amount of money you have available. Interest rates, petrol prices, inflation are some examples of economic factors. Regardless of what industry you operate in, if there is a sharp increase in the interest rate, it will have an impact on your organisation.

▸ Technological factors
  ▪ When technology changes it influences the way in which we produce, distribute, sell and market our products. The typewriter was completely replaced by the computer – a technological change that influenced all industries and even households. Should your competitors employ the latest technology that enables them to produce a product faster and more cost effectively, your organisation will be in trouble if you lag behind.
▸ Political-legal factors
  ▪ Laws on minimum wages, broad-based black economic empowerment (B-BBEE), pollution, reasonable working policies, maternity leave, etc. influence every single organisation in South Africa. Apart from the way in which the political-legal factors direct the way in which we conduct business, it also impacts on the attractiveness of a country for foreign investment. If a country is in a state of constant war or political unrest, foreign investors tend to close their wallets and move on.
▸ International factors
  ▪ It is not only what we can produce and sell locally that impacts on the way in which we conduct business, but also the options that are available from overseas. Can we import certain raw materials at a lower price than to manufacture it locally? Do we have access to international products that are not yet available locally? A true entrepreneur will look for opportunities in every avenue – whether it is in importing or exporting, the international influences are always monitored.
▸ Demographic factors
  ▪ Demographic factors talk to the constitution of the nation. In the past we were used to a workforce of older men, as women were staying home and raising children. Today, women are pursuing top positions in typically male dominated industries, recently qualified, young adults are working alongside older men, not to mention the different races, religious views and political standpoints.
▸ Ecological factors
  ▪ In the simplest terms, ecological factors refer to our responsibility towards the environment. It is the responsibility of every business owner to ensure that the way in which they manufacture their goods minimises the impact on the environment they operate in. Organisations are under enormous pressure to reduce their carbon footprint and they are forced to accept responsibility for their influence on the environment.

ENTREPRENEURIAL DILEMMA

To illustrate how the market environment influences your organisation, consider the following:
▸ How will changes in customer preferences influence your organisation?
▸ What will the impact of a new competitor be? Or what will happen if your main competitor changes their strategy?
▸ How will the inability of a supplier to deliver the required input materials on time or in the right amount impact on your organisation?

Access to qualified and skilled employees will determine how efficiently you can produce products and how effectively customer needs will be met.

Distributors who fail to distribute your products to many locations or in sufficient amounts will have a direct negative impact on the sales and potential profit of your organisation.

ENTREPRENEURIAL DILEMMA

In which country in Africa would you invest your money? What does the political situation look like? On the other hand, in which country in Africa would you be very skeptical to invest money in? Think about their government and the policies that they formulate and implement.

CONCLUSION

Entrepreneurship is vital to the economic growth of any country. The successful establishment of entrepreneurial ventures leads to employment opportunities and growth in all economies. However, in order to successfully go through the entrepreneurial process, the entrepreneur needs to understand all of the aspects of the entrepreneurial process. Entrepreneurs should ensure that they know what the logical flow of the steps in the entrepreneurial process is, as well as what it entails to successfully complete each step.

What makes entrepreneurship an intricate process is the impact that the environment has on the venture. Even the slightest change in the market may have an impact on your entrepreneurial environment. It is therefore crucial that all entrepreneurs engulf themselves in their respective environments. They must know exactly what their strengths and weaknesses are in the micro environment, who the important role players are in the market environment and how the opportunities and threats in the macro environment will impact on their ventures. Only once this is clear can a venture gain a competitive advantage in the market.

SELF-ASSESSMENT QUESTIONS

1. Argue why entrepreneurship is important for any economy.
2. Explain the entrepreneurial process in your own words.
3. List and define all the factors in the micro environment.
4. Give an example of how each of the factors in the market environment can impact on a new business venture.
5. Give an example of how each of the factors in the macro environment can impact on a new business venture.
6. Define the concepts strength and opportunity in such a way that the difference between the two is clear. Do the same with weaknesses and threats.

DISCUSSION QUESTIONS

1. South Africa is facing a number of problems including high unemployment levels, slow economic growth and poverty. Explain how the outcomes of entrepreneurship can address these issues.
2. Describe what the fundamental difference between an entrepreneur and a manager is according to you.
3. Why is it important to understand the entrepreneurial process as well as what each of the steps in the process entails?
4. Lisa is the owner and manager of a popular hair salon in Bloemfontein, where she employs a total of five hairstylists. Her aim is to ensure that her salon becomes the best hair salon in Bloemfontein within the next two years. Recently the salon experienced a drop in the number of customers coming. As a result of this drop in clientele, profits also decreased. Lisa knows that she has to increase the number of customers coming to the salon, otherwise she will have to retrench some of the hairdressers that have not been performing as well as they should have. Therefore she decided to advertise a special for the salon for the coming weeks to increase the amount of customers.

4.1 Explain what factors in the market environment are evident in this scenario.

4.2 What factors from the macro environment could potentially be (a) opportunities and (b) threats to Lisa?

EXPERIENTIAL EXERCISES

1. When considering the definition of entrepreneurship, do you think you have what it takes to become an entrepreneur? Why or why not?
2. Why do you think entrepreneurship is important? Apply your answer specifically to the impact of entrepreneurship on South Africa's high unemployment rate.
3. The entrepreneurial process is a lengthy process. Do you think entrepreneurs always have the time to commit to go through these steps? What are some of the benefits that entrepreneurs can obtain from going through the entrepreneurial process, in spite of the fact that it is a lengthy process?
4. When you take South Africa's current situation in terms of the general level of education and economic climate into account, do you think the macro environment of South Africa is enabling for entrepreneurs or not? Motivate your answer.

SOUTH AFRICA: A LAND OF EXTREMES FOR ENTREPRENEURS

Cheryl-Jane Kujenga | October 4, 2013 at 12:54

CASE STUDY

South Africa presents both strong opportunities and barriers to success for local entrepreneurs. It is evident from the EY G20 Entrepreneurship Barometer report that South Africans embrace the culture of entrepreneurship, a very important element needed to propel it to success. However there are other equally important elements such as access to funding, support and education and training that need strengthening to truly build a thriving entrepreneurial society, writes Cheryl-Jane Kujenga, EY Strategic Growth Markets Leader, Africa.

The overall environment for South African entrepreneurs is one of relative extremes. It is relatively quick and cheap to start a new business, but getting the necessary registrations and compliance in place is difficult. Furthermore, it is expensive and difficult to hire and fire new workers. Similarly, there is a growing middle class of consumers providing rich opportunities, but also a vast pool of unemployed workers, creating a sharply divided market. These extremes are observable across many aspects of the overall environment for entrepreneurs locally.

Access to funding

Seventy-nine per cent of local entrepreneurs say that access to funding is difficult for them. Added to this, many believe that funding conditions are deteriorating further, whether in terms of bank lending, angel investors or initial public offerings. More positively, though, some 69% of local entrepreneurs surveyed have seen an improvement in microfinance, while 53% also report improvements in the availability of government funding. Both sources of funding are viewed by survey respondents as vital for accelerating growth in entrepreneurship.

Microfinance in particular is ideal for millions of poor, unskilled and unemployed South Africans who, despite their disadvantages, often have the talent to develop successful businesses. Local entrepreneurs point to microfinance as a key funding instrument for the long-term growth of entrepreneurship locally.

Merger and acquisition (M&A) deal activity in South Africa was on the rise through the early 2000s, but has slowed since the financial crisis. But the country still has a very high rate of M&A investment relative to national GDP. Similarly, while venture capital availability is better than the average for rapid-growth economies, sentiment in the survey is considerably worse than average, which impacts its performance.

Overall, South Africa has a highly mature financial sector, and many believe there is enough funding in the marketplace. However, funds are not made easily available to entrepreneurs, and much of the capital is often too expensive, which limits the growth of promising ventures. To help counter this, many entrepreneurs look to the government. When asked which form of funding could make the biggest difference in improving the long-term growth of entrepreneurship, entrepreneurs cite public aid and government lending as a key priority. This highlights the role that the government will need to play in supporting entrepreneurship, to complement the country's financial services sector.

Entrepreneurship culture

South Africa's business environment and culture raises challenges for local entrepreneurs. The country's performance overall is weighed down by below-average scores on innovation metrics, such as the number of scientific and engineering articles published, spending on research and development (R&D) and the number of researchers in this area. Patent applications, which provide another measure of innovation activity, fell by 24% in South Africa between 2008 and 2011. This implies that South Africa's research institutions are unlikely to produce a large number of innovations with a commercial application in the near term, a fact that undermines prospects for the country's innovation-led start-ups.

Despite these weaknesses, South Africa's entrepreneurs believe their culture encourages entrepreneurship: 70% of those surveyed believed this. It is possible that a high level of media attention on entrepreneurs and entrepreneurship being seen as a strong career choice, rather than academic, corporate or institutional strengths, have fuelled this impression. Still, exceptionally high proportions of local entrepreneurs indicated that various measures – from promoting their role as job creators, to getting more start-up success stories publicised – could have a strong impact on cultural perspectives of entrepreneurship.

Tax and regulation

South Africa has strong start-up and taxation compliance procedures, in contrast to other members of the so-called 'BRICS club' of rapid-growth markets. In terms of tax and regulation, the country puts in a good performance against both mature and rapid-growth G20 economies. Although difficulties and bureaucracy remain, it is relatively easy, quick and cheap to start a business, and the time spent on taxes is in line with mature economies, making this a relative strength for the country's entrepreneurial ecosystem. Nevertheless, local entrepreneurs are still keen for greater support in complying with regulations, and 42% point to the need for an agency to assist in this area.

A bigger challenge emerges when companies move beyond the start-up phase. The cost of firing workers is a notable detractor, and highlights the ongoing need for labour-law reform in the country. Out of the 144 countries tracked by the World Economic Forum, South Africa is 143rd on hiring and firing practices, 140th for flexibility of wage determination and last on the measure of cooperation in labour-employer relations.

From a regulatory perspective this is the most worrying feature of the South African economy for entrepreneurs. New businesses cannot afford to comply with these burdensome labour laws, and many businesses will remain small or fall into the informal sector to avoid them. Regulatory reforms or tax credits could relatively easily help ease hiring terms, especially for the previously unemployed or for young workers, while incentivising firms to hire more freely.

Education and training

South Africa spends more on education (as a percentage of GDP) than most G20 countries and significantly more than most other rapid-growth economies. However, South Africa's education system is in clear need of reform, which raises difficult questions about how effectively education funding is being deployed.

The country has low tertiary education enrollment and a low proportion of the workforce educated to a degree level. This means many of the more advanced entrepreneurial ventures simply don't have access to the skills they need to thrive.

Furthermore, at a more general level, entrepreneurs clearly believe that more could be done to improve the public's view of entrepreneurship in the country. About one in two respondents pointed to the need for more efforts to promote success stories about South Africa's entrepreneurs, as a key measure for achieving this.

In the shorter term, though, more could be done to bolster informal learning and training schemes in order to help bridge at least some of the gap. There are encouraging signs, based on the sentiment from our survey, that the private sector is helping to pick up the slack here. For example, through stronger corporate engagement with start-ups; 62% of those polled think access to such schemes has improved in recent years, compared with 36% across the G20 overall.

Coordinated support

South Africa's entrepreneurs report improved access to various support structures, including business incubators, mentor programmes, industry-specific training programmes, entrepreneurial workshops and corporate engagement with start-ups. All this is encouraging news, particularly in terms of business incubators, as these are considered by local entrepreneurs to be the single most

important tool for strengthening the future of entrepreneurship in South Africa.

The perception of network-related elements of coordinated support, such as clubs, associations, chambers of commerce and small business administration, where only a minority of entrepreneurs noted improvements, is less encouraging.

Among G20 countries, access to educators is falling most sharply in South Africa, with 30% of respondents reporting a deterioration in the past three years. This contrasts with competing rapid-growth markets that are reporting strong improvement. Some 61% of respondents from India report an increase in access to educators, while Russia (57%), Turkey (57%) and Indonesia (55%) follow the same trend. This again highlights the need for wider educational reform, while suggesting that informal learning and mentorship opportunities will remain vital in the years ahead.

Of the G20, South Africa does seem significantly more enthusiastic about tailored support for female entrepreneurs. As far back as 1998, for example, the Government set up the Technology for Women in Business initiative to help empower women within the technology sector. This shows recognition of the value of more targeted entrepreneurial support.

Source: This article is an extract from the 'EY G20 Entrepreneurship Barometer 2013 Country Report – South Africa'. [Online]. Available: http://www.ey.com/Publication/vwLUAssets/The_power_of_three_-_SA/$FILE/EY%20G20%20 Entrepreneurship%20Barometer%202013%20Country%20Report%20-%20South%20Africa_Low%20Res.pdf

1. When considering the case study above it is clear that the macro and market environment has a significant impact on entrepreneurship. Identify all the factors from the macro and market environment that you note in the case study.

2. Do you consider the above-mentioned aspects in the case study as strengths and weaknesses or opportunities and threats? Motivate your answers.

3. How can going through the steps of the entrepreneurial process assist entrepreneurs to identify possible threats and opportunities, as noted in the case study.

SUGGESTED WEBSITE LINKS

http://www.referenceforbusiness.com/management/
Mar-No/New-Product-Development.html

http://www.ybl.co.za/
south-africa-doesnt-entrepreneurs-entrepreneurs-2/

http://sbaer.uca.edu/publications/entrepreneurship/
pdf/01.pdf

http://www.gobookee.org/
significance-of-entrepreneurial-environment/

http://www.gsb.uct.ac.za/
files/2012GEMSouthAfricaReport.pdf

REFERENCES

Hisrich, RD, Peters, MP, & Shepherd, DA. *Entrepreneurship*. 6th ed. New York: McGraw-Hill Irwin. [Online]. Available: http://sbaer.uca.edu/publications/entrepreneurship/pdf/01.pdf [28 October 2013].

Miller, C. 2014. *Types of entrepreneurs*. [Online]. Available: http://resourcefulentrepreneur.com/types-of-entrepreneurs/ [2 March 2014].

New Product Development. [Online]. Available: http://www.referenceforbusiness.com/management/Mar-No/New-Product-Development.html [7 November 2013].

Nieman, G. & Nieuwenhuizen, C. 2009. *Entrepreneurship: A South African Perspective*. Van Schaik: Pretoria.

Phitidis, P. 2013. *Seven types of entrepreneurs*. [Online]. Available: http://www.aurik.co.za/business-accelerator/blog/seven-types-entrepreneurs/#sthash.DKDLISg3.dpuf [2 March 2014].

ProductivitySA. 2010b. *Turnaround Solutions 2009/2010*. Midrand, South Africa: Productivity SA. 25–27.

Smith, D. 2010. *Exploring innovation*. McGraw Hill: Berkshire.

Top 10 South African entrepreneurs. [Online]. Available: http://www.mweb.co.za/Entrepreneur/ViewArticle/tabid/3162/Article/7017/Top-10-South-African-entrepreneurs.aspx [7 November 2013].

Turtin, N. & Herrington, M. 2012. *Global Entrepreneurship Monitor 2012*, The UCT Centre for Innovation and Entrepreneurship. [Online]. Available: http://www.gsb.uct.ac.za/files/2012GEMSouthAfricaReport.pdf [19 August 2013].

von Oetinger, B. 2005. Nurturing the new: Patterns for innovation. *Journal of Business Strategy*, 26:29–36.

Zhoa, F. 2005. Exploring the synergy between entrepreneurship and innovation. *International Journal of Entrepreneurial Behavior & Research*, 11(1):25–41.

CHAPTER 2

The entrepreneurial mindset

Karen Booysen

LEARNING OUTCOMES

On completion of this chapter you will be able to:
▶ Explore the historical development of entrepreneurs
▶ Explore the development of an entrepreneurial culture in South Africa
▶ Discuss the major resources available for exploring the entrepreneurial mindset
▶ Describe entrepreneurial characteristics
▶ Discuss and understand the impact of entrepreneurial risks.

OPENING CASE STUDY

An entrepreneurial mindset is often characterised by the ability to consistently build and develop oneself, a willingness to learn and grow both personally and in starting and expanding a new adventure, task or tool. This is also enhanced by commitment and a 'never give up' attitude.

These are just some of the characteristics of an entrepreneurial mindset. If you can achieve this mindset, it allows you to focus on your dreams and goals, thus becoming a very important tool. An entrepreneurial mindset will enable you to follow your life's passions. In addition it has the most wonderful benefit of financial and time freedom if you commit and give it the attention it deserves to achieve this kind of success.

1. Do you think you have what it takes to become an entrepreneur – reminding yourself that there is always room to become even better in every aspect of your life?
2. Which characteristics do you think are the most important for an entrepreneur? Do you posses these characteristics or do you have a plan to acquire them?

INTRODUCTION

Entrepreneurship involves knowing what people need and starting a venture to fulfil that need. It starts in the mind of the entrepreneur and motivates the entrepreneur to start, set up and grow a business. Entrepreneurship is about people and their need to buy a product or to use a service (Allen, 2010).

High levels of formal-sector entrepreneurship are at the economic heart of any country. Without such high levels of entrepreneurship, there are not sufficient producers and sellers of goods, providers of services, generators of income, or income-generating opportunities for both job seekers and prospective entrepreneurs. Bannock, Baxter, and Davis (2003) indicate in this regard that entrepreneurs fulfil a very important function to ensure economic growth and development, namely that they are alert to gaps in the supply of goods and services not identified by others and are able to mobilise resources to provide such goods and services to the benefit of consumers and the economy as a whole. Entrepreneurship is thus important for societies to generate economic growth and ensure economic and socio-economic development. In this regard, Porter (1990) noted in his well-known book, *The Competitive Advantage of Nations*, that entrepreneurship is at the heart of economic advantage. For the purposes of this book, this means that a large pool of entrepreneurs is required to benefit a society by increasing the size of the economic pie, taking on board employees, and providing high-quality products and services to customers.

In South Africa, as is true for most developing countries, there is a huge shortage of entrepreneurs. This is especially true for entrepreneurs in the formal sector. The view commonly expressed is that South Africa has too few people with entrepreneurial qualities. As a result, the South African economy performs poorly because only a very limited number of people succeed as entrepreneurs. Although the importance of higher levels of entrepreneurship for the well-being of South African society is emphasised, it is important to note that entrepreneurs seldom initiate business ventures with the primary aim of benefiting the society in which they live. Entrepreneurs tend to be people who recognise business opportunities and marshal the necessary resources to exploit these opportunities for personal gain (Bannock, Baxter and Davis, 2003). They also do so as a very exciting alternative to working for someone else.

In general, South Africans are not socialised or educated to become entrepreneurs, but rather to enter the labour market as employees. In this role they become consumers of existing jobs instead of creators of new jobs. This is still the trend, despite the very low labour-absorption capacity of the South African labour market, and the large number of unemployed and underemployed people among the economically active population.

Among those who become entrepreneurs, many do so because they cannot obtain employment in the formal sector of the economy. From this it is evident that many people who become entrepreneurs are not doing so because of a highly developed need to be successful businesspeople or to serve customers with innovative products and services; they start their own business in order to survive financially. Ligthelm (2005) shows in this regard that the second economy has become the entrepreneurial destination of many economically active South Africans who are not able to obtain jobs in the formal sector of the economy. He claims that informal businesses created by such entrepreneurs are the result of efforts to escape unemployment and poverty rather than 'the exploitation of a dynamic or prosperous business opportunity' (Ligthelm, 2005).

The aim of this chapter is to give a clearer idea of the development and characteristics of entrepreneurs. The chapter begins with a brief overview of the historical development of entrepreneurs followed by a discussion around developing a culture of entrepreneurship. The entrepreneurial mindset as well as the

---

ENTREPRENEURIAL DILEMMA

Entrepreneurs versus managers

Many companies have risen to be the brand name of the year. Others promise to deliver the best service or to be the most customer-orientated. Yet if and when the founder leaves the business, it often does not do so well anymore. Why is this?

Businesses start with a solution to a problem. The business starts to grow and matures. The founders then leave the business in the hands of capable managers. Examples include Apple and Starbucks. The founder of Apple, Steve Jobs, had to return to revive the company. Chairman Howard Schultz returned to Starbucks as CEO, explaining that 'Starbucks has lost its edge, evolving from a culture of entrepreneurship, creativity, and innovation to a culture of mediocrity and bureaucracy'.

The lesson that can be learned here is to 'never lose focus of what your customer wants'. It seems true that once the entrepreneurial mind leaves the business, the company results are usually predictable.

Source: Donnelly (2008).

successful characteristics and typical risks associated with entrepreneurs will also be discussed. The chapter ends with a list of sources that can be explored for further information about great entrepreneurs.

2.1 History of entrepreneurship

According to Mayo and Hausler (2014) the history of product innovation and entrepreneurship can be divided into three stages, namely:
▸ Product-oriented or technology-pushed stage
▸ Market-led stage
▸ Dual-drive stage

In the post-World War II era Americans were coming off wartime shortages and were in the mood to buy the many goods that manufacturers produced. Engineers, who were more product oriented than consumer oriented, designed new products that might or might not find places in consumers' hearts and minds. This was a product-oriented process in which

the market was considered the receptacle for products that emerged from the firm's research and development efforts.

However, competition escalated and consumers became more sceptical and selective about the types of products they purchased. Marketers found it increasingly difficult to rely on persuasive sales techniques to move products. Retailers grew restless when these products did not move off shelves as quickly as planned. Companies had to know more about their target markets. What were the wants and needs of the people who were buying their products? How could their firm satisfy these wants and needs?

The second stage was marked by the emergence of the market as the driver of innovation. Instead of being technology-driven, new product development evolved into a market-led process in which new products emerged from well-researched customer needs. The new product development process was placed in the hands of marketers who knew consumers' wants and needs. Customer demand 'pulled' the product through the development process.

Modern new product development is a blending of these two orientations into a 'dual-drive' approach to innovation. Companies recognise that innovation is a complex process that requires sound investment in research and development, as well as significant marketing expertise that focuses on satisfying consumers' wants and needs.

The rapid pace of change that engulfed businesses toward the end of the twentieth century put an even greater burden on companies to build adaptive capabilities into their organisations. Global competition means there are more competitors capable of world-class performance. This has made competition more intense, rigorous, and aggressive than ever before (Mayo and Hausler, 2014).

2.2 Developing an entrepreneurship culture in South Africa

Every country, including South Africa, has a core group, or base, of high-impact entrepreneurs – that is entrepreneurs who are successful and have an impact on the South African and global economies. How a country supports, celebrates, and develops that 'base' determines its culture of entrepreneurship and ultimately, the future of its economy (Fal, Sefolo, Williams, Herringtong, Goldberg and Klaasen, 2009).

South African society does not appear to support entrepreneurs who have failed. People disassociate themselves from them, banks shut them down and the press demonises them. This culture, as can be expected, is not conducive to fostering greater entrepreneurial activity and should thus be confronted.

An important component of peoples' desire for free enterprise is determined by whether they view, consciously or unconsciously, wealth as being finite or infinite. When people look at wealth as being infinite they tend to look for opportunities to create more wealth for themselves and others around them. They will look for creative and innovative ways to develop products and services to be able to increase their wealth. People looking at wealth as being finite will tend to focus their energy on gaining access to the finite riches and look at the world as consisting of '*haves*' and '*have nots*' in which they want to be part of the '*haves*'. South Africa has both and should focus on fostering the first type of people (Fat, et al., 2009). Unfortunately corporate careers are still more desirable in South African society where mathematics and science academic achievements and corporate careers are still honoured more than success as an entrepreneur.

Fal, et al. (2009) furthermore indicates that as South Africans seek to develop a culture of entrepreneurship, they need to build on pre-existing values and behaviours rather than try to emulate foreign habits and beliefs regardless of what the local norms are. Local entrepreneurial ventures and entrepreneurs should be used to develop local norms and values that potential entrepreneurs can follow.

Entrepreneurship is the answer to the many social ills South Africa faces right now, and the longer it takes to imbed a wider and deeper culture of entrepreneurship the greater the danger will be that the painfully gained South African democracy will fail. Some of the reasons mentioned in the study for the gap between men and women in entrepreneurship are women's propensities to: want to spend more time with their families, want to avoid the stress of employing too many people, have less education, and experience more difficulty accessing capital due to marriage contract formulations (Fal, et al., 2009).

Developing an entrepreneurial culture in South Africa will contribute towards an increase of entrepreneurial activities. Small business growth has often been linked to economic growth, the creation of employment and the alleviation of poverty. South Africa can learn from the experience of other countries to foster its own culture of entrepreneurship: celebrating role models, promoting an effective venture capital and private equity community, providing structures for entrepreneurial education and skills-support. However, local norms must also be taken into account.

SOUTH AFRICAN SUCCESS STORY

Inner City Ideas Cartel
Schuyler Vorster started Inner City Ideas Cartel (ICIC) in the inner city of Cape Town, which offers scalable offices and co-working spaces for the entrepreneur who needs an environment that is conducive to productivity and opportunity by encouraging the presence of like-minded people.

Vorster indicates that the need for this type of space exceeded his expectations. Within the first three months of starting the ICIC, all the available spaces were booked out and he ended with 60 names on a waiting list. The working space is available on request and can be rented for as long as the entrepreneur needs it – whether for an hour, a day, a week, month or longer.

Vorster said that he wants to bring people together that can offer each other support and business opportunities while promoting productivity. The majority of entrepreneurs renting space are between the ages of 24 and 40 years.

According to Vorster offices like ICIC exists all over the world and are popping up all over Cape Town and he is planning to expand due to the growing demand.

To what extent do you think Schuyler Vorster contributes to the development of an entrepreneurial culture in Cape Town?

Source: Brand-Jonker, 2014.

2.3 Entrepreneurial mindset

In order to cope with the trials and tribulations that pave the entrepreneurial journey, entrepreneurs must have an innate frustration at normality and a strong belief that they can offer beneficial products and services to society (Fal, et al., 2009). Regardless of how hard you endeavour, no form of success happens overnight. Whether it is in your studies, being employed or establishing your own business, it takes hard work, commitment and relentless self-evaluation and self-improvement. Most of the truly successful entrepreneurs will astound you with their stories of the road to success. Imagine trying, unsuccessfully for 9 999 times before eventually succeeding! Does it sound crazy? Well, just thank Thomas Edison for his perseverance for the comfort we can now experience due to light bulbs. Most of these famous entrepreneurs are actually ordinary people who have used their minds in extraordinary ways. Acquiring an **entrepreneurial mindset** on your path to entrepreneurship is vital to the success of your venture.

DEFINITION

What exactly is an entrepreneurial mindset? An entrepreneurial mindset can be defined as: 'A specific state of mind which orientates human conduct towards entrepreneurial activities and outcomes. Individuals with entrepreneurial mindsets are often drawn to opportunities, innovation and new value creation'.

Although there are many different opinions on how to aptly define the entrepreneurial mindset, according to Pettit (2009) the underlying theme always remains the same. It represents individuals who actively seek to improve their way of thinking and apply it to new opportunities. Actually, it is the primary difference between people who are self-employed and those who are true entrepreneurs.

This might sound like six of the one and half a dozen of the other, but business owners definitely fall into two separate categories 1) those that are self-employed and 2) those who are entrepreneurs (Pettit, 2009).

Individuals who are self-employed are the people with talent or skill, who realise that there are people who are willing to pay for their expertise. So they employ themselves rather than work for someone else. They get business cards, stationery, possibly an office. They begin marketing their services and after a while they have some customers. After a while, they find themselves working too many hours, constantly trying to fill the pipeline with new prospects, and sometimes wondering if they've bought themselves a glorified job. They can't take too much time off because without them there is no business or income (Pettit, 2009). Even franchisees, who have the support of a proven system, can find themselves in this category. Certainly many home-based businesses, consultants, coaches, info-preneurs and service professionals end up on this treadmill. We're talking about talented professionals – people who, like you, work hard and deserve success! Unfortunately, a majority of business owners fall into this category.

Figure 2.1 The entrepreneur's line of thinking

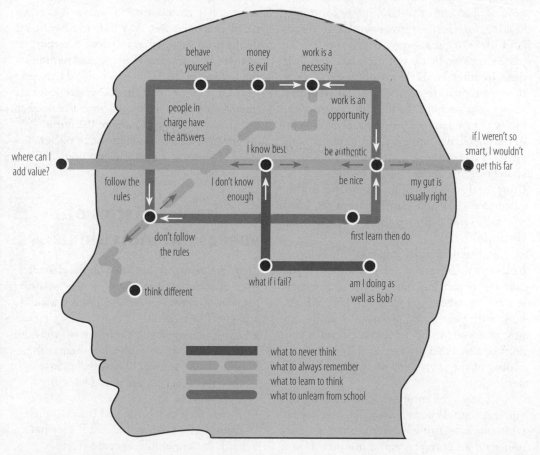

Source: Adams, 2012.

The entrepreneurs, on the other hand, are the business owners who seem to grow their businesses effortlessly, and maintain steady growth (Pettit, 2009). You talk to them and although they work hard, they make time to spend with their family or are off for a three-day weekend at the beach or somewhere in the bushveld. They even make time for a vacation somewhere in South Africa or even overseas. They do charity work and participate in activities with their family or friends. What do they know that the self-employed do not?

They have gained the entrepreneurial mindset. According to Pettit (2009) an entrepreneur is a great strategist and a master at getting others excited about helping them grow their business. They know they need to develop multiple profit centres in their business, not just one or two, so they're constantly looking for creative opportunities to do so. And some of those profit centres need to be passive income that is not dependent on their time. In other words they're not always selling time for money. In addition, the entrepreneur knows how to make the most of every opportunity to bring in new prospects, convert them to paying clients, and get them to buy repeatedly. That means carefully planning, strategising, measuring results against expectations and re-adjusting. It means taking calculated risks and learning from the ideas that fail – and there are always ideas that fail (Pettit, 2009).

An entrepreneurial mindset can be compared to travelling with public transport. If you take the wrong bus route, you will obviously not end up where you planned to be. It is the same with your thinking. If you continuously program your mind to think a certain way, don't be altogether too surprised if you keep on ending at the same (not where you planned) destination.

Of course, the entrepreneurial mindset and entrepreneurial characteristics are two inseparable concepts. Entrepreneurial characteristics underpin an entrepreneurial mindset. If you

EXAMPLE 2.1

How do your characteristics influence your thinking? For example – if you are optimistic, how do your thoughts and actions differ from those who are pessimistic?

have certain characteristics, you are bound to think a certain way.

There is a lot of discussion (and confusion) surrounding the characteristics of people who are considered entrepreneurs versus those who are considered non-entrepreneurs. However, there is no 'foolproof recipe' that separates entrepreneurs from non-entrepreneurs. It isn't a checklist that you can go through and automatically expect success as an entrepreneur. The same is true for any other occupation. To be successful in any occupation, you need a certain set of characteristics. Any individual with the desire to be successful must have a certain set of characteristics. Therefore, instead of limiting the following characteristics only to entrepreneurs, it is argued that these characteristics are important to any individual with the need to be successful and to rise above the norm.

The next section outlines the characteristics most often associated with entrepreneurs.

2.4 Characteristics of successful individuals

There are many lists available on the characteristics of entrepreneurs. Therefore the following list is by no means exhaustive, but it is accurate and apt (Duffy, 2012):

▶ *Passion*. They absolutely love what they do; it energises them and makes them come alive. It doesn't feel like work, because they feel that they are doing what they were born to do.

▶ *Belief*. Their self-belief and belief in their ideas enables them to succeed. They have faith in their ability to succeed and proceed when others doubt their ideas.

They believe they can make it work and never allow their circumstances to place a limit on their potential.

▸ *Courage.* They have the courage to take on new challenges, to follow their instincts and to go boldly where no one has gone before.

▸ *Determination.* Highly successful entrepreneurs have great determination. They are determined to make their ideas work, no matter how difficult. They are determined to nurture their ideas and watch them flourish.

▸ *Instinct.* They are good at making decisions, tuning into their gut feeling and weighing up consequences in a heartbeat. The more decisions they make, the better they become at decision making.

▸ *Calculated risk taking.* They are prepared to take risks and step outside their comfort zone to get what they want. Interestingly, a lot of their decisions are calculated risks.

▸ *Vision.* They begin with a dream of what they really want to achieve and they set clear goals and objectives. From that, they strategise, plan and act on what they want to achieve. They inspire others to focus on achieving results.

▸ *Discipline.* They are brilliant at getting things done and this takes commitment, hard work and dedication. They get up early, work late and never give up until they get what they want.

▸ *Resiliency.* They have failed in the past and they know that they will fail again in the future. They are not afraid of it. They have learned great lessons from their failures.

They turn the situation around to make it work for them. In fact, other innovations can even emerge from failures.

▸ *Adapt.* They are early adapters and quick to respond to changes that affect their business. They are not afraid of change, not afraid to adapt to unforeseen circumstances. They understand that change is a certainty and face whatever life throws at them with courage and hope.

▸ *Inspire.* They motivate and inspire others to achieve results. They recognise and nurture talents and qualities in others.

▸ *Learn.* They are always willing to learn and invest in their own personal development. They attend seminars, network and rub minds with like minds. They seek out others who share their passions and build relationships with people who support and encourage them. They have great mentors and coaches and work on ways to continually improve. They grow daily, and never fail to make use of every opportunity.

▸ *Internal locus of control.* This implies that entrepreneurs have a stronger desire to be in control of their own fate. They believe that their actions have consequences and they are in control of their own behaviour.

▸ *Need to achieve.* The need to achieve can emerge in various ways: high energy levels to chase goals, confidence that success will be achieved, and a clear measurement of success.

▸ *Need for autonomy.* This is the need of an individual to be independent and to do things 'their way'.

ENTREPRENEURIAL DILEMMA

It is often said that an entrepreneur needs to have the right qualities and characteristics to make a success of his or her business. Do you think that this is true? How many of the characteristics of highly successful entrepreneurs do you identify in yourself? Are there some you feel are stronger than others? Are there any of the characteristics of highly successful entrepreneurs that you would like to further develop?

However, one would like to shorten the list and that is perhaps why Bygrave and Zacharakis (2011:95) identified what they called the *10 Ds* which, according to them, represents the most important characteristics of successful entrepreneurs. These 10 Ds are:

▸ *Dream.* Entrepreneurs have a vision of what the future could be like for them and their businesses. And, more importantly,

Table 2.1 Test for locus of control

TEST FOR LOCUS OF CONTROL			
1	When things go right do you assign it to 'good luck'?	Yes	No
2	Do you believe in the saying 'where there is a will there is a way'?	Yes	No
3	Do you often feel that you have no say in what it is that you want to do?	Yes	No
4	Do you think that you have to start a business because everybody thinks it is the right thing to do due to low employment levels in SA?	Yes	No
5	If you have failed at a task do you pass the blame?	Yes	No
6	Are you the kind that will try something new even though it is scary?	Yes	No
7	When you do a job well is your pleasure in a job well done satisfaction enough?	Yes	No
8	Even though people tell you 'it cannot be done', do you have to find out for yourself?	Yes	No
9	Do you think it is important for everyone to like you?	Yes	No
10	If you want something do you go for it or do you wait for someone to give it to you?	Yes	No

Source: Adapted from Hisrich and Peters (2002:67).

Table 2.2: Test for risk taking

TEST FOR RISK TAKING			
1	Do you like to gamble?	Yes	No
2	If you are afraid of bungee jumping will you still attempt it?	Yes	No
3	Do you need to know the answer before you will ask a question?	Yes	No
4	Do you like to try new products or restaurants?	Yes	No
5	Have you done something risky in the last six months?	Yes	No
6	Will you only attempt something if someone else has successfully done it before?	Yes	No
7	Can you walk up to a total stranger and strike up a conversation?	Yes	No
8	When driving will you take an alternative road just to see what is there?	Yes	No
9	Do you take water and a jersey with you whenever you travel?	Yes	No
10	Have you ever arrived at a party uninvited?	Yes	No

Source: Adapted from Hisrich and Peters (2002:69).

they have the ability to implement their dreams.

▶ *Decisiveness.* They don't procrastinate. They make decisions swiftly. Their swiftness is a key factor in their success.

▶ *Doers.* Once they decide on a course of action, they implement it as quickly as possible.

▶ *Determination.* They implement their ventures with total commitment. They seldom give up, even when confronted by obstacles that seem insurmountable.

▶ *Dedication.* They are totally dedicated to their businesses, sometimes at considerable cost to their relationships with friends and families. They work tirelessly. Twelve-hour days and seven-day workweeks are not uncommon when an entrepreneur is striving to get a business off the ground.

▸ *Devotion.* Entrepreneurs love what they do. It is that love that sustains them when the going gets tough. And it is love of their product or service that makes them so effective at selling it.

▸ *Details.* It is said that the devil resides in the details. That is never truer than in starting and growing a business. The entrepreneur must be on top of the critical details.

▸ *Destiny.* They want to be in charge of their own destiny rather than dependent on an employer.

▸ *Dollars.* Getting rich is not the prime motivator of entrepreneurs. Money is more a measure of success. Entrepreneurs assume that if they are successful they will be rewarded.

▸ *Distribute.* Entrepreneurs distribute the ownership of their businesses with key employees who are critical to the success of the business.

The great thing about this lies in the fact that all characteristics are actually strengths or weaknesses – and strengths and weaknesses are completely under the control of the entrepreneur. If you lack some of the characteristics typically centred in entrepreneurs, it is under your control to acquire or improve these characteristics!

However, if your characteristics are not necessarily the deciding factor on whether you will become an entrepreneur or not, what is? The answer lies in the influences of external factors on would-be entrepreneurs.

The impact of the market and macro environment on the entrepreneur was already discussed in Chapter One and these factors have a major impact on the startup and success of any entrepreneurial venture. But there are several additional factors to pay attention to on the way to entrepreneurship. These factors are referred to as the background of entrepreneurs. The importance of these background factors is that they shape our thinking and the way in which we view the world. This in turn has a significant impact on our characteristics.

> **ENTREPRENEURIAL DILEMMA**
>
> Are you a risk taker or not? How was this influenced by you family environment or work history?

> **ENTREPRENEURIAL DILEMMA**
>
> How many close friends do you have? Do they have additional friends with whom they perhaps share one class or a hobby? A successful entrepreneur taps into even the widest networks to promote the business or to lobby support.

2.5 The risks to the entrepreneur

Few, if any, entrepreneurs have escaped failure and, apart from risking money, they also risk their reputation. Successful entrepreneurs only take calculated risks and are, therefore, not gamblers who will risk everything for the chance of success. They are willing to take risks, but calculate the risk carefully and thoroughly, and will do everything possible to avoid failure. When getting together an entrepreneurial team of co-founders and shareholders, entrepreneurs persuade others to share inherent financial and business risks with them. Creditors and customers are also included, since they might advance credit and payments.

Kuratko (2010) lists a number of critical risk areas (identified by Liles, 1974 and Vinturella, 2006) that are referred to as 'the dark side of entrepreneurship'. These are summarised in Figure 2.2 and described below.

2.5.1 Financial risk

When deciding to start a venture, the entrepreneur often does not know the outcome. Money is invested in the business. Good financial decisions need to be made and good cash-flow management practices need to be followed to minimise financial risk and financial pitfalls. Financial pitfalls, when your business is doing

EXAMPLE 2.2

Background factors that influence entrepreneurs

Various studies have been conducted on what background factors play a role in the success of entrepreneurs in starting and managing an entrepreneurial venture. The following background factors seem to contribute to the success of most of the high-impact entrepreneurs:

1. Family environment

   Children often follow in the footsteps of their parents. It is common to hear children boast about becoming the best lawyer on earth or the kindest doctor ever after they have seen dad successfully arguing a big case or mom caringly tend to a patient. The same goes for the children of entrepreneurs. They see the long hours and hard work, but they definitely also note the freedom of being your own boss and being in charge of what happens.

2. Education

   Although there are many people that argue that education crushes creativity, the bottom line remains that you will operate in an environment that constantly changes, is filled with ruthless competition, changing economic situations and technological capabilities. If you do not have the necessary knowledge to successfully negotiate terms with a supplier or to analyse the latest economic trends, be ready to pay big salaries to people who can.

3. Age

   Typically the age at which men tend to start an entrepreneurial venture is between 25 and 35 and for woman it is between the ages of 30 and 45. It is reasonable to assume that individuals between the ages of 25 and 30 have obtained a tertiary education and therefore feel empowered to take on the world in terms of establishing their own venture. At the age of 35, most men have not yet started a family and therefore they experience more financial freedom – not only in the sense of the expenses of raising children, but also in terms of not endangering the future of young children with the possible failure of a business venture.

   However, there are many people who start their first ventures while they are still at school, or as first-year students at higher education institutions. Thus it seems regardless of your age, the most important thing is to be aware of opportunities when they come by and not be intimidated by a young age.

4. Working history

   Entrepreneurs quite often have some working experience as a salaried employee in the field of their venture. It always helps to learn a little about business and the industry before putting your money in. This enables you to identify the mistakes that other people make or areas in which you can improve when you venture into this industry with your own money and time.

5. Family and professional contacts

   Family contacts could entail anything from the rich uncle with an open wallet to the aunt who has years of experience in the industry you want to venture into to the niece who is a rep and has a lot of contacts for you. The support that you get from your family and friends when things go wrong or the accolade you receive from people who are genuinely proud of you is a great source of inspiration.

   Professional contacts represent the network into which you can tap to get full access to every possible person who can help you make a success of your venture. The successful entrepreneur does not only consult his or her own network contacts, but makes contact with the networks of every person that they meet.

Figure 2.2 Risks impacting on entrepreneurship

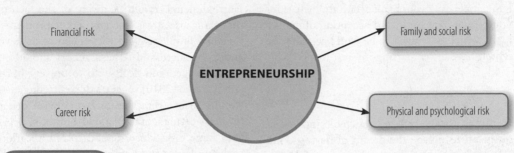

EXAMPLE 2.3

Discover if you have the mindset of an entrepreneur with this assessment from the Small Business Administration. Not only will it help you evaluate your readiness, but it also will help you identify if you have the personality, characteristics and skills to go out on your own.

Questions to ask yourself

▶ Have you ever worked in a business similar to what you are planning to start?
▶ Would people who know you say you are well-suited to be self-employed?
▶ Do you have support for your business idea from your family and friends?
▶ Have you ever taken a course or seminar on starting and managing a small business?
▶ Have you discussed your business idea, business plan or proposed business with a business coach or counsellor, such as a faculty advisor, SCORE counsellor, Small Business Development Centre counsellor or other economic advisor?
▶ Do you have a relative, friend or mentor who is an entrepreneur?

Evaluate your personality characteristics

The more questions you answer favourably, the more prepared you are mentally to begin.

▶ Are you a self-promoter?
▶ Are you a self-starter?
▶ Do you plan and organise well?
▶ Can you handle pressure?
▶ Are you comfortable with risk?
▶ Are you physically healthy?
▶ Can you work with opposite personalities?
▶ Are you passionate about your product or service?
▶ Is your drive strong enough?
▶ Are you encouraged by setbacks/challenges?

▶ Are you competitive?
▶ Are you optimistic?
▶ Can you handle criticism well?
▶ Are you patient?
▶ Are you decisive?
▶ Have you considered how the business will impact on your family and if you have their support?

Trait similarities of successful entrepreneurs

How many traits do you have?

▶ Persistence
▶ Desire for immediate feedback
▶ Inquisitiveness
▶ Strong drive to achieve
▶ High energy level
▶ Goal-oriented behaviour
▶ Independent
▶ Demanding
▶ Self-confident
▶ Calculated risk taker
▶ Creative
▶ Innovative
▶ Vision
▶ Commitment
▶ Problem-solving skills
▶ Tolerance for ambiguity
▶ Strong integrity
▶ Highly reliable
▶ Personal initiative
▶ Ability to consolidate resources
▶ Strong management and organisational skills
▶ Competitive
▶ Change agent
▶ Tolerance for failure
▶ Desire to work hard
▶ Luck

Source: Bienkowski, 2013.

well, include: accepting loan options from your bank, increasing your bank overdraft, increasing your credit card limit, and accepting offers for loans which only need to be paid back later or which have lower starting interest rates.

2.5.2 Career risk

At times a stable job with a stable income is given up to pursue the dream of having one's own business. The entrepreneur is removed from the formal employment sector. Should the business fail, formal employment becomes a problem as the re-employed entrepreneur will then need to start from the bottom again to build a career. Having been autonomous, it is often difficult for the re-employed entrepreneur to adjust to being managed and to following instructions, policies and procedures.

2.5.3 Family and social risk

Entrepreneurs also face a family and social risk. Starting a new venture brings uncertainty for the family. Sacrifices needs to be made in terms of time, money available, holidays and at times the family relocates to start the new venture. Social alienation may result, as the new entrepreneur finds himself or herself working long hours and even weekends. If these concerns are not dealt with upfront, strain is placed on the entrepreneur and the support of family and friends might dwindle as the entrepreneur focuses on dealing with hardships while building the business.

2.5.4 Physical and psychological risk

Entrepreneurs also put themselves at physical and psychological risk. Due to the long hours entrepreneurs allocate to their business, entrepreneurs often do not make time to eat healthily and to exercise regularly. Physical and psychological health is vital to enable the entrepreneur to take care of both day-to-day and long-term business concerns, and is important to the long-term survival of the business as well as the long-term wealth of the family. Entrepreneurs should be aware of the factors that can cause stress (such as people problems, financial problems, and their need to achieve and to be successful). These factors should be acknowledged and dealt with to prevent burn out. Kuratko (2010) suggests that entrepreneurs should ensure that they network with other business owners, take planned holidays, delegate some tasks, ensure good communication with employees and family members, and exercise regularly and eat healthily.

CONCLUSION

Entrepreneurs are influenced by their environments. Whether it is the economic situation of South Africa, a new competitor in the market or the environment in which they were raised, it has an enormous effect on the entrepreneur. Just as some individuals are natural athletes due to their family background, entrepreneurs are also very much influenced by their background. Our families and the experiences we have in life shape and mould us into becoming the adults that we finally are. Does this mean it is impossible for someone to become an entrepreneur if neither of their parents were entrepreneurs? Not at all! Perhaps they saw an amazing opportunity for change in their current employment. Certain events in life push us into a direction that we might not have considered previously, but regardless of where life takes you, you need the right characteristics for the right situation. Even if you are delivered to the doorstep of an excellent opportunity, if you do not have the passion or commitment to explore the opportunity, nothing will come of it. Therefore your background and characteristics need to link to finally form a true entrepreneur!

SELF-ASSESSMENT QUESTIONS

1. Describe what you understand by the term 'internal locus of control'. Why is this characteristic important for entrepreneurs?
2. List and discuss the various risks that entrepreneurship entails.
3. Do you think that the age of an individual really has such a big impact on whether that person becomes an entrepreneur or not? Motivate your answer.

DISCUSSION QUESTIONS

1. List the characteristics that are essential for entrepreneurship. Which three of these do you think is the most important? Motivate your answer.
2. How does the background of entrepreneurs influence them? For each of the factors mentioned in the chapter, indicate how that impacts on the entrepreneur.
3. What do you think has the biggest impact on entrepreneurs – their background factors or their characteristics? There is no right or wrong answer, your motivation to your answer is key!
4. Which of the risks to entrepreneurship would deter you from considering entrepreneurship as a career option? How do you think this risk can be minimised or overcome?

EXPERIENTIAL EXERCISES

1. Go through the list of questions in Example 2.3 above and answer each of these questions. Discuss your answers with your friends – do they think your perception of your own entrepreneurial abilities is correct? Do you have what it takes to become an entrepreneur?
2. In conjunction with Question 1, identify the characteristics that you possess. When considering entrepreneurship as a career, are these characteristics strengths or weaknesses?
3. Think of a well-known person that you admire regardless of whether they are sport stars or TV personalities. Why do you admire this person? What characteristics do they have that enabled them to achieve success? Can these characteristics relate to entrepreneurship?
4. Do you think we can use our background as an 'excuse' for not achieving success? Consult all the theory in this chapter before you answer this question and thoroughly motivate your answer.
5. In your opinion, why do you think our surroundings play such a vital role in our lives? What is the perception of entrepreneurs in your community and in our society? Do you think the perception of the community will have a big impact on entrepreneurial intentions? Why or why not?

CAPSICUM CULINARY STUDIO TURNS 10

Cheryl Nesbitt started Capsicum Culinary Studio in 2003 in Cape Town with only four students and today, Capsicum Culinary Studio proudly boasts a national footprint. These include six campuses at major centres in South Africa: Cape Town, Durban, Johannesburg, Pretoria, Boksburg and Port Elizabeth.

Cheryl studied hotel management at the Witwatersrand Hotel School in Johannesburg and gained eight years of hotel experience at the Protea Hotel Group. She left the Protea Hotel Group in 1991 as a deputy general manager to start Country Catering, an extremely successful events management and catering company. After seven years, Cheryl sold the business and ventured into the world of training and education. She used this experience in starting Capsicum Culinary Studio.

While many entrepreneurs grow their businesses organically, and surprise themselves by where they end up, this is not what Cheryl did. She used her experience to plan, research and create a vision of what she wanted to achieve. A combination of goal-setting, careful planning and comprehensive research, together with a natural entrepreneurial flair and eye for opportunity, have helped Cheryl to discover an unmet need for a reasonably priced and reasonable time-commitment cooking

CASE STUDY

school. She's nothing if not thorough and set about conducting comprehensive market research on hotel management schools, drawing a comparative analysis between them and the chef training schools. The exercise gave her important insight into the market demands in each sector by using two criteria for choosing a school: accreditation and price. She plotted all of the schools that existed on a graph with these two axes and found that there was a huge gap in the market for a competitively priced chef school that was properly accredited.

Today, Capsicum has more local and international accreditations and associations than any other chef training institute in South Africa and has obtained a national presence with a R13 million turnover in just five years after start-up.

At the time of the start-up Cheryl had four students ready to enrol and had just a few short months to find and stock the premises so that Capsicum could open its doors as a fully equipped chef training college in January of 2004. She borrowed R60 000 from her parents, R60 000 from a friend and cashed in her provident fund of R30 000 and her husband's insurance policy of R20 000. They found premises in Cape Town but because they were so inexperienced, they ended up spending R40 000 on renovations. She learned from this experience and now gets landlords to pay for those types of changes and upgrades. The work paid off and lectures started on 26 January 2004.

As is the case with many growing businesses, it was in opening a second branch that Cheryl learned an important lesson. Flush with the profit from her two training ventures, she opened the Johannesburg school in July which ended up being a mistake. The main reason was that most potential students are inclined to start their studies in January, not many start in the middle of the year.

The company sank its funds into setting up the new branch, but didn't get the student intake it had anticipated. It then battled with overall cash flow during that year – especially the first six months of operating the Johannesburg school. To help the business through this difficult period, Cheryl sold her house and invested R1 million into Capsicum. She also learned from her mistake; since then, all new branches open in January.

And although the business model has remained the same over this time and Cheryl has made certain changes in line with the company's growth, of which costing is just one. Cheryl indicated that they were very cheap in the first year but that it served their purpose because they were new and needed to attract students and build up credibility. However part of Capsicum's vision has always been to remain affordable which it manages to maintain as they are still the most affordable private chef school in South Africa.

Cheryl's advice to aspirant entrepreneurs is that networking can make all the difference to their business and that they should find the time to meet other people, even if it's the last thing they think they have time for. Being an entrepreneur can be very lonely and involvement in various organisations and networks can help to find solutions to common entrepreneurial problems.

In addition, it provides a network of professionals they can trust and who they can even call on for advice.

She says that entrepreneurs should invest in training – for their staff and for themselves. She also advises entrepreneurs to focus on strategic planning and to know what they want to achieve, to conduct research and develop a plan and then work on this plan.

Source: Developed from documents on the website of Capsicum Culinary Studio. [Online]. Available: http://www. entrepreneurmag.co.za/advice/success-stories/case-studies/capsicum-culinary-studio-cheryl-nesbitt/, http://www. capsicumcooking.com/home/articles/celebrating-10-years-in-culinary-education and http://www.capsicumcooking.com/ capsicum-heritage [3 March 2014].

1. What entrepreneurial characteristics does Cheryl display? Motivate your answer.
2. What factors from Cheryl's background influenced her in this case study? Motivate your answer.

3. Critically discuss the critical risk areas that Cheryl has to evaluate.

SUGGESTED WEBSITE LINKS

http://eu.wiley.com/WileyCDA/WileyTitle/productCd-EHEP001747.html

http://growvisibilitywithme.com/entrepreneurial-mindset/

http://www.inc.com/michael-gerber/traits-of-a-truly-entrepreneurial-mindset.html

REFERENCES

Adams, D. 2012. *How To Develop An Entrepreneurial Mindset*. [Online]. Available: http://www.bitrebels.com/business-2/develop-an-entrepreneurial-mindset/ [14 August 2013].

Allen, KR. 2010. *Launching New Ventures*. 5th ed. Boston: Houghton Mifflin.

Bannock, G, Baxter, RE. & Davis, E. 2003. *The Penguin Dictionary of Economics*. London: Penguin.

Bienkowski, S. 2013. *Quiz: Do you have the entrepreneurial mindset?* [Online]. Available: http://www.success.com/article/quiz-do-you-have-the-entrepreneurial-mindset [3 September 2013].

Brand-Jonker, N. 2014. Werkneste open vir Entrepreneurs. Hier broei koel idees uit. *Die Burger*, 5 Februarie 2014. [Online]. Available: http://www.dieburger.com/sake/2014-02-05-hier-broei-koel-idees-uit [15 February 2014].

Bygrave, W. & Zacharakis, A. 2011. *Entrepreneurship*. 2nd ed. Hoboken, NJ: John Willey & Sons, Inc.

Donnelly, B. 2008. The CEO's entrepreneurial dilemma. [Online]. Available: http://www.paramuschamber.com/documents/TheCEOsEntrepreneurialDilemma.pdf [28 February 2011].

Duffy, S. 2012. *12 Characteristics of a Highly Successful Entrepreneurial Mindset*. [Online]. Available: http://www.greatmindsinspire.com/archives/67 [20 August 2013].

Fal, M, Sefolo, T, Williams, A, Herringtong, M, Goldberg, J. & Klaasen, M. (Eds). 2009. *The Entrepreneurial Dialogues: State of entrepreneurship in South Africa*. [Online]. Available: http://www.sabkickstart.net/index.php/forum/thought-leadership/108-dialogues.html [3 March 2014].

Hisrich, RD. & Peters, PM. 2002. *Entrepreneurship*. 5th ed. New York: McGraw-Hill.

Kuratko, DF. & Hornsby, JS. 2009. *New Venture Management: The Entrepreneur's Roadmap*. New Jersey: Pearson Education.

Ligthelm, AA. 2005. *Measuring the Size of the Informal Sector in South Africa*. Pretoria: UNISA.

Mayo, CM. & (revised by) Hausler, D. 2014. *New Product Development*. [Online]. Available: http://www.referenceforbusiness.com/management/Mar-No/New-Product-Development.htm. [3 March 2014].

Pettit, J. 2009. *The entrepreneurial mindset*. [Online]. Available: http://www.smallbusiness-bigresults.com/entrepreneurial-mindset.htm. [March 2014].

Porter, ME. 1990. *Competitive Advantage of Nations*. New York: Free Press.

part two

The entrepreneurial process

CHAPTER 3

Creativity and generating new business ideas

Isa van Aardt & Clinton Massyn

LEARNING OUTCOMES

On completion of this chapter you will be able to:
▸ Describe creativity and how it manifests itself
▸ Understand the myths surrounding creativity as well as the reality about these myths
▸ Identify the barriers to creativity and how they can be overcome
▸ Understand the creative process and its development, and describe the entrepreneurial creative process
▸ Identify and use the sources that can be utilised when identifying new product or service ideas
▸ Perform the initial screening of business ideas and opportunities.

OPENING CASE STUDY

The entrepreneurship process is a complex endeavour carried out by people living in specific cultural and social conditions. For this reason, the positive or negative perceptions that society has about entrepreneurship can strongly influence the motivation of people to enter into entrepreneurship. Societies benefit from people who are able to recognise valuable business opportunities and who perceive that they have the required skills to exploit them. If the economy in general has a positive attitude towards entrepreneurship, this can generate cultural and social support, financial and business assistance, and networking benefits that will encourage and facilitate potential and existing entrepreneurs (Xavier, et al., 2012:18).

1. Do you agree with the statement that entrepreneurship is a complex endeavour? Why do you say that?
2. What effect do you think a negative attitude of the economy in general towards entrepreneurship will have?

INTRODUCTION

Most aspiring entrepreneurs believe their initial idea and inspiration requires the most important creative thinking. Experienced entrepreneurs will tell you that the initial idea is the easy part, and that the implementation of the idea, the establishment of the venture and the competitive business marketing usually present the real creative challenges.

This chapter deals with creativity and the myths surrounding creativity. Creativity will be defined and the models of creativity will be discussed. The chapter will end with a discussion of some of the techniques that can be used for generating new business ideas. The next section will present a definition of creativity followed in this chapter.

3.1 Creativity

Creativity has various different definitions. For one person creativity means being artistic, for others it is the practical implementation of a workable idea. When the bicycle was first sold, it was seen as both creative and innovative. The same happened with cellphones, the Internet, even the way that houses are built. Every business starts with a dream that is converted to an idea and then implemented. The process of moving from the business dream to the implementation of that idea has certain common stages.

Tams (2002) describes creativity as being of the utmost importance to succeeding in the knowledge economy. In the knowledge economy, wealth is created by turning data into information, knowledge, and judgement. Whereas competitiveness in the industrial age was found in physical resources, such as coal, timber, or gold, in the knowledge economy, wealth is created by creativity (Tams, 2002). The rise of creativity as an economic force over the past few decades has brought new economic and social forms into existence and is still evolving (Florida, 2002:23).

3.1.1 Creativity defined

Providing a definition for **creativity** that will satisfy everyone is not an easy task. Perhaps Albert Einstein gave the most accurate description of creativity when he said: *'Creativity is seeing what everyone else has seen and thinking what no one else has thought'* (Trautmann, 2011).

Naiman (2014) describes creativity as the act of turning new and imaginative ideas into reality, which involves two processes: thinking, then producing. She furthermore indicated that innovation is the production or implementation of an idea and that if you have ideas, but do not act on them, you are imaginative but not creative (Naiman, 2014).

Franken (2007) defined creativity as 'the tendency to generate or recognize ideas, alternatives, or possibilities that may be useful in solving problems, communicating with others, and entertaining ourselves and others'.

These descriptions and definitions all have the same aspects in common:

▸ Looking at things differently – this includes generating new ideas, alternatives or solutions.
▸ Implementation – this is making the idea a reality by producing either a product or service.
▸ Addressing a gap – this could be a problem, customer need, etc.

⌐ DEFINITION ⌐

For the purposes of this book creativity is described as the process of developing and implementing ideas that are both novel and useful and address a gap in the market.

3.1.2 Addressing the market gap

When addressing the **market gap**, the entrepreneur should use various techniques such as:

▸ Defining or identifying the need using analytical methods to ensure precise

identification of the problem or need and even identifying a response to the need
▸ Transforming problems into opportunities that will help the entrepreneur to look at the problem or gap as an opportunity that can be addressed – this will aid the entrepreneur in the development of a business idea
▸ Breaking down any prior assumptions and making new connections for new ideas

▸ Strategic assessment where possible future outcomes must be predicted and all possible outcomes should be identified, so that the entrepreneur will be aware of possible threats as well as of solutions that lead to the most desirable results.

When using the above-mentioned techniques, the entrepreneur should not only use logic, but should also follow his or her intuition. Creativity is seen as the most important

SOUTH AFRICAN SUCCESS STORY

NQ Jewellery Design Services

Nqobile Nkosi is the proud owner of NQ Jewellery Design Services, the first black-owned jewellery manufacturing and retail business in Soweto. The business uses precious stones such as silver, gold, platinum and diamonds to manufacture jewellery.

Nqobile's journey in the jewellery manufacturing industry started in 2007 after he attended an 18-month training course in jewellery manufacturing and design. 'I started the business with the seed capital that I made by selling cakes, biscuits and soft drinks on the streets of Soweto. However, due to limited funds and equipment, when the business was established we mainly repaired jewellery and manufactured jewellery on a small scale', he says.

With the business loan that Nqobile acquired from the National Youth Development Agency (NYDA), he managed to purchase additional equipment and material and also used it for working capital. 'We also received immense assistance and donations from Paul Spurgeon Designs and the British jewellery trade members', Nqobile elaborates.

Nkosi and Spurgeon formed a partnership to launch the Cornerstone project. The Cornerstone project is aimed at empowering disadvantaged and marginalised people, primarily from the African continent.

Their lives were poles apart and yet their hearts and minds met. The coming together of these two people identified the huge need for work and dignity through gainful employment. It also highlighted the abundance of natural resources within this great continent that for so long had supplied the needs of the worldwide jewellery market and yet had eluded them for various reasons.

Plans were made to initiate a training and employment programme based on giving individuals the skills, dignity and income to survive the ravages of poverty. Then, early in 2010, the first ever jewellery shop was opened in the township of Soweto and Cornerstone was born. History was made!

Today the business has trained and employs four people in their Soweto workshop. Over the years the business has received numerous accolades such as, the Gauteng Business Leader of the Year Award in 2008, the Jet Community Regional and National Award in 2009 and the SAB Kick Start Award in 2012.

Source: Compiled from Dlamini (2012), Ngewu (2013), Weldon (2014), Paul Spurgeon (2013) and NYDA (2014).

ingredient in starting a new venture or creating new products and (or) services in existing businesses. An example of this is Nqobile Nkosi, who creates unique jewellery that is sold in the European market. Read Nkosi's success story – *NQ Jewellery Design Services*.

3.2 Myths and realities surrounding creativity

Most people think creativity is divinely inspired, unpredictable and bestowed on only a lucky few. **Myths** about creativity are misleading. One of the most popular myths is that only certain people can be creative. However, creativity is vital in business; far too important to be left to a special cadre of 'creative people'.

DEFINITION

A myth is a widely held, false belief or idea about an event or topic (Oxford Dictionary).

Burkus (2014) did extensive research on the myths of creativity and this research helps to demystify what is behind the forces and processes that drive innovation – a very important element of entrepreneurial ventures. Burkus (2014:6) indicates that we do not need to rely on belief in an outside force to generate great ideas. With the proper training, anyone with a common-sense mindset grounded in reality can deliver creative and innovative new ideas, projects, processes and programmes.

The myths and realities surrounding creativity are described in Table 3.1.

3.3 Barriers to creativity

When you ask a group of people 'How many of you are creative?' you seldom get a unanimous response. Many people are not creative simply because they do not regard themselves as being creative. As indicated in Table 3.1 below, a number of myths exist around this perception (Myths 1, 2 and 3), yet the reality of these myths is that all people are creative. The reason why the majority of us do not believe that we are creative is due to certain barriers that stand in the way of using our creative abilities. Some of these barriers have been developed in our environments, cultures, and even our education systems. The challenge is

Table 3.1 Myths surrounding creativity and the truths about these myths

MYTH	REALITY
Myth 1: Creativity is limited to a small number of people. In other words, most people don't want to be creative, couldn't do it if asked and would be very uncomfortable in an environment where creativity is expected of them.	Every human being is creative – by our very nature, every person is endowed with an incredible capacity for innovation, as we have an innate capability to evolve and adapt. Creativity depends on experience, knowledge, technical skills, talent, ability to think in new ways, and the capacity to punch through uncreative spells.
Myth 2: Only creative people always have good ideas.	Everybody has good ideas but few of us act on them – that's the difference! New venture ideas are usually a natural outgrowth of an individual's education, work experience and hobbies, and most entrepreneurs succeed by pursuing ideas that relate to their personal criteria and values. A person, who recognises social problems, addresses them and wants to do something practical to counter them, is something of an artist.

MYTH	REALITY
Myth 3: Creative people are born that way.	Creativity is a combination of knowledge, experience and even technical skills. Everybody can be creative.
Myth 4: Analytical thought and creative thought are fundamentally different.	New ideas often emerge from the juxtaposing of existing information in the parts of the brain that we associate with more 'rational' processing and analytical thought. Creativity can be the result of systematically assembling, analysing, and challenging data to develop new possibilities for the future.
Myth 5: Money is a creativity motivator.	Various research projects done on creativity suggest that money isn't everything and that rewarding creativity may lead to unhealthy competition among employees.
Myth 6: Time pressure fuels creativity.	Although high-pressure situations may lead to creative ideas from some people, relaxed situations and environments tend to spur ideas in the majority. Time pressure stifles creativity because people can't deeply engage with the problem. Creativity requires an incubation period; people need time to soak in a problem and let the ideas bubble up.
Myth 7: Creativity is about making great leaps of imagination.	The creative process relies on the ongoing, painstaking, development of fresh perspectives and the nurturing of initially small ideas in order to gradually create something significantly innovative.
Myth 8: Competitive situations foster creativity better than cooperative situations.	Competition causes lots of ideas to be generated and sometimes companies create an environment where the employee with the best idea is rewarded. While this method does work, it works for all the wrong reasons. By keeping ideas to themselves, employees don't allow ideas to be refined by anyone else's input. They just work silently on their own and hoard up ideas for the opportune moment. Collaboration gives an extra something to even the best ideas. Without it, the idea is limited by just one person's perspective. It could have been helped along by a few more minds.
Myth 9: There are plenty of ideas around – the important part is to put them into practice.	In fact, there are lots of ideas in the sense of impressions and thoughts that come to your mind. But generating a new and innovative idea is a totally different operation. These types of ideas or concepts are not easily available.
Myth 10: Fear forces breakthrough.	Creativity is positively associated with joy and love and negatively associated with anger, fear, and anxiety. People are happiest when they come up with a creative idea and are more likely to have a breakthrough if they were happy the day before.

Source: Adapted from Baumgartner (2005), Bishop (2005), Breen (2004), Burkhardt (2009), Faltin (2001), Florida (2002), Gilkey (2008), Tan (1998), Wasu (2010), Davies (2013) and Andrews, 2014.

not only in identifying these barriers, but also in suggesting ways in which these barriers can be overcome.

Table 3.2 below provides a list of **creativity barriers** and what can be done to overcome them.

Table 3.2 Barriers to creativity and strategies to overcome them

BARRIER	OVERCOMING STRATEGIES
Barrier 1: Fear of failure. This includes the fear of making a mistake or of taking risk. It could also be a desire for security and order and could become a resistance to change. People find security in the status quo as things are then more predictable.	Conduct the difficult experiments first and never be afraid to explore something new. Treat intuition as real. Develop an understanding of success by sharing your and others' visions.
Barrier 2: Negative beliefs and habits. This includes an inability to tolerate ambiguity, believing that creativity is only for others, only seeing the negative side of the economy, and the tendency to focus on the negative aspects of problems and to expend energy on worry.	Some people seem naturally creative and some uncreative. Most people are in reality quite capable of being creative by developing creativity techniques through training in creativity skills, such as lateral thinking, mind mapping and creative problem solving. Develop the capacity not to focus on the problems, but to look for solutions and listen to others. Live a creative life by speaking something new into existence.
Barrier 3: Making assumptions. This barrier is based on the thought: 'If it isn't broken, don't fix it'. Usually this barrier is the result of a preference for judging ideas rather than generating them and an inability to relax and put the problem aside for a while to gather information, and the desire to succeed quickly. Stereotyping takes place, where assumptions are made without proper knowledge or background about the situation.	Everything can be improved, and people who say they can't, often only say that because they don't have the energy to try something new. Approach the problem from an interdisciplinary point of view and be prepared to listen to others and modify your view in the light of new information.
Barrier 4: Following rules. This is a tendency to conform to accepted patterns of belief or thoughts – the rules and limitations of the status quo. The thought is: 'This is how we have done it in the past and no other way will work!' When rules, regulations and procedures become ends in themselves, they will be applied rigidly in every situation, even where it is not appropriate.	Develop an understanding of the limits of current approaches and procedures, and develop an ability to seek new approaches and consider why you think they might succeed.
Barrier 5: Environment not willing to risk. There is a lack of support for, or understanding of, new ideas in the environment (the organisation, friends, or family). Challenging the status quo or asking questions is frowned upon as it poses financial risks.	Develop the freedom to do things differently and the ability to take risks by seeking help in the development of new ideas, and participating in open discussions, and the expression of ideas. Make it safe to take responsible risks and ideas will flow.
Barrier 6: Lack of financial support. In this case, solutions or ideas are always shot down because the lack of financial support kills creative thinking.	Create ideas for the ideal situation and then plan for ways to fund the best idea based on potential income that can be generated.

BARRIER	OVERCOMING STRATEGIES
Barrier 7: Cultural barriers. Were you raised to believe that certain topics are 'none of your business' and certain actions 'impertinent'? If these feelings cause you to feel 'out of bounds', you'll avoid investigating a wide range of phenomena and your curiosity will shut down. You may even close off your unconscious and all the creative potential it holds.	Generate ideas by engaging in conversation with people who don't share your point of view or background. It's a collaborative conversation, in which something new opens up through the process of dialogue. Do the opposite of what you are used to doing and get out of your comfort zone.

Source: Adapted from Bonkowski (2008), Duncan (2010), Evans (1993), Faltin (2001), Mauzy and Harriman (2003), Nieman, Hough and Nieuwenhuizen (2003), and Tan (1998).

3.4 The creative process

Creativity is widely acknowledged as an important force in shaping the changes that take place in the economic environment and in the development of new products, services, and business ventures. In this section, the developments and changes that occurred in applying creativity as a process used in the development of new business ideas will be discussed.

3.4.1 Theoretical developments in the creative process

One of the earliest models of the creative process is attributed to Graham Wallas (1926) who proposed that creative thinking proceeds through four phases:

1. *Preparation*, which involves consciously studying a task and trying to attack it logically by standard means.
2. *Incubation*, which is when the conscious and subconscious mind mull over the problem in hard-to-define ways.
3. *Illumination*, also called the 'Eureka step', which involves seeing a new synthesis.
4. *Verification*, or revision, which includes all the work that now follows.

Rossman (1931) examined the creative process via questionnaires completed by 710 inventors and expanded Wallas' original four steps to seven, which are:

1. *Observation* of a need or difficulty
2. *Analysis* of the need

3. A *survey* of all available information
4. A *formulation* of all objective solutions
5. A *critical analysis* of these solutions for their advantages and disadvantages
6. The birth of the new idea – the *invention*
7. *Experimentation* to test out the most promising solution, and the *selection* and *perfection* of the final embodiment.

Alex Osborn (1953), the developer of brainstorming, embraced a similar theory of balance between analysis and imagination in his seven-step model for creative thinking:

1. *Orientation* – identifying the problem
2. *Preparation* – gathering pertinent data
3. *Analysis* – breaking down the relevant material
4. *Ideation* – piling up alternatives by way of ideas
5. *Incubation* – letting up, to invite illumination
6. *Synthesis* – putting the pieces together
7. *Evaluation* – judging the resulting ideas.

The systematic combination of techniques for directed creativity and techniques for analysis continues as a strong theme in several, more recently proposed models, such as the creative problem solving (CPS) model (Parnes, 1992; Isaksen and Trefflinger, 1985) which includes six steps:

1. Objective finding
2. Fact finding
3. Problem finding
4. Idea finding

5. Solution finding
6. Acceptance finding.

For the purposes of this book, six steps in the entrepreneurial creative process have been synthesised from all the models above; these are outlined in the next section.

3.4.2 The entrepreneurial creative process

The six steps in the entrepreneurial creative process have been compiled from the various theories discussed in the section above:

1. *Preparation.* This step concentrates on analysing the problem or situation to ensure that the correct questions are being asked. During this step you need to decide on the type of business, product or service you want to be involved in.
2. *Information gathering.* Once you know what will be done, you should gather as much information about yourself and about the problem or situation that you have described in the first step. Keep a journal close by and write down thoughts, feelings, things you see, things happening around you – start by writing a new idea of the day. A journal will help you structure and develop the habit of thinking of new ideas.
3. *Idea generation.* Once you know the problem you want to solve (creating a new business, developing a product or service offering), you are ready to start generating possible solutions or ideas. It is at this phase that the conscious and subconscious mind are working on the problem or situation, making new connections, separating unnecessary ideas, and looking for other ideas. This is the phase that most people mess up the most with distractions and the hustle and bustle of daily lives. Modern life, with its many beeps, buzzes, and distractions, has the strong tendency to grab the attention of both our subconscious and unconscious mind and, as a

result, the creative process stops and is replaced by more immediate concerns. It is tempting just to accept the first good idea that you come across. If you do this, you might miss many even better solutions or ideas. While you are generating solutions, remember that other people will have different perspectives on the problem, and it will almost certainly be worth asking for the opinions of your friends, colleagues or other specialists as part of this process.
4. *Evaluation of ideas.* Only at this stage do you select the best of the ideas you have generated. It may be that the best idea is obvious. Alternatively, it may be worth examining and developing a number of ideas in detail before you select one. During this step, you can apply different decision-making and assessment techniques to help you to choose between the ideas or solutions available to you. When you are selecting a solution, keep in mind your own or your organisation's goals. Making a decision on the right idea or solution becomes easy once you know these. The different evaluation techniques will be discussed later in this chapter.
5. *Implementation* (innovation and invention). This phase is the one during which the idea you have been developing,

EXAMPLE 3.1

A practical way to generate business ideas is to walk down the street where you live. Look at the houses and surroundings in the street and ask the following questions:

▸ Are the houses neat or do they need some paint or other maintenance?
▸ What do the gardens look like?
▸ Are the sidewalks neat or unkempt?
▸ How many houses are being used for home businesses? What type of home businesses?
▸ Are children playing outside?

Use this information to think of possible products or services that can be developed.

preparing and incubating sees the light of day. During this stage, you will plan your business or plan the resources needed to implement the business idea or product within your existing organisation.

6 *Experimentation.* This step is needed to help you to test out the most promising idea by creating the business and opening your doors, packaging the product and testing it in the market, developing your service, and making it available to customers.

In the next section we provide practical guidelines to apply the entrepreneurial creative process to recognising business opportunities.

3.5 **Sources of product or service ideas**

Where does an entrepreneur come up with the idea for his/her business? In practice there are many ways in which the business opportunity and idea is first identified. Sometimes luck plays a big part; at other times there is a role for approaches that encourage deliberate creativity. In today's world of technology, which is the result of the creative mind, one tends to look at technology as the best source of business ideas. While it could be argued that technology may help with some idea generation, it certainly does help with capturing and evaluating ideas. The best source of business ideas is creativity that sometimes requires us to break away from technology. Reading a book, taking a long walk, exercising, talking to various people, and other common tasks usually lend themselves to better ideas than technology ever could.

When looking for a viable business opportunity, the entrepreneur should look for the following:

▶ *An idea.* A great product, an untapped market, and good timing are essential ingredients in any recipe for success.

▶ *An opportunity.* Entrepreneurs spot, create, and exploit opportunities in a variety of ways.

▶ *Where the next frontiers lie.* One fascinating opportunity for entrepreneurs is outer space which could include satellites for automobile navigation, tracking trucking fleets, monitoring flow rates or leaks in pipelines, testing designer drugs in the near-zero-gravity environment, and using remote sensing to monitor global warming, spot fish concentrations, and detect crop stress for precision farming.

▶ *The process of evaluation.* This could include different methods, trial and error, and scientific or economic methods of evaluation.

In this section we will look at where to find and how to generate ideas, identify opportunities, and provide guidelines for evaluating the different opportunities in order to identify the most viable opportunity.

Many people dream of starting up their own business, but they don't know where to begin. The first step in making your dreams a reality is to come up with the right business idea, which can either be a product or service.

Product and (or) service ideas can come from a number of sources. The aim is to be open to any suggestion and to be creative in developing these ideas. Most people already have an idea in mind when thinking about starting up a new business. Usually, their ideas will have some connection with their own interests, skills or experience.

However, if you are unsure about what you want to do, there are a variety of sources that could inspire you to come up with a good idea. The following resources are mostly used:

▶ *Personal skills, passions, imagination and talents.* One of the first places to start when looking for business ideas or opportunities is to look within you. To discover your passions, skills, what you are good at or what business to start, you can begin by asking yourself the following questions:

- What skills or talents do you possess?
- What are your hobbies? What are you passionate about?
- Do you possess a skill that people are willing to pay for? (Martins, n.d.)

Hobbies and interests are also a rich source of business ideas, although you have to be careful to avoid assuming that, just because you have a passion for collecting rare tin openers, there is a ready market from people with similar interests! Many people have tried to turn their hobby into a business and found that it generates only a small contribution to household income (Riley, 2012).

▶ *Talking to family, friends or other shoppers.* To come up with an idea that meets people's needs, there's no better way than by talking to people – your family, friends and even shoppers in areas that interest you. You can constantly investigate your own needs or those of your close relatives and friends to generate ideas. Any need that is not satisfied by existing products or services can become a business idea. Be aware of complaints about existing products and services to determine their shortcomings and what should be improved. This is a useful way of generating ideas for new substitute products that will provide solutions for these needs. Although the terms 'needs' and 'wants' are sometimes used arbitrarily, there is a fine distinction between the two. Our needs make up our survival kit while our wants are the desires we have for non-essentials such as cars, electronics, holidays and high-fashion clothing. Most people strive for better conditions for themselves, their family, and sometimes also their community, their nation and the whole world and these would include wants (The Times 100, 2014). Our wants are infinite. This is just as true for the relatively wealthy as it is for the poor. Needs are easier to define

but vary according to a person's age, physical environment, health and many other factors (The Times 100, 2014).

The South African success story – *Dial-a-Nerd* discussed on the next page shows how the needs and wants of family and friends can contribute towards the successful implementation of a business idea.

▶ *Current or previous experiences.* Many ideas for successful businesses come from people who have experience of working in a particular market or industry. Work experience could provide better and more detailed understanding of what customers want; knowledge of potential or existing competitors, pricing, and suppliers; information on the market which may result in a reduction in the start-up market research that should be conducted. Simply observing what goes on around you can be a good way of spotting an idea. Often an idea will be launched in another country and has not yet been tried in other, similar economies.

▶ *Government assistance services for small businesses.* Ideas could also come from assistance and support rendered by the government, specifically the Departments of Trade and Industry, Science and Technology, and Arts and Culture, or by organised business institutions, such as Business South Africa (BUSA) and its related business associations such as the *Afrikaanse Handelsinstituut* (AHI), the National African Federated Chamber of Commerce (NAFCOC), the South African Chamber of Business (SACOB) and the Black Management Forum (BMF), or by financial institutions and other businesses, such as Absa, Standard Bank, First National Bank and Edgars. The majority of these organisations have a section dealing with small businesses and entrepreneurs, and have valuable links and information that can be used to develop product and service ideas. These

SOUTH AFRICAN SUCCESS STORY

Dial a Nerd

Colin Thornton founded Dial a Nerd in 1998 at the age of 19. His first clients were friends and family and his first computer repair room the garage of his parent's home. By focusing on home users and offering a very high level of service, he occupied a niche at the time. This helped Dial a Nerd grow into the business it is now.

At that time computers were not as prevalent as they are today and the Internet was something that only nerdy people had, and even then it was slower than a leisurely walk to the local library. But Colin knew that the Internet was about to boom, and the IT industry would soon explode with possibilities.

Over the years many people have come on board to help spread the nerdiness throughout the country – Colin's brother, Aaron, joined him to assist with the ever increasing responsibilities of sales and management. In the process Colin met Roberto Caprio who took Dial a Nerd to Cape Town, where they now have three branches. Phil Case helped spread Dial a Nerd to the north of Johannesburg, starting Dial a Nerd Bryanston.

Dial a Nerd also developed beyond a home computer support company when Andrew Burns and Xavier Nel decided to help out small to medium businesses with the same care and concern they have always had for their home based customers. They started Network Nerds, now known as Dial a Nerd Business.

The business has grown to have a presence in most of the major South African cities, with five branches and over 70 staff members countrywide. It has over 40 000 customers consisting of home-based computer users and small to medium-sized businesses. Over the years Colin recognised that there were a few staff members that were essential to his business and to retain them he offered them shares as a way of ensuring Dial a Nerd's longevity. There are now six shareholders who own the business, most of whom are still active in its management.

Source: Nerdworks (Pty) Ltd. 2013. Dial a Nerd History. [Online]. Available: http://www.dialanerd.co.za/who-we-are/history/ [6 Jan 2014]. Reprinted by permission of Dial a Nerd.

organisations will be discussed in more detail in Chapter 6.

▶ *Mass media.* The mass media is a wonderful source of information, ideas and often opportunities. Magazines, TV stations, cable networks, radio, newspapers and Internet resource sites are all instances of mass media. Just take a careful look at the commercial advertisements in newspapers or magazines and you will discover businesses that are for sale.

Also, articles in the printed press or on the net, or documentaries on television may report changes in consumer needs or fashions. For instance, you may read or hear that people are now extremely interested in healthy eating or physical fitness. You may also discover advertisements calling for the provision of certain services depending on specific skills. Or you might find a new concept for which investors are needed, such as a franchise.

▶ *Keep up with current events and be ready to take advantage of business opportunities.* Societal happenings, events and trends are also sources of business ideas. If you read and watch the news regularly and have the conscious intent of discovering business ideas, you will be amazed at how many business opportunities your brain will generate. Keep up with current events because it will assist you to identify market trends, new fads, information about industries and sometimes new ideas that have business possibilities and potentials (Martins, n.d.).

▸ *Visits to trade shows and exhibitions.* Exhibitions are usually held to make industry and (or) the public aware of the different products and services that are available. The prospective entrepreneur could use such exhibitions to gain information that can be used to develop new or alternative products or markets. The Franchising Association of South Africa (FASA) organises an annual exhibition of the different franchises that operate in South Africa. These exhibitions could provide an entrepreneur with the opportunity to assess and compare the various franchising opportunities. This may lead to a decision to buy into a franchise or to develop a business idea into a franchise.

Foreign countries often have exhibitions to promote business opportunities within their country. This may lead to the development of a product or service that can be marketed to them.

▸ *The Internet and online research.* The Internet is an invaluable source of information. Not only does it provide information on existing businesses and their products and (or) services, but it also proves useful when investigating new developments in products and services. Furthermore, the Internet can be used to determine what financial and other support is available to potential entrepreneurs. Links on the various websites could also indicate national and international business needs that can be further investigated.

▸ *Identifying gaps in the market for new or improved products and services.* To develop winning ideas, you need to concentrate on a specific target market and analyse and brainstorm business ideas for services that the group would be interested in. The key to arriving at business ideas for a new product or service is to identify a market need that has not been met (Martins, n.d.).

▸ *Libraries* are an underestimated source of product and service ideas. One can obtain information on existing products in newspapers, popular magazines, subject-related magazines, research reports, and postgraduate research dissertations. Prospective entrepreneurs may also find it helpful to page through advertisements and discussions on products and services in local, national, and international magazines and newspapers to formulate business ideas. This can trigger thoughts on better ways to satisfy the need that the product or service attempts to meet.

▸ *Using creative thinking*, one can either use the same need to develop a new product or think of ways to adapt the product to make it unique, or even think of a better way to sell the same product. Prospective entrepreneurs can use research reports and dissertations to gather information on

EXAMPLE 3.2

The Internet has become one of the foremost means of communication and because most people have access to a computer and the Internet, it has become easier to reach large masses of people all over the world. Using information technology it is possible for people looking for a market to find a way to sell products they manufacture themselves, such as clothing, jewellery, art and crafts. Online advertisements are present on almost every website which makes it easy for consumers to find products and services by small business owners. Furthermore, anyone can launch their own website and start promising businesses without having to concern themselves with expenses such as office space or commuting. This is making the need for physical offices obsolete.

needs and problems that exist in industry that could lead to the development of a specific product or service, as well as to the development of a new business such as a consultancy.

This section dealt with where to find new business ideas. In the next section, we look at the methods used to develop and implement these ideas.

3.6 Methods for generating new product or service ideas

A number of methods have been devised to help aspiring entrepreneurs to generate viable business ideas. Some of these **creativity techniques** are discussed below.

3.6.1 Accumulation of knowledge

Successful business ideas or creations are usually preceded by investigation and information gathering. This should involve extensive reading of magazines, newspapers, journals and books, conversations with others working in both related and unrelated fields, and attending workshops and meetings. It is essential to investigate possible business opportunities in different geographical areas while gathering information, since valuable perspectives and information could be lost if the focus is restricted to too small a geographical area. Travelling to new places could also add to the pool of knowledge that one develops when searching for new business ideas.

3.6.2 Observation

By simply observing your environment, you could generate viable business ideas. Find a new use for something by looking at things differently or look for gaps in the marketplace. By doing this, you could perhaps identify once-successful products and services that could be recycled in a new way or find new ways of doing something. The development of computer software is an example of taking successful products and improving them by adding features.

Visit successful businesses in neighbouring cities or towns and determine whether you could do likewise in your area. Alternatively, investigate the possibility of setting up a business in a neighbouring area that may need specialised services.

Look at things that have been successful in the past but are not done any more and you may find a business idea that could be improved on. Think, for example, of the unisex hairdressers in the major cities today compared to the erstwhile all-male barbershops with sturdy leather and steel chairs and shelves adorned with a variety of bottles holding hair and shaving lotions. Could these not be upgraded a little and reintroduced with a modern feel?

3.6.3 Brainstorming

Brainstorming is a relatively simple technique that can be used when two or more people are involved in the generation of ideas. It helps to overcome pressures for conformity that may stifle the development of creative alternatives, since it utilises an idea-generating process that encourages the formulation of alternatives while withholding any criticism. In a typical brainstorming session, the people involved sit around a table. The facilitator or group leader states the objective or problem in a clear manner so that it can be understood by all participants. Members then 'free-wheel' as many alternatives as they can to realise the objective or solve the problem. No criticism of any idea is allowed, and all the alternatives are recorded for later analysis and discussion. Since brainstorming is merely an idea-generating mechanism, the techniques discussed below could be used to expand on these further by offering ways to arrive at a preferred solution.

According to Tague (2004:96–99) the following considerations should be applied during brainstorming sessions:

▸ Judgement and creativity are two functions that cannot occur simultaneously. That is the reason for the rules about no criticism and no evaluation.

▸ Laughter and groans are criticism. When there is criticism, people begin to evaluate their ideas before stating them. Fewer ideas are generated and creative ideas are lost.

▸ Evaluation includes positive comments such as 'Great idea!' That implies that another idea that did not receive praise was mediocre.

▸ The more the better. Studies have shown that there is a direct relationship between the total number of ideas and the number of good, creative ideas.

▸ The crazier the better. Be unconventional in your thinking. Don't hold back any ideas. Crazy ideas are creative. They often come from a different perspective.

▸ Crazy ideas often lead to wonderful, unique solutions, through modification or by sparking someone else's imagination.

▸ Hitchhike. Piggyback. Build on someone else's idea.

▸ When brainstorming with a large group, someone other than the facilitator should be the recorder. The facilitator should act as a buffer between the group and the recorder(s), keeping the flow of ideas going and ensuring that no ideas get lost before being recorded.

▸ The recorder should try not to rephrase ideas. If an idea is not clear, ask for a rephrasing that everyone can understand. If the idea is too long to record, work with the person who suggested the idea to come up with a concise rephrasing. The person suggesting the idea must always approve what is recorded.

▸ Keep all ideas visible. When ideas overflow to additional flipchart pages, post previous pages around the room so all ideas are still visible to everyone.

3.6.4 Nominal group technique

The nominal group technique is often used during the decision-making process as a method to generate and prioritise ideas. All group members must be present and are required to operate independently. It is necessary to have paper and pens or pencils for each member, a flipchart, and marking pens. This technique could be used by entrepreneurs to identify and evaluate business ideas by using friends, relatives or any other group of people.

After the subject to be discussed has been clarified, the following steps can be used in the nominal group technique (Tague, 2004:96–99):

1. Each member writes down his or her ideas on the problem independently before any discussion takes place.

2. After this step, each member presents one idea at a time to the group without any discussion. Each member takes his or her turn, going around the group until all ideas have been presented and recorded on the flipchart. It is important that no discussion or questions on the ideas should take place during this step.

3. After all the ideas have been recorded, the group members discuss the ideas for clarity and also start to evaluate each one. In the evaluation, the group should look at aspects such as desirability of outcome, feasibility, cost and resources involved, and compatibility with the aim or problem. All other criteria against which the ideas must be tested should be developed during this step.

4. Each member of the group now independently assigns a rank to the ideas. The idea with the highest aggregate ranking will determine the decision to be made.

3.6.5 **Delphi technique**

The Delphi technique is similar to the nominal group technique, except that the members are not required to be physically present, which makes this technique complex and time consuming. The steps used in the Delphi technique are similar to those used in the nominal group technique, but with carefully designed questionnaires used in each step. After each step, the data are collected at a central location, transcribed, and reproduced. When using the Delphi technique, steps two and three of the nominal group technique can be repeated more than once since the results of each step typically trigger new solutions or ideas. The Delphi technique is usually applied in existing corporations rather than used to develop ideas to start a business.

3.6.6 **The incubation of ideas**

You should never underestimate the value of allowing your subconscious thoughts to mull over the tremendous amount of information in the development of creative ideas. By keeping yourself occupied with activities totally unrelated to the subject, the idea might just fall into place. Allowing your subconscious mind to take over often stimulates creativity. Such activities include engaging in routine and often mindless activities (such as mowing the lawn or painting a wall), exercising (both indoors and outdoors), playing (with the children, board games, building puzzles or playing sports), meditating or just sitting back and relaxing. Daydreaming, practising hobbies, and working in a more relaxing environment can also help to encourage the formulation of ideas.

Read the dilemma box below and consider how an aspiring entrepreneur might use these methods to generate new business ideas.

It is important to prepare carefully for creative sessions by ensuring that all materials are available and, by sending reminders before the sessions, ensuring that all those invited will be present and know when and where to meet. Otherwise, a creative session may not result in generating useful ideas that could lead to a viable business opportunity.

It is useful to apply a variety of creativity techniques and to combine them in such a way that the limitations of one can be compensated for by the strengths of another. This will result in the generation of a variety of plausible business ideas and opportunities that can be utilised.

Once an aspiring entrepreneur has generated a number of possible ideas for a new business, he or she should screen those ideas to find the best alternative. This process is described in the next section.

ENTREPRENEURIAL DILEMMA

Generating ideas to start a new business

Peter de Wit wanted to start a business after completing his BCom. He lives in Bothaville and did some research in the town and found that the unemployment rate among young people in Bothaville and surrounding towns and villages is high. Peter wants to do something about it. To be successful, he attended all the required training offered by the Services Seta and also completed all the required assessments to become an accredited trainer. He wanted to move out of Bothaville as he would really like to work in one of the metro cities in South Africa, but realised that the need in his hometown is high and is not sure how many accredited trainers are available in Bothaville. He needs to look for a place to start training but is not sure how to go about choosing the right venue. He is also not sure if training would be the only solution and does not even know whether he should perhaps provide other products or services to add value. Suggest ways in which Peter could find and generate ideas that would help him to decide what best to do.

3.7 Initial screening of ideas

The entrepreneur should do a close follow-up of the ideas to screen and identify the good and bad features of each alternative. This will ensure continuous improvement of the overall idea-generating process. In this context, the opinion of each of the participants is important.

The purpose of doing an initial screening is to exclude ideas that will not have any chance of success and allow only those ideas that have some element of viability and marketability through to the final evaluation. According to Youssry (2007:20–21) the initial screening can be done by categorising potential ideas and opportunities according to any of the following:

▸ *Perception of desirability.* This refers to an element of personal bias of the entrepreneur and entrepreneurial team about ideas perceived as more desirable, a bias based on the perceived economic consequence of the idea (will it be profitable or not), the type of venture that will be needed to develop the idea into a viable opportunity (technology driven, manufacturing, construction, service, etc.), personal preferences (experience, likes and dislikes, etc.), and the level of support that will be needed to follow or implement the idea (e.g. from family, peers, colleagues, mentors, and others).

▸ *Perception of feasibility.* This reflects the entrepreneur's or entrepreneurial team's beliefs in their ability to put together the required human, social and financial resources to implement the ideas or opportunities. That belief does not come from prior experience as such, but from the resulting expertise that helps entrepreneurs to overcome potential pitfalls, such as misreading the market or forming unrealistic expectations.

▸ *Propensity to act.* This is the innate tendency to act on any idea or business opportunity. This may be different for the entrepreneur and the members of the entrepreneurial team. When propensity to act is low, entrepreneurial intentions are unlikely to develop, and perceptions of desirability become sole predictors of intentions. On the other hand, when propensity to act is high, the quantity of prior entrepreneurial experience, in addition to perceptions of desirability and feasibility, directly influences intentions.

During the categorisation process, the entrepreneur and his or her team should classify the ideas into those that would be worthwhile following and those that should be rejected offhand. Those entrepreneurial ideas that pass this initial screening have innovation at the core and have proved – theoretically – to provide a competitive edge. The next step has to be idea *evaluation.* While idea development is a process of *opening up* to new horizons and contents, idea or opportunity evaluation is a process of focusing and going into details. Without opening up, we will not get an innovative part in our business idea; without refining, we will not get the idea to run smoothly in real life.

For some, coming up with a great business idea is a gratifying adventure. For most, however, it is a daunting task. The key to coming up with a business idea is giving customers something they want or, more importantly, filling an unmet need. The purpose of starting a business is to satisfy customers who are the ultimate users of your goods or services. In coming up with a business idea, do not ask 'What do we want to sell?' but rather 'What does the customer want to buy?'.

The screening of new business ideas is perhaps the most difficult step for entrepreneurs in the process of establishing a new business venture as it requires time and effort. However, it is an essential part of the process and if not enough time and effort are spent on this process, you may find yourself in a position of either not having a marketable product or service, or trying to sell an idea without knowing whether or not there is a need for the product or service. If you have not gone through this process of testing the viability of your business idea, it will also have an effect on finding the right sources of support, financial and other, as well as identifying the resources that you will need to start the business successfully.

CONCLUSION

As discussed in this chapter, ideas can come from various sources and you need to be creative to come up with an innovative business idea. Furthermore, prior experience accounts for a large number of new business ideas as many people generate ideas for industries they are already working in, or have experience in. The business idea is seen as the starting point of a new business venture and, to identify business ideas that could be turned into viable business opportunities, the entrepreneur should go through a number of processes. This chapter dealt with those processes, namely the sources for and methods to identify product and service ideas, and how to screen all the product and service ideas in order to identify the most viable idea that could be used to establish a viable business.

The next chapter will focus on the process of evaluating the ideas or business opportunities in order to establish which would be the most viable one to implement.

SELF-ASSESSMENT QUESTIONS

Multiple-choice questions

1. Which one of the following aspects does the different descriptions and definitions of creativity not have in common?
   a. Looking at things differently – this includes generating new ideas, alternatives or solutions.
   b. Talking to people – sharing all your dreams and aspirations.
   c. Implementation – this is making the idea a reality by producing either a product or service.
   d. Addressing a gap – this could be a problem, customer need, etc.
2. Which of the following statements is the reality of the myth that money is a creativity motivator?
   a. Creativity is a combination of knowledge, experience and even technical skills.
   b. Rewarding creativity may lead to unhealthy competition.
   c. Everybody has good ideas but few of us act on them.
   d. Creativity is positively associated with joy and love.
3. Which of the following statements describes the creativity barrier 'Following rules'?
   a. Certain topics are 'none of your business' and certain actions 'impertinent'.
   b. Fear of making a mistake or taking a risk.
   c. Conforming to accepted patterns of belief or thoughts.
   d. A lack of support for or understanding of new ideas amongst your friends and family.
4. Which one of the following is the third step in the entrepreneurial creative process?
   a. Preparation
   b. Idea generation
   c. Implementation
   d. Information gathering
5. To come up with an idea that _____, there is no better way than by talking to people.
   a. meets people's needs
   b. meets your talents
   c. uses your experience
   d. is on the Internet
6. What advice will you give to someone who wants to start a business venture, but is constantly told that the business venture will not succeed?
   a. Do the difficult experiment first and then explore others.
   b. Approach the venture by creating an ideal situation and then look for funding.
   c. Develop a capacity to focus on the problem and get solutions by listening to others.
   d. Find people that will support you, although they might not share your point of view and move out of your comfort zone.

7. You were told that only creative people have good ideas and you do not regard yourself as creative. What is the truth about this statement?
    a. Everybody has good ideas as creativity is based on education, experience and your environment.
    b. Financial incentives will lead to the creation of new ideas.
    c. You are most likely to come up with good ideas if you are under pressure.
    d. Keeping to yourself will help you to create new ideas.
8. Why is it important to incubate ideas?
    a. Incubation allows your subconscious thoughts to mull over information in developing creative ideas.
    b. Incubation allows the entrepreneur to identify the geographical area.
    c. Incubation builds on someone else's idea.
9. _____ reflects the entrepreneur's or entrepreneurial team's belief in their ability to put together the required human, social and financial resources to implement the ideas or opportunities.
    a. Propensity to act
    b. Perceived beliefs
    c. Perception of feasibility
    d. Perception of desirability
10. Successful ideas or creations are usually preceded by investigation and information gathering.
    a. True
    b. False
11. When addressing the market gap the entrepreneur should transform opportunities into problems.
    a. True
    b. False
12. According to the Oxford Dictionary a myth is a widely held, true belief or idea about an event or topic.
    a. True
    b. False
13. By simply observing your environment, you could generate viable business ideas.
    a. True
    b. False
14. Our wants make up our survival kit.
    a. True
    b. False
15. Myth 7 is that creativity is about making great leaps of imagination.
    a. True
    b. False

DISCUSSION QUESTIONS

1. Provide a definition for 'creativity' and indicate the implication that this definition has for the entrepreneur.
2. Identify the creativity barriers and indicate what can be done to overcome each barrier.
3. Identify the different myths surrounding creativity and provide the truth regarding each myth.
4. Identify and discuss the steps in the entrepreneurial creative process.
5. What should an entrepreneur look for when looking for a viable business idea?
6. List the sources of business ideas that an entrepreneur could use.
7. To what extent can talking to family, friends or other shoppers and government assistance services for small businesses contribute towards new business ideas?
8. Discuss the methods that could be used to generate product or service ideas.
9. Illustrate the differences between the nominal group technique and the Delphi technique for identifying business ideas.
10. Discuss the process one can follow to do an initial screening of business ideas or opportunities.

EXPERIENTIAL EXERCISE

1. Read the success story of Nqobile Nkosi presented earlier in the South African success story box and find additional information on him on the Internet. In which of the steps discussed above would you place the following actions he followed:
   a. Attending training in jewellery design
   b. Selling cakes, biscuits and soft drinks on the streets of Soweto
   c. Establishing the initial business by mainly repairing jewellery and manufacturing jewellery on a small scale
   d. Forming the partnership with Paul Spurgeon
   e. Appointing and training employees

The activities listed below should be completed in a small group. The aim is to apply creative techniques to a situation.

2. There are various techniques to generate ideas. Use brainstorming to solve the following problem:
   The handlebars of the bicycle do not work well.
3. Do individual research on any additional creative techniques and explain the technique to your group.
4. A friend approaches you with his need to start a business, but he has no idea what to do. He has been selling beds and mattresses in a retail store in Nelspruit, Mpumalanga. He would like to move to the town in which he was born, Komatipoort, but is not sure what type of business he should start up. He has saved sufficient funds to buy a small delivery vehicle with some extra cash to spare. He would like you to help him to identify some business ideas that he could think about. Provide guidelines on how he should go about doing this.

MEDICAL DIAGNOSTECH (PTY) LTD

If South Africa is to improve its competitiveness in the global economy and create more jobs, it must foster more innovative entrepreneurs such as Ashley Uys. He is the founder of Real World Diagnostics and Medical Diagnostech (Pty) Ltd, a company that develops and markets affordable and reliable medical test kits for malaria, pregnancy, syphilis, and HIV/Aids for Africa's rural poor. These test kits can also help detect six different types of drugs, including cocaine, tik and dagga. The company's malaria test kit can reportedly detect all strains of malaria and indicate within 30 minutes whether the malaria treatment provided is effective. Far more significant is that each test kit costs R4, effectively bringing reliable malaria diagnosis into the hands of millions of people for whom living with the threat of the illness is an everyday reality.

Unique technologies give Medical Diagnostech products superiority in terms of sensitivity, specificity and stability. This has been independently confirmed internationally and the tests have been found to perform to the most demanding standards. As a result, its products are trusted by companies that are leaders in their respective markets. They are also committed to competitive pricing and have been servicing clients for over five years and their local and international client base is growing rapidly.

Uys exemplifies how industry, the government and universities can partner to improve innovation. After graduating with a BSc honours in biotechnologies from the University of the Western Cape (UWC) in 2003, Uys enrolled in a two-year incubation internship, run by Wits University, the University of Cape Town (UCT) and Acorn Technologies – a Cape Town-based incubator which, at the time, was funded by the Department of Trade and Industry but has since been absorbed by the Technology Innovation Agency.

He was then placed in a host company, Vision Biotech, where he was able to hone his skills, while the incubator paid half his salary. Initially he spent two days a week working on his business idea, slowly stretching this as his sales picked up, until he was spending the bulk of his time on his own business.

CASE STUDY

At the time, Uys was the only one in his class of 13 to opt to start a new enterprise during the internship. The remainder chose to write business plans on how they would assist existing companies. 'I always wanted to be in business and be my own boss', says Uys. 'I always wanted to be an entrepreneur, but I wanted to stay in science'.

On completion of his internship, he set up Real World Diagnostics in 2006 and moved temporarily to UWC, which gave him office space, and then to Muizenberg, where he set up a small factory.

Instead of looking around for venture capital investments to fund the large capital outlay he needed for developing new tests, he opted to start small, initially just marketing his products and those of others, while outsourcing the manufacturing to a third party.

The only equity he has given away has been that in his manufacturing company, Medical Diagnostech (Pty) Ltd, where he has given 14% to a UCT professor, with whom he consults, and the remainder to one of his lab technicians, Lyndon Mungur.

In 2008, he won the national leg of the SAB Kickstart Competition and with it R200 000 in prize money and a further R125 000 in grant money, which he ploughed back into his business. With the cash flow he generated from distributing his products, as well as the cash he won through SAB Kickstart, he was able to start buying laboratory and injection-moulding equipment to manufacture his own products, until he was able to afford his own factory space.

In 2011, he exported more than 2.5-million malaria test kits to Pakistan, Papua New Guinea and other countries via a distributor to the World Health Organisation. He also sells his kits to Alpha Pharmacies and local wholesaler Pinnacle Pharmaceuticals.

He says his new factory will allow him to manufacture about 20-million test kits a year, once Medical Diagnostech received ISO (International Standards Organisation) accreditation (ISO13485);

they started shipping new HIV kits into the rest of Africa. He claims it is just him and his former host company that manufacture rapid test kits in Africa; the remainder of the African companies in the sector simply assemble kits shipped in from overseas.

Kits cost between R4 for a simple pregnancy test and R23 for a full drug-abuse test that can test for five different types of drugs and can produce results within five minutes. Uys says the tests are 99.9% accurate, but that it is still necessary to have results confirmed by a medical laboratory. Along with the kits, he also produces a battery-operated breathalyser, which he sells mainly to pharmacies as well as to SAB, which distributes them to staff.

Uys is now looking ahead. He says that within the next five years he wants to be able to manufacture his own antibodies – which are used in rapid tests, along with antigens – as now he has to import them from the US. When he is able to do this, he will be able to develop kits for any test possible.

He's also developing a pre-diabetes test, which will allow someone to make the necessary lifestyle and diet changes before the onset of diabetes.

Uys says he has gradually built up his business, which has allowed him to reinvest income from sales into his business. Many business owners often make the mistake of dipping into their business's income to cover personal expenses, but Uys is firmly against this: 'At the end of the day, the only time your lifestyle should go up is when the company makes enough money to increase your salary'.

The best way for the country to develop more innovative businesses, he believes, is to have universities help commercialise intellectual property through business centres and incubators, with the support from the government to help start a business. 'That's where it all starts – formal education and then the support of the government to start your own venture'.

Source: Developed from Medical Diagnostech (Pty) Ltd (n.d.) and Timm (2012).

1. How did Ashley Uys go about finding a gap in the market for his business idea?
2. Do you think there were any barriers to creativity that Ashley had to overcome when he started his business?
3. What sources did he use to come up with his business idea?

SUGGESTED WEBSITE LINKS

http://www.shell-livewire.org/business-library/
generating-ideas/
http://www.creativityatwork.com/2014/02/17/
what-is-creativity/
http://www.mindtools.com/pages/main/
newMN_CT.htm
http://www.businessballs.com/brainstorming.htm
http://1000advices.com/guru/creativity_entrepreneurial.
html

REFERENCES

Andrews, C. 2014. *The 3 myths about creativity in business.* [Online]. Available: http://www.theguardian.com/media-network/media-network-blog/2014/jan/17/3-myths-creativity-in-business [4 March 2014].

Baumgartner, JP. 2005. Ten creative myths. [Online]. Available: http://www.jpb.com/creative/article_creative_myths.php [1 August 2011].

Bishop, K. 2005. Creativity Myths, 17 March 2005. [Online]. Available: http://enzinearticles.com/?Creativity-Myths&id=21178 [1 August 2011].

Bonkowski, F. 2008. Breaking barriers to creativity: Five strategies for third agers. [Online]. Available: http://www.selfgrowth.com/articles/Breaking_Barriers_to_Creativity_5_Strategies_for_Third_Agers.html [10 December 2010].

Breen, B. 2004. The six myths of creativity. [Online]. Available: http://www.fastcompany.com/magazine/89/creativity.html [5 January 2011].

Burkus, D. 2014. *The Myths of Creativity: The Truth About How Innovative Companies and People Generate Great Ideas.* San Francisco, CA: Jossey-Bass.

Burkhardt, V. 2009. Creative Myths: Interview with Keith Sawyer, author of *Explaining creativity: The science of human innovation,* 29 March 2009. [Online]. Available: http://www.ideaconnection.com/open-innovationarticles/00106-Creativity-Myths.html [5 January 2011].

Davies, A. 2013. *6 Myths about creativity.* [Online]. Available: http://www.huffingtonpost.com/2013/11/29/be-more-creative-creativity-myths_n_4343699.html. [4 March 2014].

Dlamini, P. 2012. *Soweto jewellery bound for London.* [Online]. Available: http://www.sowetanlive.co.za/news/business/2012/05/14/soweto-jewellery-bound-for-london [10 March 2014].

Duncan, C. 2010. How to be creative and productive in every stage of a project. *Productive Flourishing: Strategies for Thriving in Life and Business.*

23 August 2010. [Online]. Available: http://www.productiveflourishing.com/how-to-be-creative-and-productive-in-everystage-of-a-project/ [20 December 2010].

Evans, JR. 1993. Creativity in MS/OR: Overcoming barriers to creativity. *Interface,* 23(6):101–106.

Faltin, G. 2001. Creating a culture of entrepreneurship. *Journal of International Business and Economy,* 2(1):123–140.

Florida, R. 2002. *The Rise of The Creative Class: And How it's Transforming Work, Leisure, Community and Everyday Life.* New York: Basic Books.

Franken, RE. 2007. *Human Motivation.* 6th ed. Independence, KY: Cengage Learning.

Gilkey, C. 2008. Demystifying the creative process. *Productive Flourishing: Strategies for Thriving in Life and Business.* 29 September 2008. [Online]. Available: http://www.productiveflourishing.com/demystifying-thecreative-process/ [5 January 2011].

Isaksen, SG. & Trefflinger, DJ. 1985. *Creative Problem Solving. The Basic Course.* Buffalo, NY: Bearly Publishing.

Martins, AT. n.d. *Sources of Business Ideas.* [Online]. Available: http://www.mytopbusinessideas.com/sources-of-business-ideas/. [25 March 2014].

Mauzy, J. & Harriman, R. 2003. *Creativity, Inc. Building an Inventive Organization.* Boston: Harvard Business School Press.

Medical Diagnostech (Pty) Ltd. n.d. *Medical Diagnostech: About Us.* [Online]. Available: http://www.medi-tech.co.za/ [4 February 2014].

Naiman, L. 2014. *What is creativity?.* [Online]. Available: http://www.creativityatwork.com/2014/02/17/what-is-creativity/. [26 March 2014].

Nerdworks (Pty) Ltd. 2013. *Dial a Nerd History.* [Online]. Available: http://www.dialanerd.co.za/history.php [6 Jan 2014].

Ngewu, A. 2013. *He's a diamond in the rough.* [Online]. Available: http://www.citypress.co.za/business/hes-a-diamond-in-the-rough/. [11 March 2014].

Nieman, G, Hough, J. & Nieuwenhuizen, C. 2003. *Entrepreneurship: A South African Perspective.* Pretoria: Van Schaik.

NYDA. 2014. *Beneficiary Stories.* [Online]. Available: http://www.nyda.gov.za/media-centre/beneficiary-stories/Pages/NYDA-supports-Soweto%E2%80%99s-first-black-owned-jewellery-manufacturing-business.aspx [11 April 2014].

Osborn, A. 1953. *Applied Imagination.* New York: Charles Scribner.

Parnes, SJ. 1992. *Sourcebook for Creative Problem Solving.* Buffalo, NY: Creative Education Foundation Press.

Paul Spurgeon. 2013. *Cornerstone.* [Online]. Available: http://www.paulspurgeondesign.co.uk/page/cornerstone [11 April 2014].

Riley, J. 2012. *Starting a business - sources of business ideas.* [Online]. Available: http://www.tutor2u.net/business/gcse/enterprise_sources_business_ideas.html [25 March 2014].

Rossman, J. 1931. *The Psychology of the Inventor.* Washington DC: Inventor's Publishing.

Tague, NR. 2004. *The Quality Toolbox.* 2nd ed. Milwaukee: ASQ Quality Press.

Tams, E. 2002. Creating division: creativity, entrepreneurship and gendered inequality. A Sheffield case study. *City,* 6(3):393–405.

Tan, G. 1998. Managing creativity in organizations: A total systems approach. *Creativity and Innovation Management,* 7(1):23–31.

The Times 100. 2014. *Marketing Theory - Needs and wants.* [Online]. Available: http://businesscasestudies.co.uk/business-theory/marketing/needs-and-wants.html#axzz2xBKGmwzg [27 March 2014].

Timm, S. 2012. *Science innovation passes business test.* [Online]. Available: http://www.bdlive.co.za/business/management/2012/12/10/science-innovation-passes-business-test [11 March 2014].

Trautmann, M. 2011. *25 Creativity quotes.* [Online]. Available: http://celestra.ca/25-creativity-quotes/ [26 March 2014].

Wallas, G. 1926. *The Art of Thought.* New York: Harcourt Brace.

Wasu, S. 2010. Myths about creativity. 25 March 2010. [Online]. Available: http://tickledbylife.com/index.php/ myths-about-creativity/ [5 January 2011].

Weldon, R. 2014. *Soweto jeweller is a symbol of hope for South Africa.* [Online]. Available: http://www.gia.edu/research-news-soweto-jeweler-symbol-hope-south-africa [9 March 2014].

Xavier, SR, Kelley, D, Herrington, M. & Vorderwulbecke, A. 2012. *Global Entrepreneurship Monitor. 2012 Global Report,* Massachusets:Global Entrepreneurship Research Association.

Youssry, A. 2007. *Social Entrepreneurs and Enterprise Development.* August 2007. Alexandria, Egypt: Sustainable Development Association.

CHAPTER 4

Opportunity recognition and evaluation

Isa van Aardt

LEARNING OUTCOMES

On completion of this chapter you will be able to:
▶ Understand the foundations for opportunity evaluation
▶ Explain the role of cognitive biases and heuristics in opportunity evaluation
▶ Understand the different criteria used by venture capitalists to evaluate new venture proposals
▶ Identify the characteristics of successful products and services
▶ Determine how new ideas can be analysed to filter out those that are obviously not feasible or marketable
▶ Assess the viability of product and service ideas
▶ Develop and implement a screening guide that can be used to establish which product or service ideas should be pursued.

OPENING CASE STUDY

There is a huge difference between a business and a hobby. Would you work for free in a factory, a store or as a receptionist for a business? Then why would you look at starting a business from which you don't want or expect to make money?

However, to start the business you must have an idea that will work. Choosing the kind of business that will work for you takes a lot of thought, as there are a number of important factors to consider. To ensure that the business is viable, you need to find a product or service with a market that you can develop. In other words, you need to be selling something that people want or need.

But for your business to be competitive, you also need to have the necessary skills. The business should also suit your personality; otherwise you will soon lose enthusiasm for the venture.

When you have a product or service that you want to turn into a business, ask yourself the following two simple questions:
1. Do you know of someone that wants to buy the product or service that you want to develop?
2. Do you have a business idea that fits your skills or do you have to develop new skills?

INTRODUCTION

For many entrepreneurs the evaluation stage of creativity will be the most difficult as during this stage opportunities will be tested against economic and other realities, which sometimes results in letting go of a dream. This stage requires entrepreneurs to be brutally honest; they must assess whether the opportunity that they have identified is just a good idea or a truly viable business opportunity. Opportunities must be perceived as both desirable and feasible so that entrepreneurs can be motivated to act and mobilise resources to pursue them.

So how do entrepreneurs and small business owners decide if an idea is a feasible business opportunity or purely an idea? This is very important given the nature of often high uncertainty, low information and the hurried decision-making process surrounding the start-up phase.

Entrepreneurs are innovators who start a business that will create new or improved products or services usually with the aim of meeting unmet needs and growing and expanding the business. To do this, they need knowledge of the market that they want to serve and the products and (or) services offered in that market. However, many entrepreneurs find themselves in situations that are new and unpredictable, often due to a lack of knowledge resulting from not accessing historical trends, past performance, and other information about the market and its products or services. This will have an effect on their ability to evaluate opportunities, which could be solved by developing an opportunity evaluation scorecard. By using an opportunity evaluation scorecard, entrepreneurs will not need to rely on their own cognitive biases and heuristics (mental short cuts). Instead, they will develop a higher risk perception and therefore be more risk aware and more realistic about ideas. By evaluating an opportunity thoroughly, entrepreneurs will be able to assess the perceived opportunity before investing large sums of money and time.

The process of idea generation was discussed in detail in Chapter 3. This chapter will focus on the characteristics of viable products and services (opportunity recognition), and the processes involved in evaluating and selecting those opportunities that can be developed into viable products and (or) services.

4.1 Foundations of opportunity recognition and evaluation

> **DEFINITION**
>
> Baron (2004:A1) defines a viable business opportunity as 'a perceived means of generating economic value that has not previously been explored and [is] not currently being exploited by others and meets a need or desire'. From this definition (Baron, 2004:1A), three central characteristics emerge, namely:
> ▸ Potential economic value, which refers to the potential to generate profit
> ▸ Newness, including a product, service or technology that did not exist before
> ▸ Perceived desirability, referring to the moral and legal acceptability of the new product and (or) service in society.

At the foundation of opportunity recognition and evaluation lies the development of a **viable business opportunity** that will enable the entrepreneur to make a profit, be creative and meet a need within the market. In developing a viable business opportunity, the entrepreneur will have to use their cognitive abilities (cognitive approach) and develop objectivity (the ability to let go of their personal biases, likes and dislikes) in order to be able to recognise and deal with risks in their pursuit of the most viable opportunity.

4.1.1 The cognitive approach to opportunity recognition and evaluation

The **cognitive approach** deals with the entrepreneur's preferred way of gathering, processing, and evaluating information (Allinson et al., 2000:35). Opportunities usually emerge from complex patterns of changing conditions in technology, the external environment (economic, political, social, and demographic) and the personal situation of the entrepreneur. The entrepreneur will use his or her cognitive skills to gather, process, evaluate, and use the information from these changing conditions to recognise and evaluate viable opportunities.

> **DEFINITION**
>
> The cognitive approach refers to the knowledge structures that entrepreneurs use to make assessments, judgements or decisions involving opportunity evaluation, venture creation, and growth (Mitchell, et al., 2004).

4.1.2 The role of cognitive biases and heuristics in opportunity evaluation

How entrepreneurs evaluate their possible opportunities will influence the venture creation processes and potential future funding. Without some form of opportunity evaluation, entrepreneurs would not choose to take up the opportunity. According to Human et al. (2004:20), the evaluation criteria used reflect values that influence expectations of the venture, personal goals, and effort exerted. Entrepreneurs tend to exhibit systematic cognitive biases and overestimate their chances of success. **Cognitive biases** are common types of mental short cuts used to make judgements about opportunities and the business (Simon et al., 2000:113). An illustration is that 81% of entrepreneurs believe that their ventures will have at least a 70% chance of succeeding, even though 50% to 71% of all new ventures discontinue after five years (Cooper et al., 1988:99). (For a counter argument, see Myth 8 in Chapter 2.)

> **DEFINITION**
>
> Cognitive biases are mental simplifications made by entrepreneurs that help them to connect information, to identify opportunities, and to deal with hurdles when starting and growing a firm but which can interfere with the ability to be impartial, unprejudiced or objective when interpreting reality (Mitchell, et al., 2004).

Entrepreneurs who believe that they are able to predict how well the business will do and perceive a low probability of failure, are likely to view a new idea as an opportunity that is feasible and worth considering. According to Busenitz and Barney (1997:12) **heuristics** refers to simplifying conditions individuals use to make decisions, particularly in uncertain and complex conditions. An example may be using marketing information from one source, even if it is outdated, to make decisions on the size of the market or to assume the time and effort it may take to develop the software needed to deliver a specific technology-driven service. Busenitz and Barney (1997) found that entrepreneurs use heuristics more extensively in their decision-making processes than managers in larger organisations. Le Roux (2005:51) defined heuristics as 'non-rational decision rules or cognitive mechanisms that simplify an entrepreneur's decision-making processes. When judgemental heuristics lead to suboptimal outcomes, they are termed biases. Le Roux (2005) explains that these simplifying approaches enable entrepreneurs to seize opportunities by providing decision-making short cuts in complex settings.

> **DEFINITION**
>
> Heuristics refers to simplifying strategies that entrepreneurs use to manage information and reduce uncertainty in decision making.

The use of heuristics or short cuts can some-times be efficient in that they aid judgements without tremendous information-processing cost. Therefore, according to Le Roux (2005:52), a venture that might not be accepted if more rational decision-making rules are used, might be started if heuristics are applied.

While some have shown that people's cog-nitive biases affect their decision to start a business venture (Simon et al., 2000:37), it is not certain whether entrepreneurs exhibit the same cognitive biases. The quality of decision making, in the risk-charged environments that entrepreneurs often face, can be improved with a better understanding of risk and its role in opportunity evaluation (Forlani and Mullins, 2000).

While it is obvious that individuals are more likely to make risky decisions when they perceive less risk, little is known about the antecedents of risk perception (Tat Keh et al., 2002:126; Sitkin and Weingart, 1995). Even though there are many possible cognitive factors, Simon et al. (2000) argue that the biases of overconfidence, planning fallacy, belief in the law of small numbers, and an illusion of control directly influence risk perception and the decision to start a business venture.

4.1.2.1 Risk perception

Choosing whether an idea is a viable opportu-nity involves judgements made under conditions of uncertainty and complexity (Das and Teng, 1997:70; Allinson et al., 2000:36). Closely con-nected with uncertainty is **risk**, which is the probability that an entrepreneur will not be able to successfully turn an idea into an opportunity. An entrepreneur who fails in turning an idea into an opportunity could incur financial losses. As such, perceived risk is an important aspect of how entrepreneurs evaluate available ideas.

Le Roux (2005) describes risk perception as the subjective judgement of the amount of risk inherent in a situation. Risk perception has been found to differ between entrepreneurs and non-entrepreneurs. When entrepreneurs decide whether an idea is actually an

> **DEFINITION**
>
> Risk perception is the subjective assessment of the chance of occurrence of a risk or about the extent, magnitude, and timing of its effect(s).

opportunity, it will usually require judgements under complex or uncertain conditions. For this reason perceived risk plays a major role; when the perceived level of risk is low, the entrepreneur tends to evaluate the opportunity in a positive manner. Risk perception may explain why some people become entrepre-neurs and others do not. However, the risk perception of the business and cultural envi-ronment within which the entrepreneur operates will also play a role in his or her risk perception as illustrated in Example 4.1.

> **EXAMPLE 4.1**
>
> **South Africa's risk perception**
>
> While society's attitudes towards entrepreneurship may be favourable, South Africa's fear of failure rate of 31% may reflect the reality as to why only 14% of the country's population intend to pursue a business opportunity. An honourable action, i.e. taking a risk to venture out on one's own, is dismissed by the individual's community if failure is the end result. Potential entrepreneurs may therefore be disincentivised from taking a risk if they fear humiliation by their peers. GEM's findings prove that fear of failure is a disincentive: of the 36% who perceive there to be good business opportunities, 31% fear failure, and of those only 10% have entrepreneurial intentions (Xavier, et al., 2012:34).

Entrepreneurs have a tendency to combine business situations with cognitive categories that propose more positive attributes (greater strengths versus weaknesses, opportunities versus threats, and potential for future perfor-mance improvement versus deterioration). Therefore when an entrepreneur pursues an opportunity that would be ignored or neglected by a non-entrepreneur, it may be due to the entrepreneur's perception of a positive outcome rather than a difference in the predis-position towards risk.

4.1.2.2 Overconfidence

Overconfidence refers to the failure to acknowledge or recognise the limits of personal knowledge, skills and experience (Simon et al., 2000:113) and this leads to overestimation of one's certainty regarding facts. This bias is especially common in ill-structured decision situations, such as deciding whether to introduce a new product. Overconfidence can occur because individuals base their certainty on the ease with which they can recall reasons for confidence. Due to their initial overconfidence, these individuals do not revise their initial estimates after receiving new data, and have a tendency to seek supporting evidence rather than disconfirming evidence (Russo and Schoemaker, 1992:10).

> **DEFINITION**
>
> Overconfidence creates a state of mind where entrepreneurs underestimate possible dimensions of potential outcomes not because they do not assess them as important but rather because they overestimate their ability to deal with those when and if the time comes (Salamouris, 2013).

4.1.2.3 Planning fallacy

Planning fallacy occurs when there are strong tendencies to underestimate the amount of time needed to complete a given project, the amount of resources needed, or the amount of work that can be achieved in a given time (Baron, 1998). Planning fallacy tends to operate strongly in situations that are unique, filled with doubts, and where there is a necessity for a focus on the future. For example, in the evaluation phase of decision-making, planning fallacy is future orientated. According to Tat Keh et al. (2002:130) an opportunity in the intertemporal markets (that is the potential of the existing market that the entrepreneur envisages in the future) does not yet exist except in the mind of the entrepreneur; the entrepreneur must forecast future prices of goods and resources and use intuitive judgement to gauge market potential. These

forecasts of future outcomes are often anchored on plans and scenarios of success rather than on past results, and may possibly be overly optimistic.

> **DEFINITION**
>
> The planning fallacy is a cognitive aspect related to errors in planning, that is, the tendency to believe that one can achieve more in a given period of time than one is really is capable of (Sánchez, et al., 2011).

4.1.2.4 Belief in the law of small numbers

According to Simon et al. (2000:113), belief in **the law of small numbers** occurs when an entrepreneur uses a limited number of informational inputs (a small sample of information) to draw firm conclusions.

For example, an entrepreneur may decide that all members of the 12-to-15-year-old age group prefer mustard on their potato chips because his son, who is 13 years old, as well as all the members of the under-15 rugby team at his school like mustard on their potato chips. Tat Keh et al. (2002:130) argue that a small population may not be representative of the total population. The reason for this is that a small sample usually lacks predictive validity. Therefore, entrepreneurs who display a belief in the law of small numbers may make the mistake of being overly certain of their conclusions.

> **DEFINITION**
>
> The law of small numbers refers to a judgemental bias where a small sample of information is used to predict an outcome for a larger population.

Keh et al. (2002:130) explain that entrepreneurs do not utilise large random samples since they are rarely obtainable and they do not have resources to engage in systematic data gathering. A stronger belief in the law of small numbers, together with primarily positive information, is prone to induce a more than usually optimistic view of the business enterprise, and thus lower perceived risk. This in turn might lead to entrepreneurial failure as is evident in Example 4.2 *The danger of using small samples.*

4.1.2.5 Illusion of control

According to Simon and Houghton (2002:113) **illusion of control** occurs when the entrepreneur overemphasises the degree to which his or her skills can increase performance in situations where chance plays a great part and skill is not essentially the deciding factor. This usually occurs when they believe that they can control largely uncontrollable events and that they can accurately predict the outcome of the events. Entrepreneurs with this bias have a higher expectancy of personal success than objective probability would warrant, as they usually think that their skills are superior to those of others.

> ## DEFINITION
>
> Illusion of control occurs when the entrepreneur overestimates his or her ability to control events that are not actually within his or her control.

The illusion of control may play a part in a variety of strategies. According to Simon and Houghton (2002), an active information search may lead to entrepreneurs becoming more involved and making more choices. Giving up the illusion of control allows an entrepreneur to focus on their impact – the decisions and actions that shape their company. This is illustrated by examples discussed in Example 4.3 below.

According to Tat Keh et al. (2002:131), there are two reasons why the illusion of control persists. The first is that, when individuals are encouraged to take charge of their environment, the resulting sense of competence may lead to a sense of power over the uncontrollable. The second reason is that skill and chance factors are strongly connected and it is generally difficult to discriminate between chance and skill elements.

Entrepreneurs should guard against heuristic and conceptual biases as they may impact on their ability to identify the best viable business opportunity which may result in choosing an opportunity that can lead to business failure. Biases may also result in entrepreneurs not addressing the critical criteria that venture capitalists or investors consider when looking to invest in first-time entrepreneurship ventures as discussed in the following section.

The South African success story of Nick Kaoma and Mzoxolo Gcwabe – *Head Honcho Clothing* illustrates first-time entrepreneurs who were successful in establishing their unique clothing brand in the South African market because they identified and grabbed an opportunity and used their abilities to develop a unique product.

> ## EXAMPLE 4.2
>
> **The danger of using small samples**
>
> Identifying the right sample as a basis for decision making is a difficult task for many first-time entrepreneurs. What they should realise is that not everyone in the world, sector or industry is their customer. There is a big difference between the way men and women buy, between the poor and the rich, and the old and young. If entrepreneurs try being everything to everyone they will land up being nothing to everyone! Faced with the daunting question of who and how many people to include in a sample when one wants to establish whether an idea is viable or not, many entrepreneurs tend to restrict themselves to a small sample. In most cases, the entrepreneur only asks friends or family their opinion about a new business idea when he or she thinks they will give positive feedback. This is especially dangerous where none of the friends or family who were asked form part of the potential target market. So the entrepreneur pitches the idea to the wrong people and they all love it. Based on the positive response, the entrepreneur then starts the business and, after only a few months, has to close the doors, not understanding why the business has failed.

EXAMPLE 4.3

Giving up illusion of control by adding value

When faced with situations where the entrepreneur would like to have complete control, but is not able to, the entrepreneur could develop and implement certain strategies and actions to not lose control. The following are examples of such situations:

▸ An entrepreneur cannot make customers buy his or her products or services, but can decide what features to add, how much to charge and how to resolve customer service issues.

▸ An entrepreneur cannot make investors put money in his or her business, but can provide potential investors with the proper information to make a decision, and develop negotiation skills to work through valuation and other issues with the investor.

▸ An entrepreneur cannot make employees and contractors do his or her bidding but can be clear about resources, goals and timelines, and maintaining consistent expectations on both sides.

SOUTH AFRICAN SUCCESS STORY

Head Honcho Clothing

Head Honcho Clothing is a burgeoning Cape Town-based clothing company that was founded in November 2008 by Nick Kaoma and Mzoxolo Gcwabe. They officially launched the business in November 2008 and laboured on it for a year before they launched their first range. What inspired them to start the company was the simple desire to create something magical that reflects the spirit of their times. As fans and consumers of everything urban and street, they felt that South African street-wear lovers were being short-changed in terms of quality and originality. Nick watched the game from the sidelines for seven years while silently lamenting the half-heartedness that epitomised the approach from many local brands.

The company has grown its product line from just t-shirts and caps a season ago to include cardigans, varsity jackets, hoodies, shirts, tank tops and dresses for ladies.

Their mission as a brand is to blaze a new trail, pioneer new fashion techniques and discover new ways of interacting with young urban South Africans. Their objective is not only to produce attractive fashion, but also to ensure that the clothing is embedded with a core underlying message.

Head Honcho is now available at Shesha and selected Sporscene stores (6th Ave Group, 2014).

▸ 1. Which cognitive biases and heuristics do you think Nick Kaoma and Mzoxolo Gcwabe had to overcome in establishing their clothing business?

4.2 Venture capitalists' evaluation criteria for new ventures

The focus of this book is on entrepreneurs who will start new ventures, usually for the first time. It is thus important to note that first-time entrepreneurs tend to evaluate initial opportunities, and will usually also apply for funding, *prior* to opportunity exploitation. However, venture capitalists, who invest in these first-time ventures, usually evaluate an investment opportunity *after* the entrepreneur has decided which opportunities to exploit. Investors, therefore, evaluate the opportunity based on detailed calculations of market potential and profit estimates as well as all the factors that will contribute towards the success of the venture.

Bishop and Nixon (2006:29) indicated that, when evaluating business opportunities, first-time entrepreneurs most commonly use the following significant criteria, in order of frequency:

▸ Potential growth in the target market
▸ Demonstrated market acceptance
▸ The likelihood of a ten times return on assets in the next five to ten years
▸ The entrepreneur's ability to react well to risk.

In contrast, the criteria investors (venture capitalists) identified as being the most important focus on the knowledge, skills, and abilities of the entrepreneur. In a study by Bishop and Nixon (2006), they found that each inexperienced first-time entrepreneur used a set of opportunity criteria that differed from the set used by venture capitalists. They argue that the reasons for this may include differences in the timing and purpose of the decision and (or) different levels of prior-evaluation experience.

The majority of investors will look at the following aspects when they consider new venture proposals:

▸ *Experience and a good management team.* Although it is not necessary to have a complete team, investors need the entrepreneur to illustrate determination and ambition to achieve their long-term and short-term goals. Investors usually look for a team dedicated to growing an exceptionally successful business and having the knowledge, experience, and track record to do so.
▸ *Proprietary product or service.* Investors look for highly differentiated, unique, and significantly superior products and services. A clear analysis should explain why customers will purchase the company's product or service rather than purchase a competing alternative.
▸ *Marketability.* Venture capitalists are most likely to invest in a business that addresses customers in large, growing markets that can be identified and accessed economically.
▸ *Personal commitment and involvement of the entrepreneur.* The ability to work with the investors and their commitment to the business will be assessed. This is illustrated by personal investments in the business by the owners, taking low salaries, and being receptive to inputs from the investors.
▸ *Openness and honesty.* Investors want to be able to trust the entrepreneur with their money. Any indication that the entrepreneur tries to mislead the investor, such as inflating the financial calculations or projections of the marketability of the products or services, will probably be found out during the due diligence process.
▸ *Knowledge and experience.* It is important for the entrepreneur to do extensive research on the market – of both competitors and customers. The entrepreneur should be able to answer any questions about the industry with complete understanding and insight. Venture capitalists tend to back businesses in which they have an interest, and prefer to invest in sectors in which they have experience.
▸ *Realistic financials.* Investors expect to see a business plan that paints a realistic financial picture of the anticipated growth of the company. If the plan is overly aggressive and not consistent with growth in the industry, it may be shelved. Be realistic with financial projections, and be prepared to explain calculations and assumptions. In the case of a new venture that cannot provide specific figures based on the past performance of the business, figures from the industry or competitors are required to be provided where and when possible. These figures can carry more weight than assumed projections and are usually perceived as adding an element of reality to the proposal.
▸ *Exit plan.* Having an exit plan is critical to investors, as it assures them of the possibility that they will get their money back, hopefully with a healthy return. In the exit plan, the entrepreneur should outline the long-term plans for the business including the type of ownership, and the possibility of becoming a public company, merging

with or acquiring another business, buying out existing partners, turning the business into a franchise or developing a family business that will go from parent to child, and what will happen to the business in case of the death of the entrepreneur. Venture capitalists usually look for a high return and an exit strategy of approximately three to seven years.

▸ *Return rate on investment (ROI)*. Investors look for a high return on their capital. Anything below the existing interest rates that they could earn from financial institutions and other investments will be of no interest to them. The annual return, sometimes as high as between 40% and 50%, should reflect the risks involved in providing seeding or other funding.

▸ *Intellectual property*. A trademark, copyright or patent can be attractive to the investor as it creates a clear barrier to entry and secures a competitive advantage.

In the light of the criteria identified above, it is important for first-time entrepreneurs to be sure about the products and (or) services they want to offer in order to provide evidence of their experience or even potential experience as well as all necessary information in all of these areas. If they are not able to do so, investors may perceive them as having risky investment potential. Entrepreneurs need to focus on these criteria when evaluating opportunities and include evidence of it when applying for start-up venture capital. As such, developing evaluation decision aids might help entrepreneurs to improve in this process regardless of their experience levels.

In the next section we will look at how product and service ideas can be evaluated and screened so that the most viable opportunity can be identified and exploited.

4.3 Opportunity assessment and screening

The criteria that are used by venture capitalists when evaluating the applications for funding they receive from first-time entrepreneurs could serve as one of the bases for developing assessment criteria in the assessment and screening of ideas and opportunities. In this discussion, we will first discuss the characteristics of successful product or service ideas. The aspects that contribute towards the feasibility and marketability of the product and service, followed by the personal characteristics of the entrepreneur and the entrepreneurial team that could add to the success of business opportunities, are then highlighted. The discussion will conclude with guidelines on the development and utilisation of an idea screening guide in the evaluation of different product or service ideas.

4.3.1 The characteristics of successful product or service ideas

The products or services that an enterprise sells will play a major role in whether they succeed or not. The right product or service can propel your business to fortune, while the wrong product or service can even make your most exhaustive efforts unprofitable. It is thus important to identify the characteristics or attributes of the potentially excellent product or service. The list below has been adapted from Ryan (2003:117, 120–125) and Rogers and Shoemaker (1971:50–51):

▸ *The new product or service should fulfil a need or want* and should convince the buyer that one of his or her needs is being satisfied. An immediate benefit should thus be associated with the product or service. Does the product or service ease a pain, fulfil a dream, make life easier, or make life better? If not, start searching for a product or service that does.

▶ *The new product or service should have either a niche-market appeal or a mass-market appeal.* When catering for a **niche market** it will not be products or services that appeal to everyone, but to a pre-determined group (such as publishing a medical handbook or doing consultation in chaos theory). The advantage is that there will be generally less competition; that gives you the opportunity to develop your expertise and price it accordingly. Marketing these products and services can be done by means of trade magazines, journals, and word-of-mouth. It may furthermore be easier to develop brand recognition. When catering for the **mass market** you should realise that there will be strong competition as well as new developments of similar products and services. Mass-market products and services (such as Bioslim, Bauer pots and pans, Abflex and Outsurance) can be marketed via the Internet and infomercials. It remains true that the product or service should have a relative advantage over existing products or services by introducing unique features or values. If there is no advantage at all, do not even think of developing the product or service.

▶ *The product or service must render an income and profit.* The aim should be that the income from the products or service divided by cost of the goods or service sold should at least be at a 2:1 ratio. A ratio of 5:1 or more is optimal.

▶ *The product or service should be replenished or repurchased by the customer on a regular basis*, thus bringing about continuous sales. Some products or services are single-sale items, such as vacuum cleaners, beds, ladders, cars, interior-design consultations, and so on. It is also more difficult to build a business selling these as more money and time is spent trying to attract new customers. Should you have a choice, look for those products and services that can be sold many times to the same customer, such as health products, cellphone services, beauty products, food and beverages, and so on.

▶ There should be compatibility with existing attitudes and beliefs and a drastic change in the buyer's behaviour should not be necessary. The perceived value of the products and services should fit in with the buyer's attitudes and beliefs. Aspects such as quality, after-sales service, design, convenience, and packaging and labelling should emphasise the perceived value of your product or service. If this is true, then you should be able to increase your price without a decrease in sales and net profits.

▶ *The product or service should be simple so that the buyer will understand it.* If the innovation is complex and the buyer has difficulty understanding how to use it, it may not be bought.

▶ It should be easy to communicate the results or benefits of the new product or service to potential users.

▶ *The product or service should be made available to potential customers for a trial period* without risk or obligation to purchase. Samples can be distributed or trial users could be identified to allow potential customers to use the new product or service.

▶ *The product or service should be readily available* once the buyer decides to make the purchase. If it is not available, the sale will in all probability be lost forever.

When using these characteristics to screen potential ideas, the entrepreneur should assess whether or not the different ideas reflect the said characteristic. Only those ideas that have more than four of these characteristics should survive the screening test. Those ideas that do not survive could be shelved, to be adjusted at a later stage when new ideas are again being generated. It does happen that you may have more than one idea and are faced with which one to choose as illustrated in the dilemma box below.

4.3.2 **Feasibility of products or services**

A second screening test should be the feasibility of the product or service. The technical requirements for producing a product or service should be identified and evaluated as well as the technical skills of the entrepreneur or the venture team in relation to the product or service. The following aspects should be included in the screening test:

▶ The product or service. The entrepreneur needs to ask the following questions in this regard:
  - Can the product or service work?
  - Is the product or service legal?
  - Will the venture make or buy what it wants to sell, or will it combine these two strategies?

- Is the design functional and attractive in appearance?
- Is the design flexible? Could the external features of the product be modified to meet the demands of customers?
- Is the material used durable?
- Is the product reliable and safe, ensuring performance as expected under normal operating conditions and posing no potential dangers under these conditions?
- Is the maintenance of the product easy and inexpensive?
- Is the equipment used in the manufacturing of the product available or must existing equipment be adapted to manufacture the product?

▶ The skills of the entrepreneur and (or) venture team. During screening the following should be assessed:
  - Does the entrepreneur or venture team have the skills to make the product or provide the service?
  - Can the entrepreneur recruit and afford suitable personnel?
  - Does the entrepreneur understand the market for the product or service?
  - Does the entrepreneur know how to sell the product or service?
  - Does the type of business require a formal qualification for its venture team (such as electricians, estate agents, legal professionals, etc.)?
  - Does the entrepreneur understand budgeting, cost control, credit management, and managing debtors?

4.3.3 **Marketability**

The test for marketability can be divided into four categories, namely customers, competitors, suppliers and marketing of the product or service. It is not the aim of the screening test to draw up a complete marketing plan, but to make the entrepreneur aware of aspects that could influence the decision to develop a potential venture into a feasible business. Each of these categories is discussed below:

▶ Customers. To assess the viability of the idea as far as the customers are concerned, the following questions should be asked:
  - Who are the customers likely to be, e.g. private persons or trade and industry?
  - Where are the customers situated and how will they be serviced?
  - Is there an initial customer with a specified need? Is the size of this market large or small?
  - What are the dominant characteristics of the customers with regard to age, income level, buying habits, and so on? Are the customers prone to brand loyalty?

▶ Competitors. Ignoring the competitors or potential competitors is one mistake that could have a direct influence on the viability of a business idea. The mere fact that there are competitors could be an indication that the market is large enough to absorb a new product. The following questions need to be asked:
  - How many competitors are operating in the market and do they have a competitive advantage?
  - Will the product or service provide a competitive advantage?
  - Will the competitors react to a new entrant and, if so, how?
  - Will any initial competitive advantage that may be gained by offering a new product or service be maintained?
  - How will prices be set and how will they compare with those of the competition?

▶ Suppliers. Suppliers can play a vital role at the start-up stage of a new business venture. They could add to the competitive advantage of the products or services that will be offered or make it impossible to deliver. The following questions could be asked:
  - Will a specific supplier be needed for the planned venture?

  - Do the present suppliers have exclusive contracts with existing businesses?
  - Is there any supplier who can offer the required products or services for the planned venture?
  - Will such a supplier add to the competitive advantage of the planned product or service with regard to cost, timing, and quality?
  - Are the suppliers local, national or international?

▶ Marketing of product or service. To inform potential customers of the products or services you plan to offer, the marketing of those products or services should be evaluated by answering the following questions:
  - Will the product or service need special selling skills or a special sales team?
  - How much will be spent on advertising and selling?
  - What share of the market will the venture capture?
  - What advertising media will be used and will these be the same as those used by competitors?
  - What distribution channels will be used – wholesale, retail, direct agents or mail?
  - Is the physical location of the venture important in selling the product or delivering the service?
  - Can any orders be obtained before starting the venture?
  - Can the product or service be sold via infomercials or the Internet, is it aimed at the mass market or does it need a more specialised marketing campaign?
  - Will the sale of the product or service be influenced by seasonal changes or trends in the market?

4.3.4 The entrepreneur and entrepreneurial team

In the evaluation of the entrepreneur and business, it is necessary to link it to the aspects that the venture capitalist will use in their evaluation of the proposed business plan discussed in Section 4.2. The following should be included in any evaluation of business ideas or opportunities:

▸ *Personality and personal preferences.* Venture capitalists evaluate the commitment and ambition of the entrepreneur and entrepreneurial team as they see these as contributing to the success of any entrepreneurial venture. The questions to ask are:
  ▪ Is there a good match between the requirements of the business and what the founders want out of it?
  ▪ Do the investors have any personal preferences regarding what type of product or service will be delivered or the area within which the business will be situated?

▸ *Skills.* Certain skills are often attributed to new venture success (Human et al., 2004:69), including:
  ▪ Business skills – functional, technical, and persuasion and (or) motivation skills
  ▪ Interpersonal skills – communication, listening, conflict management, and networking skills
  ▪ Creative problem-solving and change management skills.

▸ *Traits and attributes.* Successful entrepreneurs typically exhibit certain traits, which can include the following:
  ▪ Achievement and opportunity orientation
  ▪ A strong sense of personal responsibility and control
  ▪ Tolerance for risk and ambiguity
  ▪ Proactiveness and innovativeness
  ▪ Resilience, energy, and good health.

▸ *Relevant experience.* There are three kinds of experience when it comes to start-ups (Human et al., 2004:69):
  ▪ Previous entrepreneurial or leadership experience – experience of either starting a business or in management in a related type of business
  ▪ Industry experience – experience in the industry related to the proposed business venture
  ▪ Educational experience – business-related qualifications or attendance of business-related training courses.

▸ *Synergy.* This refers to the extent that the entrepreneur or entrepreneurial team reflects the skills and understanding that will be necessary to the success of the venture. Questions to ask in assessing this are:
  ▪ Does the founding team have complementary skills that offset each other's weaknesses, and does there appear to be a clear understanding of team member roles?
  ▪ If an individual proposes the concept, does he or she show enough understanding to identify key roles or skills needed for a balanced founding team?

▸ *Exit plans (harvesting).* The exit plan should include what will happen to the business in the case of the death of the entrepreneur. It is essential that the alternative business opportunities should be evaluated according to possible exit or harvest options as this will have an impact on the long-term survival of the business venture. As indicated in Section 4.2, some of the options could be:
  ▪ Establishing a private company that will offer shares to the public in order to expand
  ▪ Merging with or acquiring another related or even unrelated business
  ▪ One of the founding members or partners buying out existing partners
  ▪ Turning the business into a franchise (see Chapter 8 for details)
  ▪ Developing a family business that will allow for the business to be handed down from parent to child (see Chapter 7 for a description of the types of business ownership).

The more experience, education, and skills the entrepreneur and entrepreneurial team have and the higher the synergy between them, the greater the probability of success. Ideally, entrepreneurs should have all three types of experience. Human et al. (2004:69) argue that experience in the industry, or knowledge and experience with the technology used to produce or provide the product or service, has been commonly associated with success and often builds important credibility early on.

4.3.5 Resources

The main resources for new ventures include financial, social, human, physical, technological, and organisational (Human et al., 2004:69). Getting the required resources has been at the forefront of opportunity evaluation for more than a decade and plays a big part in deciding whether or not to start a business. Human et al. (2004:67) suggest that the evaluation of start-ups should include questions regarding who will have to be hired, and when and how they will be found and recruited. These questions should be asked not just be for labour, but for all business resources. The following aspects should be included in evaluating the resources needed for each alternative idea or opportunity to enable the entrepreneur to identify the most viable option:

▸ *Accessibility of resources.* How accessible are the resources that are needed for the start-up? The entrepreneur should not only identify the different resources required, but also where, how, and when they can be acquired. It is important to identify, develop, and maintain solid relationships with important suppliers of the required resources.

▸ *Optimising resources.* One of the dangers of obtaining the required resources at all costs is that the new venture may not be able to afford these resources in the long term. This is especially true regarding scarce or special resources. It is thus important to make sure that all unnecessary expenditures are eliminated and only those resources which are vital to the business should be obtained, and that any optional resources should be omitted. Optimising resources should support the most viable opportunity.

▸ *Sustainable advantage.* A sustainable advantage refers to the situation where the entrepreneur is able to retain an initial competitive advantage over a long period of time and not only for the first month or year after starting the business. Nando's is an example of a business which has maintained its competitive advantage in the chicken fast-food industry, by not only keeping to its initial recipe of *peri-peri chicken*, but also continuously adding flavours for those customers that do not like to eat *hot and spicy food*, but prefer the *flame-grilled* cooking method. The question to ask is whether the necessary resources for sustainable advantage are available or whether an initial competitive advantage will be sufficient to face future competition. It is also important to establish whether the venture will be able to generate sufficient financial resources to keep cash flow positive for a year if profits do not materialise in that time. Entrepreneurs need to develop sustainable advantage through resources that are rare or of value to the market or competitors.

▸ *Type and nature of the industry.* The type and nature of the industry within which each of the alternative products or services will be sold may influence the decision of whether or not to start the business. The factors that could play a role include the availability of resources, the size of the investment needed, competition, and the projected ability of the business to survive mistakes made in the early stages. According to Human et al. (2004:69), opportunities which require unique technologies (computer technology or software, and machinery and equipment) and capital-intensive ideas (manufacturing) have a learning curve which can require heavy, ongoing investment in marketing and education long before revenues occur.

▶ *Capital requirements.* Entrepreneurs should establish the capital requirements needed to implement each of the various ideas or opportunities. Some will have low to moderate capital requirements and would thus need less investment funding. This is likely to make them more attractive than those ideas that will have higher capital requirements.

People often find the idea of entrepreneurship or starting a business attractive until they realise the personal investment, sacrifices, and other commitments necessary for success (Human et al., 2004:69). That is why it is important to generate alternative ideas (as discussed in Chapter 3) before evaluating each alternative to identify the most viable and appropriate opportunity to follow. One way in which to evaluate ideas and opportunities using specific criteria is with an idea-screening guide.

4.4 The idea-screening guide

In this section we will discuss how to identify the best idea or the ideas most likely to be successful, using some of the aspects discussed previously. The idea-screening guide is an instrument that can be used for choosing between different ideas to find the one or two that can be pursued.

The first step in developing the screening guide is to establish the criteria to be used. These could differ for each entrepreneur and even for various products or services. After the criteria have been established, a weighting (one to 10) should be assigned to each criterion to give a sense of its importance. If it is extremely important, it should be given a weighting of nine or 10. A criterion of very low importance would be given a weighting of one or two.

These scales could be qualitative (one is no flexibility in the market and 10 is total flexibility in the market) or quantitative (one is an income lower than R50 000 per annum and 10 is an income of R10 million per annum).

Each idea should then be evaluated against the different criteria and be given a rating (one to 10) to indicate how well it meets each criterion. If the idea fulfils all possible requirements of a criterion, it would receive a rating of 10. On the other hand, if it only partially satisfies the requirements, it might receive a four or a five. The weighting of the criterion must now be multiplied by the score obtained for the idea. This must be done for every criterion and the score for each idea must then be added. The idea with the highest total score should be your tentative first choice.

While identifying weightings and scoring may at first seem somewhat subjective, it is an extremely effective technique for those who can dissociate themselves from their personal biases and arrive at a logical evaluation of each alternative idea or business opportunity. If the alternative that you assume should be the proper choice turns out to have a low score, you should re-examine the weighting of each criterion. Analyse your instincts to gain a better understanding of which criteria are really important to you. If, after rescoring, your alternative still scores lower than the others, perhaps your 'gut feeling' may be wrong.

Table 4.1 is an example of a venture-screening guide that could be used in the evaluation of ideas for products or services.

From the example in Table 4.1, it can be seen that linking to another consultant would be the best option and starting the business at home would be the next best option. The weakest option would be to start with a new office. The two most viable ideas could be combined (i.e. linking up with other consultants while working from home), thus building up clientele to enable the entrepreneur to begin the process of starting his or her own business.

One word of caution – because the assigning of weightings and scores is very subjective, it could easily be abused by giving higher weightings or scores to a predetermined favoured project or idea. The biased weightings or scores could easily skew the numbers and thus sabotage the screening process. It is therefore important to keep an open mind when making the evaluation. It would also help to do the evaluation in a group or ask a partner to help you in the evaluation process. The main objective of screening various business ideas or opportunities is to identify those opportunities that will most likely be successful and render profits in the long run.

The idea-screening guide is one useful method of evaluating alternative ideas or business opportunities. Depending on the number of screening stages employed, one or more screening methods may be used. It is important to remember that the screening methods may be categorised as qualitative and quantitative. More qualitative (yes or no) methods may be employed in the primary stages of screening and more quantitative methods utilised later. Criteria or questions asked may be further classified or weighted on the basis of *must* objectives (or criteria) and *want* objectives. The

Table 4.1 Venture-screening guide for the development of a human resource consultancy

CRITERIA	WEIGH-TING	IDEA 1: WORK FROM HOME		IDEA 2: LINK TO EXISTING CONSULTANCY		IDEA 3: START OWN OFFICE	
		RATING	SCORE	RATING	SCORE	RATING	SCORE
Start-up capital required is low	9	8	72	4	36	2	18
Premises are accessible	4	3	12	7	28	7	28
Cost of premises is low	9	8	72	3	27	2	18
Ample parking is available	7	4	28	7	49	6	42
Competition is limited	9	9	81	3	27	6	54
Products and services can be easily expanded	9	4	36	6	54	6	54
Products and services offerings readily available	8	5	40	8	64	5	40
Marketing to customers in place	8	4	32	8	64	4	32
Equipment to render services is available	6	3	18	7	42	3	18
Entrepreneur skilled in product or service	8	8	64	8	64	8	64
Entrepreneur has business skills	6	5	30	5	30	5	30
Customers in medium income group	9	5	45	7	63	5	45
Should be financially viable	8	5	40	7	56	5	40
TOTAL SCORE	100		570		604		483

must objectives will reflect those things that the entrepreneur cannot or will not omit, such as previous experience, objectives and goals, technology, or financial requirements. On the other hand, *want* objectives would reflect personal preferences, which will usually be reflected in qualitative methods. The particular method used will be based on realism, flexibility, capability, ease of use, and cost considerations.

Ideas can be processed through the screening process individually or in batches, depending on possible time constraints, whether an even flow of ideas into later stages of the new product development process is important, and whether or not there are advantages to processing several ideas at a time (Rochford, 1991:292). The ideas that are discarded from the screening process should be saved as alternatives to be picked up when selected ideas are either passed on to later stages in the new product development process, dropped, or additional resources are made available. Market or technological changes can occur which can change the viability of previously rejected ideas.

CONCLUSION

The majority of entrepreneurs rely on their cognitive processes when evaluating an opportunity. Most first-time entrepreneurs are not aware of the venture-screening process or criteria used by venture capitalists. By using a venture-screening guide, entrepreneurs can be assisted in the process of evaluating opportunities. As a result, they will be able to make a more informed choice and evaluate opportunities from perspectives they might have otherwise have thought to be unimportant or irrelevant. Screening guides can also help the entrepreneur to save time and money by making sure that all the important information is considered, and avoiding quick, costly decisions.

Using a venture-screening guide can also increase an entrepreneur's risk perception and help the entrepreneur to be more realistic when evaluating opportunities. The framework of an evaluation instrument is mostly designed to allow entrepreneurs to evaluate a business idea against high-potential and low-potential venture criteria, with a goal of helping investors identify high-potential opportunities while screening out low-potential ones.

SELF-ASSESSMENT QUESTIONS

Indicate whether each of the following statements is true or false:

1. Overconfidence refers to the failure to acknowledge or recognise the limits of personal knowledge, skills, and experience and this leads to overestimation of one's certainty regarding facts.
2. In order for a product to be successful it does not need to be replenished or repurchased by the customer.

Multiple-choice questions

3. Which one of the following is not one of the criteria that venture capitalists use to evaluate new proposals?
   a. Proprietary product or service
   b. Personal commitment and involvement of the entrepreneur
   c. Ten times return on assets in the next five to ten years
   d. Return on investment
   e. Knowledge and experience of the entrepreneur
4. _____ refers to the extent to which the entrepreneur or entrepreneurial team reflects the skills and understanding that will be necessary to the success of the venture.
   a. Experience
   b. Skills
   c. Synergy
   d. Traits or attributes
5. Suppliers can play a vital role at the start-up stage of a business venture by adding to:
   a. The potential geographical site of the business
   b. The competitive advantage of the product or services that will be offered
   c. The external sources of the investors

6. To inform potential customers of the product or services you plan to offer, the marketing of those products should include the following:
   a. Where is the business located?
   b. What share of the market will the venture capture?
   c. Is the business seasonal?
7. A viable business opportunity can be defined as:
   a. A means of generating economic value that has previously been explored and is not currently being explored
   b. A means of generating economic value that has not previously been explored and is currently being explored
   c. A means of generating economic value that has not previously been explored and is not currently being explored
   d. None of the above
8. _____ are common types of mental short cuts used to make judgements about opportunities and the business.
   a. Cognitive approaches
   b. Cognitive biases
   c. General biases
   d. Heuristics
9. Which one of the following is not a planning fallacy?
   a. Belief in the law of small numbers
   b. Illusion of control
   c. Failing to plan
   d. None of the above
10. Which of the following aspects that investors look for when they consider new venture proposals can be described as 'a realistic financial picture of the anticipated growth of the company'?
    a. Experience and a good management team
    b. Exit plan
    c. Openness and honesty
    d. Realistic financials
11. Which one of the following is not a question to ask when assessing the viability of the idea as far as the customers are concerned?
    a. Will the product or service provide a competitive advantage?
    b. Who are the customers likely to be?
    c. What are the dominant characteristics of the customers?
    d. Is the size of the market large or small?

DISCUSSION QUESTIONS

1. In your own words describe what is meant by a viable business opportunity.
2. Describe the role that cognitive biases and heuristics play in the evaluation of a business opportunity.
3. Discuss the aspects that investors will look at when they consider new venture proposals.
4. Identify and discuss the characteristics of successful products and services.
5. What are the characteristics of successful products and services?
6. How can one assess the feasibility of product or service ideas?
7. What factors will influence the marketability of ideas?
8. Identify and discuss how the entrepreneur and his team should be evaluated when considering the viability of a product or service.
9. What are the aspects that should be included when evaluating the resources needed for each alternative idea or opportunity to enable the entrepreneur to identify the most viable option?
10. Describe the role that the idea-screening guide plays in choosing between different ideas.
11. Discuss the assessment of the viability of product and service ideas.

EXPERIENTIAL EXERCISE

1. Identify a successful enterprise in your area and request an interview with the entrepreneur, business owner or manager. Ask what it took for him or her to turn dreams and ideas into a profitable and successful business. Ask him or her to explain the process(es) that they used when they had to evaluate their ideas. (Tip: If the entrepreneur is too busy to see you, ask if you can fax or email your questions.)
2. Read the entrepreneurial dilemma box – *Which business to start?* Develop a screening guide for both the business ideas, namely:
   a. a drama school and
   b. an entrepreneurial accounting and marketing support business.

3. Make a list of how the screening guides for the two businesses differ.
4. Use the information that you obtained from your interview with the entrepreneur in Question 1, and combine it with the screening guides you developed in Question 2, to formulate a plan for developing your own product or service.

IFIX

Julie Alexander Fourie started iFix in 2006 to ease iPod owners' frustration at the lack of service available through traditional Apple repair channels. He says: 'It started in my dorm room in Wilgenhof in Stellenbosch University in 2007, I broke my iPod, fixed it, then fixed a few friends' iPods, and then placed an ad in the Cape Ads; and it sort of just took off from there' (Maake, 2014).

Satisfied friends soon referred numerous iPod owners in search of repairs and the first full-time technician was hired.

After six months working from a garage, iFix opened its Cape Town branch and more staff were hired full-time to serve Cape Town's burgeoning iPod and iPhone owners. For two industrious years, iFix operated on a drop-off system at the legendary Mabu Vinyl record shop in Cape Town. To satisfy demand in Gauteng, shops were opened in Johannesburg and Pretoria (ifix, n.d).

According to Fourie one of the key differentiating factors in iFix's success has always been the beautiful and awesome people that work for, and with them. 'From top management to the newly employed receptionist we always try to help, where help is needed' (ifix, n.d.).

The company is also involved in the development of the community and have launched an initiative to put its cleaning staff's children through school. The donations received by the iCare Project have enabled them to put these children in schools were they can learn to speak English and have a chance at a decent education. It's in a position where they have access to proper schooling facilities and aftercare services (ifix, 2013).

The company has expanded its offering to other Apple devices as well as some Samsung gadgets.

The company employ 80 staff in the eight stores they opened in the Western Cape, Gauteng and KZN and have done work for major clients like FNB, DionWired and Santam (Nsehe, 2014).

1. Do you think using an idea-screening guide would have helped Fourie when he initially started iFix? Why?
2. What criteria would you suggest Fourie could use in such an idea-screening guide?

CASE STUDY

SUGGESTED WEBSITE LINKS

http://www.seda.org.za/Pages/Home.aspx
http://www.bransoncentre.org/southafrica/home.html
http://www.bizmag.co.za/hot-opportunities/
http://businessowl.co.za/
http://www.kwikwap.co.za/index.php

REFERENCES

Allinson, CW, Chell, E. & Hayes, J. 2000. Intuition and entrepreneurial behavior. *European Journal of Work and Organizational Psychology*, 9(1):31–43.

Baron, RA. 2004. Opportunity recognition: A cognitive perspective. Academy of Management Best Conference Paper 2004ENT: A1–A6. [Online]. Available: http://faculty.insead.edu/andersonp/VOBM_MAYJUN2005/Anderson%20VOBM%20readings/Session%202%20 How%20venture%20opportunities%20are%20screened/Baron,%202004.pdf [1 August 2011].

Bishop, K. & Nixon, RD. 2006. Venture opportunity evaluations: Comparisons between venture capitalist and inexperienced pre-nascent entrepreneurs. *Journal of Developmental Entrepreneurship*, 11(1):19–33.

Busenitz, LW. & Barney, JB. 1997. Differences between entrepreneurs and managers in large organizations: Biases and heuristics in strategic decision-making. *Journal of Business Venturing*, 12(1):9–30.

Cooper, AC, Woo, CY. & Dunkelberg, WC. 1988. Entrepreneurs' perceived chance of success. *Journal of Business Venturing*, 3(1):97–108.

Das, TK. & Teng, BS. 1997. Time and entrepreneurial risk behavior. *Entrepreneurship Theory and Practice*, 22(2):69–88.

Forlani, D. & Mullins, JW. 2000. Perceived risks and choices in entrepreneurs' new venture decisions. *Journal of Business Venturing*, 15(3):305–322.

Human, SH, Clark, T, Baucus MS. & Eustis, AC. 2004. Idea or prime opportunity? A framework for evaluating business ideas. *Journal of Small Business Strategy*, 15(1):61–79.

ifix. 2013. *iCare Charity Project: Keeping it close to home.* [Online]. Available: http://ifix.co.za/keeping-it-close-to-home/ [29 May 2014].

ifix. 2014. *About us.* [Online]. Available: http://ifix.co.za/about-us/ [29 May 2014].

Le Roux, I. 2005. Entrepreneurial cognition and the decision to exploit a venture opportunity. PhD. University of Pretoria, South Africa.

Maake, M. 2014. *SA makes strong showing on Forbes list of promising young entrepreneurs.* [Online]. Available: http://www.citypress.co.za/business/sa-forbes-list-promising-young-entrepreneurs/ [29 May 2014].

Mitchell, R. et al. 2004. The Distinctive and Inclusive Domain of Entrepreneurial Cognition Research.. *Entrepreneursip: Theory and Practice*, 28(6):505-518.

Nsehe, M. 2014. *30 Most Promising Young Entrepreneurs In Africa 2014.* [Online]. Available: http://www.forbes.com/sites/mfonobongnsehe/2014/02/04/30-most-promising-young-entrepreneurs-in-africa-2014/ [29 May 2014].

Rochford, L. 1991. Generating and screening new product ideas. *Industrial Marketing Management*, 20:287–296.

Rogers, EM. & Shoemaker, F. 1971. *Communication of Innovation.* New York: The Free Press.

Russo, JE. & Schoemaker, PJH. 1992. Managing overconfidence. *Sloan Management Review*, 33(2):7–17.

Ryan, PMA. 2003. Zero to one million: How to build a company to one million dollars in sales. [Online]. Available: www.zeromillion.com [1 August 2007].

Salamouris, IS. 2013. How overconfidence influences entrepreneurship. *Journal of Innovation and Entrepreneurship*, Volume 2:8.

Sánchez, JC, TC. & Gutiérrez, A. 2011 . The entrepreneur from a cognitive approach. *Psicothema*, 23(3): 433–438.

Simon, M, Houghton, SM. & Aquino, K. 2000. Cognitive biases, risk perception and venture formation: How individuals decide to start companies. *Journal of Business Venturing*, 15(2):113–134.

Simon, M. & Houghton, SM. 2002. The relationship among biases, misperceptions and introducing pioneering products: Examining differences in venture decision contexts. *Entrepreneurship: Theory and Practice*. 27(2):105–124.

Sitkin, SB. & Weingart, L. 1995. Determinants of risky decision-making behaviour: A test of the mediating role of risk perceptions and propensity. *Academy of Management Journal*, 37(6):1873–1592.

Tat Keh, H, Der Foo, M. & Chong Lim, B. 2002. Opportunity evaluation under risky conditions: The cognitive processes of entrepreneurs. *Entrepreneurship Theory and Practice*, 27(2):125–148.

Xavier, SR, Kelley, D, Herrington, M. & Vorderwulbecke, A. 2012. *Global Entrepreneurship Monitor. 2012 Global Report*, Massachusets: Global Entrepreneurship Research Association.

part three

New venture creation

CHAPTER 5

Information technology for SMEs

Elana Swanepoel

LEARNING OUTCOMES

On completion of this chapter you will be able to:

▶ Explain the term 'technology'
▶ Distinguish between information-technology management and information technology
▶ Explain how to obtain promised benefits from information technology
▶ Discuss business information risks associated with information technology
▶ Describe how to plan for information technology as a business grows
▶ Describe the basic principles when selecting technology products and services
▶ Explain how to implement and coordinate business technology and avoid wasting money.

OPENING CASE STUDY

When information technology issues are discussed in South Africa, a concern is raised about the ability of the consumer who has implemented cloud and cloud-based back-up, to access these systems when and where needed. In South Africa the challenge is twofold: First, the lack of bandwidth or rather, bandwidth is too limited, and second, it is too expensive for broad implementation. With adequate bandwidth at a reasonable price, cloud computing would become more attractive to the consumer.

Another issue is the fact that the existing technology infrastructure of many consumers is outdated. These consumers need to realise that it is no longer necessary for them to own their own technology infrastructure as cloud computing entitles them to infrastructure services on demand without investing in state-of-the-art technology infrastructure. Consumers would need to make a mental paradigm shift, replacing a physical technology infrastructure with a virtual technology infrastructure.

Whereas cloud computing has removed the operational responsibility of managing own information assets from the organisation and deposited it on cloud-optimised infrastructure, with proven solutions guaranteeing up-time and data security, it remains the responsibility of the organisation to ensure that the data is protected from both a recovery and compliance perspective.

1. Have you or would you consider cloud computing for your company?
2. What are the advantages of cloud computing?

INTRODUCTION

At every stage of small business development, the smart entrepreneur periodically considers whether it is time to add technology and specifically information technology (IT) to the business tools. Even if you are not familiar with the field of information technology yet, the odds are that you already use technology of some type to help run your business. Many entrepreneurs have launched their business from a single laptop or desktop computer. In recent years, the Internet has opened up a global marketplace for each business. So what piece of equipment does your business need to access those millions of potential clients? The speed of today's technological changes makes it an impossible and hopeless task to focus on specific makes and models of equipment in this chapter as they will soon be replaced by others. Instead, this chapter will focus on the basic information technology needs of a small business and how the right choices can substantially increase business productivity and profitability.

A small business that masters IT techniques can offer services, products, and customer relations that can rival those offered by much larger companies. IT is now offered as an academic major at universities and a degree in IT is offered by many universities or further education and training colleges around the globe.

5.1 Technology

Technology affects all of us and our surroundings in so many ways. The word comes from the Greek words *tekhnē*, which means 'skill' or 'art' or 'craft', and *logos*, 'the study of a discipline or knowledge'. The term is also generally applied to specific areas of study such as environment technology and, as in our case, business technology. Technology examples include the smartphone, the iPod/tablet, the Internet, running shoes, cars, and so on – the list is long and endless. The use of technology to assist today's business owner to run and manage his or her business is a skill in itself.

5.2 Information-technology management versus information technology

It is important to understand the distinction between information-technology management and information technology.

5.2.1 Information-technology management (ITM)

DEFINITION

Information-technology management (ITM) is the integration of information systems, technology, and business management for two purposes: to use information systems to solve business problems, and to assist new product development and enterprise management.

It focuses on the human as well as the technological elements of information systems. It is the 'big picture' because it includes the needs of information users, the value of information and technology, and addresses the entire spectrum of technology.

5.2.2 Information technology (IT)

DEFINITION

Information technology (IT) includes the people, processes, hardware, and software that determine the flow of information within an organisation.

Business managers are currently reformulating the way they manage IT. Traditionally, IT success was measured in terms of IT parameters like up-time, capacity, and processing speed. It is now widely thought that if information technology is expected to deliver business value, IT should be measured in core business terms such as revenue growth and profitability.

Today's technology moves at lightning speed and this implies that IT is a rapidly changing arena. Mobile, wireless, and pervasive computing are some of the fastest growing areas for business right now. IT addresses all of the technology resources of the firm and plans how to manage these in accordance with the company's needs and priorities. These resources include investments such as computer hardware, software, data, networks, and data centre facilities, as well as the staff who are hired to maintain them. Managing this responsibility within a company requires the basic management functions such as budgeting, staffing, organising, and controlling, plus technology elements such as change management, software design, network planning, technical support, and others.

5.3 The benefits of information technology

The first step to positioning your business for promised benefits is to become well informed about the field of information technology. Business owners can feel they are at a slight disadvantage when making technology decisions because the playing field seems to favour the IT vendors and the consultant. The only way to level this field is to approach an IT purchase as carefully and thoughtfully as you can. Keep in mind that the primary purpose of information technology is to create value for the business through the use of technology. This requires that you align the technology with your business strategies. This also further requires the business management and the technology management to work together as a creative collaborative team.

> **DEFINITION**
>
> Business-information alignment occurs when a business organisation is able to use IT effectively to achieve its business objectives – typically those are improved financial performance or marketplace competitiveness.

Value to your business comes not only from the IT tools you select, but also from the way that these tools are used in the organisation. So business-information alignment includes business transformation in which organisations redesign how work is accomplished to realise efficiencies made possible by new IT – creating an organisational change-management component.

Business-information alignment usually requires work because business and IT professionals within an organisation often experience infighting owing to a lack of understanding of each other and failure to produce the desired results which leads to blaming. This rift often results in expensive IT systems that do not provide a sufficient return on investment. The search for business-information alignment often must include efforts to establish trust between business and IT professional groups and a method for consensual decision making

5.4 Business-information alignment risks

Henderson and Venkatraman (1993), the founding fathers of **business-information alignment**, state that the objective of business-information alignment is to manage three separate risks associated with information technology projects:

▸ **Technical risk.** Will the system function as it should?
▸ **Organisational risk.** Will individuals within the organisation use the system as they should?

▶ **Business risk.** Will the implementation and adoption of the system translate into business value?

Unless all three risks are managed successfully, business value is at risk. The most efficient way to mitigate these risks begins at the human resources office. Who you hire to be your IT professional(s) is key to risk management. The success of the company relies on their effectiveness and ability to reduce outages, mitigate threats, and prevent damage to the network. They can advise on access control, network security, data integrity, asset management, and software acquisition and development. Each of these is an essential element of the business's success. It is critical to hire the right people for the IT team. Some necessary qualities for the IT team members are:

▶ *Adaptability*. IT professionals should be able to react differently to each individual problem.

▶ *Knowledgeable of latest technologies and trends*. They should understand new technologies and, if they notice something that could benefit the business, they should provide advice.

▶ *Consistently back up data*. Good IT employees make back-ups a daily or weekly routine and are able to switch over to the backed-up data quickly. If they do not back up your data frequently enough, a break in the system could spell disaster for the business.

▶ *Aware of new vulnerabilities and threats to the system*. The IT employees need to keep up with new system threats and have a clear understanding of their impacts and how to mitigate them. One security breach can cripple a business.

▶ *Have contingency plans in place*. IT professionals should have a set of general responses to anything that could go wrong on the network. It provides them with basic steps to solving problems that can be combined with their quick thinking.

▶ *Trustworthy*. The most important personal quality is trust. If the network is compromised from an inside threat, it does not matter how secure it is from the outside world. Management should know the background of all IT professionals to decrease the likelihood that they would damage or steal data for another company.

The IT management team can make or break a business. An effective team will provide excellent security and minimise outages. Having a very capable IT team is a critical hiring decision.

5.5 Information technology and planning

How can technology help the small business that is experiencing growing pains? Information technology (IT) is often labelled as the blanket solution for all business ailments, which it is not. Keep in mind that a strong business relies firstly on a strong business plan. The value you will realise when you add IT always depends on its alignment with your business strategies. When do you need an IT system and how do you integrate IT as a small business grows?

A business is a system of people skills and resources that are held together by information. People and resources coordinate and perform processes and follow policies by using business information. The information is the common element that holds the business together. When the business is small, with a few employees and resources, sharing business information is easy. Processes are easy to track and policies are easy to follow. Often individual judgement is relied upon in a small team. As demand and the business grows, the number of employees and resources increase. It becomes more difficult to follow ideal processes and policies need to be defined clearly to ensure quality. Information becomes more difficult to track as the business grows. This causes the rate of growth to slow down. This is the right time to change your business system and add information technology. When IT is added to business information, it enhances the ability of the system to perform. However, simply adding technology to the old system of old processes and old policies will not be a major improvement. As the business adds the technology, it must put in place updated processes and policies that redesign how work is accomplished in order to realise efficiencies made possible by the new IT. Together these can deliver enhanced performance.

The three basic abilities that technology brings to the business system are:

▸ *Data (reusable information).* Technology converts information into data. With technology, information is captured when it is generated and not when it is required for use. This gives all members of the order team instant access to customer requirements without having to ask the sales person or the customer.

▸ *A logical workflow model.* Technology brings logic to the business system. The processes and policies can be codified into programming logic called a workflow model or flowchart. These help to ensure that the tasks and actions that are part of the process are performed in the correct sequence by the right employees using the right resources. It also ensures that policies are followed.

▸ *Network (to 'virtualise' the enterprise).* Technology brings the network to the business system. When the business expands to multiple locations, the information backbone of the enterprise can distribute the data to each location or division. Technology can provide international access to a single database source and still be practical and cost effective. Besides integrating data and workflow across multiple locations or divisions, networking can integrate the business workflow with the extended system. This includes suppliers, business partners, agents, distributors, and customers.

The IT-enabled business system ideally consists of:

▸ *A data-management system.* The **data-management system** creates templates that capture information from all sources in the business system. Using the data-management capabilities requires processes to be modified so that the extra effort of entering information into the data-management system is built in. Policies need to ensure that no significant business event escapes the system undocumented. The technical solution needs to be built in a way that minimises the effort of entering all the information in the system and must be easy to use.

▸ *A workflow-management system.* The workflow-management system consists of a model that maps out various tasks and actions that are required to be performed in various scenarios. Policies are converted into rules, responsibilities, roles, and permissions. With a workflow model, the processes and policies may change over a period of time to minimise the learning curve for each employee.

▸ *A network-integrated solution.* If the workflow involves significant interaction between multiple divisions of the enterprise that are geographically distant, then the technical solution and processes need to be networked. Choose technology that makes databases and workflows across multiple locations seamless and transparent. Systems may need to be tuned and evolved based on the speed and availability of the network. Policies need to be written for integrating external business partners such as suppliers, agents, and distributors. Customers can also be given the ability to directly tap in to the workflow of the business and participate in the solution design and delivery process.

Technology uses data, logic and networking to enable processes that are designed to deliver enhanced performance. The business processes and policies should be redefined or tuned to take proper advantage of the new IT system.

5.6 Basic principles when selecting information technology

The first principle of making the right choice in this sprawling marketplace is to do your homework. The IT system must fit the needs of your specific business and budget. Carefully assess your needs. Small-business computer systems include hardware and software. These systems collect and store information relating to the business, including financial transactions. Ask for assistance in making the selection from at least one other associate. The IT manager is a good choice to find the system that complements the business. When selecting information technology, explore:

▸ *Facts*. Business computer systems can be large or small depending on a company's operations. If the business plans to expand operations in the near future, you should examine a computer system to see how easily it will upgrade for these new operations.

▸ *Features*. Most business-software applications will have multiple modules, like purchasing, production, accounting, payroll, and others. Software that allows business owners to customise the number of modules in use may have lower upfront costs for the application.

▸ *Considerations*. Software applications may have a limited number of user accesses for each company. Also enquire about the fees for technical support and upgrades. These typically result in ongoing costs for the company depending on the manufacturer.

Systems-management software (SMS) can run a complete or major part of a company's IT system. There are many different types of systems and it is nearly impossible to find one that works for every business. You should compare the software for a specific task when considering different options by following the steps shown in Figure 5.1.

As shown in Figure 5.1, the steps involved in selecting the most appropriate software for your business are:

▸ *Identify available industry software*. First, identify software products that service your business's particular market. If the market is a veterinarian's practice, for example, then narrow your SMS search to products that service that industry. Start with a list of possible software suppliers and types for the specific sector your business services.

▸ *Compare like features*. When you compare software, compare only features that are alike to make an accurate, objective analysis.

▸ *Rate the features*. Rate the good and the bad features of the software in terms of

Figure 5.1 Software option considerations

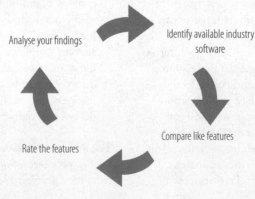

their importance to your business. For example, you could rate processing speed as more important to you than data accuracy. Use a rating system of one to five (where five is the most important) to rank the importance of the features.

▸ *Analyse your findings.* Consider the products with the highest ratings. Once you have chosen the features necessary for your systems-management software and rated their importance, list the features. For each feature, give a score for how well it performs. Multiply that by the importance ranking you gave it. After each feature for a specific product is scored, compare the totals for each product that you considered and determine which scored the highest. This will give you a guideline that will help you to decide.

5.7 Implementations of information technology

The most straightforward way to accomplish the implementation and coordination of technology is to work directly and cooperatively with your IT manager before the business purchases the equipment and software. Also consult non-industry sources such as www.consumerreports.org for the annual evaluation of computer systems. The goal is for this technology to run smoothly and enhance your business productivity and profitability. During the comparison stage, always rate the technical support and the warranty offered by each product. Strong technical support will be an important element in the successful launch of the system components.

As a business relies more on the underlying IT infrastructure, it is crucial that the IT supports the business plan. When developing an IT plan for your business, you must identify the IT capabilities the business needs. For example, a law or medical office or a brokerage firm should prioritise security while a service firm that relies on communication with customers should prioritise central messaging and collaborative software.

The dilemma in establishing a quality culture in an organisation when involved in data management is explored in the Entrepreneurial dilemma – *Data management and cleansing – not about the data.*

As shown in Figure 5.2 businesses ventures must establish a solid backbone with servers, networks, and switches. The right hardware and software selection can mean the difference between a system that is fast, secure, and reliable and a system that could become a costly problem. When selecting a server or a workstation, plan ahead. As the size of the business increases, the same server that can handle 10 to 15 users logged into it can suddenly become overloaded, slow and non-responsive when another 10 computers are added to the network. It is always less expensive to buy hardware that can handle future expansion than to pay double the price in the near future because you did not foresee the growth. Try to remain open minded and be careful not to be mislead by unbelievable deals.

Last year's server model is less expensive now, but it may also become obsolete faster than a more current model. Technology moves

Figure 5.2 Relationship between the business venture and technology

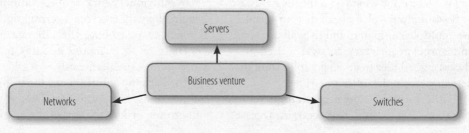

ENTREPRENEURIAL DILEMMA

Data management and cleansing – not about the data

I meet with many IT teams that are trying to establish a data quality culture within their organisations. In most cases they express a common concern: 'The business people aren't interested in solving data problems! We don't get buy-in from senior management for data governance!'

The axiom 'you can't see the wood for the trees' is apt when considering their approach to data management and data cleansing. They see so many issues caused by poor data that they assume these will be obvious to everyone. So the problem they are trying to address becomes 'poor data quality' – rather than the business issue (or issues) the data is affecting.

This common mistake has resulted in business people questioning the business value of data management projects, sometimes with a lot of money being spent, but ultimately, they do not yield any results and are perceived to be pointless. This is more than often due to data management projects that are frequently driven by technologists who do not speak the 'business language'.

After all, data management is not about the data. It is about addressing the business issues caused by data and improving the business outcome.

It is vital to partner with a data management professional that understands the business language, and how the technology can deliver results that can be linked back to business issues.

For example, a data person may ask for a budget to 'improve address data quality', assuming this is the business driver. After all, address inaccuracies are the cause of many issues.

In these cases, the business driver is not to better address data quality. A project that asks for budget to 'reduce overall debtor's days by x%', or to 'cut the volume of returned mail by y%', is far more likely to get attention – and budget – from business, than a project intended to 'improve the accuracy of addresses'.

Of course, this approach can lead to duplication of effort.

Pragmatic data governance assists to ensure that overlapping business goals are addressed by the same project, rather than having many tactical projects that may impact negatively on each other, or waste resources repeating a task that has been delivered by another project.

Experience can help to link the business and IT goals, creating that all important business buy-in and support.

Source: Alleman, G. 2012. Data management and cleansing – not about the data. iWeek, 18 July 2012: 17.[Online]. Available: http://www.iweek.co.za/viewpoints/data-management-and-cleansing-not-about-the-data Reprinted by permission of ITWeb Online.

1. What has been your experience with data management projects?
2. Do you support the statements made by the author?

quickly. It is also not necessary to purchase the best system available. Match your IT needs with your business goals. For example, it is a waste of money to buy a server that is equipped to render Pixar movies in record time if you only want to run the domain controller and email. Determine what you want the hardware to do and always plan ahead. If your business has multiple computers and they all use email and some proprietary software, then it is always a good idea to develop a solid computer network inside the office.

If the business runs a centralised server, users can log in and have certain accesses granted to them. Having a centralised server allows for managers to keep tabs on what employees can and cannot do, as well as monitor workstations and update the company's proprietary software from one centralised location. Rather than installing the software on each individual workstation computer and keeping up with everyone's version numbers, it is much easier to have the software installed centrally or to push the updates to all the workstations simultaneously.

The **back-up solutions** for the business are an increasingly important asset. As your business grows, so does the size of the archives and the everyday data. Always plan in advance when choosing a back-up solution. It is much less expensive to plan ahead than to have to replace or rebuild your entire back-up infrastructure to expand the system. If the company's data is left on the server and the important company files are not backed up anywhere else, it could be a disaster if a power surge hits or a hard drive breaks. It is highly desirable to have the data backed up in more than one place. Good options to consider are off-site back-ups as well as a local, in the office back-up server.

It is always a good investment to purchase equipment with the ability to expand as the business grows. Develop a strong working relationship with the IT manager or IT team to match the hardware and software you purchase with the strategic needs of your business.

The South African success story below shows how the design and development of IT software can be a lucrative option for an entrepreneur.

SOUTH AFRICAN SUCCESS STORY

Pearl Valley Golf Estate

Pearl Valley Golf Estate is a prestigious lifestyle estate situated in one of the most beautiful parts of South Africa. In keeping with this status, it offers a Jack Nicklaus Signature golf course, which was voted one of the top five courses in the country. It has hosted the South African Open Championship, the second-oldest open in the world, several times with distinction. APC was introduced to Pearl Valley's Management Team by Olipro, APC's PBX and VOIP partner.

The challenge

Pearl Valley required a reliable bandwidth link on the estate to run data, VOIP and a network of security cameras. The existing fixed-line infrastructure on site did not meet their current and future communications requirements for the business. APC also needed to provide a stable and reliable link to connect the sites, which are several kilometres apart in mountainous terrain. Finally, the solution needed to be competitively priced, providing high-quality service and reach. Cost savings also needed to be specified, to offset the capital outlay for a standalone network. The solution needed to provide independence from a fixed-line provider, allowing greater freedom for the future and to allow for easy expansion of the network.

The solution

APC designed, priced and presented a solution to the customer for approval. This was based on a desktop model, and later confirmed by on-site testing, prior to installation. In order to accommodate the complexity of linking over a mountain, the installation was split into two phases.

Once APC SA had received confirmation from the client, the first phase of the project was completed within a week, including the successful installation of all devices and testing of the links. The second phase was more complicated due to the location of the links being over 40 kilometres apart and separated by a mountain. In order to achieve the connection, APC successfully negotiated mounting a link on a tower on the mountain and connecting to a suitable ISP, from which the required level of bandwidth could be delivered.

Talking about the installation, APC SA manager, Damon Palframan, commented: 'A further aspect of consideration was the approval required to allow for the mounting of two radio units on the Simonsberg and La Farge towers. From a technical perspective, the design and planning for the installation of these two antennas on a structure with existing wireless links was key to the success. Despite these difficulties, APC was able to achieve a connection speed in excess of 10 Mbps.'

The result

The customer's business requirements were fully met by APC's solution. By utilising VOIP, the customer achieved a reduced cost of incoming and outgoing calls.

Due to the consistent bandwidth made available by the solution, the sharing of data, transferring of files and live streaming from the Internet were all made possible. The internal connection was also enabled to run the CCTV (security camera network) between the sites.

Without ongoing monthly maintenance fees associated with leased line connectivity, the client will achieve ROI in 2.5 years and has full possession of the line and equipment, vital for expanding the connection should the need arise.

Pearl Valley also plans to install a third phase of the project that will include internal WiFi at the clubhouse and potentially PTMP in the future to the residents on the estate.

Source: APC Solutions SA (2013:76). Reprinted by permission of Entrepreneur Magazine South Africa.

5.7.1 New trends

One more basic principle that will help you to avoid spending money on the wrong products is to find a news source for technical advice that has a style that you enjoy listening to or reading. It does not have to be full of jargon but should serve to keep you up-to-date on new trends and products for small business IT. One of the new trends that is currently hot is the invention of '**cloud computing**'. Cloud computing is a new off-site delivery model for IT services. It provides computation, software, data access, and storage services for your business. The user does not know the physical location of the cloud and can access these services from anywhere through the Internet. Cloud computing users will not have the upfront expense of buying hardware, software, and services because they will pay a provider only for what they use. This fee is usually based on resources consumed, like electricity, or is a time-based subscription fee. Other benefits of this approach are low barriers to entry, shared infrastructure and costs, low management overhead, and immediate access to a broad range of applications. Generally, users can terminate the contract at any time. However, there are fears that business security can be breached when company material is processed 'in the cloud'. Only time and the feedback of many users of the cloud system will inform us whether this is a minor or major development in the business information technology field.

A variety of hosting solutions are available, for example (Telkom, 2013):

▶ *Basic hosting*: Basic hosting is ideal for customers who have their own internal IT expertise and require a highly available off-site data centre facility to host their IT infrastructure. Basic Hosting also offers flexible Internet access bundles making this service deal for Web-facing Application Servers, E-Commerce solutions and Web servers.

▶ *Managed hosting*: Managed Infrastructure Hosting is designed to provide a centralised service, alleviating some of the major hassles companies face from IT today. Managed Hosting is perfect for companies that want to outsource the IT infrastructure that supports their business applications. The service provider takes over the responsibility of the day-to-day operations associated with keeping the infrastructure available. This allows you to focus on the applications that add value to your business.

▶ *Dedicated virtual hosting*: This service allows a customer to consolidate a number of physical machines into virtual machines running on a smaller physical server footprint hosted in the service provider's data centres. The latter manages the underlying hardware infrastructure and fully licences, manages and monitors VMware and instance operating systems. The customer can focus on the applications that add value to their business.

▶ *Shared virtual hosting*: This service allows you to buy the processing capacity you need and not the underlying hardware. The service provider will provision Virtual Machines according to a customer's processing capacity needs. This allows multiple customers to share the underlying hardware. Customers purchase the processing capacity they need without worrying about the cost and complexity of the underlying hardware. Virtual Servers can be configured according to customer requirements, including but not limited to Virtual Web Servers, Virtual Database Servers and Virtual Application Servers.

Technology will continue to offer more tools for IT, including the latest model of 'cloud computing'. Although your business interests may not be focused on technology, the field of IT deserves the attention of every emerging small business. Adapting some form of information technology for your business will allow you to launch your business from a much more even playing field than any time in the past. South Africa has also moved towards 'cloud computing'. The big advantage here is that many companies do not need to make huge capital investments anymore and the cost of communication for a business is reduced to operation cost only. Cloud computing may also reduce operating cost by a further 30%. The upgrading of the system to the latest technology also becomes part of the deal. It is estimated that about 50% of South African businesses with a telephone extension system are considering replacing their PBX-switchboards with digital services.

CONCLUSION

This chapter has introduced the discipline of the information technology field on small business development. When aligned with your business strategies, technology can improve your productivity and profitability substantially. Choosing the right technology tools and designing how to use them often requires teamwork between two usually disparate groups – the business management and the IT professionals. Building a cooperative team around IT is highly desirable. It is imperative for the small-business owner to understand the risks associated with information technology and how to plan for information technology when their business grows. Although models will keep evolving in IT, the principles will remain relatively stable and business owners should be aware of how to avoid wasting money on information technology.

SELF-ASSESSMENT QUESTIONS

Multiple-choice questions

1. Which one of the following qualities that IT team members should have is the most important personal quality?
   a. Adaptability
   b. Knowledge of the latest technologies and trends
   c. Aware of new vulnerabilities and threats to the system
   d. Trustworthiness

2. The IT-enabled business system ideally consists of a data management system, a workflow management system and a _____.
   a. talent management strategy
   b. network-integrated solution
   c. public relations plan
   d. staff reporting chart
3. When a business owner selects information technology for the business, he or she should explore facts, features and considerations. Which one of the following is not a fact, feature or consideration?
   a. Upgrades
   b. Customisation of multiple modules
   c. Marketing impact
   d. Fees for technical support
4. To select the most appropriate software for your business you need to follow four steps. Comparing the features of the software is which step?
   a. Step 1
   b. Step 2
   c. Step 3
   d. Step 4
5. Customers who have their own internal IT expertise and require a highly available off-site data centre facility to host their IT infrastructure should consider _____.
   a. basic hosting
   b. managed hosting
   c. dedicated virtual hosting
   d. shared virtual hosting

EXPERIENTIAL EXERCISE

Go to the Telkom website, specifically Telkom business: all services and products (Telkom, 2013) (http://business.telkom.co.za/enterprise/all-products/). You will find an alphabetical list of services:

1. Scan through the list of services. Are there any services which you are currently not using but which could enhance the efficiency of your business?
2. Did you explore broadband availability, disaster recovery, hosting solutions, ISP value-added services, LAN connect and network solutions?
3. What is the most basic information that you need to keep record of to manage your business effectively?
4. Is the hardware and software that you acquired for your business adequate to assist you with the managing of your business information?
5. What additional or upgraded 'tools' to assist you with the management of information technology do you need to acquire to provide for your expanding business?

DISCUSSION QUESTIONS

1. Are there any risks associated with information technology?
2. Describe the three basic abilities that technology brings to the business system.
3. Discuss the basic principles that should be considered when deciding on an information technology system.
4. Explain why back-up solutions are necessary.
5. When a business grows, its demand for efficient systems increase. How would you plan for your information technology to provide for business growth?

HP THIN CLIENTS HELP TRANSFORM CUSTOMER EXPERIENCE, BOOST SALES

'Technology is contributing to what we think is a great customer experience now and HP thin clients are an integral part of our in-store technology platform', said Robert Fort, vice president for information technology and divisional CIO, Guitar Center, Westlake Village, California.

Guitar Center has long been an iconic retailer serving the needs of music enthusiasts. Now the keys are jamming at the sales counter as well with the latest in HP thin client technology ringing up sales. This new addition is part of the company's smartstore initiative. The chain has deployed more than 3 400 HP thin clients in more than 200 stores nationwide. They are helping to speed up transactions, provide Internet access for customers, and more.

Peace, love and guitars

The Guitar Center story dates back to 1959, a small appliance and home organ store in Hollywood, California. A few years later, the company began handling VOX guitars and amps, and within the decade had redirected its mission. The company has continued to grow over the years, earning the distinction of being the largest musical instrument retailer in the world. It's a place where budding musicians can go to get a hands-on experience with new products and learn about them from knowledgeable sales staff. Guitar Center now operates more than 200 stores nationwide. Technology didn't keep pace with the chain's growth, however. For years, each store worked from a 'Deal book' – literally a book with the pricing and other information sales staff needed in order to make a sale. Then back in the early '90s Guitar Center deployed a point of sale (POS) system with Wyse green-screen terminals in the stores. Transaction processing was handled by a minicomputer back at the company's headquarters.

Fast-forward nearly two decades. Guitar Center had grown dramatically but the green-screen terminals were still in Guitar Center stores. 'Customers in our stores would come in to get their hands on the best and latest musical instruments and systems, and then have their sale rung up on a museum piece', explains Fort. Guitar Center created a vision to use new technology to enhance the customer experience and close sales against rising competition.

Smartstore technology

That's when Guitar Center launched the smartstore technology initiative. Its mission: to provide the infrastructure, technologies and processes to support an iconic and profitable customer and employee experience. 'There were people throughout the company that had great ideas for improving our operations, and they affected everything in the store', Fort says. 'Smartstore is our way of pulling all that together'. A key element of the smartstore initiative is deployment of HP thin clients. They not only replace the green screens to become Guitar Center's new POS, but also provide store employees with a state-of-the-art technology platform to do other parts of their jobs. And they give customers in-store Internet access to enhance the customer experience and help Guitar Center close more deals. Fort notes that computers have changed the way retailers do business. Smartstore was designed to make Guitar Center competitive with even the most tech-savvy retailers. 'Customers are much more knowledgeable before they come into the store today. They use Internet tools to do their research first, and we have to have the same tools available in our stores', he says. Guitar Center evaluated thin clients in the marketplace and chose HP t5730 thin clients based on their features and capabilities, as well as HP's reputation. 'HP thin clients are very progressive', notes Todd Lyche, vice president for enterprise architecture. 'They have many ports, a dynamic operating system with Windows® embedded standard 2009, and an attractive price point. The Windows® embedded platform provides the familiar Windows® environment for both staff and customers. And we were also attracted to HP because it clearly was emerging as a great company with a commitment to thin client computing'. Ease of management was another important consideration. Guitar Center's staff uses HP Device manager (HPDM) to remotely manage the thin clients. HPDM enables Guitar Center to schedule night reboots of all thin clients, obtain event logs and security audit files, and remotely manage the thin clients with firmware updates and software patches. 'Device manager has been a powerful central console for our help desk to manage all of the HP thin clients we've deployed', says Lyche.

Source: Hewlett-Packard (2013).

1. What were the main reasons why Guitar Center decided to upgrade their information technology?
2. What was the effect of the improved POS system?
3. Would in-store access to web-based competitive pricing information increase customer participation in a price-matching guarantee?
4. Would providing Internet access improve customer service?
5. Would a special order website broaden available inventory and increase special order sales?

SUGGESTED WEBSITE LINKS

Institute of Business Management and Information Technology: www.ibmit.co.za

The Information Technology Association of South Africa: http://www.itweb.co.za/office/ita/profile.htm

SITA - the South African State Information Technology Agency that provides IT (Information Technology), IS (Information Systems) and related services: www.sita.co.za

Institute of Information Technology Professionals South Africa: www.iitpsa.org.za

South African Directory of Information Technology: http://www.rainbownation.com/directory/index.asp?category=156

REFERENCES

Alleman, G. 2012. Data management and cleansing – not about the data. *iWeek*, 18 July 2012:17.

APC Solutions SA. 2013. Case study: Pearl Valley Golf Estate. Press release 30 July 2013. [Online]. Available: http://www.itweb.co.za/index.php?option=com_content&view=article&id=66111#prcontacts [27 October 2013].

Henderson, J.C. & Venkatraman, N. 1993. Strategic alignment: Leveraging information technology for transforming organisations. *IBM Systems Journal*, 32(1):472–484.

Hewlett-Packard. 2013. *HP thin clients help transform customer experience, boost sales*. [Online]. Available: http://www8.hp.com/ca/en/campaigns/thin-client-solutions/why-thin-clients.html <http://www8.hp.com/ca/en/campaigns/thin-client-solutions/why-thin-clients.html> [13 October 2013].

Telkom. 2013. Telkom business: all products and services. [Online]. Available: http://business.telkom.co.za/enterprise/all-products/ [27 October 2013].

CHAPTER 6

Entrepreneurial strategy

Isa van Aardt

LEARNING OUTCOMES

On completion of this chapter you will be able to:
▶ Define and explain why strategic management is important to the entrepreneur
▶ Describe the steps in the strategic management process
▶ Define and develop the mission statement of a venture
▶ Discuss the analysis of the external environment of a venture
▶ Discuss the analysis of the internal environment of a venture
▶ Apply the TOWS-matrix as a tool for developing strategies for the venture
▶ Explain how the best strategies could be identified
▶ Explain how the entrepreneur could ensure the implementation of strategies
▶ Discuss the importance of the allocation of resources to ensure the execution of strategies
▶ Discuss the evaluation of strategies and their implementation.

OPENING CASE STUDY

Many small construction companies spend all their time and energy bidding for and servicing large projects. This is understandable as on paper, the figures attached to these projects look extremely tempting and are sometimes seen to promise prosperity. However, this single focus leads companies to become simply project-based operations, making them highly susceptible to a feast-or-famine situation. When their single big project is finished, many such companies do not have a pool of smaller projects that will sustain them until the next big opportunity arrives. The single project focus must be avoided by dedicating time to continually looking for new opportunities, even when at work on a large project (Raiz, 2013).

1. How do these companies change their strategy from a single big project strategy to one of sustainability?

2. What disadvantages may implementing a single project strategy hold other than creating the possibility of a feast-or-famine situation?

INTRODUCTION

Success and failure is a normal part of business process but effective networking, adequate skilling, mentoring, developing good business acumen and sound principles and practices coupled with a high degree of business integrity and strategic planning will ensure that the prevalent environment does not perpetuate a culture of failure but rather a winning culture (Department of Trade and Industry, 2005).

When we talk about strategic management, the focus is on what an enterprise or new venture is trying to achieve in the long run and when and how this should be achieved. Strategic management is often associated only with large corporations that wish to implement changes, such as introducing new products or product lines, implementing a new organisational structure, going inter- or multinational, and (or) retrenching part of or even the entire staff complement. In fact, strategic management is not associated with entrepreneurship. This is a very short-sighted view of entrepreneurship and also of planning a new venture.

The strategic goal of any entrepreneur should be to gain a competitive advantage over competitors delivering unique products or services that customers will purchase and value, and to do it in such a manner that the service rendered is better than that of competitors. This could be obtained by implementing cost leadership, differentiation or focus strategies, and strategies aimed at customer service, corporate social responsibility and adhering to and implementing broad-based black economic empowerment (B-BBEE) legislative requirements to become a preferred supplier. An entrepreneur who operates without a strategy will flounder in the marketplace and eventually go out of business when more focused competitors are better able to meet the needs of customers. Without a strategy, entrepreneurs are likely to misallocate resources and fail to coordinate their actions.

This chapter will focus on strategic planning and how it will help the entrepreneur in planning his or her new venture. It will, furthermore, aim to give a concise guide to the process of strategic planning and gaining a competitive advantage. Further information can be obtained from the books on strategic management listed in the bibliography at the end of the book.

6.1 Importance of strategic planning for the entrepreneur

Entrepreneurs are managers. They manage more than just an organisation; they manage the creation of a 'new world'. This new world offers the possibility of value being generated and made available to the venture's stakeholders (owners, investors and employees). This value can only be created through change, including change in the way things are done, change in organisations and change in relationships. Entrepreneurs rarely stumble on success. It is more usually a reward for directing their actions in an appropriate way towards opportunities. Effective entrepreneurs know where they are going and why they are going in the direction they are taking. They focus on the achievement of specific goals. In order to move from the dream to the reality of a successful business, the most effective tool that is available is entrepreneurial **strategic management**. Everything an entrepreneur does when starting a new venture can be directly linked to strategic management. In drawing up a business plan, the entrepreneur should:
- Identify his or her product and type of business (mission statement)
- Identify market potential and main competitors (external audit)
- Identify the management team and personnel (internal audit)
- Identify the best location for the venture (strategy identification and implementation)
- Draw up a financial, marketing, human resource and operational plan (development of policies and objectives)

- Comment on the possibility of success (strategy evaluation)
- Continuously research and develop strategies, products and services (competitive advantage).

6.2 The process of entrepreneurial strategic management

Strategic management consists of four phases:

- *The strategy-formulation phase.* This comprises the first six steps in the process of strategic management:
  - Development of the business mission
  - Analysis of the external environment
  - Analysis of the internal environment
  - A swot analysis
  - Development of long-term objectives
  - Generation of alternative strategies
  - Choice of the strategy or strategies to pursue.
- *The strategy-evaluation phase.* This involves assessing the strategic fit and includes two aspects:
  - Analysis and review of external and internal forces

- Evaluation of strategies using an innovation and financial risk matrix (the entrepreneurial strategy matrix).
- *The strategy-implementation phase.* This involves the implementation of the strategies through:
  - The development of policies and annual objectives
  - The allocation of resources so that the formulated strategies can be executed
  - Measuring performance
  - Taking corrective action, such as changing the strategies if necessary
  - Continuous evaluation and adaptations of strategies, goals and objectives.
- *Sustainable competitive advantage.* This involves gaining competitive advantage through:
  - Cost leadership strategy
  - Differentiation strategy
  - Focus strategy
  - Customer service
  - Corporate social responsibility
  - B-BBEE.

The strategic management process is illustrated in Figure 6.1.

Figure 6.1 The strategic management process

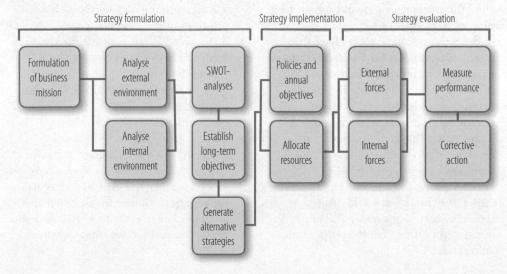

6.3 Strategy formulation

There are a number of steps in the process of formulating a business strategy, including: developing the business mission, analysing the external and internal environments, conducting a SWOT analysis, developing objectives and generating alternative strategies, and choosing those to pursue.

6.3.1 Development of the business mission

Strategic decisions are made to achieve objectives. The guideline or constraint for both these objectives and strategies is the mission of the enterprise or new venture. The mission only answers the question 'What business are we in?' but also identifies:

▶ The target market (the customers or clients to be served)
▶ The needs of the target market, which determine the products and services that will be offered
▶ The means, products and technologies by which these products and services will be achieved, or what will be required to deliver the right products or services to the customers or clients identified.

When developing a mission for the new venture, the entrepreneur should refrain from developing a statement that:

▶ Reflects sentiments (e.g. 'We have three basic beliefs: respect for the individual, the pursuit of excellence and service to customers') since this is hardly a guide to developing objectives and strategies
▶ Uses words that cannot be measured (e.g. 'to be the leading and most successful provider of services to customers') since their meaning is poorly defined
▶ Focuses on making a profit (e.g. 'to make a satisfactory profit') since this aspect should be seen as the result of doing things right rather than the purpose for doing them.

The mission should provide a framework for the objectives of the venture and should be clear so that it will be understood by and acted upon by everyone related to the venture.

The mission statement will not only aid the entrepreneur in charting the future direction of the venture, but will also compel him or her to think about the nature and scope of present operations, and to assess the potential attractiveness of future markets and activities.

Mission statements can vary in length, content, format and specificity. The mission statement is the most visible part of the strategic management process and, because it will direct the entrepreneur in establishing the new venture, it should reflect the following nine components (David, 1995:97):

▶ *Customers.* Who will buy the products and services on offer?
▶ *Products or services.* What are the major products or services that will be offered?
▶ *Markets.* Where will the entrepreneur compete?
▶ *Technology.* Is manufacturing or computer technology a primary concern of the planned venture?
▶ *Concern for survival, growth, and profitability.* Is the entrepreneur committed to economic objectives such as expansion and growth in profits?
▶ *Philosophy.* What are the basic beliefs, values, aspirations and philosophical priorities of the entrepreneur?
▶ *Self-concept.* What is the distinctive competence or major competitive advantage of the venture?
▶ *Concern for public image.* Will the venture be responsive to social, community, and environmental concerns?
▶ *Concern for employees.* Will they be perceived as a valuable asset of the firm? Although the entrepreneur may start out as a sole owner, this will seldom remain the case in the long run. Thinking about employees at an early stage will only add to the competitive advantage of the venture.

6.3.2 **Analysis of the external environment**

To respond to or even anticipate changes in the environment in which he or she plans to start the new venture, it is essential that the entrepreneur should have a sound knowledge of the business environment in which he or she plans to start a business. In the analysis of the **external environment**, the entrepreneur will be able to identify threats and opportunities that could be used in the development of his or her products and (or) services. In developing a sound knowledge of the environment, the entrepreneur will definitely have a competitive advantage over those who do not develop such knowledge or even ignore the environment. The mission statement should also be flexible enough to adapt if changes in the environment demand it.

In the analysis of the external environment, the entrepreneur should make a study of the following factors:

▸ Social and cultural
▸ International and national economic
▸ Physical
▸ Technological
▸ Communications and infrastructure
▸ Administrative and institutional
▸ Legal and political
▸ Competitive.

6.3.2.1 **Social and cultural environment**

Social and cultural changes have a major impact on virtually all products, services, markets and consumers. Trends in this environment are shaping the way we live, work, produce and consume, and could also shape a new type of consumer with the need for different products and services. New strategies may also be required to address the new needs.

Currently between 75 and 77 million people are added to the global population each year. There are now around six billion people sharing the planet, and many population experts predict that this may increase to at least eight to 10 billion before global growth stabilises between 2020 and 2050. During the past century, South Africa's population grew rapidly, from five million in 1902 to about 44 million in 2001, and to about 45.8 million in 2003 (Van Aardt and Schacht, 2003:5). According to Van Aardt and Schacht (2003), population growth is at present declining due to rapidly declining fertility rates and the HIV/Aids pandemic. While it was expected in the late 1980s that the South African population would have reached the 80 million mark by the year 2020, a population outcome for 2020 of less than 50 million is now expected (Van Aardt and Schacht, 2003:5).

Although the population growth rate is at present much lower than expected earlier, it is important to remember that nearly half the population is already living below the minimum subsistence level. This leaves government and civil society with the challenge of ensuring that there is adequate water supply, food production, jobs, schools, housing, and so on available for people being added to the population through births and immigration (Van Aardt and Schacht, 2003).

The following challenges that may have an effect on business and the products and services they deliver have been identified by a number of researchers and economic advisors (Van Aardt and Schacht, 2003, Leibbrandt, Woolard, Finn, & Argent, 2010, De Kock, 2012, Parsons, 2013 and The World Bank, 2013):

▸ A rapidly growing population, placing a strain on resources and the provision of services with nearly 50% of the populace living below the minimum subsistence level. Spatial divides hamper inclusive development and exclude the poor from fronts of developments.

▸ An exceptionally low labour-absorption capacity of the formal sector of the economy where more than 40% of the economically active population did not have a formal job. Simply put: Too few people have work.

▸ A grossly unequal distribution of wealth and income in South Africa together with the legacies of apartheid which would not easily be eradicated, especially in the short to medium term. The bottom half of the income distribution was reserved for black South Africans and poverty was dominated by black South Africans.

▸ Very high levels of functional illiteracy and generally a low educational level of the populace. The quality of school education for black people is poor. South Africa is rated by the World Economic Forum (WEF) as 143 and 140 out of 144 countries included in the global competitive index (GCI) with regards to the quality of maths and science education and quality of educational system respectively (The World Bank, 2013:189)

▸ Infrastructure is poorly located, inadequate and under-maintained and insufficient to foster higher education growth. This includes housing- and electricity-provision backlogs, inadequate health care provision, especially with regard to the rural areas and in the light of the HIV/Aids pandemic.

▸ Corruption and crime levels are high. According to the WEF, South Africa is rated 134th out of 144 countries with regards to the business costs of crime and violence (The World Bank, 2013:189).

▸ Low levels of capital and labour productivity and high labour-unit costs impeding South Africa's ability to become globally competitive.

▸ Public services are uneven and often of poor quality. The failing public health system exacerbates the widespread disease burden.

▸ The low economic-growth rates and per-capita incomes. The economy is overly and unsustainably resource-intensive.

▸ The broad spectrum of inequalities between various population groups – South Africa remains a divided society.

▸ Since 2010, South Africa's performance in Macroeconomic Environment has decreased significantly from 43rd in 2010 to 69th in 2012. On the same note the country's performance Labour Market Efficiency has also dropped from 97th in 2010 to 113th in 2012 (De Kock, 2012:4).

▸ Low levels of entrepreneurship and high levels of poverty in the informal sector.

▸ Legislation with regard to, among other things, labour, broad-based black economic empowerment (B-BBEE) and business.

▸ The ageing of the white, Indian, and coloured population and the increasing youth of the black population.

However, some of the positive aspects that should be considered are:

▸ South Africa has made improvements in property registration, intellectual property protection, efficiency of the legal framework in settling disputes and in challenging regulations and the strength of auditing and reporting standards (De Kock, 2012 and The World Bank, 2013).

▸ Financial Market Sophistication in South Africa is high (rated as 3rd in the world) especially with regard to the availability of financial services, financing through local equity market, regulation of securities exchanges and soundness of the banking system (The World Bank, 2013).

▸ It is interesting to note that South Africa ranks 15th in the world in terms of Quality of Air Transport Infrastructure (The World Bank, 2013).

▸ South Africa has the most advanced economy on the African continent. Its geographical position provides an ideal gateway to sub-Saharan Africa.

▸ Economically, South Africa is considered to be an emerging market with an abundant supply of natural resources.

6.3.2.2 International and national economic environment

The political and legal dimensions establish the boundaries of the economic environment that sets the stage for business activities. The economic factors that should be considered are:

▸ Patterns of economic growth
▸ Inflation
▸ Stock-market activities
▸ The financial rate of return
▸ Foreign-exchange rates.

Both the national and international economic environments should be studied because they can have a direct impact on the establishment of the venture. The establishment of the BRICS group in September 2010 is a group of leading emerging economies playing a key role in the world development platforms. It consists of Brazil, Russia, India, China and South Africa. The group has received overwhelming global attention since the inception of the original BRIC group in 2009 and it has been playing a critical role across the globe and aims to remain an important driving force of global economic growth. The establishment of trade agreements or free-trade areas also has a direct effect on an entrepreneur who plans to compete internationally, manufacture a product or render a service that can be obtained on the international market. The European Community (EC) has created a unified and borderless economy through political agreements between many sovereign nations in Europe, and the North American Free Trade Agreement (NAFTA) has created a free-trade area between Mexico, the USA, and Canada. Being part of such a free-trade agreement has the advantage that it is easier to conduct business, and consumers may enjoy the benefits of increased efficiency and greater access to an array of products and services. The people outside the free-trade zones face stiff tariffs for importation of their products and services,

EXAMPLE 6.1

Glimpses of hope during the downturn

Amid increasing costs, lower economic growth and looming business regulations, the mood among many business owners is one of increased concern for the future.

SA Chamber of Commerce and Industry (Sacci) chief executive, Neren Rau, said the mood among his members was 'fairly low' with many struggling to comply with existing regulations and concerned about new regulations in the pipeline and about rising costs. Despite the low mood, business owners continue to hope for the best, with small business financiers Business Partners' SME Index indicating that 71% of business owners surveyed in the first quarter remained confident that their businesses would grow in the next 12 months – in line with confidence levels recorded in the fourth quarter of last year.

Business at Alan Cogill's firm, which manufactures tooling equipment for the printers serving the wine sector, is looking good. Much of the printing sector has been hit hard by slower economic growth, but because Cogill largely supplies printers that make labelling on wine bottles, business has grown – on the back of the recent spike in wine exports led by the weak rand. He says his firm's monthly turnover is up 20% over the same period last year.

Business advisor Ed Hatton of Marketing Director said the present economic downturn is an ideal time for business owners to look at improving their business – by sharpening the quality of their goods and services while keeping prices low. Business owners should ensure that they offer quality in everything from deliveries made on time to parking that is accessible, he said, adding that a great point of sales service with knowledgeable advisors rather than just sales people is essential.

He said the biggest mistake that business owners made during the recent recession and the poor recovery that has followed, has been to assume that they could just carry on as normal without upping their game.

Source: Timm, 2013.

which increases prices artificially. If South Africa is included into any of the existing trade agreements, this might bring with it the advantage of easier business, but may have the greater disadvantage of products and services being dumped on the South African market at far lower prices. The international economy should, however, not only be restricted to the USA, Europe, and other developed economies, but should also include southern Africa, South America and other developing countries.

Example 6.1 *Glimpses of hope during the downturn* illustrates how entrepreneurs can use new strategies and unique products to ensure business survival.

6.3.2.3 Physical environment

Environmental problems such as global climate change, ozone depletion, El Niño, deforestation, the extinction of species, soil erosion, desertification, acid rain, toxic waste, water pollution, and noise pollution have been at the top of the international agenda for a number of years. The World Summit on Sustainable Development, which is held every 10 years, was held in South Africa in 2002 and most of the discussions held at the summit included these issues and how to deal with them in future. A key challenge for most industries is to discover how the development of sustainable industries, such as tourism, technology, and education, can contribute to the move towards a sustainable global economy. This should incorporate the need to combine sound economic development with the protection of natural resources, the need to analyse the trade-offs between native cultural integrity and the benefits of employment, and the need to understand the impact of rapid climate change on prime development areas, such as the coastlines and wetlands.

'Eco-friendly' has also become a buzz word and, although the concepts of sustainability and eco-friendliness are often spoken of as though they are synonymous, this is a misconception. Sustainability relates to the impact that an industry will have on the environment, whereas eco-friendliness involves the physical environment acting as the central focus of the product offering in a way that appeals to consumers' environmental interests and concerns. For instance, a grading system has been developed to assess whether or not a tourism destination meets the requirement of being an eco-tourism destination. This grading system not only indicates that the tourist destination meets the requirement of natural-resources preservation, but also that it has a waste-management programme and a wild-life preservation programme, has done community-impact assessments prior to development, and caters for all environmental interests and concerns. This grading system may also be applied to all industries to assess whether or not production and other processes meet the same requirements and that products are eco-friendly and will not harm the environment. Many enterprises also state that neither animals nor humans were harmed in the development of their products.

Health and safety also play a role in the physical environment and its effect on business. It is thus essential that one should be aware of the health-and-safety risks that may result from changes in the physical environment. The recent outbreak of foot-and-mouth disease in parts of South Africa had an effect not only on tourism, but also on the import and export of meat products.

6.3.2.4 Technological environment

In the last two decades, the technological environment has changed significantly in both the global and local context. In many industries, new process technologies have become relatively more important than new product technologies since better processes could lead to the production of better and less costly products. Here the Japanese are the world leaders as they are known for taking products invented or manufactured elsewhere, and producing them at a far lower cost through process improvements (Bounds et al., 1995).

Trends in technological advancement will revolutionise business practices and also create market opportunities. Technological trends such as shorter product life cycles, miniaturisation, automation, unmanned factories, robotics, miracle drugs, lasers, satellite networks, fibre optics, biometrics, electronic fund transfers, and computerisation, will affect the efficiency of organisational processes and products. Through computers and the Internet, the world has shrunk to fit into our living rooms or offices and references are even being made to the 'Flat World' (Friedman, 2006). International markets have been opened through the Internet, but international competitors have also entered the South African market.

Technological developments represent major opportunities and threats to the entrepreneur. Such advancement can create new markets, cause the proliferation of new and improved products and services, change cost structures and manufacturing processes, and even render existing products and services obsolete. Technological changes can reduce or eliminate cost barriers between businesses, create shorter production runs and create shortages in technical skills. No company or industry today is insulated against emerging technological developments. The aim should be to be in the driving seat as far as technological developments are concerned, which requires determination dedication and funds.

As far as technological development is concerned, South Africa is experiencing extremely high levels of development in the urban areas, but little in the underdeveloped rural areas. Building products around sophisticated technologies for the national markets sometimes means limiting oneself, since there are areas in South Africa that do not have electricity and running water. However, these circumstances could lead to opportunities. The electrification of all households, even mud huts, is one of the opportunities identified by Eskom and strategies have been developed around this opportunity that will lead to job creation and an increased standard of living for many South Africans.

6.3.2.5 Communications and infrastructure environment

The communications and infrastructure environment is important as it is the area in which you have to let others know of your existence and assess whether or not others will be able to reach you. The availability of communications infrastructure, such as radio, television, printing press, electronic and telecommunications will have an effect on your ability to communicate your products or services to potential customers, liaise with suppliers, and even assess your competitors. If you do not know what communication media are available to inform your customers and which your competitors use, you will not be able to communicate effectively with your customers. You must also know the most appropriate media to use.

Other infrastructures that will have an effect on a business are:

▶ *Transport.* It is important to move people and products around the world quickly, punctually, safely, and comfortably. Infrastructure to serve all major forms of transport continues to expand with the network of countries, cities, and towns served by air travel, and high-speed road and rail links.

▶ *Accommodation.* This not only refers to the accommodation of people in hotels and guest houses, but also to office accommodation for business enterprises. The cost of this accommodation should be a consideration when planning your business.

▶ *Support facilities.* This refers to the support facilities other than transport that a business enterprise will need, such as libraries, educational, recreational, and sports facilities.

6.3.2.6 Political and legal environment

The political climate is of the utmost importance since it can influence all the other components of the economic system. Political stability and the ideologies and aims of the governing political party have both a direct and an indirect effect on many enterprises. An entrepreneur could lose his or her entire investment if a dictatorial regime were to take over the government and seize all private enterprises or assets as property of the state.

The government is also an important guiding factor in economic activities – it can encourage or discourage investments in the various sectors of the economy and it can either attract or discourage foreign investments. Incentives are offered to entrepreneurs by government in the form of tax reductions or even tax holidays for a certain period. The information for such incentives can be obtained directly from the Department of Trade and Industry (dti) or from its agents in the various provinces of South Africa.

National legislation or policies issued by the government should also be taken into consideration when planning a venture. These include the various labour laws, company laws, financial guidelines and policies, as well as laws and policies regarding manufacturing and environmental issues. The various laws that the entrepreneur should consider will be discussed in Chapter 17.

Provincial and local governments also play a major role for businesses in their area – either by means of legislation or incentives – and this should be taken into consideration when planning the venture or its expansion.

As far as international trade is concerned, the dti could furnish valuable information regarding international businesses that want to invest in South Africa. Guidelines on what must be considered when one wants to compete on the international market can also be obtained from the dti. When entrepreneurs plan to trade internationally, the political stability and legal factors of the respective countries must also be taken into consideration.

Read how Tskakani Masia, a young woman from Polokwane, used her skills to build a business into a success story and also support young entrepreneurs achieving their dreams in *Young entrepreneur now helping others*.

6.3.2.7 Administrative and institutional environment

For any form of business, the environment will contain a wide range of institutions that can influence the operation and development of a business. Other than the government, the following institutions may have an influence on most entrepreneurial ventures:

▸ *Trade unions.* Trade unions may have an influence with regard to wage rates, skills levels, union bargaining power, transport services and the majority of unfair labour practices. You should not disregard the influence of trade unions as this may have a negative effect on your business. In the manufacturing industry, a strike among workers could lead to the closure of a factory.

▸ *Academic institutions.* Academic institutions may not only contribute towards the skills level of your workers, but the work of academics may also influence the decision-making processes, product development, service delivery, marketing, and so on.

▸ *Local government.* The local government may have requirements for production, service delivery, waste management, and registration that you will have to adhere to and should take into consideration when planning your venture.

▸ *Consumer groups.* This refers to groups such as the Consumer Council and other consumer groups that watch over the interests of consumers. These groups also assist consumers with purchasing decisions.

▸ *Special-interest groups.* These groups may try to influence an industry or business on an issue-by-issue basis and include groups relating to the environment, rights for specific sections of the population, cultural heritage, and rural development.

▸ *Law-enforcement agencies.* The high crime rate in South Africa and the desire among businesses to prevent crime levels acting as a deterrent to customers has brought business and law-enforcement agencies closer together. It has also led to the

---

SOUTH AFRICAN SUCCESS STORY

Young entrepreneur now helping others

A young woman from Polokwane has proven that age is no impediment when it comes to building a successful business, and then assisting others in developing their own enterprises.

At 37, Tsakani Masia has achieved the dream of many an entrepreneur – she has established a thriving business, and after completing BSSA business skills training courses, is now also a network facilitator for the Black Business Supplier Development Programme (BBSDP) of the Department of Trade and Industry (the dti). In order to accomplish this assignment, NBE has recruited qualified staff to administer the activities of this programme.

Tsakani was only 30 when she founded Nakiseni Business Enterprise (NBE) in 2004. Her company started off supplying stationery and catering, but as it grew, expanded into construction and trucking, and more recently, the manufacture of cleaning products. A subsidiary, Norchem was established to do this. The factory is based in Shayandima Industrial area in Thohoyandou. The target market for the products are street vendors, individuals, offices for public and private, hotels, car wash businesses etc. The long-term plan for this subsidiary is to export its products to neighbouring countries, and to package them in smaller quantities in order to have a diverse market.

In 2008, Tsakani's business excellence was rewarded when Norchem won a category award in the then FNB Enablis Business Launchpad competition, the biggest contest of its kind in Africa. In 2009, the young go-getter won the enterprise development category in the Vhembe District Municipality Youth in Business Competition.

Tsakani underwent BSSA business skills training between September 2010 and January 2011. 'Since then, my business has really taken off. We were taught how to run and grow a business, how to read financial statements, and how to ensure a business is profitable', she says.

'Before the training, I was just making sure I wasn't running at a loss, but now, I understand how to actually make a profit. My business turnover has increased markedly since the training', she says.

Nakiseni Business Enterprise now employs 50 people and has ventured into the food industry and security services in order to diversify its income sources and in order to contribute to the economy. NBE has opened a Galitos franchise store in Lephalale at the Marula Mile complex. The security service is a new portfolio for the company, which has been accredited by PSIRA, and complies with all the requirements for the security sector.

What gives Tsakani the most satisfaction, however, is being able to assist other entrepreneurs through the dti's BBSDP, a cost-sharing grant aimed at assisting enterprises in improving their competitiveness and sustainability.

'After the BSSA training, I was accredited by the dti as a BBSDP network facilitator. We've since then submitted applications for grants from around 30 enterprises to the dti.'

Source: Developed from BSSA, (n.d.).

development of a number of security businesses that work with shopping centres and malls to prevent crime in the area.

▸ *Organised commerce.* This is made up of organisations or associations that exist to support businesses in their development as well as to become a combined voice to government on all levels. Some of the biggest associations in South Africa are the AHI, NAFCOC, SACOB and the BMF (see the discussion in Chapter 7). All these organisations have a section dealing with small businesses and entrepreneurs and have valuable links and information that can be used to develop product and service ideas. Another association that is directly involved in franchises is the FASA (see Chapter 8), which renders support in the development or buying of a franchise.

6.3.2.8 Competitive environment

The competitive environment includes all the external forces that directly impact on the decisions and actions of the entrepreneur and which are directly relevant to the achievement of the organisation's goals and objectives. The main forces that make up the competitive environment are competitors, customers and suppliers.

Competitors

Collecting and evaluating information on existing or potential competitors is essential for the entrepreneur. Data about industrial trends can be obtained from institutions such as Markinor, Research International and the Bureau of Market Research (BMR) at UNISA, as well as from market-research results from educational institutions such as universities, universities of technology, and colleges. Customer and supplier meetings, trade publications, industry conferences, exhibits, expos, and the Internet are also useful sources of information on the product and service offerings of competitors. What should be obtained is information about competitors' new products and services, future offerings, price strategies, warranties and customer service offered, and about internal operations. Rather get too much information than too little.

When looking at information obtained about competitors, the long-term consequences of competitive actions should be anticipated. Failure to do so can be quite costly. For example, during the 1980s, IBM failed to pay close enough attention to the environment in which it operated. It did not fully appreciate the impact of microcomputers on the mainframe computer business, which it dominated at the time, and in which it had very high profit margins. Such margins insulated the company from problems and absolved it from the need to pay close attention to the competitive environment in which it operated, and as a result it became bloated and bureaucratic. By the 1990s though, with increasingly powerful chips such as the Intel 486 and Pentium microprocessors, it was clear that microcomputers, not mainframes, were the future, and that many companies could make and sell PCs equally as well as IBM could. The problem was that with IBM's huge overheads, the company could not price its machines competitively. This made it possible for companies with lower costs to grow into successful microcomputer companies, resulting in huge layoffs and a redirection of IBM's efforts towards microcomputers, leveraging the company's size and technological expertise across markets in ways it had not done in the past (Bounds et al., 1995).

Customers

One of the sources of ideas identified in Chapter 3 is an unsatisfied need or want. One major goal of an entrepreneur should be to earn customers' loyalty by satisfying or pleasing them with high-value products and services, and doing so to a greater extent than competitors. To do this well, the entrepreneur should use market-research techniques to learn as much as possible about the problems and needs of his or her customers. Learning about customers is perhaps the most important element of external environment analysis. The entrepreneur should accept that customers are going to purchase what they believe is in their best interest, and not those of the company. Even when the entrepreneur is the sole supplier of a product or service, he or she needs to act as if this were not the case and try continuously to improve customer value, which will attract more customers and help to ensure the venture's place in its market. If the entrepreneur knows his or her customers or potential customers and their needs and wants, it will be easier to develop strategies to address them.

Customers can be divided into two major groups, namely individual and corporate customers. **Individual customers** are those who buy on the open market and are usually more sensitive to price. They are also prone to brand loyalty, but could be persuaded to buy a new or alternative product through advertising and intensive marketing strategies. Quality is equally important, but if an alternative product with similar quality is available, price would persuade them to buy the alternative. Price strategies are thus often used to persuade the individual customer to buy a product. Some examples of the success of using price strategies are the free upgrade to a bigger car (1600 cc, 1800 cc, 2L or diesel) offered by Citroën when you buy a Citroën C2, the zero per cent interest strategy used by Toyota for the Corolla, and the inclusive car service package offered by Diahatsu on the Sirion and Terrios. Individual customers are furthermore subdivided into various categories, such as age, gender, education, income, geographical distribution, and buying patterns. Each of these categories may dictate different marketing strategies. When analysing the customer, the entrepreneur should consider where the product or service has to be delivered, when the customers want the product, and the payments and warranties linked to the product or service.

Corporate customers are more likely to emphasise quality and quantity, and the ability to deliver, rather than price. This does not mean that they are totally insensitive to price fluctuations, but merely that they will be willing to pay a higher price for better quality.

Suppliers
Suppliers play a major role in the supply and cost of raw materials, products or services. When entering the market, the entrepreneur should not ignore the suppliers and their ability to affect the market. It is in the best interests of both to assist each other with reasonable prices, improved quality, and the development of new services, reduced inventory costs and long-term advantages for all. The ability to deliver must also be assessed. It may be that the supplier also has to deliver to competitors and for that reason the entrepreneur must be sure that the supplier will be able to provide for the total demand. According to Bruwer and Plaatjies (1999) part of the success of an entrepreneur depends on the supplier's ability to ensure:

▸ Good quality raw materials
▸ Excellent service, such as timely delivery and after-sales service and support
▸ Reasonable pricing.

6.3.3 **Analysis of the internal environment**

The entrepreneur needs to undertake an analysis of each functional area that exists within the venture, such as research and development, marketing, sales, management, production, and finance. Other important aspects of the **internal environment** include the organisation's infrastructure, such as information systems to support decision making and communication. Not all of the functional areas are applicable to all ventures. The entrepreneur who plans to manufacture a product would include research, development, and manufacturing, while the entrepreneur planning a service venture, such as a consultancy, would concentrate on the marketing function and marketing research, which would provide him or her with the necessary information to develop the business.

With the analysis of the internal environment, it is far easier to use a checklist of questions as an aid to determining specific strengths and weaknesses in the functional area. A strength would be suggested by a 'yes' answer to a specific question, while a 'no' answer would probably suggest a weakness. Figure 6.2 below provides questions that could serve as a guide for an internal analysis.

Figure 6.2: Questions for internal analysis

Management
1. Is the entrepreneur the sole owner and (or) manager of the venture? If 'yes', does he or she have adequate managerial training? What about experience?
2. Is the venture managed by an entrepreneurial team? If 'yes', are its members adequately trained as managers? Do they have adequate experience as managers?
3. Do the managers delegate authority or do they make all decisions themselves?
4. Is the manager or entrepreneur available to members of staff if they have problems?
5. Are the members of staff motivated by management through reward and control mechanisms?

Finance
1. Did the venture raise start-up capital? Is the repayment of this debt adequate and on time?
2. Can the venture raise essential short-term capital?
3. Can the venture raise essential long-term capital through debt or equity?
4. Did the venture realise its projected profits? Are the profits adequate for expansion?
5. Does the venture have a positive cash flow?
6. Does the venture have sufficient working capital?
7. Are capital budgeting procedures effective?
8. Are the members of staff responsible for financial management adequately trained?
9. Does the venture use outside financial consultants? If 'yes', is this cost-effective?

Information systems
1. Does the venture have an information system? If 'yes', are the data regularly updated?
2. Has an information-systems officer been appointed within the venture? Is he or she adequately trained?
3. Does the venture make use of an outside consultant? If 'yes', is it cost-effective? Is the information system adequate?
4. Is the information system user-friendly?
5. Is training provided for users of the information system?
6. Are there effective controls for entry into the venture's information system?

Personnel
1. Is there a personnel department in the venture? Are the members of staff adequately trained and experienced?
2. Does the venture make use of outside personnel consultants? If 'yes', is this cost-effective?
3. Does the venture have an adequate number of staff members? Are they adequately qualified and experienced?
4. If members of staff are employed, are job descriptions and job specifications clear?
5. Is the morale of the employees high?
6. Is employee turnover and absenteeism low?

Marketing and sales
1. Does the market for the product or services have growth potential?
2. Has the projected market share of the venture been realised? Has it increased since the business was started?
3. Are the available channels of distribution reliable and cost effective?
4. Does the venture have an effective sales department or section?
5. Is market research being conducted? If 'yes', are the results followed up?
6. Are the product quality and the related services good?
7. Are the services rendered of good quality and competitive?
8. Are the prices of products or services competitive?
9. Are the promotion and advertising campaigns effective?
10. Does the venture make use of outside promotion and advertising consultants? If 'yes', is it cost effective?

11. Are adequate resources and funds allocated to marketing?
12. Are the members of staff in marketing and sales adequately qualified? Do they have adequate experience?

Production and purchasing

1. Are the suppliers of raw materials, parts, and other products reliable and reasonable?
2. Are the production facilities, equipment, and machinery adequate and in good condition?
3. Are the offices adequate and in good condition?
4. Are quality control policies and procedures in place and effective?
5. Are inventory-control policies and procedures effective?
6. Does the venture have technological skills?
7. Are the members of staff in production and purchasing adequately qualified?

Research and development (R&D)

1. Does the venture have R&D facilities? If 'yes', are the members of staff trained or qualified for the specific product and are the facilities adequate?
2. Does the venture make use of outside R&D consultants? If 'yes', is it cost effective?
3. Are adequate resources and funds being allocated to R&D?
4. Are the present products and their related technologies competitive?

Communication

1. Is there communication between the different functions?
2. Are information and other meetings being held for all stakeholders?
3. Are all members of staff informed of managerial decisions and how these affect them?

6.3.4 SWOT analysis

The purpose of gathering data and conducting internal and external analyses is to establish an information base from which strategic plans will emerge. Well-conceived plans ensure that the internal processes and capabilities of the venture match or are in line with the requirements, opportunities, and threats in the external environment. This match is referred to as a **SWOT analysis**, which is a review of the organisation's strengths, weaknesses, opportunities and threats. An organisational strategy will be more successful if there is a favourable match between the internal strengths and weaknesses of the organisation's processes and its external opportunities and threats.

DEFINITION

SWOT analysis is a review of the organisation's strengths, weaknesses, opportunities and threats.

6.3.4.1 Opportunities and threats

The external analysis should result in the identification of external opportunities and threats affecting the venture. An opportunity can be defined as 'a favourable situation or good chance that exists in the market which could be exploited for a profit, thus an occasion to make an improvement or to create new possibilities'. A threat can be defined as 'an indication of an undesirable situation that exists in the market which could lead to a loss or to smaller profits, thus anything that might hurt the venture's ability to serve customers while making a profit'. Each of the factors studied in the analysis of the external environment could present either an opportunity or a threat. In the political environment, higher taxes, whether income or value-added tax, could be a threat to the entrepreneur, while the Reconstruction and Development Programme (RDP) could furnish opportunities for the development of low-cost housing. There may be an opportunity in the economic environment if the disposable income of individuals increases due to economic growth and the lowering of bond and lending rates of banks, while higher bond and lending rates could be a threat. The entrance of international competitors is a threat, while the opening up of international markets is an opportunity.

> ## DEFINITION
>
> An opportunity can be defined as 'a favourable situation or good chance that exists in the market that could be exploited for a profit.
>
> A threat is an indication of an undesirable situation that exists in the market that could lead to a loss or to smaller profits.

6.3.4.2 Strengths and weaknesses

As indicated before, the internal analyses result in an identification of the **strengths** and **weaknesses** of the venture. Strengths refer to any resources or abilities to which the entrepreneur has access in order to take advantage of an opportunity or to fight off threats. Strengths may be a highly skilled workforce, a reputation for high-quality products and services, effective management, financial resources, growth in market share, and products protected by patents. Weaknesses refer to deficiencies in the resources and processes available to the entrepreneur or the venture that will render the entrepreneur or the venture vulnerable in the marketplace. Weaknesses may include deficient research and development capabilities as well as inadequate production facilities, personnel, and finance.

> ## DEFINITION
>
> Strengths refer to any resources or abilities to which the entrepreneur has access in order to take advantage of an opportunity or to fight off threats.
>
> Weaknesses are deficiencies in the resources and processes available to the entrepreneur or the venture that will render the entrepreneur or the venture vulnerable in the marketplace.

6.3.5 Development of objectives

The objectives developed for the venture should promote and be consistent with the mission. Although a venture will have a single mission, it will have multiple objectives because of the many aspects involved in contributing towards achieving that mission. Both long- and short-term objectives need to be developed since the time frame of a mission is usually three to 10 years. Some of the objectives may even be in conflict with one another. For example, an entrepreneur may have as an objective the expansion of his or her marketing department to address the greater need for marketing, but have a further objective of not expanding the total number of staff members in the venture. The entrepreneur might then move staff from another department to marketing, so that both objectives could be realised.

6.3.6 Generation of alternative strategies and choosing those to pursue

The purpose of the internal and external analyses is to gather data that could be used in developing alternative strategies for the venture. Strategy is sometimes defined as 'the match an organization makes between its internal resources and skills and the opportunities and risks created by the external factors' (David, 1995:199). The internal and external analyses thus serve as the input information for the matching and decision-making stage of the strategic process.

There are numerous techniques that can be used during the matching and decision-making stage. It is not possible to discuss all of them in one chapter, but the reader is advised to consult the books on strategic management listed in the bibliography at the end of the book. For the purposes of this book, the TOWS-matrix will be discussed. The TOWS, or Threats-Opportunities-Weaknesses-Strengths, matrix is an important matching tool that will aid the entrepreneur in the development of four types of strategies:

▶ *Strength–opportunity strategies (SO).* The internal strengths of the venture are used to address the external opportunities, trends, and events. An example is using the surplus financial resources of a venture to open a second shop or outlet in another city, where a growing market for the product has been identified.

▶ *Weakness–opportunity strategies (WO).* Strategies aimed at improving the internal weaknesses by taking advantage of external opportunities, trends, and events. An example of a WO strategy is taking over a supplier of raw materials to ensure the best prices of products in the market, with the aim of increasing market share. The weakness of input costs that are too high is addressed in this case, while the opportunity of higher market share can be obtained.

▶ *Strength–threat strategies (ST).* These are aimed at using the internal strengths of

Figure 6.3 TOWS-matrix for a training consultant

		STRENGTHS (S)	WEAKNESSES (W)
		1 Skills with regard to training 2 Quality products and services 3 Dynamic business 4 Mission is clear 5 Trained consultants 6 Low overheads 7 Management has drive and passion	1 No marketing skills 2 Financial planning and control 3 Limited mobility 4 Lack of skills regarding disadvantaged groups 5 No knowledge of people to contact 6 Lack of administrative skills and infrastructure 7 Uncertainty regarding contracts
OPPORTUNITIES (O)	1 Link-up with the RDP 2 Empowerment of workers 3 Unused market opportunities 4 Link-up with schools, technical colleges, universities of technology, universities and other training institutions for projects 5 Contracts with large businesses 6 International money for development	1 Contact NGOs working in the area of literacy training (S1,S5,S7,O1,O2,O3) 2 Form cooperative agreements with schools (S1,S2,O4) 3 Form cooperative agreements with the Tshwane University of Technology and UNISA (S1,S2,O4) 4 Form cooperative agreements with the University of Pretoria (S1,S2,O4) 5 Marketing the business using letters of reference from existing contracts (S1,S3,O5)	1 Identify and contract consultants in other areas by means of contracts with universities, universities of technology, etc. (W4,O3) 2 Use marketing skills of businesses with which cooperative agreements have been formed (W1,O3) 3 Contract with universities of technology to use third-year students for administrative support under supervision 4 Appoint administrative assistant on part-time basis and purchase necessary infrastructure
THREATS (T)	1 Unknown competitors 2 Everyone wants to link up with the RDP 3 'Fly-by-nights' 4 Tertiary institutions have larger support	1 Negotiate with tertiary institution to accredit courses (S2,T4) 2 Compile a document on the skills of consultants to use in marketing (S5,S1,T1,T2,T3)	1 Establish price structure so that quotations will be clear (W2,T1–4)

the venture to avoid the threats identified in the environment. An example is using surplus financial resources to develop products that will be biodegradable when the emphasis on environmentally compatible products becomes a threat to existing products.

▶ *Weakness-threat strategies (WT)*. These refer to defensive tactics aimed at reducing internal weaknesses and avoiding environmental threats. Disregarding these types of strategies could cost the entrepreneur dearly, since it could lead to a fight for survival, to retrenchments or bankruptcy or even liquidation.

When deciding which strategies to follow, the entrepreneur could list each of the strategies identified in the TOWS-matrix (Figure 6.3). He or she could then rate the importance of the strategies on a scale from one to five, (one being the most and five the least important). This will result in a prioritised list of strategies that could be implemented. Input from others is advisable for this step as this could facilitate making the final decision. Once this has been done, the strategies identified as those that should be pursued should be listed for evaluation. Figure 6.3 is an illustration of a TOWS-matrix that was drawn up for a training consultant.

6.4 Strategy evaluation

The evaluation of strategies is the second phase in the strategic process. During the evaluation, the strategies that have been developed should be measured to establish whether or not they will have the desired effect. The evaluation is a two-step process. The first step of this phase is to review the external and internal factors, and the second is to measure the strategies against an innovation and financial risk matrix (the entrepreneurial strategy matrix).

6.4.1 Review the external and internal factors

The first step of the evaluation is to review the external and internal factors. This is done to establish whether the strategies that have been developed will address the strengths, weaknesses, opportunities, and threats that have been identified. It is also done to ensure that the initial analysis of the external and internal factors was extensive enough.

6.4.2 Entrepreneurial strategy matrix

The second step of the evaluation is to classify the proposed strategies in terms of their associated innovation and risk. The **entrepreneurial strategy matrix (ESM)** was developed by Sonfield and Lussier (Sonfield et al., 2001). The model is a situational model suggesting strategies and actions for both new and ongoing ventures based on the level of innovation and financial risk associated with the venture and its strategies. In the application of the matrix, 'innovation' is used to describe those strategies that will lead to the creation of new, unique and different products and (or) services and 'financial risk' describes the probability of incurring a major financial loss.

Figure 6.4 illustrates the entrepreneurial strategic matrix as adapted for the purposes of this book.

In the application of the ESM, each proposed strategy should be assessed and placed in the appropriate cell of the matrix. This will then provide the proposed actions to apply during the implementation or even abandonment of the strategy. For example, strategies that have low scores for both innovation and financial risk could be implemented with minimal effort (using existing resources), but the entrepreneur would then need to accept limited financial gain and growth potential.

Figure 6.4 The entrepreneurial strategy matrix

INNOVATION	High	**High Innovation/Low risk** ▶ Move quickly ▶ Protect innovation by means of patents or copyright ▶ Implement financial control systems, contracts, etc. to protect investments and costs	**High Innovation/High risk** ▶ Reduce risk by implementing controls on operating cost and investment ▶ Protect innovation ▶ Consider outsourcing high-investment operations ▶ Consider joint-venture opportunities
	Low	**Low Innovation/Low risk** ▶ Implement with existing resources ▶ Accept limited financial gain ▶ Accept limited growth potential	**Low Innovation/High risk** ▶ Increase innovation to create a competitive advantage ▶ Develop strategies to reduce risk ▶ Use business plan and objective analysis ▶ Minimise investment and investment costs ▶ Consider franchise options ▶ Consider abandonment
		Low	**High**
		RISK	

Source: Adapted from Sonfield et al.,(2001:166) Sonfield, M, Lussier, R, Corman, J. & McKinney, M. 2001. Gender comparisons in strategic decision-making: An emplirical analysis of the entrepreneurial strategy matrix. Journal of Small Business Management, 39(2):166 Copyright © 2002, John Wiley and Sons, Inc. Reprinted by permission of John Wiley and Sons, Inc.

ENTREPRENEURIAL DILEMMA

Deciding to start a business

Ray was an early starter on the road to entrepreneurship while still at school at Hatfield Primary. His first idea came to him during a school fundraiser for Comic Relief. People were paying 50c a time to see if they could score a penalty past him. He realised that there was some money to be made from this scheme and the entrepreneurial penny dropped. He continued to get people to take penalties for money during normal school hours, and turned the scheme into a regular earner.

As he grew older, Ray became interested in music. He gained inspiration from other people's music which later led to his producing his own songs. He worked as a DJ a school functions while attending Boys High. Ray worked at various jobs and saved money to purchase the equipment he would need for music production This included working in Germany for a summer, at a time when Ray's father was living there. It proved to be a great opportunity for Ray. He developed greater independence and earned money cutting the grass on an airfield. The money he made from odd jobs enabled him to buy music production equipment.

Ray feels that some of his personality traits were pushing him towards becoming his own boss. A love of music and a strong dislike for being told what to do led Ray to take steps to become an entrepreneur. He feels that owning his own business is a way of truly being in control of his future.

After having a number of part-time jobs, Ray realised he would prefer to be his own boss. He wanted to combine his love for music with business. Ray's key motivation is not to make money; he wants to achieve something personally (to be the creator of a successful organisation) while also being involved in something he loves. However, he knows nothing about the business environment or developing goals and objectives and would like to have a sound strategy before he starts his business.

1. What would you advise Ray to do to develop a strategic plan for his business?

6.5 Strategy implementation

Implementing the chosen strategies is the third phase in the strategic management process. During this step, the policies for each function (such as human resources, production, finance, and marketing) and annual objectives must be developed in line with the chosen strategies and long-term goals. Resources should be allocated to achieve the strategies and goals, to measure performance, and to evaluate and correct strategies, objectives, and goals continuously.

6.5.1 The development of policies and annual objectives

The strategic management process does not end when the entrepreneur decides which strategy or strategies to pursue. These strategies should be translated into action. What the entrepreneur must remember is that successful strategy formulation does not guarantee successful strategy implementation, and that both require equal effort.

The first step is to establish annual objectives. These are essential for strategy implementation because they:
▸ Represent the basis for allocating resources
▸ Are major instruments for monitoring progress toward achieving long-term objectives
▸ Establish priorities within the venture.

The annual objectives should be measurable, consistent, reasonable, challenging, clear, characterised by an appropriate time dimension, and linked to rewards. These factors are important because objectives will break the various strategies that have been identified down into smaller parts. If one of the strategies identified is the establishment of a second shop or outlet in Cape Town, for example, it should be broken down into annual objectives that can

be followed. Examples of annual objectives derived from such a strategy are:
▸ Identification of a location in Cape Town by March of the given year
▸ Identification of personnel needed in the outlet by March of the given year
▸ Production plan for the outlet by March of the given year – including equipment needed and shop layout
▸ Identification of possible suppliers in the Cape Town area by March
▸ A financial analysis of the outlet and its needs by September
▸ Finalising the buying of equipment and shop layout by September
▸ Opening of the outlet in Cape Town on 1 December.

Developing objectives and communicating them to the various stakeholders will ensure that the strategies will be implemented. Changes in the strategic direction, however, are not that simple and do not occur automatically, therefore it would be necessary to develop policies to make the strategy work. Policies are specific guidelines, methods, procedures, rules, forms and practices established to support and encourage work toward the stated goals (David, 1995). Not only will policies aid the entrepreneur in identifying who will be responsible for what, but they will also help him or her in making decisions. A few examples of areas for which policies could be developed are:
▸ Affirmative-action employment
▸ Using outside consultants for specific areas
▸ Negotiation with labour unions – directly or indirectly
▸ Training and development of personnel
▸ Recruitment of personnel through employment agencies, universities, universities of technology and (or) newspapers
▸ Working and compensation for overtime work
▸ Using one or more suppliers
▸ 'Moonlighting'

▸ Sexual harassment
▸ Smoking
▸ Insider information.

6.5.2 The allocation of resources

All entrepreneurs have at least four types of resources that can be used in achieving the desired objectives: financial, physical, human, and technological resources. At the core of every strategy is the way in which entrepreneurs employ their resources and abilities to generate something of value for someone else.

6.5.3 Performance measurement

An important step in the implementation of strategies is measuring the strategies against certain criteria to establish whether or not they have been successfully implemented. The following criteria can be useful in the evaluation of the strategies:

▸ *Suitability*. The extent to which a strategy fits the situation identified in the strategic analysis and the way in which it would sustain or improve the competitive position of the venture.
▸ *Internal consistency*. The strategy that is implemented must be consistent with the various parts of the organisation. The internal strengths should support the strategy and the weaknesses addressed by it. The various resources needed to implement the strategy should be available. The strategy should also be supported by the organisational culture of the venture.
▸ *Realistic*. The plan should be achievable, even if it is challenging.
▸ *Focused on strategic problems*. The strategy addresses the key problems revealed through earlier analyses.
▸ *Capable of solving key sub-problems*. The strategy addresses minor problems and symptoms of company deficiencies.
▸ *Customer benefit*. The strategy will add value for customers.

▸ *Stakeholder benefit*. The strategy will add value for the stakeholders.

6.5.4 Corrective actions and strategy alignment

When implementing strategies, it is vital to take corrective action where needed. If, for example, it was found that there are not enough skilled members of staff to support the strategy, action could be taken to acquire the necessary personnel. If a growth strategy is implemented and it is found that additional funds will be necessary to bridge the initial stages, steps could be taken to obtain bridging finance.

6.5.5 Continuous evaluation of strategies

The entrepreneur should implement an annual review of strategies, goals, and objectives to ensure that the continuously changing needs of customers are addressed, changes in technology are implemented, changes in legislation are adhered to, new innovations are implemented and potential for growth is seized to the advantage of all stakeholders.

6.6 Obtaining sustainable competitive advantage

During the final stage of strategic management the aim is to obtain a competitive advantage by means of continuous strategic development. **Competitive advantage** is gained when a firm acquires attributes that allow it to perform at a higher level than others in the same industry. Firms can obtain a competitive advantage by implementing value-creating strategies, not simultaneously being implemented by any current competitor. These strategies need to be rare, valuable, and non-substitutable.

⌐ DEFINITION ⌐

Competitive advantage is the strategic advantage one business entity has over its rival entities within its competitive industry.

Sustainable, competitive advantages are advantages that are not easily copied and, thus, can be maintained over a long period of time. The competition must not be able to do it right away or it is not sustainable. According to Porter (1980) there are three generic strategies that an entrepreneur can use to gain a competitive advantage, namely cost leadership strategies, differentiation strategies and focus strategies. Developing a sustainable, competitive advantage in the South African business environment, strategies require aspects such as designing and developing unique products or services, a reputation for customer service, and multiple sources of advantage such as social responsibility and acquiring B-BBEE status. Other aspects that could lead to sustainable competitive advantage are customer loyalty, the development of excellent distribution channels and good vendor relations.

⌐ DEFINITION ⌐

Sustainable competitive advantages are long-term advantages that are not easily duplicable or surpassable and which allows an organisation to outperform its competitors.

6.6.1 Cost leadership strategy

This generic strategy calls for being the low-cost producer in an industry for a given level of quality. The firm sells its products either at average industry prices to earn a profit higher than that of rivals, or below the average industry prices to gain market share. In the event of a price war, the firm can maintain some profitability while the competition suffers losses. Even without a price war, as the industry matures and prices decline, the firms that can produce more cheaply will remain profitable

for a longer period of time. The cost leadership strategy usually targets a broad market (Porter, 1980:35–37).

Some of the ways that firms acquire cost advantages are by improving process efficiencies, gaining unique access to a large source of lower cost materials, making optimal outsourcing and vertical integration decisions, or avoiding some costs altogether. If competing firms are unable to lower their costs by a similar amount, the firm may be able to sustain a competitive advantage based on cost leadership.

Firms that succeed in cost leadership often have the following internal strengths:

▸ Access to the capital required making a significant investment in production assets; this investment represents a barrier to entry that many firms may not overcome.
▸ Skill in designing products for efficient manufacturing, for example, having a small component count to shorten the assembly process.
▸ High level of expertise in manufacturing process engineering.
▸ Efficient distribution channels.

⌐ EXAMPLE 6.2 ⌐

McDonald's

The restaurant industry is known for yielding low margins that can make it difficult to compete with a cost leadership marketing strategy. McDonald's has been extremely successful with this strategy by offering basic fast-food meals at low prices. They are able to keep prices low through a division of labour that allows it to hire and train inexperienced employees rather than trained cooks. It also relies on few managers who typically earn higher wages. These staff savings allow the company to offer its foods for bargain prices.

Source: Scilly (n.d.).

Each generic strategy has its risks, including the low-cost strategy. For example, other firms may be able to lower their costs as well. As technology improves, the competition may be able to leapfrog the production capabilities, thus eliminating the competitive advantage. Additionally, several firms following a focus strategy and targeting various narrow markets may be able to achieve an even lower cost within their segments and as a group gain significant market share.

6.6.2 Differentiation strategy

A **differentiation strategy** calls for the development of a product or service that offers unique attributes that are valued by customers and that customers perceive to be better than or different from the products of the competition. The value added by the uniqueness of the product may allow the firm to charge a premium price for it. The firm hopes that the higher price will more than cover the extra costs incurred in offering the unique product. Because of the product's unique attributes, if suppliers increase their prices the firm may be able to pass along the costs to its customers who cannot find substitute products easily (Porter, 1980:37–39).

Firms that succeed in a differentiation strategy often have the following internal strengths:
▸ Access to leading scientific research.
▸ Highly skilled and creative product development team.
▸ Strong sales team with the ability to successfully communicate the perceived strengths of the product.
▸ Corporate reputation for quality and innovation.

The risks associated with a differentiation strategy include imitation by competitors and changes in customer tastes. Additionally, various firms pursuing focus strategies may be able to achieve even greater differentiation in their market segments (Porter, 1980).

6.6.3 Focus strategy

The **focus strategy** concentrates on a narrow segment and within that segment attempts to achieve either a cost advantage or differentiation. The premise is that the needs of the group can be better serviced by focusing entirely on it. A firm using a focus strategy often enjoys a high degree of customer loyalty, and this entrenched loyalty discourages other firms from competing directly (Porter, 1980:39–40).

Because of their narrow market focus, firms pursuing a focus strategy have lower volumes and therefore less bargaining power with their suppliers. However, firms pursuing a differentiation-focused strategy may be able to pass higher costs on to customers since close substitute products do not exist.

Firms that succeed in a focus strategy are able to tailor a broad range of product development strengths to a relatively narrow market segment that they know very well.

Some risks of focus strategies include imitation and changes in the target segments. Furthermore, it may be fairly easy for a broad-market cost leader to adapt its product in order to compete directly. Finally, other focusers may be able to carve out sub-segments that they can serve even better (Porter, 1980).

6.6.4 Customer services

Given enough time and money, your competitors can duplicate almost everything you've got working for you. Even if you've got things patented, trademarked or cloaked in multiple layers of secrecy, your competitors can see what you deliver, what you get done and the core pieces of how you do it. Even if they can't duplicate what you do exactly, they can get close enough to hurt you – or take it to the next level and render your processes obsolete or hire your best employees (Bradt, 2012). The only thing they can't duplicate is your culture.

In sustainable, winning cultures, behaviours (the way we do things here) are inextricably linked to relationships, informed by attitudes, built on a rock-solid base of values, and completely appropriate for the environment in which the organisation chooses to operate (Bradt, 2012).

Customers will often remain with a brand or service they have loyalty towards, even though the company does not offer the cheapest or most effective product or service. Focus on building strong relationships with your customers and delivering a great customer experience and service. Ensure that products and services are delivered in time and at the highest quality. Rather under-promise and over-deliver than over-promise and under-deliver.

6.6.5 Corporate social responsibility (CSR)

According to Porter and Kramer (2006:83) successful businesses need a healthy society. Education, health care, and equal opportunity are essential to a productive workforce and safe products and working conditions not only attract customers but lower the internal costs of accidents. Porter and Kramer (2006:83) also indicated that a healthy society ultimately creates expanding demand for business as more human needs are met and aspirations grow and also that a healthy society needs successful entrepreneurs.

An entrepreneur can use CSR strategies to go beyond best practices, choosing a unique position by doing things differently from competitors in a way that lowers costs or better serves a particular set of customer needs while serving the society within it operates. Nestlé's approach to working with small farmers exemplifies the symbiotic relationship between social progress and competitive advantage (Porter & Kramer, 2006:90). The Kraal Gallery in Stellenbosch applied CSR strategies to gain a competitive advantage by employing and training township women as hand weavers and is driven by a vision to create 1 000 jobs for women, empowering them through skills transfer and a real share in the business, and weaving a platform for the transformation of grass-roots society through stable employment and a decent quality of life.

6.6.6 Broad-based black economic empowerment (B-BBEE)

Broad-based black economic empowerment (B-BBEE) is a strategic issue that is facing businesses of all sizes in South Africa. It is the government's initiative to promote economic transformation in order to ensure meaningful participation in the economy and business by black people, which includes Indian, African, and coloured persons who are South African citizens by birth or by descent or who were naturalised prior to 1993. B-BBEE has become one of the key strategic business imperatives for any business aspiring to grow and expand its asset base in the contemporary South African business environment. There is no legal requirement for private sector businesses to comply with the provisions of the Broad-based Black Economic Empowerment Act 53 of 2003 and Codes of Good Practice on B-BBEE (Department of Trade and Industry, 2007). However, businesses that operate under licence from the government and businesses that source their work from the government and state-owned enterprises are expected to contribute to the achievement of the objectives of B-BBEE. Private sector businesses that seek to get involved in private-public partnerships are also expected to contribute to the achievement of the objectives of B-BBEE.

In terms of the Broad-Based Black Economic Empowerment Codes businesses with a turnover of less than R5 million qualify as Exempted Micro Enterprises (EMEs) that are exempt from measurement in terms of the dti's Codes of Good Practice for BEE (Department of Trade and Industry, 2007). However, an entrepreneur with a turnover of less than R5 million can achieve sustainable competitive advantage above competitors that also qualify as EMEs by developing strategies to achieve B-BBEE in order to obtain contracts from businesses while contributing towards their B-BBEE rating. The legislation regarding B-BBEE will be discussed in more detail in Chapter 17.

> **DEFINITION**
>
> B-BBEE is the government's initiative to promote economic transformation in order to ensure meaningful participation in the economy and business by black people.

CONCLUSION

Although strategic planning is not usually associated with the establishment of an entrepreneurial venture, the entrepreneur could gain from doing an extensive strategic analysis of his or her environment before taking the plunge. The value of strategic management to the entrepreneur will also become more important when the venture grows faster than was initially expected.

This chapter provided clear guidelines regarding the entrepreneurial strategic process consisting of strategic planning, the evaluation of strategies, the implementation of those strategies and developing strategies to obtain sustainable competitive advantage. Using the entrepreneurial strategic matrix, the entrepreneur would be able to choose the strategies that are both innovative and will render the lowest financial risk, yielding the highest financial return on effort and investment.

True entrepreneurs know that every obstacle can be overcome if they want it badly enough. True entrepreneurs also know that they can achieve their goals with well-planned, achievable, bite-sized steps within the concept of his or her overall vision. They will be able to take the inevitable setbacks and disappointments and turn them to their advantage.

SELF-ASSESSMENT QUESTIONS

Multiple-choice questions

1. The strategic goal of any entrepreneur should be to deliver goods and services to customers that they will purchase and value, and to do it in such a way that the service rendered is better than that of the competition.
   a. True
   b. False

2. In the analysis of the _____, an entrepreneur will be able to identify threats and opportunities that could be used in the development of his or her products and (or) services.
   a. external environment
   b. internal environment
   c. strengths
   d. research capacity

3. An entrepreneur must remember that successful strategy formulation should lead to successful _____, and that both require equal effort.
   a. risk reduction
   b. innovation
   c. strategy implementation
   d. resources.

4. An important step in the implementation of strategies is measuring the strategies against certain criteria to establish whether or not they have been successfully implemented. Which one can be described as: the extent to which a strategy fits the situation identified in the strategic analysis and the way in which it would sustain or improve the competitive position of the venture?
   a. Internal consistency
   b. Suitability
   c. Realistic
   d. Focused on strategic problems

5. Which one of the following is not one of the generic sustainable competitive advantage strategies identified by Porter?
   a. Customer service strategy
   b. Focus strategy
   c. Differentiation strategy
   d. Cost leadership strategy

DISCUSSION QUESTIONS

1. Define and explain why strategic management is important to the entrepreneur.
2. Describe the phases and steps in the strategic management process.
3. Identify the aspects that should be included in the mission statement of a venture.
4. Discuss the factors that should be considered when doing an analysis of the external environment of a venture.
5. Discuss the factors that should be included in an analysis of the internal environment of the venture.
6. Illustrate how the TOWS-matrix could be used as a tool for developing strategies for the venture.
7. Explain how the best strategies could be identified.
8. Explain how the entrepreneur could ensure the implementation of strategies.
9. Discuss the importance of the allocation of resources to ensure the execution of strategies.
10. Discuss the evaluation of strategies and their implementation.
11. Define sustainable competitive advantage.
12. Discuss the generic competitive advantage identified by Porter.
13. Discuss how B-BBEE can be used as a sustainable competitive advantage strategy.

EXPERIENTIAL EXERCISE

South Africa is at present experiencing different trends in the economy. Some economists say that we have reached the end of the economic downturn, while others say that the downturn is still not over. Conduct some research on the Internet or in the library and find some of these contrasting views. Compile a report of at least five pages describing the different viewpoints and how the different views may affect an entrepreneur's strategic planning.

THE KRAAL GALLERY

The Kraal Gallery is a family-owned business with the goal of economic empowerment and provision of long-term jobs for South African women. This business plans to achieve this objective by offering an eight-month paid training period to women during which they are taught all the relevant skills needed to be employed by the company. After passing the final examinations, women are offered a job in a department of the company that suits their personal skills, talents and preferences. From then on the women get paid on the basis of their output, thereby learning to take responsibility for their own financial budget. The project was initiated by Frank Daniel, and is now managed by Frank and his two sons, Nic and Alexander Daniel (Helmreich, 2009).

Kraal is an Afrikaans word for a protective enclosure for humans and their valuables.

The Kraal Gallery (TKG) creates the finest handwoven rugs, tapestries and related articles in South Africa. Their vision is to weave products of the highest export quality combined with unique and aspiring designs making The Kraal Gallery the market leader in this niche field. Although TKG is predominately known for weaving rugs, the weavers also weave: baskets, tapestries, screen dividers, iPad sleeves, laptop sleeves, portfolio bags, kiddie's bags, sling bags, cushions, lamp shades, deckchairs, slippers, backpacks, yoga mats, picnic throws, fashion accessories, straps, placemats, table runners and other ad hoc items (Daniel, 2013:16).

TKG is a nationally registered service provider that offers learners an extensive German-adapted master weaving course. This course has been refined and created to suit the practical and social needs prevalent in South Africa and provides each learner with a holistic set of skills that can be used anywhere in the industry. A learner with no prior experience or learning can achieve export quality weaving by the time she or he completes the eight-month NQF level 2 training course under the supervision of the management team. TKG is proud of the excellently low rates of attrition and high quality of weavers.

Built on the backbone of 30+ years of experience in hand weaving and textiles, TKG's strategy is to build a profitable, scalable business that delivers economic benefits to all stakeholders involved with special emphasis on the financial and social empowerment of the weavers.

TKG's focus is holistically based on design, function and the human element. Its passion is to weave artistic items by harnessing the talents of women from isolated communities within South Africa. The TKG team has dedicated their knowledge and personal funding to create a model which is both economically sustainable and socially progressive.

TKG's dream is to showcase the talents of the weavers and to become a household name in modern hand woven design, colour and individual artistry that stretches into homes locally and abroad.

The Kraal team is driven by a vision to create 1 000 jobs for women, empowering them through skills transfer and a real share in the business, and weaving a platform for the transformation of grass-roots society through stable employment and a decent quality of life. The programme is impact driven, but with an understanding that sound business practices will ensure sustainability and longevity and the success of Africa's finest weavers.

At present the Kraal team operates in Stellenbosch, Somerset West, Hout Bay and Genadendal. It aims to combine the different cultural influences of each region into a common vision and then to present the finer details to the people of the world. The most recent project has recently begun in the rural Western Cape town of Genadendal. This town is steeped in heritage and was the first town to offer human rights to the indigenous people of Southern Africa. A fitting place to revive a work once started. Genadendal Hand Weavers (Brand: The Kraal Gallery) recently won 'Social Enterprise of the Year 2013 – Western Cape, for the work done in this community.

TKG markets its products by means of the following outlets:

1. Stellenbosch store which is the flagship. This store encapsulates the essence of the brand. Within, customers see, touch and feel the brand. Working, functional, neat – and open six days a week. A unique store that boasts not only fine products but also their combined story in creating change in South Africa. When visiting Stellenbosch one is immediately compelled to touch art and artistry. A moving, breathing, weaving haven that fosters creativity and showcases it in a high-end retail experience.

2. Firlands store – HQ which houses the nucleus of design and administration. All NPD (New Product Development) is done and tested here. Spinning (which is a production process of yarn) for the Masana Wool rugs is also conducted here. Cotton sourcing and deliveries of materials are sent to Firlands. Firlands has over 500 rug designs on record and as many in tapestry design – and numbers are growing and catalogued daily. Visitors literally make a short turn off the N2 and begin their visit to this store which is clearly visible from the road.

3. Genadendal/Greyton factory outlet which is open five days a week.

4. Hout Bay market which is a trendy small market trading from Fridays to Sunday every week. It offers a consistent cash flow and awareness of the products.

5. Retail stores are cherry-picked clients that carry Kraal stock. Most clients purchase stock from the company directly, but some have consignment agreements. All Kraal stock carries a leather tag with company and brand iconography embossed in the leather. This ensures that end-user clients can find where and how the products are made. A strong focus remains with ethical and environmental best practices.

6. Online trading by means of The Kraal Gallery website.

Source: Developed from Daniel (2013), The Kraal Gallery (n.d.), Fayerman (n.d.) and Helmreich (2009).

1. Develop a mission statement for The Kraal Gallery.
2. Conduct a SWOT analysis for the Kraal Gallery and identify at least four strategic goals.
3. The Kraal Gallery is planning to include the women in the West Coast areas of the Western Cape. Identify some of the opportunities and threats that it may face in doing this and develop strategies using their strengths and weaknesses to grasp the opportunities and face the threats.
4. What are the strategies that the Kraal Gallery can implement to give them a competitive advantage?

SUGGESTED WEBSITE LINKS

http://www.brandsouthafrica.com/research-analysis
http://smallbiztrends.com/2011/09/small-business-strategies-for-entrepreneurs.html
http://onlinelibrary.wiley.com/journal/10.1002/%28ISSN%291097-0266
http://www.entrepreneur.com/grow/businessstrategies/
http://jom.sagepub.com/content/29/6/963.abstract
https://www.youtube.com/watch?v=fVOViKEC2YY
https://www.youtube.com/watch?v=m3TTABvPCKY
https://www.youtube.com/watch?v=kqPwDGKtDvo
https://www.youtube.com/watch?v=GS-LR2a9_G0
https://www.youtube.com/watch?v=OA9Djd4SvQ8

REFERENCES

Bounds, GM, Dobbins, H. & Fowler, OS. 1995. *Management: A Total Quality Perspective.* Cincinnati: South-Western Publishing Co.

Bradt, G. 2012. *Corporate Culture: The only truly sustainable competitive advantage.* [Online]. Available: http://www.forbes.com/sites/georgebradt/2012/02/08/corporate-culture-the-only-truly-sustainable-competitive-advantage/ [October 2013].

Bruwer, P. & Plaatjies, D. 1999. *Entrepreneurship and Business Management.* Revised ed. Observatory: Future Management (Pty) Ltd.

BSSA. n.d. Young entrepreneur now helping others. [Online]. Available : http://www.bssa.co.za/

success-stories/young-entrepreneur-now-helping-others [October 2013].

Daniel, A. 2013. *The Kraal Gallery Entrepreneurship Award August 2013,* Gordons Bay: The Kraal Gallery.

David, FR. 1995. *Concepts of Strategic Management.* Englewood Cliffs, N.J.: Prentice-Hall.

De Kock, A. 2012. *Working Paper 1 – October 2012. WEF GCI 2012/13 Report: Analysing performance and implications for South Africa,* Johannesburg: Brand South Africa.

Department of Trade and Industry. 2005. *Integrated Strategy for the Promotion of Entrepreneurship and Small Enterprises,* Pretoria: The Department of Trade and Industry.

Department of Trade and Industry. 2007. *Broad-based Black Economic Empowerment Act (53/2003): Codes of Good Conduct on Black Economic Empowerment.* Pretoria: Government Printers.

Fayerman, I. n.d. *Highschool. South Africa Part 1. The Kraal Gallery.* [Online]. Available: http://projectexplorer.org/hs/za/kraal.php [Accessed October 2013].

Friedman, TI. 2006. *The World is Flat: The Globalized World in the Twenty-First Century.* Updated and expanded ed. Rosebank, South Africa: Penguin Books.

Helmreich, C. 2009. *Social Entrepreneurship in South Africa: The Kraal Gallery – A Development Project and its impact on women's lives,* Wörth: Bachelor thesis for the obtainment of the academic degree Bachelor of Arts in International Management at the University of Applied Sciences Deggendorf.

Leibbrandt, M, Woolard, I, Finn, A. & Argent, J. 2010. *Trends in South African Income Distribution and Poverty since the Fall of Appartheid.* s.l.:OECD Publishing.

MTN logo: Copyright © 2013 Mobile Telephone Networks. All rights reserved.

Parsons, R. 2013. *The National Development Plan - getting down to business?* Potchefstroom (Gauteng): AHI.

Porter, ME. & Kramer, MR. 2006. Strategy and Society: The Link Between Competitive Advantage and Corporate Social Responsibility. *Harvard Business Review,* December, 84(12):78–92.

Porter, ME. 1980. *Competitive Strategy: Techniques for analyzing industries and competitors.* New York: Free Press.

Raiz, A. 2013. Dangers small construction companies should look for. *Small Business Connect,* September:5.

Scilly, M. n.d. *Examples of cost leadership & strategy marketing.* [Online]. Available: http://smallbusiness.chron.com/examples-cost-leadership-strategy-marketing-12259.html [October 2013].

Sonfield, M, Lussier, R, Corman, J. & McKinney, M. 2001. Gender comparisons in strategic decision-making: An empirical analysis of the entrepreneurial strategy matrix. *Journal of Small Business Management,* 39(2):166.

The Kraal Gallery. n.d. *The Kraal Gallery. Our Story.* [Online]. Available: http://www.thekraalgallery.com/hand_woven_tapestries/about-us/our-story.php [October 2013].

The World Bank. 2013. *Insight Report. The Africa Competitiveness Report 2013,* Geneva: World Economic Forum.

Timm, S. 2013. Glimpses of hope during the downturn. *Small Business Connect,* September, Issue 1:4.

Van Aardt, CJ. & Schacht, A. 2003. *Demographic and Statistical Overview, 1994–2004.* Research Report.

CHAPTER 7

Business start-up

Isa van Aardt & Wesley Clarence

LEARNING OUTCOMES

On completion of this chapter you will be able to:
▶ Identify and discuss the aspects determining the capacity for survival of a new venture
▶ Discuss the necessity for a market strategy for the entrepreneur when starting a venture
▶ Discuss how competitors can influence the entrepreneur in his or her decision to start a venture
▶ Identify and discuss the resource needs of the entrepreneur and how the size of the prospective enterprise could influence the entrepreneur
▶ Identify and discuss the location factors to be considered when starting a venture
▶ Identify and discuss the various forms of ownership available for new ventures
▶ Discuss the factors affecting the entrepreneur's choice of ownership of the new venture
▶ Identify and discuss the business support systems available to entrepreneurs
▶ Identify and discuss the challenges entrepreneurs face during start-up.

OPENING CASE STUDY

Many business ideas fail to be developed successfully as the entrepreneur does not consider all the aspects of planning the growth of his or her idea. Consider for a moment the circumstances that entrepreneurs find themselves in once they have started trading or some form of start-up activity. As the business gets underway, there will be a greater need to operationalise the activities. Issues such as the presence of competitors, resources that are needed to be successful, the location of the business and the support systems all form an important part of business creation. Important decisions about these issues need to be made. When taking these considerations into account, the entrepreneur should have a long-term orientation and understanding of the business's needs. A short-term orientation would imply that the decisions surrounding these variables might not be made with a future perspective in mind.

There are many important considerations that will be highlighted in this chapter for entrepreneurs to take into account. To assist the entrepreneur, many questions can be asked that can contribute to the entrepreneur finding greater direction and developing the business. The following two questions are key considerations for the entrepreneur:
1. What type of enterprise fits my personal needs?
2. Which sources of business support do I have access to?

INTRODUCTION

The previous chapters dealt with the development of business ideas and testing those ideas for feasibility. This chapter deals with the process of establishing a business enterprise. A business venture does not come into being on its own. It is usually the result of people or entrepreneurs who identify a need for a product or service (opportunity), and utilise that opportunity, while at the same time accepting the associated risks.

The decision to start a business venture is a momentous one. The opportunities that may be derived from the need for products or services can vary from providing a new service to producing an entirely new product, or even taking existing services or products to areas where they have previously not been available. An opportunity could also be spotted by identifying a service that could be offered in a manner different to the one in which it is currently available, such as offering only a takeaway facility instead of a restaurant.

No matter which business opportunity or idea you have decided to develop into a business venture, the first obstacle to overcome is to obtain a demand for your services. This would take the form of some form of exchange between the entrepreneur and a client, resulting in a sale or agreement to fulfil a specific task for remuneration. The successful long-term utilisation of an identified opportunity through the establishment of a business enterprise requires the proposed enterprise to be profitable enough to be able to survive.

According to Cronje et al. (1997), a new venture's capacity for survival can be determined by investigating the following aspects:

▸ Characteristics, traits, and abilities of the prospective entrepreneur
▸ Market and a marketing strategy
▸ Evidence of any competitors
▸ Specific resource needs of the venture, including human resource needs
▸ Size of the proposed enterprise

▸ Where the venture will be located
▸ What business form the venture will take.

7.1 Characteristics, traits, abilities of the prospective entrepreneur

The first question that the entrepreneur should answer is whether he or she possesses the characteristics, traits, and other essential abilities to utilise the opportunity identified by the need to establish an enterprise.

In Chapter 2, the mindset and typical characteristics of successful entrepreneurs were discussed. Such characteristics include a need to achieve, a need for autonomy, an internal locus of control, and the willingness to take calculated risks. Other personal traits and abilities that the entrepreneur should consider are educational level, intellectual capabilities, ethical and moral standards, nurturing qualities, willingness to accept responsibilities, a reward and excellence orientation, optimism, the ability to organise, state of health, practical experience, personal family situation, and personal preferences. The nature of the opportunity identified may dictate that one or more of these factors will play a vital role in the eventual success of the venture. These should, therefore, be thoroughly considered before the final decision is made to start the proposed venture.

7.2 The market and a marketing strategy

Many entrepreneurs make the mistake of starting a business with potential clients in mind, but without sufficiently testing the market. Determining the extent of the need for a product or service that the entrepreneur wants to offer is probably the single most important factor in determining the future success of the prospective venture. This need be reflected not only in the present market, but also in the potential market for the relevant product or service. The entrepreneur should, therefore, do proper market research before establishing what his or her share of the market could be. The following questions (among others) should be asked (Cronje et al., 1997:33):

▶ Is the proposed product or service the first of its kind?
▶ Do similar or even the same products or services already exist? (This must be established for both existing and proposed products and services.)
▶ If the prospective product or service is an entirely new concept, should a demand for it be stimulated from scratch?
▶ What characteristics do the potential consumers of the product or service have?
▶ What is the extent of the potential market and what is the potential share of the prospective enterprise in that market?
▶ What has the growth pattern of the market been in the recent past?
▶ What is its future growth potential?
▶ What is the nature and extent of the existing and potential competition (including substitutes) in the market?
▶ What possibility does the prospective enterprise have for capturing and retaining a share of the market?

> **DEFINITION**
>
> Market research is any organised effort to gather information about target markets or customers.

It could be that the idea for the venture was the result of a change in the technology of an existing product, such as computer software, which resulted in a change in computer hardware or the development of other software programs. The market for the existing product can then be used to establish the market potential for the new products. Market research and the strategic marketing plan will be discussed in more detail in Chapter 14.

7.3 The presence of competitors

One mistake an entrepreneur should not make is to assume that there is no competitor for the product or service that he or she is about to offer. When establishing the presence of competitors, the entrepreneur should obtain answers to the following questions:

▶ Are there any competitors offering the same product or service, and if not, what is the possibility that a competitor could emerge?
▶ What is the possibility that a substitute for the product or service may be developed?
▶ What share of the market does the competitor have?
▶ What is the pricing policy of competitors?
▶ What effect will the development of the proposed venture have on the suppliers of such competitors?

The analysis of competitors is essential, since strategies should be developed to address this problem. Do not make the mistake of simply looking at similar or related products or services, but also look at substitute products or services. An example of a substitute product would be polyethylene terephthalate (PET) plastic containers competing with glass or aluminium containers.

7.4 Resource needs

For the entrepreneur, **resource needs** can be divided into four broad categories:

▶ *Operating resources.* This refers to the facilities that allow people to do their jobs. In the case of a service or retail venture, these resources will be the required site, buildings, office or shop equipment and layout, and vehicles. When manufacturing a product, these will also include machinery, factory equipment and layout, tools, and raw materials. Details regarding the operations management are discussed in Chapter 15.

▸ *Human resources.* The human resources of a venture will include all the personnel who are directly or indirectly involved in rendering the service, manufacturing, and (or) selling products. Both skilled and unskilled workers will have to be identified when planning the venture. Details regarding the human resources function are discussed in Chapter 16.

▸ *Financial resources.* Financial resources include resources that take the form of, or can be readily converted into, cash, which will enable the entrepreneur to obtain the necessary operating and human resources. It is necessary to determine the nature of these resource needs and investigate alternative ways of obtaining the necessary financial resources. Details of financial resources will be discussed in the section dealing with the Financial Plan (see Chapters 11 and 12).

▸ *Technology resources.* Technology resources include resources that support the production process, computer technology, the Internet and email, special recipes developed by the entrepreneur, and patents. It is essential to determine the nature of these resources and also assess the time frame of replacement as it will have a direct effect on the funding needs. Chapter 15 deals with technology and information management.

The nature of the business venture, and the services and products that it will offer, will determine resource needs. The ways of satisfying these needs may vary between extremely complicated and relatively simple processes. For example, the establishment of a large publishing company or car-manufacturing plant will be a more complicated process than setting up the offices of a consultant who works from home.

Another aspect that could have an effect on the products or services that the entrepreneur plans to offer is the availability of suppliers of the physical and financial resources. This could have a direct effect on the establishment of the venture as well as on the pricing of products or services.

7.5 The size of the proposed enterprise

Most entrepreneurial ventures start relatively small and then, if it is desirable and possible, expand gradually. The prospective entrepreneur should, however, reflect on the extent of his or her initial activities. There may be various factors that render a definite minimum or maximum level of activities preferable or even imperative. Cronje et al. (1997:39–40) identify the following aspects that may have an influence on deciding on the initial extent of the activities of the new venture:

▸ Availability of raw materials, equipment, labour, capital, and managerial skills
▸ Current size of the market
▸ Optimum level of production (the volume of production that will ensure the lowest cost per unit) and
▸ Minimum volume required to ensure that costs and income are matched (the so-called break-even point).

7.6 The location of the business

DEFINITION

The location usually refers to the premises that will be needed to produce the products or render the services.

Making an informed and calculated choice of location is of extreme or even vital importance, since the success of an enterprise may depend thereon. Depending on the nature of the product or service that is to be offered, the entrepreneur should, for example, decide whether the enterprise needs to be located near its market or its sources of raw materials. It must be decided whether it should be in the vicinity of other competitive enterprises, located in the city centre, the suburbs, a rural area, in existing industrial areas or anywhere the entrepreneur prefers. These are referred to as location factors.

The most important location factors that the entrepreneur should consider are:

▶ *Sources of raw materials.* Where, in what quantities, and at what prices are the most important raw materials available? What is the quality thereof? The number of suppliers and their prices, the cost of transporting these raw materials to the point of location, and their durability should also be taken into account.

▶ *The availability of labour and other human resources.* Where and at what cost is adequate labour of the right type available in terms of, for example, levels of training, type of skills and experience, development potential, and productivity?

▶ *The proximity of and access to the market.* Here consideration should be given to aspects such as potential advantages over present competitors, the current extent and the potential development of the market, the durability of the finished products, the consumers' need for rapid deliveries, after-sales service and personal contact, and the possible entry of competitors and substitute products or services into the market.

▶ *The availability of transport facilities.* This includes the possibility of using own transport, the suitability of roads, and limitations on private transport. It also includes aspects relating to the use of hired transport by rail, air, road or water. The transport costs of raw materials in relation to finished products, as well as the cost of transport of finished products to consumers, should also be considered.

▶ *The availability of power and water at a reasonable price.* The most suitable type of power, such as electricity, steam or gas, may be necessary for the supply of mechanical power, heating, cooling, lighting, and so on. Water could also be used in the process for supplying steam, the removal of waste, cleaning or even as a raw material in certain production processes, such as with the manufacturing of soft drinks or beer.

▶ *The availability of a site and buildings.* These should be of the required size and appearance, with the necessary facilities and possibilities for extension. The price at which the premises can be purchased, rented or developed, the cost of extensions or necessary improvements, should also be considered. Attention should also be given to accessibility for suppliers of raw material, customers, and employees, as well as the attractiveness of the surroundings and the presence of unpleasant, harmful or even dangerous neighbouring enterprises, such as abattoirs, chemical or explosives plants or other factories.

▶ *The availability of capital.* This need not necessarily have a direct effect on the choice of a specific location for the enterprise but can still play a role where the suppliers of capital (owners, partners, shareholders, private moneylenders, development corporations, dti or other financial institutions, for example) set specific conditions or express certain preferences in this regard, or where capital is such a limiting factor that it necessitates the choice of the cheapest location for the enterprise.

▶ *The attitude, regulations, and tariffs of local authorities.* The aspects that have to be considered in this regard are, for example, the attitude of local authorities to industrial development, including possible concessions for encouragement, as well as health regulations, building regulations, property rates, water and electricity tariffs, and the availability and costs of other municipal services.

- *The existing business environment.* This could influence the establishment of the proposed venture by, for example, the provision of repair and maintenance services, as well as the availability of spares, banking, postal, and other communication facilities. The extent to which the proposed venture could provide repair and maintenance services to other businesses in the area, if such services are not available, should also be considered.
- *The social environment.* This relates to the provision of satisfactory housing, educational, medical, recreational, and shopping facilities for employees of the proposed enterprise.
- *The climate of the region.* Some production processes require a particular climate, which can influence the recruitment and retention of personnel and encourage productivity.
- *Central government policy.* This may encourage or discourage the establishment of certain types of enterprises in specific areas in a direct or indirect manner through, for example, tax concessions. Funding from the dti for the establishment of a venture in a rural area should also be considered.
- *The personal geographical references of the prospective entrepreneur and his or her family.* The factors that could play a role here are the availability of schools, familiarity with the area, the necessity of moving house, security or other uncertainties.

ENTREPRENEURIAL DILEMMA

Chris's dilemma

Chris had always been interested in living healthily and eating a balanced diet. He often started his morning at the nearest gym, 25 kilometres from his home. He also thought about how convenient it would be to have a gym closer to the area in which he lived. When he saw a new mall being developed approximately five minutes from his home, he immediately thought about opening up a gym inside the new mall and becoming a business owner. He also thought about franchising the gym in the future thereby becoming a wealthy business owner. A local gym equipment supplier offered him a 10% cash discount as he was liquidating his gym equipment-import business and offered to help Chris find temporary storage for the goods. Chris decided to draft a resignation letter to his employer before the end of the week that he saved in his personal folder, on his work computer. He then decided to make contact with the developer of the mall who he felt could tell him if there would be space for the gym at the mall. He was sure that he could make a profit after the first six months and felt pleased with himself.

1. If you were a friend of Chris, what advice would you give to him?

Should more than one location have been identified, each one should be assessed according to the above factors and the most suitable one then chosen. This assessment would be a relatively easy task if all the location factors played an equally important role in the location of a specific enterprise, and if all such factors could be quantified in monetary terms. Unfortunately, this is not always the case. All the applicable factors should nevertheless be considered when selecting a location. To assist with this, various models have been developed which can be used when assessing location factors that can be expressed in monetary terms, as well as those that will be assessed subjectively in the choice of a location. Consequently, the overall influence of all applicable location factors on each of the potential locations can be quantified and the most advantageous location determined.

Assuming that a proposed enterprise is considering **two alternative locations**, A and B, the following procedure for making the most advantageous choice can be followed:

- *Step one:* The first step is to establish the location factors applicable to the proposed business enterprise. These could be different for each business venture. Let us assume that for the proposed business enterprise, the location factors that will have a direct impact on the decision are transport costs, competition, acceptance by the community, office rent, electricity tariffs, and personal preferences.

▸ *Step two:* After the appropriate location factors have been established, a weighting (one to five) should be assigned to each factor to indicate its importance. If it is extremely important, it should be given a weighting of five (one being lowest, three and four moderate).

▸ *Step three:* Calculate, as accurately as possible, the cost per location factor for both locations. The factors that cannot be quantified should be evaluated against the requirements set for a specific location factor, and be given a rating (zero to 10) on how well it meets the criterion. If the idea fulfils all possible aspects of a criterion, it would receive a rating of zero (no disadvantages). On the other hand, if it only partially satisfies the criterion, it might receive a four or five, and, if it does

not satisfy requirements, a nine or 10 (a large disadvantage).

▸ *Step four:* List the information gathered in steps one to three in a table (see Table 7.1).

▸ *Step five:* Calculate the disadvantages connected with each location and determine the ratio between the disadvantages of both locations (see Table 7.1).

▸ *Step six:* Decide on the best location.

7.7 Types of ownership

When starting a business venture, the prospective entrepreneur has to consider in advance what **type of ownership** to choose. In South Africa, new ventures and other business enterprises mostly take the form of sole proprietorships, partnerships, companies (profit and non-profit companies), and co-operatives.

Until the promulgation of the new Companies Act 71 of 2008, which came into force on 1 April 2011 (the dti, 2010a), close corporations were also one of the forms of business enterprise. The main influence of the

Table 7.1 A comparison and calculation of two location options

	LOCATION FACTOR			CALCULATION OF DISADVANTAGES	
	Location A	Location B	Weight	Location A	Location B
Transport cost	R12 000	R10 000	5	60 000	50 000
Competition	5	3	3	15	9
Community acceptance	3	4	1	3	4
Rental cost	R20 000	R21 000	3	60 000	63 000
Electricity cost	R9 000	R8 000	2	18 000	16 000
Personal preference	2	5	5	10	25
Total value of disadvantage				138 028	129 038
Ratio of disadvantage					1.07 to 1

Note: The disadvantages associated with location B are fewer than those associated with location A.

Companies Act is that the Companies and Intellectual Property Commission (CIPC) will no longer register new close corporations or allow a company to convert to a close corporation, although the uninterrupted and continued existence of existing close corporations for an indefinite period of time is catered for (CIPRO, 2008). The establishment of close corporation as type of ownership will thus not be discussed. Read what the CIPC (formerly called CIPRO) says about the changes in the Companies Act.

EXAMPLE 7.1

Close corporations transitional arrangements in the new Companies Act

The new Companies Act provides for the co-existence of the new Companies Act and the Close Corporations Act 69 of 1984 with amendments to the latter to harmonise the laws as far as practicable to avoid regulatory arbitrage. The new Companies Act as the legislative framework for forming and maintaining small companies, which has drawn on the characteristics of the Close Corporations Act, is sufficiently streamlined and simplified as to render it unnecessary to retain the application of the Close Corporations Act for the formation of new corporations.

However, it is recognised that existing close corporations should be free to retain their current status until such time as their members may determine that it is in their interest to convert to a company. Therefore, the Act provides for the indefinite continued existence of the Close Corporations Act, but provides for the closing of that Act as an avenue for incorporation of new entities, or for the conversion of companies into close corporations, as of the effective date of the new Companies Act.

Basically it means that CIPRO [now CIPC] will: 'continue to maintain the Close Corporations register indefinitely as far as membership, addresses, Accounting Officer, etc. amendments are concerned, but will no longer register new Close Corporations as at the full implementation of the New Companies Act' and 'not allow a company to convert to a Close Corporation as at the effective date of the new Companies Act'.

Source: CIPRO (2008).

The type of ownership has to be suited to the particular circumstances, objectives, requirements, and personal characteristics of the entrepreneur. In choosing the type of ownership when staffing the venture, the entrepreneur should remember that the original form chosen can be changed at a later stage if the circumstances, objectives or requirements of the venture change. The correct choice before establishing the venture can eliminate many problems, formalities, and expenses that may otherwise occur at a later stage.

7.7.1 Factors affecting the choice of the type of ownership

The choice of the type of ownership is important as the various alternatives have different implications for the owner and could influence various future management decisions. The following considerations should be taken into account:

▸ *The legal (juristic) personality of the venture.* This refers to whether or not the venture is a legally independent person that can own assets in its own name, can conclude contracts, and can also sue or be sued in its own name. Some of the characteristics of a legal person or entity are that:
  ▪ It exists independently
  ▪ Changes in membership have no influence on the existence of the legal entity
  ▪ If a member dies, it remains in existence and does not dissolve
  ▪ It has its own assets and obligations, and the members are not responsible for the debts of the legal entity.

▸ *The liability of the owner.* This is closely connected with the previous aspect and refers to whether or not the owner can be held liable for any outstanding debts of, and claims against, the venture.

▸ *The extent to which the owner has direct control.* Does the owner have control and (or) authority over the activities of the venture, over the utilisation of its assets and the distribution of its profits?

▶ *The ability of the venture to acquire capital on its initial establishment and with further expansion.* Here factors such as the permitted number of owners, their liabilities, and authority in management play a role.

▶ *The possibilities of a change in ownership.* This refers to the ease with which an owner can transfer his or her interest or share in the venture to someone else when he or she wishes or is obliged to withdraw from the enterprise. In this regard, the term 'existence' or 'continuity' of the venture also comes into consideration.

▶ *The legal requirements regarding the establishment, management, and dissolution of the venture.* These include the requirements of professional associations, such as those for engineers, architects, medical professions, and others, as well as the tax liability of the venture and its owner.

The most important characteristics, advantages, and disadvantages of sole proprietorships, partnerships, companies and close corporations will now be discussed briefly in terms of the preceding key considerations.

7.7.2 Sole proprietorship

DEFINITION

A sole proprietorship (or sole trader) has only one individual owner, who is usually the manager.

In a sole proprietorship, the owner has no partners and his or her venture is not registered as a company or close corporation, both of which would be registered with only one member or shareholder. Sole ownership has no independent legal personality and consequently cannot exist independently of the owner.

The assets of the venture belong to the owner, who remains personally liable for all the debts of and claims against the venture. The owner may therefore lose all his or her personal possessions if the venture is unable to meet its obligations.

The owner has full control and authority over the activities of the venture and receives all the profits. Usually he or she acts as manager and can make decisions freely about the way in which it is run. As a result, the venture can easily adjust to changes. On the other hand, a sole proprietorship can, depending on circumstances, make exceptionally high demands on the management skills and personal freedom of the owner.

One of the drawbacks of sole proprietorship is that the possibilities of acquiring capital are limited. Often the amount of capital at the disposal of the owner is the only capital available and it could be insufficient, especially when expansion is necessary. Heavy dependence on loan capital may lead to the owner being forced to relinquish control, authority and freedom of action.

There are usually few problems with the transfer of ownership in sole proprietorships. The proprietor may decide to sell at any time (if, of course, a buyer can be found), close down the business or transfer ownership to someone else. The continuity of the venture is furthermore linked to the life-span or legal capacity of the proprietor. In the event of his or her death, declared insolvency or incapability to sign contracts, the venture is usually ended.

Regarding the legal requirements, a sole proprietorship enjoys many advantages since it does not have to comply with any particular legal requirements in its establishment, practice or dissolution. However, a sole proprietor does need to register with the following institutions (for details, see Chapter 17):

▶ The South African Revenue Service (SARS) for tax matters (value-added tax (VAT)) and employee income tax
▶ The Department of Labour for staff matters, such as the unemployment insurance fund and compensation for occupational injuries and diseases
▶ A local municipality for matters relating to the business premises

▶ Companies and Intellectual Property Commission (CIPC) for business name registration, trademark registration, and other intellectual property matters.

With regard to taxation, it has already been indicated that all the profits of the venture belong to the proprietor and are, therefore, taxed only once in his or her hands as an individual. Depending on the taxable income of the owner and the prevailing tax laws, a sole proprietorship may entail greater tax advantages for the owner than any other form of ownership.

Since the sole proprietor is not a legal entity, bank accounts should be opened in the name of the business owner. To keep this account separate from his or her personal bank account, the name of the owner followed by 'trading as' and the name of the business registered with CIPC should be used.

A sole proprietorship is preferable in the case of a really small venture that renders some kind of service to the community, where the owner prefers to remain in sole control and where expansion is neither contemplated nor possible.

7.7.3 Partnerships

A **partnership** comes into being when two or more people decide to conduct business together and decide against registering as a company or close corporation. In many respects a partnership is similar to a sole proprietorship, and many of the disadvantages of a sole proprietorship are, therefore, also applicable to a partnership.

> **DEFINITION**
>
> A partnership can be described as a contractual relationship between two or more persons (known as partners), but usually not more than 20, who practise a lawful business to which every partner contributes, with the objective of making a profit to be distributed among them.

As with sole proprietorships, partnerships do not have a legal personality and all transactions, contracts or agreements are entered into by the partners in their personal capacities and not by the partnership. All the partners bear equal responsibility for debts incurred and are jointly and severally liable for claims against the partnership, irrespective of which partner was responsible for them and whether or not the other partners were aware of their being incurred. The personal belongings of the partners are, therefore, not safeguarded at all.

Unless otherwise agreed upon, the partners have joint control and authority over the venture. This can obviously lead to problems, particularly in the event of disagreements and, in this respect, a partnership is less adaptable to changing circumstances than a sole proprietorship is. The fact that more than one person has a say in managerial issues may improve management since the knowledge, expertise, and skills of more people can be drawn upon. At the same time, this presents an opportunity for the division of labour and specialisation, with the additional advantage that the individual partners are subjected to less personal stress than is the case with the owner in a sole proprietorship.

The chances of acquiring capital are usually better for a partnership than for a sole proprietorship. This is primarily because there are more people to make contributions and to provide security for credit. Transfer of ownership is generally more difficult with a partnership, once again because more people are involved. In addition, the provisions of the partnership contract, should there be one, must be complied with. On the other hand, it may be easier for a partner to sell his or her share in a partnership than it is to sell a sole proprietorship. This could be due to the fact that partnerships are better equipped to acquire capital, have better management systems, and have recourse to the division of labour and specialisation, and experience less personal stress.

An existing partnership can be dissolved when any of the following occurs:

▶ By mutual agreement between the partners
▶ The retirement or death of one of the partners
▶ The addition of a new partner
▶ A partner being declared insolvent
▶ A partner being declared contractually incompetent
▶ The partnership being declared insolvent, in which event the individual partners are, of course, also declared insolvent.

As far as legal requirements are concerned, there is little difference between a partnership and a sole proprietorship. The only significant difference is a written partnership agreement that makes provision for matters such as the nature and aims of the venture, capital contributions by the individual partners, distribution of profits, management, and dissolution. Although not legally compulsory, it is recommended that such a document be drawn up. As with the sole proprietorship, each partner is taxed in his or her personal capacity in respect of the total income that he or she earns from the partnership. The partnership per se has no liability in this regard.

Partnerships may be ordinary or extraordinary. With extraordinary partnerships two types can be distinguished, namely:

▶ *The anonymous or sleeping partnership.* In this partnership two or more people agree to do business collectively, with one or more of the partners remaining anonymous. The anonymous partner(s) also shares in the risks of the venture and has access to the financial records but may not get involved in the management of the business.
▶ *The commanditarian partnership.* A member of this type of partnership invests financially in the business and shares limited liability in the enterprise. The partners share in the profits and losses that are generated in accordance with their contribution.

7.7.4 Companies

> **DEFINITION**
>
> A company may be regarded as a more advanced form of ownership in which the drawbacks of sole proprietorship and partnership, especially insofar as these concern unlimited liability and the ability to acquire capital, are eliminated.

The legal aspects of the company are regulated by the new Companies Act of 2008 (hereafter referred to as the 'Companies Act').

In South Africa, two types of companies can be distinguished, namely for-profit companies and non-profit companies (Companies Act, 2008).

7.7.4.1 A for-profit company

A **for-profit company** is incorporated for the purpose of financial gain for its shareholders and is divided into the following:

▶ *State-owned company* that is owned by the state or municipality and must appoint a registered auditor. The name of a state-owned company must end with the expression 'SOC Ltd.'.
▶ *Private company* that is not a state-owned company and is prohibited to offer any securities or shares to the public. The transferability of its securities or shares is restricted and usually occurs only upon approval from the board of directors. A private company must appoint at least one director and the number of shareholders varies from one to 50 persons – as long as the authorised number of shares is not exceeded, there are no limitations to the maximum shareholders. The name of a private company must end with the expression 'Propriety Limited' or its abbreviation '(Pty) Ltd.'.
▶ *A personal liability company* is a private company where the directors and past directors are jointly and severally liable, together with the company, for any debts and liabilities of the company as are or

were contracted during their respective periods of office. A personal liability company must appoint at least one director and the name must end with the word 'Incorporated' or its abbreviation 'Inc.'.

▸ *A public company* must appoint at least three directors and a registered auditor. It can offer its shares to the general public and must convene annual general meetings with its shareholders. Public companies must make certain information, such as financial statements, shareholding, and names of directors, known to the public (Companies Act, 2008). The name of a public company should end with the word 'Limited' or its abbreviation 'Ltd.'.

7.7.4.2 A non-profit company

A **non-profit company** is a company that is incorporated for a public benefit and the income and property are not distributable to its incorporators, members, directors or persons related to any of them. A non-profit company is not required to have members, but must appoint at least three directors. The company name should include the expression 'NPC'.

7.7.4.3 Description of companies

A private company, personal liability company or non-profit company is not required to comply with the extended accountability requirements set for a public or state-owned company, except to the extent that the company's memorandum of incorporation provides otherwise.

Both private and, to a greater extent, public companies are subject to a number of legal requirements and limitations. A company has a legal personality, and its assets and liabilities are therefore separate from those of the owners (shareholders). The personal assets of the shareholders consequently do not form part of claims that may be made against a company. The liability of the shareholders is limited to the amount paid by them for their share capital. If this share capital has not been paid in full, the shareholders may, in the case of a claim against the company, be expected to pay

their shares in full. This is, however, their maximum liability.

The control and authority over the activities and assets of a company essentially rest with two bodies, namely the board of directors and a general meeting of members. The operational management of a company is usually entrusted to the board of directors in terms of the articles of the company, while the general meeting of members is authorised to amend the articles and is consequently able to bring about a redistribution of power between itself and the board of directors.

Usually directors are appointed by a general meeting of members, and their functions and powers are set out in the articles. These functions and powers are practiced jointly by the directors (as the board of the directors) through a majority vote. The board of directors may, if it has been authorised accordingly by the articles of association or the general meeting, delegate some of its functions and powers to a managing director.

The only way in which the members of a company can voice their opinions on the way in which the company is run or managed is by voting at a general meeting of members, which has to be held annually. In principle, a member's voting power is linked to the number of shares he or she has in the company, and decisions at the general meeting are normally taken by the majority vote.

As with a partnership, a company has the advantage of more people having an input regarding its management style, thereby providing more varied management skills and experience. Once again, this extended authority may, however, have the disadvantage of delayed decision making when consensus cannot be reached.

A company has definite advantages over a sole proprietorship or partnership with regard to the opportunities for acquiring capital, and this applies particularly to a public company. This is due to the fact that the general public is invited to invest capital in such a company, and members of the public are usually prepared to do this because of the legal personality the company has, the limited liability it entails, and the strict legal requirements the company has to adhere to. For the same reason, financial institutions are more willing to invest funds in a company than in a sole proprietorship. The possibility of obtaining capital can be facilitated by shareholders and particularly directors, should they be prepared to provide additional security for loans in their personal capacities. This often happens in practice.

A private company has **perpetual succession** meaning that the business can continue even in the event of any of the members (shareholders) passing away. The transfer of ownership in a public company takes place by the unlimited and free transfer of shares through selling shares on a private basis or on the stock exchange. The transfer of shares usually has no influence on the activities of a venture, and consequently the venture has an unlimited life-span.

Shares in a private company are not freely transferable and their manner of transfer is stipulated in the company's articles of association. The transfer is usually subject to the approval of the board of directors, and it is, therefore, necessary for the shareholder who wants to sell his or her shares to sell them to someone who is acceptable to the board of directors. In practice, this usually means relatives or friends, but it should not be difficult to find someone suitable if a company is profitable. The transfer of shares in a private company also usually has little influence on the activities and, therefore, the continued existence of the venture.

A company is subject to many more legal requirements than a sole proprietorship or partnership:

▸ Establishment and registration of a company. The requirements of the Companies Act (2008) have to be complied with, including registration of the memorandum and articles of association as well as payment of registration fees.
▸ Requirements regarding accounting practices, financial reports, auditing,

minutes, membership register, and so forth, have to be complied with.
▸ Requirements regarding the rights, powers and duties of directors and other office bearers, in respect of which the relevant provisions of the articles of association also have to be adhered to.
▸ Legal requirements concerning the dissolution or liquidation of a company.
▸ The company and its shareholders are taxed. The company pays a fixed percentage of its pre-tax profits as income tax, while shareholders have to add part of their profit from the company (company dividends based on their shareholdings) to their taxable incomes that leads to the so-called double taxation on company profits.

7.7.4.4 Other forms of ownership

The following two forms of ownership are not regarded as common alternatives available to the entrepreneur when considering setting up an enterprise. Due to the distinctive characteristics of a co-operative, it is not an alternative type of ownership that can be considered by the prospective entrepreneur, and will therefore not be included in the discussion of the alternative types of ownership that follow.

Co-operatives
Co-operatives, which may be established in terms of the Co-operatives Act 14 of 2005, are a type of ownership with limited possibilities of utilisation. Co-operatives are established to achieve certain economic advantages for their members through joint action. These co-operatives are usually found in the rural farming communities and operate as marketing and (or) supply organisations for products, goods, and services primarily to their members.

Trusts
Trusts have primarily been formed to protect the assets of its beneficiaries and as a legal entity under which to conduct business. A trust offers its members limited liability and reduced costs while looking to make a profit

and further the objectives of the trustees. A trust may not exceed 20 members.

As in the case of the previous types of ownership, the laws and regulations governing the formation of the business types changes occasionally along with the potential benefits its members derive. It is best to keep updated of the proposed and actual changes as they occur.

Table 7.2 is a summary of the main forms of ownership discussed above, based on the factors influencing the choice of business ownership.

Table 7.2 Summary of types of ownership

FACTOR	SOLE PROPRIETOR	PARTNERSHIP	PRIVATE COMPANY	PUBLIC COMPANY
Legal personality	Not a separate legal entity	Not a separate legal entity	Separate legal entity	Separate legal entity
Membership	1	2–20	1–50	Unlimited
Liability of owner	Individually liable	Jointly and severally liable	Limited liability	Limited liability
Registration	Local authority	Local authority	The registrar (CIPC)	The registrar (CIPC)
Legal requirements	Limited to different trade licences	Limited to different trade licences	Comprehensive registration process	Comprehensive registration process
Control by owner	Control and authority rests with owner	Joint control and authority	Control and authority rests with board of directors and members	Control and authority rests with board of directors and members
Taxation of profit	Individually taxed on profit whether it is drawn or not	Partners are taxed on profit whether it stays in the business or not	Profit taxed at a fixed rate, dividends declared are currently tax free	Profit taxed at a fixed rate, dividends declared are currently tax free
Taxation of salaries	Any amount distributed is seen as income and taxed	Salaries plus partners' share of profit is taxed when paid	Salaries paid to members are taxable and deducted by company – salaries must be reasonable	Salaries paid to members are taxable and deducted by company– salaries must be reasonable
Change of ownership	Owner may decide to sell at any time	By mutual agreement of partners	Shares can be sold by mutual agreement of members	Shares can be sold freely on the open market
Life of business	Continuity linked to the owner – cease to exist at death, insolvency or incapability of owner	Terminated by death, withdrawal or insolvency of a partner	Unlimited – does not end with death, withdrawal or insolvency of a member	Unlimited – does not end with death, withdrawal or insolvency of a member
Ability to acquire capital	Limited to owner's assets and outside borrowing	Limited to partners' investments and outside borrowing	Limited to shareholders' contribution, new shareholders, and outside borrowing	Limited to shareholders' contribution, new shareholders, and outside borrowing

7.8 **Business industries**

The total economy consists of industrial sectors that produce products and services and have been grouped together in the Standard Industry Classification (SIC). The SIC is a classification of economic activities of industries. A **business industry** consists of establishments engaged in the same or a closely related kind of economic activity based mainly on the principal class of goods produced or services rendered. The term 'industry' is used in the widest sense to cover all economic activity from the primary industries of agriculture, forestry, fishing, and mining to the rendering of social, recreational, cultural, and personal services (Stats SA, 1993; the complete SIC can be accessed at http://www.statssa.gov.za/additional_services/code_lists.asp).

The SIC is also used in the Small Business Act 102 of 1996 as amended (Small Business Act, 1966) to support the classification of an entrepreneurial venture as a very small (micro-), small or medium enterprise. The SIC's schedule (the revised schedule can be found in the National Small Business Amendment Act 26 of 2003:8–10) is divided into columns containing: the different sectors and subsectors of the SIC (Column 1), the size or class of the venture (Column 2), and the criteria according to which the size classes are measured (Columns 3, 4, and 5).

There are a total of ten different sectors, each with subsectors, but for the purposes of this book we will focus only on five: manufacturing, service, retail, IT industry, and Internet or e-business.

7.8.1 **Manufacturing**

The manufacturing sector provides a locus for stimulating the growth of other activities, such as services, and achieving specific outcomes, such as employment creation and economic empowerment. This platform of manufacturing presents an opportunity to significantly accelerate the country's growth and development.

Manufacturing in South Africa is dominated by the following industries:
▶ Agri-processing
▶ Automotive
▶ Chemicals
▶ ICT and electronics
▶ Metals
▶ Textiles, clothing, and footwear
▶ Construction.

7.8.2 **Service**

South Africa has an extensive and well-developed professional services industry. The services industry is characterised by the delivery of intangible services, sometimes combined with products. The services industry consists of (among others) the following:
▶ Advertising, including print, radio, television, outdoor advertising, and the Internet. The allocation of new private radio and TV licences in recent years has increased advertising options and led to increased competition within the industry.
▶ A variety of Professional bodies associated with the service industry.
▶ Marketing and market research organisations, including a number of international companies.
▶ The South African legal system, comprising a number of court structures and legal professions such as attorneys and advocates.
▶ Financial and insurance services, offering commercial, retail and merchant banking, mortgage lending, insurance, and investment. Our financial sector is highly developed and technologically advanced.
▶ Accounting service companies. The trend is for these companies to adopt a multidisciplinary approach and offer ancillary services, such as management consulting, legal services, and IT consulting.
▶ Hospitality and tourism services
▶ A variety of other services such as consulting services, office administration, hairdressing and cleaning services.

7.8.3 **Retail**

The South African retail environment is a vibrant and creative space for both emerging and established businesses. The wholesale and retail sales sector is cashing in on a sustained spending spree by the country's increasingly prosperous consumers. A retailer is defined as an enterprise deriving more than 50% of its turnover from the sale of goods to the general public for household use.

The retail industry is divided into four size groups, namely: large and medium enterprises, and small and very small (micro-) enterprises. The size of the enterprise is usually calculated based on the business's income and number of employees. The majority of entrepreneurs will start a business in the retail industry.

7.8.4 **IT industry**

The IT industry includes telecommunications services, telecommunication equipment manufacture, computer hardware manufacture, packaged software development, and IT professional services (e.g. consulting). This is an important sector that provides a highly innovative backbone to all industry participants.

7.8.5 **Internet or e-business**

Growth in e-commerce in South Africa is fuelled by the realisation that online procurement and supply-chain management can trim costs and improve customer relationships. Moreover, many of the largest companies in South Africa, such as financial institutions, mining, chemical, and manufacturing businesses, conduct business globally and have thus kept pace with the demands of global customers. Procurement marketplaces continue to grow, enabling vendor sourcing, order and transaction processing, and system integration. Chapter 22 will provide more information about this sector.

7.9 **Business support systems**

As indicated in Chapters 1 and 2, the failure rate for small businesses is particularly high. Most businesses that fail do so within the first few years. The reasons for failure are extremely varied, although there appears to be one common theme, namely that the entrepreneurs did not make sufficient use of the **sources of support** at their disposal. According to Meredith et al. (1982), the information and assistance required to help entrepreneurs survive and grow are widely available and should be used.

Why do entrepreneurs often ignore business support mechanisms? The reason for this is that they value their independence and the freedom to make their own decisions. Furthermore, suggestions from other people are often resented because they are perceived as interference. However, such an attitude may be foolish when considering the following views expressed by Meredith et al. (1982:176):

‣ Ideas and information usually come from different sources. By discussing problems with other people, the entrepreneur obtains many ideas on how to solve problems, as well as information that could be useful in solving problems.
‣ By obtaining contributions from different sources, the entrepreneur can improve his or her decision-making abilities. The more information the entrepreneur obtains, the better able he or she will be to make good decisions.
‣ After the entrepreneur has made use of specific sources of support or information, he or she will be more likely to use such sources in future with positive effect. Should the entrepreneur show that he or she appreciates the support being given by outside sources, it becomes more likely that such sources of support will, in future, go out of their way to be of assistance.

▶ The entrepreneur will, by listening to other people and using their advice and support, learn that he or she does not have all the right answers, and that people and institutions outside his or her business will be able to help when help is required. In this way, such sources of support can function as a social and institutional safety net for entrepreneurs.

As indicated above, the entrepreneur can obtain support from a broad range of individuals and institutions. In the discussion that follows, the sources of such support are indicated together with the potential assistance each one can provide. The supporting role and functions of financial institutions are discussed in Chapter 15. Other sources of support that are available to entrepreneurs are divided into three categories, namely:
▶ Personal
▶ Institutional
▶ Professional.

7.9.1 Personal sources of support

A personal support system consists of your personal knowledge and skills base, friends, family, business, and other associates who will provide support during hard times. For the entrepreneur, such a support system is invaluable because it provides a personal safety net, a sense of security, and advice and assistance when these are required (Pithey, 1993). Various personal support systems are available.

7.9.1.1 Personal knowledge and skills

The experience, technical skills, and qualifications relevant to the business activity that you want to start are very important. You must be able to deliver professional standards of work to keep customers satisfied. When you apply for start-up finance, financial institutions will be more inclined to lend you the venture capital if you have strong qualifications and ample business experience. Certain businesses, such as those in design-related or artistic fields,

and those in the service industry, such as the performing arts and tourism, require exceptional ability and technical skills training.

Business skills are also important in that the skills will aid you in all the phases of the new venture. Ideally, you should acquire some basic knowledge of the principles of business management and administration, including marketing, strategic planning, personnel administration, sales, and basic accounting before you start your business. You need not be an expert in all these fields, but having some basic knowledge will support you in dealing with the business, as well as in obtaining professional support.

7.9.1.2 Support from friends and relatives

Many of those who successfully start their own businesses have the backing, perhaps only moral support, of friends and relatives. As an entrepreneur, you will be under pressure, need to work long hours and will probably not be able to take leave for the first few years. Your family must be prepared for the impact that this may have on family life. Ensure that they can accommodate the risks that self-employment may bring, especially in terms of lower income in the initial stages as well as the implications of the business failing.

Friends and relatives could also support the entrepreneur by making funds available for the start-up and even during some of the later stages of the business. Should this occur, be sure to enter into a valid business contract so that all aspects of the funding are addressed, namely shareholding, repayment, and involvement in the business, as well as participation in the management of the business.

Another source of support that friends and relatives can provide is experience, know-how, and even business opportunities. They can assist with some of the various complexities that will be encountered when starting a new business. Share your ideas with friends and relatives, and they may even pass business on to you, which is particularly important during the start-up phase as it takes time to build up a customer base. One of the best ways of marketing is word of mouth. Friends and relatives could be especially valuable resources as their networks are often extensive and supportive.

7.9.1.3 Support from other entrepreneurs

Due to the fact that many problems are common to businesses, prospective entrepreneurs may learn valuable lessons from more experienced entrepreneurs who have successfully dealt with such problems in the past. Entrepreneurs working together in co-operatives and franchises have the highest business success and survival rates, which is an indication of the value of the support that entrepreneurs give one another. The value of an entrepreneurial network lies sharing the following:

▸ Knowledge about the development of the business plan
▸ Knowledge about the industry that the entrepreneur wishes to enter when starting the business
▸ Knowledge about the pitfalls that the entrepreneur may face during the various growth phases of the business
▸ Business and management acumen in starting and managing a specific type of business.

7.9.1.4 Support from suppliers

Suppliers want the businesses that buy from them to survive, as their failure would mean losing customers. Suppliers would, therefore, assist entrepreneurs by providing advice on management, giving extensions on credit, and making recommendations on improving the business.

7.9.1.5 Support from employees

Since skilled entrepreneurs cannot run their business operations single-handedly, they need competent employees to assist them. Well-qualified, experienced, and highly-skilled employees who are committed to your business are an asset that should be valued and utilised as much as possible. In addition, such skilled employees, who can run the business on a day-to-day basis, allow the entrepreneur more time to plan and attend to long-term issues. Some entrepreneurs also appoint employees with specialised skills to include such expertise in the workplace. The support rendered by these employees is invaluable to a successful business.

7.9.1.6 Support from customers

Due to the fact that customers are the recipients and users of the products and services supplied by entrepreneurs, they are able to give feedback with regard to the quality and utility value of the products and (or) services being provided. Through customer feedback, an entrepreneur will also be able to identify the strengths and weaknesses of his or her business operation.

Read about the role played by personal sources of support in contributing towards the start-up of an unusual South African business in *Cape Town entrepreneur gets tails wagging*.

7.9.2 Institutional sources of support

Institutional sources of support refer to support provided by the government and related organisations, by professional and business associations, and by educational institutions. These organisations provide valuable support with regard to generating and protecting ideas, training, interaction with other related businesses, and in some instances also financial support. An overview of a number of different institutional support systems follows.

7.9.2.1 Support from the Department of Trade and Industry (dti)

One of the strategic objectives of the dti is to increase the contribution of small enterprises to the Gross Domestic Product (GDP) in South Africa (Calitz, 2005). The divisions that focus mainly on stimulating and facilitating the development of sustainable competitive enterprises (by providing effective and accessible incentive measures) are The Enterprise Organization (TEO) and the Enterprise

---

SOUTH AFRICAN SUCCESS STORY

Cape Town entrepreneur gets tails wagging

Chantel Fourie has taken her love for dogs and turned it into a profitable business that is visibly appreciated by the community of Atlantis. She started studying Biodiversity and Ecology at the University of Stellenbosch, but had to end her studies after two years due to personal factors and attended a training programme at the Raymond Ackerman Academy. Fourie's time on the programme proved to be the key that unlocked her potential and kick-started her entrepreneurial journey and she opened the Doggie Tail Dog Parlour from her home in Atlantis in 2007. She spent months doing market research and, after drawing up a comprehensive business plan, was granted a R25 000 loan from the Academy to start her business.

Raising the capital, however, was not the only challenge that Fourie faced. There was little encouragement from her community and she was forced to rely on her own convictions to give her strength.

'Many people openly discouraged me from opening a dog parlour, saying that people in Atlantis don't love their dogs and there was no market for it,' explains Fourie. 'But I live in Atlantis and I'm crazy about dogs so I knew they were wrong. I did conduct a market survey just to be sure though!' she says.

Doggie Tail Dog Parlour is the first dog grooming business in Atlantis and its surrounding areas. Fourie has proved her doubters wrong and now spends every day spoiling the pets of animal lovers in her community and beyond. She has about 30 to 45 regular clients and many others who come in less frequently.

Chantal notes: 'My portfolio of clients is growing all the time and there is a great potential for profit, even though I'm not quite out of the red yet. When clients see that I really love animals and care about their dogs' happiness, they always come back again. Starting your own business is never an easy journey but being a part of the Raymond Ackerman Academy has definitely helped to even out many of the bumps'. 'Good ideas and drive are not enough to build a successful business – you need the business acumen to complement these other elements. I was given the opportunity to tap into world-class expertise and realise my full potential. I intend to do exactly that!' she says.

Source: Herrington et al., (2009:9–10).

Development Unit. The TEO consists of the following business units:

▶ *Incentive Administration Business Unit,* which is responsible for the administration of 11 incentive schemes of which the following are available to entrepreneurs:
  ▪ Small, Medium Enterprise Development Programme (SMEDP) – in manufacturing and tourism
  ▪ Skills Support Programme (SSP)
  ▪ Competitiveness Fund (CF)

▪ Black Business Supplier Development Programme (BBSDP).

▶ *New Incentive Development Unit,* which is responsible for the continuous review of existing incentives and development of new appropriate incentives that support the dti strategy.

▶ *Business Development and Aftercare Business Unit,* which facilitates the accessibility of the dti incentive offerings by establishing and maintaining a database of enterprises that have been assisted and increasing the number of enterprises that benefit from the incentives (Calitz, 2005).

The Enterprise Development Business Unit is responsible for creating an enabling environment for small, micro-, medium-sized and co-operative enterprises to contribute to the country's GDP and employment. This responsibility entails the development of legislative frameworks, policies, strategies, and programmes aimed at lowering the barriers for entry and stimulating the participation of these enterprises in all sectors of the economy. The unit implements its mandate through a range of institutions directly funded by the dti and, therefore, has a responsibility to evaluate and monitor the performance of such institutions. The unit is composed of the Enterprise Development Unit and the Co-operatives Development Unit. The Enterprise Development Business Unit is mainly responsible for co-ordinating, managing, and monitoring the implementation of the country's national strategies for the promotion of small businesses and co-operatives. The emphasis is on assisting small businesses and co-operatives enterprises to access finance, skills, markets, manufacturing support, technology, infrastructure, and other related support measures.

7.9.2.2 Support from other government-related institutions

The majority of these institutions are part of the dti Group of Institutions, which includes the following relevant to the needs of the entrepreneur (Calitz, 2005:5–7):

▶ The *Industrial Development Corporation (IDC)* is a state-owned development finance institution that promotes entrepreneurship through the building of competitive industries and enterprises based on sound business principles. The corporation is subject to the provisions of the Industrial Development Corporation Act of 1940, as amended, and certain sections of the Companies Act.

▶ The *Small Enterprise Finance Agency*, also known as SEFA, was established in 2012 as a result of a merger between the South African Apex Fund, Khula Enterprise Finance Limited and the IDC. The primary purpose of the merger was to establish and grow SMMEs and thereby contribute to job creation and economic growth.

▶ *Khula Finance* was founded in 1996 under the dti, and specialises in ensuring the enhanced availability of loan and equity capital to small, medium and micro-enterprises. Finance is made available by:
  ▪ Offering loans, guarantees, and seed funds to retail funding intermediaries in need of capital, risk sharing, and capacity.
  ▪ Offering guarantees and equity capital directly and indirectly to small, medium, and micro-enterprises.
  ▪ Providing assistance and guidance on financing and opportunities.

▶ The *National Youth Development Agency* represents a partnership between three state-owned agencies: the IDC, SEFA, and the NYDA. It is aimed primarily at job creation through the provision of professional training and mentoring.

▶ *National Manufacturing Advisory Centre Co-ordinating Body (NAMAC)* provides manufacturing, information and related business-development services through a range of support programmes to small, medium, and micro-enterprises.

▶ *National Empowerment Fund (NEF)* and the IDC empower historically disadvantaged people through the wider ownership, control, and management of certain income-generating assets in terms of the National Empowerment Fund Act 105 of 1998.

▶ *National Enterprise Promotion Agency (Ntsika)* was established under the National Small Business Act 102 of 1996 as a Section 21 company to provide non-financial support services for small, medium and micro-enterprises. Ntsika provides access to training, information, capacity building, counselling, markets, and technology.

▸ *Small Enterprise Development Agency (Seda)* is an agency of the dti. Seda was established in December 2004, through the National Small Business Amendment Act 29 of 2004. It is mandated to implement government's small business strategy, design and implement a standard and common national delivery network for small enterprise development, and integrate government-funded small enterprise support agencies across all tiers of government. Seda's mission is to develop, support and promote small enterprises throughout the country, ensuring their growth and sustainability in coordination and partnership with various role players, including global partners, who make international best practices available to local entrepreneurs.

▸ The *Companies and Intellectual Property Commission (CIPC)* – which was formerly known as the Companies and Intellectual Property Registration Office (CIPRO) – is the result of the successful merger between the former South African Companies Registration Office (SACRO) and the South African Patents and Trademarks Office (SAPTO). CIPC has the strategic goal of positioning itself among the top five registration offices in the world and offers the following services to the entrepreneur:

- The registration of companies
- The registration of copyright
- The registration of designs
- The registration of patents
- The disclosure of corporate information.

7.9.2.3 Support from the small-claims courts

The small-claims courts have been a great source of support to small businesses, because such courts eliminate the financial burden of litigation and are far less costly than magistrates'

courts. The clerk of the small-claims court, furthermore, assists entrepreneurs by drawing up the necessary documentation. The maximum amount that can be claimed in the small-claims court is R15 000 (Department of Justice and Consitutional Development, 2014).

7.9.2.4 Support from associations

A number of business and other associations exist in South Africa that could serve as support systems to the entrepreneur and small businesses. It is impossible to discuss all these associations, but the following are the most pertinent:

▸ *Black Management Forum (BMF)* is an independent non-governmental initiative dedicated to placing black managers on an equal footing with managers from other backgrounds and environments. The organisation cultivates attitudes, beliefs, motivation, and competency in both black managers and white managers and business leaders who will be conducive to the profitable growth of the South African economy. The main activities of the organisation involve policy advocacy, mainly in financing, empowerment of women and labour issues, as well as the facilitation of opportunities for members through tender advice and professionals' services.

▸ *Business Unity South Africa (BUSA).* The Black Business Council and Business SA merged in October 2003 to create Business Unity South Africa (BUSA), the country's first properly unified business organisation. BUSA is a confederation of SA chambers of commerce and industry, professional and corporate associations, and uni-sectoral employers' organisations. BUSA represents South African business on macro-economic and high-level issues that affect it at the national and international levels. Its function is to ensure that business plays a constructive role in the country's economic growth, development, and transformation and to create an environment in which businesses of all sizes and in all sectors can thrive, expand, and be competitive.

▶ *Minara Chamber of Commerce* is a formally constituted organisation formed in May 2000 to represent and assist South African Muslim businesses and entrepreneurs. The chamber's activities and objectives are based on the need to provide a formal voice and guiding vision for Muslim business. The constitution and workings are based on an adherence to an Islamic Code of Conduct and Ethics.

▶ *National African Federated Chamber of Commerce (NAFCOC)*. NAFCOC's mission is to meet the challenges and opportunities that arise in South Africa, as the leading independent, non-profit business-support organisation that primarily, but not exclusively, serves the interests of broad-based black economic empowerment (B-BBEE) companies and small, medium, and micro-sized enterprises (SMMEs). NAFCOC also aims to facilitate the growth of the economy by ensuring fast-tracked economic transformation and broad-based empowerment that will result in job creation and poverty alleviation.

▶ The *Afrikaanse Handelsinstituut (AHI)* is a multi-sectoral employer organisation, involved in all sectors of the economy except primary agriculture. The organisation was established in 1942 and is one of the principal employer organisations in the country, representing members of trade, industry, mining, financial institutions, and a variety of service organisations. The AHI's head office is situated in Pretoria, with offices in the nine provinces of South Africa.

▶ The *South Chamber of Commerce (SACOB)* addresses all the economic, social, and political issues that affect the business community. SACOB is apolitical and sees itself as 'the voice of business'. It ensures that this voice is heard where it matters – where it is necessary to protect the interests of business, at local, regional, and national levels.

▶ *Foundation for African Business and Consumer Services (FABCOS)*. The main activities of the organisation involve policy advocacy, mainly in financing, empowerment of women, and labour issues, as well as facilitating opportunities for members through tender advice and professionals' services centres. The current membership base of FABCOS consists mainly of micro-enterprises and companies in the informal sector.

▶ *Chamber of Commerce and Industry of South Africa (CHAMSA)* was established on 11 October 2003, as the independent umbrella body of the four national chambers, namely the AHI, FABCOS, NAFCOC and SACOB. CHAMSA's mandate is to create and sustain a business environment in which business can grow and prosper, to facilitate broad-based economic empowerment and to improve the conditions under which business operates.

7.9.2.5 Support from educational institutions

The majority of educational institutions, both in higher education and in further education and training, offer training courses in business venture creation and all aspects of starting and managing a small business. Some of the institutions have centres for entrepreneurship that also offer support in the development of business plans, consultation on starting and managing a small business, and accounting and legal support.

7.9.3 Professional sources of support

Although professionals such as consultants, lawyers, and accountants have to be paid consultation fees, their advice can help an entrepreneur dramatically improve profits and long-term stability. Furthermore, by means of informal discussions with them, entrepreneurs can obtain a lot of valuable information for free by asking the right questions (Meredith et al., 1982:178). The support you can obtain from professionals is discussed in more detail below.

7.9.3.1 Support from consultants

Business consultants are helpful during the process of developing a business plan and also in providing specialised support such as information technology. It is possible to outsource some of the business functions, such as human resource management, payroll administration, recruitment, and financial management to various consultants until such a time as the entrepreneur can afford to appoint full-time staff to perform these functions.

7.9.3.2 Support from lawyers

Lawyers are required to assist with all the legal aspects surrounding a business, such as contracts, labour legislation, and regulations. In this regard, lawyers have to advise, assist, and (or) represent entrepreneurs. Meredith et al. (1982) are of the opinion that an entrepreneur should establish a good working relationship with a lawyer as his or her services may be required at various times during the life-cycle of the business. Such support, advice, and (or) services of lawyers may be necessary in the following instances (Meredith et al., 1982:181):

▸ When spending a lot of money
▸ When a lawyer representing a possible future plaintiff contacts the entrepreneur
▸ When a reasonable compromise in respect of a business problem cannot be reached
▸ When entering into contracts
▸ When making decisions regarding taxes
▸ When someone's help is needed to make sense of legislation and (or) regulations
▸ When a person (customer or supplier) believes that you have acted in an improper, dishonest or illegal manner.

7.9.3.3 Support from accountants

To be able to make good business decisions, you need reliable information on the financial position of your business. It is the role of an accountant to gather financial information and present it in an easily understandable format. From the financial statements prepared by an accountant, the manager of a small business should be able to assess how his or her business is faring.

The advice, assistance, and support of an accountant is of particular value to the entrepreneur during the start-up phase of the business, when he or she can support the entrepreneur by setting up an accounting system that will suit the needs of the business. As an entrepreneur's business grows, he or she will need more accounting support from highly qualified accountants (that is, chartered accountants). Such accountants are necessary for handling tax payments in particular, and to monitor the financial status of the organisation.

Further areas in which an accountant can be of assistance to entrepreneurs are as follows:

▸ Helping with setting up partnerships
▸ Assisting with the registration of a business
▸ Designing financial records and financial reports for the business
▸ Developing, implementing, and monitoring credit systems
▸ Making suggestions with respect to prices, the control of costs, and the handling of taxes.

7.9.3.4 Support from agents

There are various agents who can be sources of support to the entrepreneur, including insurance agents, estate agents, and sales agents. Insurance agents could ensure that a business is adequately insured to reduce risk as far as possible, and to create the greatest possible financial safety net for the entrepreneur. Insurance agents can also advise business managers on insurance issues, assist with obtaining the necessary insurance cover, and continuously evaluate the insurance needs of a business. Risks to be insured against include liability, fire, fraud, unrest-related damage, and theft.

Estate agents can support the entrepreneur in finding the most suitable location for the business, give advice on the rental or purchasing decision, and assist with any property-related matters.

Sales agents can become an extension of the work force of the entrepreneur during the start-up phase of the business by working on a part-time and commission basis to sell products or services. When the business is able to employ full-time employees, the sales agent can be involved in training the new salespeople.

7.9.3.5 **Support from franchisors**

When entrepreneurs are franchisees, the franchisor continuously assists, advises, and otherwise supports the entrepreneurs (see Chapter 8 for more detail). Franchisors assist franchisees in the following ways:

▸ Selecting the business site for the franchise
▸ Participating in the franchisee's negotiations to lease business premises
▸ Assisting in designing and modelling the franchisee's outlet
▸ Guiding the franchisee when he or she selects equipment
▸ Participating in the opening of the business
▸ Providing ongoing assistance and support to the franchisee throughout the life-cycle of the franchise unit.

Such ongoing support includes monitoring the franchisee's performance, providing additional training, conducting market research, developing products, and advertising. In many instances, the franchisor's support can result in a person with very limited business skills running a successful operation.

7.9.3.6 **The Franchising Association of South Africa (FASA) as a support system for franchises**

The Franchising Association of South Africa (FASA) is aimed at developing and safeguarding the business environment franchisees find themselves in by providing a safe and ethical environment to operate in. FASA can be contacted with any question relating to franchising. Should FASA be unable to assist, FASA will refer you to a relevant specialist in that area.

7.10 Challenges during start-up

Being a successful business owner requires more than a brilliant idea and hard work. You also need to learn how to manage and grow your business. As an owner, you'll face numerous challenges and your ability to meet these challenges will be a major factor in your success (or failure) as a business owner. The following are challenges that you may face during start-up:

▸ *You might not enjoy it.* For example, you may find that once you start your business as a butcher, you do not enjoy working with raw meat every day. At this stage, you could decide either not to continue with the venture or to bring in a person to help you. When you own a business, you *are* the business. If you are going to devote the time and energy needed to transform an idea into a successful business, you need to have a passion for your work. You should believe in what you're doing and make a strong personal commitment to your business.
▸ *Survival is difficult.* You might be able to start a business on the basis of a great idea, but find it difficult to manage and nurture the business. You need to have a good understanding of the functional areas of business – accounting, finance, management, marketing, and production – or surround yourself with people who can help you. Small businesses feel mistakes more strongly.
▸ *Not enough knowledge about the business.* Successful businesspeople know what they

are doing. They are knowledgeable about the industry in which they operate (both as it stands today and where it is headed in the future), they know their competitors, distributers, and suppliers, as well as how to attract customers. They also understand the impact of technology on their business.

▸ *Misuse of funds.* As a business owner, you'll be under constant pressure to come up with the money to meet payroll and pay your other accounts. You should not fall into the trap of taking money out of the company for personal use. You need to manage your cash flow (money coming in and money going out), control costs, and collect money owed to you. You can have an excellent idea, a brilliant marketing approach, and a talented management team, but if you run out of cash, your career as a business owner could be very brief.

▸ *Losing control of work and personal time management.* A new business owner can expect to work 60 hours per week. If you want to grow a business and have some type of personal life at the same time, you will need to give up some control. The divorce rate among start-up entrepreneurs is high owing to the fact that they spend so much time on the business. You need to develop time-management skills and learn how to delegate responsibility.

▸ *Inability to manage people.* The ability to hire, keep, and manage good people is crucial to business success. As your business grows, you'll depend more on your employees. You need to develop a positive working relationship with them, train them properly, and motivate them to provide quality goods or services.

▸ *Growth creates new challenges.* You might think that a sales increase would be a good thing. Often it is, but sometimes it can be a major problem for a new entrepreneur. When a company grows, the owner's role changes. The owner needs to delegate

work to others and build a business structure that can handle the increase in volume. Some owners do not make the shift and are sometimes overwhelmed. Start-up often requires high performance, cheap labour, while growth requires higher wages to hire people who are sometimes less dedicated than the founders.

▸ *A lack of customer focus.* A major advantage of a small business is the ability to provide special attention to customers, but some small businesses fail to seize this advantage. This may happen if the owner does not anticipate customers' often-changing needs or fails to keep up with changing markets.

▸ *Poor control.* It is essential for the entrepreneur to keep accurate records and good financial control of the business. Many entrepreneurs have an aversion to record keeping which could result in financial and production loss. Entrepreneurs often spend money without focusing on fundamentals such as financial control, customers, and creating value.

CONCLUSION

It is clear from the preceding discussion that the establishment of a venture should not be handled in a haphazard way. There are various aspects that require analysis and serious consideration if the prospective entrepreneur wants to prevent exposing his or her proposed venture to unnecessary risk. The nature and extent of the proposed venture and the knowledge, insight, and experience of the prospective entrepreneur will determine whether he or she will have to make use of expert opinions, and it may be short-sighted to be too cost aware in this regard.

The chapter also dealt with the common types of business, of which four were discussed: the sole proprietor, partnerships, profit companies and non-profit companies. Co-operatives and trusts were mentioned as these two structures do exist and in some instances can be useful. The factors that influence the establishment of any of these forms of businesses were also discussed.

Furthermore, the sources of support available to the entrepreneur when starting and building his or her new venture were outlined in this chapter. These sources of support have been divided into three main categories, namely personal, institutional and professional sources of support. The personal sources of support include friends and relatives, other entrepreneurs, and persons or groups with whom the entrepreneur will work after starting the business venture. The government and government-related institutions, as well as organised business associations and institutions are examples of institutional sources of support. All of them can play a valuable role in either providing access to information, support structures, networking, funding, education and training or the registration of the business. Professional sources of support include those with specialised qualifications and experience who are able to support the entrepreneur in starting and managing a successful business venture.

One of the biggest challenges facing the entrepreneur is to identify a good business idea. This process is much more involved and difficult than most prospective entrepreneurs anticipate. Once a viable business idea has been identified and developed, the next challenge is to develop a sound and successful business, which requires enormous support. The support of friends and relatives in business is not always thought of as a good idea, but this model has many success stories. In some cultures, such as the Jewish, Indian, Chinese, and Greek cultures, this is seen as the only way in which to start a new business. Drawing on the experience of skilled entrepreneurs, family members and local community is a useful starting point to establishing a business venture.

SELF-ASSESSMENT QUESTIONS

Multiple-choice questions

1. What is the common reason for why businesses fail?
   a. The entrepreneur did not make use of the small-claims courts registration.
   b. The entrepreneur did not make sufficient use of the available sources of support.
   c. The entrepreneur did not make use of estate agents in obtaining information about geographical locations.
2. Which of the following does not play a role in determining a new venture's survival?
   a. The specific resources needs of the venture, including human resource needs.
   b. The presence of any competitor.
   c. Overcoming the demand for your service.
   d. Where the venture will be located.
3. Which of the following is an advantage of being a sole proprietor ?
   a. Limited liability of the business owner
   b. Ability to accumulate capital
   c. Owner has locus of control
   d. Ease of business creation
4. Which of the following government related institutions do not provide support to the entrepreneur?
   a. Foundation for African Business and Consumer Services
   b. Afrikaanse Handelsinstituut
   c. Business Unity South Africa
   d. a and c
   e. b and c
5. Which of the following are typically business start-up challenges?
   a. Sufficient knowledge about the business environment
   b. Inability to manage employees
   c. Exponential business growth
   d. All of the above
   e. None of the above

DISCUSSION QUESTIONS

1. Identify and discuss the aspects determining the capacity for survival of a new venture.
2. Discuss why a marketing strategy is necessary for the entrepreneur when starting a venture.
3. Discuss the ways in which competitors can influence the entrepreneur in starting a venture.
4. Identify the resource needs of a new venture and how these could influence the entrepreneur with regard to starting a venture.
5. In what way can the size of the prospective enterprise influence the entrepreneur when starting a new venture?
6. Discuss the most important location factors to consider when starting a venture.
7. What factors should a potential entrepreneur consider before selecting the most appropriate form of ownership for a new business?
8. Compare the advantages and disadvantages of a sole ownership and a partnership as types of ownership.
9. Identify and discuss the various types of industry in South Africa in which you can start a business.
10. Identify and discuss the reasons why entrepreneurs often make use of assistance and information provided by others.
11. Give examples of each of the following sources of support available to entrepreneurs:
    a. Personal
    b. Institutional
    c. Professional
12. Discuss the role that business associations can play in supporting entrepreneurs.
13. Use the Internet and business newspapers to identify at least five sources of support other than those discussed in this chapter.
14. Discuss the various challenges the entrepreneur faces when starting a new business venture.

EXPERIENTIAL EXERCISE

Karin Stander owns a restaurant in Brooklyn in Pretoria and has appointed five staff members: one chef and four waiters. She is in the process of expanding her business and plans to have 55 permanent staff working for her eventually: two restaurant managers, who will help her during the two working shifts in the restaurant; three chefs, who will work in shifts; three cooks, who will also work in shifts; five additional kitchen staff; two cleaners and 40 waiters. She also wants to appoint at least 10 temporary waiters per shift.

Her present turnover is approximately R75 000 per month, and she believes that, after the extension, her monthly turnover may increase to R350 000 or more. She wants to know how her business will be classified according to the Small Business Act.

Conduct an Internet search to obtain the Small Business Act 102 of 1996 as amended in 2003 and provide Karin with the following information:
1. The business sector or subsector that her business is in.
2. The classification of her business and the reasons for that classification.
3. List and describe five key criteria Karin should consider in her proposal.

INTENTIONAL ENTREPRENEUR: BUKIWE NDENGEZI

As far back as she could recall, Bukiwe was always passionate about fashion. Since Grade 3 she knew that she wanted to study fashion. Luckily she was fortunate enough to attend a primary school that had a passionate art teacher, who encouraged her mom to allow her to attend an art centre on Saturdays. When she eagerly announced to her parents her ambition of pursuing a career in fashion, they welcomed it with no fuss. They always believed that she should follow her passion. Bukiwe's mother understood perfectly the challenges of pursuing a career considered 'less desirable' as she too had a similar life story.

Bukiwe's parents believed that a good education would stand her in good stead and that no door would be closed to her in the future. Her high school friends thought that she was insane to choose to become 'a struggling artist'. While

CASE STUDY

many of her friends spent an extra year, post matric, improving their mathematics mark for their more academic careers, she found herself blissfully carving out a life in fashion design at CPUT. During her tertiary education she worked at various boutiques as a sales assistant to earn some pocket money, which is when she fell in love with retail. It was here that Bukiwe learnt how to charm and style customers and was exposed to visual merchandising. In her third year of study, she was given an opportunity to work part-time as a visual merchandiser at Woolworths, which turned out to be the key that unlocked her future dreams.

After a year of being at Woolworths, she found herself doing trend research, which made her realise that she would rather pursue fashion buying than designing. She was asked to do numerous trend presentations, and some styling and fashion PR opportunities also presented themselves. In the future, she intends to have her own buying, trend, styling and PR agency as there seems to be a missed opportunity in the market since no company offers all of these services to their customers. As an entrepreneur she regards herself as 'under construction' and she is inspired by successful female entrepreneurs in the industry.

Source: GEM 2012. Turton, N. & Herrington, M. Global Entrpreneurship Monitor 2012 South Africa.

1. As a friend of Bukiwe who has studied business management, assist her by providing advice regarding the type of ownership that would be most appropriate for her. Also suggest to her the advantages and disadvantages of each type of ownership form available.

2. Name and discuss the sources of support that Bukiwe is able to utilise in starting and managing her venture.

3. What additional sources of support could she consider?

SUGGESTED WEBSITE LINKS

Companies and Intellectual Property Commission: http://www.cipc.co.za/

Franchise Association of South Africa: http://www.fasa.co.za/

Small Enterprise Development Agency: http://www.seda.org.za/Pages/Home.aspx

SA Companies Act 71 of 2008: http://www.justice.gov.za/legislation/acts/2008-071amended.pdf

Stellenbosch University Business School: http://shortcourses.sun.ac.za/

School of Business and Finance, University of the Western Cape: http://www.uwc.ac.za/faculties/ems/sbf/Pages/default.aspx

Graduate School of Business, University of Cape Town: http://www.gsb.uct.ac.za/

Wits Businesss School: http://www.wbs.ac.za/

REFERENCES

Calitz, G. 2005. Promotion of Access to Information Act: Section 14 Manual. 29 April 2005. The dti: Sunnyside, Pretoria. Reference Number: 7/4/1/1.

CIPRO. 2008. Close Corporations transitional arrangements in new Companies Bill. Issued by Legal and Regulatory Services, 11 July 2008. [Online]. Available: http://www.cipro.co.za/notices/notice_cctransitionbill.htm [11 January 2011].

Cronje, GJ de J, Du Toit, GS, Mol, AJ, Neuland, EW. & Motlatla, MDC. (Eds). 1997. *Introduction to Business Management*. Johannesburg: International Thomson Publishing.

Department of Constitutional Development. 2014. [Online]. Available: http://www.justice.gov.za/scc/scc.htm [21 July 2014].

Department of Trade and Industry. 2010a. Department of Trade and Industry Press Release. The new consumer protection act and companies act to come into force on 1 April 2011.Issued by Communication and Marketing, the dti. 28 September 2010. [Online]. Available: http://www.cipro.co.za/notices/2010_10_01_Update_on_implementation_of_the_new_Companies_Act,2008.pdf [11 January 2011].

GEM. 2012. [Online]. Available: http://www.gemconsortium.org/docs/assets/uploads/1366887171GEMSouthAfrica2012Report.pdf [4 July 2014].

Herrington, M, Kew, J. & Kew, P. 2009. *Global Entrepreneurship Monitor: 2008 South African Report*. Cape Town: Graduate School of Business, University of Cape Town.

Meredith, GG, Nelson, RE. & Neck, PA. 1982. *The Practice of Entrepreneurship*. Geneva: Geneva International Labour Office.

Statistics South Africa. 1993. Standard industrial classification of all economic activities (SIC). [Online]. Available: http://www.statssa.gov.za/additional_services/sic/sic.htm [1 August 2011].

Turton, N. and Herrington, M. 2012. *Global Entrepreneurship Monitor 2012 South Africa*. The UCT Centre for Innovation and Entrepreneurship.

CHAPTER 8

Franchising

Isa van Aardt

LEARNING OUTCOMES

On completion of this chapter you will be able to:

▶ Understand the meaning of the term 'franchising'
▶ Briefly discuss franchising in South Africa
▶ Describe the different franchising variants
▶ Identify and discuss the different franchising models
▶ Understand and describe how franchises are classified in South Africa
▶ Compare and discuss the advantages and disadvantages of franchising
▶ Discuss how prospective franchisees can evaluate a franchisor and franchising opportunity
▶ Indicate what services the franchisor provides to his or her franchisees
▶ Describe and understand the reasons for franchising a business
▶ Assess whether or not franchising a business is the best option for expansion
▶ Identify and describe the steps to be followed when franchising a business
▶ Understand and discuss the financial considerations when franchising a business venture
▶ Discuss how prospective franchises can be evaluated by a franchisor
▶ Identify and discuss the elements of ongoing support to be given to the franchisee
▶ Understand and describe the impact of the Consumer Protection Act 68 of 2008 on franchising
▶ Understand the concepts of taking a franchise global.

OPENING CASE STUDY

With the influx of big-name businesses such as Burger King and Walmart entering the South African market, franchising has become a popular way for many people to start their own enterprises. It offers a tried-and-tested business idea, with products that are usually well-known to consumers. This takes most of the start-up risk out of the equation, and allows the franchisee to get on with running the business and fine-tuning the profit-making performance. Of course, all this comes at a price – and many franchisors (the company selling you the franchise) insist that you must bring some of your own money to the table, and not just get loans from the bank. The total cost of setting up a franchise these days is seldom below a million rand; the costs usually include initial (set-up) costs, upfront fees to the franchisor, an ongoing management service fee, and a contribution to the franchisor's advertising fund. The essence of a franchise is that every part of the business is mapped out for you, and the support offered is meant to help you fit into the key standards and procedures that should lead to success. Some entrepreneurs might find this model a bit restrictive, as it may not allow much room for creativity. Such entrepreneurs would be better off trying their own 'thing' – and facing the risks that come with that (Crankshaw, 2013).

1. Do you think you have what it takes to become a franchisee?
2. Do you know what franchises are available in South Africa?
3. How would you know which one is for you?

Source: Crankshaw, P. (2013, December). How to buy a franchise. Small Business Connect (4):8.

INTRODUCTION

The concept of franchising is not new. According to Illetschko (2000), early records indicate that a simple form of franchising was used in China around 200BC. Ask any South African about franchising, and the most likely response would be to talk about Wimpy, Kentucky Fried Chicken, McDonald's or Steers. McDonald's is sometimes associated with the origin of franchising, but although McDonald's may have perfected the concept, franchising did not originate from McDonald's.

The Singer Sewing Machine Company is generally believed to have been the first company to make use of a franchising distribution system to sell and service its products in the early 1800s. The company used a network of salespeople and dealers to distribute and service Singer sewing machines in a particular region. These salespeople and dealers paid a fee for the right to do just that. Although this distribution system was changed a decade or so later, it is still considered to be the birth of franchising as we know it today (Illetschko, 2000).

When an entrepreneur wants to start a new business by buying a franchise or to develop his or her business into an effective franchise, it is essential that the concept is understood at the outset and applied with skill, care, and consistency. Franchising has been compared to a set of precision tools that can deliver the expected performance in the hands of a skilled craftsman (Illetschko, 1997b).

This chapter is aimed at providing guidelines and tools that will help the entrepreneur not only to understand the concept of a franchise, but also to aid him or her in buying a franchise or developing an existing business into a successful franchise. More detailed information can be found in the Illetschko sources that are provided in the bibliography and available at the FASA offices.

8.1 Definition of franchising

The word 'franchise' originates from French and refers to privilege or freedom. It can be seen as giving people the opportunity and freedom to own, manage, and direct their own businesses without having to do so unaided. A broad definition of a franchise is a system in which 'a licensor ... grants a license to franchisees to use the trade name and an entire or part of a business format' (Gordon, 2006:3).

DEFINITION

The Franchising Association of South Africa (FASA) defines franchising as an arrangement between two parties, where the one is selling or granting a privilege (franchisor) and the other is purchasing or receiving the privilege (franchisee) to do business using the name and idea of the first party (FASA, 1998:2).

8.2 Franchising in South Africa

Franchising has grown in popularity in most countries and is widely seen as an exciting way of starting a new business or expanding and developing an existing business. In South Africa, it is also seen as a way of boosting economic growth and job creation. Of the more than 530 franchise concepts that exist in South Africa, around 86% were developed locally (BizConnect, 2012). This is in contrast with many other countries outside the USA, where foreign brands tend to dominate the market.

Franchising in South Africa contributes in the region of R256 billion each year to our country's gross domestic product and it is estimated that around 12% of retail sales in South Africa are through franchised businesses (BizConnect, 2012). In fact, the retail and direct marketing sector is the biggest employer of all franchised systems in South Africa, with more than 117 000 employees (BizConnect, 2012a).

The Franchise Factor® 2012 (Franchize Directions, 2013), a survey of the South African franchising sector conducted by Franchize Directions, which monitored the sector from the period 1 March 2010 to February 29th 2012, shows that the franchising sector has proven resilient despite the recent economic turmoil. According to the survey, the sector consists of 568 franchised systems and 30 483 business units, grew an estimated 53 066 new jobs, 2 053 new businesses and contributed R356.28-billion to the South African economy. The franchise sector also contributed 11.85% to GDP during the survey period (Franchize Directions, 2013). This study furthermore indicated that there was a slight decrease in the number of franchised systems since the survey was last conducted due to the 'exiting' of 77 franchised systems while only 69 new franchised systems were introduced (Franchize Directions, 2013).

8.3 Types of franchising

According to Whichfranchise (2014b) franchising comes in two variants, namely business-format franchising and product and trade-name franchising.

8.3.1 Business-format franchising

In a **business-format franchise**, the franchisor offers the franchisee a clearly defined package of deliverables and services. Included are, for example (Whichfranchise, 2014b):
- A strong corporate identity including the use of trademarks and logos.
- A complete system of conducting the business at optimal efficiency.
- Hands-on assistance with site selection, store layout and design, sourcing of equipment, hiring and training of staff, initial promotional activities, sourcing of products and more.

In return for access to this package of services, the franchisee pays an upfront fee, also known as an initial fee, usually upon signing the franchise agreement. Furthermore, the franchisee agrees to pay continuing fees to the franchisor in exchange for ongoing business assistance in the widest sense of the word.

Business format franchising is by far the most popular franchise format, and opportunities are available in many different industry sectors, including (Whichfranchise, 2014b):

▶ quick service and sit-down restaurants
▶ automotive services
▶ real estate agencies
▶ business services
▶ home repair services
▶ convenience stores and other retail outlets, to name just a few.

The **business-format franchise** is the most popular form of franchising today.

> **DEFINITION**
>
> The business-format franchise describes a relationship between the franchisor and franchisee where the latter is licensed to operate a proven business concept using the franchisor's name in accordance with its standardised, fine-tuned package which includes the products to be sold as well as the trademarks, logos, decor, promotional material, and menus of products (BusinessDictionary.com, 2014a).

In this type of franchising, the franchisor will need a larger infrastructure to manage and control the franchisees since the employees of the franchisor are required to make regular visits in order to maintain good relationships and monitor adherence to standards and provisions.

The franchisee becomes the owner of the business once the rights to the business format have been purchased and paid for. This implies that he or she cannot be dismissed should he or she not perform. On the other hand, the mere fact that the franchisee owns the business could serve as motivation to perform and to respond to market needs.

For the franchisor, this type of franchise holds the advantage that less own capital is required to expand the network as it is not tied up in establishing a business outlet in each region. The expansion is, in reality, financed by the capital of the franchisee. Examples of this type of franchise are Wimpy,

and Spar, where patrons of these enterprises will have the same experience wherever they are in South Africa with regard to the products as well as the decor, menus (where applicable), and promotions.

8.3.2 Product and trade-name franchising

In a product and trade-name franchise, the franchisee is expected to focus on the franchisor's product range. Warranty policies, service levels and, at least to a certain extent, the appearance of the outlet, are controlled by the franchisor. Apart from initial training, national advertising support, and service-related staff training schemes provided by the franchisor, franchisees will generally not receive operational support as the franchisor has limited involvement in the running and management of the business. This implies that the franchisee has more autonomy in the day-to-day running and systems he or she uses, but less direct support. In this relationship, the franchisee is not allowed to sell a competitive product and operates under the trade name of the franchisor.

The franchisor provides trademarks and logos, national advertising campaigns and a limited range of initial and ongoing support services. In return, the franchisee is obliged to purchase a specified product, or range of products, exclusively from the franchisor. This type of franchising does not always require the payment of ongoing fees, although fees and royalties have to be paid for the use of the franchisor's trademarks, trade name, logo and national advertising campaigns.

Due to the clear advantages that business-format franchising offers franchisors and franchisees, a growing number of existing product and trade-name franchises are converting to fully-fledged business format franchises.

Product and trade name franchising has largely been found wanting at present. To a certain extent, it continues to be used in industry sectors such as automotive, petroleum and soft drink distribution (Whichfranchise, 2014b).

> **DEFINITION**
>
> A product or trade name franchise is an arrangement in which a supplier (franchisor) supplies a product family to a dealer (franchisee) who may also take on the identity (brand name) of the franchisor (BusinessDictionary.com, 2014b).

8.4 Franchise models

Prospective franchisees should familiarise themselves with the various franchise models that exist within South Africa before they start looking at specific opportunities and investigate their advantages and disadvantages.

8.4.1 The development model

This is the franchise model the franchisor selects for the expansion of the network. During the early years when franchising became established, every franchise was granted as a unit franchise. Even today, this model remains the most popular by far. However, other models have been developed and some franchisors take a mixed approach to expansion.

8.4.2 Company-owned unit

Before there can be a franchise, the aspiring franchisor must test the concept in the market. The company-owned unit is the only way to test market acceptance and iron out all possible glitches, be they in the realm of product development, branding, processing, distribution or installation. Most franchisors retain at least one unit indefinitely, for several reasons:

▸ It serves as a model unit and training ground for new franchisees.

▸ Product modifications and improvements to systems can be tested before being released into the network.
▸ Profits generated in a company-owned store are the franchisor's to keep. Returns from franchised units are limited to a small percentage of sales. This prompts some franchisors to operate several units for their own account, especially if these can be clustered around head office to simplify control.

8.4.3 Joint venture

A franchisor may enter into joint venture agreements with prospective franchisees. The business is set up at arm's length, with the franchisor retaining a stake. This model can be attractive for several reasons:
▸ An individual who displays potential to operate the business successfully but cannot raise sufficient funds to acquire a franchise outright can do so over time.
▸ A company or CC is set up and awarded the franchise.
▸ The individual obtains a small stake in the business at the outset, with the balance held by the franchisor, or a third party investor.
▸ The individual manages the business and receives a modest salary.
▸ The same individual is entitled to acquire additional shares in the business over time. This is often funded from retained profits.
▸ The franchisor can expand into a new area with the help of an individual who is determined to make the best of the opportunity.
▸ This model is ideally suited to BEE initiatives, for example by offering deserving employees an opportunity to acquire a stake in a business immediately and own it outright over time.

8.4.4 Unit franchise

The unit franchise is the classic franchise format. The franchisee makes an investment into one unit and this is the full extent of the initial agreement. At a later stage, a unit franchisee may be offered an opportunity to invest into additional units, thereby becoming a multi-unit franchisee. This is, however, at the franchisor's discretion, usually subject to performance criteria.

8.4.5 Conversion franchise

A conversion franchise is in essence a unit franchise. The only difference is that instead of recruiting a franchisee and setting him or her up in a newly established business, the franchisor recruits an established operator into the network. Following a complete makeover, the business operates as a franchise, trading under the network's brand and using its systems and procedures.

8.4.6 Fractional franchise

This is also a standard unit franchise except that the franchisee occupies premises within an established business. This method of expansion is best suited to concepts that stand to benefit from available synergies. This type of franchise is explained in Example 8.1 below.

EXAMPLE 8.1

A fractional franchise exists where a car-wash facility and a convenience store occupy part of the forecourt of a petrol station. Ideally, the three businesses will retain their distinctive corporate identities and will operate as independent business units. However, they share the same customer base with the garage and stand to benefit from customers crossing from one to the other for add-ons. Moreover, these businesses' management, marketing activities and administration can be partially or fully shared (Whichfranchise, 2014b).

8.4.7 Area developer

The area developer acquires the right to develop the brand within a defined geographical area. Most often, this takes the form of the developer setting up a predetermined number of branches in the area and operating them for its own account.

8.4.8 Regional master franchisee

A regional master franchisee acquires the rights over a defined area from the franchisor and rolls out the franchise through a mix of company-owned stores and sub-franchisees. As far as sub-franchisees are concerned, the master franchisee assumes many of the rights and obligations of the franchisor.

8.4.9 Master franchisee

In most instances, a master franchisee contracts with a foreign franchisor to act as the local franchisor in the target country, or a defined area within the target country. The master franchisee usually assumes all the rights and obligations of a franchisor. This means that the master franchisee is responsible for testing of the local market, franchisee recruitment and training, initial and ongoing franchisee support and quality control.

8.4.10 Retail franchise

In a retail franchise, the franchisee will generally occupy retail premises and sell products or services. The business depends totally on the location of the premises, with sales coming from walk-in consumers. In this situation, the franchisee will:

▸ Sell a product or service to end-users.
▸ Operate from locations with high foot traffic like shopping malls.
▸ Depend on walk-in customers for sales.
▸ Manage the business during retail hours, often stretching into long days and weekends.

▸ Deal with the public; this requires the franchisee to be a people person.
▸ Manage people as in most instances, staff will have to be employed.

In some cases, prior experience in the type of business is essential.

8.4.11 **Management franchise**

In a management franchise, the franchisee is expected to market and manage the business while trained staff carries out the actual business activity. A good example of such a business is a plumbing repair franchise. Orders are obtained via the telephone and trained repair teams carry out the work at customers' premises. Many business-to-business activities are handled in a similar manner, except for the fact that a travelling sales force will be employed.

8.4.12 **Simple operator franchise**

Two types of this franchise format exist, namely the manual and executive franchises. In both instances, the franchisee carries out the work him/herself. In the case of the manual franchise, this usually involves the carrying out of a trade, or the selling and supply of products or services. It may be a mobile set-up and could be home-based or operated from small office premises.

The executive franchise usually involves the carrying out of a professional service or the sale and supply of products that require professional input and/or user-support and troubleshooting. The business could be home-based or operated from small office premises. The type of work is executive, examples are bookkeeping services, tax advice, business consulting, training or the supply of comprehensive office solutions for small businesses.

Both formats will require the franchisee to:
▸ Acquire the expertise required to sell and install a product or perform a service.
▸ Work on his/her own, at least initially. As the business grows, it may become

necessary to employ staff and the franchise could develop into a management franchise.
▸ Market the franchise locally to generate a steady flow of business.
▸ Conduct much of the business via the telephone and through electronic communication facilities.
▸ Be mobile, perhaps van-based and undertake administrative chores from home. On occasion, small industrial premises may be necessary.

The manual level franchisee may on occasion wear a uniform that reflects the network's corporate identity. The manual franchise will deal with the public as well as with businesses whilst the executive franchise will mainly deal with the business and sometimes with the public. Manual level franchisees have flexible business hours whilst executive franchisees will work regular office hours.

8.4.13 **Investment franchise**

In this franchise format a wealthy investor, often a corporate entity, makes a substantial investment in a franchise without having any intention of working in the business. Management of the franchise will be delegated to an executive team that is responsible for day-to-day operations. This format is used, for example, in the hotel business. It is not very popular with franchisors of smaller concepts. The reason for this is that the physical presence of the owner 'behind the counter' is what customers want. Experience has also shown that the owner's presence makes the business successful.

8.4.14 **Tandem franchising**[1]

Parker and Illetschko (2007:280) describe **tandem franchising** as an 'empowerment mechanism with a strong focus on mentoring'.

---

1 The term 'tandem franchising' is the intellectual property of Eric J. Parker.

DEFINITION

Tandem franchising can be seen as an add-on to the traditional business-format franchise. It occurs when the franchise starts out as a joint venture that may start to give a small stake in a business to a deserving employee that he or she operates jointly with a mentor chosen by the franchisor.

Profits are earmarked for the purpose of allowing the candidate to purchase additional shares until he or she becomes the sole owner. Tandem franchising is particularly well suited to the implementation of sustainable BEE initiatives (Illetschko, 2005).

8.4.15 Social franchising

Social franchising can be seen as an important means to add value to the franchise package, in that the social franchise is geared towards the achievement of social goals rather than profit-making goals (Parker and Illetschko, 2007).

DEFINITION

Social franchising focuses on meeting social goals and not making a profit.

SOUTH AFRICAN SUCCESS STORY

Social franchising format is a proven business system

In a ground-breaking move that will see franchising play a major role in growing the economy, the Jobs Fund has partnered with the Hot Dog Cafe to train and mentor 372 cadets over a three-year period.

Of these, 310 will be gainfully employed and of these 60 will become business owners.

The R17m funding from the Jobs Fund will be matched by more than R18m from the Hot Dog Cafe's other funding partners, namely R5m from the Public Investment Corporation's (PIC) Isabaya Fund, which manages the Government Pension Fund; R9.7m from the National Empowerment Fund, a women's empowerment fund established by Old Mutual; and R3.9m from the Masisizane Fund. All these entities have a vested interest in encouraging entrepreneurship, skills training and in job creation. The PIC will also provide sites to the Hot Dog Cafe enabling the initiative to realise the targeted number of jobs.

'PIC has allocated about R60bn towards projects which will have a positive impact on the development of our country. The proposed projects have many positive aspects including the development of SMEs, the promotion of entrepreneurship culture, skills development and the creation of jobs', says the PIC's Roy Rajdhar.

The Hot Dog Cafe's successful bid was based not only on the inherent success of the business format of franchising but also on the success of its past entry-level empowerment initiatives. According to Derek Smith, joint MD of Hot Dog Cafe, over the past few years the Hot Dog Cafe group initiated 11 cadet programmes with more than 150 entry-level candidates qualifying and gaining employment, with 40 of those becoming successful franchisees.

'About 90% of the beneficiaries of the Hot Dog Cafe franchise system are from previously disadvantaged backgrounds. Our job creation model proves that with franchising's structured approach, a comprehensive training programme, and strong mentoring backup, we can reduce unemployment', comments Smith (James, 2013).

Source: James, A. 2013. BDlive. Cadet programme a boost for economy, job creation. Reprinted by permission of Times Media.

This is due to the fact that the target market of social franchising would not be able to pay market-related prices for a product or service. However, the franchise should be sustainable and must operate according to sound commercial principles. At the outset, grants and donor funding will be necessary to get the venture off the ground, but dependency on such assistance should be systematically reduced until the franchise eventually generates adequate profits for it to become self-sufficient (Illetschko, 2005). An example of this type of franchising is the Hot Dog Café's youth initiative in collaboration with the dti. Read about the Hot Dog Café in the South African success story – *Social franchising format is a proven business system.*

8.5 Classification of franchises

The days when franchising was the domain of fast-food operators are gone for good. Although food franchises continue to play a major role, many other industry sectors have recognised the advantages of franchising their businesses. In South Africa, franchises are currently classified under 14 main headings ranging from automotive products and services to retailing and direct marketing concepts, namely:

▶ *Automotive franchises.* These franchises can specialise in a number of different areas, from detailing to glass repair.
▶ *Building, office and home services*: These franchises deliver construction and building maintenance services to private and commercial property owners.
▶ *Business to business services*: Franchises in this category deliver professional services to existing businesses that include services such as advertising, financial and legal services.
▶ *Children's franchises*: Franchises focusing on the needs of children are becoming increasingly popular as business owners look to provide services that benefit the physical and mental wellbeing of children, such as child care, child education, clothing, entertainment, and fitness.
▶ *Cleaning franchises*: These franchises focus on residential or commercial cleaning.
▶ *Computer, Internet and cellular*: The Internet has become a necessity for the average South African. Almost everyone has access to a computer, and the need for computer technology and Internet services will continue to grow for the foreseeable future.
▶ *Education and training*: These franchises provide education and training in specialised fields.
▶ *Fast food and restaurants*: These franchises include many of the latest trends, such as coffee shops, smoothies, and low-carb options. Yet it also includes everyday restaurant and food franchises like fast food, pizza, pies, salads, sandwiches, ice cream, and more.
▶ *Health, beauty and wellness*: These franchises range from hair salons, tanning and diet franchises to fitness, medical and health franchises.
▶ *Pet services*: From doggy day care and pet grooming franchises to pet supplies and dog training businesses, there's a wide variety of high-demand opportunities available for you in the pet services business and no previous industry experience is necessary.
▶ *Real estate and property*: Residential and commercial property management is one of the fastest growing segments of the franchising industry. Other opportunities include business brokerage, property consulting, home financing, leasing, home inspection and more.
▶ *Retail*: Retail franchises cover every product in the book. If you have a specialty interest, you can find a retail franchise in your particular niche.
▶ *Sport and recreation*: The sports and leisure franchise enthusiast has never had more ways to work in their favourite pastime.

From golf to rugby to fitness, these franchises offer a fun and rewarding career.

▶ *Travel and tourism*: Travel and tourism franchises encompass all aspects of vacations and business trips. Travel franchises help the traveller with transportation via car rentals or cruise ships and lodging through booking motels, hotels and vacation homes.

An example of a real estate and property franchise is provided in Example 8.2 below.

8.6 Advantages and disadvantages of franchising

There are various reasons for people entering into franchise contracts instead of starting their own businesses outside this franchise context. The advantages for the franchisees are as follows:

▶ *Ongoing advice, training, research, and development*. When starting the franchise business, the franchisor provides knowledge and business expertise, and is a continuous source of support in the running and management of the business throughout the duration of their business relationship. Both initial and ongoing training is provided to a new franchisee, which helps to prepare him or her in all aspects of the business. In addition, the franchisor is in a position to provide ongoing research and development, including obtaining information from the franchisee on changing customer needs, thus contributing to new product or product ranges and services.

▶ *Reduced capital outlay with increased profits*. Franchising provides the entrepreneur with the opportunity to participate in a large business operation, while allowing the capital that he or she has invested to be used optimally. In some instances,

---

EXAMPLE 8.2

Huizemark: you're home!

While there are many franchise models that aren't suited to entrepreneurially-minded franchisees, veteran real-estate franchise, Huizemark, actually embraces them. Established in 1962 by Pieter Hamman, Huizemark or De Huizemark as it was originally known, has cultivated an enviable ability to steer itself clear through the various property industry storms that so often characterise this profession. Huizemark has had its fair share of success and endured tough conditions over its 50 years yet has continued to adjust and evolve and has come out the stronger for it. In 1994, Andre Hamman and Bryan Biehler purchased the brand from Pieter Hamman and found that the existing business model no longer matched the market needs and to survive and thrive it needed to be adjusted. The first step was to simplify and change the strategy by keeping the core brand, De Huizemark, and selling off, consolidating or closing all the companies in the original group, including the holding company. The aim was to grow the brand and support their franchisees as best they could.

Known for its distinctive orange colour, De Huizemark changed its name to Huizemark in July 2005 whilst adopting a dynamic corporate identity and innovative approach to real estate. Their 'new' brilliant orange colour is immediately visible and makes them stand out from the crowd! Their identity, design and qualified property professionals, together with a service orientated approach, spells success for their buyers, sellers, agents and franchisees.

Their brand platform represents the Huizemark Way and encompasses their franchisee interaction with home office, their franchise network and more importantly, their customers' property buying and selling experience. In fact, the brand has grown from 23 franchisees to 43 since the market crash, attesting to not only its staying power, but how well the business as a whole is run.

Source: Compiled from BizConnect (2014) and Huizemark (2014).

franchising makes it possible for people with limited capital to become small formal-sector business people by lowering the cost of entry at that level. Operating under the guidance of the franchisor, the entrepreneur can expect to reach break-even far sooner than if he or she were left to learn by trial and error.

▸ *Brand awareness.* The franchisor provides the franchisee with access to an established network, a proven name, and trademark that attracts customers and provides the franchisee with a niche market that has already been penetrated. As far as the franchisor is concerned, a wider geographical spread of a franchise operation secures heightened awareness of its product in contrast to those of independent competitors. Combined with this, the uniformity of the franchised outlets affords it a far greater impact on the target market, which benefits both the franchisor and franchisee.

▸ *Buying power.* On an ongoing basis, a franchise provides the owner of a small business access to the buying power of a large business. The buying power usually results in better prices and discounts that can be negotiated for most items, including stock, corporate clothing, corporate stationery, lighting, fixtures and fittings, and even insurance packages.

▸ *Infrastructure.* In addition to the buying power, the entrepreneur also benefits from the service infrastructure such as central marketing, IT expertise, proven systems, and procedures undertaken and provided by the franchisor. The combined infrastructure can, for example, be used to achieve a more effective marketing strategy by maximising the ad spend of the group and obtaining better prices for advertising.

▸ *Business synergy.* Buying a franchise means becoming part of a network where all members work together for the benefit of the whole. All franchisees contribute to and share in ideas to the benefit of the franchise. Because franchisees are ultimately working for themselves, they are motivated to make it a success.

▸ *Increased success rate.* Franchisees have a much better chance of business success than non-franchisees who start up their own businesses. The reason for this is that management and training systems are in place to enhance effectiveness and efficiency, which in turn reduce the risk of failure.

▸ *Exit strategy.* A successful franchise could ensure excellent resale value to an established business. With its infrastructure in place, it is seen as a more viable purchase option to prospective buyers than a stand-alone proposition in the marketplace. This is not only true for the franchisee, but also for the franchisor (Day, 1993; Illetschko, 2002; Rodkin, 1996; Vaughn, 1979, Whichfranchise, 2014a).

However, there are certain disadvantages involved in being a franchisee, namely:

▸ The franchisee is not completely independent. Franchisees are required to operate their businesses according to the procedures and restrictions set forth by the franchisor in the franchisee agreement.

▸ These restrictions usually include the products or services that can be offered, pricing and geographic territory. For some people, this is the most serious disadvantage to becoming a franchisee.

▸ In addition to the initial franchise fee, franchisees must pay ongoing royalties and advertising fees.

▸ Franchisees must be careful to balance restrictions and support provided by the franchisor with their own ability to manage their business.

▸ A damaged, system-wide image can result if other franchisees are performing poorly or the franchisor runs into an unforeseen problem.

▸ The term (duration) of a franchise agreement is usually limited and the franchisee may have little or no say about the terms of a termination.

▸ The services provided by the franchisor to the franchisee can be expensive, or in some cases non-existent.
▸ The franchise contract may have been formulated in such a manner that it protects only the rights of the franchisor, to the detriment of the franchisee.
▸ Although there is a support structure to help the franchisee, he or she may still fail because of cash-flow problems and (or) inexperience.
▸ The franchise business that looked so attractive to potential franchisees may turn out to be a fad or, even worse, the franchise arrangement might be a vehicle for fraud.
▸ The satisfaction experienced by many franchisees is, in many cases, negated by the fact that franchisors do not fulfil their initial undertakings and because of the less than expected prestige associated with the job.
▸ The trade name is not always of value because customer satisfaction with the product or service (irrespective of the name) soon becomes more important than the trade name (Matshotyana, 2011).

8.7 Finding the most suitable franchise

Before people become involved in a franchise business, they have personal preferences with respect to products and (or) services that may influence their choices. Many people get involved in pizza franchises because they love pizza, while others get involved in sports-shop franchises because they love watching or participating in sports events. The question is: Where can a prospective entrepreneur obtain more information regarding franchising opportunities? Perhaps the following can serve as a guideline for the identification of such opportunities:
▸ The *Franchising Association of Southern Africa (FASA)* is a trade association for franchisors, franchisees, and the professional organisations that service the franchise industry. If the association is unable to attend to a query immediately, it will refer you to the relevant specialist.
▸ *Advertisements in newspapers and magazines.* The majority of the business sections of regional and national business newspapers have a section in which they advertise various franchising opportunities. These advertisements usually give general information about the franchising opportunity and the contact person, but will seldom furnish information about the financial outlay required.
▸ *Personal referrals.* Opportunities can be discovered by word of mouth or by making enquiries about existing businesses that are successful. Successful franchisees are a valuable source of information with regard to franchising opportunities. Many franchisee outlets will carry advertisements on other potential outlets.
▸ *International Franchise and Entrepreneurs Expo (IFE).* There is nothing better that face-to-face interaction for getting the best results and FASA's IFE is a dedicated franchise show aimed at achieving this. A cross-section of opportunities is displayed under one roof and visitors to these expos have the opportunity to discuss the various franchise opportunities with senior employees of the franchisor. Information on the expos can be obtained from the secretariat of FASA.

8.8 Evaluating a franchising opportunity

There are certain aspects that you have to be aware of when deciding which franchise business you would like to buy into. Illetschko (2002:60–65) identified numerous such issues, which are outlined below.

8.8.1 Initial screening

Compile a list of all the franchises that you are interested in and visit a few outlets, familiarise yourself with the product range, and investigate the history of the company – get to know something about it. Set up a meeting and discuss aspects such as whether the area of your choice would be available, an estimate of the total investment required, and the industry. When you have reduced the numbers in your shortlist, set up a follow-up meeting and request the Disclosure Document (discussed in Section 8.11.1), which will provide you with most of the information that you will need. Be aware that as you are screening the franchisor, he or she will be doing the same with you, so be open and cooperative and allow him or her the same courtesy. After you have done the initial screening and decided on the franchise you would like to join, you should start with a more in-depth study.

8.8.2 Assess the franchisor's history

Determine how many franchises have already been sold and how long they have been operating. Talk to existing franchisees to determine how they experience the franchise business, the franchisor, and their own franchise operations. Pilot testing of the franchise should have been done over a reasonable period, and preferably in various parts of the country, to ensure that the success of the concept is not an isolated occurrence or short lived. At least one unit of the franchise should preferably still be in possession of the franchisor, to ensure that new concepts are tested and to provide training ground for new franchisees and their staff.

When a franchise is one of the first to be sold and the initial fee for obtaining it is unrealistically high, the prospective franchisee needs to be particularly cautious. Here he or she would have to scrutinise the franchise business carefully to determine the following:

▸ The chances for business success
▸ Whether the franchise fee is justified
▸ The potential long-term profitability of the business
▸ Whether the franchisor is really good at marketing and purchasing.

8.8.3 The product or service

To be viable, the franchise concept (product or service) should give the franchisee the opportunity to add value to the concept, such as the cooking process in the case of a fast-food outlet, or the printing to be undertaken in an instant-print centre franchise. The product or service that forms the core of the franchise should furthermore distinguish itself in some way from those offered by competitors. Once the product is offered as a franchise, it should have a clearly defined and well-established market and the franchisor should continuously strive to improve the product or service and broaden its consumer appeal. Items to be purchased in the operation of the franchise should be readily available on the open market, and where items are subject to patents, the franchisor should ensure that it has necessary consent to use such patents.

8.8.4 Financial aspects

It is a prerequisite of franchising that the franchisor is financially stable, and this should be verified during your investigation. Sound financial projections that show the expected trading results of the unit for the forthcoming two or three years should be available to prospective franchisees. If these are based on assumptions that may or may not materialise, ask the franchisor to provide you with a set of financial statements based on the actual performance of a unit that is comparable in as many respects as possible, including location, size, and demographics of the surrounding area. Establish the various fees payable to the franchisor in advance so that you can do your own financial planning, since you have to provide the necessary capital for the establishment and operation of the unit. The financial information provided by the franchisor should give a clear indication of the total capital requirement and attendant cash flow, and could be used to obtain a loan or other financial support.

8.8.5 Market research

As the prospective franchisee, you should conduct market research to determine whether there is a market for the franchisor's services and (or) products and obtain a copy of the franchisor's market research report for the area to which the franchise opportunity pertains. This will enable you to assess whether the franchisor is providing a business opportunity based on sound market information or on a 'gut feeling' or assumption that its products or services will be in demand in the area in question. It is also important to investigate the product of the franchisor, with a special focus on the projected lifetime of the product. There is no point in buying a franchise that deals with products that are not in high demand or that have a limited life-span. The prospective franchisee should also ensure that the franchisor is in possession of all the necessary documentation to allow it to use any registered patents and (or) trademarks.

8.8.6 Change of ownership

It is imperative for the prospective franchisee to establish the course of events should any of the following occur:

▸ He or she wants to sell the franchise
▸ He or she or the franchisor dies
▸ There is disagreement between the franchisee and the franchisor
▸ He or she wants to renew the franchise contract at the end of the franchise term
▸ The franchisor encounters financial difficulties.

8.8.7 Franchisee support

Determine the franchisee support that is provided, what is offered in the way of initial assistance and support, as well as support in

---

ENTREPRENEURIAL DILEMMA

Watch out for unscrupulous franchisors

The single biggest way for franchisees to protect themselves against unfair practices by unscrupulous franchisors is to seek legal advice before signing any agreement. So says franchise attorney, Esmari Jonker, of SWV Inc 'Franchisees are willing to pay R500 000 or more for a business, but they do not want to spend a couple of thousand rand to seek legal advice', says Jonker.

The unwillingness to spend on legal fees could cause a franchisee to end up in a legal battle that could cost him or her R100 000 or more and which could take up to a year or two to resolve. A common spin-off of the lack of legal advice sought, according to Jonker, is that franchisees subsequently realise that they are responsible for all kinds of costs in addition to the royalties that they are required to pay to the franchisor.

A common spin-off of the lack of legal advice sought, according to Jonker, is that franchisees subsequently realise that they are responsible for all kinds of costs in addition to the royalties that they are required to pay to the franchisor. Or, in other cases, franchisees discover that there are certain restrictions that have been placed on them and that they are only able to source products from the franchisor directly or from one of the franchisor's suppliers, despite being able to buy the goods at a fraction of the cost from a different supplier.

'These examples are all a result of the agreement not specifying anything, but instead providing only high-level wording', says Jonker.

1. How would you go about to ensure that you are not taken in by an unscrupulous franchisor?

Source: Small Business Connect, 2013:10. © 2014 Small Business Connect. All Rights Reserved. Reprinted by permission of Small Business Connect.

the long term. The franchisee should expect at least the following:

▸ The operations-and-procedures manual, which should contain the procedures the franchisee is expected to follow in the operation of his or her unit

▸ Assistance in finding the right franchise facility

▸ Guidance during the establishment of the unit and the provision of the necessary specifications to ensure that the new unit conforms to the network's image in every detail

▸ Adequate training of the franchisee and key staff

▸ Continuous advertising and promotion of the brand name

▸ The availability of a franchisor's field force that can provide good business advice and is able to support the franchisee during a downturn.

The entrepreneurial dilemma – *Watch out for unscrupulous franchisors* illustrates the importance of obtaining legal advice during the process of analysing a franchise before signing a franchise agreement.

8.9 Franchising a business

While buying a franchise is one of the options for starting a new business venture, this does not imply that franchising is a separate type of ownership to those discussed in Chapter 7. A franchise describes the way in which a business is packaged to enable expansion. Franchises could still be partnerships or companies (as discussed in Chapter 7) with all the associated legal implications (see Chapter 17).

8.9.1 Preliminary planning

Before considering franchising as an option to expand an existing business, the prospective franchisor should do detailed planning and painstaking groundwork. Prospective franchisors are often too eager to go out and sign up the first franchisee they find. This should be avoided, as it is only through patience and perseverance that you may one day be able to join the ranks of the Steers and McDonald's of this world. Parker and Illetschko (2007:243–244) indicated that the following should first be evident:

▸ The existing business has been operating profitably for at least one year and compelling evidence shows that it is ready for expansion.

▸ There are clearly defined and optimised operating guidelines and practices pertaining to the production, handling, and delivery of the product or service as well as business-management systems required to control these operations.

▸ Business processes have been standardised, simplified, and documented so that it is possible for an inexperienced person to be trained to use them within a reasonably short period.

▸ A brand has been created and registered which should either be well established or show realistic potential for rapid development.

▸ There exists a well-defined market for the product or service and a clear indication that the demand for the product shows a sustainable upward trend.

▸ The target-market population for the product or service is big enough and the market is structured in such a way that the establishment of new delivery points in quick succession will be commercially viable.

▸ It may be difficult to copy or imitate the product or service due to some aspect of uniqueness intrinsic to the product or service – this will limit the possibilities of flooding the market with imitations.

▸ The growth potential and profit margins within the industry are sufficiently robust to enable the prospective franchisor, as well as future franchisees, to earn attractive returns.

▸ The prospective franchisor has made sizable investments in the establishment of franchise infrastructure and is prepared to take a long-term view with regard to expected returns.

▸ The prospective franchisor recognises and accepts the fact that building a successful network of franchises depends on creating win-win outcomes for the franchisor and the franchisee so he or she will also be committed to entrenching the principles expressed in the FASA Code of Ethics and Business Practices.

▸ Before the franchise is launched, the franchisor should have operated at least one pilot outlet as a company-owned outlet to continuously test the viability of the operation.

8.9.2 Establish network potential

According to Parker and Illetschko (2007), the franchisor should establish the marketing potential of the franchising network in detail and that it should culminate in the creation of a network-expansion plan. Depending on the type of business in question, the franchisor has to decide whether it will grant franchises for a particular location only or for an entire territory. The allocation of territories is fraught with difficulties and will remain a problem for some time to come. Established franchisors have the advantage that they could use historic data to make educated guesses as to the true potential of an area, but even this method is far from certain. New franchisors do not have historic data to rely on but work with estimates based on observation of similar businesses in the area. This emphasises the importance of doing thorough market research before embarking on a franchising venture. The following should be considered in the development plan:

▸ Identifying the target areas for expansion and assessing the potential of each of these target areas

▸ Ranking the areas according to potential – the franchisor should give due cognisance to possible logistical constraints that may negatively impact his or her ability to service and support franchisees in any of these areas

▸ Timelines and milestones for the development plan, with due consideration of commercial realities that may impact the development plan

▸ Careful planning should take place to guard against over-saturation of an area.

8.9.3 Financial projections

Starting a new venture is usually associated with the development of a sound business plan setting out the way in which a business is expected to operate, and making projections from pro forma financial statements including the profit and loss account, and cash flows for the first three to five years of operation. This should also apply when starting a franchise network but it is very rarely done. It is thus advisable that the entrepreneur who wants to develop his or her business venture into a franchise network should develop a sound business plan, and also address the different costs and projected income related to the franchise. The establishment of a franchise infrastructure requires a substantial initial investment by the franchisor.

8.9.4 Setting up franchise fees

The following **franchise fees** that should be set up by the franchisor:

▸ *Upfront fee.* An initial or upfront franchise fee is a lump sum that is payable when signing the franchise agreement and reflects the licence payment. This includes the right to use the trademark and access to technical expertise, initial training, operating systems, management procedures, and trade contracts. This fee does not include equipment, shop fittings, stock or other items needed to prepare the franchised business for trading (Illetschko, 2005:31–37). According to Standard Bank's Franchise Division the average upfront fee can range from about R106 000 up to around R350 000 (BizConnect, 2012). A guideline on how this upfront fee can be calculated is reflected in Table 8.1.

Table 8.1 Formula for the calculation of upfront fees

STEP 1	STEP 2	STEP 3
Work out estimated costs to be incurred during the preparation phase. Include professional fees etc.	Compute the total cost as per step 1 and divide it by the projected number of units to be established during the first three years of operation	The result of this calculation is the initial fee to be charged per franchisee
Add costs projected for the next three years of marketing the franchise, recruiting franchisees and providing them with initial training and support		
Add costs projected for the next 3 years of site selection services and set-up assistance		
Add goodwill (arbitrary figure that should be commensurate with the brand value)		

Source: Illetschko, K. 2012. Reprinted by permission of the author.

▶ *Renewal fee.* Some franchisors charge a renewal fee when the initial franchise agreement comes to an end and the franchisee wishes to extend it. This may not be justified in view of the fact that the upfront fee serves to reimburse the franchisor for costs incurred in creating the franchise and helping the franchisee get started, while the same costs may not be applicable on renewal of the agreement.

▶ *Ongoing fees.* The following ongoing fees have been identified (Illetschko, 2005):
  ▪ A management service fee (sometimes referred to as a royalty) paid for the right to use the franchisor's name and for the latter to provide ongoing management-support services such as training, advice, guidance, marketing strategy, an operations manual, and research – the fee is frequently computed as a percentage of turnover on a pre-determined regular and ongoing basis, and less frequently as a percentage of the purchases or indeed a fixed monthly fee.
  ▪ Additional income could be derived from aspects such as the cost to rent, build or equip an outlet or purchase the initial inventory.
  ▪ Income from product supplies under a compulsory purchase arrangement and mark-ups on products and confidential rebates that the franchisor receives from suppliers to its network – these will be applicable when the franchisee is contractually bound to purchase certain goods either from the franchisor or from sources prescribed by the franchisor.
  ▪ Some franchisors offer administration and accounting services to their franchisees in return for a fee.

When calculating the franchise fees, mark-ups, and the like, the franchisor should take care to ensure that the franchisees are given a fair chance to generate reasonable profits for themselves after market realities have been taken into account. If the franchisor is only concerned with his or her own survival, the franchise network will not prosper in the long term and the franchisor will only have himself or herself to blame for its eventual demise.

▸ *Network marketing fund.* Most franchise networks require franchisees to contribute to a central marketing fund operated by the franchisor on behalf of the network. These funds are earmarked for product advertising to the benefit of the network. The units owned by the franchisor will gain equally from group advertising campaigns and it is reasonable to expect that they should make contributions at the same rate as the franchised units. Advertising fees may be paid as a fixed amount or as a percentage of turnover, and are paid on a regular and continuous basis.

8.10 Franchisee recruitment: A five-step approach

A five-step approach to franchisee recruitment is suggested by Illetschko (2005:94–95).

8.10.1 Generate enquiries

In order to make potential franchisees aware of the franchising opportunity you have to offer, the following can be done to generate enquiries about your specific franchise:

▸ Develop a franchisee-information folder to introduce your franchise to prospective buyers and their professional advisors
▸ Introduce and present your franchise at seminars and exhibitions – use an information pamphlet for this purpose
▸ Compile an introductory visual presentation (on DVD)
▸ Offer to speak at small-business events and provide the press with information about your franchise
▸ Advertise in newspapers and magazines, and with FASA.

8.10.2 Set follow-up procedures in motion

Recruitment advertising may damage your brand if you let any enquiry go unanswered. It is best to have a system in place to deal with enquiries promptly and professionally. This system should include:

▸ Determining who will deal with initial enquiries – the person should be professional, informed, and able to access the appropriate response
▸ Keeping a record of every franchise enquiry and prompt response, regardless of the manner in which it was received
▸ Keeping track of promising enquiries until negotiations have either been successfully concluded or terminated
▸ Reacting in writing when further information is requested by enquirers, thanking them for their interest, and enclosing the concise information, which should include a questionnaire for completion by the enquirer
▸ As soon as the questionnaire has been returned, look into the applicant's background, financial standing, and any references provided. Acknowledge receipt and start the follow-up process by inviting the applicant to attend an initial interview should he or she be a suitable candidate. Emphasise that this initial interview will not place any obligation on either of you. If the prospect is unsuitable, send a formal letter thanking him or her for the interest shown, while stating that you do not wish to pursue the matter further.

8.10.3 Invitation to a meeting

During the personal meeting it is essential that you give the applicant in-depth information about your business opportunity, show him or her a company-owned unit, and discuss the necessary investment in broad terms. Encourage him or her to ask questions but do not offer detailed financial information at this stage. Assess his or her potential for your organisation.

8.10.4 Enter into concrete negotiations

If both you and the applicant feel positive about the negotiations, the applicant should be offered the comprehensive information folder. On receipt of the folder, the entrepreneur should sign the Initial Undertaking (which should be dated to record the receipt of the Disclosure Document). If negotiations stay on track, you can agree on the location of the unit, and prepare customised financial projections and statements pertinent to the territory under negotiation, taking the earnings requirements of the franchisee and other specifics into account. Encourage the prospect to discuss the Disclosure Document, financial figures, and Franchise Agreement with professional advisors, and stress the confidentiality obligations.

8.10.5 Formal agreement

The formal franchise agreement can be signed once all the details have been finalised. This could be done in the office of a professional adviser nominated by the franchisee. After the agreement has been signed, the following should be done:
▸ Bank the cheque for the upfront fee
▸ Schedule the franchisee's training
▸ Set the 'start-up assistance package' in motion.

8.11 The franchise package

The triangle that makes up the **franchise package** comprises three important elements: the Disclosure Document, the Franchise Agreement (or contract), and the Operations and Procedures Manual (FASA, 2006:86–87).

8.11.1 Disclosure Document

FASA requires its members to provide prospective franchisees with a **Disclosure Document** that gives all the relevant information about the company and the franchise opportunity (FASA, 2006). Although it is the responsibility of the franchisor to ensure that the prospective franchisee receives a copy of the Disclosure Document, it is in the self-interest of all prospective franchisees to insist on receiving a copy.

The Disclosure Document contains information on the following (FASA, 2006:10):
▸ Directors' and key executives' business experiences
▸ Company's track record
▸ Description of the franchise
▸ Initial investment required
▸ Ongoing payments due to the franchisor
▸ Termination, renewal, goodwill or assignment of agreement
▸ Number of existing franchisees and their success rates
▸ Franchisor's assistance in selecting approved sites
▸ Training and support guaranteed to the franchisee
▸ Financial information about pilot operation
▸ Financial data on the franchisor
▸ Certificate from auditor or accountant on business being a going concern
▸ Confirmation of directors on viability of the system
▸ Total investment required (indicating all costs).

8.11.2 Franchise Agreement

Potgieter (1997a:16) describes a **Franchise Agreement** as the 'founding document, in terms of which the franchisee is licensed to operate the franchised business in accordance with a predetermined business system'. FASA (2006:10) describes the Franchise Agreement as 'the legal contract which sets out the arrangement between the person buying the franchise (the franchisee) and the person selling it (the franchisor)'.

The Franchise Agreement is drafted by the franchisor and its representatives, with the objective of protecting the business and ensuring standardisation of the franchises.

According the FASA (2006), it is important to understand the nature of the Franchise Agreement as it defines the relationship between the franchisor and franchisee for the duration of the agreement. Most Franchise Agreements are complex and tend to favour the franchisor whose business and rights need to be carefully protected. The franchisee should seek legal advice before signing the agreement, to ensure that the clauses are not so demanding that they stifle his or her enthusiasm for running the franchise as a business.

The following aspects should be covered by the Franchise Agreement (FASA, 2006:10):
▸ Parties (signatories) involved in the agreement and their relevant objectives
▸ Period of the agreement and the right to renew or extend the contract
▸ Set-up requirements such as obtaining finance, renovating the premises, shop equipment, legal obligations, and so forth
▸ The rights to sell or transfer ownership of the franchise
▸ Obligations to the franchisor, such as buying supplies or services
▸ Construction and functioning of the franchise – hours of business, look and feel, and so on
▸ Terms and conditions for termination of the contract (breach of contract)
▸ Description of exact training and support offered
▸ Precise price, commissions, and rental fees involved
▸ Precise boundaries of the territory awarded, if any
▸ Functioning of the franchise: management, involvement of franchisee, and right to sub-franchise

▸ Operating systems guiding and driving the franchise
▸ Accounting system to be used
▸ Description of your heir's rights in the event of your death
▸ Definitions of all terminology that will be used repeatedly throughout the document.

The franchisor may require that the franchisee records upfront, prior to the execution of the agreement, that he or she:
▸ Has read the provisions of the agreement and fully understands them
▸ Has been advised by the franchisor to obtain independent legal advice on the terms of the agreement
▸ Has not relied on statements or representations made by the franchisor, its employees or agents, other than those recorded in the agreement and Disclosure Document
▸ Understands that none of the assistance rendered by the franchisor should be construed as a warranty for the successful conduct of the franchised business
▸ Understands that the success of the franchised business depends largely upon the abilities and efforts of the franchisee to operate it successfully (Potgieter, 1997b).

8.11.3 Operations and Procedures Manual

Parker and Illetschko (2007:245–246) describes the **Operations and Procedures Manual (OPM)** as 'the document that ensures operational consistency throughout the network'.

The OPM manual is sometimes referred to as the franchisee's bible, and must have a hands-on approach to the franchise so that it can be referred to and utilised daily, and should be regularly updated by the franchisor.

The OPM should include the following:
▸ *An introduction to the franchise.* This covers the general business and related industries that the franchise is operating in, the products or services and franchise concept,

and the work ethic and strategies, including the mission statement, philosophy, and overall long-term goals of the franchise.

▸ *Step-by-step guidelines.* These address the specific legal and statutory requirements, as well as specific location requirements that the franchisee must adhere to. These include lease negotiations, fixtures and fittings, security, hiring of staff, setting up of systems and control, corporate colours, logos, initial launch, and promotional requirements (Rodkin, 1996).

▸ *The production equipment.* This refers to equipment that is necessary to run the business, detailing the specific functions of each piece.

▸ *All details regarding stockholdings, systems and controls, as well as pricing methods.* The product or service to be sold should be detailed in exact specifications and customer requirements. This is often the most-used section of the operations manual and should thus cover all possible details to aid the franchisee and his or her staff. The details that should be provided include aspects such as initial stock levels, product range, pricing policies, minimum stockholding, stock ordering, receiving, assembly and distribution, and administrative and reporting requirements (Rodkin, 1996).

▸ *The business operation where the franchisee is obliged to meet specific operational standards.* This includes working hours, dress code, security and cash procedures, the level at which the franchisee should keep the premises maintained and in good order, the standard of cleanliness desired, set standards of service and product quality that the franchisee should meet, general standards of operation, standards regarding inventory levels, and the right of the franchisor to evaluate whether the franchisee meets the expected operational standards (Vaughn, 1979).

▸ *The accounting and administration system to be used.* This is usually the franchisor's accounting system or one that is totally compatible with that of the franchisor. As far as the accounting for the franchise unit is concerned, the franchisee is obliged to invite a certified annual audit at his or her expense and the franchisor is granted the right to audit the books of the franchisee. Furthermore, it is expected of the franchisee to provide the franchisor with a copy of his or her tax return as well as periodic financial reports (Vaughn, 1979).

▸ *The duties of the franchisor.* This information refers to providing support and advice.

▸ *Industrial relations.* This information addresses the terms of hiring and dismissing staff and the exact procedures to be followed in this regard, the relevant labour laws which should be adhered to and the necessary employment and termination letters sent and received, the fact that the employees need to undergo specific training programmes provided or prescribed by the franchisor, and the conduct of staff when dealing with customers.

8.11.4 Cooling-off period

A cooling-off period of 14 days must elapse between the day the prospective franchisee receives the Disclosure Document and a copy of the Franchise Agreement, and the day on which any binding agreement can be entered into or on which the franchisor may accept any payment from the franchisee. This cooling-off period favours both the franchisor, by eliminating individuals who have not planned thoroughly, and the franchisee, by eliminating pressure to buy.

8.12 Start-up assistance package

Once the Franchise Agreement has been signed and the upfront fee paid, the prospect has turned into a franchisee. This may be his or her first business venture and he or she may be experiencing doubts about it. In order to address this, a comprehensive start-up assistance package, prepared in advance, should now be set in motion to guide the franchisee toward the successful opening of his or her business. Five key aspects should be addressed in the start-up package (Illetschko, 1997a; 2005).

8.12.1 Pre-opening assistance

The franchisee is responsible for providing the necessary finance for the completion of the unit, while the franchisor could assist in developing an overall action plan that lists the things that need to be taken care of before opening day. It would be advisable for the franchisor to oversee the process to ensure that the new unit will be completed on time and conform to group standards in every respect. This type of pre-opening assistance would furthermore ensure that the franchisee does not overspend or take short-cuts in fitting out the unit, which in the long run could have dire cost effects.

8.12.2 Statutory requirements

The franchisee will require guidance with regard to licensing requirements and should also be assisted with preparing the necessary registrations with the South African Revenue Service, the Unemployment Insurance Fund, and other statutory bodies.

8.12.3 Staff selection and training

Any new business franchise will need to employ staff. This aspect is addressed in the section on the OPM in this chapter (see Section 8.11.3). However, the franchisor's hands-on involvement in the selection of the initial staff complement is essential. Depending on corporate policies, training of new staff could be carried out either at the franchisor's premises or those of the franchisee. Even if the franchisee is responsible for staff training and has been prepared for this during his or her initial training, the franchisor could provide hands-on assistance during the initial staff-training sessions.

8.12.4 Moral support

The franchisor should fully support the franchisee, especially during the first few weeks after opening. A representative of the franchisor should spend time at the premises of the franchisee in order to ensure that:

▶ Everything works as expected
▶ The staff are competent
▶ The franchisee is capable of doing the job
▶ Information about any opposition is available and the whole aspect of starting a new business venture is less daunting for the franchisee than it appears to be.

This is essential to build up the franchisee's confidence and self-assurance in running the business.

8.12.5 Opening promotion

The franchisor should design, develop, and provide promotional material that will make the target market aware of the opening. Special offers designed to attract customers should be advertised in the local press and in the window of the premises, where applicable. The franchisor should make artwork available to the franchisee for standard advertisement and other material that could be customised to suit the new outlet. This will ensure that the corporate identity is upheld, while the franchisee is spared the inconvenience and expense of having to arrange for artwork.

8.13 Ongoing franchisee support

Once the new franchise is operational, the obligations of the franchisor are far from over. For the success of the network and its own profits, the franchisor should provide ongoing support to the new franchisee. This could be done by a representative of the franchisor and should involve some of the important aspects (Illetschko, 1997a; 2005) listed below.

8.13.1 Training

A training schedule should be available. Depending on the complexity of the business, the training period could vary from a few days to several months. The duration of the training is not really as important as the time allocated, and should be used appropriately. The contents of the training programme should be planned well in advance and the person responsible for training should be available for the duration of the training. The franchisee and (or) any of his or her staff members should also show commitment and interest in the training.

8.13.2 Group-purchase arrangements

If the franchise involves a product, the franchisor is likely to be the supplier of the product or its components. Alternatively, group-buying arrangements could be made on behalf of the network. Whatever the arrangements, it is essential that the franchisee derives real benefit in some form of savings or profit.

8.13.3 Marketing and advertising

This is perhaps the most important ongoing benefit that the franchise has to offer the franchisees. Advertising is usually financed through advertising fees that are levied upon all franchisees and supplemented by equal contributions from the franchisor's own outlets. Regional or national advertising is funded by the advertising fund and the fact that this is done for the group as a whole contributes to the franchisor being able to negotiate the best prices for all types of advertising media. Below-the-line advertising could also be used and funded by the advertising fund. This will ensure that shop posters and giveaways are the same throughout the network. Advertisements placed by a specific franchisee in his or her local newspaper should be funded by the particular franchise, over and above the compulsory contribution to the advertising fund.

8.13.4 Trouble-shooting

Initially the franchisee is bound to encounter routine problems which, due to a lack of experience, he or she may be unable to solve unaided, and may have to turn to the franchisor for assistance. Prompt assistance will go a long way toward cementing a franchise relationship. As the franchisee 'matures' and gains confidence, the basic problems will be dealt with. The need for replacement staff to deal with emergencies will, however, always exist. Such emergency staff could be drawn from the training section or the company pool. The franchisor could also employ one or more relief managers to be sent out to franchises according to a pre-determined roster, enabling a franchisee to take annual leave without having to temporarily close down his or her unit. Other types of trouble-shooting could involve providing technical support where needed, and charging out rotation staff to allow for slack periods or when franchisees fall ill.

8.13.5 Market and product research

To commission formal market research to be carried out by an outside company is not always affordable or feasible. However, the franchisor should use its network to gain information and formulate it into an appropriate strategy to build up the brand name of the network.

Franchisees should be encouraged to monitor customer response and competitor activities by means of user-friendly questionnaires provided by the franchisor. The franchisor should add its own outlet's feedback to the returns from the franchisees and report back to all franchisees on any findings. The importance of having an own outlet for market research cannot be emphasised strongly enough. This outlet could be used by the franchisor for testing new products and ideas, before distributing these to all the franchisees in the network.

8.13.6 Administrative systems

The franchisor or its representative should help the franchisee set up the necessary administrative system. All aspects of the daily running of the business, such as the petty-cash float or checking whether there is fresh water in the coffee maker, should be covered by means of checklists.

8.13.7 Communication

The interaction that is possible in a franchise network helps to relieve the loneliness that is usually characteristic of a self-owned business venture started by an entrepreneur. Communication could add to the success of the total network through the exchange of ideas. The franchisor could enhance this success by providing formal and informal channels of communication.

8.14 Competition legislation and franchising

The existing competition legislation (Competition Act 89 of 1998) regulates competition matters in South Africa. The Act has been designed to prevent the following anti-competitive conduct, both horizontal and vertical, and the abuse of a dominant position. The implication of this is that the Act has impacted on several of the essential franchise practices such as:

▶ *Price-setting agreements.* Franchisors must ensure that no sanction, penalty or disincentive is meted out to franchisees that do not comply with recommended prices.

▶ *Tying arrangements.* Franchisors may not insist that the franchisee should agree to enter into a range of other agreements. Franchisors may, however, require the use of goods and services that meet certain standards. If they want to prescribe the source, they must apply for exemption from the Act.

▶ *Exclusive dealing.* The Competition Commission recognises the fact that provisions for purchasing exclusively from or dealing in goods provided by the franchisor or specified provider are permissible when they protect the franchisor's know-how, intellectual property and other skills, and protect against free-riding. However, franchisees may not be prevented from dealing with third parties if goods of a similar quality are available and the franchisor's trademark will not suffer harm.

▶ *Territorial restrictions.* Where territorial restrictions on trading and granting exclusive territories to franchisees have as their purpose the desire to create an effective network to the benefit of all the franchisees in the network, it may be seen that these benefits outweigh any anti-competitive effect. However, franchisors need to apply for exemption if they want to introduce such restrictions if they cannot prove this.

▶ *Clauses protecting know-how and other intellectual property.* This refers to restricting franchisees from engaging in a similar trade, business or occupation during the relationship between the franchisor and franchisee (restraint of trade). In general, this is acceptable if it is intended to protect a legitimate interest. However, upholding such restraint of trade in the franchising context within South Africa has been difficult, and this aspect is governed by the Act (Woker, 2007).

The Competition Commission has issued statements recognising the benefits that franchises offer, the unique situation that arises from the franchise relationship, and the clauses of the Franchise Agreement. It does not automatically view these as anti-competitive but will examine each case on its merits. In spite of this, cases brought to the attention of the Competition Commission still led to fines (see Parker and Illetschko, 2007). This led to the fact that the Competition Commission issued a Franchise Notice in 2005 to inform franchisors and franchisees about the impact of the Competition Act 89 of 1998 on their activities and arrangements to enable them to comply with the Act (the complete Franchise Notice can be accessed at: http://www.fasa.co.za/competition_commission/preface.html).

8.15 The CPA and franchising

With franchises becoming a common phenomenon worldwide, regulation of the industry has become inevitable. South Africa's legislature has initiated this regulation through the Consumer Protection Act 68 of 2008 (the CPA), which was signed into law on 24 April 2011. Traditionally, franchisors had the strongest bargaining position when negotiating franchise agreements. A balance was sorely needed. Franchise Agreements now have to comply with the requirements of the CPA. The terms and conditions of Franchise Agreements have been substantially altered resulting in a shift of some power to the franchisee (Rhoodie & Scriba, 2011).

The following is a list of some of the prescribed information every Franchise Agreement must contain, although this list is not exhaustive (Rhoodie & Scriba, 2011) (D'Amico, 2011) (Singh, 2014):

1. A notice on top of the first page of the agreement must refer to the 10-day cooling-off period franchisees are entitled to and state the relevant section of the Act.
2. The franchise agreement must contain provisions preventing the following:
   a. Unreasonable or overvaluation of fees, prices or other amounts;
   b. Conduct which is unnecessary or unreasonable in relation to risks to be incurred by one party;
   c. Conduct that is not reasonably necessary for the protection of the legitimate business interests of the franchisor, franchisee or franchise system.
3. As a minimum, the agreement must include:
   a. the name and description of the goods/services that the franchisee is to sell or provide;
   b. the obligations of the franchisor;
   c. the obligations of the franchisee;
   d. description of the business system;
   e. the territorial rights granted to the franchisee described in detail;
   f. details of initial and ongoing training and assistance;
   g. details relating to the advertising fund;
   h. the effect of the termination or expiration of the franchise.
4. Information about the franchisor's directors, members or equivalent officers.
5. Full particulars of the financial obligations that the franchisee incurs in terms of the franchise agreement or otherwise related to the franchised business.
6. Any direct or indirect benefit a franchisor stands to receive from prescribed suppliers due to supplying to its franchisees or the franchise system must be disclosed in writing with an explanation of how it will be applied. Clearly, franchisors are now required by law to disclose any rebates

that they receive from suppliers and how they intend to apply them.

Although certain of the points are traditionally found in the average competently drafted Franchise Agreement, franchisors will now need to check and audit their Franchise Agreements so as to ensure that they are compliant. The regulations may of course be updated from time to time and franchisors will therefore need to remain abreast with any such new or updated regulations. Further, if any written explanation of a term or section is given, this must be legally correct, failing which the franchisor risks being bound to an incorrect explanation (Singh, 2014).

As a minimum a disclosure document must contain (Singh, 2014):

▸ The number of individual franchised outlets
▸ The growth of the franchisors turnover, net profit and the number of individual new franchised outlets for the immediately preceding year;
▸ A statement of confirmation that the franchisor is able to pay its debts as and when they fall due;
▸ Written financial projections of the franchised business or of franchises of a similar nature, together with particulars of the assumptions upon which these representations are made.

8.16 International franchising

Many an entrepreneur is awed by the thought of taking his or her business to a foreign country, perhaps because he or she considers that South Africa has nothing to offer a foreign country. This is not true, since an increasing number of South African franchisers have managed to transplant their franchise concepts successfully in foreign countries. However, starting a franchise internationally is not as simple as inviting a prospective licensee to your local operations, handing him or her a set of manuals, perhaps taking him or her to a game reserve or two, and then quickly and easily earning a lot of strong foreign currency. To succeed in the long term, certain things need to be done first.

8.16.1 Assess feasibility

If the franchise business is relatively new and the franchisor is already stretched for capacity and resources, it is advisable to stay clear of international franchising until the situation has changed. If the franchise is strong enough, an international department, complete with its own staff and budget could be set up. This implies additional investment in the company-owned franchise, as well as recruiting and training additional staff to deal with international marketing research, legislation, and even language.

8.16.2 Develop a master license

A **master license** is essentially a franchise that grants the licensee the rights to open up businesses in an entire country, instead of conferring territorial rights over a specific site or territory. The licensor, in this case the franchisor in South Africa, sells the license to the master licensee in another country. This master license usually entitles the licensee to operate for his or her own account and to sell franchises to others. The master licensee has to pay an initial license fee, plus a share of any initial fees charged to local franchisees, in exchange for these rights. In addition, any ongoing management service fees collected are shared between the licensee and the original licensor or franchisor. Under current legislation, master license transactions require the prior approval of the South African Reserve Bank.

8.16.3 Assess the country

There is more to selling a master license than merely signing an agreement and handing over some manuals. The exercise entails many trips to a foreign country, both initially and on an ongoing basis. Your resources will be heavily drawn upon and, therefore, it is essential to assess the following aspects of the foreign country:

▸ Is the size of the potential market big enough?
▸ Will sufficient people be interested in buying the franchise from a master licensee and is there a sufficiently large pool of end-users to provide ongoing support?
▸ Are the attainable margins sufficient to cover expenses and will this leave a profit for both your licensee and yourself?
▸ Is the prospect suitable?

8.16.4 Investigate the licensee

Once satisfactory answers to the above questions have been obtained and the decision has been made to move into the foreign country, the individual (or company) wishing to purchase the master license has to be investigated. This could be done by assessing the following:

▸ Is the licensee who he or she claims to be, and does he or she have the ability, in the broadest sense of the term, to make the offered franchising concept successful?
▸ Do his or her business ethics appear to mesh with those of the franchisor and its network?
▸ Will he or she be willing and able to uphold the system of the franchise and franchise network?

EXAMPLE 8.3

Coffee shop brand, Vida e Caffé, says their next stop is Ghana

High-flying South African coffee bar brand Vida e Caffé is on an African expansion drive to complement its 70 local outlets and others already operating in Angola, Mauritius and the United Kingdom. Plans are now underway to open stores in Ghana and Botswana, with other Western markets – notably Australia and the USA – also being eyed by the Cape Town-based brand that started in 2001. The heart of the concept is a European-style sidewalk espresso bar that serves high-quality coffee and pastries. 'Vida e Caffé' means 'life and coffee' in Portuguese.

The Vide e Caffé brand, while successful in shopping centres and retail areas, has typically done well in corporate environments. It owes this to the fact that people are often willing to go outside the building they work at in search of a quality brand of coffee. Furthermore, an established coffee shop in a corporate building can become a popular meeting point for those looking for a more relaxed environment to discuss business.

Managing director of Vida Grant Dutton said that they plan to expand Vida e Caffé into Ghana and Botswana by the end of the year. Currently, the brand already has 72 stores in South Africa, four in Mauritius, one in Angola and two in London. Dutton said that Vida e Caffé, would like to be the first to bring a slice of the European coffee culture to African streets.

The first Angolan Vida e Caffé store was established just over a year ago, and Dutton said the uptake they received there was very impressive. While there are plans to further expand their presence in Angola, Dutton said that the market can be challenging, mainly because it is expensive. For example, property leases are expensive, and the logistical issues surrounding transporting fresh produce into the market can be costly too.

Dutton said that he is also interested in expanding to markets such as Mozambique, Zimbabwe, Kenya and Zambia. He noted that, because each African country is so different, they still have a lot to learn about each market but their strategy is to partner with strong operational partners and be the first to market in these countries, especially as a coffee culture is starting to develop in these regions. Depending on the region, Dutton said that they make use of a master franchise model for their international expansion.

Source: Adapted from Douglas (2013) and AMC Editorial Team (2013).

8.16.5 Involve support systems

Although one can build a local franchise operation without the help of professionals in the various disciplines, this should not be done when planning to move into the international playing field. The following professional support systems should be involved as soon as possible during the planning process:

▸ Legal professionals with international links and knowledge of international legislation, and who are able to give valuable advice during the planning and implementation phases. They could also be involved during the ongoing support phase.

▸ Training consultants with international links and expertise who could be involved in setting up training manuals, and even giving the initial and ongoing training support.

▸ Financial consultants with expertise in international accounting principles who could be involved in internationalising the accounting and administrative systems of the franchise network.

▸ FASA, which is a member of the World Franchise Council and is in contact with many franchise associations around the globe, including the International Franchise Association, Washington DC in the USA. Several of the affiliate members of FASA maintain databases on foreign countries where correct advice at the outset is bound to save time and money in the long run.

An example of a South African franchise that is also successful internationally is Vida e Caffé. Read some comments from the managing director of Vida e Caffé, in Example 8.3.

CONCLUSION

There is a strong future for franchising in South Africa. Franchising is an effective way of setting up entrepreneurs in their own businesses with the support they require to be successful. When considering buying into a franchise network, the entrepreneur should evaluate such a franchise before making a final decision. This chapter provides guidelines for such an evaluation that could be a useful tool in running the business.

Entrepreneurs, who are interested in starting a franchise business, should carefully assess the franchising opportunity and should use the advice of experts, lawyers, and accountants in this process. FASA is the best organisation to contact to obtain information on the process and franchise opportunities, and other advice on how to go about buying into a franchise system.

This chapter furthermore deals with the aspects that an entrepreneur should consider when planning franchising his or her business concept in order to expand it. It is not possible to cover all the details on how to franchise your business in one chapter. A more detailed discussion can be found in *How to Franchise your Business* 4th ed. (Illetschko, 2005).

The chapter also provides the entrepreneur with guidelines regarding the franchise package that he or she could expect from a franchisor when buying a franchise. The franchise package includes:

▸ The Disclosure Document, which gives all the relevant information about the company and the franchise opportunity

▸ The Franchise Agreement, which deals with the legal aspects pertaining to the contract between the franchisee and franchisor

▸ The OPM which provides the franchisee with guidelines for the day-to-day operations of the franchise business.

The effect that the Competition Act and the Consumer Protection Act have on franchising as well as international franchising is also discussed.

SELF-ASSESSMENT QUESTIONS

Multiple-choice questions

1. A product or trade-name franchise reflects the relationship between the franchisor and franchisee where the latter is licensed to operate a proven business concept using the franchisor's name in accordance with the standardised, fine-tuned package.
   a. True
   b. False

2. Which one of the following statements describes the fractional franchise?
   a. A way to test market acceptance and iron out possible glitches.
   b. An investment in one unit that is the full extent of the initial agreement.
   c. A unit franchise that occupies premises within an established business that stands to benefit from available synergies.
   d. The franchisee is expected to market and manage the business while trained staff carry out the actual business activity.

3. In the classification of franchises _____ can be described as the franchises that specifically focus on the needs of children?
   a. computer, internet and cellular franchises
   b. children's franchises
   c. education and training franchises
   d. fast food and restaurant franchises

4. Why is it important to test a new business idea, when considering buying a franchise?
   a. Prospective franchisees hope to gain knowledge in formulating the business concept.
   b. Prospective franchisees hope to gain from the experience, reputation and track record of the franchisor.
   c. Prospective franchisees expect the franchisor to help in setting up the business.
   d. Prospective franchisees hope to gain knowledge in formulating and implementing the plans.

5. The Competition Act has impacted on several essential franchises practices. Which one of the following is not one of these practices?
   a. Price-setting agreements
   b. Territorial restrictions

c. Development of franchise agreements
   d. Exclusive dealing

6. According to the CPA a notice on top of the first page of the franchise agreement must refer to a 12-day cooling-off period franchisees are entitled to.
   a. True
   b. False

7. In setting up an international franchise, it is important to keep a number of matters in mind. Which one of the following does not apply?
   a. A master licence has to be developed.
   b. If the franchise business is relatively new and is already stretched for capacity and resources, it is advisable to stay clear of international franchising.
   c. Under current legislation, master license transactions do not require the prior approval of the South African Reserve Bank.
   d. Training consultants with international links and expertise can be involved in setting up training manuals and give training support.

DISCUSSION QUESTIONS

1. Identify and discuss the different franchise variants.
2. Discuss and compare the two different types of simple operator franchises.
3. Identify and discuss the classification of franchises in South Africa.
4. Identify and discuss the various advantages and disadvantages of franchising.
5. Discuss the various costs involved in owning a franchise.
6. Discuss the various sources of franchising ideas.
7. Identify and discuss the different criteria that can be used to evaluate a franchisor and franchising opportunity.
8. What services should the franchisor provide to his or her franchisees?
9. Discuss the reasons for an entrepreneur deciding on franchising his or her business concept.
10. Identify and discuss the steps to be followed when franchising a business venture.

11. Discuss the financial considerations the entrepreneur has to take into account when franchising a business venture.
12. Discuss the ways in which prospective franchisees can be evaluated by a franchisor.
13. Identify and discuss the essential franchise practices that the Competition Act impacts on.

14. What are the minimum aspects that a disclosure document must contain as part of the requirements of the Consumer Protection Act?
15. Identify and discuss the steps the franchisor has to follow when closing the franchise sale.

EXPERIENTIAL EXERCISE

Whether new or experienced members of the franchise community, many agree that the key to a healthy and enduring business is satisfied customers. Without them, no business would survive. So what's the one thing some of today's budding franchise businesses are doing to keep customers returning? Providing relief. Yes, it may sound strange, yet the reality is that many individuals of the general public are, whether we like it or not, regularly facing some challenge or another. Be it unsatisfied appetites, a car out of service, a messy house and little time, or any other random hurdle, many often seek ways to beat the daily challenges they face. Franchise businesses across the country do their best to problem solve for customers in their respective segment and many do an excellent job of it, which leads to long-term success.

Conduct research on the Internet to find franchises in South Africa that may provide relief from the following challenges:
1. Developing business plans
2. Safety and security needs
3. Building low-cost timber housing
4. Finding a long-lost family member or friend
5. Setting up a romantic dinner for two in your own home.

Write a report on your findings that should cover the following aspects:
▸ Identify the number of franchises available to address each of the above challenges.
▸ Choose a franchise for each challenge that you think will address your needs the best, describing the franchise and providing reasons why you have chosen the specific franchise.

PAWS AND SNOUTS PET SHOPS

The Paws and Snouts pet shops franchise was started by Deon Vermaak, a veterinarian working in Centurion. He started the first shop in a new shopping centre in Eldoraigne, called Eldo Village, which was situated near his practice. Although Deon sold cat and dog food in his practice, customers were only able to make purchases at his practice during his open hours. To give customers more convenient access to his pet food for longer hours, he decided to start a shop selling his pet food. The name of the shop, Paws and Snouts, was the result of a family discussion on what it should be named. Although the shop sold all brands of

pet food, especially focusing on cat and dog food, it specialised in the high-quality brands that sold for much higher prices, such as Vet's Choice and Eukanuba. In addition, Paws and Snouts sold food for all pet types as well as pet-related products and gifts. Within three months, the shop broke even and two months later its profits started to soar. Deon decided to open two more Paws and Snouts pet shops: one in an existing shopping centre, Centurion Mall, and the second in a new shopping centre. Deon's wife, Magda, became involved in the day-to-day management of the

CASE STUDY

three shops while he ran a growing veterinary practice.

Deon and Magda want to expand and have had requests from developers in other areas in Centurion, Pretoria, and even Midrand to open a Paws and Snouts pet shop. However, Magda feels that opening three more shops will add to her already heavy workload and that she would not be able to effectively control all the aspects of three additional shops. She and Deon sat down and decided to investigate the possibility of expanding Paws and Snouts by turning it into a franchise. Magda was a lecturer at the University of Johannesburg before she became a full-time manager of Paws and Snouts. With her knowledge of teaching and developing teaching manuals, she would be able to develop the training manuals and other documents required in expanding Paws and Snouts into a franchise system. One matter that has always frustrated Magda is recruiting the right staff and identifying staff members that could be trained to become

managers in the three existing shops. She feels that she could use these skills to train and support the owners of the franchise outlets of Paws and Snouts and would be able to recruit staff to help her in this function.

1. What are the steps that Deon and Magda, the present owners of Paws and Snouts, should follow to develop it into a franchise system?
2. Deon and Magda read about the Consumer Protection Act and need advice on what they should do to ensure that they meet all the requirements in the development of their Franchise Agreement. Advise them of these requirements.
3. What documents other than the Franchise Agreement should be included in the package that they provide to prospective franchisees? What information should be included in each of these documents?
4. What are the steps that Deon and Magda should follow to enter into the African market?

SUGGESTED WEBSITE LINKS

http://www.whichfranchise.co.za/
http://www.franchisezone.co.za/
http://www.franchisedirect.co.za/
http://bizconnect.standardbank.co.za/sector-news/franchising/
http://www.fasa.co.za/
http://www.safranchisewarehouse.co.za/
http://www.bowman.co.za/eZines/Custom/ConsumerProtection/Newsflash/ConsumerProtectionRegulations.html

REFERENCES

AMC Editorial Team. 2013. African Marketing Confederation *The coffee brand that's living the life of 'Vida'.* [Online]. Available: http://www.africanmc.org/index.php/knowledge-portal/item/84-the-coffee-brand-thats-living-the-life-of-vida [23 June 2014].

BizConnect. 2012. Standard Bank BizConnect. *How to tell when the price is right. Accurately evaluating franchise costs.* [Online]. Available: http://bizconnect.standardbank.co.za/sector-news/franchising/how-to-tell-when-the-price-is-right.aspx [6 June 2014].

BizConnect. 2012a. Standard Bank Biz Connect. *Franchising in SA: A home-grown success story.* [Online]. Available: http://bizconnect.standardbank.co.za/sector-news/franchising/franchising-in-sa-a-home-grown-success-story.aspx [12 June 2014].

BizConnect. 2014. Standard Bank BizConnect. *Huizemark: Changing with the times.* [Online]. Available: http://bizconnect.standardbank.co.za/sector-news/franchising/huizemark-changing-with-the-times.aspx [23 June 2014].

BusinessDictionary.com. 2014a. BusinessDictionary.com. *Business format franchising.* [Online]. Available: http://www.businessdictionary.com/definition/business-format-franchising.html [16 June 2014].

BusinessDictionary.com. 2014b. BusinessDictionary.com. *Product franchise.* [Online]. Available: http://www.businessdictionary.com/definition/product-franchising.html [18 June 2014].

Crankshaw, P. 2013. How to buy a franchise. *Small Business Connect* (4):8.

D'Amico, M. 2011. D'Amico Incorporated Attorneys. *Franchisors beware – update your franchise agreement!* [Online]. Available: http://www.damico.co.za/legal_article_details.asp?ARTICLE_ID=8 [12 June 2014].

Day, J. 1993. *Small Business in Tough Times: How to Survive and Prosper*. Amsterdam: Pfeiffer.

Douglas, K. 2013. *Coffee shop brand, vida e caffé, says their next stop is Ghana*. How we made it in Africa. [Online]. Available: http://www.howwemadeitinafrica.com/coffee-shop-brand-vida-e-caffe-says-their-next-stop-is-ghana/27495/?fullpost=1 [23 June 2014].

FASA. 1998. *Franchising*. Johannesburg: Franchise Association of Southern Africa (FASA).

FASA. 2006. *FASA's 2007 Franchise Directory*. Bruma: Franchise Association of Southern Africa (FASA).

Franchise Finder. n.d. *The Consumer Protection Act - Part III: The CPA and Franchising*. Franchise Finder Online Directory of Franchises and Business Opportunities in South Africa. [Online]. Available:http://www.franchisefinder.co.za/Article%20Archive/consumer-protection-act-part-three.shtml [8 June 2014].

Franchize Directions. 2013. *Franchising weathers the economic storm*. Bizmag.co.za [Online]. Available: http://www.bizmag.co.za/franchising-weathers-economic-storm/ [17 June 2014].

Gordon, B. 2006. *The Standard Bank Franchise Factor®*. September 2006. Franchise Directions.

Huizemark. 2014. *About Huizemark*. Huizemark.com. [Online]. Available: http://www.huizemark.com/about--us [23 June 2014].

Illetschko, K. (Ed.). 1997b. *Let 18 Experts Tell You How to Franchise Your Business and Unleash its True Potential*. 2nd ed. Johannesburg: Franchise Association of Southern Africa (FASA).

Illetschko, K. 2002. *How to Evaluate a Franchise*. 2nd ed. Johannesburg: Franchise Association of Southern Africa (FASA).

Illetschko, K. 2005. *How to Franchise Your Business*. 4th ed. Johannesburg: Franchise Association of Southern Africa (FASA).

Illetschko, K. 2012. *How to Franchise Your Business*. 6th ed. Johannesburg: Franchise Association of Southern Africa (FASA).

James, A. 2013. BDlive. *Cadet programme a boost for economy, job creation*. [Online]. Available: http://www.bdlive.co.za/Feeds/BusinessDay/2013/08/15/cadet-programme-a-boost-for-economy-job-creation [13 June 2014].

LC Solutions. 2011. *Consumer Protection Act: Impacts on Franchising*. Legal & Commercial Solutions. [Online]. Available: http://www.lcsolutions.co.za/2011/03/24/consumer-protection-act-impacts-on-franchising/ [5 August 2013].

Matshotyana, Z. 2011. *Franchise opportunities*. Smart Cape Business [Online]. Available: http://www.smartcape.org.za/business/business-advisory/franchise-opportunities.html [23 June 2014].

Parker, E. & Illetschko, K. 2007. *Franchising in South Africa: The Real Story*. Northcliff, South Africa: Frontrunner Publishing.

Potgieter, F. 1997a. The franchise agreement. In FASA (Ed.). *The 1998 Franchise Book on Franchising (Incorporating the Franchise Opportunities Handbook 1998)*. Johannesburg: Franchise Association of Southern Africa (FASA).

Potgieter, F. 1997b. The franchise agreement. In Illetschko, K. (Ed.). *Let 18 Experts Tell You How to Franchise Your Business and Unleash its True Potential*. 2nd ed. Johannesburg: Franchise Association of Southern Africa (FASA).

Rodkin, B. 1996. *The Franchisor's Handbook. A Practical Guide to Franchising in South Africa*. Johannesburg:

Rhoodie, L. & Scriba, B. 2011. *Franchise agreements and the Consumer Protection Act*. DLA Cliffe Dekker Hofmeyer. [Online]. Available: http://www.cliffedekkerhofmeyr.com/en/news/press-releases/2011/franchise-agreements-and-consumer-protection-act.html [8 June 2014].

Singh, S. 2014. *The Consumer Protection Act poses significant challenges to weaker franchises*. Durban Chamber of Commerce and Industry. [Online]. Available: http://durbanchamber.com/profiles/blogs/the-consumer-protection-act-poses-significant-challenges-to [12 June 2014].

Small Business Connect. 2013. Watch out for unscrupulous franchisors. *Small Business Connect* (3):10.

Vaughn, CL. 1979. *Franchising: Its Nature, Scope, Advantages and Development*. Lexington: Lexington Books.

Whichfranchise. 2014a. *What is a franchise?* Whichfranchise.co.za. [Online]. Available: http://www.whichfranchise.co.za/what-is-a-franchise/ [17 June 2014].

Whichfranchise. 2014b. *What are the different franchise types?* Whichfranchise.co.za. [Online]. Available: http://www.whichfranchise.co.za/different-franchise-types/ [17 June 2014].

Woker, T. 2006. Understanding the relationship between franchising and the Competition Law. *FASA's 2007 Franchise Directory*. Bruma: Franchise Association of Southern Africa (FASA).

CHAPTER 9

Business ethics and social responsibility

Hanneli Bendeman

LEARNING OUTCOMES

On completion of this chapter you will be able to:
▶ Define the terms 'ethics' and 'business ethics'
▶ List ethical issues with which a business may be confronted
▶ Distinguish between strategic, work, and ethical values
▶ Discuss the impact of an entrepreneur's personal ethics on the venture
▶ Identify and discuss ethical dilemmas that arise in the course of operating a venture
▶ Understand the function and importance of a 'code of ethics'
▶ Discuss the creation of an ethical culture in an organisation
▶ Define 'social responsibility'
▶ Discuss the different approaches to social responsibility as well as the areas of social responsibility and how the entrepreneur could address each one.

OPENING CASE STUDY

Setting up a business takes a lot of courage as an entrepreneur often has to venture into unknown decision-making territory with only his or her skills, knowledge, financial resources and own value system. Acting consistently according to these values can be referred to as entrepreneurial integrity.

In the journey to business success, the temptation to engage in unethical practices can become very strong. Too often, companies place profit ahead of all other considerations, engaging in dubious practices and creating a culture devoid of business ethics. This can cause irreparable harm to both the business itself and its customers. An ethical business culture can be defined by several key components, which places reliable companies above those that will do anything for a buck.

1. What, in your view should be regarded as a priority for a healthy economy, ensuring that all businesses pay taxes or to strengthen the economy through tax relief for small entrepreneurs?

2. Discuss the statement: 'Bread now, ethics later' as an excuse used by entrepreneurs to indulge in dubious business practices.

INTRODUCTION

How does one justify the increasing poverty and vulnerability of a growing section of the population amid a growing economy and a prosperous business sector? The reasons for poverty are complex but could it also be that business people are only interested in generating profits and living in luxury, while their employees are paid extremely low wages and living in poverty?

Over the past few years of democracy, South Africa has acquired many of the ingredients of prosperity, such as the freedom and protection granted by the constitution and various sophisticated pieces of legislation, policy-making institutions, and institutions to give effect to the execution of such policies.

There is an increasing realisation that any business venture is part of the community in which it operates and that the success of the business depends on the prosperity of the society and the sustainability of a mutually beneficial relationship between the business and the environment. This is because land, labour, consumers, and some of the input of the business come from the community in which the business operates.

The survival of a newly established venture is sometimes closely linked to the survival of the community. A venture that opens in a rural community will not survive if there are no jobs for the members of that community, and if they do not have the ability to pay for what is on offer. If, however, the owner of that venture creates jobs for members of that community and even helps these people to start other business ventures, the community will thrive, and so will the business venture. To ensure their survival, businesses should plough efforts back into the society.

Business decisions have to take into consideration issues such as air, noise, and water pollution, preventing the wastage of natural resources, considering disadvantaged groups and their needs, assisting in improving race relations, and offering fair living wages. The King III report promotes the 'stakeholder inclusive' model of governance where the legitimate interests and expectations of stakeholders, such as the society and environment, are considered when deciding what is in the best interest of the company (*King Report on Governance for South Africa, 2009*).

The entrepreneur's responsibility includes rendering products and services that are of acceptable quality, dealing professionally with employees, and making good business decisions.

This chapter deals with the establishment of business ethics and the social responsibility of the business venture.

9.1 **Business ethics**

Business ethics focus on the responsibility of the organisation towards stakeholders as well as the underlying values that impact on the behaviour of individuals in the workplace. **Business ethics** can be defined as being 'about identifying and implementing standards of conduct that will ensure that, at a minimum level, business does not detrimentally impact on the interests of its stakeholders' (Rossouw and Van Vuuren, 2006:4). However, it is important to realise that business decisions are made by individuals (entrepreneurs) and that these decisions have an impact on others, including both internal stakeholders (employees) and external stakeholders (customers, suppliers, shareholders, society, and the environment).

The ethical issues confronting any business might differ from industry to industry and from business to business. According to David (1995:19), ethical issues that have an effect on business decisions could include issues such as:

▶ Product safety
▶ Employee health and safety
▶ Sexual harassment
▶ HIV/Aids in the workplace
▶ Smoking
▶ Affirmative action and empowerment of employees

▸ Waste disposal
▸ Foreign business practices
▸ Cover-ups
▸ Takeover tactics
▸ Conflicts of interest
▸ Employee privacy
▸ Inappropriate gifts to influence business decisions
▸ Security of company records.

The list above is by no means exhaustive and it is not possible to give a comprehensive discussion of each of these ethical issues and how they may affect the decisions of the entrepreneur in the scope of this chapter.

There is a huge responsibility on the entrepreneur to provide a safe workplace, where consistency in decision making ensures fairness, where there is no favouritism or nepotism, and where employees are provided with the opportunity to grow, develop, and thrive in a caring and professional work environment.

9.2 **Values**

Any business should formulate values or standards to tailor organisational behaviour (Rossouw and Van Vuuren, 2006:220). There are three types of values: strategic, work, and ethical values. These values are often defined in the company's value statement or vision and mission statement. The **strategic values** normally deal with the direction the business needs to go to achieve its goals. The **work values** are defined in the behaviours required from employees to achieve the business's short- and medium-term goals and the **ethical values** reflect the integrity required from employees and management.

Table 8.1 provides a list of generic values and a description of each in the business context. The list is by no means exhaustive, but it gives an overview of a selection of values and possible behaviours associated with the values required for sustainable business relationships.

Table 9.1 Generic values in the business context

STRATEGIC, WORK AND ETHICAL VALUES	
VALUE	**DESCRIPTION OR DEFINITION**
ACCOUNTABILITY (Work and ethical value)	To make commitments, take responsibility for and deliver on commitments, be judged against our commitments, be transparent and report on our performance
RESPONSIBILITY (Work and ethical value)	Taking responsibility for personal choices, admitting mistakes and failures, realising mutual dependence, and embracing responsibility for the impact of our business on all stakeholders
CARE and COMPASSION (Responsibility flows into care and compassion) (Ethical value)	Feeling and exhibiting concern and empathy for others; investing in people and creating an empowering environment through development, support, valuing diversity, and giving recognition and rewards
DIVERSITY (Associated with respect and care) (Ethical and work value)	Value our people, value diversity, ensure there is no discrimination, ensure equal opportunities for personal and professional growth, reward on merits, ensure a fair and respectful environment
RESPECT (Forms the basis of diversity, accountability, integrity, and corporate citizenship) (Ethical value)	Respect our people (diversity), respect our shareholders' interests by respecting work time and resources (diligence), respect our customers' needs, privacy, and dignity, respect the environment and society (corporate citizenship)
EXECELLENCE (Strategic value)	Moving beyond minimum accepted standards by continuously improving products, processes, and staff to deliver outstanding performance

STRATEGIC, WORK AND ETHICAL VALUES	
DILIGENCE (Work value)	Putting in a lot of effort and hard work, taking great care, doing tasks in detail, maintaining highest standards, being disciplined, using skills and knowledge to obtain maximum results in required time frames
INNOVATION (Work value)	Innovate to be competitive, push the boundaries, break new ground, encourage and reward innovation and creativity
INTEGRITY (Professionalism) (Ethical and work value)	Acting consistently with principles: Telling the truth (honesty) Keeping promises (commitment) Standing up for what is right (moral courage) Balancing the interests of all stakeholders (fairness and respect) Using company time and resources only for business purposes (diligence)
TEAMWORK (Trust is a prerequisite) (Strategic and work value)	Business interests above self interests; creates a sense of belonging and identity; belonging brings meaning for group, individuals, and stakeholders; belonging elicits normative forces that compel players to live up to the values of the team and go the extra mile in search of excellence
TRUST (Outcome of business with integrity) (Ethical value)	Trust is the bond in business relationships; it ensures a sustainable competitive advantage, makes things predictable, brings people together, and ensures a good reputation, honesty, accountability, and reliability
CORPORATE CITIZENSHIP (Strategic and ethical value)	Pursuit of commercial success in ways that honour values and respect people, communities, and the natural environment; not only fulfilling legal expectations, but also going beyond compliance and voluntarily investing in human capital, the environment, and relationships with stakeholders

It is important that an entrepreneur chooses values appropriate for his or her specific business and clearly specify the behaviour associated with living out that specific value.

9.3 The personal ethics of the entrepreneur

The entrepreneur plays a major role in establishing the initial code of ethics that have to be implemented within the venture. The integrity, or human character, of the entrepreneur often has a lasting impact on the character and reputation of the business. An entrepreneur is regarded as someone with integrity when he or she consistently adheres to a set of ethical standards and uses these standards as a basis for making decisions. Integrity is associated with values such as honesty, reliability, fairness, consistency, care, loyalty, and professionalism. The following are only a few examples of how values are essential to a sustainable business:

▶ *Honesty.* Honesty in all business dealings creates trust, and trust is the most important requirement for sustainable business relationships. Legendary entrepreneur Warren Buffet put it this way: 'Trust is like the air we breathe. When it's present, nobody really notices. But when it's absent, everybody notices'. Honesty entails that entrepreneurs should not distort the truth by deliberately lying, misrepresenting facts, cheating or misleading, even if they are doing so to protect their own interests. An entrepreneur who is dishonest is likely to be inclined to cover up incorrect decisions and business mishaps, lie to customers about products and services, and keep important information from business partners, employees, customers, and shareholders.

▸ *Reliability.* Reliability of the entrepreneur impacts on the perception of the reliability of the product. If the entrepreneur is not reliable, can a customer trust the product? Entrepreneurs should be true to their word and ensure that promises, propositions, and contractual obligations are kept. For example, if the entrepreneur promises to pay his or her employees on a weekly basis, but does not do so, this undermines his or her reliability as a businessperson and employer. It is better to renegotiate a contract if you see that it is not possible to keep it as originally negotiated, than to revoke it.

▸ *Fairness.* Business practices, labour relations and personnel practices such as promotions, dismissals and remuneration should be fair and based on competence and not on personal preferences or favouritism. Being fair means that the entrepreneur should always conduct himself or herself in such a way that the rights and interests of others are not wrongfully impaired. This would also mean that the entrepreneur should not discriminate between employees on the basis of race, gender, religion or sexual orientation.

▸ *Consistency.* Consistency creates trust as employees and customers get used to the fact that the entrepreneur can be counted on to take the same decisions under the same circumstances. If one employee is disciplined for a specific misconduct then all employees must be disciplined for this type of misconduct with no exception to the rule.

▸ *Loyalty.* Loyalty is related to reliability because it implies that the entrepreneur

will not place his or her own interests before those of the venture. This would include for example, reinvesting the profits from the business in the venture and the employees working for it. However, loyalty should not be used to favour a long-time supplier over a more deserving supplier during the tender process. There should be caution not to use 'loyalty' as an excuse for unethical business practices such as nepotism, favouritism, and unethical procurement practices.

EXAMPLE 9.1

Recognise your own fallibility as a leader, know your limits, and beware of the myth of immortality

Entrepreneurs often are horrified at the thought of leadership succession. The founders of great firms such as Google, Cisco, Amgen, and Microsoft have known that they would need to prepare for a day when they could no longer be the lone day-to-day internal boss, primary external ambassador, and symbolic cultural icon. The founder of the original (pre-Starbucks) coffee house chain, Chock-Full-o-Nuts, started his first café on Broadway's 43rd Street in 1923 and was a great national success. Sadly, sixty years later, as a dying man who had been flat on his back for two years at Massachusetts General Hospital in Boston, he still clung to the job of leader of the enterprise – his full-time physician serving as acting president.

Even if a leader shows the diligence and loyalty that is clearly evident in this example, by not ensuring proper leadership succession and allowing more competent and better leaders to take better care of the business, the lack of responsibility could be to the detriment of the business and stakeholders.

'All individual leaders, no matter how charismatic or visionary they are, eventually die, and all visionary products and services – all great ideas – eventually become obsolete'.

Source: Collins and Porras (2000:1–2).

1. Why is it ethical to ensure leadership succession for a business? Identify the parties who are affected by the proper leadership succession of a business.

9.4 Operating the venture and ethical dilemmas

The daily operation of the venture often brings an entrepreneur face to face with ethical dilemmas. This means that the entrepreneur has to balance his or her own needs with the needs and interests of the other stakeholders. These dilemmas do not only relate to the products and services rendered, but also to other aspects of the business such as advertising, personnel, natural resources, and community interests.

Depending on the nature of the business and the specific sector of the economy the following ethical issues could be addressed in a code of ethics (see Section 9.6) or in company policies and procedures.

▶ *Safety of products and (or) services.* When deciding on the type of product or service to develop or render, the entrepreneur should carefully consider the safety of the product and (or) service to ensure that there are no harmful effects on customers, employees or the environment. A business supplying unsafe products and (or) services risks costly lawsuits and a bad reputation, and may not be sustainable in the long run. Special care must be taken if the users of the product and services are vulnerable, such as children or the elderly, and are at risk.

▶ *Quality and price of products or services.* The entrepreneur should ask the following questions: Is the product quality as good as has been claimed or could it be that the ignorance of the consumer is being exploited? Is the price of the product or service a reflection of its value and quality? If the real quality of the product is inferior to the claimed quality, customers could start to complain, and may even take legal action against the business. This will make it very difficult for the business to survive in this economic climate.

▶ *Advertising.* Advertising requires honesty and integrity. Even if businesses are legally allowed to advertise, it does not necessarily mean that they advertise ethically. For example, if a business decides that youth under the age of 21 is their target market, and research reveals that the youth of today are angry, violent and rebellious, it would be unethical to capitalise on that anger and rebelliousness. Slogans such as 'communicate with your friends in ways your parents will not understand' or 'take control of your life' and 'don't ask for permission from those who don't know' – referring to parents and teachers – could be seen as inciting the youth to be unruly

ENTREPRENEURIAL DILEMMA

Contaminated medication

The Johnson & Johnson group faced a dilemma when they discovered that some Tylenol capsules had been opened and the ingredients mixed with cyanide resulting in the deaths of eight people. The group showed integrity when they recalled 31 million containers of Tylenol instead of trying to cover up the problem at the expense of more of their customers. Even though the company was not to be blamed for the deadly altering of the ingredients, they withdrew the product from the market at a cost of close to $2.5 billion in revenue. They also redesigned the packaging so that in future the capsules cannot be tampered with. The company's credo (value statement) states that its foremost responsibility is to the people who use its products.

How would you have handled a similar problem?

Source: Adapted from Hoyk, R. & Hersey, P. 2009. The Ethical Executive: Avoiding the Traps of the Unethical Workplace.

and undisciplined. This type of marketing is clearly questionable.

▶ **Comparative** advertising is now legal in South Africa, but it is still not allowed to give incorrect information about competitors when advertising a product. Examples of **competitive** advertising can be found in the advertising campaigns of Mercedes and BMW or between Pepsi and Coke. In both these instances, it is implied that the one product is better than the other without stating facts that can be challenged as lies or untruths. Ethically, advertisements should aim to give correct information about a product and service, and not mislead the consumer or cause him or her to make incorrect assumptions about a product.

(DEFINITION)

Competitive advertising involves a promotional technique in which an advertiser claims the superiority of its product over competing product(s) by direct or indirect comparison. If other products are mentioned by their name (and not as 'brand X', 'brand Y', etc.) the owners of those brands may challenge the fairness of the comparison in a court. Also called 'comparative' or comparison advertising.

▶ *After-sales service and warranty.* A large number of products and services available in the market fail to include after-sales service. The entrepreneur should aim to retain customers, and one of the most effective ways to achieve this aim is to offer after-sales service such as maintenance, training, advice, and upgrading of certain technologies. Deciding not to offer after-sales service should be communicated to customers, however this could become an ethical dilemma if the product or service on offer needs after-sales care or service or special training. Do not promise what you cannot deliver and be honest about delivery time. Some businesses take a long time to repair or replace a product

on warranty and this practice destroys the reputation of the business.

▶ *Dealing with employees.* Dealing with employees in an ethical manner is a prerequisite for any entrepreneur. Their health and safety should be protected, their working environment, family responsibilities, and emotional and spiritual well-being should be taken into consideration and consistency and fairness should be maintained at all times. Unfairness or inconsistency is not only counter-productive, but it can also be costly when an employee takes a case of substantive or procedural unfairness to the Commission for Conciliation, Mediation and Arbitration (CCMA).

▶ Employees' culture, religion, and values should be respected at all times and they should never be instructed to do anything unethical or illegal. Despite good intentions, paying employees' speed fines, for example, will send a message that you do not care about the safety of your employees and that they will not be held responsible for not obeying traffic rules and putting their lives – and the lives of other road users – in danger. Another example is if the employees are provided with money to pay for bribing traffic officers or border officials. The personal values of the employees should also be considered. If an employee objects to drinking alcohol, the entrepreneur should respect this and not force him or her to attend social functions where alcohol could be abused. The entrepreneur could also decide not to allow alcohol at social functions, in order to accommodate such an employee. Each employee's freedom of choice and privacy should be protected by the entrepreneur and guidelines to this effect should be included in the code of conduct for the business.

▶ Some unethical behaviour can only be committed by management because it is committed by those in positions of power.

Examples of such behaviour are favouritism, nepotism, unethical procurement, autocratic management styles, and disregard for employees' time and needs. Such practices create a culture of fear in an organisation where employees are afraid to speak up and feel powerless and alienated. They often react by misusing company time and resources, do only what they are instructed to do, have a 'don't care' attitude, become obstructive, and may even try to sabotage the business. It is often said that: 'a fish rots from the head' which means that it is management that creates the (un) ethical culture in any organisation.

9.5 Creating an ethical culture in a small business

Ethics in large companies are formally managed with ethics officers, formal ethics programmes, and various policies and procedures. Ethics in a small business can be implemented and monitored in a simple, practical manner because there is much less bureaucracy. This does not mean that small businesses do not have a need for clear ethical standards, but rather that ethics and standards are enforced and promoted more informally. The process starts with the way in which the business is run internally and how staff members are treated. The corporate culture is often an extension of the owner's personality and employees, customers, and suppliers quickly notice unethical behaviour. Such unethical behaviour creates a bad reputation and, in the world of small businesses, an operation's sustainability is often dependent on its reputation. An entrepreneur who loses a business can always start again, but one who loses his or her reputation compromises any future chances to start again.

Customers talk about their experiences with businesses. If a product or service is of good quality, customers will market the business for you. However, if the business delivers substandard goods and services or if the entrepreneur acts inconsistently or unethically, customers will criticise that business in an instant using the media, the Internet or even social networks such as Twitter and Facebook.

Government imposes many rules and regulations on businesses, such as Black Economic Empowerment (BEE), affirmative action, substantive and procedural fairness when dealing with labour relations, health and safety regulations which must be adhered to, and many more. However, these rules and regulations cannot ensure ethical behaviour. For example, a small company may act unethically by appointing an unskilled worker as a director just to be able to obtain a specific BEE status required to tender for a state contract.

The best thing an entrepreneur can do is to lead by example.

9.5.1 The moral development phases and ethical modes of businesses

Businesses without an ethical foundation are likely to go through various moral development phases. Rossouw and Van Vuuren (2006:44–57) describe the moral development phases and associated ethical modes which these businesses typically experience.

9.5.1.1 **Phase one: The immoral mode**

This phase can be referred to as the 'bread now, morals later' phase. If the government and society are perceived as being unethical and the business world is described as 'dog eat dog' and 'survival of the fittest', then entrepreneurs may call unethical behaviour 'good business' and justify unethical decisions with statements such as 'the business of business is business and not ethics'. In this mode, little regard is shown for fair competition requirements, customers or the environment and various methods are used to try to get around some of the sometimes perceived restrictive legal and policy requirements such as not appointing employees permanently for fear of the costs of complying with the substantive and procedural fairness requirements of labour legislation.

9.5.1.2 **Phase two: The reactive mode**

This phase usually starts when the entrepreneur realises that he or she is doing a lot of 'damage control' because of the fact that things have gone wrong and that it is beginning to impact on the profitability of the business. He or she becomes aware of the need for policies and procedures or a code of ethics to provide guidelines for behaviour because of one or more of the following:

▶ A scandal
▶ Loss of clients or contracts due to unethical behaviour
▶ Costs incurred through unethical practices such as elaborate gifts, hospitalities, and bribes to get or influence customers or suppliers
▶ Punitive CCMA arbitration awards against the company due to unfair labour practices.

However, in this mode, these policies and procedures are just tokens or a gesture of ethical intent and are not necessarily enforced. A company in this phase is very susceptible to ethical scandal and risks credibility problems with stakeholders.

9.5.1.3 **Phase three: The compliance mode**

In this mode, once the entrepreneur realises that unethical behaviour endangers the profitability and sustainability of the business, he or she will start to take ethics seriously. There is a bigger commitment to ethics and there is often a rule-based approach to ethics. Mechanisms are put into place to enforce policies and procedures: audits are done, unethical behaviour is punished through disciplinary and grievance procedures, and people are held responsible and accountable. In addition, measures are put in place to create awareness of ethics, such as ethics training programmes, ethics advice lines, and even an ethics hotline. The entrepreneur

makes a clear commitment to values and business with integrity. A problem arises when people in the business become so compliant that they begin to believe that everything that is not forbidden is allowed. For example, if the company bursary policy does not specifically state that employees cannot use the company printer to print out study material and assignments or that company stationery and paper is not part of the study assistance offered by the company, then employees might assume that they are allowed to use and misuse company property for personal studies.

9.5.1.4 **Phase four: The integrity mode**

In a mature organisation, ethical values are internalised and there is a value-based approach to ethics. The focus shifts from a reactive mode of punishing unethical behaviour to the promotion and rewarding of ethical behaviour. Employees do not look at management for ethical guidance but have a 'what can I do to make this company better' approach. There is no finger pointing and more individual responsibility and accountability, stakeholder engagement, and internalisation of company values. Company values are well defined and internalised and decisions are based on integrity and create trust and sustainability. The rewards of decisions consistently based on care, trust, professionalism, loyalty, and diligence become evident in terms of profitability, sustainability, and customer loyalty.

Not all visionary companies began life with a well-articulated core ideology or a set of well-defined values such as those shown by Johnson & Johnson. Many large and successful companies, such as Hewlett-Packard and Motorola, did not formalise their business ethics and values until after the company had solidly passed the initial start-up phase, often a decade or so after founding, but usually before they become big companies. In the early stages, most visionary companies focused on getting the business going and their ethical values only became clear as the company evolved. However, the earlier an entrepreneur

EXAMPLE 9.2

Example of a strategy to create an ethical culture in a small business

As a small business manager, you should instil in your people a set of moral guidelines and expectations that they can follow when making business decisions and taking action. However, an ethical business culture does not happen by chance and it is important that the entrepreneur understand the logic and methodology of the process and what it entails.

1. Determine the minimum level that your ethical business approach should aim to achieve.
2. Build a set of ethical standards to follow when making business decisions and consider the impact of decisions on the long-term sustainability of your business.
3. Implement your ethical standards by clearly and effectively communicating your expectations to your employees.
4. Develop an ethical code of conduct that can be distributed to employees.
5. Develop a method of monitoring compliance with the standards.
6. Encourage open discussion of ethical dilemmas amongst employees.
7. Change employee's attitude from simply looking at making short-term profits to working towards sustainable objectives.
8. Never reward performance without considering if the way in which objectives are achieved was ethical. Use the code of conduct as a guideline in this regard.
9. Lead by example.

Source: [Online]. Available: http://toolkit.smallbiz.nsw.gov.au/part/17/85/369 Reprinted by permission of Small Biz Connect at University of Western Sydney.

can sit down and apply his or her mind to the ethics and values of the business, the better (Collins and Porras, 2000:7).

9.6 Developing a code of ethics

The first decision that the entrepreneur should take is whether to make a distinction between the business's code of conduct and its code of ethics. In the South African context, the **code of conduct** could refer to the disciplinary code, which is also a document that spells out conduct requirements with associated penalties in accordance with Schedule Eight of the Labour Relations Act: Code of Good Practice: Dismissal (Act 66 of 1995). The **code of ethics**, however, should not be punitive or rule based, but should rather be inspirational and based on the company's strategic, work, and ethical values.

DEFINITION

A code of ethics is a written set of guidelines issued by an organisation to its workers and management to help them conduct their actions in accordance with its primary values and ethical standards.
Read more: http://www.businessdictionary.com/definition/code-of-ethics.html#ixzz2rXLGgMRP

Figure 9.1 provides a framework for a stake-holder-based code of ethics that can be used by the entrepreneur to establish a code of ethics within his or her own enterprise.

Figure 9.1 indicates that ethics is about what is good for the company as well as for the stakeholders. The guidelines in the code of ethics apply to both the employees and the managers of the company. They are guided by the company values, the code of ethics, and company policies and procedures in terms of their behaviour requirements towards the stakeholders. Figure 9.1 clearly shows that the values, the code of ethics, and the policies are there to deal with ethical dilemmas and to

Figure 9.1 The framework for a stakeholder-based code of ethics

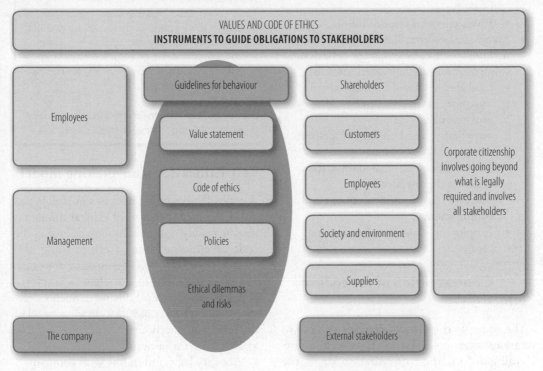

prevent ethical risks from endangering the sustainability of the company.

The guidelines in the code of ethics should focus on behaviour expected from all employees and managers towards both internal stakeholders (co-workers) and external stakeholders (customers, society, suppliers, and shareholders).

Ideally, the founder of the business, the entrepreneur, should sit down and formulate a value statement that contains the strategic, work, and ethical values on which he or she wishes to base the business. This value statement will normally form the preamble to the business's code of ethics.

9.6.1 The structure of a code of ethics

A code of ethics could take many forms, but there are a number of items that will usually appear, including:

▸ *Preamble.* The preamble is usually written by the CEO, founder or the entrepreneur and is based on the values as discussed in the previous section.

▸ *Application of the code.* A section in the beginning of the code usually indicates to whom the code applies. The code usually applies to management and employees and it could include or exclude suppliers or contractors.

▸ *General obligations.* This could be followed by broad general guidelines for all employees and managers based on the values.

▸ *Specific issues.* The code of ethics will then deal with various risk areas identified within the specific industry or business, such as:
- Conflict of interests
- Giving and receiving of gifts
- Sexual harassment
- Compliance with laws
- Customer service
- Health and safety
- Confidentiality of information

- Dealing with government and tender procedures
- Environmental responsibilities.

▶ *Specific stakeholders.* Some codes could include specific guidelines for behaviour towards various stakeholders, such as:
  - Customers – based on the value of 'customer satisfaction and professionalism'
  - Suppliers – based on fair competition and best value for money
  - The environment – based on sustainability and protection
  - Society – based on involvement and commitment
  - Employees – based on fairness and care.

9.6.2 Contravention of the code of ethics

The code of ethics could include reference to various other policies and also a section providing information on what to do if the guidelines in the code are not followed. Reference is often made to the disciplinary code and the available ethics resources, such as a whistle blowers' hotline or the grievance procedure (see Section 9.7).

Read the practical example in the box below and decide how you would react in each situation.

EXAMPLE 9.4

A code of ethics and policies and procedures are only guidelines: A practical example

Your newly appointed driver is driving your new delivery truck. He is aware of your company policy stating that company vehicles are only to be used for official business and not for private use. While busy with a delivery one day, his wife calls him to inform him that she has gone into labour. She had phoned an ambulance an hour ago but it has not arrived and she is beginning to panic. He phones the office but the phone is engaged. He phones you directly on your cellphone, but only gets through to your voice mail.

What will your reaction be in each case below?
1. The driver is so scared of you and the company policies that he does not go to assist his wife and his wife and the baby die.
2. The driver decides to go to his wife's assistance immediately. The delivery is late and the client is very upset.

Use the ethics decision-making model in Section 9.6.3 to see if it helps you to arrive at an ethical decision.

9.6.3 Ethics decision-making model

A code of ethics only serves as a guideline and given the fact that not all ethical dilemmas may be readily resolved through following the code of ethics, a code of ethics could also include an ethical decision-making tool such as a set of questions to ask when an employee is faced with an ethical dilemma. Such a decision-making tool could include some or all of the following questions:

▶ What are my options?
▶ Are they legal and in line with company policies and procedures?
▶ Is it consistent with my own and company values?
▶ Can I tell my friends, co-workers or family about this?
▶ How will it look on the front page of the newspaper?
▶ How will I feel once I have behaved in this way or taken this decision?

It might be helpful to include some universal principles in a code of ethics such as the importance of the preservation of life at all times. However, at times we need to consider which decision will hold the greatest good for the greatest majority.

The most important ingredient for the success of any code is that there should be buy-in from the employees. Employees may resist a code of ethics that has been drawn up unilaterally by the entrepreneur but they are far more likely to adhere to a code if they have been consulted and asked for their input.

EXAMPLE 9.5

An ethical decision-making model

- ▶ Step 1: Identify the problem.
- ▶ Step 2: Identify the potential issues involved.
- ▶ Step 3: Review relevant ethical guidelines.
- ▶ Step 4: Know relevant laws and regulations.
- ▶ Step 5: Consult.
- ▶ Step 6: Consider possible and probable courses of action.
- ▶ Step 7: List the consequences of the probable courses of action.
- ▶ Step 8: Decide on what appears to be the best course of action.
- ▶ Step 9: Be prepared and willing to take full responsibility for the consequences.

It is extremely important that you keep your immediate supervisor and all involved parties informed during this process. After you have made your decision, take some time to reflect on the process and to review what you have learned with a trusted supervisor or colleague.

1. Do you think this model is helpful in the resolution of ethical dilemmas?
2. What are the main points of criticism against this model and how might the model be improved?
3. Try applying this model to the ethical dilemma faced by the driver in Example 9.3.

9.7 Ethics resources

In addition to creating an ethical culture and drawing up a code of ethics, businesses should inform staff members of the various resources and mechanisms available to them to deal with ethical risks.

9.7.1 Ethics officer (ombudsman)

Big businesses go a step further after drawing up a code of ethics by appointing an ethics officer who monitors and reports on the business's compliance to the ethics code. In a small business, an ethics officer is not usually required. Instead, the role of creating an ethical culture and ensuring ethical compliance usually falls on the entrepreneur, who can delegate that responsibility to someone in human resources or finance. This person would need to be a person of integrity who is trusted by all.

9.7.2 An ethics hotline (whistle-blowers' hotline)

Bigger companies might find it necessary to obtain the services of an external supplier to provide an anonymous reporting line for more serious cases of wrongdoing. The external service provider will ensure that the identity of the reporter is kept confidential. They are under an obligation to investigate the matter reported and provide feedback to the **whistle blower** on progress made in the investigation. The final report will be provided to the board.

DEFINITION

A whistle blower is a person who exposes unethical behaviour, wrongdoing/misconduct, alleged dishonest or illegal activity in an organisation.

9.7.3 An ethics advice line

It is also advisable to make provision for a confidential ethics advice line where employees who are faced with an ethical dilemma can send an email or make a phone call to get advice on how to deal with such a dilemma. For example, if an employee is offered a gift or hospitality and he or she is not sure if it is in line with the gift policy to receive the gift, the ethics advice line can be contacted for advice. An employee who has received a study bursary from the company could also phone the advice line to check whether or not it would be acceptable to print out study material or assignments on the company printer. The ethics advice line can be contacted for advice to ensure that employees do not break company rules or unknowingly contravene policies. The ethics advice line is not anonymous but is purely there for guidance.

9.7.4 Line managers

Line managers and supervisors are key role players in dealing with ethical dilemmas. When employees are faced with an ethical dilemma they often approach their first line supervisors for advice. A supervisor needs to ensure that the advice given is legal and based on company policies and procedures. Employees often find themselves in a disciplinary enquiry having to deal with the outcome of behaviour based on poor advice from a supervisor. An unethical supervisor might not testify on behalf of the employee and will simply deny having given such advice but an ethical supervisor needs to be willing to support the employee if he or she gets into trouble and (or) causes reputational harm to the company.

It is very important for an entrepreneur to ensure that all employees are aware of the ethical values of the business and that they know that ignorance is not an excuse. Employees should know that they will be held accountable for their decisions and for the outcomes of their behaviour.

9.8 The social responsibilities of entrepreneurs

Business activities have an impact on society and entrepreneurs should use their resources to benefit people outside the business context. An organisation's social responsibility programme can help to improve relations with employees and the community. The more an organisation is seen to care for its employees, the greater the opportunity for cooperation rather that conflict (Nel et al., 2005). The entrepreneur has an obligation to the community in which the venture operates because so much of the input into the business comes from the community.

9.8.1 Stakeholders

Entrepreneurs have a social responsibility towards the business's internal and external stakeholders.

9.8.1.1 Environment

The natural environment is one of the critical areas of social responsibility and includes issues such as waste disposal and the pollution of water, air, and any natural resources. There has been a global outcry against the production and disposal of hazardous material and products and legislation has been developed to regulate all activities that could have a negative effect on the natural environment.

9.8.1.2 Customers

Entrepreneurs could adopt an attitude of social responsibility towards their customers. In adopting such a stance, the entrepreneur should know that there are four basic customer rights:

▶ The right to safe products and services
▶ The right to be informed about all relevant aspects of products and services
▶ The right to be heard in the event of a complaint
▶ The right to choose what to buy.

Socially responsible ways of dealing with customers include training employees in customer relations, providing after-sales service for all products and services rendered, and ensuring that products and services are safe and pose no danger to the health of customers.

9.8.1.3 Employees

The social responsibility of the entrepreneur towards his or her employees should extend to their families and the communities from which they come. Treating employees fairly, respecting their dignity and basic human needs, and making them part of the team could go a long way towards having a satisfied workforce. Including their immediate families in some of the benefits, such as education and training, medical aid, and social activities, could further enhance that satisfaction. The majority of larger businesses offer study loans to children and spouses, and even literacy training to spouses who cannot read or write. These are some ways in which the social responsibility towards employees from previously disadvantaged groups could be addressed. Offering equal opportunities and putting an empowerment policy in place that encourages applicants with the potential to do a job to be appointed instead of those who have specific experience in a similar job, can also be undertaken as ways of contributing to social responsibility towards employees. Preferential employment could also be used where the venture can employ the locals first before an outsider is considered for the position. Large organisations may have institutionalised social responsibility by means of an employee wellness programme (Nel et al., 2005).

9.8.1.4 **Investors**

Investors could be the co-owners or other persons who have provided financial backing to the entrepreneur. Maintaining a proper accounting system, providing information on the financial situation of the venture, and reinvesting any profits would address this responsibility. Actions such as insider trading, illegal stock manipulation, cover-ups, accepting inappropriate gifts, and withholding financial information, could have a detrimental effect on the relationships with investors. To be socially responsible towards investors, the entrepreneur should operate within the ethical code of conduct and be as transparent as possible.

9.8.1.5 **Suppliers**

The venture can also put in place a preferential procurement policy to support local suppliers. The 'global village' means that social responsibility extends beyond the borders of the country for the simple reason that most businesses are multinational and benefit from other countries. A company can show its social responsibility by refusing to do business with

a supplier from a country that has a poor human-rights record, for example.

9.8.1.6 **The general social welfare of a community**

It is an accepted norm now for entrepreneurs to be involved in the general social welfare of the community in which they do business. Involvement in health and education, contributions to charities and other related associations, and even contributions to sports development could put the company in good stead with customers. The entrepreneur could also become involved in actions aimed at correcting some of the political and social wrongs that exist, such as Business Against Crime or Lead South Africa.

A socially responsible business is more sustainable than one that shows no concern for the stakeholders, because it is supported by the community as a valuable contributor to the well-being of the community.

9.8.2 **Different approaches to social responsibility**

The level of commitment to social responsibility differs from organisation to organisation. While some companies dedicate a significant amount of time and resources to corporate citizenship, other companies barely scratch the surface with minimal compliance. Speeter (2009) identifies five different approaches to social responsibility.

▸ *Obstructionist approach.* This is a management approach that views social responsibility as an unnecessary cost item. The company also behaves irresponsibly and often illegally. Such an approach sees no relationship between the company and social or environmental community issues and sets only profit-based corporate goals.

▸ *Defensive approach.* This is a non-strategic, 'management by crisis' approach to social or environmental concerns. Although management ensures basic compliance

SOUTH AFRICAN SUCCESS STORY

Free State chicken project empowers community
Samona Naidu
5 March 2014

Grain Field Chickens, with the help of R130-million in state backing, has boosted its production from 9 000 to 130 000 chickens a day since 2012, while creating over 1 000 new jobs for people in and around Reitz in South Africa's Free State province.

During a visit to the Grain Field Chickens abattoir last week, President Jacob Zuma said this was 'great news for many families in the area. Another good story ... is that workers here at Grain Field own 23% in the business.'

He added that the people behind the project had been innovative and had not sat back and waited for the government, which had stepped in 'only at a later stage' with funding and technical assistance.

'This is the story of how you were able to take a difficult situation, like the economic recession, and turn it around into an economic and social success', he said. 'The Grain Field Chicken project proves that South Africa is a much better place to live in now. There are more opportunities that did not exist before, especially for black people'.

Grain Field MD Sas Kasselman said the company's employees were also beneficiaries of a 23.1% stake in the abattoir. 'This makes the project's success a personal success for the beneficiaries as well. It creates a social responsibility amongst employees'.

'Job growth and skills development sharing is extremely crucial to the growth of any project of this magnitude', Kasselman said. 'We ensure that employees on various levels are trained, and they in turn share their training and transfer skills to their fellow workers. It is a continuous learning environment at the abattoir'.

Employee training
An employee who has benefited from this training is Adolphina Mojatau. The 40-year-old mother of two, formerly of Bloemfontein, is now a quality supervisor at the abattoir after a year-and-a-half of skills training.

'I am very proud of what I have achieved and I am grateful to be able to work on a project that ensures the best quality for our consumers', she said.

Mojatau said a typical day at the abattoir meant slaughtering almost 50 000 chickens during the day shift and another 50 000 on the night shift.

'My team makes sure that every chicken that enters our receiving bay undergoes an antimortem. This is where we check that the chickens have no diseases, and they are healthy for consumer consumption', she said. 'It is a tough job, but we have to ensure that South Africans get the best quality product on the shelves'.

Mojatau has completed various training programmes in health and safety, food safety management, hazard training, meat inspection and examination and internal auditing and administration. She is also an internal training officer, and shares her story of growth with new employees at the abattoir.

'In such a short time, I have been promoted three times. This is not a company that one enters as a general worker and stays put for years at that level. The opportunity for growth is endless. That is what motivates me, and allows me to inspire others working here', she said.

According to Mojatau, many South Africans, especially those in the rural areas, do not know much about the poultry industry and the opportunities it offers.

'Government is providing so many opportunities, but people cannot sit back and wait for a job to fall into their laps, they must be active and open to new challenges', Mojatau said.

Grain Field Chickens supplies local and neighbouring markets and national stores across South Africa.

Job-creation funding was provided by South Africa's Department of Labour through the Unemployment Insurance Fund and the Industrial Development Corporation.

Source: SAnews.gov.za [Online]. Available: http://www.southafrica.info/business/success/abattoir-050314. htm#ixzz2wWQ2Nirp

with environmental, labour, safety, and health regulations, the focus is also mainly on the profit motive. Any corporate social responsibility initiative is only tolerated for the fact that it is a great marketing tool to attract more clients.

▶ *Strategic or accommodative approach.* A corporate social responsibility plan is developed with a dedicated budget, but in a highly compartmentalised manner. Social responsibility objectives are incorporated into the business mission, values and vision, and initiatives are selected that positively affect business outcomes, such as environmental efficiency or socially responsible product lines.

▶ *Assimilated approach.* All the stakeholders are involved in determining the various social and environmental needs. The social responsibility goals are incorporated into all business operations and policies. Benchmarks are established and tracked internally and within the industry.

▶ *Altruistic approach.* The primary corporate mission is focused on creating a better society or environment, and products and services are aligned to fulfil the corporate social responsibility mission. Marketing and communications are dedicated to enhancing community, national or global awareness of causes, and there are even attempts to affect public policy.

Although the above approaches might be only of academic interest for entrepreneurs, they can serve as a guideline to initiate the conversation of how to move to the next level. It is important to realise that a business can and should continue to evolve to achieve a higher level of social and ethical responsibility.

CONCLUSION

The ethics of entrepreneurship is essentially about behaviour that is honest, fair, and transparent. If the entrepreneur is a person with integrity, his or her personal values will set the tone for the ethical climate in the business. Any new entrepreneur is advised to draw up a value statement that will guide the employees and managers of the new venture in their decision-making processes. As the business grows and assumes a more complex business model, it becomes necessary to also draw up various policies and procedures and a code of ethics based on the business risks and the values as identified by the entrepreneur.

When necessary, various ethics resources can be provided such as an ethics officer, a whistle-blowers' hotline and an ethics advice line. Ethics awareness training for all employees should also be considered. Businesses tend to go through various ethical modes as they mature and develop. Ethics may need to be managed differently at each stage and the business's code of ethics and ethical culture may also need to change in response. No business operates in isolation, and businesses need to be sensitive to the needs of the society and ensure that they deal with all the stakeholders in a fair, transparent, and responsible manner. A positive relationship between a business and its environment, based on mutual respect and social responsibility, is a requirement for a successful and sustainable business.

SELF-ASSESSMENT QUESTIONS

Multiple-choice questions

1. The willingness to report unethical behaviour through a whistle blowing line or an ethics hotline is determined by a trade off between which two values?
   a. Fairness and honesty
   b. Honesty and loyalty
   c. Diligence and dignity
   d. Fairness and loyalty
   e. Justice and trust
2. Which one of the following values is not an ethical value?
   a. Accountability
   b. Integrity
   c. Teamwork
   d. Respect
   e. Trust
3. Laws, rules and regulations can ensure ethical behaviour.
   a. True
   b. False
4. In which mode of managing ethics does the entrepreneur find himself or herself if ethical values are internalised and there is a value-based approach to ethics?
   a. Immoral mode
   b. Reactive mode
   c. Compliance mode
   d. Integrity mode
5. The ethics advice line is:
   a. Anonymous and the advice must be followed
   b. Managed by an outside consultant
   c. The same as the ethics hotline
   d. Not anonymous but is purely there for guidance
   e. An instrument to enable management to find out what employees are up to

DISCUSSION QUESTIONS

1. Discuss the difference between an ethics helpline and a whistle-blowing hotline.
2. List the stakeholders involved in managing ethics in the workplace.
3. Explain how strategic, work, and ethical values manifest in the workplace.
4. Discuss the impact of an entrepreneur's personal ethics on the venture.
5. Identify and discuss the various modes of managing ethics in organisations.
6. Discuss the requirements to implement any code of ethics successfully in an organisation.
7. Discuss the creation of an ethical culture in an organisation.
8. Define 'social responsibility', discuss the areas of social responsibility and how the entrepreneur could address each one.
9. Discuss the various approaches to social responsibility.
10. Develop your own ethics decision-making model for a business.

EXPERIENTIAL EXERCISE

Use the South Africa success story about Grain Field Chickens to discuss the following:
▶ Identify the stakeholders in this business when it comes to ethics.
▶ Which mode of managing ethics would you say this organisation finds itself?
▶ Formulate the vision and mission of the organisation based on the information in the case study.

▶ Identify the values that you think are driving this organisation. Formulate a value statement for the organisation.
▶ Draw up a short code of ethics.
▶ Decide how you are going to implement the programme:
  ▪ Who will deal with ethical issues (e.g. HR, finance, the CEO, and ethics officer, etc.)?
  ▪ Do you think it is necessary to have an ethics hotline or an ethics helpline? Give reasons for your decision.

▪ How will you promote the code of ethics, the values, and the ethical culture (e.g. live out values every day, ethics talk, ethics as an agenda point on monthly staff meetings, etc.)?
▪ Will you reward ethical behaviour? If yes, how?
▪ How will you communicate with employees (e.g. by email, a website, banners and posters, monthly newsletters, training, etc.)?
▶ Write a concluding paragraph on the integrity of this organisation.

HELPING AN EX-EMPLOYEE

An owner of a lodge had an argument with an employee. The employee left and told fellow workers that he didn't want to work at that employer anymore. He had insurance that would cover his debt at a local furniture store in case he lost his employment due to dismissal. He wanted the employer to give him a letter stating that he was dismissed to be able to claim against the insurance company to cover the debt of the furniture.

1. If you were the employer, would you give the employee a letter stating that he was dismissed if you knew what he needed the letter for?
2. Discuss the various values that would come into effect if the employer assisted the employee.

CASE STUDY

SUGGESTED WEBSITE LINKS

http://www.sciencedirect.com/science/article/pii/S0022103113001352

http://www.darden.virginia.edu/web/uploadedFiles/Darden/Faculty_Research/Directory/Full_time/Harris_Sapienza_Bowie_2009.pdf

Ethics and entrepreneurship Jared D. Harris, Harry J. Sapienza, Norman E. Bowie, *Journal of Business Venturing* 24 (2009) 407–418: http://www.sciencedirect.com/science/article/pii/S0883902608000748

Entrepreneurship, innovation, and corruption Sergey Anokhin: http://www.sciencedirect.com/science/article/pii/S0883902608000748> and William S. Schulze <http://www.sciencedirect.com/science/article/pii/S0883902608000748>

Journal of Business Venturing: <http://www.sciencedirect.com/science/journal/08839026>, Volume 24, Issue 5 <http://www.sciencedirect.com/science/journal/08839026/24/5>, September 2009, Pages 465–476.

Special Issue Ethics and Entrepreneurship: http://www.sciencedirect.com/science/article/pii/S0883902608000505

Self-regulation and moral awareness among entrepreneurs Peter Bryant: <http://www.sciencedirect.com/science/article/pii/S0883902608000505>

Journal of Business Venturing: <http://www.sciencedirect.com/science/journal/08839026> . Volume 24, Issue 5 <http://www.sciencedirect.com/science/journal/08839026/24/5>, September 2009, Pages 505–518

Special Issue Ethics and Entrepreneurship: http://www.ehow.com/info_7756044_code-ethics-entrepreneurs.html

The Code of Ethics for Entrepreneurs By Jagg Xaxx, eHow Contributor: http://www.entrepreneurship.org/resource-center/core-values-for-ethical-entrepreneurship.aspx

Core Values for Ethical Entrepreneurship Michelle Benjamin, Founder, President and CEO, Benjamin Enterprises Inc.: <http://www.benjaminenterprises.com> http://www.ethicsandentrepreneurship.org/wp-content/uploads/2009/08/Hicks-What-Business-Ethics-Can-Learn.pdf

REFERENCES

Collins, CJ. & Porras, JI. 2000. *Built to Last: Successful Habits of Visionary Companies.* 3rd ed. London: Random House Business Books.

David, FR. 1995. *Concepts of Strategic Management.* Englewood Cliffs, N.J.: Prentice-Hall.

Hoyk, R. & Hersey, P. 2009. *The Ethical Executive: Avoiding the Traps of the Unethical Workplace.* London: Kogan Page.

King, ME. (Chair). 2009. *King III Report on Governance for South Africa*, 1 September 2009. [Online]. Available: http://african.ipapercms.dk/IOD/KINGIII/kingiiireport/ [1 August 2011].

Nel, PS, Swanepoel, BJ, Kirsten, M, Erasmus, BJ. & Tsabadi, MJ. 2005. *South African Employment Relations. Theory and Practice.* Pretoria: Van Schaik.

Rossouw, D and Van Vuuren, L. 2006. *Business Ethics.* 3rd ed. Cape Town: Oxford University Press.

Speeter, L. 2009. Checklist: What's your level of corporate social responsibility? *The Altruistic Marketer: Fostering Corporate Excellence for the Greater Good.* [Online]. Available: http://altruisticmarketer.wordpress.com/2009/0/26/checklist-what%E2%0%99s-your-levelof-corporate-social-responsibility/ [24 February 2011].

CHAPTER 10

Basic financial concepts

Stefan Bezuidenhout

LEARNING OUTCOMES

On completion of this chapter, you will be able to:
▶ Describe the purpose of accounting
▶ Explain the basic accounting cycle
▶ Define 'entity' and explain the concept
▶ Explain the purpose of financial statements
▶ Define and classify income, expenses, assets, equity, and liabilities
▶ Prepare an elementary statement of comprehensive income (income statement) and statement of financial position (balance sheet)
▶ Discuss the duality concept
▶ Describe the users of financial statements and their information needs
▶ Discuss the management of assets, equity and liabilities
▶ Discuss the use of financial ratios and how they can help you to manage your finances
▶ Conduct a financial-ratio analysis
▶ Discuss the use of the balanced scorecard as a financial performance management tool
▶ Name and discuss the various sources of finance and the circumstances in which they can be used.

OPENING CASE STUDY

In today's world, it can be said that everything revolves around money. If you embark on starting your own venture, it can be a venture that is for-profit or even a venture that is a non-profit organisation. In the end, it does not matter which type of venture you will be starting, you will have to work with money. You must have the basic knowledge of financial terminologies and concepts in order to survive in the business world. Ask yourself, do you really know what assets, equity, liabilities, income and expenses are? Have you heard about financial statements? What is the purpose of these statements? What financial knowledge do you need in order to analyse and manage your finances? It is important to realise

that the financial statements in this chapter will not correspond with the precise formats as prescribed by the International Financial Reporting Standards (IFRS). The purpose of this chapter is not to provide information on how to do accounting, but rather to understand certain financial concepts that an entrepreneur will use, not only to complete the financial plan, but also in making certain financially orientated decisions.

1. Do you think an entrepreneur should have a basic knowledge and understanding of financial terminologies and concepts?

2. Where do you think an entrepreneur will apply his or her knowledge of financial terminologies and concepts?

INTRODUCTION

In this chapter we will look at the meaning of accounting and what role it plays in an entity's financial activities. In order to understand various financial terminologies we will also look at the various financial statements you may encounter on your journey and explore where these terminologies are used in these statements. We will further explore who the various parties are that can also make use of financial information. This chapter will also look at the management of finances, providing information on the analysis of financials in order for you to make better decisions so that you can manage your finances better. Lastly, this chapter will provide you with various sources that you can make use of if you need to obtain additional funds to finance your capital requirements.

10.1 Accounting

DEFINITION

Accounting can be defined as a continuous scientific process that involves bookkeeping and reporting.

Accounting is a science because every transaction that is recorded can be analysed. It is a continuous process because once the accounting cycle is complete, it starts all over again, as is illustrated in Figure 10.1.

Accounting can be divided into two domains, namely, **financial accounting** and **management accounting**.

DEFINITION

Financial accounting is the reporting on financial activities to external users of financial information.

Financial accounting is a medium through which financial information is communicated to interested parties of the business entity by means of three primary statements, namely, a statement of comprehensive income (income statement), a statement of financial position (balance sheet), and a statement of cash flows (cash-flow statement). These statements assist in decision making at different levels. Financial accounting caters thus mainly for external users of financial information.

DEFINITION

Management accounting is the reporting on financial activities to internal users of financial information.

Management accounting, on the other hand, is concerned with reporting on specific activities inside the business and caters mainly for internal users of financial information These users are primarily the internal management and operational personnel of the business entity. They require a wide variety of financial information in order to manage the entity on a day-to-day basis.

SOUTH AFRICAN SUCCESS STORY

Learning the language of business is important
Visit the following site for an interesting article on how scientific ideas were transformed into financial reward: http://www.entrepreneurmag.co.za/advice/success-stories/entrepreneur-profiles/governance-value-creation-massive-business-growth/

Figure 10.1 A basic accounting cycle

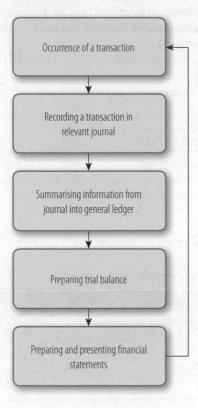

An accounting cycle, as is depicted in Figure 10.1, is completed within a financial year. A financial year is any 12 months following one another. For example, business entities such as sole proprietorships and partnerships may choose a financial year that runs from 1 March to 28 February to streamline their personal income earned period with the South African Revenue Service (SARS) period for personal income tax returns. Companies may choose, for example, to have their financial years running from 1 July to 30 June, also for tax purposes.

DEFINITION

An entity means an economic unit that operates separately from other units and whose financial statements are recorded separately from any other unit.

An **entity** can be a person, partnership, close corporation, company or charitable organisation. The economic activities of an entity are measured in monetary terms.

Accounting firstly involves bookkeeping, which refers to the recording of each transaction in its relevant journal(s). Secondly, accounting involves reporting, which refers to the reporting on an entity's:
▸ Financial performance
▸ Financial position
▸ Cash flow.

Financial reporting is usually done by preparing and presenting financial statements.

10.2 **Financial statements**

DEFINITION

Financial statements are used to report on that entity's financial performance, financial position, and cash-flow situation.

This information is useful for economic decision making by a broad range of users who are not in a position to demand reports tailored to meet their particular information needs.

Three primary **financial statements** are used for reporting purposes:
▸ Statement of profit or loss and other comprehensive income (income statement)
▸ Statement of financial position (balance sheet)
▸ Statement of cash flows (cash-flow statement).

The example statements provided below are independent of each other.

10.2.1 The statement of profit or loss and other comprehensive income (income statement)

To report on the financial performance of an enterprise, a statement of profit or loss and other comprehensive income is prepared and presented. This statement reflects the financial information of an entity that relates to its income and expenditures in order to determine whether a profit or loss has been realised over a specific financial or accounting period, usually at the end of an enterprise's financial year. An example of a very basic format of a statement of profit or loss and other comprehensive income for a sole proprietorship is illustrated in Table 10.1.

10.2.1.1 Defining the elements of a statement of profit or loss and other comprehensive income (income statement)

From the statement of profit or loss and other comprehensive income, as illustrated in Table 10.1, **income** and **expenses** can be defined as follows:

DEFINITION

Income can be defined as the increases in economic benefits during an accounting period in the form of an increase or inflow of assets, or otherwise the decrease in liabilities that leads to an increase in equity.

Table 10.1 Statement of profit or loss and other comprehensive income for a sole proprietorship

MAKHADO GENERAL DEALER	
Statement of profit or loss and other comprehensive income for the year ended 30 June 2014	**R**
Sales (or fees received in the case of a service-delivery enterprise)	1 500 000
Cost of sales (not applicable in the case of a service-delivery enterprise)	(1 200 000)
Gross profit (not applicable in the case of a service-delivery enterprise)	300 000
Other income	160 000
Rent income	120 000
Interest income	40 000
Other expenses	(131 400)
Water and electricity	(14 400))
Rates and taxes	(12 000)
Depreciation	(10 000)
Salary and wages	(60 000)
Telephone	(10 000)
Stationery (consumed/used)	(5 000)
Repairs and maintenance	(5 000)
Insurance	(15 000)
Finance cost (Interest expense)	(24 000)
Profit /(loss) for the year	304 600

The definition of income excludes increases because of owners' contributions. In layperson's terms, this means that an income is any money that was earned in an entity during a specific accounting period, whether the money has been received or not. Examples of this term can be seen in Table 10.1.

⟮ DEFINITION ⟯

Expenses can be defined as the decreases in economic benefits during an accounting period, in the form of an outflow or decrease in assets, or otherwise the increase in liabilities that leads to a decrease in equity.

The definition of **expenses** excludes decreases because of distributions to owners. This means that an expense is any money that was spent or is due to be spent in the operation of an entity during a specific accounting period. Examples can be seen in Table 10.1.

⟮ DEFINITION ⟯

Gross profit is the profit that was made on the trading activities of a trading entity.

Gross profit is therefore the profit that remains after the cost of getting the goods to be sold (cost of sales) is subtracted from the sales (cost price + profit) earned from selling those goods.

⟮ DEFINITION ⟯

Profit is realised when all the expenses are subtracted from all the income, and the income exceeds the expenses.

⟮ DEFINITION ⟯

Loss is realised when all the expenses are subtracted from all the income but, in this case, the expenses exceed the income.

The primary objective of any profit-making business is to make a profit. Even a non-profit organisation has a primary objective of ensuring that its income exceeds its expenses to realise a surplus of funds.

10.2.2 **The statement of financial position (balance sheet)**

The statement of financial position is prepared and presented to report on the financial position of an enterprise at a particular point in time. It reflects the financial wealth of the entity in terms of the assets owned by the entity and the interest of various parties in these assets. The statement of financial position is also based on the **duality concept**.

⟮ DEFINITION ⟯

The duality concept can be defined as the assets of an entity are equal to the equity and liabilities of the entity.

In layperson's terms, this is known as the constitution of accounting and entails that the money generated, either from inside the business (owner's capital contribution) or outside the business (through long-term loans from banks and (or) from creditors), must be equal to where the money has been applied (assets). This is illustrated in Figure 10.2.

The fundamental accounting equation shown in Figure 10.2 is based on the duality concept, which is illustrated in Figure 10.3.

An example of a basic format of a statement of financial position for a sole proprietorship is illustrated in Table 10.2.

Figure 10.2 The constitution of accounting

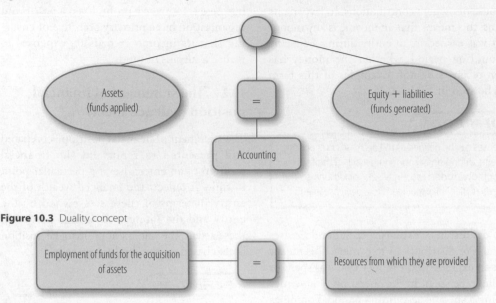

Figure 10.3 Duality concept

| Employment of funds for the acquisition of assets | = | Resources from which they are provided |

10.2.2.1 Defining the elements of a statement of financial position (balance sheet)

From the statement of financial position (balance sheet), as illustrated in Table 10.2, **assets**, **equity**, and **liabilities** can be defined as follows:

> **DEFINITION**
>
> Assets are resources that are controlled by an entity as a result of past events, from which future economic benefits will flow to the entity.

In layperson's terms, this means that an asset is something that an entity owns or possesses. Assets are divided into **non-current assets** and current assets.

> **DEFINITION**
>
> Non-current assets can be defined as assets that will not be converted into cash within the following 12 months.

Examples of non-current assets can be seen in Table 10.2. Previously, these assets were also known as fixed assets as they form part of the entity for a long period of time. Examples of these assets are: land and buildings, vehicles, machinery and equipment, and furniture. From the above-mentioned examples, it is clear that non-current assets are rather expensive assets within an entity, and therefore, it is of utmost importance that an entrepreneur considers his or her financial position before a non-current asset is obtained.

An entrepreneur has to determine the quantity of non-current assets required as well as the purchasing price of the assets. The entrepreneur must also determine whether it will be cheaper to purchase or to hire the non-current asset. When land and buildings are purchased, it is important to remember that land seldom loses value. Land usually appreciates in value and then the entity gains value in terms of its non-current assets.

The cost of a non-current asset is calculated in terms of the cash (or equivalent monetary value) necessary to purchase the asset, as well as all the additional expenses that may be

Table 10.2 Statement of financial position for a sole proprietorship

MAKHADO GENERAL DEALER	
Statement of financial position as at 30 June 2014	**R**
ASSETS	
Non-current assets	1 014 000
Property, plant, and equipment	1 000 000
Investments	14 000
Current assets	2 140 600
Inventories	1 300 000
Trade receivables	250 000
Other current assets	85 600
Cash and cash equivalents	505 000
Total assets	3 154 600
EQUITY AND LIABILITIES	
Equity	804 600
Non-current liabilities	1 736 000
Long-term loan	1 736 000
Current liabilities	614 000
Trade and other payables	350 000
Current portion of long-term loan	264 000
Total equity and liabilities	3 154 600

EXAMPLE 10.1

Determination of the cost price of premises

Mboneni Cellphone Traders acquires a premise that consists of an existing building at a cost of R250 000. Mboneni Cellphone Traders's intention is to erect a cellphone wholesale store on this site. According to the agreement of sale, the agent's commission of 10% (R25 000) is payable by the purchaser. Transfer and other legal costs pertaining to the transaction amount to R15 000. The cost of demolishing the old building is R18 000, while material from the demolished building is sold for R5 000. The cost of excavating the site for erection of the new building is R35 000. Mboneni Cellphone Traders raised a mortgage bond of R450 000 to purchase the land. Bond charges of R45 000 are still payable.

The cost price of the site can now be determined as follows:

	R
Net purchase price	250 000
Plus: Agent's commission	25 000
Plus: Transfer and other legal costs	15 000
Plus: Net demolition costs (R18 000 – R5 000)	13 000
Equals: Total cost price	303 000

necessary to get the asset into a condition and location so that it is ready for use. These expenses include the purchase price, legal costs, transport costs, and installation costs. Financing costs on loans raised to acquire the asset are not included. Maintenance costs must also be distinguished because these costs will be written off as an expense. The determination of a cost price is illustrated in Example 10.1.

Equipment, furniture, and vehicles depreciate in value (lose value), and the entrepreneur must make provision for the depreciation of the value of these non-current assets. The depreciation of non-current assets is tax-deductible, provided the amount of the depreciation meets certain guidelines set down by the South African Revenue Service (SARS). When depreciation is claimed as an expense for tax purposes, it is known as a wear-and-tear allowance. SARS prescribes rates of wear-and-tear allowances for different assets. Historically, these rates are applied on the diminishing balance depreciation method as shown in Example 10.2. The Example 10.3 thereafter illustrates the straight-line depreciation method.

The method where depreciation is calculated on the historical cost (or historic depreciable amount) is called the straight-line depreciation method (see Example 10.3). Using the straight-line depreciation method, the carrying amount of the truck would be reduced to zero after three years. Using the reducing-balance method, the carrying amount

EXAMPLE 10.2

Example of the diminishing balance depreciation method

You bought a new heavy-duty truck at the beginning of your financial year for R1 200 000. You have estimated that you will use the truck for a period of three years (useful life), and you have not estimated what the truck will be worth at the end of its useful life (there is thus no residual value).

If we had to calculate depreciation for the three years at 30% per annum, the depreciation per annum will be calculated as follows:

		R
Cost price of new vehicle		1 200 000
Depreciation deduction in the first year:	R1 200 000 x 30% =	(360 000)
Depreciation deduction in the second year:	(R1 200 000 – R360 000) x 30% =	(252 000)
Depreciation deduction in the third year:	(R1 200 000 – R360 000 – R252 000) x 30% =	176 400
Carrying amount (book value) of the vehicle after three years	R1 200 000 – R360 000 – R252 000 – R176 400 =	411 600

The diminishing balance method requires that depreciation is calculated on the current carrying amount of the asset, and not to its historic cost. The carrying amount (book value) is also known as the assets net realisable value, which means that it represents an estimated amount of what the asset is worth at a specific point in time. The carrying amount is calculated as the cost price of an asset less all the accumulated depreciation. It is important to remember that an asset is depreciated over the useful life that the asset will have in your entity and that depreciation will be calculated from the date that the asset is ready for use.

---

of the assets is reduced by a smaller amount each year, thus implying that the carrying amount approaches but never actually reaches zero.

Since April 1993, SARS has allowed taxpayers to use the straight-line depreciation method, without making a special application.

The other side of the matter should also be taken into consideration. Higher allowances lead to lower profits, but cash, not profits, is what creates value. Financial markets have been shown to react positively when firms change their methods of calculating allowances, in such a way that a higher cash flow results.

Many firms believe that the economic life of their assets differs from that implied by the rates allowed by SARS. These firms will depreciate some or all of their assets at rates different from the wear-and-tear rates. By choosing, for example, a lower rate for depreciation, which they show in their published accounts, they will reflect a higher profit figure. These firms, therefore, need to keep two asset registers: one reflecting the carrying amount of the assets for tax purposes, and the other reflecting the carrying amounts as per published accounts.

It is important to remember that the carrying amount of an asset can differ substantially from its actual market value. If an asset is sold in the market, and the market price (selling price) is higher than the carrying amount, the business must pay tax on this difference. The reason for this is that the asset was over-depreciated, and this must be recaptured when the asset is sold. If the carrying amount exceeds the market value, then the difference is treated as a loss for tax purposes. This is a tax saving for the business.

An entrepreneur has to decide how much capital is needed to finance its non-current asset needs, and also weigh this up against its long-term liabilities.

EXAMPLE 10.3

Example of the straight-line depreciation method

You bought a new heavy-duty truck at the beginning of your financial year for R1 200 000 (the same value as used in Example 10.2). In this case, the straight-line method of deducting depreciation will be used. If depreciation is calculated over three years at 30% per annum, the depreciation per annum will be as follows:

		R
Cost price of new vehicle		1 200 000
Depreciation deduction in the first year:	R1 200 000 x 30% =	(360 000)
Depreciation deduction in the second year:		(360 000)
Depreciation deduction in the third year:		(360 000)
Carrying amount (book value) of the vehicle after three years		120 000

From a cash flow perspective, this is a better method to use, as higher wear and tear allowances result in the early years. Cash inflows received earlier are more valuable because of the time value of money. Firms should thus prefer to use the straight-line method whenever possible.

DEFINITION

Current assets are those assets that can be converted into cash within the following 12 months.

Current assets are also known as operating assets and form part of the enterprise for a short period of time. Examples can be seen in Table 10.2.

DEFINITION

Equity is the remaining interest in assets after liabilities (obligations) have been deducted from assets. It also represents an owner's interest in assets against which creditors have no claim.

An example of equity is where an owner has contributed capital to the business to get the business up and running. It is however important to remember that any income will lead to an increase in equity, while any expense will lead to a decrease in equity. The equity to be included in a statement of financial position can also be calculated by using a statement of changes in equity. A simple example (for a sole proprietorship) is provided in Table 10.3.

Table 10.3 Statement of changes in equity for a sole proprietorship

MAKHADO GENERAL DEALER	
STATEMENT OF CHANGES IN EQUITY FOR THE YEAR ENDED 30 JUNE 2014	**R**
Capital: Balance at the beginning of the financial year	500 000
Capital contributions made during the year	0
Drawings made during the year (for the owner's personal use)	0
Profit for the year (as was determined in the statement of comprehensive income)	304 600
Capital: Balance at the end of the financial year	804 600

> **DEFINITION**
>
> Liabilities can be defined as present obligations that arose from past events and the settlement thereof will cause an outflow of future economic resources.

In layperson's terms, liabilities can be described as the debt of an enterprise, which the enterprise will need to pay back in future. Liabilities are also divided into non-current and current liabilities.

> **DEFINITION**
>
> Non-current liabilities can be defined as obligations that will not be paid back within the following 12 months.

An example of non-current liabilities is a long-term loan, such as a mortgage bond.

> **DEFINITION**
>
> Current liabilities are those obligations that will be paid back within the following 12 months. These liabilities are also known as operating liabilities and form part of the enterprise for a short period of time. Examples can be seen in Table 10.2.

10.2.3 The statement of cash flows (cash-flow statement)

Information about the changes in cash and cash equivalents of an enterprise for an accounting period is presented in the enterprise's statement of cash flows. Cash flows are inflows and outflows of cash and cash equivalents. An example of a basic format of a statement of cash flows for a sole proprietorship is illustrated in Table 10.4.

The example above is based on the direct method where the operational activities of the business are investigated directly. The statement of cash flows consists of three sections:
▸ Cash flows from operating activities (A)
▸ Cash flows from investing activities (B)
▸ Cash flows from financing activities (C).

Section A (cash flows from operating activities) investigates the operational activities of the business directly. It determines how much cash was received from clients through selling activities (not only from cash sales but also determining how much cash was received from debtors to whom goods were previously sold on credit). It further determines how much cash was paid out towards getting stock from suppliers or repaying suppliers for earlier credit purchases. Cash received from other income items during the entity's operation and cash paid towards expenses in order for the business to operate are also recorded in this section.

Section B (cash flows from investing activities) determines the amount of cash that was spent on investing in the business and also how much cash was received from selling some of these investments. The investments that are referred to here are, firstly, those items that will form part of an enterprise's non-current assets. It is generally accepted that an owner invests in his or her business if new or additional land, buildings, equipment, furniture, and vehicles are purchased for the business. The business can now utilise these non-current assets to help generate economic benefits. When these assets are sold or disposed of, any proceeds (not the profits or losses made, but the full selling price that was received as cash) must be recognised and disclosed in this section. Secondly, there can also be money paid for other (normal) non-current or long-term investments made, such as fixed deposits or monies received from such long-term investments. These are all recorded in this section.

In Section C (cash flows from financing activities) the cash paid or received for capital contributions or loans are recorded. Only the long-term loans or non-current liabilities are taken into account in this section. In layperson's terms, this section investigates the non-current sources of finances that may be internal, through the capital contributions of the owner, or external, through long-term loans from, for example, financial institutions.

Table 10.4 Statement of cash flows for a sole proprietorship

MAKHADO GENERAL DEALER		
STATEMENT OF CASH FLOWS FOR THE YEAR ENDED 30 JUNE 2014	**R**	
Cash flows from operating activities	739 000	A
Cash received from clients	1 873 000	
Cash paid to suppliers and employees	(1 150 000)	
Cash generated by operations	723 000	
Interest received	40 000	
Interest paid	(24 000)	
Drawings by owner	0	
Cash flows from investing activities	(260 000)	B
Purchase of property plant and equipment:		
– Additions for expansions	(200 000)	
– Replacements	(60 000)	
Proceeds from sale of investment	0	
Proceeds from the sale of property, plant and equipment	0	
Cash flows from financing activities	(24 000)	C
Increase in capital contribution	0	
Increase in loan	0	
Payment of loan	(24 000)	
Net decrease in cash and cash equivalents	455 000	A + B + C
Cash and cash equivalents at the beginning of period	50 000	
Cash and cash equivalents at end of period	505 000	

The statement of cash flows thus presents a picture to the users of financial statements of the sources of the enterprise's cash as well as indicating where cash has been applied or paid out. It also helps users of financial statements to get a better idea of an entity's liquidity.

10.2.4 The users of financial statements

To determine the nature of the information needs of the various parties interested in an enterprise, it is important not only to understand the function of information, namely to support decision making, but also to know who the users are. The users of financial information are summarised in Figure 10.4.

What types of information can be explored?

▶ *Qualitative information.* Information that is not expressed in numeric terms.
▶ *Quantitative information.* Information that is expressed in a numeric format. Quantitative information can be divided into financial and non-financial information.

Figure 10.4 Users of financial information

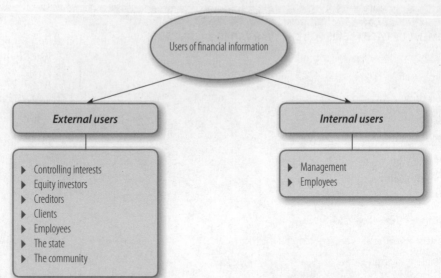

- *Financial information.* Information that is expressed in a numeric format that is of a financial nature. This can be divided into monetary and non-monetary information.
  - ○ *Monetary information.* This is financial information expressed in terms of a currency (e.g. rands).
  - ○ *Non-monetary information.* This is financial information that is not expressed in currency, but in terms such as financial ratios, percentages, quantities, and so on.
- *Non-financial information.* Numeric information that is not of a financial nature.

10.3 Financial management

Management in general involves planning, leading, organising, and controlling the enterprise's activities. With the management of an entity's finances these activities all take place with the focus on the financial affairs of the enterprise. The aim is not only to maximise an entity's profits but also to maximise the returns on what was invested in the entity in the form of the return on investment (ROI) and the return on equity (ROE).

10.3.1 The management of assets

Remember that assets are defined as resources that are controlled by an entity as a result of past events and from which future economic benefits will flow into the entity. This means that an enterprise's resources or assets need to be managed to ensure that they will enable the enterprise to generate an income.

10.3.1.1 The management of non-current assets

All non-current assets (land, buildings, equipment and machinery, furniture and vehicles) must be managed in such a way that the optimal use can be obtained from them, which will enable the entity to generate optimum future economic benefits.

For example, a pie-baking enterprise will need an oven in order to bake the pies. The oven will form part of equipment and is a non-current asset as it will be used by the entity for a period longer than the coming 12 months. The pies baked in the oven can then be sold to customers for the business to generate an income (economic benefits). If the business does not manage and account for the use of the oven effectively and efficiently, there will be inconsistencies in the quantity and quality of the pies baked. As a result, the business will not perform optimally (efficiently and effectively) at baking pies for income and the profits and returns on invested capital will not be maximised.

10.3.1.2 **The management of current assets**

The current assets can consist of the following: inventory (stock), debtors, and cash and cash equivalents.

▸ *Inventory* (stock) is an asset that is purchased for resale purposes. The inventory must be managed in such a way that:
  ▪ It does not cost too much money to store it (storage or warehousing costs)
  ▪ Perishable goods are not retained on the shelves for too long as the entity will lose money if the goods perish
  ▪ The turnover rate of inventory is satisfactory, meaning that stock must come into the entity and be sold regularly so that it is converted into sales, as quickly as possible
  ▪ An optimum level of stock must be kept to insure that there is always stock on hand. An inventory system like the first-in-first-out (FIFO) or just-in-time (JIT) systems can be decided upon to help in this regard.
▸ *Debtors* are created once sales have been done on a credit basis. It is very important that potential debtors' creditworthiness is determined before goods are sold on credit. The creditworthiness of a potential debtor refers to his or her willingness and ability to pay the outstanding debt. Certain entities only rely on information that is obtained from credit bureaus. Credit bureaus, such as the Information

Trust Corporation (ITC), can only report on defaults and judgements of people or businesses that have already happened elsewhere. This is helpful, but what if a potential debtor is not blacklisted? It does not mean that the potential debtor has an excellent credit record and is really creditworthy. To determine a potential customer's creditworthiness, a credit vetting process must be done. The following need to be taken into account:
  ▪ The character of the applicant, particularly the willingness of the person or entity to pay as agreed
  ▪ The capacity of the applicant, referring to the applicant's ability to pay
  ▪ Capital, which is the financial strength of the applicant
  ▪ Collateral, referring to the security that an applicant can offer in case of default
  ▪ Climate (condition), which describes the circumstances in which the entity is running its business
  ▪ Credit history, referring to the way the applicant has managed accounts in the past
  ▪ Common sense or good judgement, which refers to your own experience and observation.
▸ A credit policy must be developed and needs to cover the following:
  ▪ How much credit will be allowed?
  ▪ To whom will credit be allowed?
  ▪ What will the credit terms be?
  ▪ What procedures regarding the collection of outstanding fees will be followed?
  ▪ How do you retain your 'credit' customers?
▸ The main components of a credit policy are vested in the credit terms and the credit risk. An enterprise has to decide how much credit risk it is willing to accept. This then needs to be built into the enterprise's credit policy and should be reflected in the enterprise's credit terms.

▶ Debtors' outstanding monies need to be collected as soon as possible, as the cash from debtors can help to pay for other expenses and help to make payments to creditors. The longer it takes to collect monies from debtors, the more difficult it becomes. Remember that a sales transaction is not a concluded sales transaction, until the money is in the bank.

▶ *Cash and cash equivalents.* The continuous process of turning over cash into inventory and turning over debtors into cash leads to the inflow and outflow of cash in an entity. The actual amount of cash, because of the operational risk factor, is unknown. A lack of synchronisation between these movements of cash leads to the unavoidable keeping of cash assets. How much cash an entity needs to have available can only be determined once it is clear why the enterprise wants to have cash available. Three motives for keeping cash readily available are:

- The transaction motive: to finance current transactions for the continuation of the production or operational process
- The provision motive: to provide for unforeseen circumstances, since too little cash on hand can lead to illiquidity and the entity can fail, but too much cash on hand can cause an entity to lose interest on an investment that could have been made
- The speculative motive: entities can keep cash on hand to benefit from price changes and interest rate changes. For example, items may be sold at special prices or profitable short-term investments may be made. An objective decision is almost impossible and will depend on the judgement of the individual entrepreneur.

▶ It is very important for an entrepreneur to prepare a cash budget to plan the inflows and outflow of cash, and then to keep to this plan in the operation of the business.

10.3.1.3 The management of equity

Part of the primary objective of an entity is to maximise the returns on what was invested in the entity in terms of the return on investment (ROI) and the return on equity (ROE). An entity's equity and finance structure must always be managed in such a way that there is a good return on what was invested into the business. Remember that the higher the risks, the higher the returns, but one has to play it safe to ensure that the investment made into the entity will yield in a growth on that investment. One has to carefully find a balance between the risks and the returns involved. The optimal capital structure is reached at the point where the weighted average cost of capital is minimised, thereby maximising the entity's value.

10.3.1.4 The management of liabilities

Having credit, whether non-current or current, implies that you are building your own credit record. This means that you are building on your own creditworthiness. Liabilities must be managed in such a way that your creditworthiness and credit records are not jeopardised. An entrepreneur must always try to be in good standing with his or her credit providers. If credit providers are convinced about your creditworthiness and loyalty, you can make use of them in the future and also enjoy benefits such as lower interest rates and greater bulk-trade discounts and greater settlement discounts. An entrepreneur has to realise that when debt is obtained, there is always the added-on cost of interest. Try to negotiate debt with the minimum additional costs involved. Also remember, when negotiating credit terms, an entrepreneur has to try to obtain payment terms that are greater than the collection terms of monies from debtors. The cash collected from debtors can assist in paying the accounts of creditors.

10.3.1.5 Financial-ratio analysis

Financial-ratio analysis involves the methods of calculating and interpreting financial ratios to assess an enterprise's performance and status in relation to that of other entities or to itself over time. Financial ratios can be divided into four basic groups: liquidity ratios, activity ratios, debt ratios, and profitability ratios. Liquidity, activity, and debt ratios primarily measure risk whereas profitability ratios measure return.

Liquidity ratios

The liquidity of an entity is measured by its ability to commit itself and to satisfy short-term (current) obligations as they come due. It refers to the solvency of an enterprise's overall financial position. There are three basic measures of liquidity.

▸ *Net working capital.* This is calculated by subtracting the current liabilities from the current assets and is used to measure an entity's overall liquidity.
  - Net working capital = current assets – current liabilities
  - This figure is not useful for comparing the performance of different entities, but is quite useful for internal control purposes.
▸ *Current ratio.* This is one of the most commonly cited financial ratios and it measures an entity's ability to meet its current obligations. It is expressed as follows:

$$\text{Current ratio} = \frac{\text{Current assets}}{\text{Current liabilities}}$$

The current ratio of Makhado General Dealers will be:

$$\frac{\text{R2 140 600}}{\text{R614 000}} = 3.49$$

A current ratio of 2.0 means that the current assets of an entity exceed or will cover the current liabilities of an entity at least twice. A current ratio of 2.0 is occasionally cited as acceptable, but it depends on the industry in which an entity operates.

▸ *The quick (acid-test) ratio.* The acid-test ratio is similar to the current ratio except that it excludes trading inventory, which is generally the least liquid current asset. The generally low liquidity of inventory results from two primary factors:
  - Many types of inventory cannot easily be converted into cash (be sold) as they may be partially completed items, obsolete items, special-purpose items, and so on
  - Inventory items are typically sold on credit, which means that they become an income receivable prior to being converted into cash.

The acid-test ratio is calculated as follows:

$$\text{Acid-test ratio} = \frac{\text{Current assets} - \text{inventory}}{\text{Current liabilities}}$$

The acid-test ratio for Makhado General Dealers will be:

$$\frac{\text{R2 140 600} - \text{R1 300 000}}{\text{R614 000}} = 1.37$$

An acid-test ratio of 1.0 or greater is usually recommended, but it depends on which industry the entity is operating in. The acid-test ratio provides a better measure of overall liquidity only when an entity's inventory cannot easily be converted into cash. If inventory is liquid, the current ratio is a preferred measure of overall liquidity.

Activity ratios

Activity ratios are used to measure the speed with which various accounts are converted into cash or sales. Liquidity measures are, in general, inadequate because differences in the composition of an entity's current assets and liabilities can significantly affect an entity's liquidity. Five different ratios can be used to measure an entity's activity.

▸ *Inventory turnover rate.* This ratio measures how long it takes for the trading inventory (stock) to be converted into cash. The ratio is calculated as follows:

$$\text{Inventory turnover rate} = \frac{\text{Cost of inventory sold}}{\text{Inventory}}$$

The inventory turnover rate for Makhado General Dealer will be

$$\frac{\text{R1 200 000}}{\text{R800 000}} = 1.5$$

An inventory turnover of 40.0 for a grocery store would not be uncommon, whereas a common inventory turnover for an aircraft manufacturer would be 5.0.

The inventory turnover rate can also be converted into an average age of inventory by dividing it into the number of days in a year (365). If a business has an inventory turnover rate of 40, the average age of inventory would be 9.125 days ($365 \div 40$). To determine whether the calculated inventory turnover rate is good or bad, it needs to be compared to the norm of the industry in which the entity operates.

▸ *Debtors' collection period.* This ratio measures the average age of accounts receivable (trade debtors) and is useful when determining or evaluating credit and collection policies. The debtors' collection period can be calculated as follows:

$$\begin{aligned}\text{Debtors' collection} \\ \text{period} =\end{aligned} \frac{\text{Debtors (trade)}}{\text{Average sales per day}}$$

$$= \frac{\text{Debtors (trade)}}{\text{Annual sales} \div 365}$$

This ratio can add value to the management of your debtors (refer to 'debtors' in Section 10.3.1.2). You can now determine how long it takes for debtors to be converted into cash. Remember that the cash that you collect from debtors can help to pay for other expenses, including outstanding creditors accounts, and that the longer it takes to collect cash from debtors, the more difficult it becomes.

▸ *Creditors' payment period.* The average age of your trade creditors is calculated in the same manner as the average collection period of debtors:

$$\begin{aligned}\text{Creditors' payment} \\ \text{period} =\end{aligned} \frac{\text{Creditors (trade)}}{\text{Average purchases per day}}$$

$$= \frac{\text{Creditors (trade)}}{\text{Average purchases} \div 365}$$

This ratio adds value to the management of your creditors (refer to Section 10.3.1.2). Once you have determined how long your creditors' accounts have been outstanding, you can compare this to your debtors' collection period to ensure that the collection period of your debtors is shorter than the payment period of your creditors.

▸ *Non-current asset turnover rate.* This ratio measures the efficiency with which the entity has been using its non-current assets in order to generate sales. This ratio adds value to the management of your non-current assets (refer to Section 10.3.1.1). The ratio is calculated as follows:

$$\begin{aligned}\text{Non-current asset} \\ \text{turnover} =\end{aligned} \frac{\text{Sales}}{\begin{aligned}\text{Non-current assets} \\ \text{(at carrying amount)}\end{aligned}}$$

The non-current asset turnover for Makhado General Dealer will be:

$$\frac{\text{R1 500 000}}{\text{R1 014 000}} = 1.48$$

A relatively high turnover rate is preferred as it reflects greater efficiency of non-current asset utilisation.

▸ *Total asset turnover.* This ratio indicates the efficiency with which the entity uses all its assets to generate income. In general, the higher an entity's total asset turnover, the more efficiently its assets have been used. Like the non-current asset turnover ratio, the total asset turnover ratio adds value to the management of an entity's assets, but the total asset turnover measure is of greater interest as it indicates whether an entity's operations have been financially efficient. The total asset turnover is calculated as follows:

$$\text{Total asset turnover} = \frac{\text{Sales}}{\text{Total assets}}$$

The total asset turnover of Makhado General Dealer will be:

$$\frac{\text{R1 500 000}}{\text{R3 154 600}} = 0.48$$

Debt ratios

The debt position of an entity indicates the amount of other people's money being used in attempting to generate profits. Generally, the more debt an entity uses in relation to its total assets, the greater its financial leverage. Financial leverage is a term used to describe the magnification of risk and return introduced through the use of fixed-cost financing such as debt and preference share capital. This means that the more fixed-cost debt (financial leverage) a firm uses, the greater the risk and return will be. These types of ratios add value to the management of equity (refer to Section 10.3.1.3) as well as debt (refer to Section 10.3.1.4) and can also help to determine an entity's financing strategy (refer to Section 10.3).

There are two general types of debt measures: measures of the degree of indebtedness and measures of the ability to commit to debts. The degree of indebtedness measures the amount of debt against other significant statements of financial position amounts. The two most used measures are the debt ratio and the debt-equity ratio. The ability to service debts refers to an entity's ability to make contractual payments required on a scheduled basis over the life of the debt.

An entity's ability to pay certain fixed charges is measured using coverage ratios. The lower an entity's coverage ratios, the more risky an entity is considered to be. If an entity is unable to pay these obligations, it will be in default and might face blacklisting or even bankruptcy. A coverage ratio that can be used is the times interest earned ratio.

Each of these ratios is discussed in greater detail below.

▶ *Debt ratio.* The debt ratio measures the proportion of total assets financed by an entity's creditors. The higher this ratio, the more financial leverage a firm has, meaning the greater the amount of other people's money being used in an attempt to generate income. The ratio is calculated as follows:

$$\text{Debt ratio} = \frac{\text{Total liabilities}}{\text{Total assets}}$$

The debt ratio of Makhado General Dealer will be:

$$\frac{\text{R1 736 000 + R614 000}}{\text{R3 154 600}} = 0.75$$

▶ *Debt-equity ratio.* This ratio indicates the relationship between the non-current funds provided by creditors and those provided an entity's owners. It is also used to measure the degree of financial leverage of an entity and is calculated as follows:

$$\text{Debt-equity ratio} = \frac{\text{Non-current liabilities}}{\text{Equity}}$$

The debt-equity ratio for Makhado General Dealer will be:

$$\frac{\text{R1 736 000}}{\text{R804 600}} = 2.16$$

▶ *Times interest earned ratio.* The times interest earned ratio measures an entity's ability to make contractual interest payments. This ratio is extremely valuable in the credit vetting process (refer to 'debtors' in Section 10.3.1.2). The higher the value of this ratio, the more able an entity is to fulfil its interest obligations. The times interest earned ratio is calculated as follows:

$$\text{Times interest earned} = \frac{\text{Earnings before interest expense and taxes}}{\text{Interest expense}}$$

▶ The times interest earned ratio for Makhado General Dealers will be:

$$\frac{(R300\,000 + R160\,000) - R131\,400}{R24\,000} = 13.69$$

Profitability ratios

An entity's profitability can be assessed relative to sales, assets, and equity or share value. Without profits, an entity cannot attract outside capital, and present owners and creditors would become concerned about the entity's future and attempt to recover their funds. Owners, creditors, and management pay close attention to maximise profits due to the great importance placed on earnings in the marketplace.

▶ *The gross profit margin.* This ratio indicates the percentage of sales in rands after the entity has paid for its goods. The higher the gross profit margin, the better and the lower the relative cost of inventory (trading) sold. The gross profit margin is expressed as a percentage and is calculated as follows:

$$\begin{aligned}\text{Gross profit margin} &= \frac{\text{Sales} - \text{Cost of sales}}{\text{Sales}} \times \frac{100}{1} \\ &= \frac{\text{Gross profit}}{\text{Sales}} \times \frac{100}{1}\end{aligned}$$

The gross profit margin of Makhado General Dealer will be:

$$\frac{R300\,000}{R1\,500\,000} = 20\%$$

▶ *Operating profit margin.* This ratio measures the profit that is earned through the operations of the entity, and is also expressed as a percentage. This ratio does not take any financial or government charges (interest or taxes) into account. A high operating profit is preferred. To calculate the operating profit margin, the following formula is used:

$$\text{Operating profit margin} = \frac{\text{Earnings before interest and taxes}}{\text{Sales}} \times \frac{100}{1}$$

The operating profit margin for Makhado General Dealer will be:

$$\frac{(R300\,000 + R160\,000) - R131\,400}{R1\,500\,000} = 21.91\%$$

▶ *Net profit margin.* The net profit margin measures the percentage of each sale in rands remaining after all expenses, including interest and tax, have been deducted. The higher the net profit margin, the better for an entity. This ratio is commonly used to measure an entity's success with respect to its earnings on sales. The net profit margin is calculated as follows:

$$\text{Net profit margin} = \frac{\text{Profit for the year}}{\text{Sales}} \times \frac{100}{1}$$

The net profit margin for Makhado General Dealer will be

$$\frac{R304\,600}{R1\,500\,000} = 20.31\%$$

▶ *Return on investment (ROI).* The return on investment is also known as an entity's return on total assets and is extremely useful in the management of an entity's assets (refer to Section 10.3.1). This ratio, also expressed as a percentage, measures the overall effectiveness of an entity's management in generating profits (after all expenses, interest, and tax are subtracted) with its available assets. The higher the return on investment for an entity, the better. The return on investment is calculated as follows:

$$\text{Return on investment} = \frac{\text{Profit for the year}}{\text{Total assets}} \times \frac{100}{1}$$

The return on investment for Makhado General Dealer will be:

$$\frac{R304\,600}{R3\,154\,600} = 9.66\%$$

▶ *Return on equity (ROE).* This ratio measures the return earned on the owners' investment in an entity. A high return on equity will mean that the owners are better off in the entity as their wealth is maximised. The return on equity is calculated as follows:

$$\text{Return on equity} = \frac{\text{Profit for the year}}{\text{Equity}} \times \frac{100}{1}$$

The return on equity for Makhado General Dealer will be:

$$\frac{\text{R304 600}}{\text{R804 600}} = 37.86\%$$

▶ *Earnings per share (EPS).* A company's earnings per share are commonly of interest to present or prospective shareholders and management. The earnings per share represent the number of rands earned on behalf of each outstanding ordinary share. This ratio is closely watched by the investing public and is an important indicator of corporate success. This figure does not represent the amount of earnings actually distributed to shareholders and is calculated as follows:

$$\text{Earnings per share} = \frac{\begin{array}{c}\text{Profit available for}\\ \text{ordinary shareholders}\end{array}}{\begin{array}{c}\text{Number of ordinary}\\ \text{shares in issue}\end{array}}$$

▶ *Price/Earnings (P/E) ratio.* This ratio represents the amount investors are willing to pay for each rand of a company's earnings. The level of the P/E ratio indicates the degree of confidence that investors have in the company's future performance. The higher the P/E ratio, the greater the investor confidence in the company's future. The P/E ratio is calculated as follows:

$$\text{P/E ratio} = \frac{\text{Market price per ordinary share}}{\text{Earnings per share}}$$

10.4 **Financing capital requirements**

An entrepreneur will need money in order to make money. Every type of business will need money whether it is to start-up or for capital expenditure. An important lesson to remember is not to ask for more money than you can afford to repay. An entrepreneur will have to plan how financing will take place and, therefore, this will form part of the financial plan.

A limiting factor in obtaining finance for an entity to be successful is risk. An entrepreneur who can show his financial supporter(s) that the risk element can be controlled through careful planning and implementation of common sense management procedures will have greater success in obtaining finances. To achieve this, an entrepreneur must not only have an understanding of how to reach the sources of finance available to him or her, but must also know how to capitalise on these sources to reduce the risk factor.

An entrepreneur has to decide on what financial strategy will be followed. The primary considerations include:
▶ The combination of non-current and current external capital
▶ The combination of ordinary share capital plus reserves together with external non-current capital
▶ Financing through own internal funds.

With the National Credit Act currently in operation in South Africa, an entrepreneur has to bear in mind that commercial banks and registered credit providers will seldom provide 100% loans. The entrepreneur will need to choose and appropriate financing strategy:
▶ An *aggressive financing strategy* means that the durable capital needs will be financed through non-current credit and fluctuating capital needs will be financed through current credit.

▶ A *conservative financing strategy* entails that the total capital needs of an entity will be financed with non-current credit.
▶ The *mid-way strategy* is followed by most entities. They use a combination of non-current and current credit.

It is important to remember that whenever possible, non-current assets should be financed by long-term sources of finance. Current assets should be financed by short-term sources of money.

10.4.1 Sources of finance

An entrepreneur can obtain funds either internally or externally.

ENTREPRENEURIAL DILEMMA

Venture capital or private equity?

A small technology-based entity that wants to grow may need more money than what can be raised from operations or from borrowing from family and friends. In such a case you will need to turn to professional investors in the form of venture capital or a private equity firm that will inject cash into the entity in exchange for a share of the business.

The biggest difference is that a venture capital firm will invest, for the short to medium term, in entities at a relatively early stage of its development where the risks of failure are higher. Private equity investors, on the other hand, have a slightly lower appetite for risk. These type of investors are more likely to take a five- to ten-year view, investing in an entity that already has an established track record and can offer good returns. A private equity investor will also bring a wider range of skills onboard.

1. Which is the best option?
2. What are the risks and rewards of each type of capital?

Source: Online. Adapted from http://www. howwemadeitinafrica.com/venture-capital-or-private-equity-the-entrepreneur%E2%80%99s-dilemma/20362 [6 January 2014].

10.4.1.1 **Internal sources of finance**

Internal sources of finance mean that an entrepreneur can source the finances within the entity itself, for example:
▶ *Own equity* or capital contributions to be applied within the entity
▶ *Profits or earnings* of a current going concern at the end of an accounting period that are retained in the business
▶ *Speeding up collections from customers* can become a source of additional capital and more money will be available for the business's needs
▶ *Credit from suppliers,* who may be willing to extend interest-free credit on purchases of goods or services to well-established customers. This implies that you may be able to order, obtain delivery, and sell items before you have to pay for them.

10.4.1.2 **External sources of finance**

An entrepreneur can make use of finance that is obtained through sources outside of the enterprise to be used elsewhere within the enterprise. If funds are not available within the business, you could look to partners, co-members or co-shareholders to provide external equity. Other potential categories of equity for promising enterprises include 'angel investors', 'venture capital', 'private equity', and 'public equity'. Private equity firms provide expertise, organise financing, and often increase the debt levels of firms. Examples of public enterprises that could provide financing include the National Empowerment Fund (NEF) and Khula Enterprise Finance.

External finances can be divided into long-term finance, intermediate (mid-term) finance and short-term finance.
▶ *Long-term finance.* Long-term finance can be obtained from the following sources which are to be repaid over a period longer than five years:
  ▪ *Long-term loan* from a financial institution such as a commercial bank in the form of, for example, a mortgage

bond to obtain property, which is to be repaid over a period of 20 years

- A business entity can also issue *debentures*, where money is borrowed from the public and is repayable over a period of more than five years.

▶ *Intermediate (mid-term) finance.* This type of finance is payable within a period of two to five years and can be in the form of:

- *Leases,* which are contractual agreements between a lessee (user of an asset) and the lessor (asset owner). The lessor receives payment from the lessee for the use of the asset and at the end of the lease period the lessee has the option to either purchase the asset or to negotiate a secondary rental contract.

- *An operating lease,* which is applicable to equipment, for example, and the equipment is leased for a period that is much shorter than its normal life. After the lease has expired, the lessor may sell the equipment or remarket it. With an operating lease, the lessee has the right to cancel the lease agreement before the expiry date and an entrepreneur has to take into account that maintenance costs are frequently included as part of the lease payment.

- *A financial lease,* allows you, for example, to drive either a new or a used vehicle without having to make a substantial initial payment or deposit. The plan is exceptionally flexible, as you can negotiate your lease period from 12 to 60 months, and determine the payments that best suit your budget. Business users benefit through attractive tax benefits and deductions under this scheme and, at the end of the period, there are several options, including the ownership of the vehicle.

▶ *Short-term financing.* Short-term finances are repayable within 12 months and can be obtained from the following sources:

- *Trade credit* is credit that is extended between firms to each other in the normal course of business. The repayment terms may vary between 30 and 120 days, and the seller (supplier) may offer a settlement discount upon early settlement of the account.

- *Bank credit* allows money to be borrowed from a financial institution such as a commercial bank in the form of a bank overdraft on the business's current account. Interest is usually paid on the amount used and the interest rate is usually the prime lending rate plus additional percentage points according to the entity's risk profile.

- *Bankers' acceptance* is created when a business sells a bill of exchange to a commercial bank to be settled on a predetermined date. A bill of exchange is an unconditional order in writing addressed by one person to another, signed by the person who drafted the bill, requiring the person to whom it is addressed to pay on demand or on a specific future date a specific sum of money to the person who ordered the bill or the bearer (the presenter) of the bill. It is usually used to finance overseas trading transactions.

▶ *Factoring* occurs when an institution such as a commercial bank purchases the debtors (trade receivables) of a business at a discounted price. The institution (bank) assumes the risk of non-payment by debtors and accepts responsibility for the selection, management, administration, and collection of debts. An advantage of factoring is that an entity can get cash directly after the debtors were sold and this reduces its short-term capital required. The entity does not need to collect the outstanding monies from debtors as this function is now taken over by the financial institution.

10.4.1.3 Sources of start-up finance for entrepreneurs

Banks are not the only places that provide start-up finance to entrepreneurs. It is a matter of doing your research, having a good business plan, and then being prepared to sell yourself. Some of the institutions that are prepared to finance prospective entrepreneurs are:

▶ *Business Partners Limited*. This company is South Africa's leading investment company for small and medium enterprises (SMEs). The company invests between R250 000 and R15 million in SMEs across all sectors except farming, on-lending, and non-profit organisations. It also offers a range of support services for entrepreneurs, including property management consultants, mentors who are allocated according to a company's needs, and access to other expertise.
Contact details:
Cape Town: 021 464 3600
Durban: 031 240 7700
Johannesburg: 011 470 3111
email: enquiries@businesspartners.co.za
Internet: www.businesspartners.co.za

▶ *Commercial banks*. The commercial banks have specialist SME divisions that provide finance for qualified prospective entrepreneurs. Web pages that could be visited include:
  ▪ ABSA Bank: www.absa.co.za
  ▪ First National Bank: www.fnb.co.za
  ▪ Nedbank: www.nedbank.co.za
  ▪ Standard Bank: www.standardbank.co.za

▶ *Khula Enterprise Finance*. Khula Enterprise Finance Limited is an agency of the Department of Trade and Industry (dti) and was established in 1996 to facilitate access to finance for SMMEs (small, medium and micro-enterprises). This company also provides assistance through various delivery channels, including commercial banks, retail financial intermediaries (RFIs) and micro-credit outlets (MCOs).

Contact details: Tel: 012 394 5560/5900
Toll free: 0800 118815
email: helpline@khula.org.za
Internet: www.khula.org.za

▶ *The Industrial Development Corporation (IDC)*. The IDC of South Africa is a self-financing, national development finance institution (DFI). It was established in 1940 to promote economic growth and industrial development in South Africa.
Contact details: Call centre: 0860 693 888
email: callcentre@idc.co.za
Internet: www.idc.co.za

▶ Other useful websites include:
  ▪ www.jse.co.za
  ▪ www.dti.gov.za
  ▪ www.businesscentral.co.za/businesstips/sourcesfinance.htm
  ▪ http://touchstonecapital.co.za
  ▪ www.nefcorp.co.za

CONCLUSION

In this chapter, basic financial concepts were defined and discussed, including accounting as well as the various financial statements and their various components. Formats of financial statements were used to illustrate where and how these concepts and elements are applied. It is of vital importance for an entrepreneur to familiarise himself or herself with these basic financial concepts in order to complete the financial section of a business plan. The management of assets, equity, and liabilities were also discussed together with financial-ratio analysis and the importance of these ratios on the management of the financial aspects of an enterprise. The financing of capital requirements as well as financing strategies were discussed. The chapter closed with a description of the different sources of finance available as well as a useful list of Internet websites that were provided to assist you to familiarise yourself with the various aids available in practice.

SELF-ASSESSMENT QUESTIONS

Multiple-choice questions

Choose the correct answer for each of the questions below:

1. Income earned by an entity but not yet received will be classified as:
   a. Non-current asset
   b. Non-current liability
   c. Current asset
   d. Current liability
   e. Equity
2. To purchase on credit will be classified as:
   a. Equity
   b. Current liability
   c. Current assets
   d. Non-current assets
   e. Non-current liability
3. In which statement will you report on the increase or decrease of cash of an entity?
   a. Statement of changes in equity
   b. Statement of financial position
   c. Statement of cash flows
   d. Statement of profit or loss and other comprehensive income
   e. All of the above
4. In which statement will you report on the income earned and expenses incurred of an entity?
   a. Statement of changes in equity
   b. Statement of financial position
   c. Statement of cash flows
   d. Statement of profit or loss and other comprehensive income
   e. All of the above
5. The acid-test ratio measures:
   a. Performance
   b. Liquidity
   c. Activity
   d. Profitability

DISCUSSION QUESTIONS

1. Define accounting.
2. Define and provide an example of each of the following terms:
   a. Assets
   b. Equity
   c. Liabilities
   d. Income
   e. Expenses
3. Discuss the concept that forms the constitution of accounting.
4. Discuss the profitability ratios and how they can help you in the evaluation of an entity's financial statements.
5. Discuss why liquidity ratios are important in the analysis of financial statements.

EXPERIENTIAL EXERCISE

Visit a local drycleaner or laundromat and answer the following questions:

1. Is the business privately owned or does it belong to a franchise?
2. Does the business own or rent the premises?
3. Does the business own or rent the equipment?
4. Discuss what the business premises or equipment will be recognised as in the statement of financial position of the entity if either one if them is owned.
5. Discuss what the renting of the business premises or the equipment will be recognised as in the statement of profit or loss and other comprehensive income.

AQUA TRADERS

You are interested in taking over Aqua Traders but need to analyse and evaluate the liquidity of the entity. The bookkeeper of Aqua Traders provided you with the following calculated ratios from information available from the entity's financial statements:

	2013	2014
Acid-test ratio	0.9:1	0.5:1
Inventory turnover rate	9 times	6 times
Debtors collection period	32 days	48 days
Creditors payment period	45 days	45 days
Gross profit percentage	50%	50%

Required

Evaluate the liquidity of Aqua Traders by discussing each of the above-mentioned ratios according to the following:

a. Refer to the strong points of the entity as indicated by the above-mentioned ratios.
b. Refer to the weak points of the entity as indicated by the above-mentioned ratios.
c. Provide possible reasons for the weak points.
d. Provide possible advice on how the situation can be improved, if necessary.

SUGGESTED WEBSITE LINKS

http://www.youtube.com/
    watch?feature=player_
    embedded&v=qsDWkpKDvpE
http://www.vantagepoint.co.za
http://www.entrepreneurmag.co.za.
http://www.howwemadeitinafrica.com
http://www.gemconsortium.org

REFERENCES

Bezuidenhout, S, Cloete, M, Joynt, C, Nortjé-Rossouw, D. & Van Pletsen, L. 2013. *Accounting and Basic Financial Literacy.* 3rd ed. Pretoria: Salt and Pepper Publishing.

Gitman, LJ. 2007. *Principles of Managerial Finance.* Boston: Addison-Wesley.

Gitman, LJ. & Joehnk, MD. 2004. *Personal Financial Planning.* 10th ed. Mason: Thomson South-Western.

Myburgh, J, Fouché, J. & Cloete, M. 2013. *Accounting an introduction.* 11th ed. Pretoria. LexisNexis.

CHAPTER 11

Financial planning and forecasting

Stefan Bezuidenhout

LEARNING OUTCOMES

On completion of this chapter, you will be able to:
▶ Define 'financial plan'
▶ Discuss the purpose of a financial plan in detail
▶ Define 'financial policy'
▶ Discuss the purpose of a financial policy in detail
▶ Name and discuss the different components of a financial policy and their influences
▶ Determine a break-even point
▶ Name and discuss the various types of finance
▶ Discuss the importance of cash flow in a small business venture
▶ Define 'forecasting process' and discuss this concept
▶ Develop the three financial statements used in the forecasting process.

OPENING CASE STUDY

The function of management entails planning, leading, organising and control. Part of our personal lives also entails planning. We manage our own lives by planning the day ahead, what activities we have, when each activity should be done and sometimes how it is to be done. From a financial point of view we also plan on how we will obtain money, how we will spend our money and how much money we will have left at the end of the day.

1. Do you plan how you will obtain money?
2. Do you plan how and on what you will spend your money?

INTRODUCTION

So many things to do and so little time! In the first part of the chapter, planning as a management function will be discussed with a focus on financial planning, which is needed for an entrepreneur to accomplish his or her financial goals.

In the second part of the chapter, financial forecasting (budgeting) will be discussed. Financial forecasting forms an integral part of financial planning as it will help you to convince lenders and investors that your enterprise will be a sound investment.

An entrepreneur needs to ask the following question: Why do I want to embark on a business venture? One of the answers to this question will surely be, 'to make money'. In order to fulfil this objective one needs to plan ahead!

Planning is one function that an entrepreneur (manager) needs to exercise in order to complete the management function that also involves leading, organising, and control.

Not all entrepreneurs are excited by the idea of doing their own financial planning as discussed in *Entrepreneurs are not always interested in financial planning*.

11.1 Financial planning

DEFINITION

Planning involves thinking what and how a required outcome, result or objective should be obtained.

ENTREPRENEURIAL DILEMMA

Entrepreneurs are not always interested in financial planning

For many prospective entrepreneurs, accounting, financial figures, and financial planning are the last things they want to think about. They would rather focus on what they are really interested in, for

SOUTH AFRICAN SUCCESS STORY

Exactech Fraud Solutions – Antonio Pooe
Antonio Pooe, owner of Exactech Fraud Solutions, pursued his dream for his business without getting distracted by factors such as having no funding.

During the first eight months, his business did not make a cent. Although Antonio applied for funding through the banks, he was unsuccessful. His focus in the first two years was educating the market, creating a need and filling it.

In order to survive, Antonio knew he had to keep operating costs down and planned at least 24 months ahead to keep the business afloat.

Antonio won the SAB Kick Start programme and used the prize money to buy machinery for his lab. His advice, among other things, is: 'Only spend money on what you need. It might be great to have a flashy office but I'll keep three chairs, and until I need that fourth chair, I'm not going to buy it'.

example, providing human resources services. Although financial plans are vital to the planning and running of a business, this entrepreneur's lack of interest in finances is commonly reflected in poorly prepared financial plans.

Prospective entrepreneurs can outsource this part of the business plan, but ultimately, it is their financial and business plan for which they need to accept responsibility. They should at all times be actively involved in the preparation of the financial plan in order to be fully informed about what their financial plan entails.

In a book, Beyond the Business Plan by Simon Bridge and Cecilia Hegarty, ten reasons are provided why not to write a business plan first:

1. A new venture is a means, not an end.
2. Don't start by committing more than you can afford to lose.
3. Pick a domain where you have some experience and expertise.
4. Carry out reality checks and make appropriate plans.
5. The only reliable test is a real one.
6. Get started and build momentum.
7. Accept uncertainty as the norm.
8. Look for new opportunities.
9. Build and use social capital.
10. Acquire the necessary skills.

What are the dangers that entrepreneurs may face if they are not fully informed regarding their financial plans?

By looking at the ten reasons above, 'why not to write a business plan first', what is your opinion about financial planning?

11.1.1 The planning process

The **planning** process involves the following activities:

▸ *The identification and formulation of objectives.* An entrepreneur is required to set objectives which he or she wants to achieve over a specific period of time. An entrepreneur should think strategically (out of the box) in order to identify the long-term objective(s) that is, 'What do I want to accomplish after a period of ten years?'

These plans include the following:

- Proposed fixed asset outlays
- Research and development activities
- Marketing and product development actions
- Capital structure
- Major sources of financing.

After setting the long-term objectives, an entrepreneur should focus on the mid-term objective(s) that is: What do I want to accomplish after five years in order to reach my long-term objective?

After the mid-term objectives have been set, an entrepreneur should now focus more on operational or short-term objectives. An entrepreneur should now look at the day-to-day operations to set objectives that must be obtained within the following 12 months so that he or she can obtain the mid-term objectives, which will lead to obtaining long-term objectives. These plans involve:

- Sales forecasts
- Various statements (budgets).

▸ *Gathering all the necessary data.* An entrepreneur should conduct research. To set the necessary objectives, an entrepreneur should, for example, investigate the economic environment in which the business will be established so that he or she can determine the latest and possible future economic trends, not only of that particular industry, but also of the country as a whole.

- The entrepreneur should also ensure that the data collected are valid and relevant, that is, that they are a true reflection of an enterprise's financial operations and can be used as a basis for forecasting. An enterprise can have up to three different financial records:
- To satisfy the South African Revenue Service
- To satisfy creditors
- To 'personally know what the financials of the business are'.

When you conduct your research, do not settle for anything less than the actual financial records (i.e. to know personally what the financials of the business are).

Market research should also be conducted to establish the market trends of the particular enterprise to determine profit margins, pricing options, service quality, and so on.

Financial options should be investigated, for example, deciding which type of financing will be used by the enterprise and whether it is better to obtain assets by financing them or by providing the necessary money out of one's own pocket. Other decisions need to be made regarding how much of the enterprise's capital will be own capital and how much will be borrowed capital.

An entrepreneur should also investigate which financial institution will have the best deal on interest rates, not only for borrowing purposes but also for saving or for investment purposes.

These are only some of the research topics to be considered. The entrepreneur should investigate everything holistically in order to gain a clear and general picture of what can be expected when embarking on his or her new business venture.

▸ *Analysing the data.* After all the necessary data has been collected, it should be analysed to make it meaningful information. This is done to ensure that all possibilities, implications, and possible complications are taken into consideration.
▸ *Drawing up the plan.* Using the information gathered, different plans of action must be developed to lead to the different objectives that have been set. This means that a long-term, medium-term, and short-term financial plan must be developed. The best financial plan for each time period should be selected so that it is ready for implementation.
▸ *Implementation of the plan.* The selected plans must now be implemented.

Available resources should be selected and allocated accordingly. Remember that these plans should always be re-assessed after implementation to determine whether the enterprise is still on the right track to achieve the set objectives, and corrective actions should be taken if any deviations have occurred.

11.1.2 The financial policy

DEFINITION

A policy sets out the guidelines or principles according to which an enterprise must act in obtaining its objectives.

To achieve his or her financial objectives within a certain period, an entrepreneur has to set financial guidelines. These should take into account all the different aspects that will have an influence on the enterprise's financial affairs, in order to develop a sound financial **policy** that will support the financial plan. This will contribute towards making a success of the business and achieving the objectives set.

Components that should be included in the financial policy are the following:
▸ *Forecasting and planning.* Interaction between the various business functions or departments within the business must take place as they look ahead and lay the plans that will shape the business's future.
▸ *Major investment and financing decisions.* A successful business enterprise has rapid growth in sales or funds received, which requires investments in plant, equipment, and inventory. The optimal sales growth rate (or growth rate in funds received for non-profit organisations) must be determined in order to help the decision-making process on what specific assets to acquire, and then to choose the best way to finance those assets. For example, should the enterprise finance the assets with debt, equity, or a combination of the two, and, if

debt is used, how much should be long-term and how much should be short-term?

▶ *Coordination and control.* Coordination between the different functions (departments) within the business is essential! All business decisions, whether it is marketing, or a production decision, have financial implications. Without the necessary coordination, the availability of funds may be restricted for certain departments and the control over the acquisition and use of financial resources cannot be done effectively.

Financial control consists of four steps that are:

- *The setting of standards.* An entrepreneur has to establish standards that are of a quantitative nature and use these in budgets and in determining cost structures and financial ratios. These standards may include prices, tariffs, quantities, and production time per unit.
- *The comparison of actual results with the set standards.* This is necessary in order to identify any deviations between the actual results and the set standards.
- *Evaluation of any deviations.* It is important to determine the reasons for any deviations to identify the cause of the problem that has resulted in the deviation. This will provide the entrepreneur with more clarity when performing the last step.
- *To take corrective action when necessary.* Corrective action must be taken should any negative deviations have occurred, not only to prevent future negative deviations but also to reduce the

probability that the problem(s) may recur.

▶ *Risk management.* All businesses face risks that include natural disasters such as fires and floods, uncertainties in commodity and security markets, volatile interest rates, and fluctuating foreign exchange rates. Many of these risks can be reduced by purchasing insurance or by hedging in the derivatives markets. The entrepreneur or the financial staff of the enterprise is responsible for the business's overall risk-management programme, including identifying the risks that should be managed, and then managing them in the most efficient manner.

11.2 **The financial plan**

> **DEFINITION**
>
> Financial planning is concerned with investigating the choice between two or more alternatives for reaching a specific objective and also determining how each specific goal is to be achieved.

Financial planning is an important aspect of an enterprise's operations. It provides road maps for guiding, coordinating, and controlling an enterprise's actions to achieve its objectives.

Financial planning involves the effective acquisition, use, and control of financial resources more effectively and involves an investigation into current and future needs. This is summarised in Figure 11.1.

Financial planning provides not only the specific outcomes of future activities in

Figure 11.1 Organisational planning model

Source: Gitman and Joehnk (2004).

monetary terms, but also the necessary figures to support the various choices made. For the purpose of this book, emphasis is placed on the short-term financial-planning process. The short-term financial-planning process is outlined in the Figure 11.2 flow diagram.

Short-term financial plans specify short-term financial actions and the anticipated impact of those actions. These plans usually cover a period of one to two years.

Short-term financial planning begins with the sales forecast. From the sales forecast, production plans are developed in order to determine lead times and include estimates of the required types and quantities of raw materials. Now an entity can estimate direct labour requirements, factory overhead outlays, and operating expenses. After making these estimates, an entity's statement of profit or loss and other comprehensive income and cash budget can be prepared. With the statement of profit or loss and other comprehensive income, cash budget, non-current asset outlay plan, long-term financing plan, and current period

statement of financial position, the statement of financial position can finally be developed.

11.2.1 **Factors to be taken into account in developing a financial plan**

To be able to develop a financial plan, an entrepreneur has to take the following factors into account:

▸ *The industry.* This refers to the kind of business activity upon which the entrepreneur is going to embark. An entrepreneur should investigate what other businesses are involved in the same kind of business activities, for example buying and selling furniture or providing an electrical service, to see what they are doing and how they are performing.

▸ *Competition.* An entrepreneur has to investigate whether there are any other businesses against which he or she will have to compete. An entrepreneur also has

Figure 11.2 The short-term (operating) financial-planning process

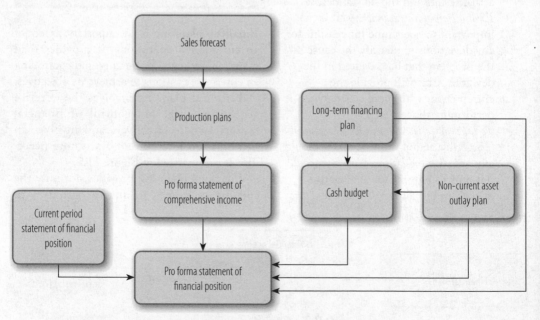

Source: Gitman, LJ. Principles of Managerial Finance, Brief edition, 1st edition, © 1998, p. 462. Reprinted by permission of Pearson Education, Inc., Upper Saddle River, NJ.

to ensure that he or she can afford to compete with competitors. Competition is healthy for a business as it leads to more realistic price settings and prevents the formation of monopolies.

▸ *The market.* If an entrepreneur knows the kind of industry in which the business will function, he or she needs to make certain that there is a genuine need for his or her product or service. If there is no need for the business's product and (or) service, there will be no income to be received from it.

▸ *Current economic circumstances.* A business's life cycle is dependent on a country's economic cycle, as depicted in Figure 11.3.

If a country's economy is in an expansion phase, it means that economic growth is happening, which implies that more money is available and more purchasing power exists among consumers. In contrast, when the recession phase is entered, economic growth decreases. As a result, less money is available, which implies that consumers have less purchasing power. A depression phase occurs when there is little or no economic growth and there is also a scarcity of funds available. This means that there is very little purchasing power among consumers.

The recovery phase, which follows the depression phase, occurs when economic growth is positive again. More money is available and consumers have more purchasing power.

Current economic circumstances are of crucial importance for an entrepreneur. These involve the trends with regard to interest rates, fuel prices, currency rates, inflation, and the factor of supply and demand. These factors will all have an influence on an entrepreneur's decision-making process. For example, if interest rates are expected to increase, and an entrepreneur has a loan with a financial institution, this will lead to a higher repayment of the loan at the end of each month, which in turn reduces the amount of cash available and the profit of the business.

▸ *Current political circumstances.* Political stability is a great attraction for any investment. Instability can scare people and business entities away, which in turn will lead to a decrease in the investment by local and foreign people and businesses. For example, if you compare the current political circumstances in South Africa to those in Zimbabwe, in which country would you choose to invest your money?

Figure 11.3 The economic cycle

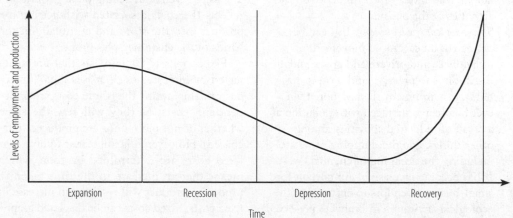

Source: Adapted from Smit, PC., et al. 1996. Economics – A South African Perspective. Kenwyn: Juta & Co, Ltd. p.370.

From time to time, governments introduce different kinds of legislation, which may restrict businesses in their activities. An entrepreneur should become familiar with the various laws that may lead to a restriction in business activities. Examples include income tax, value-added tax, currency, and labour legislation.

▸ *Technology.* The economic environment encompasses all product and services that are the end result of human skills and innovation, in the form of machinery, apparatus, procedures, and methods. An entrepreneur should be aware of all the changes in technology if the business activities rely extensively on technology. The entrepreneur should make sure that his or her business keeps track of such changes in order to stay or become more effective, efficient, and competitive.

▸ *Social environment.* Any kind of business has a social responsibility, which is to try to improve the conditions of the society in which the business functions. The role and activities of an entity in a dynamic society have to be adapted to the changing needs and expectations of that society. An entrepreneur has to take into account that the geographical distribution of his or her potential clients, and the issues surrounding skilled versus unskilled labour, will have a direct influence on the activities of the business.

▸ *The ecological environment.* This can be defined as an organised movement of individuals, and private and government institutions to preserve and protect the natural environment. Today, more than ever before, we are faced with pollution as a result of industrial activities, among other things, and the dumping of waste, including the dumping of chemical waste. It has become increasingly important for small-business vendors to ensure that the ecological environment is always preserved and protected.

11.2.2 Setting prices and the break-even analysis

The financial plan should also include a pricing strategy, as some entrepreneurs and new venture managers find it difficult to set the right prices for their products. Questions that are commonly asked are the following: Are my prices too high or too low? What is my profit margin? Am I going to make a profit?

With the help of a break-even analysis, an entrepreneur can establish at what point his or her entity will make neither a profit nor a loss (earnings before interest and tax are equal to zero or EBIT = 0). The break-even analysis is a vital tool for short-term planning as it will enable an entrepreneur to determine:

▸ The level of operations necessary to cover all operating costs
▸ The profitability associated with the various levels of sales.

11.2.2.1 Calculating the break-even point

The break-even point can be calculated using an algebraic formula or a scale graph. A venture's break-even point can be determined algebraically, using the following formula:

$$\text{Sales quantity in units } (Q) = \frac{\text{Fixed costs per unit (FC)}}{\text{Selling price per unit (P) } - \text{Variable costs per unit (VC)}}$$

The sales revenue or selling price per unit (P) reflects the costs associated with getting the product into the store and eventually in the hands of the customer, plus profit.

Fixed costs (*FC*) are costs that are unaffected by increases or decreases in volume of output. This means that these costs are 'independent' costs, as they will stay the same whether or not more units are produced (purchased). However, it is important to note that fixed costs are determined by time, which means that an increase in the time taken to produce a product will result in an increase in fixed costs. Fixed costs can be displayed graphically as in Figure 11.4.

Variable costs (*VC*) are costs that tend to increase with an increase in the volume of output or sales. Variable costs are added to the fixed costs (*FC*) to determine the total costs (*TC*), as is displayed in Figure 11.5.

Taking the sales price per unit or sales revenue (*P*) into account, the break-even point can be calculated graphically using the following steps:
▸ Determine the scale of each axis
▸ Determine and plot the fixed costs
▸ Determine and plot the total costs
▸ Determine and plot the selling price per unit

▸ Find the break-even point (at the intersection of the total costs and the sales revenue).

Figure 11.6 illustrates a graphical calculation of the break-even point. Remember that EBIT is the entity's earnings before interest and tax. Below the break-even point, EBIT is less than zero and the business makes a financial loss. Above the break-even point, EBIT is greater than zero and the business makes a financial profit.

Example 11.1 below demonstrates the algebraic calculation of the break-even point.

Figure 11.4 Fixed costs per unit remain constant regardless of the quantity produced

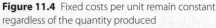

Figure 11.5 Variable costs are added to fixed costs to determine total costs per unit

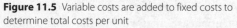

Figure 11.6 The break-even analysis

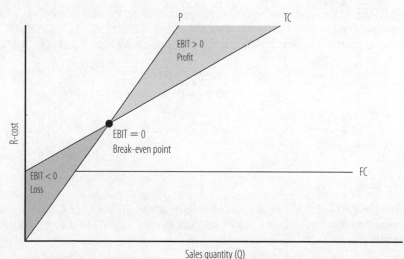

When determining the selling price of your product, you should first determine all direct and indirect costs involved in getting the product on the shelf, before the product is sold to a customer. When the costs have been established, you need to determine the break-even point to ensure that you know how many products you have to sell to begin to make a profit.

Before you add your mark-up, you also need to take into account the selling prices of your competitors because you not only want to make a profit, but you also want to have the competitive edge. Your selling price (with your profit margin included) will affect the demand for your product. If your price is too high, the potential customers will buy the same product for less from your competitors, and you will lose your customers. If you think that you do have the right price, you should determine your break-even point again, in order to determine whether you should sell more or less of the same product before you can really say that you will make a profit.

11.2.2.2 Limitations of the break-even point analysis

The break-even point analysis does have the following limitations to an entrepreneur:

▸ It is not easy to classify all costs involved as either fixed or variable costs
▸ The elements that constitute fixed or variable costs are not always constant and may change over time
▸ The break-even analysis uses units and monetary values, but excludes qualitative factors
▸ Because monetary values are used, the instability of the monetary value is not taken into account.

Once the financial plan has been developed, the entrepreneur is able to use this plan as a tool for financial forecasting or budgeting.

11.3 Financial forecasting

As discussed at the beginning of this chapter, financial planning is a very important aspect of an entity's operation and survival. Financial planning provides and formulates the

---

EXAMPLE 11.1

Example of a break-even analysis

Themba Cleaning Materials trades with cleaning materials. Themba Cleaning Materials has fixed operating costs of R10 500, variable operating cost of R250 per unit, and a selling price of R500 per unit.

The number of units which Themba Cleaning Materials must sell in order to break even can be calculated as follows:

$$\text{Sales quantity in units (Q)} = \frac{\text{Fixed costs per unit (FC)}}{\text{Selling price per unit (P)} - \text{Variable costs per unit (VC)}}$$

$$Q = \frac{FC}{P - VC}$$

$$= \frac{R10\,500}{R500 - R250}$$

$$= 42$$

The answer implies that if Themba Cleaning Materials sells 42 units at R500 per unit, no profits and no losses will be made. If the venture sells fewer than 42 units, it will make a loss. To make a profit, Themba Cleaning Materials will need to sell more than 42 units.

guidelines on how the financial goals are to be achieved. Financial plans form an entity's statement of what is to be done in the future. The financial-planning process can be broken down into five steps:

▶ *Project financial statements.* These projections can be used to analyse the effects of the operating plan on projected profits and various financial ratios.
▶ *Determine the funds needed to support the five-year plan.* This includes funds for plant and equipment, as well as for inventories and receivables, for research and development programmes, and for major marketing campaigns.
▶ *Forecast funds available for the next five years.* This involves estimating the funds to be generated internally as well as those to be obtained from external sources. Any constraints must be incorporated in the plan.
▶ *Establish and maintain a system of controls.* Control systems are needed to govern the allocation and use of funds within the entity to make sure that the basic plan is carried out properly.
▶ *Develop procedures for adjusting the basic plan.* If the economic forecasts originally used to base the plan on do not materialise, the plan needs to be adjusted.

Two key aspects of the financial-planning process are cash planning and profit planning.

Cash planning involves the preparation of an entity's cash budget, while profit planning is usually done by means of pro forma financial statements. These financial statements are not only useful for internal financial planning, but are also routinely required by existing and prospective lenders.

◖ DEFINITION ◗

A financial forecast or budget is a formal plan that indicates how you are going to use your resources to achieve your goals.

In this part of the chapter, we will take a closer look at the forecasting process and especially at the pro forma financial statements that are used as part of financial forecasting.

11.3.1 Reasons for forecasting

Why is it important for an entrepreneur to budget (forecast)? The following reasons emphasise the importance of forecasting, not only for business-plan purposes, but also for sound business practices:

▶ *Forecasting enhances the quality of planning* because it considers the future of the business and provides the course of action that will be taken by the business. This will also help the business to obtain finances from external sources, as the lending institution will have a clearer idea of what the business wants to achieve and how the business will achieve it. It also reflects whether the business will have the ability to repay the loan amount.
▶ *The control function* (which is one of the management functions) is made easier as actual results can be measured against the planned objectives.
▶ *Forecasting enhances the integration and coordination of various opinions and needs* in order to strive and work towards the common goal of the business.
▶ *The actual performance of the various departments and personnel can be measured* more easily against set targets (objectives).

11.3.2 The forecasting process

The financial-planning process begins with long-term or strategic financial plans that in turn guide the formulation of short-term (operational) financial plans.

The long-term or strategic financial plans involve planned long-term financial actions, and their anticipated financial impact. The short-term or operational financial plans involve planned short-term financial actions, and their expected financial effect.

In this chapter, we concentrate on short-term financial plans. These plans cover a one- to two-year period. Key inputs include the sales forecast and various forms of operating and financial data. Key outputs include a number of operating budgets, the cash budget, and pro forma financial statements.

After the sales forecast is developed, production plans are developed, and they take into account the preparation time and include estimates of the required types and quantities of raw materials. Using the production plans, an entity can estimate direct labour requirements, factory overhead costs, and operating expenses.

After these estimates have been made, the venture's statement of profit or loss and other comprehensive income and cash budget can be prepared. With these basic inputs, namely the statement of profit or loss and other comprehensive income, cash budget, a fixed asset outlay plan, long-term financial plan, and current period statement of financial position, the statement of financial position can finally be developed.

11.3.2.1 Information needed to prepare the financial section of the business plan

An entrepreneur will find it extremely helpful to have the following in order to complete the financial section of the business plan:

▸ *An operating budget.* The operating budget commences with sales forecasts, leading to production plans, wherein all inputs such as labour, operating expenses, materials used, and overheads must be included
▸ *The projected cash budget*
▸ *The projected statement of profit or loss and other comprehensive income*
▸ *The projected statement of financial position.*

11.3.3 The three pro forma statements used in the forecasting process

The pro forma documents needed in compiling the financial section of the entrepreneur's business plan are discussed in detail and illustrated in this section.

11.3.3.1 The pro forma statement of cash flows (the cash budget)

DEFINITION

The cash budget is a statement of an entity's planned cash inflows (money physically coming into the business) and cash outflows (money physically going out of the business), and it is used to estimate an entity's short-term cash requirements.

In the cash budget, the entrepreneur is working with the actual cash received and the actual cash that was used to pay accounts. The transaction is recorded in the month when it is really going to happen. For example, if goods or inventory are purchased on credit, the payments are recorded in the specific month when the actual payments are made, not before the time (at the time of purchase), as it is in the case of the pro forma statement of profit or loss and other comprehensive income. The same principle as with the collections of accounts receivable (accounts of debtors) is applied with the payment of accounts payable (accounts of creditors). The cash budget, therefore, ignores the accrual concept, which recognises an income or expense when it is incurred, whether or not the money has been received or paid. In a cash budget, the actual inflow (money received) as well as the actual outflow (money paid out) is recorded in the month (or year) when it was actually received or paid.

An example of a cash budget is provided in Example 11.2 below. When studying the example, keep in mind that *cash receipts* include all the entity's cash inflows in a given financial period. The most common of cash receipts are cash sales, collections of accounts receivable, and other cash receipts.

Cash disbursements include all outlays of cash by an entity during a given financial period. The most common cash disbursements are cash purchases of inventory, payments of accounts payable, rent and lease payments, wages and salaries, water and electricity

EXAMPLE 11.2

Example of a cash budget

Mary Ngobane, a financial analyst for Rama Industries, has prepared the sales and cash-disbursement forecast for the period March to July of the current year. Mary has considered market trends when she determined the sales and cash disbursement. She established that in the holiday months, Rama Industries showed growth in their sales, but as their sales increased, so did the cash disbursements. Mary also did market- and industry-related research to determine, through personal visits to companies and through sending questionnaires to companies, what the sales trends and trends with regard to cash disbursements are within the market. Mary incorporated the information obtained in the forecast as shown in the sales and cash-disbursement forecast below.

SALES AND CASH-DISBURSEMENT FORECAST FOR RAMA INDUSTRIES FOR THE PERIOD MARCH TO JULY		
Month	**Sales** **R**	**Cash disbursements** **R**
March (actual)	3 000	1 500
April (actual)	4 500	2 000
May	4 000	2 000
June	7 000	2 500
July	10 000	5 500
Total sales and cash disbursements	**28 500**	**13 500**

Mary has indicated that 40% of sales will be on a cash basis. The remaining 60% of sales are sales conducted on a credit basis. Of the credit sales, 40% will be collected during the month of sales, a further 40% will be collected in the month following the month in which the sales transaction was conducted, and the remaining 20% will be collected two months after the sale.

Rama Industries wants to maintain a minimum ending balance in its cash account of R2 000. Balances above this amount will be invested in short-term securities (e.g. a fixed deposit at a commercial bank), whereas any negative defects will be financed through short-term bank borrowing (bank overdraft). The opening cash balance on 1 May is R5 000.

The cash budget for the months May, June, and July that Mary prepared is shown below.

CASH BUDGET FOR RAMA INDUSTRIES FOR THE MONTHS MAY, JUNE, AND JULY					
	March	**April**	**May**	**June**	**July**
Actual sales	3 000	4 500			
Forecasted sales			4 000	7 000	10 000
Expected income:					
Cash sales (sales × 40%)			1 600	2 800	4 000
Collection from debtors:			960	1 680	2 400
Accounts receivable after one month			1 080	960	1 680
+ Accounts receivable after two months			360	540	480
= Total cash received			**4 000**	**5 980**	**8 560**
Less total cash disbursement			(2 000)	(2 500)	(5 500)
= Net cash flow			2 000	3 480	3 060
+ Opening cash			5 000	7 000	10 480
= Closing cash			7 000	10 480	13 540
Less minimum cash balance			(2 000)	(2 000)	(2 000)
= Surplus / (shortage) of cash			**5 000**	**8 480**	**11 540**

payments, tax payments, fixed asset purchases, interest payments, cash dividend payments, repurchases or retirements of shares, payments of loans and cash drawings. It is important to remember that depreciation, and other non-cash charges are *not* included in the cash budget, because they are representing a scheduled write-off of an earlier cash outflow.

When a *cash surplus* is reached at the end of the cash flow budget, it means that the entity will have enough cash available to commit itself to short-term obligations, and could use the money to invest or save. When a *shortage of cash* is expected at the end of the cash flow budget, the entity, has to make use of short-term borrowing sources, to be able to raise the necessary cash to commit itself to short-term obligations.

Example 11.3 below provides a cash-budget template that an entrepreneur may adjust to suit his or her needs as well as a practical exercise.

As the entity will cater mainly for business clients, 70% of all sales will be conducted on a credit basis. Credit sales will be collected as follows:

▶ 50% will be collected during the month of sales
▶ 30% will be collected one month after the original sales transaction took place
▶ 20% will be collected two months after the original sales transaction took place.

EXAMPLE 11.3

A cash-budget template and practical exercise

You are interested in purchasing Executive Dry-Cleaning. It is estimated that the business will have an opening cash balance of R120 000.

The following cash inflows are expected:

EXPECTED INFLOWS FOR EXECUTIVE DRY-CLEANING FOR THE PERIOD JANUARY TO JULY

Sales	R
Actual sales for January	30 000
Forecast sales for:	
February	25 000
March	40 000
April	47 000
May	50 000
June	70 000
July	80 000

Prepare a cash-flow budget for Executive Dry-Cleaning for the period February to July by downloading the cash-flow budget worksheet from the following website: http://southafrica.smetoolkit.org/sa/en/content/en/2889/Cash-Flow-Budget-Worksheet. Change the format to suit your needs. Your answer should look as shown overleaf.

EXPECTED OUTFLOWS FOR EXECUTIVE DRY-CLEANING FOR THE PERIOD JANUARY TO JULY

	February R	March R	April R	May R	June R	July R
Advertising	5 000	4 000	3 000	2 000	1 000	1 500
Bank service charges	300	300	300	300	300	300
Fuel	2 000	2 000	2 000	2 000	2 500	2 500
Insurance	8 000	8 000	8 000	8 000	8 000	8 000
Interest	1 000	1 000	1 000	1 000	1 000	1 000
Consumables purchased	2 000	2 500	3 000	3 500	4 000	4 500
Salaries and wages	5 000	5 000	5 000	5 000	5 000	5 000
Rent (including utilities and property tax)	25 000	25 000	25 000	25 000	25 000	25 000
Leases	1 200	1 200	1 200	1 200	1 200	1 200

EXECUTIVE DRY-CLEANING CASH-FLOW BUDGET

	February R	March R	April R	May R	June R	July R	Total R
Beginning cash balance	120 000.00	93 050.00	79 500.00	73 450.00	73 420.00	88 000.00	
Cash inflows (income):							
Accts. rec. collections	15 050.00	23 450.00	28 350.00	32 970.00	41 580.00	49 700.00	191 100.00
Loan proceeds							0.00
Sales and receipts	7 500.00	12 000.00	14 100.00	15 000.00	21 000.00	24.00	69 624.00
Total cash inflows	22 550.00	35 450.00	42 450.00	47 970.00	62 580.00	49 724.00	260 724.00
Available cash balance	142 550.00	128 500.00	121 950.00	121 420.00	136 000.00	137 724.00	
Cash outflows (expenses):							
Advertising	5 000.00	4 000.00	3 000.00	2 000.00	1 000.00	1 000.00	16 000.00
Bank service charges	300.00	300.00	300.00	300.00	300.00	300.00	1,800.00
Fuel	2 000.00	2 000.00	2 000.00	2 000.00	2 500.00	2 500.00	13 000.00
Insurance	8 000.00	8 000.00	8 000.00	8 000.00	8 000.00	8 000.00	48 000.00
Interest	1 000.00	1 000.00	1 000.00	1 000.00	1 000.00	1 000.00	6 000.00
Consumables purchased	2 000.00	2 500.00	3 000.00	3 500.00	4 000.00	4 500.00	19 500.00
Salaries and wages	5 000.00	5 000.00	5 000.00	5 000.00	5 000.00	5 000.00	30 000.00
Rent	25 000.00	25 000.00	25 000.00	25 000.00	25 000.00	25 000.00	150 000.00
Leases	1 200.00	1 200.00	1 200.00	1 200.00	1 200.00	1 200.00	7 200.00
Subtotal	49 500.00	49 000.00	48 500.00	48 000.00	48 000.00	48 500.00	291 500.00
Total cash outflows	49 500.00	49 000.00	48 500.00	48 000.00	48 000.00	48 500.00	291 500.00
Ending cash balance	93 050.00	79 500.00	73 450.00	73 420.00	88 000.00	89 224.00	

11.3.3.2 The pro forma statement of profit or loss and other comprehensive income (income statement)

> **DEFINITION**
>
> The statement of profit or loss and other comprehensive income is a statement used to anticipate whether an entity will be making a profit or a loss during a given financial year, taking into account all the income that is to be received, and all the expenses that have to be paid.

The statement of profit or loss and other comprehensive income reflects the **accrual concept**, which means that an income or expense is recognised when it is incurred during a financial period, whether or not the money has been received or paid.

The following steps may be followed to compile a pro forma statement of profit or loss and other comprehensive income:
- *Compile a sales or fees-received projection* to determine the projected income that will be earned through the core activity
- *Compile an operating schedule* to determine the amounts that will be spent on the use of materials, labour costs, and other overheads directly related to performing the core activity of the venture – after this is subtracted, the gross profit can be determined
- *Determine any other expenses* that will be incurred during the normal operations of the business
- *Calculate the projected profit* for the period.

A new venture can use the percentage-of-sales method in developing a pro forma statement of profit or loss and other comprehensive income together with the fixed and variable components of the entity's historical costs and expenses.

With the percentage-of-sales method, and distinguishing between fixed and variable costs, an entity would concentrate on its cost of goods sold, operating expenses, and interest expense, to have a clearer and in-depth view of the different costs of the entity.

> **DEFINITION**
>
> Fixed costs are those costs that do not depend on other factors and so are expected to stay the same over a relatively long period.

Fixed salaries and rent are examples of **fixed costs**.

> **DEFINITION**
>
> Variable costs do depend on other factors and so vary over a given period, and do not stay the same year after year.

Some examples of **variable costs** are commission-based salaries, wages based on the number of hours worked (normal time plus overtime), and electricity used in a production plant (the more production the higher the electricity and vice versa), fuel costs (which depend on increases or decreases in the fuel price, and whether more fuel has been used or less). Distinguishing between fixed and variable costs will help the entrepreneur to identify where savings can be introduced to increase the profitability of the entity.

An example of a pro forma statement of profit or loss and other comprehensive income is provided in Example 11.4 below.

The format of the pro forma statement of profit or loss and other comprehensive income can be explored in more detail.

The first item on the pro forma statement of profit or loss and other comprehensive income is *revenue*. This reflects the total revenue that will be received from cash as well as credit sales. If the entrepreneur is going to render a service, this item will then be called income received from services rendered.

The second item is the *cost of goods sold*. This item includes all the expenses incurred to purchase and store the inventory and to place it in the hands of the buyer.

EXAMPLE 11.4

Example of a pro forma statement of profit or loss and other comprehensive income

The marketing department of Shuttle Enterprises estimates that its sales in the year 2015 will be R144 000. Interest expense is expected to remain unchanged at R2 480 and the firm plans to pay R2 000 in cash dividends during the year. A statement of profit or loss and other comprehensive income for Shuttle Enterprises in 2013, and a breakdown into fixed- and variable-cost components of the firm's cost of goods sold and operating expenses in 2014 are reflected in the statements below.

STATEMENT OF PROFIT OR LOSS AND OTHER COMPREHENSIVE INCOME OF SHUTTLE ENTERPRISES FOR THE YEAR ENDED 31 DECEMBER 2013	
	R
Sales revenue	115 200
Less: Cost of goods sold	(85 750)
Gross profit	29 450
Less: Operating expenses	(15 670)
Operating profits	13 780
Less: Interest expense	(2 480)
Profit for the period	11 300

FIXED- AND VARIABLE-COST BREAKDOWNS OF SHUTTLE ENTERPRISES FOR THE YEAR ENDED 31 DECEMBER 2014	
	R
Cost of goods sold	
Fixed cost (40%)	34 300
Variable cost (60%)	51 450
Total cost (100%)	85 750
Operating expenses	
Fixed cost (30%)	4 701
Variable cost (70%)	10 969
Total cost (100%)	15 670

To prepare a pro forma statement of profit or loss and other comprehensive income for Shuttle Enterprises for the year ended 31 December 2015, the first step would be to determine the new fixed and variable cost breakdowns for Shuttle Enterprises for the year ended 2015, as shown in the statement below.

FIXED- AND VARIABLE-COST BREAKDOWNS OF SHUTTLE ENTERPRISES FOR THE YEAR ENDED 31 DECEMBER 2015	
	R
Cost of goods sold	
Fixed cost (stays unchanged)	34 300
*Variable cost (51 450/115 200) x 144 000	64 313
Total cost	98 613
Operating expenses	
Fixed cost (stays unchanged)	4 701
*Variable cost (10 969/115 200) x 144 000	13 711
Total cost	18 412

The pro forma statement of profit or loss and other comprehensive income for the year ended 31 December 2015 is illustrated in the statement below.

STATEMENT OF PROFIT OR LOSS AND OTHER COMPREHENSIVE INCOME OF SHUTTLE ENTERPRISES FOR THE YEAR ENDED 31 DECEMBER 2015	
	R
Sales revenue	144 000
Less: Cost of goods sold	(98 613)
Gross profit	45 387
Less: Operating expenses	(18 412)
Operating profits	26 975
Less: Interest expense	(2 480)
Profit for the period	24 495

The variable costs of the previous year are divided by the previous years' sales and then that percentage is multiplied by the expected sales of the following year.
** *Calculated answers are estimated to the nearest rand.*

The *gross profit* represents the difference between the sales and cost of sales. The more the entrepreneur has earned through sales, and the less he or she has spent on costs incurred in purchasing and storing the inventory and placing it in the hands of the buyer, the greater the profit will be. One can thus define gross profit as the profit obtained over sales, by only taking cost of sales into account, and before any other income or costs are accounted for.

Other income earned through rent, or interest received can now be added to the gross profit but these were not included in the example.

Operating expenses consist of all the expenses that it is necessary to pay to be able to operate the business. Examples include water and electricity, telephone, fuel, delivery costs, salaries, wages, stationery consumed, and so on.

With the *operating expenses* deducted from the gross profit, one can now determine the *operating profit*. This is the profit (earnings) of the business, before deducting interest and tax.

Interest is now deducted. Interest is the financing cost incurred when money was borrowed by the business or for business purposes. It is important to remember that when a loan is paid back, the payment per month consists of both the capital repayment and the interest on the outstanding amount.

The money remaining, called *retained earnings,* is money that can be retained by the business to be used when necessary by the business, for example to expand.

Profit planning is important for an entrepreneur as it enables him or her to see the overall picture and to analyse how each cost and expense item behaves in relation to changes in the level of sales. The budgeted amounts can then be used to compare with actual results, and variances can then be analysed and corrected.

Example 11.5 below provides a pro forma statement of profit or loss and other comprehensive income template that an entrepreneur may adjust to suit his or her needs as well as a practical exercise.

EXAMPLE 11.5

A pro forma statement of profit or loss and other comprehensive income template and practical exercise

New Horizons asked you to assist them in preparing a pro forma statement of profit or loss and other comprehensive income for the year ended 31 December 2015. They provided you with the following estimates of income and expense items that will be earned and incurred during the financial year ending 31 December 2015.

ESTIMATED INCOME AND EXPENSE ITEMS FOR NEW HORIZONS FOR THE YEAR ENDED 31 DECEMBER 2015	
	R
Sales	2 575 250
Sales returns	30 250
Opening inventory	1 000 000
Purchases	800 000
Freight-in	200 000
Closing inventory	1 200 000
Advertising	12 000
Bad debts	10 000
Bank charges	12 000
Contract labour	120 000
Depreciation	50 000
Insurance	100 000
Interest	14 400
Maintenance	20 000
Office expenses	30 000
Operating supplies	40 000
Payroll taxes	117 000
Permits and licenses	20 000
Property taxes	60 000
Repairs	10 000
Telephone	36 000
Fuel	50 000
Wages	260 000

Prepare a statement of profit or loss and other comprehensive income for New Horizons for the year ending 31 December 2015 by downloading the pro forma statement of profit or loss and other comprehensive income from the following website: http://southafrica.smetoolkit.org/sa/en/content/en/317/Income-Statement-Template. Change the format to suit your needs. Your answer should look as shown overleaf:

NEW HORIZON PRO FORMA STATEMENT OF PROFIT AND LOSS AND OTHER COMPREHENSIVE INCOME FOR THE YEAR ENDED 31 DECEMBER 2010		
	R	R
Revenue:		
Gross sales		2 575 250.00
Less: Sales returns and allowances		30 250.00
Net sales		2 545 000.00
Cost of goods sold:		
Beginning inventory	1 000 000.00	
Add: Purchases	800 000.00	
Freight-in	200 000.00	
	2 000 000.00	
Less: Ending inventory	1 200 000.00	
Cost of goods sold		800 000.00
Gross profit (loss)		1 745 000.00
Expenses:		
Advertising	12 000.00	
Bad debts	10 000.00	
Bank charges	12 000.00	
Contract labour	120 000.00	
Depreciation	50 000.00	
Insurance	100 000.00	
Interest	14 400.00	
Maintenance	20 000.00	
Office expenses	30 000.00	
Operating supplies	40 000.00	
Payroll taxes	117 000.00	
Permits and licenses	20 000.00	
Property taxes	60 000.00	
Repairs	10 000.00	
Telephone	36 000.00	
Fuel	50 000.00	
Wages	260 000.00	
Total expenses		961 400.00
Net operating income		783 600.00
Net income (loss)		783 600.00

11.3.3.3 The pro forma statement of financial position

The statement of financial position is a planned financial statement on a certain date to determine the financial position of the entity with respect to its capital generated and the application of capital.

In the **statement of financial position**, an entrepreneur anticipates future assets, liabilities, and the net worth position of the entity.

A number of simplified approaches are available for preparing the statement of financial position. The most used approach is the judgemental approach which entails that the values of certain statement of financial position accounts are estimated, and others are calculated. When this is applied, the entity's external financing is used as a balancing figure. This means that the amount of external financing is needed to bring the statement into balance.

A positive value for external financing required, means that, to support the entity's forecast level of operation, it must raise funds externally using debt and (or) equity financing. If the value for external financing required is negative, it means that funds are available for use in repaying debt, repurchasing stock, or increasing dividends.

Example 11.6 provides a pro forma statement of financial position template that an entrepreneur may adjust to suit his or her needs as well as a practical exercise.

The entrepreneur should remember that these financial statements are not the financial statements that will be published. These financial statements are for internal use only. They are prepared so that the financial manager or the entrepreneur can plan and establish the financial position of the venture. Therefore, these financial statements will not necessarily correspond with the Generally Accepted Accounting Practices (GAAP) standards or

EXAMPLE 11.6

A pro forma statement of financial position template and practical exercise

You are required to assist with the preparation of Entrepreneurial Business Solutions' pro forma statement of financial position as at 31 December 2015. You have been provided with the Assets, Equity, and Liability forecast for 31 December 2015.

ASSETS, EQUITY, AND LIABILITY FORECAST FOR ENTREPRENEURIAL BUSINESS SOLUTIONS AS AT 31 DECEMBER 2015	
	R
Cash	200 000
Debtors	300 000
Allowance for credit losses	30 000
Inventory	500 000
Expenses paid in advance	10 000
Vehicles	300 000
Accumulated depreciation on vehicles	10 000
Furniture	100 000
Accumulated depreciation on furniture	5 000
Equipment	200 000
Accumulated depreciation on equipment	20 000
Buildings	500 000
Accumulated depreciation on buildings	10 000
Land	1 000 000
Creditors	200 000
VAT payable	140 000
Payroll taxes payable	50 000
Current portion of long-term loan	20 000
Long-term loan	875 000
Owners equity	???
Net profit	1 250 000

Prepare a statement of financial position for Entrepreneurial Business Solutions as at 31 December 2015 to determine the amount of owner's equity that will be involved by downloading the pro forma template from the following website: http://southafrica.smetoolkit.org/sa/en/content/en/685/Balance-Sheet-Template. Change the format to suit your needs. Your answer should look as shown overleaf:

ENTREPRENEURIAL BUSINESS SOLUTIONS PRO FORMA STATEMENT OF FINANCIAL POSITION AS AT 31 DECEMBER 2015			
	R	R	R
ASSETS			
Current assets:			
Cash		200 000.00	
Accounts receivable	300 000.00		
Less: Reserve for bad debts	30 000	270 000	
Merchandise inventory		500 000	
Prepaid expenses		10 000	
Total current assets			980 000.00
Non-current assets:			
Vehicles	300 000		
Less: Accumulated depreciation	10 000	290 000	
Furniture and fixtures	100 000		
Less: Accumulated depreciation	5 000	95 000	
Equipment	200 000		
Less: Accumulated depreciation	20 000	180 000	
Buildings	500 000		
Less: Accumulated depreciation	10 000	490 000	
Land		1 000 000	
Total non-current assets			2 055 000
Total assets			3,035,000.00
LIABILITIES AND CAPITAL			
Current liabilities:			
Accounts payable		200 000.00	
Sales taxes payable		140 000	
Payroll taxes payable		50 000	
Short-term bank loan payable		20 000	
Total current liabilities			410 000.00
Non-current liabilities:			
Mortgage payable		875 000	
Total long-term liabilities			875 000
Total liabilities			1 285 000
Equity:			
Owner's capital		500 000	
Profit		1 250 000	
Total equity			1 750 000
Total liabilities and capital			3 035 000.00

the International Financial Reporting Standards (IFRS).

CONCLUSION

When planning your venture, it is essential that a financial plan should be drawn up. The financial plan should include what financial sources you are going to use, what financial policy you are going to introduce, and, most importantly, the following pro forma statements:

▸ The cash-flow budget
▸ The statement of profit or loss and other comprehensive income
▸ The statement of financial position.

For business-plan purposes, it is recommended that entrepreneurs provide figures for at least five years in advance. Provide monthly projected figures for the first and second year, quarterly figures for years three and four, and annual projections thereafter. To determine your selling price, perform a break-even analysis, and take into account all the different factors that may influence the setting of your prices. All of this is necessary to ensure that the financial management of the new venture is based on sound practice, and will ensure the survival of the entity.

SELF-ASSESSMENT QUESTIONS

Multiple-choice questions

1. What is the main purpose of budgeting?
   a. To assess the non-financial performance of an entity
   b. To value a company
   c. To plan and control the income and expenditure of an entity
   d. To help in the preparation of a five-year business plan.
2. Which one of the following will not be an advantage of budgeting?
   a. Budgets define goals.
   b. Budgets serve as a communication medium.

   c. Budgets help with the allocation of resources.
   d. None of the above.
3. The pro forma statement of cash flows is important for a potential investor as it can influence a potential investor's decision to invest because the pro forma statement of cash flows reflects:
   a. The anticipated financial performance of an entity
   b. The anticipated financial position of an entity
   c. The anticipated liquidity of an entity
   d. The anticipated investment needed in the entity.
4. The following item must not be included in a pro forma statement of cash flows:
   a. Cash sales
   b. Depreciation
   c. Expenses paid with cash
   d. Interest received on a positive bank balance that will be reflected on your bank statement.
5. Which one of the following pro forma financial statements will provide information on an entity's future financial performance?
   a. The pro forma statement of profit or loss and other comprehensive income.
   b. The pro forma statement of cash flows.
   c. The pro forma statement of financial position.
   d. The pro forma statement of changes in equity.

DISCUSSION QUESTIONS

1. Discuss the planning process.
2. Discuss the components that should be included in the financial policy.
3. Discuss the factors to be taken into account in developing a financial plan.
4. Discuss the break-even point and the importance of its inclusion in a business plan.
5. Discuss the steps involved with the financial planning process.

EXPERIENTIAL EXERCISE

You are currently a first-year student in entrepreneurship at university. You receive a monthly allowance of R500 from your parents. You need to prepare a cash budget to determine whether you will be able to cover the following monthly expenses:

	R
Car guards at university	60
Rent	1 900
Groceries	800
Cellphone costs	300
Water and electricity	200
Entertainment (social)	300
Fuel	400
Food and drinks on campus	200
Stationery	70

Additional information
1. Your parents pay for your studies and books.
2. You have an au-pair job and receive R3 000 per month.
3. You also provide maths classes to high-school students. You receive R50 per tutoring session and give four lessons each Saturday.
4. You try to save your cash surpluses in order to buy birthday presents.

Required
Prepare, according to the above-mentioned information, your own cash budget.

CASE STUDY

DECONITE TRADERS

The partially completed cash budget was taken from the records of Deconite Traders:

	NOVEMBER 2014	DECEMBER 2014
	R	R
Cash receipts	168 000	120 000
Cash payments		
Payments to creditors		(?)
Cash purchases		(?)
Other expenses	(14 000)	(14 000)

Additional information
1. Balances as at 1 November 2014:

	R
Equipment (at cost price)	80 000
Accumulated depreciation on equipment	34 000
Bank overdraft	40 000
Salaries payable	3 000

2. Extract from the statement of profit or loss and other comprehensive income for the year ended 31 October 2014:

	R
Salaries	180 000
Depreciation	4 600
Advertisements	21 500
Credit losses (bad debts)	12 000
Other expenses	168 000

3. Total sales

	REAL		BUDGET	
August 2014	September 2014	October 2014	November 2014	December 2014
R	R	R	R	R
60 000	70 000	85 000	90 000	94 000

4. Cost of sales is equal to 75% of sales
5. Debts are collected as follows:
   - 40% in the month of sales to allow debtors the benefit of receiving 12.5% settlement discount for timely payment;
   - 35% after 30 days;
   - 20% after 60 days; and
   - The rest is written off after 90 days.
6. 40% of the purchases are done on a cash basis. Creditors are paid after 30 days. Inventory on hand is maintained by monthly purchases.
7. Advertising costs are based on the budgeted monthly sales and are paid cash within the same month. The advertising cost is expected to increase from 3% to 4% on 1 December 2014.
8. The entity has five employees who receive a salary of R3 000 each per month. Salaries are paid

cash. The salaries payable for October 2014 will be paid in November 2014.
9. Other expenses amount to R14 000 per month.
10. A new computer costing R8 700 will be purchased on credit during November 2014. The amount will be paid back in three equal monthly instalments, starting on 15 December 2014.

Required
a. Prepare the cash payment section of the cash budget for the period 1 November 2014 to 31 December 2014.
b. Calculate the receipts from debtors during November 2014.
c. Calculate the credit losses (bad debts) that will be written off during the budgeted period.
d. Calculate the settlement discount that will be allowed during December 2014.

SUGGESTED WEBSITE LINKS

http://www.youtube.com/watch?feature=player_embedded&v=qsDWkpKDvpE
http://www.vantagepoint.co.za
http://www.entrepreneurmag.co.za
http://www.southafrica.smetoolkit.org

REFERENCES

Bezuidenhout, S, Cloete, M, Joynt, C, Nortjé-Rossouw, D. & Van Pletsen, L. 2013, *Accounting and Basic Financial Literacy*. 3rd ed. Pretoria: Salt and Pepper Publishing.
Bridge, S. & Hegarty, C. 2013. *Beyond the Business Plan*. Hampshire, UK. Palgrave Macmillan Publishers.
Gitman, LJ. 1998. *Principles of Managerial Finance*. Brief edition. Boston: Addison-Wesley.
Gitman, LJ. 2007. *Principles of Managerial Finance*. Boston: Addison-Wesley.
Gitman, LJ. & Joehnk, MD. 2004. *Personal Financial Planning*. 10th ed. Mason: Thomson South-Western.
Smit, PC. et al. 1996. *Economics – A South African Perspective*. Kenwyn: Juta & Co, Ltd.

CHAPTER 12

The business plan

Stefan Bezuidenhout

LEARNING OUTCOMES

On completion of this chapter you will be able to:
▶ Understand what a business plan entails
▶ Identify the various aspects dealt with in a business plan
▶ Determine the differences and similarities between a business plan and a strategic plan
▶ Formulate a business plan
▶ Understand how a business plan is implemented
▶ Identify the criteria for an effective business plan and its successful implementation
▶ Identify the pitfalls in formulating and implementing a business plan.

OPENING CASE STUDY

You could ask a student, Monique, the following questions: 'What is your purpose at the institution? Why are you studying?' Monique's response could be: 'I am at the institution to gain knowledge, meet new people and most importantly to complete my educational qualification'. A second question to Monique could be: 'How do you plan to achieve your goals or reach your objectives?' Her response may be: 'I will attend all my classes/lectures; study and work hard on a regular basis; and pass all my tests and examinations'. Monique therefore knows what her purpose is at the institution and how she plans to achieve her goals. Each and every student will have their own agenda for studying at an educational institution. When an individual decides to pursue entrepreneurship, he or she also needs to have a feasible and viable business idea, knows what the business venture is all about and how he

or she plans to develop a sustainable business venture. A business plan describes your current position, where you want to be in future and how you intend to get from the one point to the other. Just as students have different goals and objectives, entrepreneurs have different business ideas and plans. There is not only one correct recipe for a business plan and no single plan will work in all situations. A business plan is an entrepreneur's personal written road map. It provides the direction, guidance and motivation when embarking on the process of starting a business.

1. Make a list of your goals and objectives (personal, educational, social, business) for the year.
2. For each goal and objective listed in Question 1, develop a plan of action of how you will accomplish it.

INTRODUCTION

Business plans are used for various purposes such as to determine the chances of business success, to raise capital, and as a schedule for business start-up and growth. A business plan is of vital importance in today's highly competitive business world. In fact, financial institutions would generally not even consider providing financing for would-be entrepreneurs who do not have a well-reasoned business plan. Furthermore, an entrepreneur without a business plan is comparable to an aeroplane without a flight plan, that is, lacking in direction.

Even after the business has been started, the business plan plays an important role as a managerial tool. Management often uses business plans as the basis for formulating business strategies and making difficult decisions; in this instance, the original business plan constitutes a base-line document on which to plan future endeavours. A well-formulated business plan could also be a source document for management in understanding the reasoning of those who founded the business in the first place, decided on particular products and (or) services, and penetrated the markets they did.

This chapter begins with a discussion of the purpose of a business plan. This is followed by guidance on how to prepare a business plan and some detail on the aspects to include, as well as a brief discussion on international business plans. A pro forma business plan and a business plan template are provided towards the end of the chapter to clearly illustrate the structure and content of a typical business plan.

12.1 The purpose of a business plan

When focusing on business plans, it is important to remember that such documents are formulated by an individual or venture team with a specific purpose in mind, namely to start or acquire a business. When formulating the **business plan**, the individual entrepreneur or venture team has to plan for aspects that are often difficult to predict, such as the level of possible market penetration, intangible aspects such as the attitudes of potential customers and suppliers towards the business, volatile trends (future economic trends), and unforeseen circumstances such as dramatic price increases of supplies. The level at which an entrepreneur is able to anticipate such aspects accurately will have a considerable influence on the success of a venture.

> **DEFINITION**
>
> A business plan is a written road map of where a business venture is headed, what it has to do to get there, and what it will look like on arrival.

Timmons (1994), however, indicates that there are further reasons for formulating a business plan apart from those mentioned above. These include the following:

▸ The process of formulating a business plan helps an entrepreneur to work smarter rather than harder, since planning helps people to arrive at a better understanding of the risk involved in starting or acquiring a business, and to devise ways of reducing such risks; planning forces the entrepreneur to consider the future, making him or her more alert and responsive to opportunities, problems, and changes.

▸ By formulating a business plan, an entrepreneur develops and updates business strategy by assessing the efficacy of ideas and approaches.

▸ By setting goals in a business plan, an entrepreneur develops a concern for realising goals and showing progress, particularly if the goals are stated clearly and in measurable terms, thus allowing performance and progress to be evaluated.

▸ By setting realistic goals, an entrepreneur acquires a dynamic understanding of what needs to be done to start or acquire a business and manage it successfully, thus establishing a blueprint for the effective management of the start-up or acquisition process, and helping the people involved cope with a highly stressful situation.

▸ The formulation of a business plan has various positive effects on motivation in that people trying to realise attainable goals are motivated to do so.

Having a business plan, however, is not all plain sailing. Bangs (2005) shows that there are certain things that business plans cannot do, namely:

▸ *Business plans cannot predict the future.* Business plans can contain a best guess of what the future could possibly be like but they cannot predict the future. The business plans of the *Titanic* probably stated that it would sail the oceans for about 50 years, little knowing that it would not survive its maiden voyage.

▸ *Business plans cannot guarantee funding.* Although an entrepreneur may be convinced that he or she has a sure-fire winning concept, banks will not necessarily agree.

▸ *Business plans cannot raise all the money required.* Cost and sales estimates (forecasts) in business plans are often incorrect; entrepreneurs often overestimate sales and underestimate costs, leading to a situation where there is a shortfall of cash required to run the business smoothly.

▸ *Business plans cannot fool all the people all the time.* As banks and other financiers see hundreds of business plans a year, they are able to spot fallacies and confidence tricks in business plans.

Business plans also have some important negative effects of which we need to take note. Timmons (1994) indicates the following problems associated with business plans:

▸ Business plans rapidly become dated because of changing market conditions, new technologies, and product innovations.

▸ Rigidly sticking to a business plan may result in inflexibility in starting and (or) managing the business – since the future is so unpredictable, the entrepreneur needs to be flexible in dealing with challenges.

▸ There are many important events affecting a business that the formulators of a business plan cannot anticipate, thus a business plan is a blueprint of foreseeable events and can provide very little guidance if unforeseen events occur.

▸ Formulating a good business plan necessitates the use of various resources (e.g. reliable information, plenty of time, and human resources), which may not be readily available to entrepreneurs or may be in short supply. Furthermore, should such resources be available, they may be better utilised for purposes other than detailed planning, such as efforts to start up or manage a business.

Implementing or executing the business plan is key to the success and existence of a business venture. Business plans also need to be updated from time to time because they can become rapidly outdated due to changing market conditions, new technologies and products innovations. Read about this in the entrepreneurial dilemma – *Your idea is worth nothing*.

ENTREPRENEURIAL DILEMMA

Your idea is worth nothing

It's not all about the great business idea you've come up with, it's how you execute it that gives it value. When you are executing your business plan, you will be implementing a plethora of (hopefully) great ideas. And frankly, an idea is really only worthwhile when it includes some kind of execution plan. It is far more important for entrepreneurs to be 'getting things done' than thinking about an endless stream of new ideas about how they are going to change the world. Put simply, execution gets the product shipped and brings revenue in the door; revenue pays the bills and keeps you in business. It is really difficult to overstate the importance of the action in executing your plans and responding to the changing business environment. Invariably, business plans change as you adapt to the ever-changing climate around you, and the greater flow of information makes these changes occur with great rapidity. Bill Gates started out building programming languages but ended up hitting the home run when he licensed operating system software that he resold to IBM. Nokia started out in forestry, not phones; General Electric started out in domestic appliances and today makes most of its money from jet turbines, medical diagnostic tools and until recently, financial services. The lesson here is that reinvention is more important than invention and that most certainly require a powerful ability to execute within your business DNA, rather than come up with ideas. In reality, as you execute, you also learn that what you thought would be a good idea might not hold as much promise as initially anticipated. If I had to promote either the idea or the execution, I would certainly choose the latter.

Source: Adapted from Spratt (2012). © Entrepreneur Media SA (Pty) Ltd. Reprinted by permission of Entrepreneur Media SA (Pty) Ltd.

1. Besides Bill Gates, Nokia and General Electric, identify at least three other companies that were reinvented to keep up with changing market conditions, new technologies and product innovations.

12.2 Preparing a business plan

The purpose of business plans and some of the problems associated with drawing them up have been indicated. The discussion that follows will focus on preparing business plans. According to Megginson et al. (1988), there are three main steps involved when preparing a business plan.

▶ Determine the present status of a business (that is, no business has been established but the venture team would like to start or acquire one).

▶ Describe where you want to go with the business and develop objectives to take you there (that is, an entrepreneur describes how he or she will start a business and what objectives will be used to achieve this goal).

▶ Formulate an action plan to facilitate the realisation of objectives (that is, the entrepreneur formulates a plan to implement the business plan).

When discussing the preparation of business plans, an important issue pertains to who should be performing this function. In practice, we find that where an entrepreneur is the only person involved in the business, he or she personally has to prepare the business plan while drawing on the advice and input of others. Where a venture team is involved, the formulation of the business plan needs to be a team effort to ensure that all the members contribute to the plan, take ownership of it, and are committed to its successful implementation.

Although it is preferable for an entrepreneur to develop the business plan personally, many prefer to outsource it so that they can pay more attention to recruiting employees. Outsourcing the formulation of the business plan, however, may not always be such a great idea. Entrepreneurs who formulate the business plans themselves have the opportunity to explore possible outcomes of different strategies, and can come to a more in-depth understanding of the human and financial requirements of starting and expanding a business. Furthermore, they may also come to a better understanding of the business in which they want to become involved.

Having completed the first step of preparing a business plan, in other words, deciding who will formulate it, it is important that a plan of action should be decided on for formulating the business plan. According to Timmons (1994), such an action plan should encompass the following steps:

▸ *Decide on the format and outline of the business plan.* The person responsible for drafting the various sections has to be identified and the time scheduled for drafting the business plan established.

▸ *Decide on the specific tasks to be completed in starting or acquiring a business.* The entrepreneur or venture team need to make decisions regarding the priorities of such tasks and those responsible for them as well as the target dates for completion of these tasks. Thereafter the various tasks need to be broken down into easy-to-complete components.

▸ *Place the tasks to be completed on an action calendar.* This action calendar could be assessed by the entrepreneur with respect to due dates and completion of tasks.

▸ *Formulate the business plan and make adjustments to the target dates and action to be completed.* At this stage, it will be useful to have outside reviewers (e.g. consultants, business people or attorneys) review the business plan to assess the level of realism of the ideas contained in it. Outside reviewers can also act as a sounding board in developing solutions to problems.

12.3 Aspects covered in the business plan

A business plan is an important document that can take up to 400 hours or more to complete. This document is important since the effective use of human and financial resources depends on a good business plan and its successful implementation. Over the years that the many entrepreneurs and venture teams have formulated business plans, a fairly universal outline has emerged. This broad outline encompasses the following (Megginson et al., 1988):

▸ A cover sheet indicating the proposed name of the business, its address, its landline, fax or cellphone numbers, the principals involved in starting or acquiring the business, and the date when the business plan was completed

▸ An executive summary briefly setting out the business plan, indicating the major objectives, describing the products and (or) services, briefly delineating the marketing strategy, and showing some financial projections

▸ A table of contents, with the relevant page numbers, indicating the various sections, subsections, and appendices of the business plan

▸ A brief history of the business and its principals, showing the corporate structure of the business and past business successes and (or) experiences

▸ A description of the business to ensure clarity with regard to the type of business

▸ A description of the market by indicating the possible target market, showing some projections (estimates) in respect of market penetration, and providing an analysis of the competition

▸ A discussion of products and (or) services to give clarity on the products to be sold and (or) the services to be provided, the status of research and development, and an indication of patents, trademarks, and copyrights

▸ A delineation of the management and organisational structure of the business by naming the managers who will put the business plan into practice, explaining what the organisational structure will look like, and outlining the employment policies that will be followed

▸ A description of the objectives and goals of the business by indicating its manufacturing, marketing, and financial plans, revenue forecasts, and quality-assurance plans

▶ A projection of income, cash flow, and costs, including projected statements of comprehensive income (income statements) for the first few years of existence of the business, projected cash-flow analyses for the first year, projected statements of financial position (balance sheets) for the first few years, analyses in respect of projected cost–volume–profit breakdowns, and projected statements of changes in financial position

▶ Some appendices, including organisational charts, product brochures, and detailed product, marketing, manufacturing, financial, and administration analyses.

The aspects covered in the business plan are discussed in more detail below.

12.3.1 Cover sheet

The cover sheet should contain the basic information about the business, such as the names of the principals and the name of the business. Being the first page of the business plan, this page is the first to be seen by prospective investors and financiers and should look professional, thorough (attention to detail), and attractive to draw their interest.

12.3.2 Executive summary

It is important to supply an **executive summary** or statement of purpose as an overview of the business plan as good executive summaries sell ideas (Bangs, 2005). Since people who look at a number of business plans do not have the time to read each one in detail, they tend to assess the initial worth of the plan or business idea on the basis of the executive summary or statement of purpose. Should the ideas elicit the interest of the prospective investor or financier, he or she may then read the business plan in detail or assign it to other people for review (Bangs, 2005). In the

executive summary, an overview of the business plan is supplied, together with an indication of its various objectives, and how such objectives will be realised (Megginson et al., 1988).

> **DEFINITION**
>
> An executive summary is a short summary of the entire business plan that provides a clear and concise overview of the future business venture.

12.3.3 Table of contents

This may appear to be stating the obvious, but it is surprising how many business plans fail this test. A table of contents enables the reader to find the information in which he or she is interested more readily.

12.3.4 Brief history of the business and its principals

The business plan should contain information about the entrepreneur or members of the venture team, together with an indication of the contribution of each person. Prospective investors, financiers, and the future managers of the business are interested in details in respect of how the idea for the product or service of the business originated, how this product or service was developed, why it was decided to start or acquire a business, and what the process of business acquisition or start-up entailed. In cases where the business was acquired from someone else, the previous owner, and the history of the business under the original owner should be indicated. Should the business have been operating profitably in the past, this should also be indicated here.

12.3.5 Description of the business

It is of vital importance that the readers of a business plan should be provided with a basic description of the business, namely: its size, what consumer needs it will try to meet, and which products and (or) services it will provide

(Bangs, 2005). It is also useful to indicate what the entrepreneur or venture team expects from the business and compare this with customer and supplier expectations.

12.3.6 Description of the market

Focused efforts at market penetration are simply not possible if the entrepreneur does not have a clearly defined target market. A target market should be geographically and demographically well defined so that marketing efforts can be focused directly on such a market. The potential target market should also be described in terms of consumer behaviour, what proportion could be penetrated, and what would motivate its members to change brands or buy a new product or service.

Example 12.1 below provides insight into the different markets that an entrepreneur identified in the insurance sector after conducting research.

EXAMPLE 12.1

Reliance Life, an insurance company, targets markets that are under-serviced or viewed as high-risk by traditional insurance companies such as Santam, Outsurance, Hollard and Sanlam. Reliance Life identified niche, largely untapped markets. These comprise four main groups – pensioners, commuters, municipalities and unions. The other groups fall into the lower-income bracket and have also been under-serviced by the market. Under-serviced markets have great growth potential.

Source: Adapted from Pitman (2013). © Entrepreneur Media SA (Pty) Ltd. Reprinted by permission of Entrepreneur Media SA (Pty) Ltd.

12.3.7 Description of the products and (or) services

This section should provide details of the services to be rendered and (or) products to be sold. According to Timmons (1994), it is important to indicate the applications of products and services, and to describe the primary and secondary end-users of products and services supplied. Since competitive advantage is so important, unique features of products and services should be indicated. It will also be useful to supply a comparative analysis of what is currently available on the market and the new product to be sold or service to be rendered. In this regard, it can also be indicated how such unique features of products and (or) services could facilitate market penetration in competition with existing products or services. When describing products to be sold and (or) services to be rendered, the entrepreneur should also point out their weaknesses.

The present level of development of the product and (or) service needs to be indicated, together with an estimate of how much money, time, and other resources will still be required to develop, test, and introduce such a product or service. In this regard, it is also important to indicate how you may gain a favourable position in the market when introducing the product or service, and how comparative advantage against any competition could be maintained after introducing the product or service. To achieve this, an entrepreneur may want to indicate how he or she will upgrade and expand his or her products and services to ensure continuing competitive advantage (Timmons, 1994).

12.3.8 Management and organisational structure of the business

In this section of the business plan, the key management roles in the business and the people who fulfil such managerial roles are indicated. As far as other employee roles in the organisation are concerned, an organisational chart needs to be formulated to show the various roles, and how such roles are horizontally and vertically related.

Apart from describing key management roles and formulating an organisational chart, it is also important to describe the contents of the various jobs in the organisation and to indicate how these ensure effective organisational functioning (e.g. how the various jobs in the organisation contribute to the manufacture and sale of products or the provision of services by the organisation).

The business plan should also indicate how investors and directors will be organisationally related. In this regard it should indicate whether there will be other investors in the business apart from the original entrepreneur. Should there be further investors, the number of shares to be issued should be indicated, and the initial share prices shown. As far as the directors are concerned, the board members should be identified and their possible contributions to the business indicated.

12.3.9 Description of the objectives and goals of the business

According to Bangs (2005), this section of the business plan should indicate what the business will be all about, and what it aims to accomplish by formulating and implementing the business plan. To indicate what the business will be about, it is important to include a strategic plan of the envisaged future of the business, some sales forecasts, some manufacturing and retail plans, some quality-assurance plans as well as some financial plans. It may be wise to make some predictions in respect of profits, budgets, projected cash-flow sheets, and also some marketing and market-penetration objectives that are foreseen.

12.3.10 Projection of income, cash flow, and costs

It is important to indicate the projected financial results of the operations of the business. By estimating financial results, an entrepreneur can determine the **financial viability** of the business it wants to establish.

Such financial analyses also provide information to prospective investors on the returns they could expect from investing in the business, and the level to which their investment would be a safe high-yield one. The projected income, cash flow, and costs analyses are usually attached as appendices to the business plan.

DEFINITION

Financial viability provides an indication of whether a business venture will be profitable and sustainable. It determines whether the business idea will be able to generate revenue.

Entrepreneurs must clearly define their target market, understand their needs and provide an offering that will satisfy their needs. You can learn more about this topic in the success story of Luvuyo Rani, who started Silulo Ulutho Technologies.

12.4 International business plans

With the emerging global village complete with its global labour market and global marketplace, businesses are increasingly being started and acquired across national borders. A unique business plan is required as the basis for such cross-border entrepreneurship, such as an international business plan that takes into account the difficulties (e.g. cultural problems) involved in setting up a business in a foreign country.

An **international business plan** supplies a detailed analysis of competitive advantages and disadvantages related to possible competitors in the foreign country to identify actions that would optimise strengths and minimise the impact of weaknesses (Grosse and Kujawa, 1995). On the basis of such an international business plan, various decisions could be made, namely to invest in production or sales in another country, to export goods to other

Silulo Ulutho Technologies: Luvuyo Rani

In 2004 Luvuyo Rani opened Silulo Ulutho Technologies, a company that provided local teachers with refurbished computers. It didn't take long to realise that his target market did not understand the technology, and so he opened an Internet café to create a space where he could place the refurbished PCs, and provide the residents of Khayelitsha with a place to access the Internet and learn about computers. And no one came. The café was losing money fast and Luvuyo and his partners were simply hoping people would come.

'We realised we had recognised a market – but that the market hadn't recognised itself', he says. 'People need technology, but we were pitching to a market that simply didn't know how to use what we were offering'.

And so Silulo added training courses to its business model. At first the courses were ad hoc – an hour or two each day at the Internet café. It soon became clear that in trying to create a market for their products, Silulo had actually struck on a business offering the marketplace was desperate for. Today Silulo operates 18 training centres across the Western Cape. Courses run for six months at a time, 8am to 5pm. MWeb has taken notice of the business and refurbished five centres as part of its Enterprise Development (ED) programme. This second revenue stream has lower costs than the Internet café, and is more profitable.

'You can't be too precious about your business model', Luvuyo says. 'Sometimes you need to adjust your offering to suit the market. You can't expect the market to adjust to you, simply because you are offering something. Find what they want or need, and then give them a solution.'

Source: Todd (2012). © Entrepreneur Media SA (Pty) Ltd. Reprinted by permission of Entrepreneur Media SA (Pty) Ltd.

countries, to start a business in another country, to acquire a business in another country or to expand an existing business transnationally. Prospective transnational entrepreneurs and existing businesses have to decide what type of business they want to be in, how widely they want to be spread geographically and what the growth objectives of the business are. The international business plan resulting from such planning should encompass three important aspects:

▶ *An entrepreneur or existing business should have a set of overall objectives.* An example would be a computer retail business. On the basis of such overall objectives, the decision should be made whether to attempt to diversify into new products or services, expand to new geographical areas, or start or acquire further businesses in other countries.

▶ *Optimal operating strategies should be decided on.* This will ensure that the business has effective overall competitive strategies.

▶ *Any business operating transnationally has to maintain control over its widespread sections.* To effect such control, the plans of the business as well as its decisions and activities should be continuously measured and evaluated to ensure that optimal competitiveness is achieved (Grosse and Kujawa, 1995).

12.5 A pro forma business plan

Section 12.3 described the important components of a business plan and the subsections below provide a template for each of these components.

12.5.1 Cover sheet

A cover sheet will contain the following information and will be structured as follows:
1. Full name of business
2. Type of business
3. Form of ownership (sole proprietor, partnership, company)
4. Name of owner(s)
5. Full street address of business
6. Contact details: Phone, fax, email and website information
7. Date of the plan.

12.5.2 The table of contents

The table of contents reflects the content of the business plan and may look as follows:
1. **Executive summary**
2. **Introduction**
    2.1 Description of products being sold and (or) manufactured, and (or) the services being rendered
    2.2 Why the business is viable and feasible (feasibility study: market potential)
    2.3 Long-, medium-, and short-term objectives.
3. **Description of business**
    3.1 Type of ownership
    3.2 Legal requirements: licence and tax regulations
    3.3 A detailed description of the product by referring to the processes involved in manufacturing and (or) selling the product and the machinery being used
    3.4 A technical analysis of the functioning and possibilities of the machinery involved in manufacturing (if applicable)
    3.5 A description of where the business is, the facilities at the disposal of the business, the plan layout, a

comparison with competitors, leasing and buying agreements, and so on
    3.6 An outline of the educational qualifications, work experience, and training of the owner(s).
4. **An outline of the marketing plan**
    4.1 A description of target markets and clients
    4.2 A description of the buying plan.
5. **A description of the financial plan**
    5.1 A detailed statement of comprehensive income (income statement) projected for 12 months
    5.2 Break-even points and gross profit percentages
    5.3 A detailed cash-flow sheet projected for 12 months
    5.4 A detailed statement of financial position (balance sheet) projected for 12 months
    5.5 The amount of own financial contributions
    5.6 The amount of capital required and purpose of such capital
    5.7 Security available.
6. **The business structure and operational plan**
    6.1 A description of the number of employees that should be appointed, the reasons why they should be appointed, how they will be recruited, and how they will be deployed in the business
    6.2 A description of management and staff, their qualifications and work experience, their job descriptions, and their remuneration
    6.3 A description of the administration and bookkeeping system
    6.4 A description of employment policies.
7. **Summary and concluding remarks**
    7.1 A description of why the business plan will be successful
    7.2 An indication of why financing should be supplied.

12.5.3 The body of the business plan

A pro forma body for a business plan is supplied below in an easy-to-complete format.

1. **Introduction**
   1.1 A description of the product that will be manufactured and (or) sold, and (or) the services to be rendered
   1.2 Why the business is viable and feasible (feasibility study: market potential)
   1.3 Long-term objectives determined by top management
   1.4 Medium-term objectives determined by middle management
   1.5 Short-term objectives determined by supervisors.

2. **Description of the business**
   2.1 Type of ownership
   2.2 Legal requirements: licence and tax regulations
   2.3 A detailed description of the product manufactured or sold, and (or) the service rendered:
      ▶ The processes involved
      ▶ The machinery used (if applicable).
   2.4 A technical analysis of the specifics and possibilities of machinery being used (if applicable)
   2.5 An indication of where the business is located, the business facilities, a comparison with competitors, leasing and buying agreements, and so on
   2.6 An exposition of the educational qualifications, work experience, and training of the owner(s)
   2.7 A description of competitors and their products and (or) services.

3. **An exposition of the marketing plan**
   3.1 A description of target markets and clients
   3.2 The buying plan: cost estimates and estimation
   3.3 Sales promotion strategy
   3.4 Pricing policies
   3.5 The buying plan and sales.

4. **A description of the financial plan**
   4.1 A detailed statement of comprehensive income (income statement) projected for 12 months
   4.2 Break-even points determined by using values for:
      ▶ Total expenditure
      ▶ Gross profit %
   4.3 The gross profit percentage (%) based on:
      ▶ Gross profit
      ▶ Sales (turnover)
   4.4 A detailed cash-flow sheet projected for 12 months
   4.5 A detailed statement of financial position (balance sheet) projected for 12 months on December 20XX
   4.6 Own contributions: financial
   4.7 Own contributions: inventory
   4.8 Own contributions: vehicles
   4.9 Own contributions: equipment
   4.10 The amount of financing required for marketing capital and for what purpose
   4.11 The amount of financing required for machinery capital and for what purpose
   4.12 The amount of security available.

5. **The business structure and operational plan**
   5.1 A description of how many employees should be appointed, why, how they will be recruited, and where they will be deployed in the business
   5.2 The qualifications and experience of management and employees
   5.3 The job descriptions of management and employees
   5.4 The remuneration packages of management and employees
   5.5 A description of the administration and record-keeping system
   5.6 A description of the staff policy: working hours
   5.7 The staff policy: fringe benefits
   5.8 The staff policy: overtime remuneration

5.9 The staff policy: sick leave
5.10 The staff policy: medical fund
5.11 The staff policy: trade unions
5.12 Other aspects of staff policy.
6. **Summary and concluding remarks**
6.1 An indication of why the business plan will be successful
6.2 Why financing should be supplied.

Many business plan formats are available in libraries, bookstores and software. Figure 12.1 gives an example of a business-plan template from http://southafrica.smetoolkit.org/sa/en/content/en/478/How-to-Finance-Your-Business that you can download as a Microsoft Word document and use on your computer.

Figure 12.1 Business plan template

Business name Your name Today's date
SECTION 1: THE BUSINESS PROFILE
Description of my business Describe your product or service.
Targeted market and customers Describe your customer profile and why they want or need your product and (or) service.
Growth trends in this business Is the market for your product and (or) service growing or shrinking?
Pricing power Explain the unique qualities or circumstances concerning your product or service that will enable you to maintain profitable pricing.
SECTION 2: THE VISION AND THE PEOPLE
Describe convincingly that you are passionately committed to your new business and have the realism to make inevitably hard choices.
The people
Work experience related to the intended business Describe your work experience in the business you plan to start, including a list of your skills and knowledge that will be required in your business.
Personal background and education credentials Describe yourself including your education.
SECTION 3: COMMUNICATIONS
Computer and communications tools Provide a table of each piece of communications equipment you intend to use, including a description and budget for each one. You can use the following as a guide. **Resource requirements:** **Communications** Enter a description of all communications equipment. Enter a budget for all communications equipment. **Telephones** Enter a description of all telephone equipment. Enter a budget for all telephone equipment.

Pagers
Enter a description of pagers.
Enter a budget for all pagers.

Facsimile
Enter a description of all fax equipment.
Enter a budget for all fax equipment.

Computers
Enter a description of all computer equipment.
Enter a budget for all computer equipment.

Internet
Enter a description of necessary Internet providers.
Enter a budget for Internet access.

SECTION 4: ORGANISATION

Business organisation
Explain the form of business organisation you intend to use and why it is best for your business.

Professional consultants
List the names of your lawyer, accountant, insurance agent, and any other professionals.

Licenses
List what licenses you will require to go into business.

SECTION 5: INSURANCE

Insurance
List the forms of insurance coverage including costs that are anticipated.

SECTION 6: PREMISES

Location criteria
Outline your location criteria:
▶ Space requirements
▶ Future requirements
▶ Site-analysis study if needed (attach)
▶ Demographic study if needed (attach)
▶ Lease check-off list (attach)
▶ Estimated occupancy cost as a percentage of sales
▶ Zoning and use approvals.

SECTION 7: ACCOUNTING AND CASH FLOW

Accounting
Furnish, as a separate exhibit, your starting statement of financial position (balance sheet) and projected statements of comprehensive income (income statements) for the first six months to one year.

Cash-flow planning
Provide a separate exhibit of your one-year cash-flow analysis, including estimated sales, all costs, and capital investments.
Provide a checklist of all expense items for input into your cash-flow projection.

Analysis of costs
List all your costs: fixed, variable, product, delivery, and so on.

Internal controls
Explain your intended internal controls and cash controls, check signing policy, strategy for controlling shrinkage and dishonesty, and control of incoming merchandise.

SECTION 8: FINANCING

Financing strategy

Provide a chart or spreadsheet showing all of the sources of your start-up capital. Explain any government assistance or loan-guarantee programmes you intend to apply for.

If your business is for use with potential lenders, include a cash-flow projection and projected statements of comprehensive income (income statements) to show sources of repayment of loans. Be conservative in your forecasts.

List your sources of referrals to lending institutions (such as your accountant, and so on).

SECTION 9: E-COMMERCE

E-commerce plans

Describe in detail how you plan to use the Internet in marketing your product or service.

E-commerce budgeting

Provide a detailed breakdown of the costs involved in creating, operating, and maintaining your e-commerce activities.

E-commerce competition

Describe how your best competitors utilise e-commerce and your strategy to improve on their practices.

SECTION 10: ACQUISITIONS

Due diligence procedures for acquisitions

List the following:

▸ Your consulting team: attorney, accountant, banker, broker, and so on
▸ Verification of seller's revenues: how you plan to authenticate
▸ Seller's records to be inspected: financial statements, income tax returns sales backlog, cash deposit records, utility bills, accounts payable and receivable, backlog, financial comparisons of similar businesses, and so on
▸ Inspections and approval of leases and contracts
▸ Appraisals, as appropriate
▸ If a franchise, interview with randomly selected franchisees
▸ Finance plan for acquisitions: include sources, including seller financing
▸ Market conditions
▸ Value of goodwill
▸ Method of purchase: stock, assets, and so on.

SECTION 11: MARKETING

Marketing plan

Describe your overall marketing and sales strategy including how you plan to get and retain customers.

Advertising and promotion plans

Describe your plans and budgets for advertising and promotions.

Purchasing and inventory control

Create a 'how to buy' checklist.

Training policies

Describe your plans for hiring and training your sales associates.

The competition

Describe your strongest competitors and how you intend to compete with them.
Describe your competitors' shortcomings and how you can capitalise on them.

SECTION 12: GROWTH PROGRAMME
Expansion
Describe your growth plan. You might include development of a profitable pilot operation, sources of financing, cash flow, accounting system in place, incentive-compensation plan for managers, benefits package and policies, and economies of scale.
Handling major problems
Describe scenarios of adverse conditions and how you intend to respond to them. For example, how you would plan to handle a 25% reduction in sales, or new competitors, and so forth. Prepare a cash-flow projection based on lowered expectations and show how and where you would reduce costs to maintain liquidity.

Source: Downloaded from http://southafrica.smetoolkit.org/sa/en/content/en/478/How-to-Finance-Your-Business Reprinted by permission of Business Partners Limited/SME Toolkit South Africa.

CONCLUSION

Experienced business owners and managers are all in agreement that a business plan is an extremely important management tool. A business plan is a written road map of where an entity is headed, what it has to do to get there, and what it will look like on arrival.

A business plan has various uses such as setting goals and objectives, testing the feasibility of ideas, establishing and evaluating performance benchmarks, and serving as a communication tool by communicating messages to internal and external stakeholders.

It is important to keep in mind that your business plan should be reviewed. Ask someone familiar with business management and the planning process to review your business plan for completeness. Check the business plan for objectivity, logic, presentation, and effectiveness.

Remember that a business plan is a 'living' document and therefore it should be periodically updated. As your environment and objectives change, update your plan to reflect these changes or your plan may become useless.

A last comment on the business plan: include sufficient research findings and background materials. Make your business plan interesting by using your background data, your biography, charts, demographics, and research data.

SELF-ASSESSMENT QUESTIONS

Multiple-choice questions

1. There are certain things that business plans cannot do. Identify which one of the following things business plans cannot do.
   a. Business plans cannot predict the future.
   b. Business plans cannot guarantee funding.
   c. Business plans cannot raise all the money required.
   d. All of the above
2. The form of ownership of the business should best be mentioned in the _____ part of the business plan: (Please select the most correct answer)
   a. executive summary
   b. cover sheet
   c. management plan
   d. operations plan
3. Which one of the following is not an example of the purpose of a business plan:
   a. To plan a new business
   b. To transform or expand an existing business
   c. To obtain staff
   d. To obtain a loan
4. Which one of the following is true regarding the break-even point?
   a. It determines the maximum sales required to cover operating costs
   b. A point below which a profit is made
   c. Gross profit = operating costs
   d. Sales = total costs
5. Which resources are required to formulate a good business plan?

a. Reliable information and plenty of time
b. Plenty of time, reliable information and human resources
c. Human resources and reliable information
d. Plenty of time and human resources

DISCUSSION QUESTIONS

1. Briefly explain the purpose of a business plan.
2. Discuss the typical components covered in the business plan.
3. Briefly discuss how the formulation of a business plan enhances business success.
4. Explain the disadvantages associated with business plans.
5. Identify and describe the steps involved in formulating a business plan.

EXPERIENTIAL EXERCISE

Identify three entrepreneurs in your neighbourhood. Find out whether they compiled a business plan or not when they started their businesses. Make a list of the reasons why they did or did not compile a business plan. What valuable lessons can you learn from these entrepreneurs?

Download two business plans from the Internet. Compare the executive summaries of the business plans. If you were an investor, in which one of the two business plans will you invest? Motivate your answer.

Visit the following websites to extract information on business plans and guidance on starting your own business:

▸ http://www.idc.co.za/Venture%20capital.asp?frmContent=7
▸ www.fnb.co.za
▸ http://www.absa.co.za/Absacoza/Small-Business/Accessing/Small-Business-Support-Centre
▸ http://southafrica.smetoolkit.org/sa/en/category/2944/Business-Plans
▸ http://www.seda.org.za
▸ http://www.sefa.org.za
▸ http://www.thedti.gov.za
▸ http://www.entrepreneurmag.co.za

DEADLIEST START-UP SINS

Whether your venture is a new pizza place or the hottest new software product, beware: These nine flawed assumptions are toxic.

1. Assuming you know what the customer wants
First and deadliest of all is a founder's unwavering belief that he or she understands who the customers will be, what they need, and how to sell it to them. Any dispassionate observer would recognise that on Day One, a start-up has no customers, and unless the founder is a true domain expert, he or she can only guess about the customer, problem, and business model. On Day One, a start-up is a faith-based initiative built on guesses. To succeed, founders need to turn these guesses into facts as soon as possible by getting out of the building, asking customers if the hypotheses are correct, and quickly changing those that are wrong.

2. The 'I know what features to build' flaw
The second flawed assumption is implicitly driven by the first. Founders, presuming they know their customers, assume they know all the features customers need. These founders specify, design, and build a fully featured product using classic product development methods without ever leaving their building. Yet without direct and continuous customer contact, it's unknown whether the features will hold any appeal to customers.

3. Focusing on the launch date
Traditionally, engineering, sales, and marketing have all focused on the immovable launch date. Marketing tries to pick an 'event' (trade show, conference, blog, etc.) where they can 'launch' the product. Executives look at that date and the calendar, working backward to ignite fireworks on the day the product is launched. Neither

CASE STUDY

management nor investors tolerate 'wrong turns' that result in delays.

The product launch and first customer ship dates are merely the dates when a product development team thinks the product's first release is 'finished'. It doesn't mean the company understands its customers or how to market or sell to them, yet in almost every start-up, ready or not, departmental clocks are set irrevocably to 'first customer ship'. Even worse, a start-up's investors are managing their financial expectations by this date as well.

4. Emphasising execution instead of testing, learning, and iteration

Established companies execute business models where customers, problems, and necessary product features are all knowns; start-ups, on the other hand, need to operate in a 'search' mode as they test and prove every one of their initial hypotheses. They learn from the results of each test, refine the hypothesis, and test again – all in search of a repeatable, scalable, and profitable business model. In practice, start-ups begin with a set of initial guesses, most of which will end up being wrong. Therefore, focusing on execution and delivering a product or service based on those initial, untested hypotheses is a going-out-of-business strategy.

5. Writing a business plan that doesn't allow for trial and error

Traditional business plans and product development models have one great advantage: They provide boards and founders an unambiguous path with clearly defined milestones the board presumes will be achieved. Financial progress is tracked using metrics like income statement, balance sheet, and cash flow. The problem is, none of these metrics are very useful because they don't track progress against your start-up's only goal: to find a repeatable and scalable business model.

6. Confusing traditional job titles with a start-up's needs

Most start-ups simply borrow job titles from established companies. But remember, these are jobs in an organisation that's executing a known business model. The term 'Sales' at an existing company refers to a team that repeatedly sells a known product to a well-understood group of customers with standard presentations, prices, terms, and conditions. Start-ups by definition have few, if any, of these. In fact, they're out searching for them! The demands of customer discovery require people who are comfortable with change, chaos, and learning from failure and are at ease working in risky, unstable situations without a roadmap.

7. Executing on a sales and marketing plan

Hiring executives with the right titles but the wrong skills leads to further trouble as high-powered sales and marketing people arrive on the payroll to execute the 'plan'. Executives and board members accustomed to measurable signs of progress will focus on these execution activities because this is what they know how to do (and what they believe they were hired to do). Of course, in established companies with known customers and markets, this focus makes sense. And even in some start-ups in 'existing markets', where customers and markets are known, it might work. But in a majority of start-ups, measuring progress against a product launch or revenue plan is simply false progress, since it transpires in a vacuum, absent from real customer feedback and rife with assumptions that might be wrong.

8. Prematurely scaling your company based on a presumption of success

The business plan, its revenue forecast, and the product introduction model assume that every step a start-up takes proceeds flawlessly and smoothly to the next. The model leaves little room for error, learning, iteration, or customer feedback. Even the most experienced executives are pressured to hire and staff per the plan regardless of progress. This leads to the next start-up disaster: premature scaling.

9. Management by crisis, which leads to a death spiral

The consequences of most start-up mistakes begin to show by the time of first customer ship, when sales aren't happening according to 'the plan'. Shortly thereafter, the sales manager is probably terminated as part of the 'solution'. A new sales manager is hired and quickly concludes that the company just didn't understand its customers or how to sell to them. Since the new sales manager was hired to 'fix' sales, the marketing department must now respond to a sales manager who believes that whatever was created earlier in the company was wrong. (After all, it got the old sales manager fired, right?)

Here's the real problem: No business plan survives first contact with customers. The assumptions in a business plan are simply a series of untested hypotheses. When real results come in, the smart start-ups pivot or change their business model based on the results. It's not a crisis, it's part of the road to success.

Source: Steve Blank. Deadliest start-up sins, 14 May 2012. [Online]. Available: http://steveblank.com/2012/05/14/9-deadliest-start-up-sins/ [29 January 2014]. The Startup Owner's Manual: The Step-by-Step Guide for Building a Great Company by Steve Blank and Bob Dorf © 2012, K and S Ranch Publishing Division. Reprinted by permission of the author.

1. As highlighted in the chapter, an entrepreneur needs to cover a number of important aspects when compiling a business plan. Identify the aspects that are covered in the case study and motivate your answer with quotations from the case study.

2. Identify the aspects that are not covered in the case study.
3. Briefly discuss the lessons that entrepreneurs can learn from the case study regarding the precautions that must be taken when compiling a business plan.

SUGGESTED WEBSITE LINKS

http://www.idc.co.za/Venture%20capital. asp?frmContent=7
http://www.idc.co.za/finance-by-sector/business-plan
www.fnb.co.za
http://www.absa.co.za/Absacoza/Small-Business/Accessing/Small-Business-Support-Centre
http://southafrica.smetoolkit.org/sa/en/category/2944/Business-Plans
http://www.entrepreneurmag.co.za
http://www.seda.org.za
http://www.sefa.org.za
http://www.thedti.gov.za

REFERENCES

Bangs, DH. 2005. *Business Plans Made Easy*. Portsmouth: Entrepreneur Press.

Blank, S. 2012. Deadliest start-up sins. [Online]. Available: http://steveblank.com/2012/05/14/9-deadliest-start-up-sins/ [29 January 2014].

Boucher, C. 2012. Exactexh: Antonio Pooe. *Entrepreneur Magazine*. [Online]. Available: www.entrepreneurmag.co.za [5 January 2014].

Grosse, RE. & Kujawa, D. 1995. *International Business: Theory and Managerial Applications*. Chicago: Irwin.

Megginson, LC, Scott, CR, Trueblood, LR. & Megginson, WL. 1998. *Successful Small Business Management*. Plano: Business Publications.

Pitman, J. 2013. Tim Tebeila on taking a gap. *Entrepreneur Magazine*. [Online]. Available: www.entrepreneurmag.co.za [5 January 2014].

Spratt, J. 2012. Your idea is worth nothing. *Entrepreneur Magazine*. [Online]. Available: www.entrepreneurmag.co.za [5 January 2014].

Timmons, JA. 1994. *New Venture Creation: Entrepreneurship for the 21st Century*. Burr Ridge: Irwin.

Todd, N. 2012. Silulo Ulutho Technologies: Luvuyo Rani. *Entrepreneur Magazine*. [Online]. Available: www.entrepreneurmag.co.za [5 January 2014].

CHAPTER 13

Entrepreneurial management

Elana Swanepoel

LEARNING OUTCOMES

On completion of this chapter you will be able to:
▶ Identify the various business functions that could exist within a venture and briefly discuss each of these
▶ Describe the concept of entrepreneurial leadership in a business
▶ Explain the importance of teams in a business
▶ Compare the basic team types found in a business
▶ Discuss the entrepreneurial management process
▶ Explain the various managerial tasks and processes and their importance to the entrepreneur.

OPENING CASE STUDY

Selina started a placement agency for reliable, honest and experienced domestic workers, gardeners and handy men. She advertised her services in the local newspapers and distributed pamphlets to residential properties. Soon she was inundated with calls, from both people who were looking for jobs and wanted to be on her books, as well as customers seeking to employ people on her books. She and her two assistants could no longer cope with the workload and she appointed another ten employees. Each of the jobseekers had to be thoroughly vetted and tested before they could be placed on the list. She found that it was no longer possible for her to be responsible for all the tasks. She had to delegate. In addition, she found that she had to spend more time managing the business and implementing control systems. She decided to divide the employees into teams and give each team specific responsibilities and targets. Two of the three teams worked well and delivered on target. These two teams seemed to plan how to reach their targets, were good at multitasking and had fun building good supportive relationships. Selina realised that she would have to identify the problems in the third team.

1. When does an entrepreneur become a manager?
2. How does the focus of the entrepreneur change as the business grows?
3. Why do some teams function well and others do not?
4. What planning is required as the business grows?

INTRODUCTION

Any venture, irrespective of its size, has to perform certain activities and functions to enable it to achieve its objectives. Seven business functions can be identified, namely: purchasing, manufacturing or production, marketing, finance, human resources, administration, and public relations. The management functions are performed by both the owner and the managers of the venture.

There are links between management and entrepreneurial leadership. Many businesses make use of teams in the workplace. To manage a new venture effectively, the entrepreneur needs to develop and perform certain managerial tasks, including planning, decision making, organising, leading and controlling and involve management teams in these activities.

13.1 Business functions

The management of a business involves various functional areas of management. In larger enterprises, the various functions will be performed by a division or department created for this purpose. In smaller ventures, two or more of these functions may be grouped together, while for very small ventures there may be no separate divisions at all, since the owner or manager may personally take care of all the activities. To achieve the business's goals, irrespective of how the various activities are grouped or arranged, the functions should be performed as efficiently as possible. These activities could be seen as the way in which the entrepreneur or manager handles the resources of the venture to obtain the desired output, whether products or services.

The functional areas of business management are illustrated in Figure 13.1. At level one the four functional areas are those that are typically identified in a business organisation, while at level two the three functional areas are those that are classified as more generic management functions.

13.1.1 Level one functional areas

The **level one functional areas** are those functions that are typical in any business organisation.

Figure 13.1 Functional areas of business management

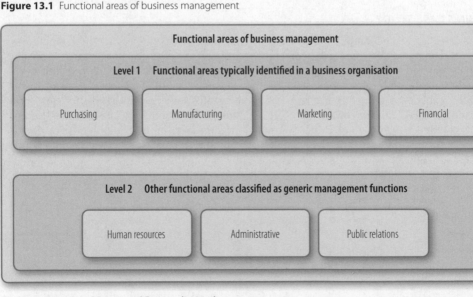

Source: Adopted from Nieman and Bennett (2006:4).

13.1.1.1 **The purchasing function**

The activities performed in the **purchasing function** revolve around the acquisition and provision of material resources for commencing and continuing the activities of the venture. The material resources may be those required for manufacturing products, such as raw material, components, machines, tools, and transport vehicles, and those needed in the operation of the venture, such as office furniture and equipment, stationery, and other vehicles. The most important activities in the purchasing function are the following:

▸ *Determining purchasing needs.* This involves establishing the quantity, quality, and type of resources needed throughout the venture.
▸ *Identifying suppliers.* The number of raw-material suppliers may decrease as suppliers merge and some cease to exist.
▸ *Negotiating with suppliers.* When suppliers are identified, the right price, discounts, delivery dates, after-sales service, and continuous supply should be negotiated with each one.
▸ *Placing and following up orders.* After negotiating with the suppliers, orders for the enquired quantity, quality, and type of materials should be placed and followed up.
▸ *Receiving and expecting items.* The items received should be measured against the quality standards set during the negotiating process.
▸ *Stock-keeping.* This should be done for the entire business to determine the volume and value of the inventory in the storerooms and on the floor at a given time, as well as to be able to meet the demand for inventories according to the quantity and quality needed.

13.1.1.2 **The manufacturing function**

DEFINITION

The manufacturing function includes the activities involved in the creation and provision of products and (or) services.

The manufacturing process is critical in that it provides the products or services that are sold and from which the venture earns revenue. These products and (or) services should address the specific needs of consumers. The following activities are included in the manufacturing function:

▸ Obtaining information on the types, quantities, and quality of the goods and (or) services to be made
▸ Production planning for the short and long term
▸ Production control to ensure that the predetermined production objectives are achieved
▸ Maintaining and replacing production equipment.

13.1.1.3 **The marketing function**

DEFINITION

The activities of the marketing function revolve around the marketing of products and (or) services that the venture provides and from which it has to earn its revenue.

The purpose of marketing is:
▸ To introduce new and unknown products to the consumer
▸ To illustrate the advantages and uses (value) of new products and services to the customer
▸ To create a larger demand for products with which the consumers are already familiar
▸ To maintain the demand for products already known to consumers.

Market-information activities

The marketing function is responsible for the identification of opportunities and threats to the venture by obtaining marketing data and transforming these into useful information for developing products and services.

Marketing opportunities can be seen as new product or service ideas to improve competitiveness, while marketing threats would include competitors' actions that may contain competitive threats. The new product or service ideas not only refer to new product or services but could also include finding new markets for existing products or services, finding new products and services for the existing markets, or even finding new products and services for new markets. Market research is necessary to make sound decisions regarding the products and (or) services to offer.

Marketing and the marketing function are discussed in detail in Chapter 14.

13.1.1.4 The financial function

During the planning and start-up phase of the venture, the entrepreneur is involved in activities linked to forecasting and financial provision for the venture. The activities of the **financial function** during the pre-start-up and start-up phases can be grouped into three categories:

▶ Activities related to the capital requirements and sources, where the initial capital requirements for the business are estimated and sources of funds are identified

▶ Activities related to the protection of investment capital or risk management, where the risk to the firm's material and human capital resources are identified and plans are drawn up to cope with it

▶ Activities related to the preparation and analysis of pro forma financial statements, where the income, cost, and profits are forecast using pro forma income statements, cash-flow statements, and balance sheets.

The financial function of the established enterprise, on the other hand, is concerned with the real flow of funds within the venture and can be divided as follows:

▶ Acquisition of funds, also known as financing, which involves both short- and long-term financing

▶ Application of funds by acquiring assets and the different production factors such as labour, raw materials, equipment, and other usable materials

---

ENTREPRENEURIAL DILEMMA

Moving beyond close family store management for independents

One of the biggest dilemmas facing the successful independent store owner, who wants to grow, is taking the big step of bringing outsiders to the family onto the supervisory management team. There are no simple answers and the move is seldom without challenges. Often faith in people on the part of the independent and on the part of the hired hand is shattered. Yet the step is essential for growth and sometimes survival.

The most critical consideration in employing an outsider is one of scale and fit. This is structuring the specific job in relation to the managerial or supervisory talent available on the market to the store – with respect to the current family management strengths and weaknesses and the contribution to store sales and profits that should result – against the costs of employing the talent.

Imagine a thriving independent store operated by the owner, with a lot of help from his wife and his retired father. The customer catchment area is growing fast and there is a lot of potential additional business to be had. Areas in his store, such as the dry groceries and the fresh departments need more attention. The owner has neither the time nor the expertise in some fresh produce areas that the management function demands. His dilemma is who to employ.

1. Should he look for a young enthusiastic person with chain store experience in fresh produce, who could grow with the business and contribute to its growth?
2. With regard to the key problem of getting more expertise in the perishables department, should he appoint a full-time qualified butchery manager?
3. Is it essential that the person is a people's person who is good with consumers? Can he teach the staff?

Source: Adapted from Wholesale Business (2014:25–27).

- Advancement of funds by giving credit to customers
- Administration of and reporting on financial matters.

The financial function and basic financial concepts were discussed in Chapters 10 and 11.

13.1.2 Level two functional areas

Level two functional areas are those that are classified as the more generic management functions.

13.1.2.1 The human-resource function

> **DEFINITION**
>
> The human-resource function consists of those activities concerned with human-resource planning and with the procurement, development, and maintenance of sufficient and capable employees, who will be able to carry out the activities of the venture as efficiently as possible.

Once the entrepreneur decides to appoint people to support and help him or her in achieving the goals set for the venture, the **human-resource function** comes into being.

Human-resource planning
Deciding on the number and type of employees required for the venture is known as human-resource planning. During the planning stage, the following activities should be performed:
- Determine the type of personnel the venture will need in the short and in the long term according to the type of training, experience, skills, and personal characteristics required to be able to do the job
- Estimate the numbers of staff needed in both the short and long term
- Assess the changes in staff needs that would be necessary when expanding the business

- Determine whether specialised staff will be needed or whether a rotation system could be implemented.

Information on other human-resource matters will be discussed in Chapter 16.

13.1.2.2 The administrative function

> **DEFINITION**
>
> The administrative function consists of those activities concerned with the collection, processing, storage, and dissemination of information that is essential for the achievement of the goals of the venture.

The collection activities should be aimed at acquiring data, which may be unprocessed and not necessarily usable facts, from the various functions within the venture and from various outside sources that publicise information that could affect the venture, such as the SA Reserve Bank, Statistics South Africa, and other institutions providing economic reviews. These data should now be transformed into useful information that the enterprise could use in decision making, planning, setting of standards, and even evaluation of the achievement of the venture (processing activities). To be easily accessible, the information should be stored in a systematic way. It should be made available to the various functions and to the entrepreneur in the form of regular reports and returns, and also to people outside the venture such as the owners, shareholders, the Registrar of Companies, and the South African Revenue Service (SARS).

13.1.2.3 The public-relations function

The **public-relations function** forms part of the marketing function.

The primary objective of an enterprise is surely to make a profit but without customers to purchase products or services from the venture, there can be no profit maximisation. Public relations are thus a necessity to attract customers. By creating goodwill and a positive image among your customers, you try to ensure that they will keep coming back to your business to purchase goods and services that they need, and that you have to offer. Word of mouth is an important tool for attracting new customers to your enterprise and should not be underestimated. By creating good customer relations with existing customers, you also create long-term loyalty to your business.

Although the public-relations function primarily concentrates on external factors and society at large, it could also play a valuable role in creating a positive image among existing and potential employees. The manager could use the public-relations section or department to communicate with the employees in the business, making it a valuable managerial tool.

13.2 Entrepreneurial leadership and teams in the workplace

To build a high-potential venture without leadership and without a team is extremely difficult. Entrepreneurial leadership and a team culture create energy and excitement, and transform ideas and dreams into tangible visions that people believe they can achieve.

By encouraging innovation, entrepreneurial leaders build confidence and breed independent, entrepreneurial thinking. The entrepreneur should also encourage teamwork – encouraging staff to accept more responsibility for the completion of tasks that were previously undertaken by the entrepreneur.

13.2.1 Entrepreneurial leadership

> **DEFINITION**
>
> Leadership involves pointing the way and getting others to follow willingly.

An entrepreneur must convey his or her vision of the firm's future to all participants in the business so that they can contribute effectively to the accomplishment of the vision. Although leaders must also engage in many routine processes, the first tasks of the entrepreneur are to create and communicate a vision for the company (Moore et al., 2010).

Entrepreneurial leadership refers to the way that you operate as the chief executive of your business, and involves three aspects (Katz and Green, 2011):

▸ *Innovation* is a key attribute of the leader of a small business as its key visionary. The owner is the person who thinks about the future of the business, including how to compete better, how to grow faster, and what new products or services to add.

▸ *Operation* is the component most closely related to the task and person elements of administrative leadership. Operation refers to the ability to manage the business as it grows.

▸ *Inspiration* stems from the reasonable expectation among employees and customers that the entrepreneur should be the business's biggest booster and champion.

Past experience is the best indicator of whether you have what it takes to be an entrepreneurial leader. If you have been a leader of a team or group and the people completed the tasks successfully and liked each other, you probably have what it takes to manage the operation.

13.2.2 The management and entrepreneurial teams

Many businesses have a team of two or more co-owners, and the trend is toward even more businesses being developed by teams of entrepreneurs.

13.2.2.1 The management team

Individuals with supervisory responsibilities and non-supervisory staff who play key roles

---

SOUTH AFRICAN SUCCESS STORY

Don't tell me … 'It's not my job'!
The most popular talk, which I have conducted up and down the country to thousands of delegates, is my teamwork presentation based on the lessons we learn from Africa's most successful team - The African Wild Dog! The only reason that they are so successful is due to the way they work as an effective team.

Firstly, the 'pack' all has the same purpose for going to work in the morning. When the wild dogs go hunting, they all focus on the same prey, as opposed to just charging at a herd of impala. They focus on one individual. Effective business teams all need to go to work and have the same purpose for being there – I suggest that it is to make the business profitable!

Just as individuals in a wild dog team have various jobs to conduct, be it digging and cleaning out the den, or perhaps watching over the pups while the rest go hunting, we have to be multi-skilled ourselves. Think about training cashiers to become sales people or merchandisers. The more multi-skilled your team members are, the more of a valued asset they become to the business. However, while they are cashiering, receiving stock, following up on debtors or serving the customer, whatever task they are doing, each and every team member must take responsibility for that task!

Another lesson we can learn from these wonderful creatures is the manner in which they care for and nurture their young. We have 'young' in our businesses; I am talking about new employees not necessarily the youngest. I truly believe that it is everybody's responsibility to assist and coach new employees – not just the responsibility of Human Resources or the Training department!

Communication must be one of the wild dog's best assets. Before they leave for a hunt they will nuzzle each other, run around and literally motivate each other with yelps and barks letting the pack know that it is time to hunt! Once they have found say a herd of impala, they instinctively as a team single out an individual as the prey for the final chase. This is noiseless communication that they all understand. In business, employees often just wait for communication to happen. Communication is omnidirectional, in other words, from the boss down, then from the bottom upwards, and side to side – co-worker to co-worker.

Did you know that even injured dogs go on the hunt? How many people do we know that will not go to work because they are not feeling too good – perhaps have a headache or some other arbitrary ailment? Now the injured dogs may not be able to keep up with the rest of the pack, but they are there, at work with their 'colleagues'. If this discipline can work in nature, then it can work in business; and what is even more amazing is that injured dogs eat first!

When out in the bush, the wild dogs have fierce competition such as hyena, lion and leopard. These competitors are much larger and stronger than the individual wild dogs, however as they stick together they manage to chase off larger predators. As you may have larger competitors in your business, if EVERYONE in your organisation sticks together to deliver world-class service and offers your customer a great experience, you can, and will, increase your business.

Finally, when the dogs get back to the den from yet another successful hunt, they regurgitate the food for those team members who did not take part in the hunt, as well as the pups. This is their way of celebrating and sharing in the rewards. Every month we receive our salary – that

is our reward for doing a job. If however, you have a stronger team, your business may produce more profits and this could lead to more rewards being shared! All the business owners that I speak to agree that the more money the business makes, the more their staff will earn.
1. What business lessons have you learnt from the way that the African Wild Dog operates?
2. Are these lessons really relevant to a small business?
3. What have you learnt from the African Wild Dog regarding team functioning?
4. Does the pack spend time bonding and communicating prior to embarking on a task?
5. Do they strategise? Do they isolate a single target and focus all their energy on the target?
6. Do they allow participation and involvement of weaker members?

Source: Bush (2011:32).

in a business make up the management team. For example, members of a management team might include a marketing manager, who oversees all marketing related activities, or a human-resources manager, who directs human-resource roles and responsibilities.

13.2.2.2 The entrepreneurial team

DEFINITION

'An entrepreneurial team consists of two or more individuals who combine their efforts to function in the capacity of entrepreneurs. In this way, the talents, skills, and resources of two or more entrepreneurs can be concentrated on one endeavour'(Moore et al., 2010:17).

The most important resource for the entrepreneurial venture is the people involved in starting up and running the venture. Many people become so involved in their endeavour to realise financial gain that they forget about their employees. The people who work for the entrepreneur in a small business can be the greatest asset if they are optimally managed, or its greatest liability if they are incorrectly managed. The following people can make up the entrepreneurial team:
▸ The co-founders
▸ The management team
▸ Employees
▸ Consultants.

13.2.2.3 Teams in the workplace
A new venture requires a lead entrepreneur with personal characteristics as referred to in Figure 13.2. However, a high-potential venture also requires interpersonal skills to foster communications and, therefore, team building. The most important aspects of a team are summarised in Figure 13.2.

13.2.2.4 Team performance
The dynamics of teams and teamwork performance are uniform regardless of the size of the business. So hiring employees with the ability to work well on team projects is both a necessity and an advantage. According to Kuratko and Hornsby (2009), teams need to follow seven critical steps to ensure quality decision making.
▸ *Define the problem.* A problem statement should incorporate observable and measurable data, and should be as exact as possible. The primary purpose of problem statements is to define the gap between the current situation and the desired result. This step can be made easier by using mind maps, brainstorming, or problem questioning.
▸ *Decide on the process to use.* Once the problem has been defined, the team must decide on the process or model by which it will find a solution. Without an agreed-upon process, the team may create overlapping work efforts and team members may become irritated. Key

Figure 13.2 An entrepreneurial team as a critical ingredient for success

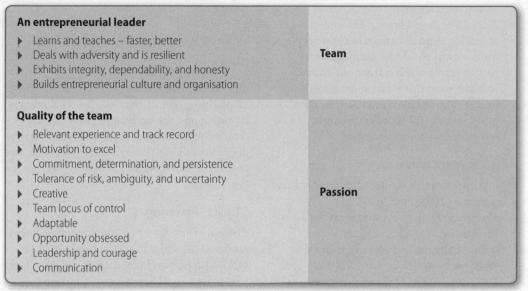

An entrepreneurial leader

▸ Learns and teaches – faster, better
▸ Deals with adversity and is resilient
▸ Exhibits integrity, dependability, and honesty
▸ Builds entrepreneurial culture and organisation

Team

Quality of the team

▸ Relevant experience and track record
▸ Motivation to excel
▸ Commitment, determination, and persistence
▸ Tolerance of risk, ambiguity, and uncertainty
▸ Creative
▸ Team locus of control
▸ Adaptable
▸ Opportunity obsessed
▸ Leadership and courage
▸ Communication

Passion

Source: Timmons and Spinelli (2009:113).

questions to answer when deciding on the process include:

- Who should be involved in the problem-solving process? Who are the critical stakeholders or experts the team needs to be part of the process?
- What tools or equipment will the team need to make a decision?
- What information and data will the team need?

▸ *Gather information.* The following questions need to be addressed:

- Does the team have accurate data that are readily available?
- Does the team need help to understand and interpret the data?
- Does the team need information that is considered private or confidential?

▸ *Make the decision.* Answer the following questions before reaching the conclusion:

- Will the whole team work on the whole problem, or will the work be divided among sub-teams?
- What decision-making style will the team use?
- What are the criteria for the solution?

▸ *Develop an action plan.* An action plan is similar to a business plan (see Chapter 12) in that it is used to track progress. It also serves to track how well the chosen solution worked. A standard action plan will answer the following questions:

- What action is required?
- Who is responsible?
- Is there a completion date?
- Does the plan contain space for marking when the action has been completed?

▸ *Audit and evaluate the decision and process.* The learning does not end when the decision has been made. Team self-analysis and feedback allow for a review of the results and the ability to learn more about both the team's cognitive processes and the problem-solving process. Future performance can be improved by answering the following questions as a team (team self-analysis):

- How well did we define the problem?
- How well did we gather information?
- What would we do in the same way next time?

- What would we not do in the same way next time?
▶ *Record and share learning.* Prior to activating team dynamics in the workplace, mechanisms should be put in place to permit teams to learn from one another and to ensure that vital information is not lost. A foundation of intellectual capital is priceless and will allow any company to remain afloat and competitive.

13.2.2.5 Team types

Specific team types, as identified by Byrd and Megginson (2009), are:
▶ *Problem-solving teams* that meet for an hour or two a week to discuss ways to improve the quality, efficiency, and the work environment
▶ *Self-managing work teams* that take over some managerial duties, such as work and vacation scheduling, the hiring of new members, and the ordering of materials
▶ *Cross-functional teams* that are formed to monitor, standardise, and improve work processes that cut across different parts of the organisation, to develop products, or to otherwise address issues calling for broad representation and expertise.

13.3 Entrepreneurial management

To manage a new venture effectively, the entrepreneur has to develop and perform certain managerial tasks, such as planning, decision making, organising, leading, and control. These functions can be divided into three main phases, namely:
▶ *Formulation of plans*, including the planning and decision-making functions
▶ *Implementation of plans*, including organising and staffing the venture, and leading and motivating staff
▶ *Evaluation of plans*, which includes the control function of the manager.

Figure 13.3 is a graphic illustration of these phases.

13.3.1 Phase one: Formulation of plans

The planning process and the actual experience of planning are critical to the entrepreneur. Planning and the exchanging of ideas can be a creative process for everyone involved. In the decision-making process, various options and possibilities are considered before selecting the best option.

13.3.1.1 Planning

Planning is the most essential function since it occurs at all stages and levels of the business and is also part and parcel of all the other tasks performed in the business. **Planning** deals with compiling a detailed business plan, thus purposefully reflecting on the goals and objectives to be achieved within a given time, the means and activities that are needed to do so, and the problems that may be encountered. It also involves drawing up the most appropriate plan of action to achieve the said objectives.

The planning process
Objectives are the specific circumstances or state of affairs that a business wants to achieve, and plans can be regarded as the way in which these objectives can be achieved. Planning is a process consisting of the following activities:
▶ Identifying and formulating objectives
▶ Gathering information
▶ Analysing the information
▶ Developing alternatives and drawing up the plan
▶ Implementing the plan.

Types of plans
The different types of plans are identified according to their time frame, organisational span, and frequency of use. The following types of plans can be identified:
▶ *Long-, medium-, and short-term plans.* These types of plans refer to the time

Figure 13.3 The entrepreneurial management process

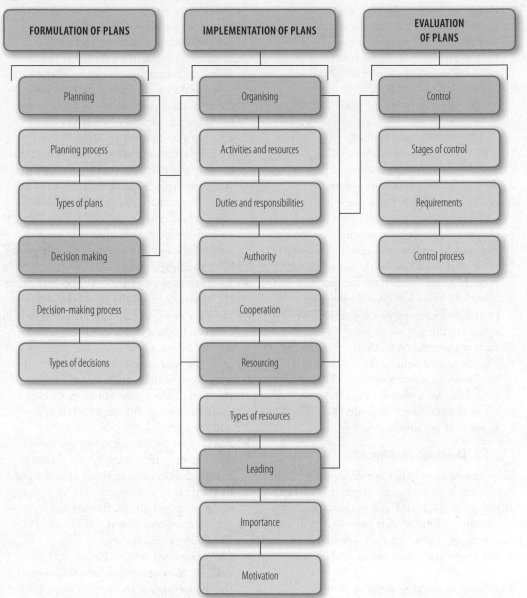

frame for which the plan was drawn up. One should not be dogmatic in saying that all long-term plans cover a period of one year or more, medium-term plans six to 12 months, and short-term plans a period of less than six months. The time frame for each of these plans must be determined by each business according to its circumstances and requirements.

▸ *Master plan and divisional plans.* A master plan is usually drawn up for the business as a whole by, or in close cooperation with, top management. It is also referred to as the total plan, overall plan or broad plan. The master plan is drawn up for a period of at least a year and covers the overall objectives for that time, as well as the contributions of the various sections or functions of the total business. The plans for the various sections or functions in the business are referred to as divisional or operating plans. Although the various operating plans cover the same time frame as the master plan, they are usually broken up into smaller time frames and groups of activities or tasks for each function, department, division, section or project.

▸ *Single-use plans or standing plans.* The difference between these plans lies in the number of times a specific plan is used. A single-use plan is normally used only once and may be a plan for a specific project or order that would probably not be repeated. It could also be drawn up for specific objectives to be achieved during a set period. Standing plans (which are also called routine plans) are used repeatedly, such as procedures, methods, programmes, directives, and policies. These plans are used without alterations or, if changes are made, the basic plan remains the same while the details are amended according to the new circumstances.

13.3.1.2 Decision making

Making sound and effective decisions is paramount for a new venture since it is directly linked to its success. Each decision made by management affects staff members and can thus strongly influence their job satisfaction, loyalty, motivation, and productivity.

The decision-making process

The decision-making process is composed of the following steps:

▸ *Identify and formulate the problem or situation.* The decision-making process begins with gaining complete clarity about the nature and extent of the situation, event or problem or, more specifically, a discrepancy between an existing and a desired state of affairs.

▸ *Collect all relevant information.* Gather as much information as possible regarding all factors and circumstances that relate to the problem or situation, and all this information should be accurate. The true facts and causes should be established and you should guard against suppositions, distractions, assumptions, and unfounded assertions, as well as placing too much emphasis on past experience.

▸ *Develop all possible alternatives.* It is at this stage in the decision-making process that you demonstrate your creativity, since all possible alternatives need to be identified. The decision maker should deliberately try to find all alternatives that may exist beyond the obvious or those that may have been used previously.

▸ *Evaluate each alternative.* When evaluating the alternatives, all the strengths and weaknesses of each alternative need to be evaluated, while being careful to guard against biases.

▸ *Select the most appropriate alternative.* This step involves the actual decision making, the final choice of the solution, or even more than one solution, which is apparently the best.

▸ *Ensure that the decision is implemented.* To implement a decision properly means to convey the decision to those affected and to get their commitment to it. One should assign responsibilities, allocate the necessary resources and clarify any deadlines or milestones.

▸ *Follow up and evaluate.* Follow up and evaluate the outcomes of the decision. If the follow-up and evaluation indicate that the desired results were not achieved, the decision-making process should be reviewed to determine what went wrong. Essentially this presents a brand new problem and requires that the decision-making process be followed again with a new perspective.

13.3.2 **Phase two: Implementation of plans**

With the implementation of plans, the entrepreneur should organise and structure the activities of the business to ensure the attainment of its objectives. An entrepreneur is also responsible for assisting employees to perform effectively in their work. In order to do this, the entrepreneur should demonstrate leadership, and be aware of factors that motivate him or her as well as other employees.

13.3.2.1 **Organising**

During the establishment of a business, the entrepreneur may create a new organisation and attention has to be devoted to organising the activities and resources of the business as a whole. This means that he or she should find the answers to the following questions:

▸ Who will do the work?
▸ How will it be done?
▸ What resources will be used?
▸ Exactly when and where will the operations take place?

Organising is the first step in implementing the plans that have been developed by the entrepreneur and involves arranging the activities and resources of the business by allocating duties, responsibilities, and authority to persons and departments or divisions. The relationships between the individuals, departments, and divisions should also be determined so that they can cooperate in systematically performing the work and achieving objectives in the most efficient way possible.

13.3.2.2 **Resources**

After establishing the organisational structure, the next step is to identify the resources that are required. For the entrepreneur, these resources can be divided into four broad categories:

▸ *Operating resources*. These refer to the buildings, assets, equipment, and stock that will be needed to achieve the goals and objectives of the business. In the case of a service business, they may include the building, vehicles, office equipment, and a specific layout. If the business sells products, it will also include the stock, shop equipment, and layout plans. When a product is manufactured, the resources will include machinery, factory equipment and layout, tools, and raw materials.
▸ *Human resources*. The human resources of a venture will include all the personnel who are directly or indirectly involved in rendering the service, manufacturing, and (or) selling products. (Chapter 16 provides guidelines for recruitment).
▸ *Financial resources*. The entrepreneur determines what financial resources are available, whether it is own capital, loan capital or investment capital. All the processes should be put into place to manage these as well as the gross and net income and cash flow.
▸ *Technology resources*. It is impossible for a business to exist today without technological resources such as computers, telephones, printers, faxes and access to the Internet and email. In establishing the organisational structure, it is also necessary to identify and obtain the necessary technological resources.

13.3.2.3 **Leadership**

Leading is probably the management task to which the entrepreneur devotes most of his or her time. Moreover, leading is a difficult and demanding task if done correctly because the entrepreneur has to supervise activities and the use of resources, including people. Leading requires the entrepreneur to interact with and address people directly. When leading, close daily contact has to be established, since instructions have to be issued, information and guidance have to be provided, plans have to be put into operation, and the execution of the work has to be supervised. Consequently, leading has a strong interpersonal character and is not only focused on activities, but equally as much, if not more, on people.

The importance of leadership for the entrepreneur

The most important reason for the entrepreneur to develop his or her leadership skills may be summarised as follows:

▶ Leadership facilitates the execution of the activities of the business
▶ Proper leadership can ensure that the execution of the work will take place as effectively and efficiently as possible
▶ Leadership has an important influence on the relationship between the entrepreneur and his or her personnel, as well as on the willingness of the personnel to work efficiently.

Motivating as part of leading

The entrepreneur needs to use leadership and motivation to encourage his or her staff members to be enthusiastic about their work. The aim of motivation is to encourage people to perform their duties to achieve the objectives of the venture and, in so doing, also address their needs. Employees will be encouraged to perform optimally if their needs are met in the process. According to Maslow (1943), human needs can be classified into five categories and have a definite rank-order priority. The five categories of needs are the following:

▶ *Physiological needs.* The need to survive is represented by a need for food, water, housing, clothes, and recreation.
▶ *Safety needs.* This refers to self-preservation needs such as protection against danger and losses, and security with regard to employment and income.
▶ *Social needs.* These consist of a need for friendship, love, acceptance, and being a member of a group or a specific society.
▶ *Esteem needs.* These are needs relating to personal success, achievement, status, self-respect, self-confidence, and self-esteem.
▶ *Self-actualisation needs.* These relate to a person's desire for self-expression, personal development, creative work, and overcoming challenges.

The entrepreneur should try to ascertain what the needs of his or her employees are and provide opportunities for satisfying those needs.

Managing individual motivation

Wickham (2001) identified the following five key elements to managing individual motivation (see Figure 13.4):

▶ *Understanding personal drives.* It is important to learn and recognise what a person wants to gain from a situation. As discussed above, individuals bring a complex mix of financial, social, and development needs to a situation. The entrepreneur can lay the ground for motivating them by involving them in the vision of the business and also by communicating to them the importance of the role that they play in this vision.
▶ *Setting goals.* People are not motivated just in the abstract sense but by doing something. The entrepreneur can motivate them by setting the goals that must be achieved. These goals should be realistic, should demand some effort from the individual, and should be achievable given the personal and organisational resources the individual commands.
▶ *Offering support.* If people are to deliver on the goals and objectives set for them, they require support in the form of ongoing encouragement, advice, the provision of resources, and authority to do the job at hand.
▶ *Using rewards.* Rewards take a variety of forms and are the means to satisfy an individual's economic, social, and developmental needs. This may imply a nod of approval, financial incentives, training and development opportunities, or increasing levels of responsibility.
▶ *A positive approach to sanctioning.* In some instances, the entrepreneur will need to resort to sanctioning individuals who fail to perform in an appropriate way. The way in which this is done will have an effect not only on the individual, but also on the

organisation as a whole. Sanctioning should be approached positively and must be seen as helping the individual to perform at an acceptable level and not as a punishment. It should focus on how performance could be improved in the future and not on wrongdoings of the past.

13.3.3 Phase three: Evaluation of plans

Plans need to be evaluated and, as the final management task, control links up with planning. Control allows for effective leadership within a set structure of the business. It also ensures the coordination and effective functioning of all activities in the business so that objectives are well implemented and pursued according to plan.

13.3.3.1 Control

> **DEFINITION**
>
> Control is that function of management that regulates the execution of plans and ensures that this is done according to the prescribed plans and standards, and that the formulated objectives are achieved.

Stages of control

Control can be exercised at one or more of the following stages:

- *Pre-control.* During pre-control the entrepreneur thinks ahead and makes provision for any contingencies that may cause any deviations, delays, mistakes, changes in the environment, and so on.
- *Concurrent control.* This takes place while the work is being done and aims to ensure that all directives and requirements of the plans are carefully adhered to. Control is thus not postponed until the work has been completed or until such time as corrective action might be too late.
- *Post-control.* This takes place only after the completion of a task or instruction. Post-control is perhaps only necessary when drawing up final financial, costing, budgetary, and other reports.

The control process

According to Marx and Churr (1985) and Cronje et al. (2004), the controlling process may be divided into the following four steps:

- *Design and introduction of the control system.* When the control system is

Figure 13.4 A framework for individual motivation

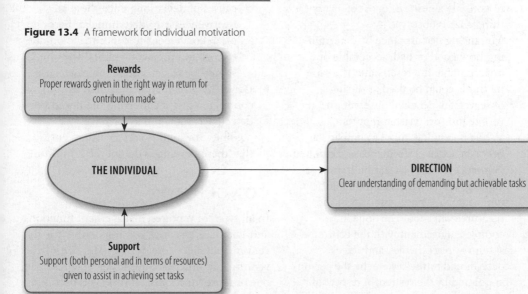

Source: Wickham (2001).

designed and introduced, the following should be adhered to:

- It should fit in with and be adapted to the planning, organising, and leadership that precede control
- It should make provision for defining control points, places, times, or stages so that control can be exercised according to a fixed procedure and with specific objectives in mind
- The criteria or standards with regard to the quality of the work that will be done and the efficiency of the execution thereof should be determined
- Control should be designed in cooperation with personnel and they should be involved in the development thereof
- The control system should be introduced and explained to the personnel.

▶ Observation and measurement of actual performance and reporting thereof. During this step the following should be done:

- Observe performance to determine what results are being obtained either personally or by listening to verbal reports or perusing written reports; with personal observation, it is essential to compile a written report on everything that is observed
- Measuring performance by determining how good or bad, acceptable or unacceptable the results are (the same methods could be used as during observation: personal observation, verbal and (or) written reports)
- While measuring, make a comparison between actual performance and planned performance, with a clear indication of any deviations, whether favourable or unfavourable – both observation and measurement should be done in complete agreement with the control system at places, times, and stages determined by the system, by the persons appointed by the system, in respect of the aspects mentioned in the system and in the units prescribed by the system

- Reporting on the findings, either verbally or in writing. Avoid writing lengthy reports that will not be read or easily understood; be concise and to the point, without omitting the necessary details that will explain the process followed and the way in which the results were obtained.

▶ *Evaluation of performance.* The next step is to analyse and evaluate the information obtained during observation and measurement of performance. This step is largely concerned with the following:

- *Assessing the importance of the deviation.* Minor deviations should not be ignored entirely, since they could be an indication of a bigger problem that will only be determined if they are investigated further. Negative deviations should be corrected, while positive deviations could be investigated for possible application at a later stage.
- *Determining the causes of or reasons for deviations.* This is often regarded as the most significant aspect of control. It is essential that the entrepreneur should not stop at the probable and obvious causes of deviations since these are relatively easy to determine and are often convenient to concentrate on due to cost and time constraints. The aim should be to determine the true causes.

▶ *Corrective action.* The last step in the control process is correcting the deviations detected as soon and as effectively as possible. The aim should also be to ensure that these deviations do not recur in future.

CONCLUSION

In all types of ventures, management functions and tasks are essential and imperative for the venture's efficient functioning. The size of the venture and other circumstances may result in one or more functions and (or) tasks becoming more important than the others. It is nevertheless essential that all functions should exist and that they should cooperate and coordinate their activities in such a manner that the overall objectives of the venture will be achieved and have a higher priority than the achievement of the functional or divisional objectives.

Teams and entrepreneurial leadership can make all the difference in venture success. Both are distinguishing features of a high-potential business. Furthermore, the existence of quality teams ensures the ability to offer employment, while contributing to the overall success of the venture.

SELF-ASSESSMENT QUESTIONS

Multiple-choice questions

1. Which one of the following activities is an important function of purchasing?
   a. Taking stock
   b. Placing advertisements
   c. Negotiating finance
   d. Selecting personnel
2. An entrepreneurial team is critical for the success of a business. Which one of the following qualities is not a quality of an entrepreneurial leader?
   a. Learns and teaches – faster, better
   b. Avoids adversity and is not resilient
   c. Exhibits integrity, dependability, and honesty
   d. Builds entrepreneurial culture and organisation
3. In which one of seven critical steps in team functioning will the team address the following question: 'Does the team need help to understand and interpret the data?'
   a. Decide on the process to use
   b. Gather information
   c. Make a decision
   d. Develop an action plan
4. In which step of the decision-making process do you demonstrate your creativity?
   a. Formulate the problem.
   b. Collect all relevant information.
   c. Develop all possible alternatives.
   d. Evaluate alternatives
5. During the control process, observation and measurement of actual performance involves _____?

a. assessing the importance of deviation
b. determining the causes of deviations
c. observing performance results
d. taking corrective action

DISCUSSION QUESTIONS

1. Discuss the different business functions.
2. Differentiate between the attributes of an entrepreneurial leader and an entrepreneurial team.
3. Explain how you would improve the effectiveness of an entrepreneurial team.
4. Explain the four management functions of planning, leading, organising and control.
5. Describe the decision-making process.

EXPERIENTIAL EXERCISE

1. You started a travel management company six years ago and now have 30 people reporting to you. Reflect on your leadership attributes. Would you consider yourself to be an entrepreneurial leader?
2. In your travel management company you have divided your staff into five teams consisting of six members. Why did you divide your staff into teams? What are the advantages of having entrepreneurial teams?
3. You have set targets for each of the five teams in your travel management company. You have watched the teams during their meetings to discuss their strategies to meet these targets. What guidance will you provide the teams to enhance the team decision-making process?
4. You have decided to expand your travel management company by opening another branch. What planning do you have to do to ensure that the launch of the new branch is successful?
5. You have appointed an operations manager in your travel management company to take control of all the operational issues. What procedures should she follow in controlling the operations?

EASTERN CAPE FEMALE FARMER NAMED AS JOB CREATOR OF THE YEAR 2012

Madelé Ferreira of Mooihoek Boerdery has been named the 2012 Sanlam/Business Partners Entrepreneur of the Year®, Job Creator of the Year. Awarded for her incredible ability to adapt and effectively thrive in a previously unfamiliar industry, Madelé's business has grown from a few hundred plants in 1998 to a multi-million rand farming enterprise today.

The business was started on a small scale when Madelé initially began farming on land that she leased from her husband. Today, the business produces spinach, leeks and strawberries on a 40 hectare farm in the Gamtoos Valley in the Eastern Cape and supplies the distribution centres of three of South Africa's leading chain store groups, namely Spar, Pick n Pay and Shoprite/ Checkers /Freshmark. Madelé currently employs 90 employees at Mooihoek Boerdery.

The farm also currently delivers strawberries to chain stores and markets in Johannesburg, Bloemfontein, Durban, Pietermaritzburg and Port Elizabeth.

Madelé says that Mooihoek Boerdery started as a little girl's dream of one day marrying a farmer and later evolved into a dream of empowering the working women on the farm. She says that building and maintaining relationships is one of the most important elements of her business as her suppliers, employees and clients are the life-blood of the business.

She attributes her faith and determination to continually better her business that brought her into contact with role players that enhanced, empowered and provided her with the necessary knowledge she needed in the fields of production methods, irrigation and good business practices.

According to Kobus Engelbrecht, a member of the 2012 Sanlam/Business Partners Entrepreneur of the Year® judging panel, Madelé stood out amongst her competition because of the number of jobs she created in a rural area where unemployment is rife. 'Not only did she create a sustainable business, but she also provides employment to people who otherwise would only have contributed towards the unemployment number.'

Source: EOY (2012:1).

1. Does Madelé exhibit the characteristics of an entrepreneurial leader?
2. To manage 90 employees, what management skills would Madelé have to use?
3. To deliver strawberries to chain stores and markets in Johannesburg, Bloemfontein, Durban, Pietermaritzburg and Port Elizabeth would require detailed planning. What planning would the owner have to focus on?
4. How do you think she is 'empowering the working women on the farm', apart from providing them with jobs?
5. To supply the distribution centres of three of South Africa's leading chain store groups, namely Spar, Pick n Pay and Shoprite/Checkers / Freshmark, Madelé would have to implement control processes. What control processes should she employ?

SUGGESTED WEBSITE LINKS

African Entrepreneurs - activating social capital: http://www.africanentrepreneur.com/pages/articles.html
Challenges facings Africa's entrepreneurs: http://news.bbc.co.uk/2/hi/business/6100180.stm
Entrepreneur of the year: https://www.eoy.co.za
My Arms Wide open - My business my community: http://myarmswideopen.org/causes/my-business-my-community.html

Overcoming challenges for young entrepreneurs: http://www.emergingstars.com/hot-tips/overcome-challenges-young-entrepreneurs-face

REFERENCES

Bush, G. 2011. Don't tell me ...'It's NOT my job'! *Supermarket & Retailer*, February, 32.
Byrd, MJ. & Megginson, LC. 2009. *Small Business Management, an Entrepreneur's Guidebook*. New York: McGraw-Hill/Irwin.

Cronje, GJ de J, Du Toit, GS. & Marais, A de K. 2004. *Introduction to Business Management.* 6th ed. Cape Town: Oxford University Press Southern Africa.

EOY – Entrepreneur of the Year. 2012. *Eastern Cape female farmer named as Job Creator of the Year 2012.* [Online]. Available: http://www.eoy.co.za/posts/from-new-ground-springs-new-growth-628 [7 May 2014].

Katz, JA. & Green II, RP. 2011. *Entrepreneurial Small Business.* 3rd ed. New York: McGraw-Hill.

Kuratko, DF. & Hornsby, JS. 2009. *New Venture Management: The Entrepreneur's Roadmap.* New Jersey: Pearson Education.

Marx, FW. & Churr, EG. 1985. *Fundamentals of Business Economics.* Pretoria: HAUM Educational.

Maslow, AH. 1943. A theory of human motivation. *Psychology Review,* July:370–396.

Moore, CW, Petty, JW, Palich, LE. & Longenecker, JG. 2010. *Managing small business: An entrepreneurial emphasis.* 15th ed. Mason: South-Western Cengage Learning.

Nieman, G. & Bennett, A. (Eds). 2006. *Business Management: A Value Chain Approach.* 2nd ed. Pretoria: Van Schaik.

Timmons, JA. & Spinelli, S. 2009. *New Venture Creation: Entrepreneurship for the 21st Century.* 8th ed. New York: McGraw-Hill/Irwin.

Wholesale Business. 2014. Back to basics: Growing pains! Moving beyond close family store management for independents. 1, 25–27.

Wickham, PA. 2001. *Strategic Entrepreneurship: A Decision-Making Approach to New Venture Creation and Managment.* Harlow: Prentice Hall.

CHAPTER 14

Marketing

Elana Swanepoel

LEARNING OUTCOMES

On completion of this chapter you will be able to:
▶ Contextualise the marketing process
▶ Explain the target market
▶ Discuss marketing strategy
▶ Describe the elements of the marketing mix
▶ Differentiate between services marketing and product marketing

OPENING CASE STUDY

This morning, what woke you up? Was it the alarm ringtone on your smartphone, the Samsung Galaxy, or your Sony radio? On which station was your radio – Talk Radio 702 or 5FM? As usual, you went for a jog wearing your Nike trainers and your Adidas tracksuit. On return, you may have met a business contact for a business breakfast at Doppio Zero restaurant. After you returned home, you took a shower and were grateful that the recently installed Cobra taps and showerhead worked well. At your office, the dress is casual and so you slipped into your Levi's jeans and a t-shirt from the Levi's store. It is a short drive to your office in your Audi A8 4.2 TDI Quattro, but the car fuel indicator's yellow light has been flickering for a few days. You stopped at the Caltex garage because it is on the way. At the office you called clients using your Samsung PABX system while your office administrator/bookkeeper printed invoices using the Sage Pastel Xpress accounting software solution for small businesses.

It is obvious, that from the moment you wake up in the morning you come across marketing. All the products that you have elected to purchase or services that you have chosen to use are as a result of marketing.

1. What is marketing?
2. Does marketing only refer to products or also to services?
3. Is marketing synonymous with selling and advertising?

INTRODUCTION

Frequently, when people talk about 'marketing', they mean 'selling' or 'advertising'. These two concepts form part of marketing, but marketing entails substantially more than 'selling' or 'advertising'. Every day you are exposed to radio and television commercials, billboards, pamphlets, brochures, sales calls and email or mobile advertisements. Of course, selling and advertising are critical marketing communication activities. If your potential customers do not know about your products or services, they would not purchase it. Without customers you would not have cash flowing into your business and without cash you do not have a business. So, targeting the right customers and ensuring that you have enough customers on a continuous basis is the fulcrum point of any business, and in particular a start-up business. Marketing involves a process that starts with the question: 'Who is my customer?' In this chapter we will explain marketing as a process consisting of five steps that starts with understanding and profiling the customer. Then we look at how to develop a package of satisfaction that provides the customers' needs and wants at an acceptable price. The different promotional and distribution options are then explored. To conclude, services marketing will be discussed as many start-up businesses focus on providing a service.

14.1 Marketing contextualised

To understand marketing you need to accept that marketing is a process. To clarify the marketing process, Amstrong and Kotler (2013) developed a simple model of the marketing process, depicted in Figure 14.1.

As you can see from this five-step model of the marketing process, it is all primarily about the customer. The first step is to understand customers, in step two and three create and deliver customer value, and in step four build mutually beneficial customer relationships. Following these four steps, the company benefits as it profits from increased sales and long-term customer equity.

14.1.1 Marketing defined

> **DEFINITION**
>
> Marketing can be defined as the 'process by which companies create value for customers and build strong customer relationships in order to capture value from customers in return' (Amstrong & Kotler, 2013:33).

Figure 14.1 A simple model of the marketing process

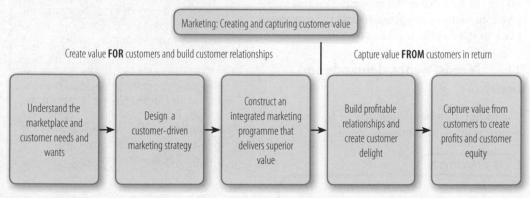

Source: Amstrong and Kotler (2013:22).

What activities are involved in such a marketing process? **Marketing** is the 'activity, set of institutions, and processes for creating, communicating, delivering, and exchanging offerings that have value for customers, clients, partners, and society at large (Approved July 2013)' (American Marketing Association (AMA), 2014:1). The AMA's definition provides some of the detail that is included in the marketing process and extends the value offerings beyond the customers and organisation to include the larger community in which it operates. From both these definitions of marketing it follows that marketing is a complex and comprehensive function that we will explore in the rest of this chapter.

14.2 The target market – the customer

When an entrepreneur decides to start a business, the first question should be: 'Who will benefit from my product or my service?' This should be followed by:

▶ How can my products or services satisfy the customers' needs and wants? The need or want is the opportunity.

▶ What opportunities exist or are likely to exist or can be created in the current and future markets?

By seeking answers to these questions, you are taking the first step in the marketing process by trying to understand customers and the market place in which your company operates.

14.2.1 Needs, wants, demands and benefits

Customer purchases are driven by human **needs**, wants and demands.

DEFINITION

A person has a need when he/she experiences a lack or deficiency.

Humans inherently have different needs. They have *physiological needs*, such as a need for sleep, food, clothing, warmth, water and air; *safety needs*, such as a need for protection against accidents, personal and financial security; *social needs*, such as the need for friendship, affection and belonging; *self-esteem or self-respect needs*; and *self-actualisation needs*.

Wants can be needs taking on a different form as they are shaped by culture, one's society, individual personality and peer pressure.

ENTREPRENEURIAL DILEMMA

What motorcar to purchase?

After specialising in advertising at undergraduate level and graduating with an MBA, Nombulelo started her own advertising company, focusing on mobile marketing. Her target market consists of large companies selling well-known consumer brands. To sell the services offered by her company, she has to arrange appointments with the marketing directors at these companies. These directors tend to be very busy. Thus, she needs reliable transport to ensure that she always arrives on time for scheduled appointments. Her current vehicle is quite old and no longer reliable. She needs to purchase a new vehicle but having just started the business, her finances are limited. She can afford a bottom-of-the-range 1.6 litre car, but she really wants a larger car, such as a Honda CR-V 2.0 or a BMW. Because of a cultural tendency to associate success with expensive cars, she is concerned about the image that the cheaper car may portray to potential clients. If the marketing directors see her driving a bottom-of-the-range car, they might think that she does not have a successful business and may decide that it is too risky to contract her services. She can approach the bank for a loan to finance the car, but they require proof of regular monthly income over a period of several months, but her business only started four months ago and she has not been able to pay herself a regular salary. She really wants the smarter car as it would also boost her self-confidence.

What would you advise Nombulelo?

Source: Author.

When consumers have substantial buying power, their wants can change into demands. They have the financial resources to demand specified or additional features or unique services because they perceive that they derive benefits from such and that value is added.

Apart from understanding the customers' needs, wants and demands, you also need to understand the market place.

14.2.2 Markets

Your target market comprises the actual and potential buyers who share a specific need or want that can be satisfied by your products or services through a process of exchange. You provide a need-satisfying offering (perceived to be of value by the customer) in exchange for the customers' money (which is of value to you). During this exchange a relationship is built with the customer.

14.3 The marketing strategy

A marketing strategy is an integral part of a company's strategic plan and contributes to the company's vision, mission and objectives. Through the marketing strategy the company develops a plan to create customer value and generate profits for the company through a customer-driven relationship. In today's competitive marketplace, to succeed and grow, it is essential that companies are customer centred.

It is impossible for your company to profitably serve all the customers in a market. Thus, you need to conduct a customer analysis

to segment the total market so that you can select the most profitable segment, and develop strategies to serve the targeted segment profitably. 'This process involves market segmentation, market targeting, differentiation, and positioning' (Amstrong & Kotler, 2013:77).

14.3.1 Market segmentation

A market consists of different types of customers with varying needs and wants. By means of market segmentation you can divide the total market into distinct groups, with each group having similar needs and wants and responding in a similar way to a marketing programme. The description of the customers in a segment is called the customer profile. Typically, four sets of criteria are used to segment a market:

1. *Geographic variables,* such as geographic region (e.g. Limpopo), size of the city (number of inhabitants), density of the population (urban, suburban, small town or rural) and climate (winter or summer rainfall, very hot and humid, or cold and dry).
2. *Demographic variables* – characteristics of existing and potential customers, such as gender, age, family size, family life cycle, personal income, household income, occupation, religion, race/ethnicity, education, language, life stage (infant, preschool, child, youth, collegiate, adult, senior), household size, marital status and occupation. Age can be subdivided according to birth era, for example baby boomers (1949–1964), generation X (1965–1976) and generation Y (1977–current), each with different buying habits.
3. *Psychographic variables,* such as lifestyle (conservative or liberal), personality (gregarious, compulsive, impulsive, ambitious, aggressive or authoritarian), social class (lower, middle or upper) and values (innovators, thinkers, achievers, etc.).
4. *Behavioural variables,* such as the purchase occasion (regular use or on special occasions only), benefits sought (economy,

convenience, prestige, speed or service), user status (non-user, ex-user, potential user, regular user or first-time user), usage rate (heavy, medium or light), loyalty status (none, medium, strong or absolute), readiness stage (unaware, aware, informed, interested, desirous or intending to buy) and attitude to product or service (enthusiastic, positive, indifferent, negative or hostile).

In relationship marketing the focus is on identifying the specific benefits sought by the customers relevant to your product or service and ensuring that your products and services comply.

14.3.2 **Market targeting**

After segmenting the market into distinct segments, you compare the different segments to determine in which segments you can contribute the best customer value while earning the highest profit, and sustaining this over a period of time. Most start-ups enter the market by serving one segment, and once they are established they expand into other segments.

To select a target market after you have segmented the market, the following five criteria should be taken into consideration (Kerin, Hartley & Rudelius, 2013:232):

1. *Market size*: Determine the estimated size of the market segment that you are interested in. Is it worth selling to? Will they buy enough of your products or services for you to operate a sustainable business?

2. *Expected growth*: If the market size is currently small but is expected to grow at a substantial rate in the near future, then it would be worth pursuing. However, if the market size is currently large but expected to stagnate, then you should carefully consider your reasons for entering such a market.

3. *Competitive position*: How many competitors are operating in the segment in which

you are interested? How strong are these competitors? Do you stand a chance against them? For example, if you are interested in buying a courier company in Gauteng, you would have to compete against well-established companies such as DHL and several others.

4. *Cost of reaching the segment*: A segment that cannot be reached by your company's promotional activities would not be an option.

5. *Compatibility with the company's objectives and resources*: A segment may appear attractive but your company may not have the resources, such as physical equipment, skilled labour or the know-how to serve such a segment. Unless you can acquire such resources timeously and at a reasonable cost, rather choose another segment that is compatible with your existing objectives and resources.

14.3.3 **Differentiation**

After deciding on a lucrative and compatible segment, you have to differentiate your products or services from those of competitors in the same segment. You differentiate your market offering to ensure that you provide benefits that are highly valued by customers. For example, if you started a motor-vehicle tracking company, how will you differentiate your product and service from those of existing companies? Have you invented a better tracking device or system? Can you guarantee 100% recovery of stolen vehicles?

14.3.4 **Positioning**

Positioning takes differentiation one step further. It involves giving a product or service a distinctive identity. The benefit that is most valued by customers is emphasised in the marketing campaigns and becomes associated with the product or service. For example, MTN, the international communications company, has positioned themselves with the slogan 'everywhere you go', in line with their new corporate vision 'to lead the delivery of a bold, new digital world to their customers' (Brands & Branding in South Africa, 2013:114)

Once you have decided on your marketing strategy and selected your target market, you can start planning the details of the marketing mix.

14.4 The marketing mix

> **DEFINITION**
>
> The marketing mix consists of a set of four marketing tools/instruments/elements, namely product, price, promotion and place (distribution) that the company designs and combines in such a way that the target market would purchase the offering.

By designing an effective marketing mix addressing the needs and wants of the target customers, the company offers buyers a clear customer value proposition (Kerin, Hartley & Rudelius, 2013). The company uses the four tools of the marketing mix, also known as the 4Ps, to influence the demand for its products and services. For each of the four tools the company develops a strategy to attain a desirable customer value proposition. These strategies are explained in greater detail in the next sections.

14.4.1 Product strategy

> **DEFINITION**
>
> The product refers to goods and/or services offered by the company to the target market to satisfy a need or want.

The term 'product' is not limited to physical goods, but could include a broad range of 'things' or activities (Ferrell & Hartline, 2014:11), such as:

- *Goods*: Goods are tangible items and can range from micro-chips to wrist watches to Airbus aircraft and include second-hand items.
- *Services*: Services are intangible products that focus on people and their assets. Services are offered by lawyers, the medical profession, accountants, consultants, courier companies, hotels, airlines, airport shuttles, plumbers, electricians, tutors and many others.
- *Ideas*: Ideas refer to issues or causes that are addressed to benefit the customer, such as those focused on by non-governmental and charitable organisations. A typical example would be the Red Cross, organisations focusing on finding a cure for cancer or assisting cancer sufferers, the Hospice, etc.
- *Information*: In our digital age, the production and distribution of information has become critical in our economy. Information is generated and distributed by websites, journals, magazines, research companies, book publishers, universities, schools, and churches.
- *Digital products*: Digital products include among others, software, music and movies.
- *People*: The marketing of people would include professions such as politicians, actors, professional speakers, athletes or celebrities. For example, soccer players are traded between clubs.
- *Places*: Not only do vacation and conference destinations market themselves but also, cities, provinces and countries to tourists, businesses and residents. A good example is the marketing of countries and cities to host the Olympic Games or the FIFA World Cup.
- *Experiences and events*: These would include events such as sporting events, (Formula 1 racing), music concerts and theme parks.

▶ *Real or financial property*: The sale of stocks, bonds and real estate can be completed either offline or online through investment companies or real estate agents.

▶ *Organisations*: With the assistance of their corporate communications departments, most organisations endeavour to create a favourable image with their target market and with the public at large.

When you develop your product/service strategy you need to consider the following:

▶ *Choice of product/service and the scope of the product/service range*. For example, if you decided to open a motor vehicle dealership in Modderfontein, which makes of cars will you be selling?

▶ *The features of the product/service refer to design, style, size, colour and functionality*. Some features can be adapted according to customer specifications, in particular when a customer demands it and is prepared to pay. A customer may demand that the six cars that he has purchased be painted to look like cheetahs in line with the company's image of speedy service, and the company will pay for the respraying of the cars.

▶ *The packaging of the product*. Packaging has a dual function – simultaneously protecting and promoting the product. The design of the packaging is an integral part of the marketing strategy as the package design can contribute to increased sales. In package design, the shape of the container, the material used, the durability and the colour would be considered.

▶ *The branding of the product*. The purpose of branding is to differentiate the product from all other similar products through the use of a brand name, term, symbol or design. A well-known car brand in South Africa is Toyota and their slogan 'Everything keeps going right – Toyota'.

▶ *Warranty*. A warranty is a promise from the manufacturer/seller regarding the quality of the product. The content of the warranty must be carefully compiled with the assistance of the legal profession. The company must choose between a full or limited warranty and the period, which is normally one year from date of purchase.

▶ *Instructions and installations*. Explicit instructions are provided to ensure that products are assembled and used correctly, and that the necessary safety precautions have been adhered to. Such instructions can also serve to indemnify the manufacturer in case of accidents, which resulted from not following the instructions. For example, when purchasing an electric stand-up AEG fan with a remote control, the fan is delivered in a box but in several separate pieces, which has to be assembled. The instructions are presented in clear steps. If one follows the steps diligently, the assembly is perfect. Where assistance with installation is required, this is usually negotiated as a separate contract.

Your product strategy should contribute to a customer value proposition that customers would find irresistible. The focus is that the target customers will purchase your product/service and not your competitor's product/service.

14.4.2 Pricing strategy

The pricing strategy is a crucial element contributing to the sustainability of the company, but it is also a complex activity to decide on the right price. To earn revenue the following equation applies:

Revenue = price × quantity sold.

To increase revenue either the price or the volume of products sold can be increased. However, price increases are subject to several factors, such as consumer demand and perceptions, as well as the pricing strategies of major competitors. In the following paragraphs key issues in pricing strategy are explained.

The company's cost structure

In setting a price you have to first determine your direct and indirect costs as your price should at least cover all the costs plus allow for a profit.

Price = total cost + profit margin,
     where total cost = direct cost + indirect costs

Direct costs typically include raw materials, components, finished goods, supplies, sales commission, transport, while indirect costs refer to administrative costs, utilities, rent, insurance, etc. In cost-plus pricing setting a price based on the average unit costs and a planned mark-up percentage, the following formula is used:

$$\text{Selling price} = \frac{\text{Average unit cost}}{1 - \text{Mark-up per cent (decimal)}}$$

One of the challenges in using this formula lies in deciding on or determining the correct mark-up percentage. Where industry norms exist, these can be used as guidelines. For example, in clothing retailing the mark-up can be 300 to 400 per cent while in grocery retailing the percentage could range in the twenties. Another challenge is the variation in the cost structure of different companies. If your company's cost structure is relatively high in comparison to others selling to your target market, you may have to accept a lower profit margin to be competitive. Alternatively, if you can produce a product at the lowest cost, it does not imply that you should sell at the lowest price. Although average unit cost is the bottom limit below which prices cannot be set for an extended period of time, other critical factors to take into consideration in pricing are market conditions and customer demand and perceptions.

Perceived customer value

The value of a product/service as perceived by the customer includes the benefits that the customer experiences from the product offering. Some of the attributes could be prestige/image, user-friendliness, solution to a problem, quality, availability and after-sales service, all adding up to customer satisfaction. The customer balances the three or four most critical attributes against the cost of securing the product/service. The customer's costs would include the price of the product (the money the customer has to pay), time and effort, and all these compared to the alternative product offerings.

> **DEFINITION**
>
> 'Value can be defined as the subjective evaluation of benefits relative to costs to determine the worth of a company's product offering relative to other product offerings' (Ferrell & Hartline, 2014:161).

Thus, in determining an appropriate price, the values prized by the target market are incorporated in the pricing strategy and highlighted in every element of the marketing programme focused on customer satisfaction and retention.

Price elasticity

> **DEFINITION**
>
> Price elasticity can be defined as the changes in customer demand following changes in price.

This means that a relationship exists between the demand for a product and the price charged for the product. It is not easy to know the elasticity of a product. Instead, companies consider changes in customer purchasing behaviour and link it to price elasticity.

In the following situations customers tend to exhibit higher sensitivity to price, which means that the price is more elastic:

▸ Substitute products are available. When customers can choose among various substitutes, they will be more price sensitive. For example, customers can choose from a range of washing powders and may change brand when the price of their favourite brand increases. In essence the products are seen to deliver the same value and the only difference is the price.
▸ Comparison of products is easy. If customers can easily compare prices of competing products, they may exhibit greater price elasticity.

In the following situations customers tend not to be sensitive to changes in price, which means that, the price is more inelastic:

▸ No substitute products are available. When customers do not have a choice of products, they will be less price sensitive. For example, when a motor vehicle goes in for repairs and engine parts for a specific make have to be replaced, the buyer does not have an option as the parts of other makes will not fit.
▸ Customers have a real or perceived need for the product or service. The product is perceived as a necessity. A young lady may insist that hair extensions would make her look prettier and would pay whatever the hairdresser charges for the hair extensions.
▸ Customers perceive specific benefits from the product. Although the product may be classified as 'expensive' the customer considers it worth it. An example would be a Rolex watch.
▸ The product is clearly differentiated from other similar products. Through branding and advertising a product can be differentiated to the extent that customers will not purchase a similar competitive product. In such instances the price inelasticity is evident. Even if the preferred product price is increased, the committed customer will still purchase the product.

To summarise, the surest way to ensure that customers are not price sensitive is by product differentiation to the extent that customers value the product and become brand loyal.

To decide on the appropriate pricing strategy, the company considers the pricing strategies of competitors. Some approaches are:

▸ *Price skimming.* When a new product is launched, the price is set high to recover the research and development costs incurred in developing the project and the promotional expenses. For example, when a new iPhone is launched, it is priced high for the first few months.
▸ *Price penetration.* A low price relative to similar products is set to gain market share and maximise sales.
▸ *Competitive matching.* The price is set at a level that matches the prices of the major competitors.
▸ *Prestige pricing.* The price is set at the top of the price range for competing products to differentiate the product as unique and of superior quality accompanied by excellent service.

Taking into consideration the type of product/service offering that you are entering the market with and having selected an appropriate price, you need to support your decisions with a promotion strategy.

14.4.3 Promotion strategy and promotion mix

Promotion reinforces the marketing strategy's differentiation and positioning.

DEFINITION

The promotion strategy involves the seller's communication of information to the potential target market and relevant others to influence their attitudes and buying behaviour (Perrault, Cannon & McCarthy, 2014).

To promote the company and its products/services, the company communicates with both existing and potential customers and relevant stakeholders. Marketing communication has a three-fold purpose:

1. To inform the target market (existing and potential customers) about the products/services. Before customers can buy a product/service, they have to know about it.
2. To persuade the customers to buy the products or services and to use such services. The product/service communication has to convince customers that this particular product/service would best satisfy their need or want.
3. To remind the customers to continue purchasing the products/services. The customer is reminded of their past positive experiences with the product/service so that they are not enticed by products/services of competitors.

The promotion mix includes different methods of communication, each with its own strengths and limitations:

▶ *Personal selling* involves the direct spoken (oral) presentation of information about a service, product or idea to potential customers. Sales staff inform the potential customers about the benefits of the products/service and obtain immediate feedback from the potential customer. The personal selling can be face-to-face or telephonically (telesales). The aim is to conclude a transaction. Personal selling can be expensive and for optimal benefit it is combined with mass selling.
▶ *Mass selling* involves simultaneous communication with a large and/or scattered target market consisting of large numbers of potential customers. Mass selling can take on two main forms:
  ▪ Advertising is paid-for communication relating to the products/services or ideas by an identified sponsor. Advertisements appear in different forms of traditional media, namely the print media (newspapers and magazines), radio, television, signs, outdoor billboards and direct mail. A new form through which to advertise is the Internet and mobile phones. Advertising is expensive. To ensure an optimum impact, you have to carefully select the media that communicates best with your target market.
  ▪ Publicity is any free communication about products/services or ideas to influence customers through the publicity media such as the press, radio and television. Since all companies seek favourable news reporting about their activities, products and services, they have corporate communication departments that provide the publicity media with favourable information about the company without paying any media costs. An additional avenue for unpaid communication is on the company's website. The communication departments of companies create and place information about products/services and solutions to problems on the company's website or a service such as YouTube. Alternatively, blogs are written to provide customers with essential information.
▶ *Sales promotion* complements personal selling, advertising and publicity by reinforcing the communication to the potential customers through the promotion activities intended to activate interest, trial or purchase by consumers. Sales promotion activities are aimed at consumers or intermediaries (wholesalers or retailers) or the company's own employees. Sales promotion activities intended for the consumer may include samples, trade shows, aisle displays, contests, frequent-buyer programmes, sponsored events, banners, streamers and coupons. Promotional activities aimed at the intermediaries may include catalogues, merchandising aids, calendars, gifts,

videos, price deals, promotion allowances, sales contests and trade shows. For the company's sales force the promotion activities may include portfolios, displays, sales aids, training materials, contests, and bonuses. Sales promotions are designed to elicit quick results.

SOUTH AFRICAN SUCCESS STORY

Techsavvy – Social media is fast becoming a valuable tool for retailers
With the social media revolution, individual customer experiences very quickly become publically shared via social networks. Social media isn't static – there is continual movement, and what people are calling 'social shopping' is predicted to boom. This will have significant implications for retailers when it comes to customer reach, marketing and brand control.

Many retailers are already implementing advanced analytics to recognise preferences, trends and buying patterns as part of their market research. However, sources that could deliver even greater customer insights such as customer service feedback, blogs, retail and shopper communications and online communications are also crucial to market research, but these tend to be drawn on less.

The major challenge isn't the amount of data available – it is interpreting the data and making business decisions based on them, that is the real trick. The way to access consumers' honest, unmediated needs and expectations (keeping in mind that one opinion that is voiced may represent thousands, and that same single voice may also influence thousands more) is to analyse digital channels such as blogs, tweets and social networks.

According to Mark Peters, Institute of Marketing Management, 'Staying close enough to customers to be able to respond to their needs is critical to the success of any supply chain. After all, what good is a supply chain if it doesn't get the product customers want to them, when they want it and the way in which they want it?'

South African winery embraces social media
South African family winery, Warwick Wine Estate, has developed quite a reputation for its innovative use of social media. Now with the imminent public share offering of Twitter on the New York Stock Exchange, Warwick managing director, Mike Ratcliffe, has taken a step forward by printing the company's Twitter handle on all Warwick's wine bottle corks.

'A cork is the first opportunity a consumer has to experience our wine before actually drinking it, so why not facilitate a conversation?' says Ratcliffe. Believed to be the first South African winery to have embraced social media to this extent, the Warwick team hopes to be able to get close to their customers and develop a real conversation with them. 'While Twitter is generally seen as a marketing tool, we prefer to use it for our in-house consumer research', says Ratcliffe.

The Warwick Wine Estate Twitter and Facebook pages are consistently amongst the most active in the wine industry and the strategy seems to be working.
1. Apart from Twitter, what other social media can Warwick Wine Estate use to enter into a dialogue with their customers?
2. Should they consider posting blogs?
3. What type of information will persuade their customers to buy more wine?

Before an integrated promotional campaign can be launched, the company has to ensure that the products/services are available at the places advertised for the customers to purchase them.

14.4.3 Place/Distribution strategy

> **DEFINITION**
>
> Place refers to the physical or virtual locations where products and services are available in the right quantities when customers want them.

As a producer of a product/service you have to make a basic but crucial decision whether to distribute directly or indirectly to the customer.

Should you choose direct distribution, you would handle the entire distribution task yourself by either opening your own outlets and/or using direct-to-customer e-commerce selling. Direct distribution enables you to maintain control of the marketing mix. By being in direct contact with your customers you can assess changes in customer attitudes and demands and adapt your marketing communication and customer services accordingly. Website-based e-commerce systems allow even small companies the opportunity to design a web page and source customers dispersed all over the world. Many large companies have a website where consumers can place a direct order.

Indirect distribution refers to the use of **marketing channels**.

> **DEFINITION**
>
> A marketing channel is 'an organized system of marketing institutions, through which products, resources, information, funds, and/or product ownership flow from the point of production to the final user' (Ferrell & Hartline, 2014:169).

Wholesalers, distributors and retailers are intermediaries that take possession of the products, whereas agents and brokers merely facilitate the distribution process. Making use of intermediaries is appropriate when consumers are spread geographically; when setting up an own distribution network would require a substantial investment in facilities, staff and information technology; when it is not possible for the producer to carry the inventory; when consumers have an established buying-from-intermediaries behaviour; when wholesalers can extend credit to consumers; and when they can serve the customer needs better and at a lower cost than the producer.

To make products available to consumers at the right time, at the right place, in the right quantities and cost-efficiently requires logistics and supply chain management.

> **DEFINITION**
>
> The marketing/distribution channel consists of a number of intermediaries (interdependent organisations) that contribute to the availability of the product/service to the consumer for use or consumption (Amstrong & Kotler, 2013:321).

Every marketing decision of a company is affected by its channel decision. The pricing will depend on whether the company decides to sell directly to consumers via the web, through boutique stores or through national chains. The extent of the promotional activities – selling and communicating with the channel partners – would depend on how much convincing, training and support the channel partners require. Even the development of new products takes into consideration the eventual distribution of the product both in the current sales environment and the future sales environment.

The length of a **distribution channel** will depend on the number of intermediaries in the channel. The following are typical examples of distribution channels:

- Producer → consumer
- Producer → retailer → consumer
- Producer → wholesaler → retailer → consumer

Distribution costs include costs relating to service/order entry, administration, transportation, warehousing and inventory. The channel intermediaries can contribute to the reduction of these costs as they are specialists in one or more of the following functions:

▸ *Offer a convenient location.* Manufacturers are geographically separated from the consumers, while intermediaries are situated in locations easily accessible to the final consumers.

▸ *Provide an assortment.* Customers want an assortment of products in one location, while the manufacturer only produces one product or a limited range. By supplying, for example, a supermarket that provides a variety of products, the manufacturer's products are included in the assortment.

▸ *Break bulk.* To benefit from economies of scale, manufacturers produce and deliver large quantities of a product. By breaking the bulk into smaller quantities, the intermediaries make it available in quantities acceptable to the customer.

▸ *Hold inventory.* Most manufacturers produce products for consumption in the future, and not on demand, except manufacturers of very large items such as large aircraft manufacturers or shipbuilders who build on order. By holding inventory, the intermediary bridges the time gap between the time of manufacturing and the time of purchase by the consumer.

▸ *Provide services.* Intermediaries in the channel, add value to the products by offering services such as gathering information about consumers, spreading persuasive communication about products, finding and communicating with potential consumers, and negotiating with customers to agree on a price so that a transfer of goods can take place. Intermediaries accept the risk of the channel activities for which they are responsible.

You are not limited to the use of one channel of distribution. To achieve the maximum degree of market exposure to the different segments in your market may require a multichannel distribution strategy. For example, a toy manufacturer may sell toys directly from its website, or to a wholesaler or to retailers such as Toys R Us. The rise in multichannel distribution is linked to the multichannel shopping behaviour of consumers. Some consumers prefer to search on websites for the desired product, while others may prefer to buy from a wholesaler or visit the retailer to physically inspect the products.

The challenge with multichannel distribution is to keep all the channel members contented. If a manufacturer sells large volumes of items directly through its website, and it results in a loss of sales by its retailers, the latter may decide not to stock the manufacturer's products at all. Thus, the management of the channel relationships becomes essential.

14.5 Services marketing

The world economies have shifted from goods production to service delivery. The types of services that are offered vary from services offered by government to not-for profit organisations to business organisations. The latter includes services offered by airlines, banks, consulting firms, hairdressers, insurance companies, lawyers, medical practitioners, real estate companies, retailers, telecommunications companies, and many others.

14.5.1 Characteristics of services

Services are differentiated from physical goods with regard to five characteristics (Fisk, Grove & John, 2014):

▸ *Intangibility.* Services cannot be touched because they lack a physical form. Services involve experiences, processes and time. You cannot inspect a service with your five senses prior to purchase. It cannot be seen, tasted, touched, heard or smelled. Thus, it may feel riskier to a customer to buy a service than a physical item. To reduce the customer's perceived risk and reluctance, marketers use information and visuals about successful outcomes of their services. For example, an architect, after he has discussed your design requirements and made some suggestions, can provide a computer-generated picture of a house that he designed.

▸ *Inseparability/simultaneity.* The service is provided at the same time that it is consumed. The service provider and the consumer are inseparably linked through the interaction that takes place during service delivery. Often, the customer becomes a co-producer during the rendering of the service. For example, when you visit a hairstylist, you may not know exactly what your hairstyle is going to look like until it is finished. During the styling you may interact with the stylist regarding your preferred colour and style. This simultaneity of production and consumption of service means that closer contact with the customer is experienced and places additional demands on services marketing as the service marketer has to manage the role of the customer in the service interaction effectively and efficiently. The people who provide the service are, in fact, the service. A customer, therefore, buys the skills of a specific person, for example an accountant, a tax consultant, an ICT specialist and entertainer.

▸ *Variability.* The quality of the service is determined by the person who provides the service, as well as when, where and how. Thus, the challenge the service organisation faces, is to standardise the quality of its service performance and provide consistent quality service. Human beings provide the services, which results in variability of service. The service organisation has to carefully select, hire and train personnel to ensure positive customer interactions, and monitor the interactions. In addition, the modern customer is quite informed and thus the progressive service organisation should consider customer skills in employee training.

▸ *Perishability.* Unlike most products, services cannot be stored for later consumption. The revenue opportunity cannot be enacted at a later time without losing revenue. For example, empty hotel beds are an example of perishability. The perishability links to the question of supply and demand on which services marketers have to focus their marketing to ensure near maximum capacity utilisation. Most service providers make use of a reservation or appointment system to direct demand, taking into consideration customer demand patterns. To increase capacity utilisation in off-peak periods, price promotions are used.

▸ *Rental/Access.* Utilising a service does not entitle the user to permanent possession, but merely to temporary possession (e.g. a hotel room) or access (e.g. to a concert).

14.5.2 Services marketing triangle

Service providers, just like manufacturing companies, use marketing to position themselves clearly in their target market. For example, ACCA claims that their accountants are 'Prepared to be different', while RMB purports 'Traditional values. Innovative ideas' and XPS promises 'We deliver'. Although services companies use the marketing mix instruments, they require more than the traditional 4Ps of marketing that focuses on external marketing. Services marketing has to add to the marketing mix two other forms of marketing, namely internal marketing and interactive marketing. The services marketing triangle consists of three major players: the company, employees and customers, illustrated in Figure 14.2.

Figure 14.2 Services marketing types

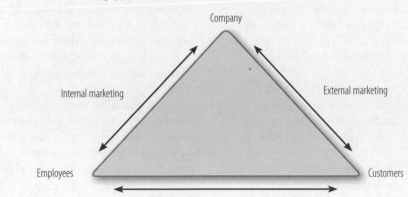

Source: Amstrong and Kotler, 2013:238.

▶ Internal marketing involves the marketing activities of the company directed at the employees who are the service providers. The marketing focuses on both the employees who are in contact with customers and the supporting staff to ensure that both are motivated to provide customer satisfaction. The goal is customer-centric service. In hiring such staff members they should be carefully selected to guarantee that they have inherently a customer orientation, in other words, a passion to serve. After appointment these employees should receive the necessary orientation in customer commitment, followed by continuous motivation.

▶ Interactive marketing focuses on interactive marketing skills required for the buyer-seller interaction during the service encounter. The service deliverer as well as the quality of the service delivery contributes to the final service quality. Thus, the service deliverer (employee) needs to be trained in the art of interacting with customers to satisfy their needs or wants. It is an art to deal with customers who have irrational demands or are frustrated for reasons not related to the company, or who have an impatient disposition, and yet give them all a successful customer experience.

▶ External marketing includes the 4Ps, namely service design, pricing, promotion and location applied to the services company, plus an additional three Ps – participants, physical evidence and the process of service assembly (Fisk, Grove & John, 2014). Participants include all the people involved in the service production and delivery. Physical evidence refers to the service environment and any tangible evidence of the service that is experienced before, during or after the service. The process of service assembly includes the entire procedure required to deliver a service. It can be depicted by a flow chart of the activities.

14.5.3 **Service quality**

Customers may perceive the exact same quality of service differently. The reason for this is that the expectations that customers have of acceptable service levels are different. For example, in a restaurant one customer may wish to have a long leisurely lunch and would not require prompt service, while the customer at the next table may have a one-hour business lunch and expects prompt service.

The service provider may define service quality as the extent to which the service features comply with the company's specifications but these may differ from the customer's expectations. Therefore, service quality must be understood from the perspective of the customer to ensure customer satisfaction and eventual loyalty.

How do customers assess the quality of a service experience? What attributes do customers consider as critical when evaluating a service? A measure of service quality, called SERVQUAL, was developed by Parasuraman, Berry and Zeithaml (1988). SERVQUAL measures the perceptions of customers of service quality using five key attributes:

▸ Tangibles – any physical facilities (e.g. appearance of hotel bedrooms), equipment (e.g. check-in machines at airports) and appearance of personnel
▸ Reliability – ability to perform the promised service dependably and accurately (e.g. PX uses the slogan 'When your business depends on it'. Thus, a customer would expect that they distribute freight on time to the correct destination and intact.)
▸ Responsiveness – willingness to help customers and to provide prompt service (e.g. 'It is not my job' is evident of no desire to assist the customer.)
▸ Assurance – knowledge and courtesy of employees and their ability to convey trust and confidence (e.g. booking a flight to Latvia and the travel agent has no idea where Latvia is)
▸ Empathy of the service provider – caring, individualised attention provided by the service provider to its customers (e.g. after making a provisional booking to fly to Tromso, Norway and waiting for the payment to be cleared, the travel agent did not confirm the booking, resulting in the booking being cancelled by the airline, even before due date. A new booking had to be made and the flight ticket price jumped from R10 500 to R21 000.)

Some customers may rank reliability higher than responsiveness, while other customers may rank tangibles higher than empathy. It all depends on the values of individual customers.

An easily quantifiable measure of quality service delivery is customer retention. If a service provider consistently delivers quality service to its customers, it is more likely to retain its customers as they are assured of receiving a value proposition. A high turnover in customers is a symptom of unacceptable levels of service quality.

Service quality can be used in the company's differentiation strategy. By delivering consistently higher quality service than its competitors, a company differentiates itself. However, it would be necessary for the company to ascertain what, according to the customers' perceptions, comprises 'consistently higher quality service'.

CONCLUSION

In this chapter we expounded the concept of marketing and its constituent parts. As business is centred on the customer, the target market and the needs, wants and demands of the customer were enlarged upon. The activities involved in a marketing strategy were detailed. The four instruments of the marketing mix, namely product, price, promotions and place were fleshed out. Owing to the growth in service industries, services marketing was explored, focusing on the characteristics of services, the service marketing mix and attributes of quality service.

SELF-ASSESSMENT QUESTIONS

Multiple-choice questions

1. What is the first question that an entrepreneur should ask when starting a business?
    a. Where can I start my business?
    b. With whom should I start my business?
    c. Who will benefit from my product or my service?
    d. What products do I have that I can sell?
2. During market segmentation you segment the market using behavioural variables. Which one of the following is not a behavioural variable?
    a. Benefits sought
    b. Purchase occasion
    c. User status
    d. Personality
3. With regard to price elasticity of products or services, in which one of the following instances would prices be more elastic?
    a. Substitute products are available
    b. Substitute products are not available
    c. The product is clearly differentiated from other products
    d. The customers perceive a specific need for the particular product
4. Mass selling involves simultaneous communication with a large and/or scattered target market consisting of large numbers of potential customers. Which one of the following is a form of mass selling?
    a. Personal selling
    b. Sales promotion
    c. Merchandising aids
    d. Advertising
5. Services are differentiated from physical goods with regard to five characteristics. Which one of the following is not a characteristic of services?
    a. Simultaneity
    b. Intangibility
    c. Storability
    d. Perishability

DISCUSSION QUESTIONS

1. Contextualise the marketing process.
2. Explain the process to identify a target market.
3. Discuss the concepts relevant when formulating marketing strategy.
4. Describe the elements of the marketing mix.
5. Differentiate between services marketing and product marketing.

EXPERIENTIAL EXERCISE

1. You have decided to purchase an existing courier business in Polokwane, based on the fact that according to the financial statements the business has been growing and has a number of established customers. How will you differentiate the services of your courier business from well-established courier companies servicing the Polokwane area?
2. On your smallholding you have built several tunnels and are successfully growing vegetables. You can grow a variety of vegetables but first you have to decide on your target market and their needs. As the smallholding is not far from Cosmo City and Diepsloot in Johannesburg, should you provide vegetables to these areas? What type of vegetables would they primarily be interested in? Maybe cabbage, spinach, carrots, onions and potatoes? Or should you consider supplying vegetables to retailers such as Fruit & Veg, Woolworths, or Pick n Pay? But what type of vegetables can you supply to them that they do not already have existing suppliers for? Identify a lucrative and sustainable target market for fresh vegetables.
3. As the owner of an Italian restaurant, how can you differentiate the Italian dishes served at your restaurant from those served at similar restaurants? How can you ensure authentic Italian cooking? Could you employ a native Italian from Italy, passionate about pizza, to teach your staff the art of making Italian pizza, using the old-school hand-rolled technique to make the pizza base? What else could you do?

4. In the *Northcliff-Mellville-Times* newspaper dated 11 April 2014 it was announced that General Nutrition Centre (GNC) has opened its first concept store in South Africa in Cresta shopping centre, Johannesburg. GNC offers a wide range of vitamins, herbal supplements, sports nutrition and slimming products targeted at health conscious consumers who want to improve their wellbeing. GNS has launched in larger Clicks stores in South Africa. Why would GNC now launch a separate concept store? Could this store be seen to be in competition with Clicks? Why did GNC decide to start their first store in Cresta, Johannesburg and not in, for example, Sandton?

5. You own a travel agency that services corporate clients. Several customers have complained about the lack of communication, as a result of which they were not fully informed about booking requirements. Some customers have lost bookings owing to the tardiness of travel agents. Taking into consideration the typical characteristics of services, how would you ensure that your employees deliver quality service as measured by SERVQUAL?

GROUNDBREAKING CONVENIENCE! FRESHSTOP AIRPORT CITY SETS THE BAR FOR CONVENIENCE STORES

CASE STUDY

FreshStop Airport City, situated 2.5 km from Cape Town International Airport, opened on 8 November 2012. The store's new approach to convenience retailing resulted in it being awarded Top International Convenience Retailer in the World. It is a huge achievement as it is the first time that a South African retailer has won this award.

Store background

Initially, the idea was that the site would house a regular fuel forecourt and convenience store partnership. But after looking more closely at the site and surrounding areas, the owners believed that the site would not only uplift the retail offering for consumers living close by, but also be an ideal destination for travellers, commuters and businesses in the area to refresh and refuel.

Store design

The design is based on the Food Lover's Market layout. The shop floor is open-plan. As you enter you walk through the fresh foods displays and into the bakery and hot food areas. Fridges that contain the Grab 'n Go selection, cold drinks and dairy products line the walls with the central area of the store housing grocery lines and snacks. A full-service Seattle Coffee Bar is situated in a prominent section of the store with coffee baristas on hand. In front of the coffee bar is a dried fruit and nuts bar, and more impulse bakery lines.

Research conducted locally revealed the need for meeting facilities and FreshStop Airport City has two conference rooms that are fully serviced with in-house catering. An outdoor eating area has also been created.

On the upper deck, first-floor level, a large seating and dining area has been established for an eat-in experience and this often serves as a meeting place for local workers and business people. The seating area is equipped with free Wi-Fi and plasma screens for those wanting to catch up on the latest news and sport. There are neat and clean toilet facilities, ample parking outside and a car wash, as well as a selection of ATMs from the four main South African banks on-site.

Main clientele

The majority of customers are those stopping to buy an item for immediate consumption, such as coffee or a snack. The lunchtime trade is the store's busiest period and also from around 16:30, when customers stop by on their way home.

Customers are also drawn from the local business area and include staff from Cape Town International Airport. There's some local trade mainly on weekends and on public holidays. 'Our customers are generally repeat customers who pop in on average about 3 or 4 times per week, so we need to change our food and fresh offering regularly', says general manager Warryn de Klerk. 'We have also noticed over the last six months that our female customers are shopping with us more often and are spending more per basket than their male counterparts. So we have changed the layout of the store and our product ranges to enhance our female customers' shopping experience', says Warryn.

Source: Bolton (2014:15–17).

Attracting customers and promotions

'We consistently run promotions on various products in-store, and these are marketed to our local customers. FreshStop continuously runs national promotions on TV, radio and in the press'.

1. Who is the target market of FreshStop Airport City?
2. Has FreshStop Airport City segmented the target market and on which segments do they focus?
3. What is their product strategy? What range of products is on offer and why?

4. How do they promote their business? What else can they do to promote their business?
5. What distribution aspects did they take into consideration? Are they only a retailer or also a manufacturer, for example the bakery?

SUGGESTED WEBSITE LINKS

South African Audience Research Foundation: www.saarf.co.za

South African Statistics: www: statssa.gov.za

South African Marketing Research Association: www.samra.co.za

Direct Marketing Association of South Africa: www.dmasa.org

Mobile Marketing Association of South Africa: www.mmasa.org

REFERENCES

American Marketing Association (AMA). 2014. *Definition of marketing.* [Online]. Available: https://www.ama.org/AboutAMA/Pages/Definition-of-Marketing.aspx [11 April 2014].

Amstrong, G. & Kotler. P. 2013. *Marketing: An Introduction.* Global edition.11th ed. Upper Saddle River, N.J: Pearson.

Bolton, T. 2014. Social media is fast becoming a valuable tool for retailers. *Wholesale business,* 1. © *Wholesale Business.* Reprinted by permission of the editor, *Wholesale Business.*

Brands and Branding in South Africa. 2013. *20th Anniversary Edition.* Johannesburg; Affinity Advertising & Publishing.

Ferrell, OC. & Hartline, MD. 2014. *Marketing strategies: Text and Cases.* 6th ed. USA: South-Western Cengage Learning.

Fisk, RP, Grove, SJ. & John, J. 2014. *Services Marketing – An Interactive Approach.* 4th ed. USA: South-Western Cengage Learning.

Kerin, RA, Hartley, SW. & Rudelius, W. 2013. *Marketing.* 11th ed. New York: McGraw-Hill.

Parasuraman, A, Berry, LL. & Zeithaml, VA. 1988. SERVQUAL: A Multi-item Scale for Measuring Consumer Perceptions of Service Quality, *Journal of Retailing,* 64 (Spring):12–37.

Perrault, WD, Cannon, JP. & McCarthy, EJ. 2014. *Basic Marketing: A Marketing Strategy Planning Approach.* 19th ed. New York: McGraw-Hill.

CHAPTER 15

Operations

Isa van Aardt

LEARNING OUTCOMES

On completion of this chapter you will be able to:
▸ Define the terms 'operations management', 'capacity', and 'capacity planning'
▸ Identify the various aspects addressed in an operational plan
▸ Identify the business facilities required by an entrepreneur
▸ Indicate the number and type of employees required by an entrepreneur to do the daily tasks in the business
▸ Discuss the planning that a small business needs to do concerning administration in the business
▸ Understand the strategies and plans to be continuously developed to ensure business success
▸ Identify the elements of planning pertaining to manufacturing and inventory management in a business plan
▸ Describe the importance of the operating cycle in business management.

OPENING CASE STUDY

When starting a business, a small business owner needs to determine their reasons for starting this business. Is it because you want a change from the nine-to-five rat race? Maybe you want to be at home more for the family, or you want to be your own boss, or you have spotted a gap in the market and believe it's a gold mine, or you want to harness your skills better.

One of the main reasons for a business being stunted is because of the owners themselves. Without systems, a business owner may find themselves in a position where only they can complete the required tasks – either because of specialised knowledge, reluctance to delegate, or because of a lack of systems or operational planning. Another reason for limited growth may be an issue of money. As they saying goes: You need to spend money to make money. This may require the business owner to take out a loan to increase their business's capacity through equipment, hiring staff (such as administrative assistants, workers, specialists and managers), opening an office or factory, management of inventory and finance, and developing strategies for survival and growth.

1. What aspects do you think are important for the survival and growth of an entrepreneurial venture?
2. What could stunt it?

INTRODUCTION

The operational plan is the entrepreneur's formulation of plans for running the business. An effective operational plan, when successfully implemented, can ensure a smooth-functioning and productive organisation. It is, therefore, extremely important that the operational plan should be well formulated and well implemented.

Few new business owners think about the cost implications and the management of the flow of their raw materials and information when they start their business. Not planning the management of these activities is a recipe for disaster. In contrast, careful planning and management can enable a business to grow and thrive relatively quickly.

This chapter gives an overview of operations management and then gives a detailed discussion of the important aspects of an operational plan. The chapter closes with an operations management plan checklist that gives practical guidance on how to draw up an effective operations management plan.

15.1 **Operations management**

Operations management deals with the planning and management of producing a product or service. It is important to indicate how the business will be structured as an organisation and what the reporting relationships will be. The management roles of people in the business should be indicated, and administrative procedures and policies should be devised as an administrative framework within which managers can run the business. Administrative systems (e.g. bookkeeping, payment, personnel records, and personnel assessment systems) need to be created and refined. Staff members will have to be trained in the use of such systems and retrained should the systems change. For example, if a fast-food outlet has three workers who report to the store manager, it will be necessary to indicate who will attend to the administrative functions such as taking stock, bookkeeping and purchasing stock.

Figure 15.1 The operations management process

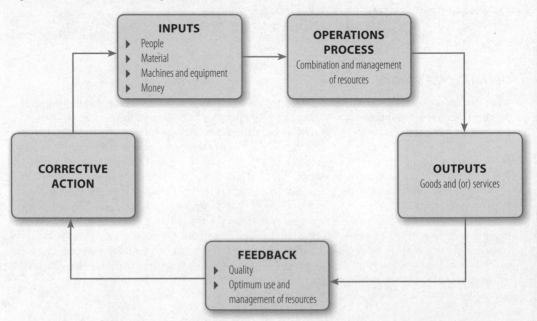

The term operations management can, therefore, be defined as the processes and procedures that are put in place to manage the resources (people, materials, machinery and equipment, and money) required to produce the products and (or) services provided by a business. Figure 15.1 illustrates the operations management process.

> **DEFINITION**
>
> Operations management refers to managing the resources necessary for the production and delivery of products and services.

As shown in Figure 15.1, the inputs are the various resources required by the new venture to start the process of delivering or manufacturing the product and (or) service. The inputs shown here are a simplified list and each business should compile its own list of input needs under the four customary headings. These resources are then combined and managed in the most effective and efficient manner. (Being effective is to get the job done well and being efficient is to use the most appropriate tools and skills to do the job in the least amount of time.) Once the product and (or) service is delivered, feedback will be received either via quality measures that have been put in place or via customer feedback.

The operations manager then uses this feedback to decide whether any changes to the process are necessary. Necessary changes might include, for example, a change in supplier due to poor quality products, training of unskilled staff, investing in the latest technology, or implementing more quality checks. Once this corrective action has been taken, the operations management process starts again. The process should be checked regularly to ensure that the process is as effective and efficient as possible.

There are times when limits are placed on the management of internal resources. For example, top management might limit or stop new appointments or require the use of particular suppliers. Management could also be limited by union agreements that prohibit job rotation (the use of a worker for another task). To deal with these limitations, the entrepreneur can devise an operations strategy or a future plan for how best to deal with available resources based on expected demand (Chase and Jacobs, 2010).

15.1.1 Operations strategy

Normally, an **operations strategy** will outline how best to balance the inputs (workforce size, working hours available, and stock) against outputs (products and services that needs to be provided) (Chase and Jacobs, 2010). For new ventures, which do not yet have an operations history, it is a challenge to know what inputs and outputs are needed and when they are needed. The entrepreneur will need to estimate the demand for his or her goods and (or) services based on the market research done before starting the venture.

> **DEFINITION**
>
> An operations strategy is a plan specifying how an organisation will allocate resources in order to meet long-term goals and is designed to maximise the effectiveness of production and support elements while minimising costs (Business Directory, 2014 and Hartman, 2014).

Over time, however, this challenge can be overcome by keeping record of what orders and requests were placed when, and the response from customers. By analysing this data after the first three months and thereafter monthly, the entrepreneur will be able to determine cycles and trends. A more accurate forecast can then be used. This will also provide the entrepreneur with information that can be used to compare the original forecasts based on market research done. Variations can be detected and analysed, and corrections can be made. Strategies that can be applied include, for example, potential subcontractors and suppliers, a production plan showing costs and projected volumes to be sold, an inventory plan (a large inventory or just-in-time stock), quality control, and inspection plans (Timmons, 1994). The new business venture owner needs to compile an operational plan to assist him or her to visualise and plan how the business will operate.

Without a clear operations strategy, a business is likely to struggle to maintain growth. Read about Collins Kubeka's struggles in the entrepreneurial dilemma – *Lenong General Road Maintenance* below.

15.2 **Operational plan**

> (**DEFINITION** \
>
> The operational plan is a highly detailed plan to achieve short-term objectives and consists of both a workflow plan and a structure for how the business is to be managed (Business Directory, 2014b).

The **operational plan** needs to be carefully formulated to ensure the effective functioning, coordination, and control of the business to optimise return on investment. An effective operational plan, when successfully implemented, can save costs, increase competitiveness, and ensure a smooth-functioning and productive organisation. It is, therefore, extremely important that the operational plan should be well formulated and well implemented.

There are several key components of an operational plan, including: the location of the business, the facilities needed for operation, the machinery and equipment needed for production or sales, the staff required, the layout of the business, inventory and stock control policies, purchasing guidelines, total quality management, maintenance plans, the operating cycle, capacity planning, and plans to boost productivity continuously to remain competitive

---

ENTREPRENEURIAL DILEMMA

Lenong General Road Maintenance

Lenong General Road Maintenance was founded by Mr Collins Kubeka in 1997 in the Ekurhuleni Metro after identifying a niche market in road construction and maintenance. Founder member and current managing director Mr Kubeka, a qualified and experienced engineer, is able to network and successfully tender and secure projects from both the public and private sectors. Lenong actively takes advantage of opportunities presented by government's enabling environment, such as the preferential procedure policy framework (PPPF), by tendering for government-related jobs. However, its main target is private-sector built environment and road projects.

Lenong's main business activities are general road maintenance, civil construction, plant hire, road-sign supplies, and road grass cutting. A preliminary inspection of Lenong's previous projects in 2011 revealed that, since inception, it had undertaken a number of medium-sized projects to the value of approximately R78 million over a 10-year period. Lenong's financial statements, however, showed that the company was in decline. Despite the increase in turnover between February 2010 and February 2011, Lenong's net loss situation had increased by 156% from negative R223 000 in 2010 to negative R571 000 in 2011.

The problems that led to Lenong's operational and financial performance in 2011 include the following:

▸ Salary and wage costs are high compared to the industry norm
▸ Reported productivity levels do not justify these high salary and wage costs
▸ The company does not have any labour relations, financial, or operational systems in place to operationalise and streamline the business; as a result, fixed expenses are very high
▸ Lenong does not have a full-time bookkeeper, so financial reporting is slow and inaccurate
▸ Most of the workers are not aware of how the business works or how to run a construction site.

1. What would you advise Lenong?
2. What plans can be put in place to turn this around?

Source: Adapted from Productivity SA (2010:21).

(Timmons, 1994; Chase and Jacobs, 2010). Each of these key aspects of the operational plan is discussed in more detail below.

15.2.1 The business location

The entrepreneur needs to specify the location of the business and the results of any location analysis that may have been conducted. According to Longenecker et al. (2008) the entrepreneur needs to discuss the advantages and disadvantages of the location in terms of the proximity of the business to suppliers, resources (including staff and materials for production or goods for resale), and customers.

The most important location factors that the entrepreneur should consider are discussed in detail in Chapter 7.

15.2.2 The facilities

The entrepreneur or the venture team needs to indicate what facilities will be required for plant warehousing, shop, and office space. Having done so, he or she needs to indicate how, where, and when the required facilities will be acquired. In this regard, it should also be shown how the necessary facilities will be obtained. For example, will they be leased or bought? Finally, an estimate should be made of when the facilities leased or acquired would have to be expanded to meet the needs of a growing business (Timmons, 1994). The ideal facilities are safe, meet the venture's operational and administrative needs, meet the legal occupational and health requirements, and fit the image that the business wants to portray to its customers.

15.2.3 The machinery and equipment

Machinery and equipment is a costly aspect of the business, but can provide the entrepreneur with a competitive advantage. The entrepreneur should carefully plan and consider the various options available before selecting the equipment and machinery needed to carry out the business operations. Machinery and equipment should be affordable and suited to the type of business. Entrepreneurs should consider the current technology available and the competitive edge the use of such equipment and machinery will provide to the business. Resale and salvage possibilities must also be taken into consideration, particularly when financing is required. The hire of machines and equipment, with the options of a full maintenance plan and future upgrades or purchase, is becoming a popular way of obtaining the latest technology without the initial full capital outlay.

15.2.4 Staff

Able and well-trained personnel are required for the smooth operation of the business. The entrepreneur needs to determine his or her staff requirements and, on that basis, formulate a staff plan indicating how many employees will be required, what their responsibilities will be, whether their employment will be full time or part time, what salaries and benefits will have to be paid to them, and what training they should undergo. When formulating the staff plan, the entrepreneur should also formulate job descriptions for each vacancy to be filled to clarify each employee's functions (Wright, 1995).

Productivity South Africa is a government-subsidised institution that creates awareness of the importance of productivity and how to create an overall environment conducive to productivity enhancement.

15.2.5 The layout of the business

The **layout** of the business should be indicated. In the case of a retail business, it is important to remember that first impressions are important to a customer, which implies that the layout should project an image of professionalism and efficiency (Wright, 1995). In addition, the layout should be effected in such a way that it will facilitate productivity and daily operational effectiveness.

15.2.6 Inventory and stock management

> **DEFINITION**
>
> An inventory is a list of all the goods required by a company to manufacture its products (such as car parts to assemble a car) or to provide a service (such as washing powder at a laundry service).

Companies keep an **inventory** to ensure that they have enough stock to produce their products and (or) provide their services. They also need to ensure that they have what they need to maintain their equipment and prevent breakdowns. An inventory of stationery and other office equipment is needed to ensure that the business is able to supply support services to the various departments within the organisation and to its outside stakeholders (such as suppliers and customers).

Retail stores also need to monitor their stock levels closely. Stock needs to be ordered, received, paid for, handled, stored, and retrieved. Damaged goods need to be returned and reordered. Stock also needs to be recounted and checked to ensure that all the stock ordered is either still available or has been used up or sold. An entrepreneur must look for ways to manage stock, including, for example, keeping the minimum stock required and reducing redundancy, theft or damage of stored goods. Slow-moving inventory items need to be identified. Stock needs to be stored and administered and will tie up money while it lies on shelves. Stock that does not provide any returns will impact negatively on the business cash flow.

The management of stock and an inventory may seem simple, but it requires skilled employees and careful administration because stock is tied-up money. Every time you see a container, truck, train, or aeroplane carrying goods, you see stock that needs to be managed (Chase and Jacobs, 2010).

15.2.7 Purchasing

> **DEFINITION**
>
> Purchasing has to do with obtaining the required materials, machines, equipment, and services from outside sources to enable your new venture to deliver its product and (or) services.

It is important for all **purchasing** to be done on time and at the right quantity and price as this affects the venture's costs and operations as well as the final price that customers are charged. Purchasing policies and practices need to be in place to assist the entrepreneur with decisions such as whether to make or buy products and (or) to deliver or hire services.

The choice of supplier or suppliers needs to be carefully considered to ensure that the quality of products and (or) services can be maintained. Factors which play a role in the selection of supplier(s) include trust and relationship building, product quality, prices and service. Mutual product development can benefit both the business and its supplier(s) as this will open new markets and business opportunities for both parties (Longenecker et al., 2008).

The South African success story – *Envirodeck* overleaf describes how Envirodeck was able to turn the company around by addressing, among other things, inventory and stock management as well as the management of suppliers.

15.2.8 Total quality management

> **DEFINITION**
>
> Total quality management requires a management system that looks at all quality aspects of the company in terms of the products and (or) services that it provides.

Envirodeck

An entrepreneur who has experienced challenges and ultimately overcame them is Warren Graver, founder and director of Envirodeck, and winner of the 2012 Small Business Entrepreneur of the Year® title. Envirodeck was established in 2004 as a supplier of environmentally friendly decking materials to the local building industry. Over the past decade, composite decks have grown in popularity as demand for 'green' products increases.

They have maintained their leading position by constantly researching and staying abreast of technologies used locally and abroad. Envirodeck began extensively marketing and distributing boards for the construction of composite decks as an alternative to traditional wooden decking after recognising an opportunity to offer sustainable solutions to the outdoor leisure market.

Envirodeck's offering stretches far beyond the supply of decking boards, however, and the driving factor behind their operations is to consciously improve the lives of their customers by adding value throughout the supply chain, from manufacture, right through to the installation of composite decks – all while contributing to a more sustainable future.

Envirodeck's success is founded on providing high-performance decking that sets itself apart from the competition. The biggest challenge of this innovative industry is providing a consistently high-quality decking product that not only performs well but also looks attractive, using inconsistent raw materials.

Warren Graver states that as a recognised pioneer in the industry, they understand the technical as well as the straightforward aspects of manufacturing, supply and installation of composite products. They have actively partnered with innovative business partners and invested in state-of-the-art technology concepts to deliver a truly evolved product to the local market. Professional contractors have come to rely on the value and consistency for which Envirodeck is known. 'We take pride in our emphasis on patented product quality and good service and we are a company that offers a truly sustainable building solution to our market and we also take an active stance towards minimising our ecological footprint'.

Graver furthermore says that Envirodeck has not always been a successful business and that he had to overcome a significant number of challenges in the early years of the business. 'I could not have made worse business decisions than in the first two years of opening the business, which was doomed by me not focusing sufficiently on market, product or supplier research'.

'The first challenge that I faced was that although I noticed a considerable gap in the market, I was unsure on how to present the product to an existing market that I had no experience in. It was also a market that was very reluctant to change to new products, as timber was traditionally the only way that decking had ever been done, and it proved extremely tough to penetrate a market when no one had ever seen or heard of such innovative products'.

Graver says that another challenge he encountered was establishing a supplier network. 'I did not do sufficient supplier research and subsequently after landing the first shipment, the supplier closed its doors. This error in judgement on my behalf meant that the initial start-up capital was quickly absorbed into obsolete inventory that would never be sold even at discounted rates'.

He also touches on the importance of managing cash flow. 'The most critical element of a start-up business is managing cash flow versus inventory management, a concept that I failed to understand and subsequently a year later I had no start-up capital left'.

However, the business was saved through continual focus on the gap in the market. Through intense global product sourcing, supplier canvassing and a life-saving loan, Graver managed to slowly recover and turn the business around so that by 2009 it had broken even.

Source: Compiled from Envirodeck (2013) and Finweek (2012). Reprinted by permission of Envirodeck. Text by Gallo Images/Finweek.

As part of a quality programme, it is important that all employees understand the direction the company intends to take. Company efforts should be directed at constantly improving their product and (or) service as well as customer relations. It is important for quality efforts in the business to be visible as they reveal progress made and reinforce the business's commitment to both employees and customers.

15.2.9 Maintenance

The regular use of machinery and equipment causes wear and tear that will lead to breakage and ultimately increased cost. Breakdowns are normally handled in a rush to get the machines up and running. As a result, there is no time to find the best prices and repairs cost more than they should. New ventures are most guilty of this practice because they often do not have the necessary cash flow to carry out **preventative maintenance** on their equipment and machines.

(DEFINITION)

Preventative maintenance refers to planned, continuous checks, service, and maintenance of machinery and equipment, including replacing faulty or worn components, before the equipment or machinery breaks down.

Maintenance is an especially important aspect of a new venture that is still trying to establish itself and cannot afford to build a poor reputation based on machine and equipment failure. Manufacturing companies in particular need to ensure that their equipment and machines are serviced on a regular basis.

If machinery and equipment are not well maintained, their overall performance and capacity capability will reduce over time. This in turn will affect product quality and can threaten the safety of operating staff. Customer dissatisfaction will also increase as orders are either late or of a poor quality.

15.2.10 The operating cycle

The lead and lag times that characterise a business should be described when planning the operating cycle. Usually, when the first activity finishes, a second activity starts. When the first activity is still running and second activity starts, this is called Lead, and the balance of time for the first activity is known as lead time. Lead time is the overlap between the first and second activity (Usmani, 2013). When the first activity is completed and there is then a delay or wait period before the second activity starts, this is called lag and the delay is known as the lag time (Usmani, 2013).

Furthermore, the entrepreneur or venture team needs to plan how operations could be maintained at higher levels during peak times (e.g. seasonal variations or demand driven by the economic cycle). This could be done by devising a back-up structure to deal with higher output catering for additional staff to be obtained at short notice, outsourcing, strategic partnerships, maintaining additional production capacity to cater for peak times, and introducing shifts during peak times. In this way, the entrepreneur is able to ensure that the production capacity of the business is well managed.

15.2.11 **Capacity and capacity planning**

Capacity is expressed in output units. For example the number of customers that can be served per hour. The entrepreneur needs to know how long it will take to make a product (from the time that the order is received to the time that the product is delivered) or provide a service. This depends on the availability and suitability of the resources of labour, materials, machinery and equipment, and money. A clear knowledge of a venture's capacity is important as it allows for careful and accurate planning.

Capacity planning is based on the output of products and (or) services required within a specific time period as well as the available staff, working hours, and equipment. Capacity planning is important as it links directly to product and service delivery times. The optimal operating level for a business is the one for which the operating process was designed and the output at which average cost is minimised. The capacity utilisation rate refers to how close a company is to its operating level (Chase and Jacobs, 2010). Expanding existing capacity is challenging as it may increase running costs or require the relocation of the business.

According to Kruger, Ramphal and Maritz (2013:230) the following very important questions must be addressed when capacity is planned:

▶ What is the amount of capacity required?
▶ What facilities, equipment, machines, and labour will be part of the planned capacity?
▶ Are the existing facilities adequate to satisfy existing and impending capacity requirements?
▶ Does the organisation predict any changes in existing and impending demand patterns?
▶ What type of capacity is required by the organisation?
▶ Should the organisation erect new facilities to meet impending demand?
▶ When and how will capacity be totalled to operations, processes, and systems?
▶ When will the organisation require the capacity?

Example 15.1 illustrates how to calculate the operating capacity of a business.

EXAMPLE 15.1

Calculating the available capacity of a business

The local garage decides to open a car wash. The owner of the garage first wants to test the market. He allocates and demarcates an area and hires two attendants. The cars will be washed manually. Besides the necessary consumables (buckets, water, soap, cloths, polish, etc.) he also provides them with a vacuum cleaner and access to power. One will wash the car and the other one will clean and vacuum the interior.

It takes approximately 40 minutes for a normal sedan motor to be washed, cleaned and vacuumed. It is possible that some clients would only like to wash and go and others would only like to clean and vacuum the interior. This implies that more cars can be serviced based on various needs.

If capacity is based on the maximum requirements, and we assume no rest breaks for the labourers, the capacity would be calculated as follows:

▶ 8 hours per day × 2 workers = 16 labour hours per day
▶ 16 hours × 60 minutes = 960 labour minutes available per day
▶ Although the vacuum cleaner is available for 24 machine hours per day, it is actually also only available for 8 hours (960 minutes) per day due to worker availability
▶ Therefore: 960 minutes available per day / 40 minutes per car = 24 cars per day
▶ The available capacity is thus 24 cars per day.

Of course, this does not happen in reality as we have to budget for rests breaks (we work with human beings) and any other contingencies (such as running out of detergents or water, a power failure, etc.). To calculate the available capacity, we should deduct roughly 1 hour per labourer for lunch, tea and normal rest breaks, leaving us with only 840 labour minutes available. The available capacity will then be 21 cars (840 minutes / 40 minutes per car) if all goes smoothly.

15.3 **Operations management plan checklist**

A pro forma operations management plan checklist, which includes possible questions that can be asked when developing the operations management plan, is provided in Table 15.1 below. It is possible to add questions to the checklist to provide for different types of products and services. Even if you are starting your business alone at this stage, the answers to these questions will provide you with an indication of how you plan to attend to some operational matters simultaneously.

Table 15.1 The operations management plan checklist

Administration
1. How will the business be structured as an organisation and what will the reporting relationships be?
2. What will the management roles of the various people in the organisation be and how will the various managerial roles fit together?
3. What will the administrative policies and procedures be? Attach such written policies and procedures as appendices to the operational plan.
4. Who will be doing what administrative work in the business? (That is, who will be taking stock, who will do the bookkeeping, who will purchase stock, and so on?)
5. Describe the administrative systems (i.e. bookkeeping, payment staff record, and personnel assessment systems) devised for the business. How will staff be trained in the use of such systems, how will the systems be implemented, and how will they be adapted to remain effective and applicable in time?
The strategy and plans
1. What potential sales does the business hope to achieve in the coming months?
2. Which potential subcontractors and suppliers could the business use and how will these subcontractors and suppliers be selected?
3. Describe the production plan of the business, showing costs and projected volumes to be sold.
4. Describe the stock control and inventory plan of the business. Will a large stock be maintained or will there be just-in-time production?
5. How will quality control be ensured? Will inspections be carried out? If yes, what will the nature of such inspections be and how frequently will they be undertaken?
Manufacturing, retail, and services
1. Describe in detail the manufacturing, retail, and service processes that will be followed in the business.
2. How will such processes be structured, i.e. what percentage of these processes will be done in-house and what percentage will be outsourced?
The location
1. Where will the business be located? Describe the location. Why was this location selected?
2. What were the results of the location analysis? Did it confirm the efficacy of the selected location?
3. What are the advantages and disadvantages of the location in terms of the business's proximity to suppliers, resources, and customers?
4. Are you familiar with provincial and local legislation, rules, and regulations pertaining to your business?

The facilities

1. What facilities will be required for plant, warehousing, shop, and office space?

2. When and where will the required facilities be obtained? Describe the process for obtaining such facilities.

3. Will the required facilities be leased or bought? What are the advantages and disadvantages of leasing and buying respectively?

4. According to your estimates, how long will it take before the facilities leased or acquired would need to be expanded to meet the needs of the growing business?

The staff

1. What are the staff requirements of the entrepreneur, i.e. how many employees will be required and what will each one of them be doing?

2. How will able and well-trained staff be recruited to ensure the smooth operation of the business?

3. What will the staff composition be in terms of full-time and part-time workers? What salaries and benefits will have to be paid to them, and what training should employees undergo to ensure that they are productive workers?

4. Formulate a staff plan and job descriptions for each of the jobs to obtain clarity on the content of each employee's job.

The layout

1. How will the business be laid out?

2. What will be done to ensure that the layout gives the customer an impression of professionalism, effectiveness, and efficiency?

3. If you set up your business from home, where will it be located, and how will you set it up to ensure that you can work from home in a professional manner?

Stock and inventory

1. What stock levels do I want to keep?

2. How am I going to control and check my inventory?

3. Do I need software to manage my inventory? If so, how much does it cost and what is the license fee?

4. How often am I going to buy stock?

5. Where am I going to keep my stock?

6. Do I have the necessary equipment and space to transport and store my stock?

7. What am I going to do with slow-moving, redundant, or damaged items?

Purchasing

1. Who are my suppliers?

2. Where are they located?

3. Am I sure I have negotiated the right quantity, quality and price for the products and services that I need to set up and run my business?

4. Are my suppliers reliable?

Total quality management

1. How am I going to perform regular quality checks?

2. What system do I have in place to ensure customer satisfaction?

Maintenance
1. Do I have maintenance plans in place for the machinery and equipment that I bought?
2. What will it cost me to implement a preventative maintenance plan compared to fixing a breakdown?
Capacity
1. How will I calculate my current capacity?
2. Can I expand my current capacity if I do not know subcontractors that I can use?
3. What are the lead and lag times that characterise my business?
4. How would operations be maintained at higher levels during peak times?

CONCLUSION

This chapter provided a basic description of operations management, which is essential to setting up and growing a new venture. The chapter also dealt with the key concepts associated with operations management: location, facilities, machinery and equipment, staff, layout of the business, inventory and stock, purchasing, total quality management, maintenance, the operating cycle, and capacity planning. The chapter concluded with an operations management plan checklist.

SELF-ASSESSMENT QUESTIONS

Multiple-choice questions

1. Operations management deals with the planning and management of producing a product and (or) a service.
   a. True
   b. False
2. In the operations management process, once the product and (or) service is delivered, feedback will be received either via _____ or _____
   a. the operations manager or marketing manager
   b. quality measures put in place or customer feedback
   c. operations strategy or operations plans
   d. customers or marketers.

3. The owner of a car wash calculates that it takes him 30 minutes to manually conduct a full wash and vacuum on one standard sedan car. He receives six cars per hour. How many helpers must he appoint to assist him with the expected demand per eight-hour day? (Exclude lunch and tea time needs at this point in the calculation.)
   a. 24 helpers
   b. 2 helpers
   c. 1 helpers
   d. 5 helpers
4. In the operational plan the entrepreneur needs to indicate what _____ will be required for plant warehousing, shop, and office space.
   a. facilities
   b. business location
   c. machinery
   d. staff
5. Keeping record of all your sales over a period of time will allow you to make a more accurate sales forecast that will allow you to do more accurate capacity planning.
   a. True
   b. False
6. A new business buys a new state-of-the-art printer. What is the available machine capacity per week (at eight hours per day for a five-day week)?
   a. 40 hours
   b. 35 hours
   c. 120 hours
   d. 8 hours

7. _____ is based on the output of products and (or) services required within a specific time period, available staff, working hours and equipment.
   a. Total quality management
   b. Purchasing
   c. Operating cycle
   d. Capacity planning

8. An administration section in the operations management plan allows the entrepreneur to plan the administration of the business. What is not included in this plan?
   a. A description of the administrative systems that will be used
   b. An indication of who will do what in the company
   c. An outline of the structure of reporting relationships, roles and responsibilities of employees to avoid duplications
   d. A plan to reduce staff

10. Why is a total quality management approach towards the business important, even for a sole proprietorship?

11. Identify the various elements that should be included in the operations management checklist. Provide some questions that should be asked with regards to stock and inventory.

EXPERIENTIAL EXERCISE

An entrepreneur would like to open a pizza outlet and has asked you to formulate an operational plan for her. Use the following questions to guide you and remember to explain each answer in full. It might be useful for you to interview the owner of an existing pizza outlet in your area to learn how his or her business operates.

1. What strategies should be formulated for the pizza outlet to ensure business success?
2. What will be the best location for a pizza outlet?
3. What business facilities will be required by the entrepreneur to run an effective pizza outlet?
4. What machinery and equipment are needed?
5. What employees will the entrepreneur require?
6. How should the administrative function of the pizza outlet be structured? Which administrative system will be used and how will the administrative work be divided among the staff?
7. Describe how the stock (e.g. stationery as well as pizza ingredients, such as flour, eggs, onions, vegetables, ham, salami, etc.) should be managed.
8. What are the health and safety requirements that need to be taken into consideration?
9. What total quality management system can you recommend to ensure quality standards are maintained?

DISCUSSION QUESTIONS

1. Explain the term 'operations management'.
2. Why is it important to have an operational plan?
3. Provide a graphical illustration and discussion of the operational management process.
4. Identify and discuss the various elements of the operational plan.
5. How do the selection of facilities, the layout of the business, the selection of machinery and equipment, and the stock you want to keep interact with each other?
6. What are the important questions an entrepreneur should address when planning capacity?
7. What are some of the factors the entrepreneur must consider when selecting supplier(s)?
8. Explain the importance of maintaining machinery and equipment.
9. Illustrate by means of a practical example what an entrepreneur needs to consider when calculating the venture's capacity.

SOUTH AFRICA'S SELF-MADE MEDIA MOGUL WITH A TWIST

Like many successful entrepreneurs, Lebo paid his dues as a salaried employee before taking the leap and starting his own business. His early career was spent at the SABC, where his love of marketing and the media industry soon set him apart as a highly talented member of the team. A lucrative offer from South Africa's first black advertising agency, Herdbuoys, soon followed, giving Lebo the chance to work with some of the best minds in the PR industry.

The decisive moment in Lebo's journey was a simple realisation – while he enjoyed his work, his true passion was partying. Already famous in his social circle for the parties he hosted at home, Lebo decided to share his passion with clients … and get paid for doing what he loved. Before long, Lebo was arranging launch parties for YFM, making (and spending) money faster than he could have dreamed, and learning the hard way how to manage his cash flow. Lebo found himself running out of money when he bought a flashy car and spent his money on parties. Once again, he had to start from scratch. He approached Penta Publications and sold media space for them. Within a year he'd left and started Corporate Fusion, which was earning R2 million in business in the blink of an eye. He bought a restaurant and turned it into the place to be in Johannesburg.

Writing off his losses and chalking it all up to experience, he went on to found the GEM Group of companies, which offer media, hospitality, and technology services to some of South Africa's largest corporates. His journey from poverty to success is an inspiration to all entrepreneurs, reminding us of the power of big dreams. GEM's strategy is to add value to their clients by extending the concept of hospitality and brand awareness through innovative channels. GEM's travel and hotels partnership with the Singer Group resulted in the establishment of its travel division, Izani Travel and Hospitality, which will evolve over time according to the needs and expectations of customers that are travelling.

Passenger transportation has become another great opportunity for the GEM Group in that they invested in Pastranscor as part of the group's integrated travel and hospitality plans. Pastranscor provides a full service passenger transportation solution for corporate, government and leisure, which spans from luxury vehicles, to yachts, air charters and luxury busses.

Technology revolution has also become a great opportunity for the group, and their partnership with Neotel to penetrate the South African telecommunication market that has opened up new doors in digital communications. They have invested many resources into the establishment of IzaniTel, their new Telecoms division that seeks to improve access to these integrated communication and technology solutions by the masses. InTouchNet is another great technology opportunity that the group has embarked on and is providing an unprecedented Wi-Fi experience in the hotel industry.

The Group is furthermore steadily increasing its interest in the property space and has partnered with Landmark Properties to provide corporate and government office space rental solutions. Their network of properties provides them with a national footprint of available office space.

As the GEM group looks ahead to sustaining its performance as an organisation, it acknowledges that it faces enormous challenges as a group of companies. Managing their partnerships, deriving value and managing resources requires much skill and planning. The world as they know it is changing. Globalisation and technological revolution are a reality and their clients have started adapting their spending habits. In a world in which there are no shared certainties, what is certain is that they will have to rise to the opportunities presented by change if they wish to continue to exceed their expectations as an organisation.

Source: Compiled from GEM (2013), MWeb (2014) and Rom (2014).

1. How can developing an operations strategy be an advantage to the GEM group of companies? What strategies do you recommend for GEM?

2. Prepare an operations plan for GEM. Compare with other advisors and debate the most appropriate plan for GEM to follow.

3. If you advise GEM to subcontract, what quality check measures can they put in place?

SUGGESTED WEBSITE LINKS

www.apqc.org

www.econ-datalinks.org

www.fedstats.gov

www.trekbikes.com

www.rockwell.com

www.apple.com

www.bmw.com

www.carnivalcruise.com

http://worldacademyonline.com/article/18/1/capacity_management.html

https://www1.eere.energy.gov/manufacturing/tech_deployment/pdfs/10097517.pdf

http://www.teamquest.com/pdfs/whitepaper/tqwp23.pdf

http://www.teamquest.com/solutions/capacity-planning/

http://www.teamquest.com/webinar/062206/062206.html (presentation)

http://www.teamquest.com/pdfs/whitepaper/tqeb01.pdf

http://www-935.ibm.com/services/us/its/pdf/g563-0339-00.pdf

YouTube

http://www.youtube.com/watch?v=w0cD26CLBA0

http://www.youtube.com/watch?v=m4NJnhekJPw

http://www.youtube.com/watch?v=Btx5s9htkRI

(All websites accessed in March 2013)

REFERENCES

ASEN. n.d. *Social enterprise feature - Iyeza Express.* [Online]. Available: http://asenetwork.org/2013/08/15/social-enterprise-feature-iyeza-express/ [2 March 2014].

Business Directory. 2014a. *Business Directory.com/Definitions/Operations strategy.* [Online]. Available: http://www.businessdictionary.com/definition/operations-strategy.html#ixzz35jXQ6JGZ [26 June 2014].

Business Directory. 2014b. *Business Directory/Definitions/Operating plan.* [Online] Available: http://www.businessdictionary.com/definition/operating-plan.html [26 June 2014].

Chase, F. & Jacobs FR. 2010. *Operations and Supply Chain Management.* 13th ed. New York: McGraw-Hill/Irwin.

Envirodeck. 2013. *Envirodeck. Company profile.* [Online]. Available: http://www.envirodeck.co.za/about-envirodeck-composite-decking/composite-decks-profile [21 March 2014]. Reprinted by permission of Envirodeck.

Finweek. 2012. *Overcoming entrepreneurial challenges.* [Online]. Available: http://finweek.com/2012/11/30/overcoming-entrepreneurial-challenges/ [21 March 2014]. Text by Gallo Images/Finweek.

GEM. 2013. *Group profile.* [Online] Available: http://www.gemgroup.co.za/index.php/group-profile?id=5 [26 June 2014].

Hartman, D. 2014. *Operations strategy for product expansion.* [Online]. Available: http://smallbusiness.chron.com/operations-strategy-product-expansion-25609.html [26 June 2014].

Kruger, D, Ramphal, R. & Maritz, M. 2013. *Operations Management.* 3rd ed. Cape Town, South Africa: Oxford University Press Southern Africa (Pty) Ltd.

Longenecker, JG, Moore, CW, Petty, WJ. & Palich, LE. 2008. *Small Business Management: An Entrepreneurial Emphasis.* International ed. Mason: Thomson Publishers.

Marx, S, Van Rooyen, DC, Bosch, JK. & Reynders, HJJ. 1998. *Business Management.* Pretoria: Van Schaik.

MWeb. 2014. *Homegrown entrepreneur: Lebo Gungulusa, founder of the GEM Group.* [Online]. Available: http://www.mweb.co.za/Entrepreneur/ViewArticle/tabid/3162/Article/12968/Homegrown-Entrepreneur-Lebo-Gunguluza-founder-of-the-GEM-Group.aspx [26 June 2014].

ProductivitySA. 2010. Lenong Road Maintenance. [Online]. Available: http://www.turnaroundsolutions.co.za/pebble.asp?relid=218 [1 August 2011].

Rom, F. 2014. *Lubu Gunguluza: Self-made media millionaire.* [Online]. Available: http://www.emergingstars.com/success-stories/lebo-gunguluza-self-made-media-millionaire [26 June 2014].

Timmons, JA. 1994. *New Venture Creation: Entrepreneurship for the 21st Century.* Burr Ridge: Irwin.

Usmani, F. 2013. *Lead time and lag time in project scheduling network diagram.* [Online]. Available: http://pmstudycircle.com/2013/02/lead-time-and-lag-time-in-project-scheduling-network-diagram/ [21 March 2014].

Wright, C. 1995. *Successful Small Business Management in South Africa.* 6th ed. Sandton: Struik.

CHAPTER 16

Managing human resources

Elana Swanepoel

LEARNING OUTCOMES

On completion of this chapter you will be able to:

▶ Define 'human resources (HR)' and 'human resource management' (HRM)
▶ Describe the human-resources strategy as business strategy
▶ Understand the role of culture, diversity, conflict, and change in the working environment
▶ Differentiate between job analysis, job description, and job specification
▶ Describe the recruitment and selection process
▶ Conduct a performance appraisal of your employees
▶ Identify changes and developments in HRM
▶ Assess the importance of making use of HR from outside the organisation or business
▶ Explain outsourcing and contracting as HR functions.

OPENING CASE STUDY

Green Buildings (Pty) Ltd is a new construction company focusing on providing building constructions with low energy consumption that are environmentally friendly. The company was established about 11 months ago with ten employees. However, the demand for 'green' buildings has increased and the owner, Peter, needs to appoint at least another ten employees. Some of his current employees have complained that they are not sure what their jobs entails as they have to complete a variety of different tasks. In addition, they all get the same monthly salary even though the tasks performed by some of them require a higher level of skill. Even the employee appointed as supervisor receives the same monthly salary as the rest. The employees have complained to Peter as they consider it unfair. In addition they are concerned that the new employees will be appointed at a higher monthly salary. Most of the employees have been in construction for several years and have experienced the volatile nature of the construction industry – some of them were retrenched when the company they worked for could not secure any construction contracts. Even though the business is growing, the morale amongst the employees does not seem to be high, judging from the increase in accidents on site. Such accidents are costly and the business owner needs to get to the root cause of the accidents.

1. Would a proper job analysis of each of the tasks performed in the company assist Peter in planning his workforce and developing a fair remuneration scale?
2. How should the business owner address the problem of increased accidents on the construction sites? In trying to get to the root cause, it is possible that conflict may arise. What conflict resolution technique should the business owner employ to ensure a win-win situation?

INTRODUCTION

Diversity, globalisation, deregulation and technology are changing the nature of jobs and the working environment. Jobs require new types of knowledge workers, new human resource management (HRM) methods to manage them, and a new focus on human resources (HR). Most new firms and smaller ventures aim to grow into larger firms and expand their workforce. As the number of employees grows, greater guidance is needed in effectively dealing with human resource issues and challenges presented by growth.

Rapid changes in the work environment can have serious implications for HRM, for example, greater awareness and appreciation of various cultural backgrounds in the recruitment, selection and promotion processes may be needed. Kuratko and Hornsby (2009) argue that the low supply of skilled and experienced labour can have a direct effect on small business survival. Small-business owners should rise to this challenge as the skill and experience levels of employees in smaller firms can sometimes be the difference between success and failure.

16.1 **Human resources concepts and functions**

Businesses are managed and staffed by people and without people, businesses cannot exist. To manage the business effectively, the entrepreneur needs to be familiar with the following HR and people-related concepts and functions.

16.1.1 **Human resources (HR)**

Employees represent a venture's human resources and are perhaps the most vital of all its operations. To build a competitive business, you need to think carefully about how to find and hire the best people available and then consider how to retain them. Honest, competent, motivated employees are the lifeblood of the small business, so it is critical for entrepreneurs to manage them competently and efficiently. Human resources include employees at all levels in the organisation, both managerial and non-managerial employees, such as factory labourers, production supervisors, sales personnel, financial analysts and engineers. To keep a company competitive, employees need to be motivated, imaginative, qualified, and dedicated (Byrd & Megginson, 2013).

16.1.2 **Human resource management (HRM)**

Human resource management comprises the following (Nel et al., 2011):
▸ The people in the organisation determine how successfully the other means of production will be applied.
▸ HRM is a purposeful action of the HR department, which aims to assist functional managers in the optimal application and utilisation of the HR under their control, in accordance with official organisational policy as well as general HRM theory and practice to achieve the goals of an organisation.
▸ Within the organisational framework of the company, the HR function manifests itself as an HR department. The HR function describes a number of ancillary

functions carried out to achieve the goals of an organisation. A HR department, responsible for the organisation's HRM activities, carries out the HR function. However, the department also gives advice and assistance to the rest of the organisation.

The human resource functions can be summarised under the following headings, according to Grobler, Wärnich, Carrell, Elbert and Hatfield (2011:12–14):

▸ Job analysis and design
▸ Recruitment, selection, induction and internal staffing
▸ Appraisal, training and development, and career management
▸ Compensation and health

▸ Labour relations
▸ Human resource information systems (HRIS), human resource research and problem solving.

16.2 Relationship of the human-resources strategy to the business strategy

The HR strategy parallels and facilitates the implementation of the strategic business plan. The HR strategy contains a set of priorities that a firm uses to align its resources, policies, and programmes with its strategic business plan. Figure 16.1 shows the relationship of the HR strategy to the broader business strategy. The model also illustrates that planning proceeds top-down, while execution proceeds bottom-up.

Figure 16.1 The relationship of the HR strategy to the broader strategy of a business

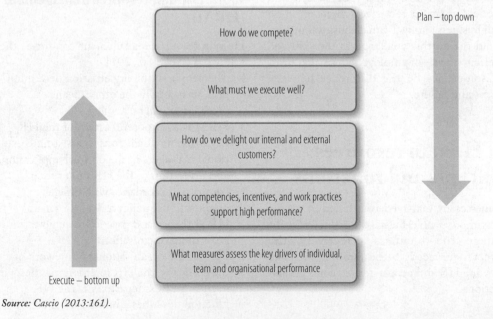

Plan – top down

How do we compete?

What must we execute well?

How do we delight our internal and external customers?

What competencies, incentives, and work practices support high performance?

What measures assess the key drivers of individual, team and organisational performance

Execute – bottom up

Source: Cascio (2013:161).

16.2.1 The management of employees

A venture changes as it grows and to manage these changes is often a complex task, one that is better undertaken with a participative style of management.

> **(DEFINITION)**
>
> A participative style of management is one in which the entrepreneur involves others in the decision-making process (Hisrich et al., 2010).

The advantages of using a **participative management style** when a firm is growing include:
▸ The complexity of growing a business and managing change increases the information-processing demands on the entrepreneur. Involving others in the decision-making process is a way of reducing these demands.
▸ Highly qualified managers and employees are an indispensable resource for generating new ways to approach current problems.
▸ If employees are involved in the decision-making process, they are more prepared and more motivated to implement the decided course of action.
▸ In most cultures, employees enjoy the added responsibility of making decisions and taking initiative, which means that a participative management style will enhance job satisfaction.

16.2.2 The development of managerial and professional employees

A small business has a strong need to develop managerial and professional employees. Whether the business has only a few employees or many, irrespective of the position of the employee, it must ensure that all the employees perform effectively and efficiently. Employees should be developed to the point where they can adequately carry out the responsibilities assigned to them. Although an entrepreneur often postpones grooming an employee for a managerial position (placement), this step is crucial to ensuring a smooth transition to the firm's management.

The establishment of a management development programme requires considering the following factors (Moore et al., 2010:537):
▸ *The need for development.* What vacancies are expected? Who needs to be developed? What type of training and how much training are needed to meet the demands of the job description?
▸ *A plan for development.* How can the individuals be developed? Do they currently have enough responsibility to permit them to learn? Can they be assigned additional duties? Should they be given temporary assignments in other areas?
▸ *A timetable for development.* When should the development process begin? How much can be accomplished in the next six months or one year?
▸ *Employee counselling.* Do the individuals understand their need for development? Are they aware of their prospects within the firm? Has an understanding been reached as to the nature of the development programme planned? Have the employees been consulted regularly about progress in their work and the problems confronting them? Have they been given the benefit of the owner's experience and insights without having decisions made for them?

16.2.3 Culture, diversity, conflict, and change

The twenty-first century is characterised by a highly competitive business environment. To manage people and maximise productivity, the entrepreneur should keep the following variables in mind that might influence people and the working environment.

16.2.3.1 Company culture

DEFINITION

Company culture is the distinctive and unwritten code of conduct that governs the behaviour, attitudes, relationships and style of an organisation.

It is the essence of 'the way we do things around here'. A company's **culture** has a powerful impact on the way people work together in a business, how they do their jobs, and how they treat their customers. Company culture manifests itself in many ways – from how workers dress and act to the language they use. A company's culture arises from an entrepreneur's consistent and relentless pursuit of a set of core values that everyone in the company can believe in. When the right culture is nurtured in a company, this can enhance a company's competitive position by improving its ability to attract and retain quality workers and by creating an environment in which workers can grow and develop.

Scarborough et al. (2009) argue that today's organisational culture relies on certain principles that are fundamental to the creation of a productive, fun, and supportive workplace, and these principles include:

▸ *Respect for the quality of work and a balance between work life and home life.* Companies must recognise that their employees have lives away from work and should offer flexible work schedules, part-time work, job sharing, telecommuting, and so on.
▸ *A sense of purpose.* Forward-thinking companies rely on a strong sense of purpose to connect employees to the company's mission.
▸ *Diversity.* Companies with appealing cultures not only accept cultural diversity in their workforce, but also embrace it and actively seek out workers with different backgrounds. They recognise that a workforce that has a rich mix of cultural diversity gives their companies more talent, skills, and abilities from which to draw.
▸ *Integrity.* Many workers take pride in the fact that they work for a company that is ethical and socially responsible.
▸ *Participative management.* Modern managers recognise that employees expect a participative management style to be part of a company's culture.
▸ *Learning environment.* Progressive companies encourage and support lifelong learning among their employees. They are willing to invest in their employees, improving their skills and helping them to reach their full potential.
▸ *A sense of fun.* Smart entrepreneurs recognise that creating a culture that incorporates fun into work allows them to attract and retain quality employees.

Companies that build their cultures on these principles have an edge when it comes to attracting, retaining, and motivating workers. In other words, creating the right culture helps a small company to compete more effectively.

16.2.3.2 Diversity

DEFINITION

Managing diversity means 'establishing a heterogeneous workforce to perform to its potential in an equitable work environment where no member or group of members has an advantage or a disadvantage'.

This remains a pragmatic business strategy that focuses on maximising the productivity, creativity and commitment of the workforce while meeting the needs of diverse consumer groups (Cascio, 2013:137).

Managing diversity is not the same thing as managing **affirmative action**.

DEFINITION

Affirmative action refers to actions that are taken to overcome the effects of past or present practices, policies, or other barriers to equal employment opportunity.

It is a first step that gives managers the opportunity to correct imbalances, injustices, and past mistakes. Over the long term, however, the challenge is to create a work setting in which each person can perform to his or her full potential and therefore compete for promotions and other rewards on merit alone.

Diversity management has become a dominant activity in managing an organisation's human resources for the following reasons:

▸ The shift from a manufacturing to a service economy
▸ Globalisation of markets
▸ New business strategies that require more teamwork
▸ Mergers and alliances that require different corporate cultures to work together
▸ The changing labour market.

16.2.3.3 Conflict

DEFINITION

Conflict can emerge in a group when the actions of one group member prevent or obstruct the actions of another person, or when there are different or inaccurate perceptions, different time horizons, or a lack of clarity of group goals.

Conflict can be seen to indicate that some ideas, thoughts, and feelings have not been shared by the group. Although several conflict-resolution techniques exist, the five different conflict-resolution techniques that are often used are:

▸ *Competing (win-lose).* I satisfy my concerns at the expense of yours. One person loses while the other wins. It should be remembered, though, that conflict is not a game to be won.
▸ *Avoiding (lose-leave).* Neither you nor I satisfy our concerns, as the style is to withdraw from any conflict situation. There is basic denial that a problem exists.
▸ *Compromising (win some, lose some).* We both give up half our concerns to come to an agreement.
▸ *Accommodating (yield-lose).* I satisfy your concerns at the expense of my own. This style means that one person gives in to the needs of the other person.
▸ *Problem-solving or collaborating (win-win).* Both you and I approach the conflict as a mutual problem, allowing us to discover alternatives that satisfy our concerns. With this approach, there is a belief that there is a solution that will satisfy both parties. The style requires both parties to trust one another and to be open with one another as to their needs and goals, while using good problem-solving and decision-making principles.

The nature and seriousness of the conflict as well as how quickly you need to resolve the conflict situation, would influence your choice in selecting an appropriate conflict resolution technique. The ideal would be to use the problem-solving or collaborating technique to reach a constructive win-win outcome. The collaborating approach does not always work, but it does provide the greatest possibility for reaching a solution that is mutually acceptable. Remember to try to control your emotions and not to let them cloud your judgement.

16.2.3.4 Change

Change can be exciting and challenging to some workers while others view change as a threat. Those who see change as a challenge are less vulnerable to stress consequences, but those who resist change succumb more easily to stress because they prefer familiar situations where they know what to expect. Many older workers find the growing number of younger workers, more females (including female managers), and a culture of transformation and diversity stressful. This problem is relevant to South Africa (Nel et al., 2011).

Change leadership
Effective change management and leadership go hand in hand. The chief executive officer (CEO) of HR Africa Labour Solutions (Krieg, 2002:25 cited in Nel et al., 2006) proposes the following approaches to change leadership:
▸ *Develop the need to change.* Nobody will change without feeling the need to change, which should be created by management utilising knowledge management.
▸ *Develop a change vision.* The top leader of the business must have a clear vision and idea where he or she wants to take the organisation.
▸ *Develop a communication strategy.* Communication is the golden rule to the change process and staff members need to be informed regularly about the progress made in change.
▸ *Communicate the vision.* The vision must be communicated to the organisation in understandable terms to prevent panic.
▸ *Get worker leaders informed.* Consult with union leaders on what is being planned for the future – the earlier the better.
▸ *Get the transformation team together.* This team should also receive the necessary power and status to make it acceptable in the organisation.
▸ *Conduct an organisational audit.* An organisation should know what it has before it can plan specific changes.
▸ *Decide on the change process strategy.* The planned process of implementing change needs to be communicated to all stakeholders to test acceptability.
▸ *Prepare both the organisation and the stakeholders.* Managers need to be developed in handling change as they need to support staff during the change process.
▸ *Implement the changes.* Leadership is meaningless without action. The use of

project teams is advisable, but teams should be selected carefully as they can make or break the change.
▸ *Remove any hindrances.* Hindrances, which may include policies, organisational structure, and (or) managers and employees, must be removed if the organisation wants its changes to last.
▸ *Mainstreaming the changes.* Changes need to be made part of the mainstream organisational process. Changes in organisational structure often need to be made when performance-management issues are implemented.
▸ *No plans or projects must be cast in stone.* Adjustments will continuously need to be made as circumstances change.

Melusi Ntumba is a successful South African entrepreneur who, through his experiences, has learned important lessons about managing people. Read about some of what he has learned in the South African success story – *Ntumba Chartered Accountants: Growing into the future.*

16.3 Human resource provisioning

For a small business to grow it requires the right number of employees with appropriate skills, experience, values and attitudes. The activities to be performed to ensure this are referred to as human resource provisioning, namely job analysis, recruitment and selection.

16.3.1 Job analysis, job descriptions and job specifications

Before an organisation can select employees, it must be able to specify the kind of work (and tasks) that needs to be done, how it should be done, the number of people needed, and the personal characteristics that are required to do the work.

Ntumba Chartered Accountants: Growing into the future

Ntumba Chartered Accountants incorporated was formed in 2001 by the founder and chief executive officer (CEO), Melusi Ntumba. The company has clients at national government and provincial level and is growing.

'We have invested a lot of our time in skills development and training of our people', says Ntumba. 'We also work very hard, are dedicated, professional and subscribe to values such as integrity, professionalism and objectivity'.

He believes that a leader should have faith in the people they lead, allow them to be creative, motivate them all the time and allow them to make mistakes as part of their learning and growth.

'Challenges we face in the immediate future include finding solutions to the shortage of skilled and experienced people within our sector, which threatens the growth of the business', says Ntumba. When it comes to finding the right people for the job, Ntumba says passion for the job they want to do, a positive attitude, problem-solving skills and innovation are all key ingredients.

Source: The Wits Business School Journal (2013). Issue 34:78–79.

16.3.1.1 **Job analysis**

Small-business owners should recognise that what they do before they start interviewing candidates for a position will determine how successful they will be at hiring winning employees. The first step is to perform a **job analysis**.

> **DEFINITION**
>
> Job analysis is the process by which a company determines the duties and nature of the jobs to be filled, and the skills and experience required of the people who are to fill them (Scarborough et al., 2009).

A job analysis entails the gathering of information about a specific job – its content, context and human requirements. From the job analysis it is possible to complete a job description and a job specification. Whereas the job description is about the actual job, the job specification is about the person that has to competently execute the job.

16.3.1.2 **Job descriptions**

> **DEFINITION**
>
> A job description is a list of the tasks, duties, activities, responsibilities, working conditions and performance results required by a specific job, as well as relationships between the job and other jobs in the organisation.

Byrd and Mcgginson (2013) state that **job descriptions** should be flexible in very small firms to give the owner more freedom in assigning tasks to available employees, whether the work fits their job description or not. Your first step is to define and describe all the tasks that will be part of the new job.

Areas that could be included in a job description are (Katz and Green, 2011):

▶ *The reason the job exists*, including an explanation of the job goals and how they relate to your position and other positions in the company.

▸ *The mental or physical tasks involved,* ranging from judging, planning and managing to cleaning, lifting, and welding.

▸ *How the job will be done,* including all of the methods and equipment to be used.

▸ *The qualifications needed,* outlining the kind of training, knowledge and skills that are necessary.

Ultimately, it is best to 'match' the job with the ideal individual who can fulfil the responsibilities of the job and grow with the business. To identify the ideal person, you need a job specification.

16.3.1.3 Job specifications

Once the job description has been completed it is possible to draft the **job specification**.

> **DEFINITION**
>
> A job specification is a written statement of the education, qualifications, knowledge, skills, personal traits, abilities, attributes and characteristics needed for a job stated in terms such as education, skills, and experience.

A job specification shows an entrepreneur the kind of person to recruit and helps to establish the standards that an applicant must meet to be hired. Like a job description, a job specification also includes the job title, who the person should report to, and a summary of the competencies required to complete the task productively. It lists educational requirements, desired experience and required specialised skills or knowledge along with the salary range and benefits. Job specifications should address the physical or other special requirements associated with the job and any occupational hazards the employee may face.

From this information you can evaluate potential employees to assess how well they match your ideal set of requirements.

Writing job descriptions and job specifications help an entrepreneur to determine whether he or she needs a part or full-time employee, whether the person should be permanent or temporary, and whether an independent contractor rather than an employee could fill the position (Scarborough et al., 2009).

16.3.2 Recruitment and selection processes

Just as organisations compete to develop, manufacture and market the best product and (or) service, so they should also compete to identify, attract and hire the best qualified and experienced people. Therefore, regardless of the size of the business or what industry it is in, the recruitment and selection of people with strategically relevant abilities is more important than ever.

The recruitment and selection processes follow the completion of the job description and the job specification and would be based on the information contained in the job description and the job specification. From the latter the personal characteristics necessary to do the work, such as competencies, knowledge, skills, and abilities are gleaned.

16.3.2.1 Recruitment

Smaller firms can outperform large businesses in attracting high-quality employees. Advertisements in regional newspapers or the use of an employment service have been traditional methods to attract and hire new talent into medium to large growing organisations. Katz and Green (2011:612) propose the following less expensive alternatives to consider when recruiting new employees:

▸ **Networking** is a relatively low-cost, although time-intensive method of recruiting. Benefits include receiving a credible critique of a potential candidate's work experience and personal character. People to network with include colleagues, business professionals, friends, vendors you have strong relationships with, alumni and advisory board members.

▸ You can also use online **social networking** sites to recruit, either by directly posting for a job or asking if people know someone who might be interested in the job that you are offering.

16.3.2.2 Selection

To reduce the risk of taking an uninformed gamble on applicants of unknown quality, an employer might (Moore et al., 2010:529–533):

▸ *Use an application form.* By using an application form, an employer can collect enough information to determine whether or not a prospect is minimally qualified and provide a basis for further evaluation. Typically, an application asks for the applicant's name, address, educational history, employment history, and references.

▸ *Interview the applicant.* An interview permits the employer to get an idea of the applicant's appearance, job knowledge, intelligence, and personality. Any of these factors may be significant to the job to be filled. To give you a sense of how such an interview can be structured, here is a sample of popular questions that might be asked:

- Give me a specific example of a time when you used good judgement and logic when solving a problem.
- Tell me about a time when you set a goal and were able to achieve it.
- Can you recall a time when you had to conform to a company policy with which you did not agree? How did you handle that situation?
- How do you typically deal with workplace conflict? Describe an experience that required you to make such an adjustment.
- Give me an example of a time when your integrity was tested and yet prevailed in a workplace situation.

▸ *Check references and other background information.* Careful checking with former employees, authorities, references, and so on, can help an employer avoid hiring mistakes.

▸ *Test the applicant.* Many kinds of jobs lend themselves to performance testing. With a little ingenuity, employers can develop practical tests that are clearly related to the job in question, and these can provide extremely useful insights for selection decisions.

▸ *Require physical examinations.* A primary purpose of physical examinations is to evaluate the ability of applicants to meet the physical demands of specific jobs. However, care must be taken to avoid discriminating against those who are physically disabled.

16.4 **Orientation**

A person should be made to feel at home in an organisation. Many new employees feel lost or nervous during their first few days on the job. To help them overcome this, managers should show them around, introduce them to people that they will be working with, and show them how their job fits into the overall mission of the business.

> ### DEFINITION
> Orientation 'is familiarization with and adaptation to a situation or an environment' (Cascio, 2013:314).

During the **orientation** period, an employee is more receptive to cues from the organisational environment than he or she is ever likely to be again. Such cues to proper behaviour may come from a variety of sources, for example:

▸ Official literature of the organisation
▸ Examples set by senior people
▸ Formal instructions given by senior people
▸ Examples given by peers
▸ Rewards and punishments that flow from the employee's efforts
▸ Responses to the employee's ideas
▸ Degree of challenge in the assignments the employee receives.

16.5 Recent developments in human resources

Change, growth, and sometimes displacement (e.g. through layoffs and restructuring) are facts of modern organisational life. Employees must realise that lifelong learning is a current and valid phenomenon that is here to stay, and it will be important for employees to stay up-to-date and to contribute positively to the overall functioning of an organisation.

16.5.1 A changing work environment

The formal employment landscape has changed drastically over the past few decades. Many organisations face the need to streamline their operations and cut back on costs, and more and more employees face significant changes in their working environments. Some of these changes include (Schiebe, 2010:44-45):

▸ *13th cheques replaced by performance incentives.* Many companies have been generously distributing 13th cheques at the end of every calendar year irrespective of whether the employee has met performance expectations or not. Since the recession (2008/9), however, the focus has shifted to the payment of performance-based incentives. These incentives are only payable if the company has met its financial targets in the first instance and, secondly, if the employee has achieved his or her performance targets.

▸ *Across-the-board increases replaced by performance-based increases.* Many companies have employed an across-the-board approach to annual salary increments. Recently, salaries tend to be reviewed taking into consideration a combination of performance measures, such as the broader economic climate, specific industry norms, company performance, and individual employee performance.

▸ *Reward for performance, not for tenure.* Companies are moving away from long-service awards towards recognising and rewarding performance not only through annual-performance incentive schemes, but also through profit-sharing schemes, company share allocations, development opportunities, global-exposure opportunities, and smaller spot awards in the form of work-life balance rewards. The number of years spent in the employ of the company also starts to become irrelevant if these employees do not continually re-invent themselves, up-skill themselves, and add significant value to the bottom line of the company.

16.5.2 The use of performance appraisal systems

DEFINITION

Performance appraisal 'is the formal, systematic assessment of how well employees are performing their jobs in relation to established standards and the communication of that assessment to employees' (Kuratko & Hornsby, 2009:243).

The purpose of **performance appraisal** is to provide both managers and employees with feedback on how well the employees are doing. These appraisals help to determine actions, such as merit pay increases, promotions, training, transfer, and discharge. In addition, in large measure, performance appraisal is the primary process for the evaluation and development of organisational personnel.

Performance appraisals should be based on an employee's job description. You cannot measure performance unless you meet certain requirements. Employee appraisals are usually based on such factors as quantity and quality of work performed, cooperativeness, initiative, dependability (including attendance), job knowledge, safety, and personal habits. While appraisals are usually done by the employee's direct supervisor, they may also be done by the affected employee, his or her peers or subordinates, or by the use of electronic devices. Employee evaluations should be related to promotions and salary increases in addition to identifying marginal workers and designing training activities for them. They can also be used to motivate employees, if the evaluations are adequately translated into rewards.

Performance appraisals are based on the assumption that employees have personal abilities and qualities that lead to job behaviours that result in work performance that can be identified and measured (Byrd & Megginson, 2013). Therefore, you need to determine which personal qualities an employee has that resulted in his or her behaving in a certain way on the job resulting in a certain level or quality of work being performed.

Although employee appraisals themselves are important, it is the feedback from them that really leads to improved performance. If it is done properly, performance appraisals can be effective ways of providing employee feedback to improve workers' performance. However, it takes planning and preparation on the business owner's part.

16.5.2.1 The use of the balanced scorecard

The appeal of the balanced scorecard has ensured a widespread adoption and use of this as a model, also in South Africa (Swanepoel et al., 2008). The balanced scorecard was conceptualised by Robert Kaplan and David Norton of Harvard University as a management system to track organisational performance, not only from the traditional reliance on short-term financial measures, but also by combining hard and soft measures together with short- and long-term ones.

The focus is not only on management accountancy bottom-line measures, but also incorporates performance measures from the following four balance perspectives:

▶ Financial (e.g. return on capital employed)

▶ The customer (e.g. customer loyalty)
▶ The internal or business process (e.g. process quality and process cycle time)
▶ Learning and growth (e.g. employee skills).

The balanced scorecard also emphasises the importance of focusing on both lagging and leading indicators, namely:

▶ Traditionally, organisational performance or measurement systems have focused almost exclusively on financial measures indicating what has happened in the past (i.e. **lagging performance indicators**).
▶ The balanced scorecard approach proposes a system that also builds in measures that focus on the future – and assesses the key success factors that act as performance drivers in the future (i.e. **the leading performance indicators**).

Furthermore, the HR scorecard is a measurement system that incorporates these same principles. A distinction is made between measuring HRM 'do-ables' (the enablers) and HRM 'deliverables' (the results that drive organisational performance). This process includes answering the following questions:

▶ What are our strategic goals for the organisation?
▶ How will we achieve these goals – what must the business strategy entail?
▶ How will we measure our performance (of strategy implementation) as we progress towards goal achievement?
▶ What type of employee behaviour and performance is required to enable us to implement the strategy successfully?
▶ What does the HR function need to do in order to enable employees to behave and perform as required (the 'enablers' or 'do-ables')?
▶ What does the HR function currently do in this regard?
▶ What needs to change?

Although human resources are traditionally given financial compensation, recent developments encourage more creative management of labour costs. One way of managing labour costs is to pay a basic salary with differing levels of commission, as the business owner did in the entrepreneurial dilemma – *Firing friends*.

16.5.3 Outsourcing

To buy products or services from other business firms is known as outsourcing. Firms can sometimes save money by buying from outside suppliers that specialise in a particular type of work, especially services such as accounting, payroll, and equipment-repair services. The expertise of these outside suppliers may enable them to provide better-quality services by virtue of their specialisation.

To adopt a strategic approach to outsourcing allows an organisation to focus more of its resources directly on generating value for its customers. However, the need for greater efficiency in both costs and execution makes it imperative not only to plan your outsourcing strategy, but also to manage it effectively. The extent to which one transfers the responsibility

for a company's function to an outside supplier can vary greatly. Specialist skills are highly valuable, but they are also costly to the business as they do not directly generate income, and thus these salaries are not cost-effective to maintain on a monthly basis. Therefore, the current move is towards the use of external business consultants who provide specialist skills, as and when a business requires them (Schiebe, 2010).

16.5.4 Contracting

When a business owner decides to utilise the services of an outside provider, care has to be taken to select the right provider and to structure such a relationship. The business owner may need to contract financial service providers, marketing consultants or labour brokers. In the case of labour brokers or temporary employment service organisations, they engage in commercial contracts with independent contractors to supply the marketplace with labour for a specific purpose. Should the business owner contract a company to manufacture specific parts, the contractor is responsible for managing the manufacturing process using his

---

ENTREPRENEURIAL DILEMMA

Firing friends

A business owner of a small but growing company offering telecommunications installation services employed two salesmen. Salesman A had been a loyal and close friend for many years and although he tried different jobs never stayed long in a job. The owner offered him a job as a salesman and he accepted. He was appointed on a low basic salary plus a high commission and received training. For a couple of months it seemed as if he was beginning to enjoy selling and was closing deals, enough to cover his basic salary. However, he never reached his targets and started complaining about petty issues. It was obvious that he was no longer interested in selling and the number of deals that he signed was decreasing. If the owner fired him, it could mean the end of many years of friendship.

Salesman B had been in the industry for a couple of years as a salesman and came highly recommended. He was appointed on a higher basic salary than salesman A, plus commission. However, after a couple of months he had not closed any significant deals. Most of the deals were very small in value. It was obvious that he was not the high performer he claimed to be.

The business was not in a financial position to carry dead wood. The two salesmen were costing the company money in salaries and were taking up space in offices that could rather be used by salespersons that would perform. What should the business owner do? Fire both salesmen, and if so when – at the same time? Should the business owner risk losing a friend?

Source: Author.

or her own equipment and workers to manu-facture and deliver.

Labour broking has become a controversial subject, with different parties having different perspectives, as debated in the *Financial Mail* article below.

Contracted vendors should add value to an organisation's work requirements. If they do not, one needs to search for alternatives that may include reverting to some work redesign and bringing back some of the work into the control sphere of the organisation. It is essential to find the right vendors, to establish contractually sound relationships, and to develop good com-mercial and general working relationships. The same principles apply if the business owner wants to use the services of consultancy firms. He or she should 'shop around' and then make a decision as to which firm to bring on board to help with certain tasks. In most instances, quotes will be requested or a tendering process may be followed (Swanepoel et al., 2008).

ENTREPRENEURIAL DILEMMA

The controversial Labour Relations Amendment Bill has stalled in parliament after more than two years of haggling over its content

This leaves the issue of labour brokers – or temporary employment services – unresolved. However, many companies have already taken steps to reduce their reliance on brokers over fears that they might have to take on casual workers full-time, at great cost.

Labour federation, Cosatu, has led the call for the complete banning of labour brokers. The bill proposed that workers employed through labour brokers should be considered full-time employees at companies where they had worked for six months. The clause applies only to workers earning below R183 000/year.

When the bill came before the parliamentary labour portfolio committee, ANC MPs voted to drop the time period to three months. The bill was due to be adopted last week, but there were too few MPs in the national assembly to make up a quorum. Parliament is now in recess so it is unclear when the bill will again be presented for a vote.

As the bill had been rigorously debated at Nedlac between government, labour and business, some saw the ANC's decision to reduce the time period as undermining these negotiations. Nedlac executive director Alistair Smith says the parties deadlocked on all amendments relating to labour brokers. Cosatu and the National Council of Trade Unions insisted on banning them while business wanted a 12-month grace period before temporary workers had to be made permanent employees. Government, with the support of the Federation of Unions of South Africa, proposed six months. Smith says it is 'unfortunate that much of the debate on labour brokering has been marked by adversarialism and political point scoring rather than more open and evidence-based engagement'.

There is substantial evidence to show that South African companies favour temporary employment over permanent jobs.

University of Cape Town economist Haroon Bhorat found that aggregate employment growth since 1994 has been driven by the financial and business services sector, as well as the wholesale and retail trade sector, and the overwhelming number of jobs created in the financial sector were driven by security services and labour brokers.

The trend is not unique to South Africa. According to the World Bank 2013 development report, part-time and temporary wage employment are now major features of industrial and developing countries. The report says temporary employees make up about 7% of SA's labour force and provide employment to an average of 410 000 workers a day.

Adcorp, South Africa's biggest labour broker by market share, says the labour broking industry has an annual turnover of around R44bn. It says that from 2000 to 2012, the number of permanent jobs declined by 1.9m while the number of temporary jobs increased by 2.6m. Adcorp labour economist Loane Sharp attributes this to an unpredictable economy, employers tending to organise activities in non-traditional ways and onerous labour legislation.

But Cosatu sees labour broking as akin to modern-day slavery because it treats workers as commodities. Its campaign against labour broking began as far back as 1999 and it has promised to continue to fight for its banning.

The ANC's capitulation in parliament is seen as gratifying Cosatu, its alliance partner, ahead of next year's general elections.

Labour brokers have been partly blamed for the strife on Rustenburg's platinum belt. They are viewed as exploitative, since the work they provide is uncertain, low paying and offers no benefits such as medical aid or pension. The three main platinum mines in Rustenburg subject to worker unrest last year were Anglo Platinum (Amplats), Lonmin and Impala Platinum (Implats). According to their 2012 annual reports, Amplats had just under 52 000 full-time and 4 434 contract workers, while Implats had 33 062 full-time employees and 15 245 contract workers. Lonmin says it now has about 27 717 permanent employees and 7 333 contractors. National Union of Mineworkers general secretary Frans Baleni says the problem of labour brokers on the platinum mines is 'huge'. 'The platinum industry is abnormal in that in some instances you can have more subcontractors than main company employees', he says.

Implats spokesman Johan Theron says it is necessary to use contractors for specialised work. For example, Implats is building three of the deepest new shafts in South Africa, which can take up to 10 years to complete. This work requires skills the miner does not have in-house, he says. Implats has reduced the number of workers it hires through labour brokers to 100–150. These workers are brought in to replace employees who are out of action for a few months, says Theron. 'We have tried over the past couple of years to minimise these kinds of workers because of uncertainty over the law. We mitigate the risk of having to give them full-time jobs by using as few of them as possible and only where necessary'.

This echoes the experience of labour lawyer Imraan Mahomed of Routledge Modise. His clients have been reconsidering their business models to see if they really need brokers or can find alternative ways to do business, either by permanently employing workers or finding ways to do without them.

Claire Gaul, head of the employment & employee benefits practice at Webber Wentzel, says her clients are concerned about the financial implications of taking on casual workers full-time. 'One client who has casuals working alongside full-time staff has restructured the workplace, including job grades, in anticipation of the legislation. So casuals would come in on a job grade on which you can afford to hire them', she says.

Baleni says the gold and coal sectors, where employers and workers negotiate centrally through the Chamber of Mines, sets a better example of how contractors should operate. When a company in these industries wants to hire a contractor it has to first convince the local union of the need for short-term, specialist jobs.

Theron says the gold industry has instituted a non-binding rule that all companies contracted to work on the mines have to pay the same as the miners pay. 'This has worked quite well in making sure unscrupulous contractors are kept out. We [the platinum sector] can learn through the chamber's experiences as they have been more successful than we have in addressing some of the challenges'.

Mahomed says the amendments to the laws dealing with labour brokers are unnecessary as many of the problems can be dealt with by better enforcement by labour inspectors of existing laws. Unions should hold employers accountable if they fail to comply with existing laws. Recent labour court judgments have shown that the courts are willing to offer protection to labour broker employees, says Mahomed. 'The labour court came down quite strongly in saying that because we have fair labour practice in the constitution, it is unlawful for a client to demand that a labour broker undermine an employee's rights to fair labour practice'. He says amendments to the Labour Relations Act will make it easier for unions to organise among labour broker employees.

But Baleni dismisses suggestions that unions should better organise such employees. 'It's a moving target. You recruit workers on a particular site, submit the stop orders, and the company or broker finds out and moves [the] workers to another site. Then you start from scratch'.

Source: Jones, G. Financial Mail. 27 June 2013. [Online]. Available: http://www.financialmail.co.za/business/2013/06/27/issue-of-labour-brokers-a-work-in-progress [10 December 2013].

EXAMPLE 16.1

The relationship between HRM practices and organisational commitment of knowledge workers. Facts obtained from Swiss SMEs.

Abstract of research conducted by David Giauque; Fabien Resenterra; Michaël Siggen.

This paper explores the effects of human resource management (HRM) practices in Swiss small-to-medium enterprises (SMEs). More specifically, the main objective of this study is to assess the impacts of HRM practices developed in Swiss SMEs upon the commitment of knowledge workers. Using data from a survey of over 198 knowledge workers, this study shows the importance of looking closer at HRM practices and, furthermore, to really investigate the impacts of the different HRM practices on employees' commitment. Results show, for example, that organisational support, procedural justice and the reputation of the organisation may clearly influence knowledge workers' commitment, whereas other HRM practices such as involvement in decision making, skills management or even the degree of satisfaction with pay do not have any impact on knowledge workers' commitment.

Source: Published in Human Resource Development International. Apr 2010, Vol. 13 Issue 2:185–205._21p. [ABSTRACT FROM AUTHOR] DOI: 10.1080/13678861003703716. (AN: 49707512).

16.6 Future trends and implications for human resources

To remain competitive, the entrepreneur should consider future trends that might impact on the working environment. Examples of such trends include, among others, leased employees, disposable managers, and free-agent workers, a trend that may grow in importance in the future. In this section some other emerging human-resource trends are explored.

16.6.1 A quality workforce

Regardless of the size of the small business, the owner(s) and (or) manager(s) need to source, employ and retain a quality workforce. For the new millennium the adequate availability of quality employees seems to be a challenge. It would not be enough to appoint quality workers; in addition, owners would have to devise retention strategies, which could include a range of perceived benefits, such as training and childcare.

Kuratko and Hornsby (2009) argue that it is apparent that small-business owners should recognise issues that need to be continually improved on if a quality workforce is desired, namely employee morale and improving employee performance.

16.6.1.1 Employee morale

Are workers doing what they should be doing? Is their morale good? Are the personnel content? Do they feel they are being treated properly? When answering these questions, owners or managers often find that their attention turns toward behavioural topics such as communication, motivation and leadership. The major reasons for employee problems can be traced to a lack of job satisfaction. Keep in mind that what is considered acceptable varies based on the type of business and industry, but the following are likely indicators of employee dissatisfaction:

▶ *Labour turnover.* Is the number of people leaving the organisation for jobs elsewhere increasing?
▶ *Productivity.* Is the cost per unit rising because of worker inefficiency?
▶ *Waste and scrap.* Is the amount of material discarded higher than it should be?
▶ *Product quality.* Are customers returning goods because they have been made improperly or do not perform as expected?
▶ *Service quality.* Are customers complaining about the service that they receive?

- *Tardiness and absenteeism.* Are employees coming to work late or staying home more frequently than before?
- *Accidents.* Has the number of accidents or injuries at the workplace increased?
- *Complaints or grievances.* Is the owner and (or) manager hearing more worker complaints, especially about minor issues? If the firm has a union, are more grievances being filed than usual?
- *Suggestions.* If a suggestion box exists, is the number of suggestions for improving morale or working conditions beginning to increase?
- *Exit interviews.* When individuals who are quitting are asked why, do they indicate dissatisfaction with the work environment?

These are not the only indices of employee morale, but they are some of the primary ones. When poor morale is indicated, the owner or manager needs to take appropriate action.

16.6.1.2 **Improving employee performance**

Two control-related areas warrant the owner or manager's special attention because they are related to employee morale. The areas are:

- *The pay–performance link.* Do those who do the best work receive the highest salaries? In many small businesses, the minimum wage is paid to newly appointed personnel, and all salaries are kept secret. The manager should try to link salary increases to performance whenever possible.
- *Teamwork.* Although some owners and (or) managers believe that they encourage teamwork, they actually promote competition which results in infighting among the personnel. The owner or manager can ensure that teamwork develops by rewarding those who are team players and reprimanding those who refuse to cooperate for the overall good.

16.6.2 **New competitive realities**

In today's world of fast-moving global markets and fierce competition, the windows of opportunity are often frustratingly brief. Cascio (2013:14–15) states that the 'three C logic' (i.e. command, control, and compartmentalised information) dominated industrial society's approach to organisational design throughout the nineteenth and twentieth centuries. However, the shift toward new forms of organisation in the twenty-first century is accelerated by trends such as:

- Smaller companies that employ fewer people
- The shift from vertically integrated hierarchies to networks of specialists
- The decline of routine work, coupled with the expansion of complex jobs that require flexibility, creativity, and the ability to work well with people (managers, software applications engineers, artists, designers, and so on)
- Pay tied less to a person's position or tenure in an organisation and more to the market value of his or her skills
- A change in the paradigm of doing business from making a product to providing a service, often by part-time or temporary employees
- The outsourcing of activities that are not core competencies of a firm (such as payroll)
- The redefinition of work itself: constant learning, more higher-order thinking, less nine-to-five mentality.

In response to these changes, many businesses are doing one or more of the following: developing new forms of organisation, restructuring (including downsizing), adopting quality-management programmes, re-engineering work processes, and building flexibility into work schedules and rules.

CONCLUSION

People are a major component of any business, and the management of human resources is a major part of every manager's job. HRM describes a network of interrelated components. Therefore, the HR function is responsible for maximising productivity, the quality of work life, and profits through the improved management of the workforce.

The workforce is increasingly more diverse with regards to race, ethnicity, language, lifestyles, religion, etc. To manage diversity and change poses major challenges to both managers and employees. The technological advances and the globalisation of commerce have increased competitiveness in the HR environment. The business owner of the new venture has to be alert to the challenges in the managing of human resources, in particular attracting, retaining and motivating quality employees to be highly productive in the workplace.

SELF-ASSESSMENT QUESTIONS

Multiple-choice questions

1. The human resource function covers a range of activities. Which one of the following is not a human resource function?
   a. Job analysis and design
   b. Operations management
   c. Recruitment and selection
   d. Compensation and health
2. It is possible to assess the level of job satisfaction in the company from several indicators. Which one of the following is not an indicator of job satisfaction?
   a. Labour turnover
   b. Waste and scrap
   c. Temperature
   d. Product quality
3. To establish a management development programme requires first determining the need for development followed by a plan for development.
   a. True
   b. False
4. The focus of the balanced scorecard is only on management accountancy bottom-line measures.
   a. True
   b. False
5. When a company decides to no longer perform an in-house function such as the payroll, but to pay specialists to perform the payroll function on behalf of the company, it is called outsourcing.
   a. True
   b. False

DISCUSSION QUESTIONS

1. Define the concept 'human resource management' and explain the purpose of human resource management.
2. Explain the seven principles that are necessary to ensure an organisational culture resulting in a productive, fun and supportive workplace.
3. What is the purpose of orientation?
4. In a small business everyone has to be fully motivated and productive. If this is not the case, the business owner needs to address it immediately. Discuss the ten indicators of low job satisfaction.
5. In the twenty-first century there is a shift toward new forms of organisation brought about by a number of trends. Explain these trends. Can you think of any other trends that are also contributing to this shift?

EXPERIENTIAL EXERCISE

As entrepreneur and human resource manager you will need to provide a competitive advantage by tapping your employees' ability to create, judge, and build relationships for managing a business, as businesses in the twenty-first century are fast paced, exciting, and full of people-related challenges.
1. Your company has grown to the extent that you now need a full-time human resource manager. Draw up a job description for the human resource manager.

2. Compile a job specification for the human resource manager from the job description.
3. Draw up an advertisement from the job description and the job specification to advertise for the position of human resource manager. Where or how will you advertise this position? What are the different options that you can use for advertising? Which one do you think would be the most effective – ensuring that a number of good candidates apply?
4. Assume that your advertising strategy worked and you received 10 applications. Explain the selection process that you will follow to guarantee that the best candidate is selected to work for your company.

5. At the end of the year you need to conduct a performance appraisal of the human resource manager. Draw up the key performance areas on which to assess the human resource manager from the job description. Remember, for each key performance area you need to stipulate a realistic and quantifiable measurement against which to measure the performance of the human resource manager. Complete the performance appraisal. Has the human resource manager performed at a satisfactory level? Does the human resource manager need any further training or development?

THE CHANGING LANDSCAPE OF CHANGE

Extracts from a report by Terry Meyer

Social networking influences the internal change processes that organisations apply. Executives no longer have the sole discretion to implement change by decree. Transparency is an essential feature of change design and implementation, especially where organisational transformation and cultural change are concerned.

It has always been the case that those involved in change should, where possible be involved in the process. What social networking does is accentuate that need. It also provides a vehicle to facilitate it. A good example of this is a process used by IBM. Using technology – such as its internal social networks and instant messaging – important issues can be discussed and debated in real time across all 450 000 employees located in over 150 countries around the world. The example cited was that the CEO had taken three days to engage with the entire organisation on the company's values. So in theory, each employee, anywhere in the world, had the opportunity to interact with the CEO or other key leaders on the values of the organisation.

This capability of large-scale engagement with stakeholders is becoming the basis for any large-scale systems change. It is also facilitating a new value system – especially among the younger generation, which places a premium on openness and transparency. However, there are implications for executives in the context of change. First, they need to adopt a mental model where openness and transparency are valued and are seen to be valued. Second, they need to recognise that it is not possible to control large-scale conversations in their organisations. Such conversations will occur across divisional, functional and geographic regions, whether they like it or not. What they need to do is help shape and influence the conversations, through the use of interactive processes facilitated by technology. Third, they need to listen to conversational trends. It is a great opportunity to hear what people are saying, rather than making assumptions about what people think.

Social media presents executives with an important opportunity to influence and communicate with employees.

Source: The Wits Business School Journal (2012) Issue 28:20–21.

1. It is said that in a small business the business owner knows his or her plans and the changes envisioned, but the employees do not. How can the business owner ensure that change design and implementation are transparent? How can you involve your employees in the change process?

2. Assuming that you honour values of honesty, integrity, work ethic, timeliness and respect, how would you ensure that your employees adhere to the same values?
3. Do you tweet or use other real-time channels for communication with your employees? If not, would using social media contribute to greater effectiveness and efficiencies in your business?
4. Are you aware of the conversations that are taking place among your employees? Are these positive conversations among diverse groups?
5. What conversations are taking place among the different cultures in your business? To what extent are the employees from different ethnic backgrounds working as a team?

SUGGESTED WEBSITE LINKS

Centre for Conflict Resolution (CCR), Cape Town, South Africa: <http://www.ccr.org.za/>

The Future of the HR professions: https://www.shrm.org/about/pressroom/Documents/future_of_hr.pdf

Outsourcing definitions and solutions: http://www.cio.com/article/40380/Outsourcing_Definition_and_Solutions

Employee Performance Appraisals Management Software: <http://www.successfactors.com/small-business/performance-appraisals/> http://www.successfactors.com/en_us/solutions/small-business/professional-edition/performance.html

SA Journal of Human Resource Management: <http://www.sajhrm.co.za/> www.sajhrm.co.za/

Institute of People Management: <http://www.ipm.co.za/>

REFERENCES

Byrd, MJ. & Megginson, LC. 2013. *Small Business Management: An Entrepreneur's Guidebook*. 7th ed. New York: McGraw-Hill.

Cascio. W. 2013. *Managing Human Resources: Productivity, Quality of Work life, Profits*. 9th ed. New York: The McGraw-Hill Companies, Inc.

Grobler, PA, Wärnich, S, Carrell, MR, Elbert, NF & Hatfield, RD. 2011. *Human resource management in South Africa*. 4th ed. Hampshire, UK: South-Western Cengage Learning.

Hisrich, RD, Peters, MP. & Shepherd, DA. 2010. *Entrepreneurship*. 8th ed. New York: McGraw-Hill.

Jones, G. *Financial Mail*. 27 June 2013. [Online]. Available: http://www.financialmail.co.za/business/2013/06/27/issue-of-labour-brokers-a-work-in-progress [10 December 2013].

Katz, JA. & Green II, RP. 2011. *Entrepreneurial Small Business*. 3rd ed. New York: McGraw-Hill.

Kuratko, DF. & Hornsby, JS. 2009. *New Venture Management: The Entrepreneur's Roadmap*. New Jersey: Pearson Education.

Meyer, T. *The Wits Business School Journal*. 2012. Issue 28:20–21.

Moore, CW, Petty, JW, Palich, LE. & Longenecker, JG. 2010. *Managing small business: An entrepreneurial emphasis*. 15th ed. Mason: South-Western Cengage Learning.

Moore, CW, Petty, JW, Palich, LE. & Longenecker, JG. 2010. *Managing small business: An entrepreneurial emphasis*. 15th ed. Mason: South-Western Cengage Learning.

Nel, PS, Van Dyk, PS, Haasbroek, GD, Schultz, HB, Sono, T. & Werner, A. 2006. *Human Resources Management*. 6th ed. Cape Town: Oxford University Press.

Nel, PS, Werner, A, Poisot, P, Sono, T, Du Plessis, A. & Ngalo, O. 2011. *Human Resources Management*. 8th ed. Cape Town: Oxford University Press Southern Africa.

Scarborough, NM, Wilson, DL. & Zimmerer, TW. 2009. *Effective Small Business Management: An Entrepreneurial Approach*. 9th ed. New Jersey: Pearson Prentice Hall.

Schiebe, L. 2010. The changing world of work. *Succeed*, September 44–45.

Swanepoel, BJ. (Ed.), Erasmus, BJ. & Schenk, HW. 2008. *South African Human Resource Management, Theory and Practice*. 4th ed. Cape Town: Juta & Co. *The Wits Business School Journal* (2013). Issue 34:78–79.

CHAPTER 17

Legal aspects

Isa van Aardt

LEARNING OUTCOMES

On completion of this chapter you will be able to:
▶ Identify and discuss the legal requirements when establishing a business venture, its registration, and its name
▶ Discuss the legal requirements for establishing a partnership
▶ Discuss the legal requirements for establishing a company
▶ Identify the procedures involved in calculating and paying income tax on income derived from ventures
▶ Discuss the principles of value-added tax (VAT) and the calculation thereof
▶ Discuss the procedures involved in registering as an employer for tax purposes
▶ Identify and discuss the aspects of a binding and legally enforceable contract
▶ Identify and discuss the aspects to consider regarding the Consumer Protection Act
▶ Identify the various legal requirements that should be adhered to when dealing with employees
▶ Identify and discuss the various insurance policies available to an entrepreneur.

OPENING CASE STUDY

If you want to start a business today it seems to be very easy. The Internet gives you access to business ideas, information about the market and area that you want to operate in, as well as about potential suppliers that you can use. You can also obtain information on advertisers to promote your business and its products or services.

A business is established to succeed and not to fail. Still, thousands fail due to a lack of knowledge about the legal aspects regarding the continuous operation of the business, dealing with staff and signing contracts.

1. What do you think is the most important legal aspect to research when starting a business?
2. Do you think it is important to pay taxes as small business?

INTRODUCTION

The majority of entrepreneurs will confirm that starting and managing a business is a challenge and sometimes very lonely. As business owner the entrepreneur has to make all the decisions and be creative in developing new strategies, but also carries all the risks and the costs that come with the trial and error of building the business, its products and/or services and markets.

When starting your own business you ideally want two people on speed dial:

▶ A mentor to serve as sounding board for ideas and plans, and
▶ A commercial lawyer to provide support in dealing with all the legal aspects that may impact the new venture.

While a mentor with goodwill to spare can still be found, commercial lawyers come at a price. Unfortunately entrepreneurs often run substantial risks by trying to avoid legal costs by foregoing legal advice, which often results in businesses being incorrectly structured or basic business agreements not being in place.

If you are thinking of opening up a business, regardless of whether it's a clothes shop or coffee shop, you will need to have a good working knowledge of the legislation applicable to your business. This is important because it will ensure that you are abiding and complying with the law rather than breaking it and facing possibly harsh consequences.

Laws are put into place to protect everyone – the customer, the employee and the company. You are not expected to be a lawyer, but being aware of the relevant legislation will help your organisation run more smoothly and avoid complications in the future, such as getting tied up in lengthy legal battles for an unfair staff dismissal etc.

This chapter provides information on the legal aspects that should be considered when choosing the type and name of the business, licensing, dealing with personnel, registering as a credit provider, complying with the requirements of BEE legislation, dealing with SARS, entering into contracts, dealing with the Consumer Protection Act (CPA), as well as legal aspects that could influence the operation of the venture. The aim is not to cover all legal aspects in detail, but rather to give an overview. The entrepreneur is, however, advised to contact a lawyer or legal consultant when making decisions concerning the venture.

17.1 The establishment of the venture

In Chapter 7, the different forms of business ownership were discussed, namely sole ownership, partnership, and the different types of companies and in Chapter 8, franchising was discussed as an option for starting a business. In this section, the legal requirements with regard to the establishment of each of these forms of business ownership are discussed, as are other aspects that should be considered when establishing a business venture. Certain general aspects regarding the registration, name, and introduction of the business venture will be discussed before we go into detail about each form of ownership.

17.1.1 Registration of the business venture

There are no specific requirements for the registration of a business venture. However, certain other types of registration may be needed before one can start a business, and this could be directly linked to the form of ownership decided on. To establish a company, one must be registered with the Registrar of Companies. A partnership is not registered, but it is established in terms of a partnership agreement that has to be drawn up before that partnership can start operating as a business venture. Sole ownership is the only form of business venture that is free from any formalities before it can start to operate.

According to Benade et al. (2003), any venture that operates as a business must be registered with the following institutions:

▸ SARS, as far as the following are concerned:
  ▪ Income tax payable on the income derived from operating as a business
  ▪ The registration of employees with regard to income tax (PAYE and SITE)
  ▪ Registering for value-added tax (VAT) purposes.
▸ The Department of Labour and the appropriate commissioners for the payment of:
  ▪ Unemployment insurance
  ▪ Worker's compensation.
▸ The local authorities with regard to:
  ▪ Licensing when trading in food or perishables, providing certain health facilities or recreation, and hawking meals and other perishables
  ▪ Ownership of a property within the boundaries of the local authority, when annual rates and taxes are payable.
▸ The local greater metropolitan substructures with regard to the payment of appropriate levies.

17.1.2 The name of the business venture

Should you wish to reserve a name for your business venture before it is established, you can apply to the **Companies and Intellectual Property Commission (CIPC)** to reserve a name on form CoR 9.1, also known as a defensive name. You may list up to four alternative names, which will then be considered for reservation in the listed order. Only one name will be reserved. In applying to reserve a name, you will prevent someone else from registering the same name. When a company is registered, its name is also reserved and may not be used by any other company. The first option, however, is cheaper than registering a company just to protect a name.

17.1.3 Registering a trademark

In terms of the provisions of the Trade Marks Act 194 of 1993, a **trademark** is a brand name, a slogan or a logo that identifies the services or goods of one person and distinguishes them from the goods or services of another. Examples include:

▸ Brand names: Capitec Bank, Samsung, Sunlight, NoMU and Mediclinic
▸ Slogans: Reaching new frontiers (SASOL); A diamond is forever (De Beers); You always get something out (Outsurance)
▸ Logos: MTN – the top brand in South Africa in 2013 (Brand Finance, 2013)

Woolworths

Nando's chicken

Gautrain

▸ Specific shapes: the Coca-Cola bottle, Toblerone chocolates
▸ Colour: Edgars' red square, MTN's yellow and blue.

When a trademark (brand name, slogan or logo) has been registered, nobody else can use that trademark, or one that is confusingly similar. If this happens, legal action may result. You can apply with the Trade Marks Registry, administered by the CIPC, to register a trademark. A registered trademark can be protected forever, provided it is renewed every ten years upon payment of a renewal fee.

(DEFINITION)

A trademark is a brand name, a slogan or a logo that identifies the services or goods of one person and distinguishes them from the goods or services of another.

17.1.4 **Publicising the business venture**

It is necessary to publicise a business venture. This should be done on a scale and in a way that is appropriate to the business. The following guidelines could be used:

▶ The full name of the business venture must be displayed outside each office or the premises where the business is operating
▶ The full name must be displayed on all notices or official publications, cheques, order forms, letterheads, delivery notes, invoices, receipts, and credit notes.

Before you can register your business, you need to decide what type of entity would best suit your needs. Different entities have different legal structures and implications.

17.1.5 **Sole proprieties and partnerships**

It is not necessary to register a sole propriety or partnership, but you will need to obtain a bank account in order to reserve a name. Sole proprieties are also subject to the same tax regulations, VAT, and levy as other legal entities.

A legal partnership agreement is a prerequisite for the establishment of a partnership. Such an agreement is a special type of contract and must thus meet the validity requirements of a contract (see Section 17.3).

17.1.6 **Companies**

As discussed in Chapter 7, until the promulgation of the new Companies Act 71 of 2008, which came into force on 1 April 2011 (the dti, 2010), close corporations were also one of the forms of business enterprises. The main influence of the Act (Companies Act, 2008) is that the CIPC will no longer register new close corporations or allow a company to convert to a close corporation, CCs will exist indefinitely and be treated as private

companies, and the Close Corporations Act 69 of 1984 will be brought into line with legislation on private companies (the dti, 2010:22).

DEFINITION

CIPC is the Companies and Intellectual Properties Commission.

Establishing a company requires certain procedures to be followed and it is thus advisable that an attorney or registered accountant with the relevant expertise should be consulted. Certain documents need to be drawn up by an attorney and lodged with the CIPC. The most important document is the company's memorandum and articles of association, which serve as the charter of the company. The memorandum of association must be signed by all its subscribers who will become the members of the company. The following must be stated in the memorandum of association:

▶ The name of the company, which must have been applied for on Form CM5 at the CIPC prior to registration
▶ A description of the main purpose of the business, with the formulation of the main objective of the company – it is important not to be too restrictive when describing the main objective of the company, but rather to give a broader definition (for example, a company planning to manufacture processed meat could rather indicate its purpose as manufacturing processed food as this is less specific and less restrictive)
▶ The amount of the initial registered share capital, divided into shares of a fixed amount – the par value (rand value) of the shares could also be indicated, but where no par-value shares will be issued, the total number of shares should be indicated
▶ Any powers or authority that the company is legally entitled to that need to be excluded or qualified
▶ The adoption or ratification of any pre-incorporated contracts must be

indicated should they exist – all contracts entered into by the entrepreneur before the establishment of the company must be mentioned

▸ Any special terms and conditions regarding the operation of the company

▸ An association clause explicitly stating the subscribers' wish to form a company and their agreement to take up a certain number of shares in the company.

The articles of association are concerned with the internal management of the company and must deal with aspects such as shares, lending powers, meeting procedures, voting rights, and the powers of directors. The articles must be set out on a prescribed form. When the company is registered with the CIPC, the following documents must accompany the original, and at least two certified copies of the memorandum and articles of association:

▸ Form CM5, stating the approved and reserved name and, if necessary, its translated and (or) abbreviated name

▸ The physical office and postal address of the company on Form CM22

▸ A proxy from each founding member, authorising another person to sign the memorandum and articles if he or she is not going to sign them personally.

These documents can only be handed in or received by one of the persons who have signed the memorandum or articles, or by a duly authorised attorney or his or her clerk.

A company may not start trading before receiving a certificate from the CIPC authorising it to do so. The following documents must be submitted to the CIPC before such a certificate will be issued:

▸ An application for the certificate to commence business (on Form CM46)

▸ A statement by the directors testifying that the issued share capital of the company is sufficient to conduct its business (on Form CM47)

▸ The particulars of the directors and other officers of the company (on Form CM29)

▸ Consent from an auditor to be the official auditor of the company (on Form CM31).

It is important to note that not all the aspects of the revised Companies Act can be covered in this book. For more detailed information, either the respective Acts, or the publications that deal with them, can be consulted. Copies of the Acts can be obtained from the offices of the Government Printer or in libraries, and electronic copies of these Acts can be obtained from the government website www.gov.za. Publications on companies can be obtained from bookshops and libraries.

17.2 South African Revenue Service (SARS)

The **South African Revenue Service (SARS)** was established with effect from 1 October 1997 by the South African Revenue Service Act 34 of 1997 (SARS Act) as an autonomous administrative organ of state within the public administration, but as an institution outside the public service. It is responsible for the collection of tax and customs revenue for national government (SARS, 2013:1). In this section, a summary of the aspects that the entrepreneur should do with regards to SARS is provided. It is not possible to cover all aspects in detail and you are encouraged to visit the SARS website at www.sars.gov.za to get up-to-date information.

17.2.1 Income tax on income derived from operating a business

In South Africa, **income tax** is payable by every individual, in the case of a sole proprietor, partner, in a partnership, as well as every individual member of all forms of company that derive a taxable income, either in the form of a profit, share or salary. The Income Tax

Act 58 of 1962 requires individuals to pay tax at a progressively increasing rate until the maximum of 40% is reached, while companies pay a rate of 28%. These rates may, however, change from time to time, and it is therefore essential that **SARS** or an accountant is approached for the most up-to-date information related to income tax.

DEFINITION

Income tax is assessed on the taxable income of individuals or members of companies in any one tax year, namely 1 March to 28 February of the following year.

DEFINITION

SARS is an autonomous administrative organ of state within the public administration, but as an institution outside the public service and is responsible for the collection of tax and customs revenue for the national government.

Income tax is assessed on the taxable income of individuals or members of companies in any one tax year, namely 1 March to 28 February of the following year. The taxable income for individuals and companies is calculated in the same way, by deducting any expenses (excluding capital expenses) incurred in the production of income during a given tax year from the gross income earned in that year. Income tax returns must be submitted to SARS each year for assessment, at the end of the tax year in February. In the case of a new business, this may sometimes be for a period of less than a full year. The financial statements must be prepared up to the last day of February, unless otherwise agreed by SARS. A person other than the company's auditor must be appointed by every company as a public officer to represent it for tax purposes.

Companies are required to make two provisional tax payments towards their tax liabilities in each year of assessment, and a third voluntary payment can be made if the taxable income of the company exceeds R20 000. Some individuals who are also classified as provisional taxpayers have to make the same number of provisional tax payments, and voluntary payments can be made if their taxable income exceeds R50 000. Two payments must be made in a financial year, namely one within the first six months, and the second at the end of the financial year (SARS, 2013).

The following expenses may be deducted from the taxable income of individuals or companies operating a business:

▸ Depreciation or wear-and-tear allowance on vehicles, equipment, and articles used in the business (the rates of depreciation must be agreed upon by SARS and may vary from year to year)

▸ A proportion of the private home expenses if part of your home is used for business purposes, including rent, rates, telephone, and cleaning costs – this concession is not normally allowed for people who earn a fixed income

▸ Revenue expenditure on scientific research done during and for the development of the business

▸ Travelling expenses incurred on behalf of the business

▸ The cost of developing, purchasing or registering a patent, design, trademark or copyright to be used in the business

▸ Rental of land, buildings, plant or machinery, and royalties for films, patents, designs, and trademarks used in the production of your income (lease premiums may be deducted proportionally over the period during which the asset has been used)

▸ Manufacturers may deduct depreciation or wear and tear of 20% per annum on a straight-line basis on plant and equipment

▸ An allowance equal to 50% of the cost of building housing for employees can also be deducted, provided that it does not exceed R6 000 per annum (the employees may also not be shareholders or relatives of shareholders)

▶ Interest paid on loans used for the production of income
▶ Any expenditure in respect of repair and pest control in buildings used for business or from which income is derived
▶ A 10% initial allowance and a 2% annual allowance on the cost of erecting buildings
▶ Any expenditure accrued from improving land or buildings that are rented for the purposes of business – the proviso being that should this expenditure have been incurred in terms of an obligation imposed under the lease agreement, it is deductible over the period of the lease or 25 years, whichever is shorter
▶ Trade debts that cannot be recovered
▶ Twenty-five per cent of the total number of debtors who are regarded as doubtful may be deducted as an allowance for doubtful debt, unless it can be shown that a debt is wholly doubtful, when the allowance is 100%
▶ A percentage reserve of any instalment sale debtor amount outstanding on the last day of the tax year
▶ Any compensation paid to Transnet resulting from losses incurred by operating a railway line for the benefit of the business
▶ Annual insurance premiums paid to cover the assets and loss of profit of the business
▶ Legal expenses paid in the course of operating the business with the proviso that these expenses are not of a capital nature
▶ The repair costs of tools, equipment and plant used in the business in the year in which the repairs occur
▶ Annual subscriptions to trade and professional associations
▶ The cost price of trading stock, which includes fixed and variable production overheads (this can be deducted at the beginning of each tax year, while that of closing stock is taxable)
▶ Finance charges relating to the assets used in a business
▶ Levy payments to the greater metropolitan structures.

The following expenses cannot be deducted from taxable income:
▶ Private, personal or domestic expenditure
▶ Expenditure that can be recovered from a third party, such as an insurance claim
▶ Income tax and interest or penalties on this amount
▶ Capital expenditure.

When the total amount of deductions exceeds the total amount of income, this is seen as an assessed loss. This amount can be carried forward to the following tax years, provided that the venture remains operational until the loss is cancelled out.

According to the proposed changes in income tax for 2010/2011, companies qualifying as small-business corporations pay tax at a graduated rate, namely 0% tax on R70 700.00 of taxable income, 7% on taxable income between R70 701.00 and R365 000.00, and R20 601 plus 21% on the amount of taxable income between R365 001 and R550 000, and R59 451 plus 28% of the amount above R550 000 (SARS 2014a).

17.2.2 Value-added tax (VAT)

Value-added tax (VAT) is tax payable to SARS and is calculated on consumption, presently at 14%. All business ventures with an annual turnover in excess of R150 000 must register for VAT, while this is optional for those with an annual turnover of less than R150 000.

DEFINITION

Value-added tax (VAT) is tax payable to SARS and is calculated on consumption, presently at 14%.

The concept of VAT relates to the person from whom SARS collects the tax. In principle, the amount of VAT on an appliance sold by a retailer for R2 000 is R280. The VAT-inclusive price is thus R2 280. Each business in the distribution chain, however, only pays VAT to

SARS in proportion to the value added by that particular business. This could be the total value or the cost of producing the product, plus the profit added to that cost, as is the case with a producer, or the amount (cost plus profit) added to the price for which it was bought by the wholesaler or retailer.

VAT should be calculated on a regular basis and returns submitted to SARS on a standardised form. A retailer who has received the amount of R2 280 for the appliance would calculate the amount of VAT payable to SARS as follows:

VAT charged to customers:	R280
Less VAT paid to suppliers:	
(wholesaler R56)	
(producer R140)	R196
VAT due to SARS:	R84

17.2.3 **Capital gains tax**

Capital gains tax was introduced through an amendment of the Income Tax Act 58 of 1962 in 2001. In terms of this Act, a '**capital gain or loss**' is the difference between the base cost of a specific asset and the consideration realised upon disposal of such an asset. Should an entrepreneur realise a net capital gain for such assets, such taxable capital gains should be included in the entrepreneur's income for the year of assessment. The inclusion rates to be used depend on the status of the entrepreneur, namely:

▸ The inclusion rate for individuals and special trusts is 0 to 10%
▸ The inclusion rate for companies is 14%
▸ The inclusion rate for small-business corporations is 14%
▸ The inclusion rate for trusts is 20%.

> **DEFINITION**
>
> 'Capital gain or loss' is the difference between the base cost of an asset and the consideration realised upon disposal of such an asset. A net capital gain for such assets is taxable and forms part of the entrepreneur's income for the year of assessment.

17.2.4 **Registration as employer for PAYE**

All businesses that employ staff must complete and submit an IRP1 to SARS to be registered as an employer. SARS will then return the following forms:

▸ IRP2 forms, which must be completed by all staff members, giving full personal particulars
▸ IRP4 forms, which are used to cover the monthly return of employees' tax, deducted according to the PAYE (pay-as-you-earn) method
▸ IRP5 forms, which are used to reflect the deductions of each employee, including annual earnings, pension, PAYE, UIF, medical aid, and so on, for the year ending at the end of February
▸ IRP5(6) forms, which are used to reconcile the stock of books of IRP5 certificates on hand
▸ IRP10 forms which are the tax-deduction tables annually sent to all employees or whenever tax rates are changed and which are used to calculate the PAYE deductions of employees.

If staff members are either younger than 62 years of age and earn R14 604 or less per annum, or older than 65 and earn R26 780 or less per annum, it is not necessary to register with SARS as an employer. According to law, an employer must apply for registration with the South African Revenue Service (SARS) within 21 days after becoming an employer, unless none of the employees are liable for normal tax. Application to register as an employer for Pay-As-You-Earn (PAYE), Skills Development Levy (SDL) and Unemployment Insurance Fund (UIF) must be made on an EMP101e form – Payroll Taxes – Application for Registration (SARS, 2014b). Where an employer expects that his total salary bill will exceed R500 000 over the following 12 months, that employer becomes liable to pay SDL and must register with SARS indicating the jurisdiction of the Skills Education and Training Authority in South Africa (SETA) within which the employer must be classified. (SARS, 2014c).

17.2.5 Registration for skills levy

Businesses are required to register with their Sector Education and Training Authority (SETA) for the skills-development levy. The skills levy amounts to 1% on the total amount paid in salaries to employees (including overtime payments, leave pay, bonuses, commissions and lump sum payments) when the payroll is more than R500 000 a year. To pay, you must register with SARS and pay the levy each month. SARS will supply the correct forms to fill in (SDL 201 return form). The levy must be paid to SARS not later than seven days after the end of every month.

You can get money back from the SETA or the National Skills Fund to use on training and developing your employees' skills. To qualify for a Skills Development Grant you must:
▸ Have paid skills-development levies
▸ Have a skills-development facilitator
▸ Follow all the rules and regulations in the Act.

17.2.6 Expanding the business tax net by means of the Small Business Tax Amnesty and Amendment of Taxation Laws Act 9 of 2006

The above-mentioned Act was introduced in 2006 to provide for the voluntary disclosure by entrepreneurs of their failure to comply with tax legislation from 25 February 2007 to 31 March 2007 (which was eventually extended to 31 May 2007).

This Act empowers the Tax Commissioner to approve applications for tax amnesty in respect of applicants who apply for tax amnesty. Applicants who receive tax amnesty are obliged to pay tax-amnesty levies – these are paid for the benefit of the National Revenue Fund.

17.3 Contracts

All business ventures are involved in numerous contractual obligations. A basic understanding of South African contract law is thus essential. In this section, some basic principles will be discussed, but it is still best to consult an attorney or legal consultant when a contract with another party needs to be drawn up or entered into.

A **contract** may be defined as any agreement between two or more persons and is binding by law. According to JurisPedia (2011), the following aspects should, however, be present in a binding contract that is legally enforceable:
▸ *Consensus.* The parties much reach conscious agreement regarding the terms and conditions to which each of them will be legally bound and have a genuine concurrent intention.
▸ *Contractual capacity.* Each party to the contract must have the capacity to act, which means that each party must be legally capable of performing the particular act which gives rise to the formation of the contract.
▸ *Physical possibility.* The terms and conditions must be realistic – thus the performance must be determinable and possible at the time of conclusion.
▸ *Legality.* The agreement must be legally possible – according to this requirement, the agreement, as well as the terms and conditions that are stipulated, must be permitted by law.

▸ *Formalities.* If formalities are prescribed for the formation of the contract, they must be observed.

The following are seen as defective contracts (JurisPedia, 2011):

▸ *Void contract,* where one of the requirements for a valid contract is absent or where no contract was concluded.
▸ *Voidable contract,* where a contract has indeed been concluded but it can be set aside on account of a defect that existed at the time of conclusion (e.g. consensus improperly obtained).
▸ *Unenforceable contract,* where a contract has indeed been concluded but it creates a natural obligation, which is recognised but not enforced by law (e.g. a wager).

DEFINITION

A contract is any agreement between two or more persons and is binding by law.

17.3.1 Entrepreneurs and the National Credit Act

The National Credit Act 34 of 2005 has a number of implications for entrepreneurs. Entrepreneurs who supply goods or services under a discount transaction or credit agreement, who advance money or credit under a pawn transaction, or who extend credit under a credit facility or any other person who acquires the rights of a credit provider under a credit agreement, need to be registered as credit providers. An entrepreneur should register as a credit provider if he or she is the credit provider under at least 100 credit agreements.

The applications of prospective credit providers are considered by the National Credit Regulator (NCR). The NCR evaluates such applications on the basis of (1) the appropriateness of registering the applicant based on specific criteria, including those set by the Broad-Based Black Economic Empowerment Act 53 of 2003, (2) the commitments made by the applicant in combating over-indebtedness, and (3) whether the applicant is registered with SARS.

Credit providers may not entice prospective debtors in any way. The Act provides strict regulations regarding the way in which credit providers may provide credit. The Act also provides consumers with a range of rights should they be unable to repay their debts.

17.3.2 Entrepreneurs and the Consumer Protection Act (CPA)

As an entrepreneur and small business owner, you can add value to your business by knowing your customers' rights and protecting them. The Consumer Protection Act 68 of 2008 (CPA), which was fully implemented on 31 March 2011, introduced new consumer rights, while also strengthening existing rights. A **consumer** for purposes of the CPA does not only refer to natural persons but also includes small businesses and franchisees in terms of a franchise agreement (South African Government, 2009:18). The CPA treats any juristic person whose asset value or annual turnover at the time of the transaction is less than R2m as a consumer (NSBC).

DEFINITION

A consumer for purposes of the CPA refers to a natural person, including small businesses and franchisees in terms of a franchise agreement. The CPA treats any juristic person whose asset value or annual turnover at the time of the transaction is less than R2m as a consumer.

The CPA applies to the sale of goods and the provision of services, provided it is concluded in the ordinary course of trade (Strachan, 2013). The entrepreneur and small business owner can earn goodwill by being sensitive to consumer needs that can lead to significant returns. It is not possible to discuss the contents of the CPA extensively and entrepreneurs are encouraged to read up on the requirements and contents of the CPA in more depth. However, some of the aspects that are important to keep in mind are the following (Cameron, 2013; Entrepreneur, 2012; National Small Business Chamber, 2013; Strachan, 2013; Wade, 2011a and Wade, 2011b):

▸ Customers have the right to cancel any pre-booking/reservation/order for goods or services without being penalised.
▸ Fixed-term agreements cannot be automatically renewed and the business should contact customers in writing between 40 to 80 days before the contract expires. Customers must be given an option to continue with the contract, to change the terms or to cancel it.
▸ Consumers can cancel a fixed-term agreement at any time, provided written notice is given at least 20 days prior to the cancellation. They are liable for payments up till the date of cancellation and a reasonable cancellation penalty can be charged.
▸ Businesses must provide an estimate or quote for customers to agree to prior to work being done. If the cost has not been acknowledged and accepted in writing, none can be charged for repairs, maintenance work or other diagnostic work done.
▸ A consumer may return unsafe or defective goods, including goods that are not of a good quality, for a period of six months from the date of purchase. No penalty can be charged to the consumer.
▸ Calculated from the date of installation, there is a mandatory three-month warranty on service providers who install any new or reconditioned part during repair work.
▸ There is no obligation on the part of a recipient to pay for unrequested goods and services.
▸ A customer who has accepted a transaction via direct marketing has five business days to rescind the transaction without reason or penalty. Written notice must be given to the supplier. Furthermore, businesses are prohibited from contacting customers at certain times, including Sundays or public holidays, Saturdays before 9am and after 1pm, and between 8pm and 8am the following day during the week. Direct marketers cannot send material to consumers unless they have confirmed (in writing) that no pre-emptive block was registered.
▸ Suppliers may not promote their products and services in a deceptive, misleading or fraudulent manner or in a way that violates dignity or is based on unfair discrimination.
▸ The Act contains standard product warranties, provides for strict product liability and makes labelling of goods and services more important. Many businesses protect themselves by having customers sign standard terms and conditions. This is in order to prevent future disputes and give the business essential protection against non-payment, product or service liability. However, the Act makes many of the terms previously included illegal or unenforceable, so businesses need to obtain a new document to properly protect their business interests and avoid administrative fines.
▸ The Act states that everything must be in plain language – all agreements must be easily understandable. Suppliers may not use false, misleading or deceptive representations to win over consumers to their products. They must also make full and honest disclosure about products, including their price. Sales that advertise goods 'while stocks last' can no longer use the same tactics, for example, if a TV is advertised for R1 000 and the consumer arrives to buy the TV as advertised, the supplier cannot offer a different TV for a different price in its place.
▸ A franchise agreement must:
  ▪ Be in writing and signed by or on behalf of the franchisee;

- Include any prescribed information, or address any prescribed categories of information; and comply with the requirements of section 22.

▶ A franchisee may cancel a franchise agreement without cost or penalty within 10 business days after signing such agreement, by giving written notice to the franchisor.

▶ Grey products need to be labelled as such.

While the bulk of the Consumer Protection Act is common sense and good business practice, complying with the Act does require a little work by business owners who should ensure that they have a strong risk management system in place. You can start by double checking all interaction and points of correspondence between your business and clients, including emails, calls, adverts, SMSs, websites and how walk-in customers are treated by staff.

You can also mitigate risk by creating templates for all correspondence. Ensure that the words 'All Terms and Conditions Apply' appear on everything. To ensure that your agreements use plain language, get someone else to read through all the business's documents with a critical eye (Entrepreneur, 2012).

17.4 **Personnel**

Certain legal requirements must be adhered to when an entrepreneur decides to employ personnel within the venture. Some of these are related to the safety of the employees, some to the general conduct of employers toward employees, while others relate to insurance issues. We will now discuss the legal aspects that should be adhered to when dealing with personnel.

17.4.1 **Compensation for Occupational Injuries and Diseases Act 130 of 1993 (COIDA)**

This Act repealed the Workmen's Compensation Act and is administered by the Compensation Commissioner. According to Finnemore (1998), COIDA provides a system of no-fault compensation for employees who are injured during the course of their employment. Employees are compensated irrespective of whether their injuries were as a result of their own negligence, or that of the employer or any other person. Accordingly, an employee may not institute a claim for damages against an employer or any other person. Three categories of disablement are addressed by the Act and the calculations of benefits payable in each are made according to a set formula. These categories are temporary disablement, permanent disablement, or death of the employee, in which case the benefits are paid to the dependants of such an employee.

17.4.2 **Unemployment Insurance Fund (UIF)**

An entrepreneur should furthermore complete and submit a UIF form, which is available from the Department of Labour. This form need not be signed and covers those employees working 24 or more hours per month. Employers must pay unemployment insurance contributions of 2% of the value of each worker's pay per month. The employer and the worker each contribute 1%. Contributions are paid to the Unemployment Insurance Fund (UIF) or the South African Revenue Service (SARS). Workers who earn more than the annual, monthly or weekly maximum earnings ceiling must also contribute to the Fund, but their contributions are worked out on the maximum earnings ceiling, which currently stands at R178 464 a year. (South African Department of Labour, 2014).

Once the venture has been registered, the UIF offices will send the following:

▶ A UIF3 form, indicating the monthly return for the premiums payable regarding UIF
▶ A UIF5 form to be used when registering new employees
▶ A UI-19 information form to be completed for every existing UIF member to be submitted to the Commissioner by the seventh day of each month if any changes occurred during the previous month; the member's employment history is recorded on this form.

17.4.3 Registration with bargaining councils

Bargaining councils have been set up for many industries and trades, with levies payable by every business operating within such industries and trades. Bargaining councils deal with collective agreements, solve labour disputes, establish various schemes, and make proposals on labour policies and laws related to the industry within which they have been established. It is the responsibility of the entrepreneur to establish whether or not the venture needs to be registered with any of these councils. If the venture has any employees, the entrepreneur is obliged to register with the council for the industry in which the venture operates. The levies apply to aspects such as holiday pay, health funds, sickness benefits, and pension or provident fund contributions.

17.4.4 Labour Relations Act 66 of 1995 (LRA)

The Labour Relations Act deals with employment relationships and collective bargaining in South Africa, which include unions, workplace forums, and employers' organisations. The purpose of this Act is the advancement of economic development, social justice, labour, peace, and the democratisation of the workplace. Its primary objectives are to include the provision of a framework for collective bargaining and to promote collective bargaining at sectorial levels. Entrepreneurs should realise that their employees have the right to form or join a trade union, to participate in the activities of that trade union, and even to hold office in a trade union. On the other hand, the Act also makes provision for the entrepreneur to form or join an employers' organisation, and to participate in the activities of such an organisation or to hold office in it. Furthermore, the Act provides that the rights of both the employee and employer in this regard may not be interfered with by any party and deals with strikes and lockouts, workplace forums, and alternative dispute resolution. It also establishes the CCMA (Commission for Conciliation, Mediation and Arbitration), Labour Court, and Labour Appeal Court as superior courts, with exclusive jurisdiction to decide matters arising from the Act.

Consider your response to this legislation and striking workers as you read the *Freedom of association* dilemma below.

ENTREPRENEURIAL DILEMMA

Freedom of association

For a company to ensure the elimination of restrictions on freedom of association within its own operations, it should first comply with national laws on freedom of association, such as the Labour Relations Act and the Basic Conditions of Employment Act. Within the guidelines of these Acts, companies should aim to create policies that responsibly respect the right to freedom of association.

In South Africa we have this freedom of association entrenched in our legislation, workers may join trade unions and if follow correct procedures may legally strike. These strikes have an effect on business enterprises.

You are starting a business, what will you do to ensure that you meet the freedom of association requirements and how will you deal with workers who want to strike?

17.4.5 Basic Conditions of Employment Act 75 of 1997

This Act deals with the establishment and enforcement of basic conditions of employment, namely:

▶ Working hours including ordinary hours of work, overtime and payment thereof, meal intervals, rest periods, remuneration for work on Sundays, public holidays, night shifts, exclusions, and emergency work
▶ Leave that includes annual leave, sick leave, maternity leave, family-responsibility leave, and exclusions
▶ Remuneration, deductions, and notice of termination
▶ Administrative obligations of the employer with regard to information on remuneration, keeping records, informing the employees of their rights, certificate of service, and exclusions
▶ Prohibition of employment of children and forced labour
▶ Variations and sectorial determinations
▶ The employment conditions commission, its establishment, composition, and functioning.

17.4.6 Wage Act 5 of 1957

This Act creates the equipment, namely the Wage Board, which may be used in establishing minimum wages and other conditions of employment. It applies specifically to those areas and industries where the employers and employees have not been organised into organisations or unions, through which agreements regulating the relationships between their members have been reached by means of negotiation. The Wage Act would thus deal with those aspects that have not yet been regulated in terms of the Labour Relations Act (Finnemore, 1998).

17.4.7 Broad-based black economic empowerment (B-BBEE)

Broad-based black economic empowerment (B-BBEE) is a strategic issue that is facing businesses of all sizes in South Africa. It is the government's initiative to promote economic transformation in order to ensure meaningful participation in the economy and business by black people, which includes Indian, African, and coloured persons who are South African citizens by birth or by descent or who were naturalised prior to 1993. B-BBEE has become one of the key strategic business imperatives for any business aspiring to grow and expand its asset base in the contemporary South African business environment. There is no legal requirement for private sector businesses to comply with the provisions of the Black Economic Empowerment Act 53 of 2003 and its Codes of Good Practice on B-BBEE (Department of Trade and Industry, 2007). However, businesses that operate under licence from the government and businesses that source their work from the government and state-owned enterprises are expected to contribute to the achievement of the objectives of B-BBEE. Private sector businesses that seek to get involved in private-public partnerships are also expected to contribute to the achievement of the objectives of B-BBEE.

> **DEFINITION**
>
> B-BBEE is the government's initiative to promote economic transformation in order to ensure meaningful participation in the economy and business by black people, which includes Indian, African, and coloured persons who are South African citizens by birth or by descent or who were naturalised prior to 1993.

The assessment for B-BBEE is done according to the Codes of Good Practice as listed in Table 17.1.

All measured businesses are assessed out of a total score of 100 points. However, various industries have established principles,

Table 17.1 B-BBEE Codes of Good Practice and their measurements

CODE	WHAT IS IT?	HOW IS IT MEASURED?
000	Conceptual Framework of B-BBEE	Carries the General Principles and the Generic Scorecard
100	Ownership	Measures effective ownership of enterprises by black people
200	Management Control	Measures the effective control of enterprises by black people
300	Employment Equity	Measures initiatives intended to achieve equity in the workplace
400	Skills Development	Measures the extent that employers carry out initiatives designed to develop the competencies of black employees
500	Preferential Procurement	Measures the extent that enterprises buy goods and services from BEE compliant suppliers as well as black owned entities
600	Enterprise Development	Measures the extent to which enterprises carry out initiatives contributing to Enterprise Development
700	Socio-Economic Development	Measures the extent to which enterprises carry out initiatives contributing to socio-economic development and promoting access to the economy for black people
800	Qualifying Small Enterprises	Measures the extent to which enterprises carry out contributions made by Qualifying Small Enterprises

Source: Department of Trade and Industry, No Date:8.

guidelines and methodologies to inform B-BBEE transformation that is specific to the environment in which they operate, these industries are (Department of Trade and Industry, 2007b):

▸ Transport Sector
▸ Forest Sector
▸ Construction Sector
▸ Tourism Sector
▸ Chartered Accountancy Sector
▸ Information and Communication Technology (ICT) Sector
▸ Property Sector Charter
▸ Agri-BEE Charter
▸ Financial Sector Charter

In terms of the Broad-Based Black Economic Empowerment Codes businesses with a turn-over of less than R5 million qualify as Exempted Micro Enterprises (EMEs) that are exempt from measurement in terms of the dti's Codes of Good Practice for BEE (Department of Trade and Industry, 2007a). They automatically qualify as 100% contributors towards BEE. However during 2009 two sector

charters were released that reduced the turn-over required for exemption as follows:

▸ Tourism & Hospitality Charter reduced the turnover required for exemption to R2.5 million for all businesses that are considered to be part of the tourism and/or hospitality industry.
▸ Construction Charter reduced the turnover required for exemption to R1.5 million for Built Environment Professionals (BEPs), these 'provide services related to but not limited to consulting engineering, architecture and quality surveying'. Contractors are considered exempt if they have a turnover of less than R5 million.

All other businesses would either fall under the qualifying small enterprises or generic enterprises.

▸ A Qualifying Small Enterprise (QSE) is a business with a turnover between R5 million and R35 million and is measured using the QSE Scorecard. Each category for a QSE Scorecard has a weighting of 25%, and only 4 needs to be measured (Department of Trade and Industry, 2007b).

▶ A Generic Enterprise is a business with a turnover of more than R35 million and is measured using the Generic Scorecard where each category has different weighting points adding up to 100. The measured entity must be rated on all 7 elements (codes of good practice) of the B-BBEE scorecard, regardless of whether they can or cannot score under a specific element (Department of Trade and Industry, 2007b). The current weighting for the elements is reflected in Table 17.2.

Table 17.2 Generic Scorecard and weights of 7 elements

ELEMENT	WEIGHT
Ownership	20
Management & Control	10
Employment Equity	15
Skills Development	15
Preferential Procurement	20
Enterprise Development	15
Socio-Economic Development	5
Total	100

Source: Department of Trade and Industry, 2007b:8.

The B-BBEE recognition levels that are awarded to business enterprises according to the scores that they obtain on the scorecards are reflected in Table 17.3.

A revision of the B-BBEE codes has been published by the dti and can be accessed at the following website: http://www.gpwonline. co.za/Pages/default.aspx. This revision will be implemented during the course of 2014 and will be discussed in more detail in the chapter on contemporary issues (Chapter 22).

17.5 Insurance

When starting a business venture, the entrepreneur has to take certain business risks, some of which are unavoidable, but others can be covered by insurance. In any business, the possibility that years of hard work may be lost due to theft, accidents or fire, should not be ignored. Insurance is usually voluntary but nevertheless important. The entrepreneur should thus develop a well-planned insurance policy that can cover these losses.

Generally, the following types of insurance against avoidable risks are available to the entrepreneur:

▶ *Personal accident and life insurance.* Some business ventures can suffer great losses

Table 17.3 B-BBEE recognition levels according to scores obtained

B-BBEE STATUS	QUALIFICATION	B-BBEE RECOGNITION LEVEL
Level 1	>= 100 Points	135%
Level 2	>= 85 but < 100 Points	125%
Level 3	>= 75 but < 85 Points	110%
Level 4	>= 65 but < 75 Points	100%
Level 5	>= 55 but < 65 Points	80%
Level 6	<= 45 but < 55 Points	60%
Level 7	<= 40 but < 45 Points	50%
Level 8	<= 30 but < 40 Points	10%
Non-Compliant	< 30 points	0%

Source: Department of Trade and Industry, 2007b:10.

should the owner, or one of the key personnel or investors, pass away or be injured during the course of duty. This type of loss can be prevented by taking out a life-insurance policy or an accident-insurance policy, which can then provide protection for a venture.

▶ *Fire and general property insurance.* This type of insurance could be taken out to cover losses suffered due to fire, vandalism, hailstorms, windstorms, explosions, rioting, lightning, and malicious damage. The entrepreneur should make sure that the insurance covers the current and not the historical replacement costs of the assets of the venture.

▶ *Burglary insurance.* This can be taken out for protection against losses that occur when forcible entry has been gained and stock, cash, and (or) assets stolen. The insurance should cover both the items stolen and the damage to the premises as a result of the intrusion.

▶ *Plate-glass insurance.* This will cover window breakage and the resulting losses.

▶ *Goods in transit.* This covers losses that occur during the transportation of goods, either collected from or delivered to customers.

▶ *Money in transit.* Unless banking is handled by a security firm, it would be advisable to take out this type of insurance as it will cover money transported to the bank.

▶ *Vehicle insurance.* This covers vehicles in case of theft or damage resulting from accidents or other events.

▶ *Public-liability insurance.* This covers injuries and losses suffered by members of the public while they are on the property of the venture.

▶ *Business-interruption insurance.* This is also referred to as insurance against the loss of profits and refers to insurance cover that can be taken out in case the business suffers losses due to fire, floods or any unforeseen event, where it will be necessary to pay taxes, interest, utilities, and the salaries of employees while the facilities are being rebuilt or repaired.

▶ *Product–liability insurance.* This is taken out to cover injury to customers arising from the use of the products or services provided by the venture.

▶ *Bad-debt insurance.* When the venture grants credit to customers, the entrepreneur could take out insurance against possible bad debts.

▶ *Fidelity insurance.* Entrepreneurs involved in giving professional advice to customers should take out insurance against any claims for loss or damage arising from dishonesty or negligence on the part of employees.

▶ *Employer's liability insurance.* Some employees will be covered by COIDA for personal injury sustained during their employment. However, an entrepreneur should take out a suitable group-accident policy for those employees whose earnings are too high to be covered by the COIDA.

17.6 Registering patents, designs, copyrights, and trademarks

According to CIPRO (2011b), a **patent** is an exclusive right granted for an invention, which is a product or a process that provides a new way of doing something, or offers a new technical solution to a problem. The patent provides protection for the owner and gives him or her the right to exclude others from making, using, exercising, disposing, offering to dispose, or importing the invention. The protection is granted for a limited period of 20 years

In terms of the South African Patents Act 57 of 1978, individuals may file their own provisional patent applications. However, it is advisable to seek the assistance of a patent attorney for support in this process. Should an entrepreneur wish to register a new invention, a patent may be registered in terms of this Act.

Also in terms of this Act, an entrepreneur can register any new invention that involves an inventive step and that is capable of being used or applied in trade and industry or agriculture. The following aspects are not regarded as an invention for the purposes of the Act:

▸ A discovery
▸ A scientific theory
▸ A mathematical method
▸ A literary, dramatic, musical or artistic or any other aesthetic creation
▸ A scheme, rule or method for performing a mental act, playing a game or doing business
▸ A computer program
▸ The presentation of information.

Where the Patents Act of 1978 caters for the registration of patents, the Designs Act of 1993 provides for the registration of designs.

A further Act in this regard is the Copyright Act 98 of 1978 that provides for copyright protection of various outputs of entrepreneurs including, among other things, literary works, musical works, artistic works, films, sound recordings, published editions or computer programs.

The South Africa success story – *NoMU* describes how Tracy Foulkes started her company and developed a national and international brand that is registered and protected.

SOUTH AFRICAN SUCCESS STORY

NoMU

Tracy Foulkes and Paul Raphaely are the heart and soul behind NoMU. Tracy's passion for flavour inspired her to start the company in December 2000 in a small cottage in central Cape Town. Her love of spices and the stylish, uncomplicated way she loves to cook is very much evident in the NoMU range of products where the emphasis is always very clearly on Quality, Consistency and Innovation with an authentic and unusually personal story attached!

Tracy was a vegetarian when she started the business and because of this, Paul suggested that, as a name for her original plan, which was to start a unique deli experience in Cape Town; she ought to have a name that could communicate some of her personality and her quirks.

Since Tracy's dream outlet would not exactly feature a massive red meat section at that time, Paul suggested that no meat would equal 'no cow' which would equal 'No-Moo.' This became 'NoMOO,' evolving into 'NoMU'! About six months later, they discovered by accident that in Japanese, NoMU loosely translates as 'to drink, swallow or savour'.

The company manufactures and exports upwards of 70 different products – many of which are savoury herb and spice blends – to some 38 countries. It also provides an expansive range of private label items to various retailers under their own brand, both locally and internationally. Apart from the herb and spice 'rubs' and 'grinders', NoMU also provides a variety of premium quality baking kits, cocoa, vanilla paste and extracts, concentrated liquid stock (called 'Fonds') but has become perhaps best known for its multi-award winning range of hot chocolates.

The company's mission has always been to disrupt any category they enter and to develop products that consistently deliver the best overall experience for the consumer, in terms of flavour and quality, at a fair price. And while NoMU has an online shop that distributes directly to the public, its primary customers are conventional retailers and overseas importers and distributors.

Tracy has become a well-respected South African food personality and businesswoman while Paul has also become a popular public speaker, sharing the brand's experiences of building a potent, credible brand on a shoestring marketing budget. The company has garnered multiple awards, including the 2013 'Western Cape Premier's Recognition Award for Established Entrepreneur,' 'Businesswoman of the Year' (2009) and the International Grand Prix for 'Excellence and Innovation in Packaging and Design' at the SIAL International Food Fair in Paris (2006). NoMU's story as an entrepreneurial case study and branding success story has also seen the brand earn critical acclaim and attention in a variety of food related television programmes, featured editorials and events.

And although the name still carries the same story for NoMU, Tracy is no longer a vegetarian...

Source: Compiled from http://www.nomu.co.za/about/story-so-far and http://www.nomu.co.za/about/why-nomu Reprinted by permission of NoMU.

CONCLUSION

An entrepreneur may have realised a dream when he or she opens the doors of the venture for the first time. This dream could become a nightmare if the legal aspects associated with the specific venture are not attended to. Although the legal requirements for establishing a sole ownership or partnership may be limited when starting out, those involved in these forms of business should familiarise themselves with all the legal aspects that may come into effect once the venture starts to operate. The legislation governing the payment of taxes and levies and contracts, as well as those related to the employment of personnel, could have a direct impact on both sole ownerships and partnerships.

The legal aspects pertaining to the establishment of companies are more complex than those concerning sole ownerships and partnerships. All the other legal requirements that apply to the day-to-day operation of a company or close corporation should be considered. Changes in legislation are made all the time and entrepreneurs are encouraged to obtain legal consultation regarding these changes, how they affect their specific businesses and how to implement it in their businesses.

Insurance against misfortune is available to all entrepreneurs operating a venture. It is not compulsory to take out any insurance, but it is advisable to do so to enable the company to survive in the long run.

SELF-ASSESSMENT QUESTIONS

Multiple-choice questions

1. When you register the name of your business with the CIPC you will still not be able to prevent someone else from registering the same name.
   a. True
   b. False
2. A _____ refers to a brand name in the sense of a product or a service rendered by a specific enterprise.
   a. product name
   b. name of the service
   c. trademark
   d. quality mark
3. Income tax is assessed on the taxable income of individuals or companies in any one tax year, namely _____.
   a. 1 January to 31 December of the same year
   b. 1 April to 31 March of the following year
   c. 1 March to 28 February of the following year
   d. 1 July to 30 June of the following year
4. The _____ introduced new consumer rights, while also strengthening existing rights:
   a. National Credit Act
   b. Consumer Protection Act (CPA)
   c. Income Tax Act
   d. Broad-based black economic empowerment codes
5. According to CIPRO a patent is an exclusive right granted for an invention, which is a product or a process that provides a new way of doing something, or offers a new technical solution to a problem.
   a. True
   b. False

DISCUSSION QUESTIONS

1. Identify and discuss the legal requirements that the entrepreneur should adhere to for the registration of the venture and its name.
2. Can the entrepreneur protect his or her product in any way?
3. What should the entrepreneur do when he or she wants to publicise his or her venture?
4. What aspects should be present to make a contract binding and legally enforceable? Is there anything that will make a contract void? Explain.
5. What does the Consumer Protection Act state with regards to customers who are buying products or services online?
6. Identify and discuss the procedures involved in calculating and paying income tax on income derived from the venture.
7. Discuss the principles of value-added tax (VAT) and the calculation thereof.
8. Discuss the procedures involved in registering as an employer for tax purposes.
9. Identify and discuss the aspects of a binding and legally enforceable contract.
10. Identify and briefly discuss the aspects that the Basic Conditions of Employment Act deal with.
11. Identify the B-BBEE codes of good practice, what they are and how they are measured. Do you think it is possible for an entrepreneur to adhere to all these codes from the point of starting the business? Explain.
12. Can an entrepreneur insure his or her business venture against all types of business risks? Identify and discuss the various insurance policies available to the entrepreneur to cover insurable risks.

EXPERIENTIAL EXERCISE

You have a retail business selling televisions, radios and other electronic products. You have bought fifteen 42" HD television sets from the wholesaler at a price of R6 500 each and are selling them at a discounted price of R10 900. According to your knowledge, the sets were produced for R2 300.

Calculate the VAT payable to SARS if you sold all 15 sets.

LERUMO LA BASADI CLEANING SERVICES

Sheila Ditsele taught high school science for many years, until the onset of an illness that left her incapable of speaking for a prolonged period. Unable to teach, she found alternative employment as a supervisor in an industrial cleaning company. Sheila made a rapid transition from classroom to management, and so impressed a manager at a client company that he suggested she go into business for herself. He persuaded her that it is not impossible and that you do not have to be rich to have your own business. She registered her company, Lerumo la Basadi cleaning services, in 2005.

In the beginning, Sheila did everything herself – recruiting and supervising labour, resolving human resources issues and marketing her services to potential clients in the region. Since those early days, Lerumo la Basadi – which means 'Spear of the Woman' – has won long-term contracts to clean offices and change-houses, and to provide laundry services to Anglo American Platinum's Pilanesburg mine and Anglo American's enterprise development initiative, Zimele's Small Business Hub office situated in Rustenburg.

Today Lerumo la Basadi has 17 permanent employees and also uses the services of up to 40 contractors to clean before and after special events, which include soccer games at the 46 000-seat Royal Bafokeng Stadium.

Sheila has received recognition for the successes her company achieved by Anglo American in 2011 and her vision for Lerumo la Basadi is one of continuous growth while continuously being committed to community upliftment and development through job creation. 'I must make a difference', she states with her usual conviction. However, she needs guidance with regards to the different legislative requirements that may impact her company.

Source: Developed from: http://www.angloamerican.co.za/sustainable-development/case-studies/developing-entrepreneurs.aspx [Accessed 19 November 2013].

1. Advise Sheila on the tax legislation that will impact her business.
2. Sheila learnt about the new Consumer Protection Act but does not know whether this act will have any impact on her as she does not market her service online. What impact would this Act have on Lerumo la Basadi cleaning service?

SUGGESTED WEBSITE LINKS

http://www.itweb.co.za/index.
    php?option=com_content&view=article&id=59047
http://www.labourguide.co.za/
http://www.labour.gov.za/DOL
http://www.sars.gov.za/Pages/default.aspx
https://www.thedti.gov.za/
http://www.dti.gov.za/economic_empowerment/bee.jsp
https://www.facebook.com/thedti

REFERENCES

Benade, ML, Henning, JL, Delport, PA, Du Plessis, JJ, De Koker, L. & Pretorious, JT. 2003. *Entrepreneurial Law*. 3rd ed. Butterworths: Durban.

Brand Finance. 2013. *South Africa Top 50*. The annual report on South Africa's 50 Most Valuable Brands. August 2013, Johannesburg: Brand Finance plc, in partnership with Brand South Africa and Brand Africa.

Cameron, N. 2013. *Does your business comply with the Consumer Protection Act?* [Online]. Available: http://businessnews.howzit.msn.com/does-your-business-comply-with-the-consumer-protection-act [November 2013].

CIPRO. 2011. Patents. [Online]. Available: http://www.cipro.gov.za/products_services/patents.asp [1 August 2011].

Department of Trade and Industry. 2007a. *Broad-based Black Economic Empowerment Act (53/2003): Codes of Good Conduct on Black Economic Empowerment*. Pretoria: Government Printers.

Department of Trade and Industry. 2007b. *Interpretative Guide to the Codes of Good Practice*. Pretoria: Department of Trade and Industry.

Department of Trade and Industry. 2010a. *Department of Trade and Industry Press Release*. The new Consumer Protection Act and Companies Act to come into force on 1 April 2011.

Department of Trade and Industry. 2010b. *The Companies Act, No. 71 of 2008. An explanatory guide*. Pretoria: Department of Trade and Industry.

Entrepreneur. 2012. The Consumer Protection Act. [Online]. Available: http://www.entrepreneurmag.co.za/advice/starting-a-business/start-up-guide/the-consumer-protection-act/ [November 2013].

Finnemore, M. 1998. *Introduction to Labour Relations in South Africa*. Durban: Butterworths.

Gautrain logo. Reprinted by permission of the GAUTRAIN MANAGEMENT AGENCY.

JurisPedia. 2011. *Introduction to the law of contract (ZA)*. March 2011. [Online]. Available: http://en.jurispedia. org/index.php/Introduction_to_the_law_of_contract_(za) [14 March 2011].

Nandos logo. Reprinted by permission of Nando's flame-grilled PERi-PERi chicken restaurants.

National Small Business Chamber. 2013. *The CPA and small businesses*. [Online]. Available: http://www.fin24.com/Entrepreneurs/Resources/The-CPA-and-small-businesses-20130314 [November 2014].

NOMU. [Online]. Available: http://www.nomu.co.za/about/story-so-far and http://www.nomu.co.za/about/why-nomu

SARS. 2013. *Taxation in South Africa 2012/13*. Pretoria: South African Revenue Service.

SARS. 2014a. *Small Business*. [Online]. Available: http://www.sars.gov.za/ClientSegments/Businesses/SmallBusinesses/Pages/default.aspx. [9 April 2014].

SARS. 2014b. *Registering for employees' tax pay-as-you-earn (PAYE)*. [Online]. Available: http://www.sars.gov.za/ClientSegments/Individuals/Taxpayer/Pages/Register-for-PAYE.aspx. [9 April 2014].

SARS. 2014c. *Skills Development Levy (SDL)*. [Online]. Available: http://www.sars.gov.za/TaxTypes/SDL/Pages/default.aspx. [9 April 2014].

South Africa, 29 April 2009. Act No. 68 of 2008: Consumer Protection Act, 2008. No 32186 ed. Cape Town: Government Gazette.

South African Department of Labour. 2014. *Basic guide to UIF contributions*. [Online]. Available: http://www.labour.gov.za/DOL/legislation/acts/basic-guides/basic-guide-to-uif-contributions [9 April 2014].

Strachan, D. 2013. *Small business and the CPA*. [Online]. Available: http://www.fin24.com/Entrepreneurs/Opinions-and-Analysis/Small-businesses-and-the-CPA-20130221 [November 2013].

Wade, B. 2011a. *The Consumer Protection Act – What to do?* [Online]. Available: http://www.ei.co.za/entrepreneur-incubator-blog/the-consumer-protection-act-what-to-do- [November 2013].

Wade, B. 2011b. *The CPA: Learner's Guide*. [Online]. Available: http://www.ideate.co.za/2011/04/11/the-cpa-learner%E2%80%99s-guide/ [November 2013].

Woolworths logo. Copyright © Woolworths Holdings Limited.

part four

Managing the venture

CHAPTER 18

Business cycles and the entrepreneur

Carel van Aardt and Patrick Naidoo

LEARNING OUTCOMES

On completion of this chapter you will be able to:
▶ Explain what business cycles are
▶ Describe the four distinguishable phases of the business cycle
▶ Provide a historical perspective on business cycles in South Africa
▶ Provide a sectoral perspective on business cycles in South Africa using financial data from different business sectors and industries
▶ Indicate the relevance of business cycles to entrepreneurs and prospective entrepreneurs
▶ Describe how entrepreneurs can ensure profitability during the different phases of the business cycles
▶ Show how entrepreneurs can incorporate business cycle forecasts in their business plans
▶ Describe how entrepreneurs can make use of sectoral business cycles to optimise their business success in the sector they are operating in
▶ Identify business opportunities using business cycle information.

OPENING CASE STUDY

This chapter provides an overview of business cycles and the entrepreneur with a specific focus on four important questions: (1) what do business cycles encompass, (2) what is the nature of business cycles in South Africa, (3) how can an understanding of business cycles facilitate business survival and growth and (4) how do business cycles influence entrepreneurs' decision making?

INTRODUCTION

No economy in the world is static. Economies experience continuous change which poses a host of challenges to entrepreneurs and businesses operating in a specific economy. These changes include, among other things, changes in the structure of demand for goods and services, changes in household, government, and business expenditure as well as the primary focus of this chapter, namely business cycles. To ensure business success, entrepreneurs should scan economic trends continuously and should be able to respond to changes in the economy. Prospective and existing entrepreneurs should use the knowledge of economic trends they acquired for their business plans, to identify business opportunities, markets, and products for their services, in conducting market planning, in deciding upon expanding their business, in making decisions about new outlets, and in calculating business risks. The most important broad economic trend that entrepreneurs need to keep track of, analyse, and forecast is business cycles. A thorough knowledge, understanding, and incorporation of business cycles in business planning will have a strong positive impact on the chance of an entrepreneur's business surviving and growing.

18.1 The nature of business cycles

Having indicated the importance of incorporating information about business cycles in business plans in order to optimise the chances of business success and growth, it is important to clearly define the term 'business cycle'. The term **'business cycle'** describes the cyclical but irregular up-and-down movements in economic activity, which are measured by fluctuations in real **Gross Domestic Product** (GDP) as well as other macroeconomic variables. Key variables such as turnover, and change in inventories and capital expenditure can be used to measure economic activity. Business cycles consist of four distinguishable phases, namely contraction, recovery, peak and slump.

▸ *Contraction* occurs when an economy is experiencing negative real growth in its GDP. **Contractions** are characterised by very low demand for goods and services (compared to periods of positive real economic growth), high levels of job losses, rising unemployment, low levels of consumer and business confidence, and increased government expenditure as a percentage of GDP to 'kick-start' the economy to move from negative real GDP growth towards positive real GDP growth.

▸ *Recovery* occurs when an economy starts to show positive real GDP growth again after a contraction. **Recoveries** take various shapes of which the so-called 'V', 'U' and 'L' shaped recoveries are most prevalent. A 'V' shaped recovery occurs when a fairly dramatic slump in real GDP growth is followed by a fairly quick recovery. A 'U' shaped recovery occurs when a slump in real GDP growth is followed by a protracted contraction before the onset of the recovery that follows. As was the case following the 2008 to 2009 recession in South Africa, economic recovery did not happen quickly giving rise to an 'L' shaped recovery during which recovery takes a very long time. Economic recoveries are characterised by low but positive real GDP growth rates, a decline in the number of job losses brought about by the recession, followed by the start of positive employment growth, and increasing levels of consumer and business confidence while government starts cutting back on increased expenditure aimed at 'kick-starting' the economy.

▸ *The peak* is the 'happy days' part of the business cycle. During the **peak** fairly high real GDP growth rates, sustained positive employment growth rates, and fairly high levels of consumer and business confidence are experienced.

▶ *The slump* phase of the business cycle follows the boom phase. The **slump** is when real GDP and employment growth rates start to decline. At the same time, consumer and business confidence levels decrease while a growing number of consumers and businesses become increasingly financially vulnerable.

DEFINITION

The term 'business cycle' describes the cyclical but irregular up-and-down movements in economic activity, which are measured by fluctuations in real Gross Domestic Product (GDP) as well as other macroeconomic variables.

The four phases of the business cycle as discussed above are shown in Figure 18.1. Note that the business cycle shown in Figure 18.1 is continuous, namely after the slump shown on the right-hand side of the figure there will be another recovery phase, followed by a peak, followed by a slump phase, and so forth.

It is very important for entrepreneurs to understand and plan for business cycles as explained in *Planning for the impact of business cycles*.

ENTREPRENEURIAL DILEMMA

Planning for the impact of business cycles

The economy is continuously changing, continuously experiencing one stage of the business cycle after the next. This makes it very difficult for any business to sustain the same product and service offerings continuously while expecting the same levels of business success. During the collapse of some financial institutions in Europe and the United States in 2008, a vast number of businesses failed because they did not sufficiently plan for the impact of business cycles on their bottom-lines. A large number of businesses also failed during the protracted recovery phase of 2008 to 2014.

1. How can an entrepreneur optimise business success during all phases of the business cycle when he or she is not sufficiently knowledgeable about business cycles and on how to make and implement strategic decisions that will make his or her business more business-cycle friendly?
2. How can an entrepreneur deal with volatility and downside risks in the short, medium and long-term?

In addition to the terms 'contraction', 'recovery', 'peak', and 'slump', another term we often hear when economists refer to business cycles

Figure 18.1 The four phases of a business cycle

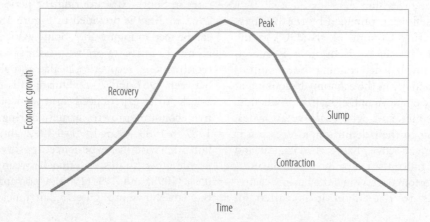

is the term 'recession'. If a contraction is severe enough then we have what is called a **recession**. Should a very long recession, taking the form of a deep trough, be experienced, economists talk of a 'depression'. A typical example of a depression is the worldwide great depression experienced during the 1930s brought about by the Wall Street Stock market crash on 29 October 1929. There is often confusion relating to the difference between a recession and a depression. This is due to there not being a universally agreed upon definition. A common joke amongst economists is: 'A recession is when your neighbour loses his job. A depression is when you lose your job'.

/ DEFINITION \
A well-known definition of a recession is a decline in the GDP for two or more successive consecutive quarters.

A well-known definition of a recession is a decline in the GDP for two or more successive consecutive quarters. However, this definition is not very popular among some economists for two reasons. The first reason is that the important variables, such as changes in the rate of unemployment and consumer confidence, are not taken into account in this definition. Secondly, this definition uses quarterly data which makes it difficult to determine the start and end of a recession.

One definition provided by the Business Cycle Dating Committee (BCDC) at the National Bureau of Economic Research (NBER) involves determining the amount of business activity in the economy by looking at things like employment, industrial production, real income, and wholesale-retail sales. According to their definition, a recession is when business activity has reached its peak and starts to fall until the time when business activity bottoms out. When the business activity starts to rise again it is called an expansionary period. By this definition, the average recession lasts about a year.

A simple definition of a **depression** comes from the Great Depression of the 1930s. A depression is viewed as a recession that lasts longer and has a larger decline in business activity. Prior to 1930, any downturn in economic activity was referred to as a depression. However, there needed to be a differentiation between a depression and the smaller economic declines that had occurred previously, hence the term 'recession' was developed. To distinguish the 2008 to 2009 world recession from the Great Depression of the 1930s, economists refer to the 2008 to 2009 downturn as the Great Recession.

/ DEFINITION \
A simple definition of a depression comes from the Great Depression of the 1930s. A depression is viewed as a recession that lasts longer and has a larger decline in business activity.

18.2 Business cycles in South Africa: A historical perspective and lessons for entrepreneurs

A graphical representation of GDP growth rates in South Africa during the period from 1961 to 2009 is provided in Figure 18.2. As can be seen in Figure 18.2, South Africa experienced quite a few business cycles (contractions, recoveries, peaks, and slumps) between 1961 and 2009. During this period, South Africa experienced eight years of negative economic growth, namely during 1977, 1982 to 1983, 1985, 1990 to 1992, and 2009, but otherwise has experienced positive economic growth rates differing between about 0.5% (1998) and 7.9% (1964). Upon analysing the data shown in Figure 18.2, it appears that the average economic growth rates for the five decades shown were as follows:

▶ 1961 to 1969: 5.8%
▶ 1970 to 1979: 3.3%
▶ 1980 to 1989: 2.2%
▶ 1990 to 1999: 1.5%
▶ 2000 to 2009: 3.6%
▶ 2010 to 2013: 2.8%

In Figures 18.3 to 18.10 the business cycles of each industry covered in the *Quarterly financial survey* (QFS) of Statistics South Africa (2014) are shown with respect to two key macroeconomic variables, namely turnover received (which includes sales and service income) and total closing inventory. Although changes in inventories are the smallest component of South Africa's GDP, they are much more important than their absolute size because changes in inventories signal changes in aggregate demand and are, therefore, indicators of future economic activity. Care should be taken when ascertaining the value of inventories – during tough times, businesses may reduce

their stocks to avoid production costs; while in boom times the additional or unexpectedly high demand for such items may mean a lower inventory level.

DEFINITION

Gross domestic product is an economic measure of the total flow of goods and services produced by the economy over a specific period of time, i.e. annually or quarterly.

18.2.1 The business cycle for the mining and quarrying industry

Figure 18.3 reflects the business cycle for the mining and quarrying industry for the 31 quarters from March 2006 to September 2013. Prior to the December 2008 quarter, there appeared to be a generally positive correlation between turnover and inventory and the two variables seem to track one another. The deviation in the December 2008 quarter can possibly be attributed to the effects of the global

Figure 18.2 Annual Gross Domestic Product growth rates for South Africa at 2005 constant prices, 1970 to 2013

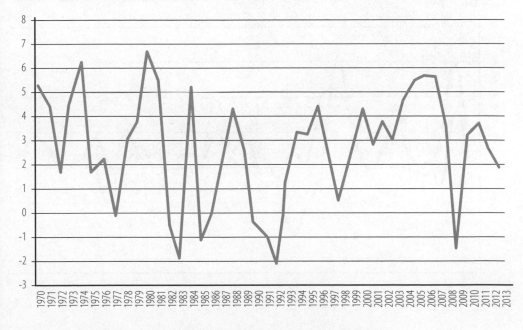

Source: Statistics South Africa (2013) 2009=-1.5%; 2010=3.1%; 2011=3.5%; 2012=2.5%.

recession during that period, and which continued to reflect difficult trading conditions. The weak demand for commodities, services, and products; the reduction in production in most industries; the drop in the average price of platinum group metals; and the decrease in average oil price represent an adverse productivity shock resulting in a recession.

Entrepreneurs considering becoming involved in the mining and quarrying sector need to take note of the relative volatility of earnings in this sector. They should also be aware that a very large capital outlay is required to set up a business in this sector and that the demand for goods and services from this sector is dependent upon the relative volatility of commodity prices on national and international commodity markets. The possible nationalisation of mines and numerous other legislative obligations are key factors to consider when becoming involved in this sector.

18.2.2 The business cycle for the manufacturing industry

There appears to be a lag effect between the turnover and inventory variables in the manufacturing industry for the period March 2006 to September 2013 (see Figure 18.4). An increase or decrease in inventory in one quarter is followed by a subsequent increase or decrease in turnover in the next quarter. The lowest level of turnover during this period was experienced in the March 2009 quarter, the 2008 to 2009 financial crisis being the most likely contributing factor. The post-recessionary period for this sector has been very difficult with some quarters showing negative turnover growth in 2011, 2012 and 2013.

Entrepreneurs becoming involved in the manufacturing industry need to note that the business cycles in this sector are very similar to those of the economy as a whole, although the contractions experienced in this sector are deeper. This could be attributed to the fact that during slumps and contractions in the national

Figure 18.3 Time series of percentage change in turnover and inventory between consecutive quarters for the mining and quarrying industry

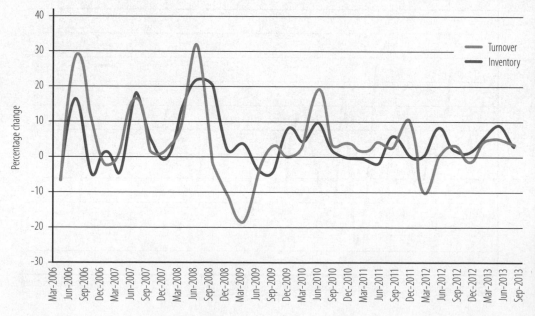

Source: Statistics South Africa (2014).

economy, people tend to cut down more on manufactured goods – especially on semi-durable (e.g. clothing) and durable goods (e.g. cars) – than on foodstuffs and personal services.

18.2.3 **The business cycle for the electricity, gas, and water-supply industry**

The business cycle for the period March 2006 to September 2013, on a quarterly basis, for the electricity, gas, and water-supply industry is provided in Figure 18.5. It appears that deep slumps and high peaks are experienced in this sectors' business cycle brought about by fluctuations in household and business demand for gas, water, and electricity. Various other factors, including the provision of basic services to all communities and the need to ensure stable provision of this service, have placed substantial pressure on the enterprises in this sector. This is especially dependent upon production and service input requirements that fluctuate

quite a lot depending on demand for goods and services.

Entrepreneurs who are considering entering the electricity, gas, and water-supply sector should note the wide differentials between peaks and slumps in this sector's business cycle that makes it very difficult to forecast future demand accurately. There are substantial cost increases emanating from this sector, and consumers face difficult choices regarding the significant increases in electricity and water costs. Furthermore, the monopolistic nature of this industry together with the large capital requirements for setting up and running a business in this sector make it difficult for new businesses to survive.

18.2.4 **The business cycle for the construction industry**

The business cycle with respect to the construction sector for the period March 2006 to September 2013 is shown in Figure 18.6. It

Figure 18.4 Time series of percentage change in turnover and inventory between consecutive quarters for the manufacturing industry

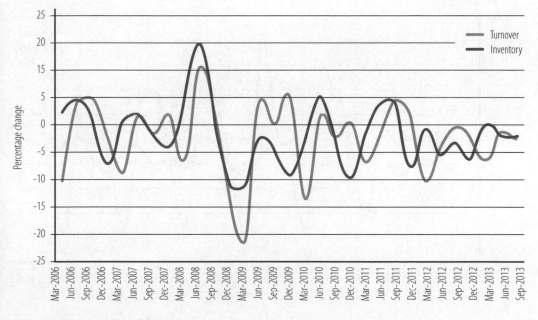

Source: Statistics South Africa (2014).

appears from this figure that very high turn-over growth rates were experienced during the period early 2006 to early 2008 with respect to the construction sector, with negative growth rates for the period thereafter. During the past decade, a large number of entrepreneurs have entered this sector as 'building contractors' or 'handymen' working on residential and (or) non-residential building contracts. Government's high level of infrastructure expenditure during the past decade, focusing on the 2010 FIFA Soccer World Cup and expanding infrastructure, also encouraged a large number of new entrants to this sector.

Prospective entrepreneurs to the construc-tion sector could take heart from the fact that there are many business opportunities in this sector, but also take note that there is great competition in this sector and should keep in mind that they should be willing to sit-out protracted slumps (i.e. Q4 2012 and Q1 2013) and contractions as reflected in Figure 18.6.

18.2.5 The business cycle for the trade sector

The number of entrepreneurs operating in the trade sector has increased dramatically over the past two decades. Such entrepreneurs work in various capacities in this sector, some are sur-vivalists operating in the informal trade sectors selling a small range of products in order to survive while they remain on the lookout for employment opportunities. Others become formal sector entrepreneurs by starting up their own outlets, buying out existing outlets or buying into franchise opportunities. As shown in Figure 18.7, as a result of the strong demand for goods by households during most of the reference period, retailers have been perform-ing well. However, the mortality rate among retail outlets is fairly high because of high levels of competition in this sector, relatively low profit margins, and the strong impact of economic slumps and contractions on this sector (see Figure 18.7).

Figure 18.5 Time series of percentage change in turnover and inventory between consecutive quarters for the electricity, gas, and water-supply industry

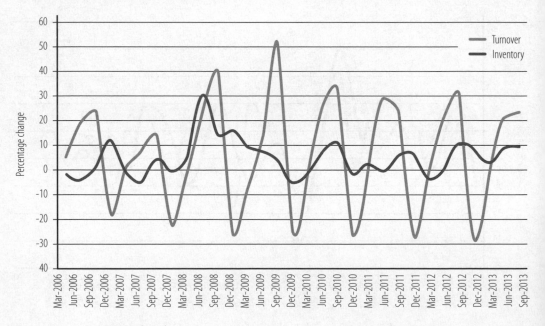

Source: Statistics South Africa (2014).

Figure 18.6 Time series of percentage change in turnover and inventory between consecutive quarters for the construction industry

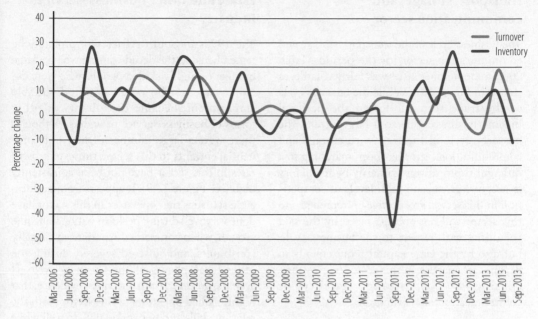

Source: Statistics South Africa (2014).

Figure 18.7 Time series of percentage change in turnover and inventory between consecutive quarters for the trade sector

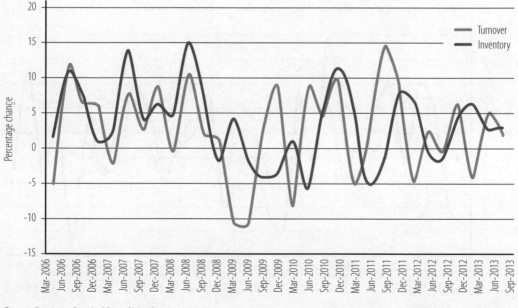

Source: Statistics South Africa (2014).

18.2.6 The business cycle for the transport, storage, and communication sector

The business cycle of the transport, storage and communication sector for the period March 2006 to September 2013 was fairly volatile, as shown in Figure 18.8. While the business cycle of the trade sector followed the national income business cycle to a large extent, the business cycle of the transport, storage and communication sector has been marching to a different drum driven primarily by regulatory issues, fuel prices, and high levels of competition in this sector. Prospective entrepreneurs to this sector will not only be faced by the said volatilities with respect to the business cycle, but also by the large capital requirements to become an operator in this sector (e.g. by purchasing a taxi, storage facility or communication infrastructure).

18.2.7 The business cycle for the real estate and other business-services industry

The 1990s in South Africa will probably be remembered as the decade during which a large number of highly skilled people, who were ex-employees or who could not find suitable employment, became consultants or other forms of business-service providers. Although there were a large number of new entrepreneurial entrants to this sector, turnover growth rates in this sector have not been consistently high (see Figure 18.9). It appears from business cycle statistics that operators in this sector have done very well during peaks in national income growth, when companies experienced capacity constraints, and suffered severely during the other three phases of the business cycle. It appears, however, from anecdotal evidence, that highly skilled operators in this sector (with the relevant skills and networks) will do well while average and below-average quality business-service providers will struggle to survive.

Figure 18.8 Time series of percentage change in turnover and inventory between consecutive quarters for the transport, storage, and communication sector

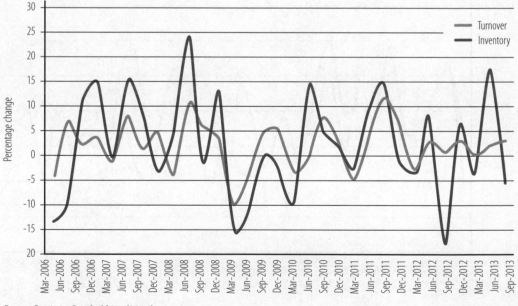

Source: Statistics South Africa (2014).

18.2.8 The business cycle for the community, social, and personal-services sector

Shown in Figure 18.10 is the business cycle for the community, social, and personal-services sector for the period March 2006 to September 2013. As indicated in this figure, prior to the December 2008 quarter an inverse relationship existed between turnover and closing inventories, as turnover increased this was accompanied by a decrease in inventory. Subsequent to the December 2008 quarter, turnover and inventory closely tracked one another indicating the possible impact of the global financial crisis and contraction of this sector experiencing limited percentage changes between turnover and inventory. Prospective entrepreneurs in this sector have to determine which market segment to pursue and the profitability thereof as this sector is mainly characterised by health and social work, sewage and refuse disposal, sanitation and recreation, and cultural and sporting activities.

Although it is important for prospective entrepreneurs to be aware of trends in the sector or industry which is most relevant to them, an overview of the trends across the different industries can also prove to be extremely useful.

18.2.9 A comparison of the business cycle trends across the different industries in the South African economy

Table 18.1 shows the percentage change in turnover per industry between the September and December quarters of 2006 to 2012. This table provides an indication of trends within the covered industries. For example, mining and quarrying shows a decreasing trend. The negative percentage growth of 10.8% between the September and December 2008 quarters for the mining and quarrying industry can be attributed to a decrease in turnover due to a cut in production as a result of weak market conditions; a decrease in volumes sold and produced; a drop

Figure 18.9 Time series of percentage change in turnover and inventory between consecutive quarters for the real estate and other business services industry sector

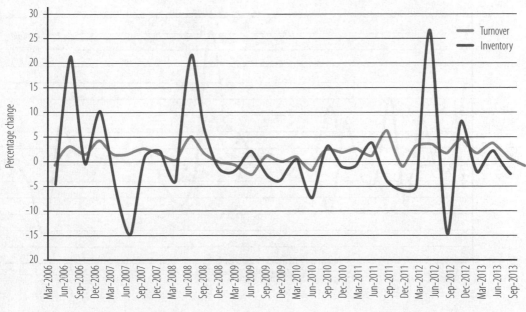

Source: Statistics South Africa (2014).

in the price of ore or alloy and average price of platinum group metals (PGMs); and the global economic slowdown linked to the recession.

Table 18.1 also shows that, over the years, there is generally a decrease in the electricity, gas, and water-supply industry between the September and December quarters, mainly due to reduced demand for electricity and lower industry production levels as some sectors shut down over the holiday period.

. The increasing trend reflected by the construction industry between these two quarters (with a peak in 2007) appears to be contracting from 2008 onwards. This trend line masks the increased activity in preparation for the 2010 Soccer World Cup. The low percentage change between September and December 2009 is attributable to market conditions the economy faced during 2008 and 2009 as well as a slowdown in projects for the 2010 World Cup as projects were being finalised.

Trade usually reflects high growth during the December quarter. The low percentage increase

during 2008 is due to the unfavourable economic climate as a result of the global recession.

Table 18.2 shows an overall increase in all industries of 2.8%, when comparing the turnover of the fourth quarter of 2012 to that of 2011.

As shown in Table 18.2, most sectors perform well in the comparative December quarters. With the exception of the 2008/9 December quarter suffering from the recession, many enterprises have higher turnovers to provide for the seasonal demand normally associated with the end of the calendar year.

As has been illustrated in this section, an awareness of the business cycle trends in the various sectors of the South African economy, as well as some understanding of their implications, can be enormously useful to the prospective entrepreneur. The next section looks more specifically at why an awareness and understanding of business cycles is so important to entrepreneurs and how entrepreneurs can apply this understanding to their business plans to ensure profitability.

Figure 18.10 Time series of percentage change in turnover and inventory between consecutive quarters for the community, social, and personal-services sector

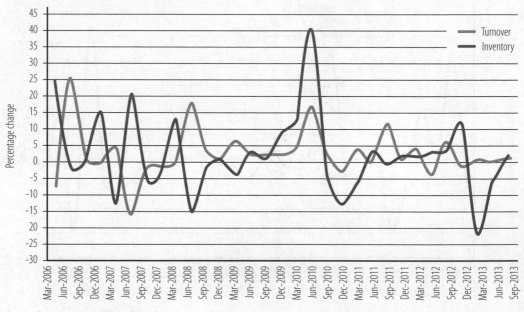

Source: Statistics South Africa (2014).

18.3 **Ensuring profitability during the different phases of the business cycle**

To ensure that their businesses remain profitable during different phases of the business cycle, entrepreneurs need a clear understanding of the effects of business cycles on the market and an awareness of broader trends in sectoral business cycles. Entrepreneurs then need to be able to apply this understanding and knowledge to their business plans to ensure that they are able to respond appropriately to the different phases of the business cycle.

18.3.1 **The relevance of business cycles to the entrepreneur**

An in-depth knowledge of business cycles is important to entrepreneurs for a variety of reasons. A failure to base business decisions on business cycles can often have disastrous consequences for entrepreneurs. An example of this is prospective entrepreneurs, who have been retrenched from their jobs during a recession, deciding to establish a business while the same recession is still underway, using the severance pay that they received from their erstwhile employers. The chance of such a new business taking off and growing during the said recession and the first phase of the recovery following the recession is very slim indeed. Other important consequences for entrepreneurs include, among others, differences during different phases of the business cycle in:

▶ The quantity of goods and services demanded
▶ The quality of goods and services demanded (buying down)
▶ The nature of goods and services demanded
▶ The types of business opportunities available (although opportunities are available during each phase).

In essence, many new entrepreneurs do not go into detail when venturing into new businesses. Many failures can be attributed to the lack of detail in business plans, business focus and mission, and goals to be achieved over the short, medium, and longer term.

The South African success story – *Clothing retailers* illustrates these points.

In addition to understanding how businesses are likely to be affected by different phases of the business cycle, entrepreneurs also need to be aware of broader industry trends across small, medium, and large enterprises.

SOUTH AFRICAN SUCCESS STORY

Clothing retailers
The large clothing retailers in South Africa have succeeded in diversifying their product ranges and services in such a manner that they benefit during all stages of the business cycle. During recessions, they conduct frequent sales, focus on cheaper non-branded goods, and ensure that they have a sufficiently large number of customers with loyalty and (or) in-house credit or retail cards who will use such credit facilities during lean times. During the recovery phase, they systematically limit the number of sales and step-up the availability of branded goods that will grow in demand as consumers have greater disposable incomes. During the peak and slump periods, marketing is stepped up to capture a maximum market share, and here especially from the sale of more expensive branded goods.

Table 18.1 Yearly percentage change in turnover per industry from September to December quarter, 2006 to 2012

INDUSTRY	SEPTEMBER 2006 – DECEMBER 2006	SEPTEMBER 2007 – DECEMBER 2007	SEPTEMBER 2008 – DECEMBER 2008	SEPTEMBER 2009 – DECEMBER 2009	SEPTEMBER 2010 – DECEMBER 2010	SEPTEMBER 2011 – DECEMBER 2011	SEPTEMBER 2012 – DECEMBER 2012
Mining and quarrying	-2.7	2.1	-10.8	-0.1	4.1	10.4	-1.3
Manufacturing	2.6	6.7	-7.3	10.0	5.4	6.8	2.6
Electricity, gas, and water supply	-18.6	-22.3	-25.2	-24.9	-26.1	-27.4	-28.3
Construction	3.7	6.5	-4.2	-0.7	-5.0	3.4	-4.9
Trade	5.4	8.3	0.8	8.1	9.1	8.1	5.7
Transport, storage, and communication	3.5	4.6	3.4	5.3	2.4	6.1	3.2
Real estate and other business services, excluding financial intermediation and insurance	5.9	1.2	-2.0	-1.8	2.0	-3.5	7.5
Community, social, and personal services, excluding government institutions	0.0	-1.7	1.0	2.3	-2.6	1.0	-1.5
All industries	3.3	5.5	-3.3	5.5	4.4	5.3	2.5

Source: Statistics South Africa (2013).

Table 18.2 Comparison of QFS turnover between the December quarters 2006 to 2012

INDUSTRY	DECEMBER 2006- DECEMBER 2007	DECEMBER 2007 – DECEMBER 2008	DECEMBER 2008 – DECEMBER 2009	DECEMBER 2009 – DECEMBER 2010	DECEMBER 2010 – DECEMBER 2011	DECEMBER 2011 – DECEMBER 2012
Mining and quarrying	23.9	26.7	-19.2	32.5	19.8	-8.3
Manufacturing	13.0	12.4	6.2	5.6	17.5	1.7
Electricity, gas, and water supply	-3.5	26.9	21.4	22.3	15.2	12.2
Construction	37.2	21.0	-3.8	-5.7	9.5	0.8
Trade	16.2	11.6	-12.4	12.7	17.4	1.6
Transport, storage, and communication	13.2	16.7	-3.6	7.0	17.3	4.2
Real estate and other business services, excluding financial intermediation and insurance	7.3	6.0	-11.6	0.0	11.3	20.4
Community, social, and personal services, excluding government institutions	-15.7	23.0	13.5	21.7	16.7	4.6
All industries	14.2	13.5	-5.3	9.4	16.7	2.8

Source: Statistics South Africa (2013).

18.3.2 **Industry turnover trends across different enterprise sizes**

Figure 18.11 reflects the **turnover** estimates for the small, medium and large enterprises within the trade industry as well as the total industry estimate for the quarters ending during December 2011 and March 2013. It appears that the industry trend is determined by the large enterprises; however, the distance between the two graphs indicates the spread of total turnover is across all size groups and not mainly large enterprises. As for the manufacturing, and electricity, gas, and water-supply industries, the small enterprises consistently reflect a greater contribution to total industry estimates than medium enterprises. The impact of smaller enterprises within the trade industry is expected to be greater than industries such as mining and quarrying due to the ease of entry.

> **DEFINITION**
>
> Turnover comprise the total sales of a specific enterprise over a predetermined period, i.e. annually or quarterly.

The trend of the real estate and business services industry as a whole is not determined solely by a particular size group as shown in Figure 18.12. This industry is characterised by various sectors and a large number of enterprises involved in a large variety of business activities (from real estate, renting of equipment and machinery to research and development activities, just to name a few). This industry includes the standard industrial classification of 'business activities not elsewhere classified' which results in a 'mixed bag' of enterprises and makes it difficult to analyse and determine the reasons for trends within the industry.

Figure 18.11 Time series of turnover for small, medium, and large enterprises within the trade industry

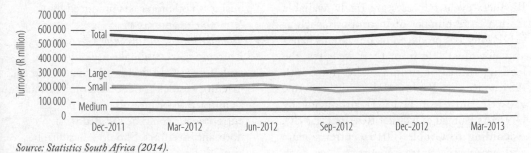

Source: Statistics South Africa (2014).

Figure 18.12 Time series of turnover for small, medium, and large enterprises within the real estate and other business-services industry

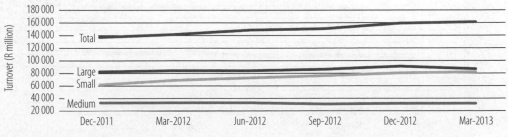

Source: Statistics South Africa (2014).

Figure 18.13 graphically reflects the trend of the community, social, and personal-services industry for small, medium and large enterprises as well as the industry as a whole. Large enterprises contribute the most to total turnover estimates for this industry. There does not appear to be much fluctuation in the trends in any of the categories. This could be due to the fact this industry is relatively small and, after electricity, gas, and water supply, is the second lowest contributor to all the industry turnover. Activities within this industry remain relatively constant and are not as volatile as the electricity, gas, and water-supply industry.

Entrepreneurs who are skilled at reading and understanding trends in business cycles in the different sectors of the economy will be better able to plan for the future. The next section explores how business cycle forecasts can be used in making business plans.

18.3.3 Incorporating business cycle forecasts into business plans

Business cycle forecasts are freely available from a large number of institutions, such as GDP forecasts produced by the various banks and downloadable from their websites, the leading indicator produced by the South African Reserve Bank, and the early economic growth indicator (EEGI) produced by UNISA's Bureau of Market Research (BMR). According to Gruble (2010), entrepreneurs and prospective entrepreneurs can use such

information in a variety of ways to optimise business success, namely:

▶ *To anticipate changes in demand and supply of goods and services.* This is required to ensure that the entrepreneur is not caught unprepared for changes in the business cycle. An example of this is the fact that many businesses globally failed to prepare for the 2008 to 2009 global contraction of business activities giving rise to many businesses having to sell or close down.

▶ *To realign capital overheads* so that scarcer capital resources could be used to ensure that the business survives while creditors are paid. During times of economic contraction, entrepreneurs need to decide whether they cut back on capital spending or increase it to gain first mover advantage during the upturn that will follow. In order for an entrepreneur to make a good decision in this regard, he or she needs to know how long the contraction will be and what form the upturn will take. Such information could be obtained from business cycle forecasts produced by reputable economists.

▶ *To make important inventory decisions.* Entrepreneurs can make use of business cycle forecasts to decide whether to add to inventory (stock) or cut back on it. Should a contraction be around the corner, an entrepreneur could be saddled with dormant inventory. Should an upturn be around the corner and inventories have

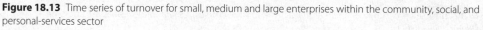

Figure 18.13 Time series of turnover for small, medium and large enterprises within the community, social, and personal-services sector

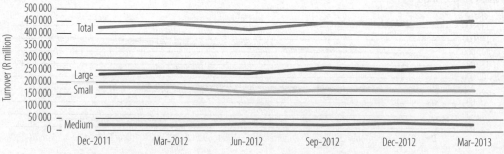

Source: Statistics South Africa (2014).

EXAMPLE 18.1

Quarterly Financial Statistics: Business size

The QFS is based substantially on larger businesses (referred to as size group 1 companies), comprising 56% of the sample, while the remaining portion of the sample consists of smaller-sized enterprises (12% size group 2, 13% size group 3 and 19% size group 4). Enterprises are allocated a size cut-off as small, medium or large according to the dti allocation points as adjusted for the QFS which are applied to the value-added tax (VAT) turnover as reported by an enterprise. These size allocation points differ across the various industries covered by the QFS, for example a large enterprise operating in the mining and quarrying sector has a reported VAT turnover above R273 million while a large enterprise operating in the transport sector has a reported VAT turnover above R182 million. Additional disaggregated information regarding estimates of small, medium and large enterprises by industry per variable is available on the Stats SA website.

Aggregate data is presented in the QFS statistical release. Tables containing disaggregated data (i.e. data broken down into small, medium and large estimates), are made available in addition to the QFS release.

In the QFS, disaggregated data has been extrapolated from aggregated data and divided and broken down into smaller size categories. This data is a critical step to gaining increased knowledge from collective data. Fully

Figure 18.14 March 2013: Per industry, small, medium and large distribution

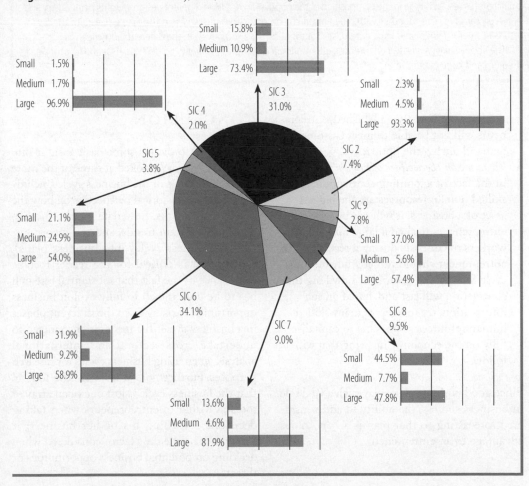

disaggregated data helps to expose hidden trends within the different enterprise size categories that may not be seen from aggregated data.

Disaggregating data is important to reveal patterns that can be masked by larger, aggregate data. Looking specifically at sub-populations can help make sure that resources are spent on the areas where they are most needed and can have the biggest impact. Perhaps most importantly, disaggregated data can help in making wiser future data analysis decisions.

The total turnover of all industries for the first quarter of 2013 was estimated at R1 615 032 million (R1.62 trillion), and the revised fourth quarter of 2012 was estimated at R1 659 654 million (R1.66 trillion). Large enterprises represented more than 68% of total turnover for both the December 2012 and March 2013 quarters while medium and small enterprises represented 9% and 23% respectively.

Figure 18.14 above indicates the small, medium and large enterprises March 2013 turnover estimates as distributed per industry. The manufacturing and trade industries represent the largest sectors contributing to the total industry turnover of R1 615 032 million, as estimated for the quarter ending March 2013.

The trade sector's estimated turnover for the quarter ending March 2013 indicates that large enterprises contributed 58.9% to total trade turnover while medium and small contributed 9.2% and 31.9% respectively. The manufacturing industry indicated that larger enterprises contributed 73.4%, followed by small (15.8%) and medium enterprises (10.9%).

Because the entire population is not surveyed, the published estimates are subject to weights in the medium to small enterprises. A change in the composition of the population results in different design weights per industry and between samples. This together with different dti cut-off points per industry and the actual nature of the sector results in small, medium and large enterprises contributing at various levels in the different industries.

The above analysis is based on turnover; other estimated variables may reflect different trends and level of small, medium and large contribution.

not been sufficiently replenished, entrepreneurs will not be able to meet customers' demand during the upturn.

▸ *To decide on the welfare of human resources* in the face of a looming contraction. Since skilled human resources are the biggest asset of a business, it will not be wise for entrepreneurs to shed a large number of workers to cut costs during a recession. An entrepreneur should rather study business cycle forecasts to determine how long the contraction will last and, based on such information, try to keep as many skilled human resources as possible to capitalise fully on the economic upswing that will follow.

Since good business plans play such a vital role in business success, the ability to add considered forecasting to that plan is an enormous advantage to an entrepreneur.

CONCLUSION

This chapter provided some basic insight into business cycles. We looked at some of the more pertinent aspects of the business cycle (including its nature, historical perspective on how the mechanism works, how data can be used to determine certain trends, and the incorporation of business cycles into business plans). However, it is critical for the reader to take cognisance of the fact that substantial research has to be undertaken to fully exploit business opportunities arising from the different phases in a business cycle. The reader is encouraged to undertake cross-sectoral and international analysis when using business cycles for research purposes. Furthermore, it is imperative to note that the business cycle is just one of an array of tools available to entrepreneurs when taking decisions regarding his or her business; it should not be the only factor considered when deciding on potential business opportunities or threats.

SELF-ASSESSMENT QUESTIONS

Multiple-choice questions

1. How many stages are there in the business cycle?
   a. Three
   b. Four
   c. Five
   d. Six
2. In South Africa, business cycles are tracked using two variables, namely:
   a. Retail growth and personal consumption expenditure
   b. Output growth and business confidence
   c. Turnover and inventories
   d. Output growth and inflation
3. Business cycles have important consequences for entrepreneurs, namely:
   a. The value, brand names, and quality of goods and services demanded differ during different phases of the business cycle
   b. The quantity, value, and usability of goods and services demanded differ during different phases of the business cycle
   c. The quantity, nature, and quality of goods and services demanded differ during different phases of the business cycle
   d. The usability, nature, and brand names of goods and services demanded differ during different stages of the business cycle
4. The reason business cycle forecasts are conducted is:
   a. To plan changes in demand and supply of goods and services
   b. To realign capital overheads so that more widely available capital resources could be used to ensure that the business survives while creditors are paid
   c. To make important sales decisions
   d. To decide on the welfare of human resources in the face of a looming contraction
5. To optimise business success, entrepreneurs should:
   a. Increase their own knowledge of business cycles and use such knowledge to strategise for optimal success during the different stages of the business cycle
   b. Only obtain business cycle information when required
   c. Look at the ways in which other businesses have coped with the different stages of the business cycle and emulate their best practices
   d. Make full use of business consultants or advisors to formulate plans for them on how to cope with the different stages of the business cycle

DISCUSSION QUESTIONS

1. What is meant by the term 'business cycles'?
2. Identify the phases of the business cycle.
3. How would you describe the historical business cycle trajectory in South Africa?
4. Would you say that the business cycles found in the various sectors differ from each other? Provide evidence for your answer.
5. Why are business cycles relevant to entrepreneurs and prospective entrepreneurs?
6. How can entrepreneurs ensure profitability during the different phases of the business cycles by making use of their knowledge of business cycles?
7. How should entrepreneurs incorporate business cycle forecasts in their business plans?
8. Describe how entrepreneurs can make use of sectoral business cycles to optimise their business success in the sector they are operating in.
9. Describe how you would identify business opportunities using business cycle information.

EXPERIENTIAL EXERCISE

Visit a business centre in your area and explain that you are working on an experiential project as part of an entrepreneurship course. Enquire from at least three business owners how they optimise business success by using their knowledge of business cycles. Your enquiry could also be done telephonically (by phoning businesses listed in a telephone directory) or online (via social networking websites, email, or a web-based discussion forum).

During your interviews:

1. Enquire whether business owners take business cycles into account in their business planning, and if 'yes', ask how they do so.

2. Find out whether they:
   a. Continually improve their knowledge of the economy and business cycles
   b. Follow economic and business trends
   c. Identify new business opportunities and (or) market segments by making use of such information

GAVIN PETERS STARTS A NEW BUSINESS

Gavin Peters is by nature not a risk taker at all. He likes to play it safe as far as humanly possible. He was born in a Karoo town, the son of a hotel clerk. His father's father was a farm worker who went out of his way to encourage his son to complete his secondary education and to obtain an office job away from the farm. Gavin's father in turn encouraged him to complete both secondary and tertiary studies and saved wherever possible to ensure that his son would have sufficient money to pursue university studies.

Gavin was fascinated by all the 'fancy stuff' the accountant did at the hotel where his father worked and decided to study accountancy after school. He completed his BCom in accounting and decided to work for a bank. His idea was to possibly return to university later to study for an honours degree in Accountancy and the Certificate in the Theory of Accountancy (CTA). These qualifications, after clerkship and the Chartered Accountancy (CA) examination, would allow him to register as a CA. He never got to study further because his job at the bank kept him very busy and he got married young leaving him with marital and later family duties that kept him very busy. He did not complain, though, because his salary and married life was good. However, the business cycle turned his fortunes around. During the 2008 to 2009 economic recession, his bank had to lay off a large number of employees to cut costs due to lower growth in banking incomes. Gavin was unfortunately one of the bank employees affected by layoffs and lost his job during the third wave of layoffs at the bank. Since he had survived the first two waves of layoffs, he had assumed that his job was safe. The worst for him was that other employers were retrenching rather than hiring, making it very difficult for him to obtain another job.

While Gavin was job hunting his wife had another idea. She encouraged Gavin to set up his own accounting business. He, however, disagreed with his wife and did not think it wise to set up a costly high-risk business in the middle of a recession. While Gavin was slowly slipping into desperation and hopelessness, his wife advertised Gavin's accounting services in the local papers. To Gavin and his wife's amazement, they found that the recession created a new type of client, namely deeply indebted people who urgently needed financial advice. While he had thought that there would only be business opportunities during the upswing and peak phases of the business cycle, it became clear that there were different accounting clients during the different phases of the business cycle.

Gavin did not actually make a conscious choice to become an entrepreneur and to quit looking for jobs. In his mind, he was only taking on accounting clients because he had to survive financially until there was an economic upswing and he could get another job. As the economic recovery continued and his services became more widely known he found his client base expanding rapidly. As the economic recovery continued he found that an increasing number of clients came to him for general accounting and tax services. Having started his business during an economic slump, he realised the importance of diversifying his service range right from the start to ensure that he would be able to attract sufficient clients during all four phases of the business cycle.

1. Based on the contents of this chapter and case study above, what would you advise Gavin Peters to do to make his new venture even more business-cycle friendly?

CASE STUDY

2. Would you say that it was wise for Gavin to start a business during a slump? If you were to start a new venture during a slump, how would you mitigate against business failure?

3. What benefits might Gavin Peters' accounting and tax-services business derive during the different phases of the business cycle?

SUGGESTED WEBSITE LINKS

Bureau for Economic Research (University of Stellenbosch): www.ber.ac.za

Bureau of Market Research (Unisa): www.unisa.ac.za/bmr

Google Scholar: www.google.com/scholar

Investopedia: www.investopedia.com

International Monetary Fund: www.Imf.org

South African National Treasury: www.treasury.gov.za

South African Reserve Bank: www.resbank.co.za

Statistics South Africa: www.statssa.gov.za

World Bank: www.worldbank.org

REFERENCES

Gruble, C. 2010. The challenge that is the business cycle, 8 February 2010. [Online]. Available: http://www.articlesbase.com/business-articles/the-challenge-that-isthe-business-cycle-1832682.html [4 August 2011].

South African Reserve Bank. 2014. Research/statistics database. [Online]. Available: www.resbank.co.za.

Statistics South Africa. 2013. *Quarterly financial statistics: December 2012 and Quarterly financial statistics online database*. Pretoria: Statistics South Africa.

Statistics South Africa. 2014. *Quarterly financial statistics: September 2013 and Quarterly financial statistics online database*. Pretoria: Statistics South Africa.

CHAPTER 19

Managing growth and harvesting

Elana Swanepoel

LEARNING OUTCOMES

On completion of this chapter you will be able to:
▸ Identify the barriers to and motivators for enterprise growth
▸ Describe the growth path through the business life cycle
▸ Differentiate between generic, internal and external growth strategies
▸ Explore the entrepreneurial orientation towards growth
▸ Discuss growing the business from a marketing, financial, management and planning perspective
▸ Evaluate harvesting and harvesting options.

OPENING CASE STUDY

Sipho noticed how much time and money his three sisters were spending on manicuring and painting their nails and decided to open a nail salon. He borrowed money from his uncle and opened his first nail salon three years ago. It was located in Johannesburg, in a Northern suburbs mall. The nail salon was an instant success as it was the only one in the mall, situated in an affluent community. He employed four well-trained nail technicians. The feedback from the customers indicated that they were highly satisfied with the courteous and professional service. About a year later, he invested the profits from the first nail salon into a second, again in a mall in Johannesburg and again it was a success. He now had eight nail technicians and two cleaners working for him and a part-time bookkeeper. In the third year he decided to open a nail salon in his hometown, Nelspruit, the first and only nail

salon. He also opened one next to a shopping mall, near the University of Johannesburg, targeting the students and university staff.

The growth in Nelspruit was disappointing. Although he had only appointed two nail technicians in Nelspruit, not enough customers used the services to cover all the costs. He had overestimated the market in Nelspruit. Although his was the only nail salon in Nelspruit, he subsequently found out that some of the hairdressers offered manicures at the hairdressing salons. It seemed customers preferred their nails to be manicured at the hairdressing salons. His fourth nail salon faced other challenges such as frequent power outages and he did not have a generator. The salons in the malls were not affected by power outages because the malls had their own generators. Then the malls decided to increase the monthly rent by 20%, much more than the

estimated budgeted amount. In addition, his uncle recalled the loan.
1. Was Sipho over ambitious in growing his business?
2. Did Sipho determine customer needs and wants in Nelspruit prior to opening a nail salon there?
3. Why did Sipho not start paying back his uncle when he showed a profit?
4. Does Sipho have any contingency plans in place for unforeseen problems?

INTRODUCTION

It is assumed that you have passed through the start-up phase of creating or recognising, shaping and successfully seizing an opportunity and that your business is registered and starting to show a profit. For a couple of years you may just have been surviving, with your business showing some growth. Now it is time for higher growth. However, not all entrepreneurs are interested in growing their business. They cannot be called entrepreneurs as the definition of entrepreneurship implies creating, enhancing and pursuing opportunities that offer long-term customer value. Thus, it implies the building of a sustainable business with a positive cash flow and expansion possibilities.

In this chapter we will briefly explore the barriers to enterprise development and the internal and external motivations for business growth. Growth will be contextualised in the business life cycle. This will be followed by the discussion of the generic growth strategies, organic and external growth strategies. For those ready to grow the business, the attributes required of the entrepreneur will be discussed. Four critical business areas that need focused attention when embarking on rapid growth, namely, marketing, financing, management and planning are explored in detail. The chapter concludes with a discussion of harvesting the business. We first investigate the reasons why an entrepreneur would consider harvesting and then discuss the various harvesting options available.

19.1 Barriers to enterprise growth

Many entrepreneurs are not interested in growing their companies and prefer a lifestyle to a growth strategy. Some of the reasons are rooted in the entrepreneurs themselves, such as internal motivation, commitment, skill and knowledge issues. One of the reasons is attitudinal – they feel that they do not have the required expertise or skills. Some entrepreneurs value their independence and ownership control, which would be diminished through external equity investment. Some entrepreneurs fear that the pursuit of a growth strategy may attract the interest of larger competitors who may try to take over their company. In such a case, either the entrepreneur may lose total control or be expected to manage a larger company with several employees – to such responsibility the entrepreneur does not aspire, or may not deem him/herself to be capable of. However, many barriers to growth are perceived to be in the external environment, with the most critical being lack of finance, no market demand growth and increasing competition. In spite of these barriers to growth, internal and external motivations for growth exist.

19.2 Internal and external motivations for growth

A number of internal and external reasons for growth have been identified by Westhead, Wright and McElwee (2011:241):

▸ *Internal entrepreneur* (and family) motivations. To satisfy an entrepreneur's need for achievement; to increase an entrepreneur's desire for control and independence; to generate a store of wealth for the entrepreneur and his or her family; to provide employment positions for family members; to ensure the survival of an independent firm that can be transferred to the next generation of family members; to spread risks across products/services and/or markets; and to make a contribution to the development of the local community where the entrepreneur lives.

▸ *External motivations*. To increase the status and legitimacy of the owner(s) and the firm in social and business networks; to ensure external resources are leveraged to address the liabilities of newness and small size; to proactively consider current and future competitive threats; and a growth and competitiveness focus that enables the firm to adapt and to remain competitive irrespective of market, technological and/or regulatory conditions.

Irrespective of the motivation for growth, the process of growth would need to be managed. When does business growth take place – at which stages of the business life cycle?

19.3 Growth and the business life cycle

The growth of a company is a continuous process as it passes through its **business life cycle**.

> **DEFINITION**
>
> The business life cycle is defined as the sequence of developmental stages that all businesses pass through during a life span.

The rate of growth varies as the company passes through the five phases of the business life cycle:

Stage 1: Nascent stage. Research and development takes place in this emergent stage during which the business idea is developed into a business opportunity following a thorough feasibility study. At this stage it is critical to clarify the value proposition that will satisfy the customers' needs and wants and determine the potential market size for the company's products and services. This stage could last a few months or even years, but the ideal is to start the business after 18 months of investigation and due diligence. During this stage no growth is recorded.

Stage 2: Start-up stage. The company establishes its existence. The business is in operation but marketing, operations and finance need further development. During this stage the risk that is relevant is termed the liability of newness, which refers to the lack of knowledge from two perspectives: by the owners about their business and by the customers about the new business (Katz & Green, 2011). This stage lasts about two to three years but it could drag on. During this stage the lead entrepreneur and the selected team make every effort to place the company on a growth trajectory. As sales and profits increase it contributes to customer, supplier, investor and banker confidence in the business. The owners should consider developing manufacturing or supplier strategic alliances.

Stage 3: Rapid growth stage. During this stage the company should show consistently improved financial performance and rising sales. The growth takes off, and is continually increasing, even exponentially. Especially for high-tech companies, this is the harvest point as it allows for the greatest leverage for selling out. During the rapid growth stage the role of the entrepreneur changes from taking full responsibility for all activities to delegating responsibility to employees. Some of the challenges are to finance large orders, operational capacity and management effectiveness. The company has to ensure that it grows at least at the same rate as the market opportunities. The profits are reinvested in the company to hire personnel and expand operations. However, it is maintained that it is during this stage that most of the new venture failures occur.

Stage 4: Maturity stage. This stage is characterised by a steady growth in sales and profits that can contribute to complacency on the part of the entrepreneur and management. After years of servicing customers, the company may take them for granted. This could result in the loss of such customers should a competitor offer them better products or prices or more personal service. How do you avoid customer complacency? This will be addressed in a subsequent section.

Stage 5: Stability stage. During this stage the growth can start declining, unless new products or services are developed to extend the company life cycle. The challenge is to extend the product/service life cycle through innovation.

To stay small is in most instances not an option as a company is more vulnerable when it is small. To overcome the various challenges experienced during the growth of the company will be addressed in subsequent sections. What possible growth strategies exist?

19.4 Generic growth strategies

As entrepreneurs immerse themselves in the establishment and development of the company, they formulate their vision and the accompanying growth strategy for the business. The entrepreneurs decide what type of business they prefer with regard to the speed of growth and the level of growth. The entrepreneur can choose among four generic growth strategies (Katz & Green 2011:641):

▸ *Lifestyle or part-time company*. These businesses stay small and make enough profit to supplement the income of the owner, but not enough to cover living expenses. The growth in these businesses stabilise when the owner has learnt the basics of managing the business. About half of all small businesses fall within this category.

▸ *Traditional small business*. These include the smallest full-time businesses and often consist of single site operations. The business generates enough profit to sustain the owner and his/her family. Growth of these businesses tends to level off once the operations have been standardised. About a quarter of small businesses fall in this category.

▸ *High-performance small business*. These businesses grow between 5% and 15% per annum often by adding multiple locations, increasing the staff compliment and through higher levels of professionalisation. They focus on maximising their profitability over the longer term. Their growth levels off and they remain manageably small. About one fifth of all businesses fall within this category.

▸ *High-growth ventures*. These companies grow at 25% or more per annum. Their goal is to become a big business. They pursue high levels of professionalisation and require external funding. About 5% of all businesses fall in this category.

ENTREPRENEURIAL DILEMMA

Battle with the big guys

Background information: Blue Label was started by Mark and Brett Levy in South Africa in 2001 after obtaining a national licence to sell prepaid airtime for Telkom. Since 2003 the company has been on a growth-by-acquisition path. In 2011 the following article appeared at the time the market capitalisation value of Blue Label was R17 billion.

Blue Label is currently experiencing a strained relationship with shareholders and partners – namely, Microsoft and Telkom. Microsoft acquired a 12% equity stake in Blue Label Telecoms around the same time the group listed in 2007. An agreement was also put in place for strategic collaboration and preferred partnerships between the Redmons software giant and the South African distribution firm.

However, rumours have surfaced about a breakdown in that relationship. Joint Blue Label CEO Mark Levy confirmed that the relations are strained in areas but has not broken down completely. 'To explain what happened with Microsoft we need to go back to how we view a partnership and how they do. The problem in those big organisations is that you get lost. Because they are so big you do not necessarily get the relationship you want. There is no real common alignment from a strategic point of view – and that is where we battle with Microsoft. We know what we want, we know where we are going – it has not changed. But we are not sure if we fulfil what their strategy is', Levy says. 'So, I would say the relationship is strained from a strategic point of view: what value we can add to them, and vice versa'.

There is a possibility Microsoft will end its relationship with Blue Label and possibly disinvest. Levy says it would be a pity if that happened, but that Blue Label is not dependent on Microsoft. 'We did not create dependencies on anyone but ourselves. So if Microsoft had to end the relationship tomorrow there is actually no inter-company dependencies – bar the licence you buy over the counter.

I think we both could get more out of the relationship. We are seeing it dilute – not breakdown. I think we have missed out on opportunities, on both sides. So we will have to work it out. But for us there was life before and there will be life beyond. We have become a very self-sufficient organisation'. Levy adds if Blue Label and Microsoft work out their difference they would need to extrapolate more value from each other.

Another potential setback Blue Label has suffered is in Nigeria, where it had an exclusive contractual relationship with troubled Telkom subsidiary Multi-links. Blue Label's Nigerian subsidiary, Africa Prepaid Services signed a 10-year agreement with Multi-links in 2008 that was cancelled last year. Telkom had been trying to renegotiate the contract and outgoing interim Telkom CEO Jeffrey Hedberg claimed Multi-links would not survive unless the agreement could be restructured.

Multi-links is a telecoms company that provides CDMA voice and data services in Nigeria, as opposed to the GEM technology used by most other operators. Blue Label had exclusive rights to distribute those services, but Multi-links announced last year it would be exiting the CDMA market. The effective termination of the agreement is something Blue Label views as unlawful and is pursuing the matter legally.

But Brett and Mark Levy are adamant they will ultimately succeed in Nigeria. Says Mark Levy: 'We had an interesting agreement with Multi-links and we did not think it delivered on its contract and we have now cancelled the contract after a lengthy debate with them. Ultimately, we will head off to arbitration to tell us who's right or wrong'.

He continuous: 'Our game plan in Nigeria was always bigger than Multi-links … what the Multi-links thing did for us was to speed up what we need to do: we need to deliver a technical solution. What existed in Multi-links historically was very paper-driven. Over the coming months we are rolling out thousands of point-of-sale devices in that region and I think Nigeria poses a massive opportunity for this group'.

Levy's argument is that the Multi-links contract was structured on commission for Blue Label, the more business it brings to Multi-links, the more money BLT makes. He says there might well be a short-term earnings blip on the radar due the Telkom breakdown. 'It's just sad we have such a disruption for nothing'.

1. Which growth strategies did Blue Label incorporate in growing their firm?
2. Should Blue Label have entered into alliances with Microsoft and Telkom?
3. What were the initial advantages of entering into such alliances?
4. Will Blue Label exit unscathed from their agreements with Microsoft and Telkom?

Source: Dingle (2011:18–19).

Whatever your preferred growth strategy your business has to grow, whether at 5% or 25%. To purposely grow a business, basically different strategies can be followed as detailed in the next section.

19.5 Growth strategies

Growth strategies can be divided into two categories, namely internal and external (Nieman & Nieuwenhuizen, 2014:310). Internal growth strategies refer to organic growth whereby the entrepreneur innovatively combines resources to expand the market of the business. The following are internal growth strategies:

▸ Investment is required for new product development, market share increase and expansion to new locations.
▸ Exclusive agreements with customers, means that your company will be the only supplier of the product or service. For example, Carlson Wagonlit Travel has an exclusive agreement with South African Breweries, and no other travel company may be used by South African Breweries staff for official travel arrangements.
▸ Licensing refers to the agreement whereby the creator of a product allows other companies to manufacture the product under licence and sell it.
▸ Alliances can be defined as the 'agreements between independent organizations who work together under an incomplete contract' (Reuer, Ariño & Ollk, 2011:6). In the 'dilemma' case, the company Blue Label had alliance agreements with Microsoft and Telkom.
▸ Dealerships refer to manufacturers supplying products to dealers for sale. For example, Toyota manufactures motor vehicles that are then sold through a dealership network.
▸ Franchising, the concept incorporates several types of franchising of which the best known is business format franchising.

For example, Nandos is a franchisor that has sold many business format franchises.

In the case of external growth strategies, the entrepreneur considers companies operating in its value chain, in other words, suppliers, customers or competitors with a view to acquire or collaborate. The entrepreneur could consider mergers, acquisitions or joint ventures:

▸ Mergers and acquisitions. An acquisition refers to the complete absorption of a company by the acquiring company. During a merger two companies become one and develop a new corporate name.
▸ Joint ventures involve two separate companies that agree to cooperate as partners for the purpose of sharing expertise, such as technology.

Each company would have to evaluate the growth options and select the most appropriate to the product and services, financial capability and long-term strategy of the company. The question arises: Does the entrepreneur have a growth orientation to drive a growth strategy?

19.6 Entrepreneur's growth orientation

Growth strategies can only be effective if they are supported and driven by the lead entrepreneur. It is thus necessary to ascertain the orientation and fears of the lead entrepreneur concerning growth.

It has already been established that entrepreneurs should have the following seven attitudes and behaviours: commitment and determination; courage; leadership; opportunity obsession; tolerance of risk, ambiguity and uncertainty; creativity, self-reliance and adaptability; and motivation to excel (Spinelli and Adams, 2012).

An entrepreneur with a growth orientation embraces calculated risk and knows that growth is generated by increasing the sales through

ENTREPRENEURIAL DILEMMA

Bringing in experience – Systems lead to success

When little-known private equity firm, Mayibuye, took over troubled, listed micro-lending firm, Blue Financial Services, it seemed a case of throwing good money after bad. Blue Financial Services had dug itself into a deep hole after a combination of rapid growth during boom years and poor financial controls and systems saw it lending but not conducting correct credit vetting or making collections. Money was going out the door but not coming back – a guaranteed death knell for businesses of any shape or size. In Blue's case, it crippled the business and turned a multi-billion rand company into one fighting for survival. During the financial crisis, businesses riding on the back of rampant growth found themselves floundering when growth and business volumes dried up.

While it is too early to pronounce it an out-and-out turnaround success, Mayibuye believes it has returned some order to the micro-lending business by bringing in established people, systems and skills from other companies in its stable.

'If you look at everything that went wrong with Blue, those were areas where the rest of Mayibuye had developed skills and technology specifically for those problems', says CEO Johan Meiring. For this reason he believes Blue will ultimately prove to be a good fit for the group.

Whether your business is listed on the JSE or is a one-person start-up, systems are important to help you as you grow. Entrepreneurs we spoke to say they were so busy trying to do business they often allowed systems to lapse – or in many cases never even had them in place. Many were so taken up with chasing potential business or servicing clients they were not sure they were actually making money and any growth was constrained by the number of hours they put in each day.

Leading international business coach, Brad Sugars, highlights the importance of using systems to change that situation. He has developed a number of rules to help entrepreneurs measure the success of their various initiatives, including advertising.

'From the day I started my newsletter, World Money Analyst, in 1974, I have kept detailed results of every ad and promotion I have run'. Sugars provided an example of a business he consulted where 90% of the sales were being generated by just 10% of the adverts. By eliminating the 90% that were not working and doubling up on the ads that were, the entrepreneur was able to spend smarter and focus on the parts of the business that were thriving.

A word of advice from the Business Partners SME (small and medium enterprises) toolkit perhaps sums up the situation best and gives entrepreneurs some food for thought: 'If the business owner understands why the business landed up in a situation where desperate measures are needed to rescue it from failure, then half the battle is already won. Too often the business owner screams for help when it is too late. It is a sad fact that more often than not the writing is on the wall, but the business owner is oblivious to those facts and carries on in the hope that things might improve.'

1. Should Mayibuye have taken over troubled, listed micro-lending firm, Blue Financial Services?
2. What contributed to the failure of Blue Financial Services?
3. What skills did Mayibuye have that could contribute to a turnaround of Blue Financial Services?
4. Why is it important to have proper systems and rules in place when growing a company?

Source: Adapted from Finweek (2011:49).

delivering a value proposition satisfying an increasing number of needs and wants of customers. The entrepreneur focuses on quality; first of all quality of product and service, supported by quality personnel who care. The entrepreneur understands that growth is the result of an innovative culture and high performance teams. They view problems as opportunities and are not bogged down by operational issues and financial controls. They deeply believe that they can succeed despite difficulties.

Do you have such a growth orientation or do you perhaps have a fear of success? Some research has isolated the fear of success on the part of the lead entrepreneur as a cause of business failure (Arkebauer, 1993:67). You may have a fear of success because you do not believe that you are worth it. Or, you are afraid that your inadequacies with regard to business capability will be revealed. Procrastination can be a sign of a fear of success. Low self-esteem is considered to be the root cause of a fear of success, coupled to not knowing what you want out of life. To overcome the fear of success you need to understand who you really are, not what you perceive yourself to be. You need to mentally counteract any self-defeating thoughts. From a base of self-trust, face the challenges/problems, but not necessarily on your own. Use your teams or consult experts outside the company. Part of self-discipline is allowing others to contribute to a team effort.

Now that you have a realistic concept of your potential, know that you are worth being successful and that success is a team effort and manageable, the 'how' of growing a business can be explored.

19.7 Growing the business

When you embark on growing your business, an integrative approach is required. You should consider the marketing, finances, management and planning simultaneously, explained in greater detail in the next sections.

19.7.1 Marketing practices to grow the business

As explained in the chapter on marketing, the point of departure is always the customers' needs and wants. When you started your business you had to create or recognise, shape and successfully seize an opportunity. The same applies when you plan to grow your business as you need to grow the customer base by either providing high value-added or value-created products and services to existing customers, or by increasing the number of new customers. From meaningful customer communication

and observation, you can establish how to solve or eliminate a problem that customers are experiencing and for which they are willing to pay. Customers' needs and wants are not static, but change with technological development and environmental changes.

Products and services
You should consider the range of products and services that would address the customers expanding and changing needs and wants. With regard to products and services, Spinelli and Adams (2012:117) have summarised the 'leading marketing practices of high-growth companies':

▸ Deliver products and services that are perceived as highest quality to expanding segments.
▸ Cultivate pace-setting new products and services that stand out in the market as best of the breed.
▸ Deliver product and service benefits that demand average or higher market pricing.
▸ Generate revenue flows from existing products and services that typically sustain approximately 90% of the present revenue base, while achieving flows from new products and services that typically expand revenue approximately 20% annually.
▸ Create high-impact, new product and service improvements with development expenditures that typically account for no more than approximately 6% of revenues.
▸ Rapidly develop broad product and service platforms with complementary channels to help expand a firm's geographic marketing area.
▸ Generate revenue flows from existing customers that typically sustain approximately 80% of the ongoing revenue base, while achieving flows from new customers that typically expand revenue approximately 30% annually.
▸ Depending on the nature of the product or service, utilise a high-yield sales force that typically accounts for approximately 60% of marketing expenditures.

Market structure

The structure of the market is determined by the number of potential customers (buyers), number of competitors (sellers), the size of the competitors, the degree of differentiation of products, conditions of market entry and exit, cost conditions and price-demand elasticity. For rapid growth the ideal would be a large number of potential customers, few competitors with none dominating the market, and substantial product differentiation.

To differentiate your company in your existing market, you need to look for gaps in customer needs and wants which are not filled by competitors or to which you could add new dimensions. If no gaps exist, you may have to create new products or services for this market. Alternatively, you may move into other lucrative markets. A market that is fragmented and imperfect or an emerging market would contain market niches that you could explore. Markets that should be avoided are those that are highly concentrated (a few major suppliers) or perfectly competitive (many suppliers, e.g. the airline industry), mature (no new developments) or declining (demand is decreasing).

Market size and growth rate

If you are selling to a market that is large and growing at about 20% per annum, you can grow your business, provided your share of the market does not threaten the major players in the market. You should not incur the wrath of the dominant competitors as they probably have sufficient cash to start a price war and force you to exit the market. When a market grows between 30% to 50%, niches emerge which can be served by new ventures. Often the major players are not interested in serving such niches and thus the new ventures are not seen to be a threat to the major supplier(s). If you can capture a high market share (about 70%) in the niche market, your company becomes a high-potential company in which investors will be interested.

Geographic expansion

If you started your business providing products and services in one specific town, your growth strategy could include opening branches in other towns in the same province, then in other provinces and eventually across the borders and the oceans (internationally). Each additional business location that you choose should be preceded by a thorough market analysis to ensure that the market demand exists, and that promotional strategies approach customers in a way that is acceptable to them. The latter is of particular importance when you expand your business across borders. The cultural differences may require that the branding be adjusted to comply with local values, tastes and laws. For example, when South African Breweries decided to sell beer in Russia, extensive research was conducted to determine an acceptable and desirable beer taste and impactful branding.

Once you have settled on the product and service growth strategy, financing needs should be addressed.

19.7.2 **Financial practices to grow the business**

In growing a business, cash is needed for marketing, equipment, inventory and additional staff. However, the cash should preferably be low-risk money; available as soon as possible and as much as is needed. These three basic principles are often ignored by the entrepreneur and management team because of a lack of expertise in financial analysis and understanding its relationship to strategy and management. The financial statements *per se* are not sufficient to inform the entrepreneur, unless the latter can identify the interdependencies between business decisions and financial structure. Such a lack of financial know-how can have dire results for the company.

In the quest for finance, the entrepreneur first has to come to terms with the financial nature of the small business:

▶ Cash flow and cash is essential for entrepreneurial finance.
▶ Timing is critical as the time periods for financial payments and transfers are shorter and more compressed. The business is subject to volatile swings from high to low to high.
▶ Capital market theories, such as the capital asset pricing model, do not apply to small companies.
▶ The high-potential entrepreneur requires not only the best possible deal but the investor who can add value in terms of knowledge, experience and guidance.
▶ Rather than a 'take-all-you-can-get' approach, the wise entrepreneur would opt for staged capital commitments whereby money is committed in stages linked to results. Such an approach contributes to the setting of realistic growth targets to the benefit of both the entrepreneur and the investor.
▶ Valuation methods, such as discounted cash flow, and financial ratios used to evaluate established companies do not provide accurate valuations of smaller unlisted companies. Instead, real value contributors are mostly intangible such as the inherent knowledge of the entrepreneur, the specialists, the management team and the network of relationships.

When the need for additional capital for business growth has been assessed and quantified, the entrepreneur can either use equity capital or debt capital.

Equity capital

DEFINITION

Equity capital is money given to the business in exchange for part ownership of the business.

Equity can be provided by the entrepreneur or others. Usually the entrepreneur is the first source of financing the business. If the entrepreneur does not have sufficient cash to finance the growth strategy, he or she may approach others, such as family members, friends, business angels, venture capitalists, public stock offerings or direct public offerings. All of them expect to gain on the investment or receive a dividend as a shareholder. It is advisable for the entrepreneur to retain as many shares in the business for as long as possible but not at the risk of impeding the growth prospects. In choosing an equity partner, great care should be taken that the partner can add value to the venture in the form of knowledge, skills, creativity, experience and networks, in addition to the money. If you opt for equity capital your business would not have to pay interest costs, you will reduce your own exposure to financial loss, and outside investors may come with new insight, ideas, more effective processes and procedures.

Debt capital

DEFINITION

Debt capital refers to money borrowed to invest in the business with a legal obligation to repay the money in the future.

Mostly small businesses make use of borrowed funds. Loans can be obtained from the South African banks. Small businesses may apply for loans to Business Partners, the Small Enterprise Finance Agency or the Industrial Development Corporation.

It is likely that your business may require more than one round of financing. It would thus be prudent to secure funding from sources that have flexibility and can expand the amount that they may lend you. It is preferable that you retain voting control, throughout.

SOUTH AFRICAN SUCCESS STORY

IT head honchos: Rapelang Rabana (CEO and co-founder of Yeigo)

How did Yeigo Communications start?
We (Rapelang with co-founders Lungisa Matshoba and Wilter du Toit) started it when we realised the corporate world was not going to work for us. We thought it would compartmentalise us and we would not have an opportunity to demonstrate our skills and do something worthwhile.

So when we started looking at ideas, we looked at solving our own immediate problems. As a student, the cost of communication is a big one. We were tired of always sending each other a 'please call me' and thought with 3G phones coming about (at that time), we could use the Internet as a communication platform. And that is really how we started exploring the idea of mobile VoIP application.

When we released our first version in 2006, this was a very new concept and there were maybe two other companies worldwide doing something similar. We were doing something that was exciting and cutting-edge, but also something to solve the cost of communication – and being entrepreneurial. It is great being in a position to do something that makes you want to get up in the morning.

Were you concerned about Skype as a competitor?
Not really. At the time Skype was very much a PC-to-PC service for a broadband Internet environment. We were in this environment that did not have widespread broadband access. We specifically wanted a solution where you would be able to VoIP on cellphones because most people had a cellphone.

Was Yeigo an instant success?
Given the environment, we did not have the marketing bucks to push Yeigo like a company funded by American Venture Capital – brands, such as Fring, which perhaps has in excess of $30 million in venture capital (VC). Not having huge investments forced us to be more efficient. It allowed us to focus more on a profitable market, whereas they could rely immediately on advertising and VC. We needed to ensure cash collection and customers that would pay us, was our main market, which is what pushed us more to the business individual.

How did the relationship with the Swiss-based TelFree come about?
We met through the market; they were coming from the perspective where they had this great network, but you could only access it via a quality Internet connection like ADSL. At the time, there were relatively few ADSL lines in the country. Their captive market was small, whereas a mobile voice application meant any cellphone 3G network could connect to the infrastructure – it was a win-win for both sides. It opened up access to their platform to many more users, and provided us with a quality back-end that could reflect well on the software.

They bought the majority shareholding in Yeigo. The company will still exist as part of the TelFree group and essentially forming most of the research and development functions for the group related to VoIP and telecoms-related software.

Given your international connection to TelFree, are there plans to expand beyond South Africa?
Definitely! For us, South Africa was the first case study and, essentially, once we have built a product and a base here, the thought was: we can now begin to replicate that. The rest of Africa is going to be very important for us, and being able to 'copy and paste' what we have done here into other countries is on the road map. TelFree has worked in most of the African countries, so there is a familiarity there with the key stakeholders to be able to facilitate an expansion once we are ready.

1. What was the source of Yeigo's business opportunity?
2. How did Yeigo finance the start-up?
3. Why was Yeigo's relationship with TelFree a win-win relationship?
4. What are Yeigo's growth plans?

19.7.3 Management practices to grow the business

Whereas during the start-up phase the marketing and operations were founder driven and controlled, with lead entrepreneurs assuming responsibility for all activities, this changes when the business enters rapid growth. For rapid growth, a power and control shift occurs as these are delegated, resulting in a sharing of leadership that frees the entrepreneur to seek new opportunities and negotiate large contracts. The commitment of the entrepreneur, management and all the staff is to grow the company for mutual gain. To ensure the success of the business, the entrepreneur and management set clear goals to pursue. They develop good relations with all the different stakeholders, namely customers, suppliers, creditors, financiers, partners, shareholders and employees, appreciating the interdependencies and the need for being effective influencers. The culture is one of mutual respect, trust and transparency.

The rapid growth phase is characterised by change and uncertainty as a result of new technologies, new customers, new competitors, new employees and new systems. In such a business environment, neither a dictatorial and dominating management style, nor a bureaucratic management style, would be appropriate.

What would be appropriate management practices for fast-growing companies?

The entrepreneur should implement the following leading management practises of fast-growth firms, identified by Timmons and Spinelli (2009:117):

▸ Use a collaborative decision-making style with the top-management team.
▸ Accelerate organisational development by assembling a balanced top-management team with or without prior experience of working together.
▸ Develop a top-management team of three to six individuals with the capacity to become the entrepreneur's entrepreneurs.
▸ Align the number of management levels with the number of individuals in top management.
▸ Establish entrepreneurial competency first in the functional areas of marketing, finance and operations.
▸ Assemble a balanced board of directors composed of both internal and external directors.
▸ Repeatedly calibrate strategies with regular board of directors meetings.
▸ Involve the board of directors heavily at strategic inflection points.

To summarise, for rapid growth entrepreneurial management is essential to deal with nonlinear and nonparametric events that characterise the entrepreneurial company. In addition decision making can be unconventional to cope with newness and its accompanying uncertainty. At times, decision making could even be counterintuitive.

19.7.4 Planning practices to grow the business

For rapid growth it is essential to plan. If you had developed a business plan during the pre-start-up phase, this business plan can be used as a base and expanded upon. Your business plan for rapid growth should indicate that you have:

▸ Created significant customer value in a large growing market, differentiating your product/services from competitors
▸ Solved a serious customer problem for which they will pay a premium
▸ Incorporated a longer-term sustainable growth path through a range of products/services
▸ Matched the founder's goals and the management team capabilities
▸ Planned to obtain early cash flow and an attractive return on investment
▸ Identified risks and developed contingency plans
▸ Set clear target dates.

The business plan is a work in progress, to guide decision making and has to be continuously updated. By involving all key staff members in the planning process, facilitates the operationalisation of the plans.

At the operational level, several leading planning practices of fast-growth firms have been suggested by Spinelli and Adams (2012:117):

▸ Prepare detailed written monthly plans for each of the next 12 to 24 months and annual plans for three or more years.
▸ Establish functional planning and control systems that tie achievements to actual performance and adjust management compensation accordingly.

▸ Periodically share with employees the planned versus actual performance data directly linked to the business plan.
▸ Link job performance standards that have been jointly set by management and employees to the business plan.
▸ Prospectively model the firm based on benchmarks that exceed industry norms, competitors, and the industry leader.

Monitoring and evaluating business performance on a continuous basis ensures that the focus is maintained and that the targets are reached.

Once the business is on a growth trajectory, it would be a good time for the owners to consider harvesting the business.

19.8 Harvesting the business

DEFINITION

Harvesting refers to the recovering of value through the sale of a company or its assets.

Why would the goal of harvesting be considered when an entrepreneur works on a business plan to start a company? The harvest goal is a long-term goal that can only be achieved if the entrepreneur creates a value-added business that would be attractive to outsiders. The entrepreneur makes many sacrifices, puts in time, money and effort into growing the business with the goal of making money from it in some future time. Harvesting a business provides a return on the investment of time, effort and money. But this is not the only reason why entrepreneurs would consider harvesting.

19.8.1 Entrepreneurs' reasons for harvesting

External factors beyond the control of the entrepreneur could force him or her or the management to consider harvesting. External factors relating to the entrepreneur could be his or her death or serious ill health, or psychological or mental breakdown. Other external factors include the loss of key expertise or threatening environmental conditions, such as continuous labour strikes.

Internal reasons for harvesting are reasons over which the entrepreneur has control:

▶ *Goal of the entrepreneur.* If the entrepreneur's goal is to make as much money as possible out of the business, he or she realises at the start of the business that if its growth is impressive, it is possible that competitors or larger companies may be interested in buying it and a substantial profit can be made. Thus, the entrepreneur sets out to grow the business rapidly for the purpose of selling it.

▶ *Pursuit of new ventures.* The entrepreneur has identified new opportunities, but to pursue these, capital is required which can be obtained by selling the existing business. This is typical of a serial entrepreneur who starts one business after the other.

▶ *Succession.* The family business owner who has decided that it is time for the next generation to take over the reins of the business may consider harvesting as an option.

▶ *Disillusionment.* If the entrepreneur started his or her own business to be his or her own boss and to have more free time, the reality may have been an eye opener. Yes, he or she is boss but with it comes the full responsibility of the business together with long hours and many challenges to overcome. After years of slaving away and growing the business, the owner may decide that he or she has had enough and consider harvesting.

▶ *Retirement.* After many years of owning and managing a business and having reached an advanced age, the entrepreneur may decide to harvest the business with the view of maximising returns.

If the decision has been made to harvest the company, the question is: 'Which harvesting strategy would be the most lucrative?'

19.8.2 Harvesting options

Several harvesting options are available and these are explained.

Outright sale

The owner sells the business to any interested buyer that can meet the asking price. The buyer may be an entrepreneur who prefers to buy an existing company rather than start a new venture and bypass the challenging start-up phase. Alternately, the buyer could be a supplier interested in forward integration, or a customer interested in backward integration, or a company in a related industry wishing to spread risk, or even a competitor. Selling to a competitor would entail providing the competitor access to confidential information and if the deal goes sour, then the owner of the business for sale is in a compromised situation.

Buyouts

> **DEFINITION**
>
> A buyout or an outright sale of a company involves the creation of a new independent company in which the ownership is concentrated in the hands of management or a private equity firm.

Five different types of buyouts are possible (Westhead, Wright & McElwee, 2011:151):

▶ *Leveraged buyout (LBO).* Either a large division of a group or a publicly-quoted corporation is acquired by a private equity firm, acquiring a significant equity stake. When a specialist LBO association is the buyer, the company that is the result of the LBO is typically controlled by a small board of directors that represent the LBO association, with the chief executive officer (CEO) the only representative from the resulting company on the board.

▶ *Management buyout (MBO)*. As the name suggests the existing management of the company secures capital to buy out the owner. When a company decides to divest in a division or subsidiary, the existing management take a significant percentage of the equity. While management retains the majority voting equity, the former owner may retain an equity stake to ensure a trading relationship continues with either suppliers or customers. This often applies to family owned businesses. Usually a small group of managers are involved in becoming equity holders but the MBO can be extended to other managers and even to selected employees, in which case it is known as a management-employee buyout (MEBO). One reason for involving employees may be because of their human capital value. Another reason is when the company is geographically widely spread and management control is difficult, for example a branch in Nigeria. The manager of the branch is included in the MEBO as he or she then has a personal interest in the growth of the branch.

The advantage of a management buyout to the business is that the management knows the business. For the owner the advantage is that he or she can exit quickly. The disadvantages are that management may have neither an entrepreneurial nor a growth orientation.

▶ *Management buy-in (MBI)*. In a management buy-in, managers from outside the firm buy equity in the firm. The risk is that these managers do not have an intimate knowledge of the nature and operations of the newly acquired business. However, if these managers are from similar businesses they bring with them knowledge of other, perhaps more effective systems and methods, and could greatly contribute to growing the business profitably. It is also possible to have a hybrid buy-in/management buyout (BIMBO) where some of the managers are from outside the firm and others are from inside the firm. Thus, the tacit knowledge of operating the business is retained while new and fresh approaches are added.

▶ *Investor-led buyouts (IBOS)*. Also known as bought deals or financial purchases the whole company or a division is acquired by a private equity firm. Either the existing management is retained to run the company or a new management team is appointed to grow the company, or a combination of existing and new managers. Stock options may or may not be offered to incumbent managers.

▶ *Leveraged build-ups (LBUs)*. Following a management buyout or buyin the company is used as a platform investment to which a series of acquisitions is added to develop a corporate group. This happens when private equity firms seek to generate returns from buyout investments. The purpose is to attract skilled and experienced management to grow the business through acquisitions.

Employee share option plans (ESOPs)

DEFINITION

An ESOP, also known as an employee stock ownership plan, is a formalised legal structure to transfer some or all of the ownership of a business to its employees through the transfer of shares.

A structure is created through which the employees can obtain shares in the firm and consequently participate in ownership of the firm. The outcome of an ESOP is that a wide spread of stock ownership among employees is created, thus they have a vested interest in the wellbeing and growth of the company. Thus, ESOPs are deemed to be a positive motivational device. The advantage of an ESOP for the owner, who wants to harvest the company, is that the owner can gradually obtain liquidity and be phased out, while management participates in the scheme and remains. ESOPs are more suitable to large companies as structuring the deal and the financing thereof is complicated. A major disadvantage of ESOPs is that the entrepreneurial spirit may be lost.

Merging with another business venture

A merger is when one company is merged into another, usually a smaller company into a larger company. The reason for the merger is to offset strengths and weaknesses. While compiling the deal the entrepreneur focuses on the pricing of the company, structure of the deal and the terms of the deal. However, other issues such as the culture mix, integration of employees, product range integration and pricing needs clarification. Employees of both companies may experience fears of job loss, unfamiliar management styles, and transfers to other divisions. Will downsizing take place? As soon as the deal is agreed to, employees need to be informed about the implications for them and the opportunities that lie ahead. Apart from the people issues, a multitude of factors relating to the marketing and operational issues need clarification. These include research and development strengths, manufacturing methods, operations management, selling procedures, distribution channels, and product or service pricing structure.

Initial public offering (IPO)

> **DEFINITION**
>
> An initial public offering refers to the first time a public sale of a stock listed on a public stock exchange takes place.

The business sells its stock to the public by listing it on a stock exchange. To take a company public may be the ultimate goal of an entrepreneur and may sound highly appealing, but after the listing the entrepreneur has to account to a myriad of shareholders for the growth of the company. The demands on the entrepreneur may escalate and he or she may wonder if it was worth it.

In this section different options to harvesting were discussed. Prior to embarking on harvesting, the value of the company has to be assessed in order to realise a fair deal. The valuation of a business is complicated and many aspects, not only financial ratios, need to be taken into consideration. It will not be discussed in this chapter and you are advised to consult a highly recommended expert in the field of evaluation of entrepreneurial businesses, which differs somewhat from evaluating a listed corporate.

CONCLUSION

This chapter attempted to broaden the understanding of business growth and what it entails. Firstly, the barriers to enterprise development were highlighted. Both internal and external motivations exist when considering business growth and these were described. The stages in the business cycle were discussed with special focus on the growth potential in each of the stages. Four generic growth strategies that could also be termed approaches to growth were detailed. This was followed by the organic and external growth strategies exposition. Before embarking on the explanation of implementing growth, it was necessary to determine if the entrepreneur had a growth orientation and if not, what fear contributed to it. The practices required for implementing a growth strategy in four business areas, namely, marketing, financing, management and planning were detailed. The chapter concluded with a discussion of harvesting the business, focusing on the reasons for harvesting and the different options for harvesting.

SELF-ASSESSMENT QUESTIONS

Multiple-choice questions

1. During the _____ in the business life cycle, some of the challenges are to finance large orders, operational capacity and management effectiveness.
   a. start-up stage
   b. rapid growth stage
   c. mature stage
   d. stability stage

2. _____ can be defined as agreements between independent organisations who work together under an incomplete contract.
   a. Dealership
   b. Licensing
   c. Alliances
   d. Franchising

3. Which one of the following is a leading marketing practice of high-growth companies?
   a. Deliver products and services that are perceived as average quality to expanding segments
   b. Create new products that are a marginal improvement on existing products
   c. Deliver product and service benefits that demand average market pricing
   d. Rapidly develop broad product and service platforms with complementary channels

4. Which one of the following financial considerations is relevant to a small growing business?
   a. Timing is not critical as the time periods for financial payments and transfers are liberal.
   b. Capital market theories, such as the capital asset pricing model, apply to small companies.
   c. The high-potential entrepreneur requires not only the best possible deal but the investor who can add value in terms of knowledge, experience and guidance.
   d. Valuation methods, such as discounted cash flow, and financial ratios used to evaluate established companies provide accurate valuations of small growing companies.

5. When an entrepreneur has a new idea for an opportunity and considers harvesting the existing business, the reason for harvesting relates to _____.
   a. succession in a family business
   b. disillusionment with business ownership
   c. the goal of the entrepreneur
   d. pursuit of a new venture

DISCUSSION QUESTIONS

1. Discuss the internal and external motivators for enterprise growth.
2. Explain the attributes of an entrepreneurial orientation towards growth.
3. Discuss growing the business from a marketing perspective.
4. Discuss the critical management practices to ensure growth.
5. Describe the different harvesting options.

EXPERIENTIAL EXERCISE

1. Your business has not been performing as you had originally planned. You are wondering what the root of the problem could be. Some months you feel confident and then sales are up. But when you feel down, the sales seem to go the same way. Read the section on growth orientation and tick all the attributes that you have for growth orientation. Be honest with yourself. Do you perhaps have a fear of success?

2. Google Rapelang Rabana and click on the 'Exclusive interview with the quintessential Rapelang Rabana founding partner Yeigo' or go to http://www.ventures-africa. com/2012/08/exclusive-interview-with-the-quintessential-rapelang-rabana-founding-partner-yeigo/ Read the interview conducted with Rapelang Rabana. What did you learn from her experiences in growing a company?

3. Your business venture to grow vegetables in tunnels, specialising in cabbage, spinach, carrots, onions and potatoes and selling to small traders in Diepsloot and Cosmo City has been highly successful. The demand for your vegetables has increased. You have covered all

available land on your smallholding in tunnels and have no more room for expansion. To grow the business you need to increase the yield or purchase or rent the land adjacent to your property, but that would be very expensive. You could consider hydroponics. However, you are toying with the idea of double-story tunnels. What do you think would be the best long-term growth option?

4. Your Italian restaurant has been highly successful since you introduced old-school hand-rolled pizza bases and authentic Italian dishes. However, your parents back in Italy are not well and would like you to return and manage the family business in Italy. What should you do with the restaurant in South Africa? You have considered selling half the shares to your cousin and he can take over the management. But you are not sure that your cousin has the appropriate management style to grow the business. How can you ensure that your cousin understands how to manage a growing business?

5. Richard Maponya owns the Maponya Mall in Soweto, but he started many years ago, opening a business in Soweto during the apartheid years. What business did he start and how did he grow his business ventures over the years? A few years ago, at the age of 91 he indicated that he planned to open a mall in Polokwane, his hometown, but that he had been faced with many challenges. Nevertheless, he remains determined to pursue this dream. Should Mr Maponya pursue this dream or should he consider harvesting his businesses?

CENTRALISATION LEADS TO ULTIMATE EFFICIENCY – THE JWAYELANI RETAIL OPERATION SHOWCASES ITS SUCCESS

A streamlined operation – from meat packing plant to convenience supermarket – is why Jwayelani has established itself as the store of choice for customers looking for quality, value-for-money and good service and situated predominately on the transport nodes of KwaZulu Natal.

The right start

Jwayelani, which means 'welcome and be happy' in isiZulu, was established in 1987 as a retail operation focused on fresh and frozen meat products. Rather than opening a number of butcheries and convenience supermarkets where the meat processing and packing takes place in-house (as is the general case), they spent five years building a 4 000m² state-of-the-art factory. 'You cannot only build a business around people, but rather you need to ensure a system to support those people. So we just built such a system first', explains Jwayelani director David Schneiderman. With 21 stores at present and R1 billion turnover per annum, it seems they have the recipe right.

Why meat really matters

For most customers, the quality and price of meat in the supermarket butchery largely determines their choice of store. Having the advantage of a centralised factory, with all of its obvious benefits, sets Jwayelani apart from its competitors. This has proven particularly important to its existing customer base, which has come to expect the same quality of product and standard of in-store experience as customers in more affluent areas.

How central works

'Following supermarket trends in Europe and the US, we believe that central is the only way to go', says Schneiderman. The benefits of improved productivity and efficiency within the system are made clear, by the simple fact that the Jwayelani stores never experience out-of-stocks. Apart from the meat plant, Jwayelani also has a centralised bakery, which produces bread and a limited number of confectionery items, and a dry good distribution centre. According to the Distribution Control (DC) manager, Trevor Coppin, their average shrinkage is approximately 0.03% per year. Around R30 million worth of stock passes through the DC each month – 'we are very efficient with turnaround time', he says. The DC system may still be rudimentary in terms of manual packing and loading, but it is adequate for the volume and number of lines present, and there is still enough space to double or even triple operations.

Convenience for commuter traffic

Situated predominately around the transport nodes, has meant that Jwayelani stores have been able to position themselves as a convenient one-stop shop. These small store formats have proven to be very attractive to the passing commuters (despite heavy competition all around), as they have come to be known as a place where shoppers can get in and out really quickly with everything they require.

Source: Adapted from Durham (2011:33–35).

1. How did Jwayelani differentiate their product and service offering to ensure growth? How do they position themselves?
2. What operational strategy differentiates Jwayelani from its competitors? Why is centralisation a strategic option?

Expansion

'We opened three stores in four months last year', says Schneiderman. 'The plan going forward is to expand the Jwayelani footprint in KwaZulu Natal, particularly along the major highway routes'. New store formats include specialised butchery offerings and entry into established shopping centres, though this has been difficult due to the restrictive exclusivity clauses placed by other supermarkets.

Supplied with the latest equipment from around the world, the meat processing and packing plant in Durban currently sees 300–350 tons of meat and chicken processed – 20% of the factory's capacity. As the group expands the volume of fresh and frozen meat and chicken will increase accordingly, 'without the need for too much more capex', says he.

3. What does their growth/expansion strategy entail?
4. Have they considered the financial cost of expansion?
5. Should Schneiderman consider harvesting? If so, what option should they contemplate?

SUGGESTED WEBSITE LINKS

Business Partners Ltd: http://www.businesspartners.co.za/about-our-finance-options/

Industrial Development Corporation - Development funds: http://www.idc.co.za/development-funds

Small Enterprise Finance Agency (SEFA): http://www.sefa.org.za/

SMEToolkit South Africa: http://southafrica.smetoolkit.org/sa/en

Venture capital service providers: http://www.businessmechanics.co.za/business-directory/page/2/?category=venture-capital-service-providers

REFERENCE LIST

Arkebauer, JB. 1993. *Ultrapreneuring: Taking a venture from start-up to harvest in three years or less.* New York: McGraw-Hill.

Brands and Branding in South Africa. 2013. *20th Anniversary Edition.* Johannesburg; Affinity Advertising & Publishing.

Dingle, S. 2011. Battle with the big guys. *Finweek,* 3 March, 18–19. Text by Gallo Images/Finweek.

Durham, L. 2011. Jwayelani - Centralisation leads to ultimate efficiency. *Supermarket & Retailer,* February, 33-35. © 2013 *Supermarket & Retailer.* Reprinted by permission of the editor. *Supermarket & Retailer.*

Finweek. 2011. Bringing in experience: Systems lead to success. 3 March 2011:49. Text by Gallo Images/Finweek.

Katz, J. & Green, R. 2011. *Entrepreneurial Small Business.* 3rd ed. New York: Irwin McGraw Hill.

Kriel, Z. 2011. IT head Honchos: Rapelang Rabana. *Leadership,* 314, April:50.

Nieman, G & Nieuwenhuizen, C. 2014. *Entrepreneurship - A South African perspective.* 3rd ed. Pretoria: Van Schaik.

Reuer, JJ, Ariño, A. & Olk, PM. 2011. *Entrepreneurial Alliances.* Upper Saddle River, New Jersey Prentice Hall.

Spinelli, S. & Adams, R. 2012. *New venture creation: Entrepreneurship for the 21st century.* 9th ed. New York: McGraw-Hill.

Westhead, P, Wright, M. & McElwee, G. 2011. *Entrepreneurship - perspectives and cases.* Essex: Financial Times Prentice Hall.

CHAPTER 20

Corporate entrepreneurship

Isa van Aardt

LEARNING OUTCOMES

On completion of this chapter you will be able to:
- ▶ Define the term 'corporate entrepreneurship'
- ▶ Discuss the different forms of corporate entrepreneurship
- ▶ Discuss the corporate entrepreneurial life cycle
- ▶ Understand the concept of entrepreneurial intensity and how it can be measured
- ▶ Understand the role of a corporate entrepreneurship culture
- ▶ List the typical characteristics of corporate entrepreneurs
- ▶ Explain the constraints placed on corporate entrepreneurship
- ▶ Explain how corporate entrepreneurship can be promoted in an organisation.

OPENING CASE STUDY

Different products and services are used by customers and each customer has a unique experience – some of which may be not satisfactory. If you work in product or service development, and a customer called you up to offer suggestions for improvements to your offering, would you listen? It is important not to ignore any feedback received from a customer; however, one can evaluate the feedback.

1. Does the customer have insights that are new or unusual?
2. Are they repeating some of the same things you've heard before?
3. What can be done to improve the product or service delivery?
4. What about developing a new product or service?

INTRODUCTION

South Africa is a relatively wealthy, politically stable country with a population of well over 50 million people. However, unemployment levels in South Africa are around 25.2% amongst adults and as high as 47.5% amongst the youth between the ages of 18 to 35 years (Stats SA, 2014) and education seems more important than wealth creation. There is no guarantee that graduates will find work in the formal sector. Part of the South African government's strategic focus is on uplifting the country as a whole by stimulating and creating sustainable employment for its citizens. The South African government view entrepreneurship as an important tool and recognise the important contribution that entrepreneurs play in the economic and social development of our country. Governments across the world, including South Africa, see small businesses as the key to addressing unemployment issues. However, South Africa does not rank highly on the global entrepreneurship monitor (GEM) report and the total South Africa entrepreneurial activity average for 2012 was 7.2% of whom 32% are entrepreneurs out of necessity (Turton & Herrington, 2012).

20.1 South Africa's need for job creation

A typical problem for job creation in South Africa is that most of the endeavours to start and set up businesses turn entrepreneurs into small-business owners. Once they are established and can provide a good standard of living for themselves and their immediate families, they often decide not to grow their businesses. Factors that contribute to this decision include a lack of finances and skills, an increase in the level of complexity, a lack of trust to take in partners, and extended-family dependence (Hewitt, 2002). There are those business owners who would like to grow their businesses but, due to the demands of the day-to-day running of their businesses, they may become stagnant and find themselves lacking innovation and time to think strategically. We also know that many entrepreneurs do not like to delegate responsibilities and give up control of their business activities. They tend to control their employees and prefer them to stay in their prescribed roles and responsibilities. As a result, these entrepreneurs wish to grow and expand their businesses on the one hand, but do not want to relinquish control or delegate responsibility on the other.

As mentioned in the introduction, South Africa is not an entrepreneurial nation but one that sees education as more important than wealth. As a result, we are a nation that creates 'jobseekers' and not 'job creators'. We are taught from a very young age to find a good, stable job that will provide a good, stable income, with a good, stable pension fund. Our nation's risk profile is low which means that many prospective entrepreneurs who see and recognise opportunities will rather seek a job than face the risks and uncertainties of setting up and starting a business. The opportunity in this lies with the smart business owner who employs such an entrepreneurial individual, who acts and thinks like an entrepreneur but who does not want to take on the risks associated with starting a business.

20.2 Defining corporate entrepreneurship

Entrepreneurship happens whenever someone identifies an opportunity, implements a new idea and develops a new product or offers a new service. 'Corporate entrepreneurship' is a term that is used to describe entrepreneurial activity within an existing business. Many other terms are used to describe corporate entrepreneurship, such as 'intrapreneurship', 'innovation management', 'entrepreneurial orientation', 'corporate venturing', and 'strategic entrepreneurship'.

Morris et al. (2008) distinguish between management and corporate entrepreneurship. Managers follow the organising, planning, coordinating, and control route. They focus and report on organisational objectives set. They collect facts, analyse them and report on progress. They also pay attention to basic managerial principles and values with a strong sense of accountability. Entrepreneurs have vision and they are willing to take calculated risks to create a future. Many organisations find it difficult to achieve balance between these two as their risk propensity lowers as their business becomes more stable because they do not want to risk their current business activities.

20.3 **Forms of corporate entrepreneurship**

According to Singer, Alpeza and Balkić (2009) corporate entrepreneurship, in the narrow sense, represents formal and informal activities whose aim is the creation of new ventures within existing organisations, creation of new business entities in collaboration with the existing organisation, or transformation of the existing organisation through strategic renewal. Two forms of corporate entrepreneurship can be identified from this description, namely:

▸ Corporate venturing which includes internal venturing and new venturing, and
▸ Strategic renewal.

These forms of corporate entrepreneurship are illustrated in Figure 20.1.

Corporate venturing involves investing in new businesses, or adding new businesses to existing businesses. Often an entrepreneur starting a new venture will happen to see other opportunities and decide to venture into them. For example, if an organisation makes canvas tents, a customer might ask whether it would be possible for the business to provide a canvas cover for her boat or car as well. If the business owner decided to follow this opportunity, he or she would still be in the same line of business, but the product range would begin to expand. This is referred to as **internal venturing**.

A different example might be a logistic organisation that is doing very well and so the business owner is looking for another business opportunity. He meets with a friend, who informs him that he obtained a contract from a telecommunications network to install cellphone towers in the Limpopo province, but

Figure 20.1 Forms of corporate entrepreneurship

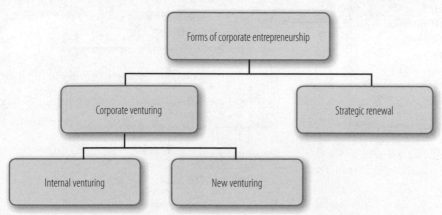

that some of his technicians left, his truck broke down, and he is struggling to meet the demands of the tender. Immediately, the business owner identifies an opportunity to partner his friend. This opportunity is outside his field of expertise, but he has the necessary finance to obtain the resources and to buy in the necessary skills. With his ability to manage the resources, he sees no problem venturing into this new direction. This is a new line of business and the forming of a new venture and is referred to as **new venturing**.

It is also necessary for organisations to revitalise themselves on a regular basis to meet the demands placed on them by the external environment. This brings us to the third form of corporate entrepreneurship and is referred to as strategic entrepreneurship.

'**Strategic renewal**' is a term used to describe a situation where the organisation needs to redefine its relationship with the external environment in order to introduce an entrepreneurial culture within the organisation. The external environment is dynamic (ever changing) due to, among other things, new government legislation, new regulations, and changes in regional or local municipal by-laws, new competitors or new technology. Organisations must continue to rely on innovation and relook at their practices to keep innovative ideas in the organisation. This will

retain talents and skills, and stimulate innovative thinking in the organisation. Organisations also need to relook at how they go about bringing new ideas into the organisation to provide fresh thinking and a new perspective to the organisation. Their internal organisation must continuously be readjusted to meet the demands placed by the external environment.

Figure 20.2 depicts strategic renewal. The external box shows some of the dimensions (government legislation, new regulations, local municipal by-laws, new competitors, and new technology) that may impact on the current venture. This in turn will lead to the redesign and restructuring of their internal practices

Figure 20.2 Strategic renewal

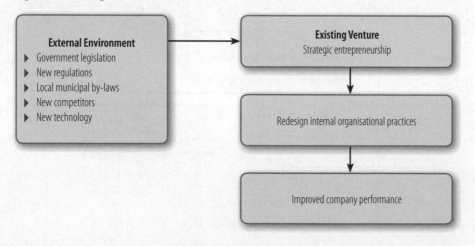

EXAMPLE 20.1

Who will lead corporate innovation? Rank or enthusiasm?

Corporate innovation and corporate venturing require new ways of looking at what is happening in the organisation as well as in the external environment. It is necessary to focus on the generation of new ideas, look at developments in technology and the market and stretch the existing boundaries of the organisation. During this process of corporate innovation directions with regard to how the innovation process should proceed, how it will be monitored and how successes and new ideas will be authorised need to be set. But who will lead the process? Should it be senior management who have the experience and credibility within the organisation, even though they might tend to be more risk averse, or should it be mid-level employees who may be the innovators themselves and have more enthusiasm to develop new things or take more risk?

1. Who do you think should take the lead?
2. Do you think that both levels could play a role in corporate innovation?

---

with the hope of increasing their business performance.

The discussion that follows will look at aspects of the corporate entrepreneurial life cycle, corporate entrepreneurial intensity, and corporate entrepreneurial culture. All these aspects play an important role when an organisation decides to strategically move in an entrepreneurial direction.

20.4 Corporate entrepreneurial life cycle

DEFINITION

A corporate entrepreneurial life cycle describes the different stages an organisation goes through as it grows, from being very creative to becoming very formal.

When a new venture is started up because an entrepreneur saw an opportunity, the business grows and the entrepreneur becomes a business owner and manager. As the business starts to grow, more people are employed. The smaller the workforce, the less formal and rigid it is. Employees share ideas and decision making is quick. Problems are dealt with effectively and efficiently. The customer base is important and

the small workforce is creative in their approach and problem-solving activities.

The greater the number of employees, the more policies, rules, and regulations need to be put in place to manage and control the business activities. The more 'red tape', the less entrepreneurial an organisation becomes. The more decision makers in the process, the less action is taken. Soon the once thriving organisation finds itself not growing, but settling in with its current products, services, processes, administrative systems, and managers and employees who think and act in the same way. Employees will do their jobs and not challenge the current way of doing things (Greiner, 1972).

20.5 Corporate entrepreneurial intensity

Morris et al. (2008:74) refer to **corporate entrepreneurial intensity** (CEI) as the degree and frequency of entrepreneurial activity in an existing business. An organisation's CEI will vary according to internal and external factors. Internal factors include the type of management structure and the decision-making routes, policies, rules, and regulations in place and external factors include competition, government legislation, and the customer base that the business needs to deal with.

DEFINITION

Corporate entrepreneurial intensity (CEI) is the degree and frequency of entrepreneurial activity in an existing business.

The frequency of entrepreneurial activity can be influenced directly by completion and market heterogeneity, whereas the degree of entrepreneurial activity depends on the availability of technology. As pointed out before, it is in the interests of the organisation to cultivate corporate entrepreneurship for its long-term survival. In order to do so, the organisation needs to recognise the individual and set up systems to enable them to risk growth, but at the same time protect the organisation from unsuccessful endeavours. Large organisations need to cultivate entrepreneurship if they want to stay competitive in both the local and the global economy. Small new organisations today are competitive, rigorous, and quick to do business.

Today, on a social level, many more individuals want to do their 'own thing' and be independent. They do not hold onto old values and also do not have the same sense of loyalty toward organisations as their parents had. Employed individuals who believe in their own talents and skills very quickly become frustrated if their ideas are not valued. They seek greater flexibility and do not operate very well in highly structured organisations. They also express themselves more freely and frequently. Due to easy access to media and information, many organisations today find themselves with a highly informed workforce. These individuals come from a convenience-orientated generation and are able to access technology (e.g. computers, the Internet, cellphone technology) and social networks that can aid a large organisation should they recognise and channel this to realise new business opportunities and markets (Hewitt, 2010). Each employee in a venture has a role to play in developing the culture of the organisation.

20.6 Corporate entrepreneurial culture

DEFINITION

Corporate culture describes the basic beliefs and assumptions about what the organisation is.

Human resource policies created to select new employees that fit with the current way of organisation thinking, often place an unintended constraint on creative thinking. In order to promote new thinking, existing organisations need, for example, to manage conflict constructively. In order for an organisation not to lose its entrepreneurial flair, it needs to provide a corporate culture conducive to promoting entrepreneurial thinking.

According to Badal (2012) there are four key steps that organisations can implement to find, support and nurture their own entrepreneurs. These key steps are:

1. **Break the silos**. Formal organisations tend to limit entrepreneurship to a few departments, such as research and development (R&D) and information technology (IT). This totally misses the mark and they should create an entrepreneurial environment across all divisions and departments. The entire organisation should be engaged in becoming more risk-tolerant and entrepreneurial. Unleashing multidisciplinary collaborative thinking will put the organisation in a better place. Furthermore, breaking silos can potentially bridge the gap between innovation and entrepreneurship. Most of the larger organisations are generally not short on great ideas; what they lack is the entrepreneurial risk taking and passion to bring the idea to the market. Uniting the genius of the idea generator and innovator with the ingenuity of the entrepreneur is what ultimately makes organisations successful.

2. **Identify and foster talent**. Not everyone in the organisation will have the innate

talent to excel as entrepreneurs or innovators and those individuals excelling should be identified across the organisation. Once identified, the traits that enable them to perform can be identified and those talents prioritised when hiring new employees. Organisations should then allocate appropriate financial and non-financial resources to support and develop these individuals and increase the probability of extraordinary performance.

3. **Create the right environment**. Just identifying talent isn't enough. Organisations must create the environment to foster it. The most successful entrepreneurial environments:

   ▸ *Are open to risk taking*. Managers and employees are encouraged to tolerate failure and accept change. This enhances a firm's capacity for breakthrough innovations.

   ▸ *Encourage trusting relationships*. This creates a culture of trust among employees and managers. Having strong relationships in the workplace also encourages employees to take risks without the fear of losing their jobs.

   ▸ *Build skills and knowledge*. Provide employees and managers with opportunities to learn and grow. Support new ideas and employee-driven initiatives.

   ▸ *Offer management support*. When senior leaders don't walk the talk, no amount of entrepreneurial efforts made by employees or middle managers will work. Senior leadership's commitment to innovation, openness to change at all levels, and most importantly, delegation of appropriate authority to managers and employees to try new ideas sends a clear message to employees that the organisation is serious about creating an entrepreneurial environment.

   ▸ *Permit access to resources*. Provide employees with resources, time, and material. Employees should know that

they have resources available to embark on new and innovative projects.

   ▸ *Maintain a supportive organisational structure*. Complex hierarchy and elaborate policies are designed to bring order, but they also constrain entrepreneurial activity. Simplify approval procedures, cut the red tape, and keep organisational flexibility.

   ▸ *Set realistic performance goals*. Entrepreneurial undertakings, by their very definition, have unknown outcomes. Set realistic timelines and reliable performance measures for entrepreneurial initiatives. Design employee reward systems that accommodate failure, tolerate ambiguity, and keep the focus on long-term outcomes.

4. **Continually assess the environment**. Regularly monitoring and measuring an organisation's progress on the entrepreneurial path is crucial. It takes time and effort to create an entrepreneurial culture. It is important to ask all employees how they perceive the organisational environment. Do they believe that organisation's leadership supports entrepreneurship? Does their day-to-day environment allow or encourage entrepreneurial thinking and action?

The right approach is to survey workers at all organisational levels. Capture each employee's opinion on the issue, and share results at the team level – that's the level at which employees and managers work together to achieve change. Continued assessment enables executives to measure progress and keep the momentum building toward an entrepreneurial environment (Badal, 2012).

The danger that organisations often encounter is that if the 'project champion' leaves the organisation, the project also fades away unless an entrepreneurial culture is entrenched in the organisation. How organisations can recognise entrepreneurial individuals and what can be done to keep innovative employees in an organisation is discussed in the next section.

The issues discussed in the entrepreneurial dilemma – *Fostering an entrepreneurial culture* are evident of how difficult it sometimes is to implement and maintain an entrepreneurial culture within larger organisations.

20.7 Characteristics of the corporate entrepreneur

As discussed in Chapter 2, common characteristics of entrepreneurs include the desire to achieve, high energy levels, independence, the need to be in control, and calculated risk taking. The corporate entrepreneur or intrapreneur can be described as a middle-class person, often highly educated with some technical background, and someone who perceives

transactions within a hierarchy as a basic relationship. The corporate entrepreneur requires freedom and access to organisation resources, is self-motivated, and wants corporate recognition and rewards. This person wants to delegate, but also does not hesitate to do what is required. He or she has self-confidence, and know how to be clever in using the system to achieve their goals. They also like to learn from their own mistakes without making their mistakes public knowledge (Morris et al., 2008). However, if their work environment is not conducive to nurturing and extracting this potential, it is a loss to the organisation. Some employees might have a great idea, but previous experience or the current corporate culture might give the impression that it is best not to make any suggestions or to try new things. The next section will discuss further constraints placed on corporate entrepreneurship.

ENTREPRENEURIAL DILEMMA

Fostering an entrepreneurial culture

It is important for organisations to find a balance between allowing enough time for creativity and innovation, and delivering on the core requirements of the business. The 'scarcity mind-set' or state of mind, where organisations become obsessed with the notion that 'resources are fixed', often prohibits creativity. The idea that a person can only succeed at the expense of somebody else's failure permeates many organisations.

This can be a big inhibitor for employees to understand the value of collaborating in order to create great products and services. The 'collaboration concept' is also lacking. Allowing participation in the workplace and enabling employees to rotate between roles brings a fresh perspective to particular problems faced in the business. Softer skills, such as independent problem solving, the ability to take initiative and action orientation are often not harnessed and sufficiently developed. These skills could contribute to the success of the organisation (Fal, Sefolo, Williams, Herrington, Goldberg & Klaassen, n.d.).

1. What can organisations do to address these issues and successfully promote a culture of entrepreneurship and innovation?

20.8 Constraints on corporate entrepreneurship

Russell and Russell (1992) discuss some hurdles that may hinder corporate entrepreneurship. Four of these elements are discussed below and then summarised in Figure 20.3.

▶ *Strategic direction.* Organisation management needs to have in their strategic long-term vision the passion that they want to nourish and foster an entrepreneurial culture. Management must see their employees as potential entrepreneurs and not be suspicious or unaware of their efforts.

▶ *Systems.* These refer to, among other things, the employment system, the remuneration system, the reward system, the costing system, the budget system, the employee recognition system, and so on. Managers are often guilty of asking employees to be innovative and creative, but then measure employee performance in tangible issues such as office hours, days of sick, telephone bills, and so on. This often leads to distrust between employees and the employer.

▸ *Structures.* These refer to the organisational and reporting structures. Many organisations are guilty of not updating their organisational and reporting structure on a regular basis (at least once every two years). Employees are placed in compartments and are not allowed to freely communicate and exchange information. Some managers are guilty of not wanting to accept or implement innovative management techniques and initiatives in their departments if these are implemented by another department. Managers who are in competition with each other may lose sight of the bigger picture. In addition, some managers are assigned entrepreneurial freedom without the required authority to carry out their activities.

▸ *Policies and procedures.* These are the organisation guidelines and rules to ensure conformity and order in the organisation. If staff members are not treated in the same way, they tend to become unhappy and feel hard done by (like children). Policies and procedure are not designed to meet the needs of an entrepreneurial endeavour in the organisation. Organisations that pursue new ventures often exclude existing policies and procedures, and design new guidelines and rules by which staff should perform.

The South African success story – *Cashless ATM extends banking's reach* illustrates how a change in organisation culture can contribute to innovations within the organisation.

The next section explores several ways in which corporate entrepreneurship can be promoted within an existing venture.

20.9 **Promoting corporate entrepreneurship**

Individuals starting a new venture are often seen to be energetic, bold, unconventional, risk-taking individuals who do not pay attention to normal structures. They identify opportunities, gather resources, and pursue their goals. The

Figure 20.3 Corporate entrepreneurial constraints

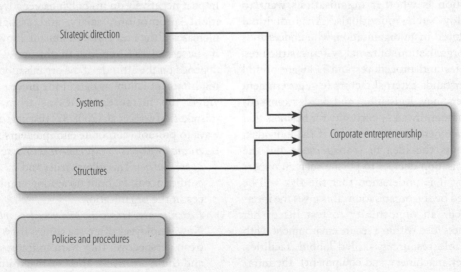

Source: Adapted from Russell and Russell (1992).

SOUTH AFRICAN SUCCESS STORY

Cashless ATM extends banking's reach

FNB applied innovative thinking and design to bring about a new solution building on the best practices of the Mini ATM but with all the power of a full ATM. The new Slimlines replace the FNB Mini ATMs.

The concept is simple, yet revolutionary. The bank gives small businesses a device that will allow customers to draw from their bank account a cash value up to R1 500. It does not matter who the customer banks with, the transaction processes like a normal ATM transaction. The customer simply presents the slip to the retailer cashier, who will in turn give the customer the full value of the cash he or she has withdrawn from the till.

The shop owner will get credited in his or her business FNB account the full value of the withdrawals for the day – same day. The additional features include biometric reader, camera and barcode scanner, which allows the bank to bring more innovation in the future.

The new Slimline is also the starting point of community banking, SMME banking and selling additional services, product and solutions to communities where building a full branch or network is not possible. This new device is the foundation to creating a bank in a shop. SASSA (South African Social Security Agency) grant recipients no longer have to travel long distances in order to withdraw funds from their SASSA accounts.

FNB plan to have 990 devices in the market by end Aug 2013. They anticipate 12 million transactions a year. This equates to 1 million transactions a month!

The transactional volumes are already exceeding all their expectations and there is a customer waiting list for these devices.

FNB has changed the way Self Service Delivery operates by enabling faster deployment to market and a new type of device (Cassim, 2013).

---

question is whether organisations want to employ such individuals. An individual employed in an organisation, who understands the organisation's internal systems, structures, policies and procedures and is aware of and understands external factors (e.g. government tenders, new legislation, and needs expressed) might identify an opportunity for business that management has overlooked. If the individual presents the idea to management and the organisation decides to pursue such an opportunity, it is understood that the risk will be carried by the organisation. This gives the intrapreneur an opportunity to test his or her business idea within a secure environment (with available resources, skilled labour, facilities, money, machinery, and equipment). The intrapreneur carries a career risk, which might

impact negatively on his or her career advancement, promotions, salary, and associated increases if the idea is not successful. However, if successful the opposite might apply. This depends on the attitude of the organisation that might accept failure as part of the process provided the intrapreneur learns from past mistakes. Morris et al. (2008:37) discuss several ways to promote corporate entrepreneurship:

▶ *Allow employees to experiment with low-risk opportunities.* This allows trust and confidence to be built up among employees in the organisation.
▶ *Listen to new employees and young people.* New employees often see things from a fresh perspective. They want to impress and think creatively. This creative thinking should be considered and exploited as it

may lead to improved administrative systems and procedures, or new products and services. Young people often bring with them quick and easy ways to solve work-related frustrations. Through their social networking, they may find creative ideas and solutions to problems that could lead to improved productivity and more efficient use of resources. Allow new employees and young people to have their say.

▸ *Recognise and reward employees for new innovations.* Corporate entrepreneurs, as new venture entrepreneurs, also appreciate recognition. Create avenues for employees to submit, take ownership of, and see through their ideas.

▸ *Provide a flow of capital.* It is important for organisations that foster intrapreneurship to have a budget for implementing new ideas.

▸ *Occasionally intentionally set unreasonable goals.* If organisations sometimes set unreasonable goals, staff will be forced to think creatively to meet such expectations. Covin et al. (2008) found that there are no mature industries, only mature managers who unthinkingly accept someone else's definition of what is possible.

Three possible reasons why entrepreneurial individuals stay employed rather than starting their own ventures are:

▸ The current resources needed are available
▸ They can operate quickly and efficiently in a given infrastructure
▸ They can operate in a secure environment (where they still have a job and an income and all resources are paid for by someone else).

Management of an enterprise can use various measuring instruments to judge how well the business promotes corporate entrepreneurship as discussed in the next section.

20.10 Measuring instruments

Several measuring instruments are available to measure the intensity of corporate entrepreneurial orientation. One such instrument was developed by Miller and Friesen (1982) and adopted by Morris et al. (2008). This instrument is a self-administered 28-question questionnaire that is completed by the owner or manager of the business. The first 12 questions in the questionnaire assess the degree of entrepreneurship in the business and the remaining items measure the frequency of entrepreneurship. The total scores for degree and frequency are then weighted. Scores across industries will differ. Covin et al. (2008) also provide a useful instrument that can be used to measure corporate entrepreneurship climate. These measurements provide a base reading that can be compared to a measurement of the effects of changes implemented. These measurements can provide the organisation with valuable information on how to change strategically to move into a more entrepreneurial direction.

White and Partners Ltd (2010) identified the following aspects that can be used to measure corporate innovation or the corporate entrepreneurship climate:

▸ Surveys that provide customers' and stakeholders, (suppliers, investors, employees) opinion of an organisation's innovativeness and its brand image – as compared to the competition.
▸ New sales to new customers – marks the rate of new customer acquisition reflecting the efforts to enhance the brand.
▸ Measurements of incidence, or rate of increase, of attractive, internally generated investment opportunities (the size of the pipeline) that come under review by management and the board.
▸ Increase in the value of intellectual property generated from internally-sourced ideas; augmented by acquisitions

of IP from other organisations. The information could be broken out by IP for existing versus new product initiatives.

▸ Share price premium attributed to the company's reputation for innovativeness.
▸ Conducting an analysis focused on employee retention and ease of attraction.
▸ Collaborations and partnerships reflecting the company's reputation for its innovativeness.
▸ The percentage-of-time key executives or board members spend on innovation as a specific topic of a meeting, seminar or workshop.
▸ Alignment between strategy and culture that supports innovation (White & Partners Ltd., 2010).

EXAMPLE 20.2

Seeds versus weeds: Separate the wheat from the chaff

Deciding on the merits of innovative ideas presents some challenges as the organisation needs to ask the question whether the new idea is worth it or not and does it have any merit. The dilemma is that some innovation projects require a considerable level of investment before merit can be determined. The ideal is to separate the seeds from the weeds when looking at ideas:

▸ Seeds – are those ideas that are likely to bear fruit and develop into new products or services or new ventures.
▸ Weeds – are those ideas that are not likely to bear fruit and which should be cast aside

1. What mechanisms can organisations use to select right innovation projects?

CONCLUSION

The chapter defined 'corporate entrepreneurship' as a term that is used to describe entrepreneurial activity within an existing business. There are many other terms that are also used to describe corporate entrepreneurship including 'intrapreneurship', 'innovation management', 'entrepreneurial orientation', 'corporate venturing', and 'strategic renewal'. A clear distinction was drawn between management and corporate entrepreneurship.

Different forms of corporate culture were briefly defined and corporate culture, as well as the importance of creating such a culture, was discussed. The chapter also described the corporate entrepreneurial life cycle and described corporate entrepreneurial intensity (CEI). The characteristics of the corporate entrepreneur were explored to provide a better understanding of how such individuals can be identified in the organisation. Internal organisation constraints and ways in which to promote corporate entrepreneurship were explored and the chapter ended with a brief discussion on how corporate entrepreneurship can be measured.

SELF-ASSESSMENT QUESTIONS

True and false questions

Indicate whether each of the following statements is true or false:

1. Corporate entrepreneurship is the same as innovation management intrapreneurship.
2. Most successful entrepreneurial organisations do not set performance goals.
3. It is important to ask all employees how they perceive the organisational environment when assessing the corporate environment.
4. There is no difference between a good manager and a corporate entrepreneur.
5. Managers concern themselves with factual information in order to plan, organise, coordinate, and control their resources, whereas the corporate entrepreneur pursues risks and sees how the organisation resources can be exploited.

Multiple-choice questions

1. Entrepreneurship can happen anywhere, however entrepreneurship that takes place inside an organisation is called:
   a. Corporate entrepreneurship
   b. Corporate venturing
   c. New venturing
   d. Strategic venturing

2. _____ exists when the product range would begin to expand in the existing business.
   a. Internal venturing
   b. External venturing
   c. New venturing
   d. Strategic renewal
3. Management differs from corporate entrepreneurship in the sense that managers focus on facts and organisational objectives, have strong managerial principles and values and _____.
   a. a strong sense of accountability
   b. a strong sense of accountability, and are visionaries
   c. a strong sense of accountability, and are moderate risk takers
   d. a strong sense of accountability, and are visionaries and moderate risk takers
4. Which of the following are forms of internal corporate venturing:
   a. A new idea of an employee is implemented to expand the current product line
   b. The business owner decides to acquire a new organisation that is not currently in the same line of business
   c. The business owner normally buys ready-made curtains and then resells to clients and he recently decided to venture into making and selling curtains himself
   d. A and B
5. The third key step that organisations can implement to find, support and nurture their own entrepreneurs is:
   a. Continually assess the environment
   b. Identify and foster talent
   c. Breaking the silos
   d. Create the right environment
6. It is important for organisations that foster _____ to have a budget for implementing new ideas.
   a. new ventures
   b. intrapreneurship
   c. change management
   d. accountability
7. An organisation loses its entrepreneurial way due to:
   a. Too few employees, policies, rules and regulations, and decision makers
   b. Too many employees, policies, rules and regulations, and decision makers
   c. The fierce external environment
   d. Loose management structures in the internal environment

DISCUSSION QUESTIONS

1. Corporate entrepreneurship has many other names, for example, intrapreneurship, innovative management, and strategic entrepreneurship. Research each of these terms, analyse them, and add any other names you discover to the list.
2. Briefly discuss the corporate entrepreneurial life cycle.
3. Explain the key steps that should be taken by organisations to establish and maintain an entrepreneurial culture.
4. Discuss the importance of corporate culture in establish and maintaining intrapreneurship.
5. Discuss in what way the characteristics of the corporate entrepreneur differ from that of the entrepreneur starting his or her own business. Conduct additional research on this difference.
6. Discuss the constraints on entrepreneurial performance in a business.
7. Discuss some of the avenues an organisation could explore to promote corporate entrepreneurship.

EXPERIENTIAL EXERCISE

Approach three organisations in your area. Ask them what programmes, if any, they have in place to foster innovative thinking amongst their employees and how they measure and reward the success of the innovative ideas implemented.

ELEMENT SIX

As diamonds are a miracle of nature, so synthetics are a triumph of science

Element Six is the global leader in the design, development and production of synthetic diamond super-materials. Part of the De Beers Group, Element Six is an independently managed global company with its head office registered in Luxembourg, and primary manufacturing facilities in Ireland, China, Germany, Sweden, South Africa and the UK.

For over 50 years, the core business has remained the synthesis and processing of synthetic diamond super-materials, a term that includes manufactured synthetic diamond and other super-materials such as cubic boron nitride, tungsten carbide and silicon cemented diamond. While synthetic diamond is well known as the planet's hardest known material, it has many extreme properties and is one of the most useful and remarkable materials. It is from carbon therefore, the sixth element of the periodic table, that the business takes its name: Element Six (De Beers Group, 2013).

Innovation is pivotal to Element Six's strategy and competitive capability. Their innovation capability is unrivalled and relentless. Through innovation, Element Six explores and develops novel applications and markets for their synthetic diamond, cubic boron nitride and tungsten carbide–based family of materials. The result: proprietary products that unlock value for their customers and end users. Their approach to innovation has a firm base in their world-class R&D capabilities. They utilise the creative input and technical and marketing insight available across the entire organisation. An important part of their approach to innovation includes partnering with specialised research institutes, customers and end users. For example, they have strong enduring partnerships with world-renowned academic institutions and third parties including the University of Warwick, Harvard University and the University of Witwatersrand.

These innovation collaborations aim to unlock the value inherent in the unique properties of the full range of their synthetic diamond, cubic boron nitride and tungsten carbide–based materials, and they protect this value with a strong patent portfolio.

Their vision for innovation is supported by an annual R&D investment commitment of over 7% of turnover, with over 200 employees around the world actively participating in innovation projects. They own about 590 granted patents and 850 pending patent applications worldwide, covering all their businesses, with about 50 new inventions being protected each year.

They never stop the process of identifying smart solutions that deliver the extreme performance their customers seek. Recent demonstrations of their innovative capabilities include:

▸ Commercialisation of silicon cemented diamond (SCD) – a new type of 3D composite material that offers customers a versatile and cost-effective super-hard material option not previously accessible.
▸ Synthetic diamond road picks developed by Element Six last up to 40 times longer than standard road picks, reducing operating costs and increasing productivity for their road construction customers.
▸ ABN900, the latest in a line of CBN (cubic boron nitride) products, tailored for single-layer tool applications, has been proven in tests to extend tool life by up to 55%.
▸ Element Six Technologies designs and builds synthetic diamond-based electrochemical reactors for the treatment of a wide range of industrial wastewaters and landfill leachates (Element Six, 2013).

1. What form of corporate entrepreneurship has Element Six implemented? Motivate your answer.
2. Discuss the extent to which Element Six meets all the requirements of a successful entrepreneurial environment within the organisation.
3. Do you think there are any constraints on the entrepreneurial performance that Element Six should be aware of? Motivate your answer.

SUGGESTED WEBSITE LINKS

http://www.sabstories.co.za/edcp-enterprise-
development-community-partnerships/
http://www.google.com/edu/rise/related_initiatives.html
http://www.google.com/entrepreneurs/initiatives/
http://iq.intel.com/where-personal-computing-is-
morphing-into-the-age-of-smart-things/
http://www.themobilityhub.com/

REFERENCES

Badal, S. 2012. Building corporate entrepreneurship is hard work. *Gallup Business Journal,* 25 September.

Cassim, A. 2013. *Slimline ATM Innovation – An African First for FNB!.* [Online]. Available: https://blog.fnb.co.za/2013/08/slimline-atm-innovation-an-african-first-for-fnb/ [23 March 2014].

De Beers Group. 2013. *As diamonds are a miracle of nature, so synthetics are a triumph of science.* [Online]. Available: http://www.debeersgroup.com/en/Operations/Element-Six/ [25 March 2014].

Element Six. 2013. *Our innovation capability.* [Online]. Available: http://www.e6.com/wps/wcm/connect/E6_Content_EN/Home/Innovation/Our+innovation+capability/ [25 March 2014].

Fal, M, Sefolo, T, Williams, A, Herrington, M, Goldberg, J. and Klaassen, M (Editors). n.d. *The Entrepreneurial dialogues. State of entrepreneurship in South Africa,* Johannesburg, South Africa: First National Bank and Endeavour South Africa.

Greiner, LE. 1972. Evolution and revolution as organizations grow. *Harvard Business Review,* July–August 1972.

Hewitt, M. 2002. Confirming influencing factors on small medium enterprise (SME) activity. [Online]. Available: http://johannesburg.academia.edu/MagdaHewitt/Papers/696094 [24 February 2011].

Hewitt, M. 2010. Management and Generation-Y: A theoretical model perspective. [Online]. Available: http://johannesburg.academia.edu/MagdaHewitt/Papers/119608 [24 February 2011].

Miller, D. & Friesen, PH. 1982. Structural change and performance: Quantum versus piecemeal-incremental approaches. *Academy of Management Journal,* 25(4):867–892.

Morris, MH, Kuratko, DF. & Covin, JG. 2008. *Corporate Entrepreneurship and Innovation.* 2nd ed. Mason: Thompson.

Russell, R. & Russell, C. 1992. An examination of the effects of organizational norms, organizational structure and environmental uncertainty on entrepreneurial strategy. *Journal of Management,* 18(4):639–657.

SAinfo. 2013. *Cashless ATM extends banking's reach.* [Online]. Available: http://www.southafrica.info/business/trends/innovations/atm-020913.html.Uy2874XIl0E#ixzz2wi7LTeSa [22 March 2014].

Singer, S, Alpeza, M. & Balkić, M. 2009. *Corporate Entrepreneurship: Is Entrepreneurial Behaviour Possible in a Large Company?.* Maribor, IRP - Institute for Entrepreneurship Research.

Stats SA. 2014. *Statistical release P0211: Quarterly Labour Force Survey, Quarter 1, 2014,* Pretoria: Statistics South Africa.

Turton, N. & Herrington, M. 2012. *Global Entrepreneurship Monitor 2012 South Africa.* Cape Town: UCT Centre for Innovation and Entrepreneurship. [Online]. Available: http://www.gsb.uct.ac.za/files/2012GEMSouthAfricaReport.pdf [19 August 2013].

White & Partners Ltd. 2010. *Step 6: Measuring and sustaining innovation.* [Online]. Available: http://www.corporateinnovationonline.com/innovative-ideas/tools/step-6-measuring-and-sustaining-innovation/ [08 June 2014].

CHAPTER 21

Decline and turnaround

Elana Swanepoel

LEARNING OUTCOMES

On completion of this chapter you will be able to:
▶ Describe the troubled business
▶ Identify and discuss the stages in business failure and the danger signs of impending trouble
▶ Explain the drivers and moderators of business decline
▶ Describe the turnaround model, including the turnaround situation, turnaround response, and turnaround strategies
▶ Understand the processes regarding bankruptcy and insolvency.

OPENING CASE STUDY

Sipho had been a partner in a large advertising agency in Johannesburg and had gained valuable experience. He decided that it was time to start his own business. He sold his shares and started a public relations agency that grew steadily over a five-year period. He was approached by Malusi and Nombulelo who owned a successful marketing company that had a turnover of R20 million the previous year. They joined forces and formed a new company to provide a full range of marketing services, including public relations and advertising. Sales were projected at R30 million for the first year of business.

They immediately expanded their workforce to 20 employees, appointing highly experienced and expensive specialists. In addition, they invested heavily in state-of-the-art equipment and upmarket offices. They expected to retain their clients from the businesses they operated prior to the formation of the new company, and

that repeat business would flow in rapidly. To their surprise, their turnover in the first year barely reached R16 million and their payroll bill was quite substantial. In an attempt to increase turnover and secure contracts they started bidding lower on advertising and public relations projects. This resulted in a slow erosion of margins. In addition, several customers started delaying payments. By the end of the second year, the company closed its doors.

1. What were the warning signs that the company could go into decline? Did they overspend at start-up phase on staff, equipment and premises?
2. What could they have done to prevent failure and to effect a turnaround? Could they have reduced their number of expensive professionals – cut the staff and hired freelance specialists, as and when needed?

INTRODUCTION

The number of businesses that underwent either voluntary or compulsory liquidation in South Africa dropped from a high of 4 133 liquidations in 2009 to 2 716 liquidations in 2012, of which 1 457 were close corporations (Stats SA, 2013:7). Although this figure excludes sequestrations and those businesses that close their doors for other reasons, it is still an indication that many businesses do not address problems until it is too late and are often slow to react to early warning signs.

Entrepreneurial businesses hover somewhere between the extremes of the success-failure continuum that influences the decisions that the managers of those businesses face, according to Pretorius (2009). He states that the environment within which the entrepreneurial business exists will naturally weed out unfit businesses, and that the ability to survive over time is a function of both a business's suitability to the current environment and its ability to adapt appropriately if the environment evolves.

The 2012 Global Entrepreneurship Monitor (GEM) for South Africa (Turton & Herrington, 2012:7) reports that whereas South Africa's total early-stage entrepreneurial activity (TEA) rate is 7.3% in 2012, the established business rate is only 2.3%. The latter is once again the second lowest in the world, a finding that is consistent in GEM South Africa's surveys. These percentages imply that many businesses do not progress from the early-stage to the established stage. The GEM defines the established business owner rate as the percentage of the 18 to 64-year-old population who are currently owner-manager of an established business, i.e. owning and managing a running business that has paid salaries, wages, or any other payments to the owners for more than 42 months.

The GEM also calculates a business discontinuance rate which is defined as the 'percentage of 18 to 64-year-old population who has, in the past 12 months, discontinued a business, either by selling, shutting down, or otherwise discontinuing an owner/management relationship with the business' (Turton & Herrington, 2012:15). A note is added to emphasise that it is not a measure of business failure rates. The 2012 GEM for South Africa focused on youth entrepreneurship and reports that the youth's business discontinuance rate (4%) is higher than its established business rate (1%) (Turton & Herrington, 2012:73).

The importance of entrepreneurial activity in economic and social development is an accepted fact. New and existing entrepreneurial businesses contribute to innovation and job creation. However, to ensure this contribution, entrepreneurial businesses should be managed in such a way that they are able to react promptly to environmental changes and not fail within the first two to four years, as is so often the case. The aim should thus not only be to increase the number of new businesses, but to provide guidelines on how to manage and grow existing businesses through troubled times to avoid failure. Guidance, especially as far as turnaround strategies are concerned, should be offered. This chapter is about the entrepreneur and the troubled business and the strategies necessary to turn a troubled business around to become successful.

21.1 The troubled business

DEFINITION

A troubled business can be described as one that is experiencing a decline in performance over an extended period of time as a result of inadequate or negative cash flow, excess number of employees, unnecessary and cumbersome administrative procedures, fear of conflict and taking risks, tolerance of work incompetence, a lack of a clear mission or goals, and ineffective or poor communication within the business (Robbins and Coulter, 2009).

Trouble can be caused by external forces over which management has no control (Timmons

& Spinelli, 2009). External forces could include drastic changes in the weather, such as a severe drought or monsoons; or natural disasters such as earthquakes. Not such drastic forces but with severe effects could include a recession, economic downturn, changes in government legislation and policies, inflation, interest rate changes, the entry of new competition, and even industry or product obsolescence. Examples of obsolete products that could not be turned around are video cassette recorders (VCRs), which were replaced by digital video discs (DVDs), which are being replaced by Blu-ray discs (BDs). But, 'if you're upgrading your DVD collection to Blu-ray, the CEO of Roku says you shouldn't bother. Roku CEO Anthony Wood predicts that Blu-ray players will be obsolete within four years' (Hickerson, 2012). Failure is not typically the fault of changes in the environment of the business, but rather management's inability to deal with these changes and to align the business and its resources to the changing realities in the environment.

The most frequently cited causes of trouble can be grouped into three broad areas, according to Timmons and Spinelli (2009):

▸ *Strategic issues.* Since failure involves the alignment or misalignment of the business and its environment, it is, by definition, about strategy. These could include misunderstanding the niche market, mismanaged relations with suppliers and customers, diversification into unrelated business areas, focusing on the product and not the market need, inadequate cash-flow planning when embarking on a big project, and a lack of contingency planning.

▸ *Leadership issues.* Since failure deals with strategy and the implementation of strategy, the choices that the leaders of the business make can either accelerate or prevent business failure. The leadership issues could include a lack of leadership skills, experience and know-how, a weak finance function, a high turnover in key management personnel, and a focus on accruals rather than cash flow.

▸ *Poor planning, financial or accounting systems, practices and controls.* Since business failure can be avoided even after a rapid or prolonged decline, the ultimate failure of the business really stems from a failure to plan, manage and control finances. Such sources of trouble could include poor pricing, overextension of credit, excessive leverage, lack of cash budgeting and management, no or poor management reporting, lack of standard costing, and a lack of standard and variance costing and reporting. Another cause could be that companies do not understand how to differentiate between fixed and variable costs.

Although the causes of trouble were categorised in the above discussion as either external or internal causes, Ropega (2011:479) points out that the 'reasons for failures cannot be treated as only one or a few separate factors entirely coming from the environment or from the inside of the organization'. An interrelationship exists between the environment and the organisation. From his research Ropega (2011) found that the most critical factor for small firms seems to be 'a very strong relationship between the company and its owner, which entails the consequences in all areas of the company, especially in the early stages of development'.

Seven warning signs indicating to business owners that their business might be in trouble are listed in the entrepreneurial dilemma – *Warning signs of business trouble.*

21.2 **Stages in business failure**

Three separate stages can be identified during business failure, namely decline, failure and turnaround (Pretorius, 2009). While it is true that 'decline' and 'failure' are often used interchangeably, it is necessary to distinguish between them, as this may influence the

ENTREPRENEURIAL DILEMMA

Warning signs of business trouble

You do not know where your next sale will come from

Having a consistent and reliable flow of customers and sales is essential for the health and growth of any business. Marketing and lead generation must be effective and ongoing to provide the flow of current and future sales needed for planning and for implementing strategy.

The business seems to be always late in delivering

It seems as if the business is continuously experiencing serious deviations from projections and time estimates in the business plan. Marshalling resources according to plan and time projections becomes impossible.

Your employees are unhappy or demoralised

The culture, environment, and atmosphere of your business will have a direct impact on your customers by way of client fulfilment, customer service, and overall productivity and quality. Unhappy and demoralised staff will not perform to the standards you want and this will have a tangible effect.

You feel like you can never be away or take a vacation

If the functioning of your business is wholly dependent on you and your presence, it will never grow further than that. You must have an effective management component in place to free you from your business enough to have a life outside of the business.

You are losing more customers than you are gaining

It does not take a rocket scientist to determine that if you are consistently losing more customers than you are winning it is simply a matter of time before you have fewer customers than you need to break even. If that trend continues you will soon be taking on water – or red ink!

The company's objectives are not clearly defined to your employees

This is a bit more insidious but still a critical sign of trouble. Imagine a soccer team where none of the players knows what the team is trying to accomplish. It is not enough to simply 'do your job' – everyone needs to know the vision, the strategy for getting there, and how they fit in with it all.

You feel financial control is slipping away

Accounting and information systems and control (purchasing orders, inventory, billing, collections, cost and profit analyses, cash management, and compiling statements of financial position) do not seem to work and no information is available when needed.

Your business is constantly in 'survival' mode

This can actually be a combination of signs and symptoms, but the general sense of it is easily recognised and can be deadly for a business owner. The daily onslaught of unpaid vendors, outstanding receivables, and lack of sales can grind away at you and take the wind out of your sails.

Source: E–Myth (2010).

strategies that will be pursued during each stage. Their strong interrelationship may also be obvious, thus requiring the exploration of both terms, as well as the term 'turnaround', to explain the differences.

21.2.1 Decline

> **DEFINITION**
>
> A business is in decline when its performance and operations slow down over consecutive periods and it experiences distress in continuing operations.

The **decline** stage is characterised by the business's, and usually management's, failure to anticipate, recognise, avoid, neutralise or adapt to external or internal pressures that threaten the business's long-term survival.

21.2.2 Failure

> **DEFINITION**
>
> A business fails when it involuntarily becomes unable to attract new debt or equity funding to reverse the decline process; consequently, it cannot continue to operate under the current ownership and management.

According to Pretorius (2009), failure can be seen as the endpoint of discontinuance (bankruptcy) and when it is reached, operations cease and judicial proceedings start taking effect. This implies that the level of business capital reaches a point where the business is no longer able to meet its financial obligations to debt holders, employees or suppliers and resorts to or is forced into bankruptcy or liquidation (Levinthal, 1991).

21.2.3 Turnaround

Turnaround occurs when a business has been able to recover from the decline stage that threatened its existence in such a way that it is able to resume normal operations and achieve performance acceptable to its stakeholders (shareholders, management, employees, suppliers, and customers). This is achieved by reorientation of positioning, strategy, structure, control systems, and power distribution. Turnaround can also be seen as a return to positive cash flow by the achievement of normal operations (Pretorius, 2009).

21.3 The drivers and moderators of business decline

> **DEFINITION**
>
> A driver is a causal factor with the ability to strongly influence the business decline, while a moderator refers to a condition that will alter the way that the driver impacts on the business decline (Pretorius, 2010).

An example of a driver is rising interest rates that may exacerbate the possibility of a venture defaulting on its loan repayment. In this scenario of rising interest rates, a moderator would be if the industry in which the venture is operating is experiencing a rapid growth rate. In spite of the rising interest rate, such a venture would still be able to honour loan repayments as it is growing with the industry and has the capital to cover the increase in interest payments.

The fact that decline precedes failure means that it is of strategic importance for business owners to be able to identify drivers contributing to decline and consequently attend to the drivers to pre-empt failure. In his study of drivers and moderators, Pretorius (2010:229-230) identified two types of drivers: core drivers and peripheral drivers, as well as several moderators. The interrelationship between the core and peripheral drivers and the moderators is illustrated in Figure 21.1. From the figure it follows that the relationships are complex with core drivers influencing peripheral drivers and vice versa, while moderators primarily influence the drivers with the exception of two drivers that also influence a moderator.

Pretorius (2010) defines the drivers and moderators as core drivers, peripheral drivers and key moderators.

Core drivers directly influence decline, they are:
▸ *Resource munificence.* This determines a firm's ability to act. When resources (human capital, financial capital, reputation, networks) are scarce or limited or non-existent, it is difficult for the business owner to respond to changes in the environment and to combat competition.

Resource munificence is influenced by leadership origin and causality.
▸ *Leadership.* This is the origin of decline in that all decline can be traced back to the ability or inability of the leadership to anticipate, recognise or respond to pending signs of eventual decline.
▸ *Causality (strategic versus operational origin) of decline.* This governs the signs, preconditions and turnaround strategy options. It is easier to identify operational causes of decline such as operational inefficiencies, incorrect resource application and managerial deficiencies, than strategic causes of decline, such as wrong

Figure 21.1 Drivers and moderators of decline

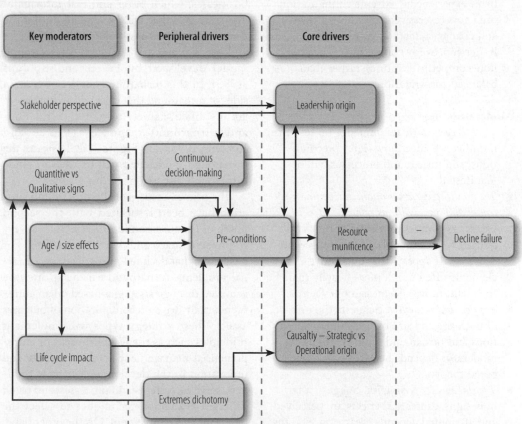

Source: Pretorius (2010:222).

market positioning, technological changes and loss of competitive advantage.

Peripheral drivers directly influence the core drivers and indirectly influence business decline, they are:

▸ *The continuous decision driver*. Postulates the influence of leader and management decisions on the visibility of signs and the configuration of preconditions, which change continuously.
▸ *Preconditions*. Determine the severity and suddenness of decline and turnaround activities. Decline is rarely caused by a single factor, but rather a set of preconditions.
▸ *The extremes dichotomy driver*. Suggests that decline is mostly associated with firms experiencing extreme configurations of factors (excessive versus slow growth and change, autocratic versus weak leadership, overly competitive versus non-competitive culture), rather than balanced configurations.

Moderators are:

▸ *The life-cycle stage*. Its influence on resource munificence affect how signs, preconditions, and turnaround processes will be manifested.
▸ *The qualitative versus quantitative nature of causes and preconditions related to decline*. Leads researchers to use metaphors and gestalts to assist them in explaining what those are. It appears that qualitative elements often weigh more heavily than the quantitative and measurable factors.
▸ *The age and size effect*. Suggests the impact of both age and size of firms on preconditions and turnaround options. This moderator depends heavily on resource-based theory.
▸ *The stakeholder perspective*. Suggests that how signs, causes and effects are perceived and attributed depends greatly on who the stakeholders are; variation is found between views of leadership, management

(board old versus new management), staff, financiers and others.

To the extent that the business owner is aware of these drivers and moderators and has a clear understanding of their effects, can he or she protect the business from failure?

21.4 The business turnaround model

The description of turnaround implies that a declining business can be turned around, while a business that has failed cannot. Legal actions are often associated with failed businesses but less often with those in decline or very small businesses, which enter and exit informally. The strategies that will be applied during the three stages of business failure will be different and are explained by using the turnaround model developed by Pearce and Robbins (1993). In this turnaround model, two main sides of turnaround that exist within businesses are identified, namely turnaround situations and turnaround responses (Pearce and Robbins, 1993:623). Figure 21.2 illustrates the turnaround model that will be used to guide turnaround discussions in this chapter.

The primary causes of the turnaround situation have been associated with the second phase of the turnaround process, the recovery response (Smart and Vertinsky, 1984). For businesses that declined primarily due to external problems, turnaround can most often be achieved through strategies based on an entrepreneurially driven reconfiguration of business assets. These strategy types will implement principles such as the establishment of entrepreneurial management teams; creativity and innovation in the development of new products, services, systems and processes; and using different evaluation techniques to select the best options to implement. On the other hand, for businesses that declined primarily due to internal problems, turnaround can most often

Figure 21.2 The business turnaround model

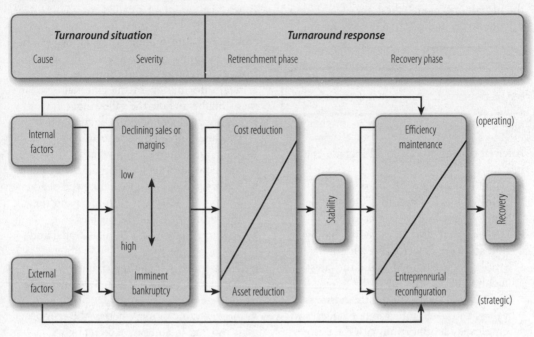

Source: Pearce and Robbins (1993:624).

be achieved through recovery strategies involving the maintenance and management of efficient existing or new business systems and activities.

> **DEFINITION**
>
> According to Pearce and Robbins (1993), recovery is said to have been achieved when economic measures indicate that the business has regained its pre-downturn levels of performance.

21.4.1 The turnaround situation

> **DEFINITION**
>
> According to Pearce and Robbins (1993), the turnaround situation exists when a business has been experiencing multiple years of declining financial performance subsequent to a period of prosperity.

These turnaround situations are usually caused by combinations of external and internal factors and may be the result of economic slowdown or downturn (external) or financial decline within the business.

> **DEFINITION**
>
> The immediacy of the resulting threat to company survival posed by the turnaround situation is known as situation severity.

Low levels of severity are indicated by declines in sales or income margins, while high levels of severity would be signalled by imminent bankruptcy (**failure**) (Pearce and Robbins, 1993).

If there is anything that is steadfast and unchanging, it is change itself. Change is inevitable, and those businesses who do not keep up with change will become unstable, with questionable long-term survivability. Situations, events or things may have a negative effect on the way a business operates and, according to the turnaround model, these are called internal driving forces and external driving forces.

DEFINITION

The internal driving forces occur inside the business, and are generally under the control of management.

Internal driving forces could include changes in:

▸ *Machinery and equipment*, such as the aging of machinery and equipment or replacement by new technologies

▸ *Technological capacity*, including hardware and software capacity and whether employees are trained to use the latest technology

▸ *Business culture*, including the business values and communication of values, and employee identification with the business culture

▸ *Management systems*, such as skills and experience of management, management turnover rate, and the management and ownership link

▸ *Financial management systems*, including pricing, costing, credit and budgeting processes, cost behaviour of management and employees, management financial reporting, cash flow, and cash budgeting

▸ *Employee morale*, such as purpose, individual development, trust and openness, employee empowerment, employee remuneration, strikes and other workforce actions.

DEFINITION

External driving forces refer to situations that occur outside of the company that are by and large beyond the control of management.

However, in order for a business to succeed and gain the competitive edge, the business must know what changes are indeed occurring, and what changes might be coming up in the future. This might be called forecasting (see Chapter 11). It is critical for businesses to do continuous information scanning or searches and then appropriate analyses of the information and data gathered. Some examples of critical information in the external environment might include the following:

▸ *Competitors and suppliers*, such as what they are doing, how the relationships with them are managed, and whether there are any new entrants looming on the horizon

▸ *Customer behaviour*, including the needs, wants and desires of customers and the marketing niche of the business

▸ *Industry outlook*, on a local, national and global perspective

▸ *Demographics*, including changes in population statistics, such as gender, race and age, and population density

▸ *Economy*, including whether the economy is moving in a negative direction or growing, expected growth and growth peaking

▸ *Political movements and (or) interference*, such as the statements regarding the nationalisation of certain businesses

▸ *Social environment*, including unemployment, the call for capacity development, and community involvement programmes

▸ *Technological changes*, such as changes that may have an effect on product development and production processes, service delivery, and other business processes

▸ *General environmental changes*, such as the emphasis on 'going green', global warming, climate change, earthquakes, and the impact of sustainable-development programmes

▸ *Government interference*, including laws, regulations, policies and so on.

Whether the driving forces are internal or external, one thing is certain for both: change will occur! A company must be cognisant of these changes, flexible and willing to respond to them in an appropriate way. External driving forces can bury a business if not appropriately dealt with. The question is how a business knows what changes are occurring so that they can deal with them in a positive way. It is never easy, but businesses that are successful include all of the above (and more) in their analyses, to develop the appropriate tactics, strategies, and best practices, to ensure successful outcomes.

The severity of the impact of the internal and external driving factors depends on their influence on the business. Owing to legislation, the majority of small businesses in South Africa have good financial reporting, but not necessarily good management reporting. If they rely solely on financial reporting to provide them with sales figures and profit margins, they will continuously rely on historic, after-the-event information. Management reports allow the business to identify problems in process and to take corrective actions where and when needed. If the impact of these changes is not controlled, it may add to the severity of the turnaround situation and may lead to imminent bankruptcy. In the next section, which deals with turnaround response, we will look at some strategic actions that can be taken to ensure a turnaround of the decline.

21.4.2 The turnaround response

> **DEFINITION**
>
> Turnaround responses include two phases of strategic activities: retrenchment and recovery.

The aim of retrenchment is to stabilise the business's financial situation by implementing a combination of cost-cutting and asset-reducing activities. When a business is in danger of bankruptcy or failure, thus representing a severe situation, it can achieve stability through cost and asset reductions and thus halt the decline process. Businesses in less severe situations can achieve stability merely through cost retrenchment (improving budgeting and costing processes or employee retrenchment) (Pearce and Robbins, 1993).

Turnarounds occur when businesses are able to persevere through performance decline, which may threaten their existence, and end this threat by implementing a combination of strategies involving skills, systems, and business capabilities in order to achieve sustainable performance recovery. This type of turnaround goes well beyond the stereotyped financial and efficiency gains resulting from certain strategic actions; rather, it encompasses a sustainable recovery from simultaneous and comprehensive changes in business's structure, strategy, systems, technology, and individual behaviour.

The primary cause of a business's downturn is usually related to internal and external factors and turnaround strategies should address the functional levels within the business related to these factors. Within the turnaround response phase, Pearce and Robbins (1993) found that:

▸ Businesses that experienced downturns caused by external factors were more successfully turned around when entrepreneurial creativity and innovation strategies and activities were implemented. A threat caused by a new entrant would thus be countered by introducing new or improved products, services or systems.
▸ Businesses that experienced downturns caused by internal factors were more successfully turned around when there was a focus on efficiency strategies and activities, such as improved financial controls and other systems, improved marketing efforts, new technology, and training of existing employees during the recovery-response phase.

21.4.3 Turnaround strategies

In the light of the above, implementing turnaround strategies should be linked both to the different functional areas within the business and entrepreneurial activities, such as creativity and innovation, within the different functional areas of the business. These could be any or a combination of the following.

21.4.3.1 Management and general administration

The management and general administration area is usually affected by internal factors and would thus require a greater emphasis among efficiency activities in the recovery response. The management and general administration efficiency activities and strategies that could be introduced to turn a business around are related to centralising managerial responsibility and restructuring according to functional area. Both represent clear attempts to gain increased control of operations and move toward simplified structures and decision-making authority restricted to the higher levels of the company. In implementing these types of strategies, the entrepreneur and his or her management team will be able to have a greater say in the way that the business is run and how finance is utilised. The South African success story below indicates the strategies that BidorBuy introduced when the bottom dropped out of the dot.com market.

SOUTH AFRICAN SUCCESS STORY

Building a multi-million rand online brand

It was the late 90s, Andy Higgins was 24, living and working in London setting up online auction sites in the UK, Germany, France and Italy for his employers, and business was booming. Having gained a huge amount of experience in the online environment, he returned to South Africa and started BidorBuy an online retailing site with a difference, it does not sell anything. It merely provides a platform to facilitate trade between buyers and sellers. Hence, set-up costs were low: no big capital expenses, no need for a building and staff could be kept to a minimum as the business was largely driven by technology. Items for sale are listed on the website and potential buyers can browse the site – no need to keep stock. Money would be earned from charging between 1% to 5% per sale and it is paid by the seller.

It was 1999, and the dot.com boom was in full swing. Caught up in the euphoria, Higgin's investors gave him $250 000 to start the business. It launched in South Africa first, but had a base in Sydney from where Higgins would launch other sites across the world.

Then in March 2000, when he and his team were preparing to launch to 12 other countries, the Nasdaq collapsed and the Internet boom came to a halt. Multi-million start-ups had reported huge losses. There was no hope of attracting further investment and no way BidorBuy was going to carve a niche for itself.

Higgins retrenched employees and put cost-cutting measures in place, just to keep the company afloat; most of the sites were shut down, except for those in South Africa and India, where the absence of competitors made it possible to continue.

Higgins had also not counted on stiff competition in Australia from the likes of eBay and Yahoo auctions about to be launched too, both backed by big local media companies. The Australian BidorBuy site was sold to eBay and 50 people retrenched. The Indian site was merged with competitor Baazee.com and the profits from the sale ploughed back into the South Africa operation. 'We had some offers to buy the company but they were way below what it was worth', says Higgins. He and his shareholders both believed he had a great product and could ride out the storm.

He had to let about 25 employees go in South Africa. He returned in August 2001 to South Africa. At one point it was only Higgins and one other person working for the company. He was not making any money and lived on savings. He put the business in maintenance mode with just a couple of hundred users and made sure expenses were minimal. It grew bit by bit. Its popularity was fuelled by the fact that there were no direct competitors in the country.

2005 was a turning point. That is when always-on Internet access began to replace dial-up. BidorBuy saw the impact of this progress as its gross merchandise value (GMV) grew between 60% and 120% every year from 2007. In 2010 it stood at R30 million per month and BidorBuy employed 25 people. It had more than 1.1 million unique visitors, 26 million page impressions and 700 000 items listed for sale every month.

Source: Entrepreneur (April 2010) Verduyn, Monique. Case Studies <http://www.entrepreneurmag.co.za/category/advice/success-stories/case-studies/> Bidorbuy: Andy Higgins <http://www.entrepreneurmag.co.za/advice/success-stories/case-studies/bidorbuy-andy-higgins/> Entrepreneur Magazine, posted July 2010. [Online] Available: http://www.entrepreneurmag.co.za/advice/success-stories/case-studies/bidorbuy-andy-higgins/ © Entrepreneur Media SA. Reprinted by permission of Entrepreneur Media SA (Pty) Ltd.

21.4.3.2 **Human resources and industrial relations**

Within the human resources and industrial relations area, downturns could also be caused by both internal and external factors. External factors usually relate to the availability of the right quality of people (labour supply and demand), the introduction of labour legislation by the government, and labour-union activities. Internal factors, on the other hand, relate to the utilisation and application of human resources within the business.

The human resources and industrial relations efficiency activities related to internal factors should be directed to increase labour and managerial productivity. This includes activities aimed at enhancing the competencies of both hourly and managerial employees as well as the allocation and utilisation of human resources. Strategies that could be developed include improving current management and employee skills, redesigning jobs (by applying job analyses and time-and-motion studies) for enhanced employee utilisation and retention, employee performance management (all related to cost reduction), and laying off employees (retrenchment). Strategies aimed at addressing external forces would focus on human-capacity development and developing effective human resource policics and procedures. Read about some of the dilemmas that a manager may face when confronted with a downsizing strategy in the entrepreneurial dilema – *Downsizing strategy dilemmas*.

21.4.3.3 **Marketing**

The marketing area can be impacted by both internal and external factors. When impacted by internal factors, the entrepreneur should focus on implementing marketing-efficiency strategies or activities that usually implies narrowing the scope of the marketing function. Strategies and activities associated with narrowing the scope include reducing the sales force, introducing a more restrictive distribution system or narrowing the geographic coverage (retrenchment strategies). Cost-reduction strategies would include focusing on the procurement of large contracts and customer orders with the thrust of the marketing effort aimed towards the marketing of fewer, more standard products to a smaller but stable customer base.

ENTREPRENEURIAL DILEMMA

Downsizing strategy dilemmas

In lean times when managers have to grapple with downsizing, they are faced with unique dilemmas in managing cutbacks. If you are asked to reduce your staff by half, who would you retrench?

▸ Obviously, you may think, one starts with the employees who have not performed according to the required standards and have not improved after training. On investigation you identified three employees who are not performing. In total you have to retrench 10 staff members. Another seven have to go!

▸ Should you retrench the newest employees who have only been with the company for a short while, based on the LIFO principle – last in, first out? But one of your newest employees is one of your highest performers?

▸ Should you consider retrenching those who are near retirement age? But they are unlikely to find other employment as a result of their age.

▸ Should you allow your retrenching strategy to be guided by the required employment equity profile?

▸ Should you retrench the ones that you are confident would find other employment easily?

▸ Should you rank your employees according to their value and contribution to your company and retain the top ranked employees and retrench the rest?

If you were asked to downsize your department and retrench half of your staff, how would you approach these dilemmas?

Source: Author.

When impacted by external factors, there should be an increased emphasis on entrepreneurial marketing activities and an increased emphasis on product quality. This could include an increase in the promotional and distribution efforts associated with the higher-quality and presumably higher-profit-margin products, especially in those segments of the product line that were considered to represent a high overall level of quality.

21.4.3.4 Engineering and research and development (R&D)

Within the engineering and research and development (R&D) functional area, increased emphasis on efficiency activities is required in the recovery response when a decline was caused by internal conditions. These would include strategies and activities focused on investing to improve the productive processes and quality of present products, thus spending on manufacturing process-oriented R&D, improving present products, and extending current equipment life. The strategic objective within the R&D functional area should be to achieve improved productivity through investing in state-of-the-art manufacturing processes and preventive maintenance on current equipment. Collectively, these activities are intended to increase the quality and quantity of present products.

21.4.3.5 Production

Within the production area, downturns caused by internal factors require greater emphasis on strategies and activities aimed at improving and maintaining efficiency of systems and processes. These could included improving inventory and materials control, consolidating production facilities, specialising in high-profit-margin and low-cost-margin products, and manufacturing on an individual-order basis. These production activities are consistent with the activities previously revealed in the marketing and engineering and R&D functional areas. The general theme is the efficient production and promotion of high-profit-margin and low-cost-margin products in stable demand patterns.

21.4.3.6 Financial management

Within the financial management area, the causes of decline could be either internal factors, such as financial mismanagement, lack of debt and cost control, and lack of profit management, or external factors, such as economic downturn and changes in government legislation and taxes. Although it may be true that giving out credit to customers may be a great selling advantage, if the repayment time is not the same or shorter than the time within which you have to pay your suppliers, this can lead to cash-flow problems, which may have a dire effect on the future of your business. Many small businesses that have contracts with larger businesses in South Africa are feeling the effects of the fact that the larger businesses have payment periods of between 60 and 90 days, which is longer than the time that they have to honour their commitments to suppliers and employees. Financial turnaround strategies would thus include improving cash-flow management and credit control, offering discounts to customers who pay cash, managing profit margins, implementing cost and budgeting management, and developing management reporting. There are various financial control mechanisms, as discussed in Chapter 11 that could also be implemented.

21.5 **Bankruptcy and insolvency**

When the severity of the turnaround situation is extreme or when turnaround strategies have been implemented without positive changes to the productivity of the business, the business owner may be faced with imminent bankruptcy, which will impact on all stakeholders of the business. Bankruptcy is a legal status of a business that cannot repay the debts owed to its creditors. In some instances, the creditors may file a bankruptcy petition against the business (involuntary bankruptcy) in an effort to recoup a portion of what is owed to them.

> **DEFINITION**
>
> Where the business owner initiates the bankruptcy due to a position of insolvency, thus not being able to repay its creditors, it is known as voluntary bankruptcy.

Bankruptcy is best approached by a comprehensive and integrated system to address issues of insolvency that will not be discussed in detail as it is best to obtain legal advice on the most appropriate process to follow for each individual business. In South Africa, there are no less than five laws governing company exit, business rescue, and insolvency procedures:

▸ Companies Act 71 of 2008 (CA) provides for the incorporation, registration, organisation and management of companies, the capitalisation of profit companies, and the registration of offices of foreign companies carrying on business within the Republic; defines the relationships between companies and their respective shareholders or members and directors; provides for equitable and efficient amalgamations, mergers and takeovers of companies; provides for efficient rescue of financially distressed companies; provides appropriate legal redress for investors and third parties with respect to companies; establishes a Companies and Intellectual Property Commission and a Takeover Regulation Panel to administer the requirements of the Act with respect to companies, establishes a Companies Tribunal to facilitate alternative dispute resolution and to review decisions of the Commission; establishes a Financial Reporting Standards Council to advise on requirements for financial record-keeping and reporting by companies.

▸ Close Corporations Act 69 of 1984 (CCA) provides for the formation, registration, incorporation, management, control and liquidation of close corporations; and for matters connected therewith.

▸ Insolvency Amendment Act 122 of 1993 (IA) governs procedures for insolvent companies, consumers, partnerships, and other juristic entities.

▸ Magistrates' Courts Amendment Act 120 of 1993 (MCA) governs procedures for administration orders.

▸ National Credit Act 34 of 2005 (NCA) regulates the process of debt restructuring for individuals (consumers) with respect to credits governed by the National Credit Act.

The multiplicity of laws and procedures adds to the legal and regulatory complexity and does not provide for seamless treatment of an insolvent. Moreover, multiple courts exercise independent, or in some cases concurrent, jurisdiction over matters. Moving from one court to another creates additional delays in the overall administration process, which is considered by some to be already too slow. Table 21.1 maps the various insolvency procedures in South Africa.

21.6 Entrepreneurial management needed in turnaround

The important parts of turnaround-strategy development and deployment are leadership, experience, and expertise. The success of a turnaround plan rests with the people on the turnaround team and their ability and willingness to incorporate the management team and key employees in the process. It is necessary to have a process structure that can achieve this. The first thing that the entrepreneurial management should do is to manage, manage, manage, and manage. This includes:

▸ *Manage the people.* The people are obviously the entrepreneur and his or her team, but also the stakeholders. They should be kept involved and informed in the process as it unfolds and develops.

▸ *Manage the process* by constantly identifying and capturing the values of the next 'quick wins' so that the plan continues to show positive results all the way through. Monitor progress and take steps to identify and deal with any slippages but also keep an eye on the overall realism of the plan. No plan survives contact with reality and as the business's circumstances change over time, so your plan also has to change. However, if it does, ensure that you communicate this change and the reasons for it to the stakeholders.

▸ *Manage the business.* Do not forget to keep an eye on the numbers and ensure that the process of change does not distract from the need to continue to manage the day-to-day business as well as, if not better, than before.

▸ *Manage the turnaround risks.* Keep an eye on the risks that you may be running while operating a business in difficulty and ensure that you cover yourself against potential problems.

To the entrepreneurial manager, the five key stages of any turnaround plan can be summarised as:

▸ *Recognising the need.* The first, and in some ways, most important step towards solving a problem are realising that you have one,

Table 21.1 Insolvency procedures in South Africa

TYPE OF LEGAL PERSON	RESCUE (RELEVANT ACT)	LIQUIDATION (RELEVANT ACT)
Business	▸ Informal workouts ▸ Compromises (CA, CCA) ▸ Business rescue (CA)	▸ Voluntary winding-up or bankruptcy (CA, CCA) ▸ Involuntary winding-up or bankruptcy (CA, CCA, IA) ▸ Insolvency, liquidation (IA)
Individual	▸ Informal agreements and voluntary compositions ▸ Debt adjustments (NCA) ▸ Administration orders (MCA)	▸ Sequestration (IA)

Source: USAID (2010:10).

how urgent it is, what is causing it, and the need to face up to it.

▸ *Being around to do it.* This essentially means that to have a future you have to survive the immediate cash crisis and quickly get a strong grip on what your business's finances are and what these are telling you about its performance, the reasons for any problems, and possible solutions.

▸ *Deciding what to do.* This involves taking an objective look at what you want to do with your business, its industry, markets, products, competitive strengths and weaknesses, and coming up with a broad picture of the key issues and your proposed strategy and priorities in the long and short term.

▸ *Generating detailed action plans.* These should describe who is going to do what, when, and with what projected results. Often you will need to do some diagnostic work, drilling down into your performance in certain cases to get a better understanding of the cause of underperformance and its remedy.

▸ *Preparing marketing plans and forecasts and (re)organising the management team.* This will allow the business to achieve the planned milestones, budgets, and objectives.

▸ *Doing it.* You need to lock in whatever support it is you need from all stakeholders (i.e. investors, partners, managers, suppliers, customers, employees, and the bank) to ensure that the plan can happen and ensure the required financial resources are in place.

▸ *Keep on succeeding.* Once your business is heading back in the right direction, keep going. Use the skills and approaches you have adapted to return it to being a successful business to ensure that it continues to prosper. Keep on using the business's numbers to assess its performance and keep the strategy and business-development plan under regular review.

CONCLUSION

This chapter dealt with the factors that cause business trouble and the stages that a business follows when in trouble. The drivers and moderators that impact on business decline were explained as well as the interrelationships among them. An entrepreneurial turnaround model is described that consists of two major phases: the turnaround situation and the turnaround response. In the description of the turnaround situation, the external and internal factors that may contribute to the turnaround situation are identified and discussed. The discussion of the turnaround response identifies which strategies would be applicable when the turnaround situation was caused by external factors and which would be applicable when it was caused by internal factors. It is evident that more entrepreneurial strategies, creativity, and innovation are necessary when the turnaround situation was caused by external factors as these would lead to improved or new products, services, systems, and procedures that would counter the threats coming from competitors, customers and other external forces. Strategies addressing turnaround situations caused by internal factors can usually be linked to efficiency of systems and processes and could include cost reduction and retrenchment. A number of turnaround strategies were identified and discussed. The discussion of business failure and turnaround issues ended with a brief discussion on bankruptcy and insolvency as well as what the entrepreneurial manager should do during situations of trouble in business ventures.

SELF-ASSESSMENT QUESTIONS

Multiple-choice questions

1. A lack of leadership skills, experience and know-how, a weak finance function, a high turnover in key management personnel, and a focus on accruals rather than cash flow are frequently cited causes of trouble that can be grouped in which one of the following areas?
   a. Financial systems
   b. Leadership issues
   c. Strategic issues
   d. Planning issues

2. Misunderstanding the niche market, mismanaged relations with suppliers and customers, diversification into unrelated business areas, focusing on the product and not the market need are frequently cited causes of trouble that can be grouped in which one of the following areas?
   a. Operational issues
   b. Leadership issues
   c. Strategic issues
   d. Financial systems

3. Since business failure can be avoided even after a rapid or prolonged decline, the ultimate failure of the business really stems from a failure to plan, manage and control finances. Which one of the following is a source of trouble relevant to this statement?
   a. Accurate pricing
   b. Appropriate cash budgeting
   c. Regular management reporting
   d. Overextension of credit

4. Which one of the following is not a core driver of business decline?
   a. Resource munificence
   b. Leadership
   c. The age and size effect
   d. Causality (strategic versus operational origin) of decline

5. When the business is insolvent, thus not able to repay its creditors, the business owner can initiate a _____.
   a. turnaround strategy
   b. turnaround response
   c. involuntary bankruptcy
   d. voluntary bankruptcy

DISCUSSION QUESTIONS

1. Explain how you would be able to identify whether your business is a troubled business.
2. Describe the different stages in business decline.
3. Differentiate between the drivers and moderators of business decline.
4. Explain how the turnaround situation differs from the turnaround response and the turnaround strategy in the turnaround model.
5. Discuss what the entrepreneurial management should manage internally during a turnaround.

EXPERIENTIAL EXERCISE

Explanation of success versus failure variables

Study the factors/variables identified by Lussier and Halabi (2010) in their research to validate a Business Success versus Failure Prediction Model. Read each factor/variable carefully and decide whether it applies to you and your business.

▶ Capital. Businesses that start out undercapitalised have a greater chance of failure than firms that start with adequate capital.
▶ Record keeping and financial control. Businesses that do not keep updated and accurate records and do not use adequate financial controls have a greater chance of failure than firms that do.
▶ Industry experience. Businesses managed by people without prior industry experience have a greater chance of failure than firms managed by people with prior industry experience.
▶ Management experience. Businesses managed by people without prior management experience have a greater chance of failure than firms that are managed by people with prior management experience.
▶ Planning. Businesses that do not develop specific business plans have a greater chance of failure than firms that do.
▶ Professional advisors. Businesses that do not use professional advisors have a greater

chance of failure than firms using professional advisors. A more recent source of professional advisors is venture capitalists.

▶ Education. People without any tertiary education who start a business have a greater chance of failing than people with one or more years of tertiary education.

▶ Staffing. Businesses that cannot attract and retain quality employees have a greater chance of failure than firms that can.

▶ Product/Service timing. Businesses that select products/services that are too new or too old have a greater chance of failure than firms that select products/services that are in the growth stage.

▶ Economic timing. Businesses that start during a recession have a greater chance of failure than firms that start during expansion periods.

▶ Age. Younger people who start a business have a greater chance of failure than older people starting a business.

▶ Partners. A business started by one person has a greater chance of failure than a firm started by more than one person.

▶ Parents. Business owners whose parents did not own a business have a greater chance of failure than owners whose parents did own a business.

▶ Minority. Minorities have a greater chance of failure than non-minorities.

▶ Marketing. Business owners without marketing skills have a greater chance of failure than owners with marketing skills.

How many of these factors/variables are relevant to you or your business? If any one or several of these variables apply to you or your business, you should seriously consider a strategy to change the situation around to avoid business failure.

ENGLISH FOR ADVANCEMENT

In 2005, Nompumezo started English for Advancement, a school for teaching English to foreign students and students from rural areas. Apart from being fluent in English and French, she is fluent in three ethnic languages and understands a few more. She learnt English while attending one of the best English schools in South Africa and completed a degree in English teaching at a reputable university in England. In addition she has certificates in TEFL (Teaching English as a Foreign Language) and TESOL (Teaching English to Speakers of Other Languages). She is passionate about teaching English and believes that if students and professionals spoke good English they would advance more rapidly.

With a large contingent of students from the rest of Africa in South Africa, as well as large numbers of young professionals not fluent in English, she was convinced that her business would succeed. She started small, operating from her home in Johannesburg, but soon realised that she had to expand. She bought a large expensive house and turned the large rooms into classrooms. Enrolment grew and she employed 20 English teachers, some on a part-time basis. She spent time developing an easy-to-follow practical and participative teaching approach

that seemed to increase success rate. It included English conversation sessions. The feedback from students was very positive.

By the beginning of 2008 she had 400 enrolled students, and then the recession hit. Student numbers declined. Her company was in serious financial trouble. She had paid little to no attention ever to formal planning, structuring the company along responsibility lines, and did not receive regular management accounting reports. Her application to the bank for a loan was rejected. She borrowed money from friends, and to some lenders she promised a high interest rate. There was still a substantial amount outstanding on the bond. She was so passionate about teaching English to uplift the youth, that she did not monitor the profitability of the business. However, she has realised that she needs assistance with a turnaround strategy, or her company will liquidate.

1. Identify and describe the internal and/or external factors that contributed to the demise of English for Advancement.

2. Which of the various turnaround strategies should English for Advancement implement to turn their situation around?

CASE STUDY

SUGGESTED WEBSITE LINKS

Turnaround strategies News & Topics: www. entrepreneur.com/topic/turnaround-strategies

7 Turnaround Strategies To Revive A Dying Business: www.naijapreneur.com

Sanlam Turnaround Plan: <http://www.sanlam.co.za/BusinessOwners> : www.sanlam.co.za/BusinessOwners: Visit Sanlam, For a Strategic Plan To Help With Your Challenges.

The Entrepreneur Magazine: http://www.entrepreneurmag.co.za/advice/starting-a-business/small-business-advice/small-business/

What are the major reasons for small business failure?: http://www.sba.gov/content/what-are-major-reasons-small-business-failure

REFERENCES

E-Myth. 2010. Seven signs that your business is in trouble. 1 September 2010. [Online]. Available: http://www.e-myth.com/cs/user/print/post/7-signs-that-yourbusiness-is-in-trouble [17 March 2011].

Entrepreneur. 2010. Building a multi-million rand online brand. *Entrepreneur Magazine.* April 2010.

Hickerson, M. 2012. Will Blu-Ray be obsolete in four years? *Slice of Scifi,* June 14: 1. [Online]. Available: http://www.sliceofscifi.com/2012/06/14/will-blu-ray-be-obsolete-in-four-years/ [27 October 2013].

Levinthal, DA. 1991. Random walks and organisation mortality. *Administrative Science Quarterly,* 36:397–420.

Lussier, RN. & Halabi, CE. 2010. A Three-Country Comparison of the Business Success versus Failure Prediction Model. *Journal of Small Business Management,* 48(3):360–377.

Pearce, JA. & Robbins, K. 1993. Toward improved theory and research on business turnaround. *Journal of Management,* 19(3):613–636.

Pretorius, M. 2009. Defining business decline, failure and turnaround: A content analysis. *Southern African Journal of Entrepreneurship and Small Business Management,* 2(1):1–16.

Pretorius, M. 2010. Drivers and moderators. Acta commerci, 222.

Robbins, SP. & Coulter, M. 2009. *Management.* 10th ed. New Jersey: Pearson Education.

Ropega, J. 2011. The Reasons and Symptoms of Failure in SME. *International Atlantic Economic Society* 17:476–483, DOI 10.1007/s11294-011-9316-1.

Smart, C. & Vertinsky, I. 1984. Strategy and the environment: A study of corporate responses to crises. *Strategic Management Journal,* 5(3):199–213.

Stats SA. 2013. Liquidations and insolvencies August 2013. *Statistical release P0043.* [Online]. Available: http://www.statssa.gov.za/publications/P0043/P0043September2013.pdf [27 October 2013].

Timmons, JA. & Spinelli, S. 2009. *New Venture Creation: Entrepreneurship for the 21st Century.* 8th ed. New York: McGraw-Hill/Irwin.

Turton, N. & Herrington, M. 2012. *Global Entrepreneurship Monitor 2012 South Africa.* Cape Town: UCT Centre for Innovation and Entrepreneurship.

CHAPTER 22

Contemporary issues

Elana Swanepoel

LEARNING OUTCOMES

On completion of this chapter you will be able to:
▸ Describe corporate social responsibility
▸ Describe corporate citizenship
▸ Differentiate between corporate social responsibility, corporate governance and corporate social investment.
▸ Discuss corporate governance
▸ Explain sustainable development
▸ Discuss broad-based black economic empowerment (B-BBEE).

OPENING CASE STUDY

Some small and medium-sized business owners are of the opinion that corporate social responsibility is not relevant to them and that it applies only to the large companies because they are the ones that pollute the environment. The large companies are perceived to have the money to spend on corporate social investment.

However, all businesses, irrespective of size should ask themselves the following questions:
1. What is the business for?

2. What are our core values?
3. Who should have a say in how we run our company?
4. Should there be a balance between the demands of shareholders and those of the other stakeholders?
5. What would the implications be if we do not head the requests of the other stakeholders and only pander to the shareholders?

INTRODUCTION

In recent years companies of all sizes, whether local or global, have tended to position themselves as socially responsible. After the end of World War II in 1945 various conceptions of corporate social responsibility surfaced. Businesses were urged to provide social benefits such as higher standards of living, contribute to economic progress, and the development of the individual. In the early days companies fulfilled social responsibilities through corporate philanthropy. Since then the concept has been refined to incorporate the triple bottom line agenda. Other concepts through which corporate social responsibility finds expression are corporate citizenship, corporate social investment, corporate governance, sustainable development and broad-based black economic empowerment. This chapter explores each of these concepts in greater depth.

22.1 Corporate social responsibility

Most companies subscribe to the concept of corporate social responsibility (CSR) and are involved in the development and implementation of corporate social responsibility frameworks, policies and practices as an ongoing process. However, few companies have fully institutionalised corporate social responsibility in their corporate policies and culture. The effective implementation of corporate social responsibility requires the vision and commitment of the business owner and the senior management team, including the board of directors.

22.1.1 Corporate social responsibility defined

Why is there such a demand for corporate social responsibility? If you take into consideration that the turnover of some companies is greater than the gross domestic product of some countries, it is obvious that they wield substantial economic power. This power can result in the company's operations causing harm to human health (e.g. asbestos mines), human society, political governance and the natural environment (e.g. toxic effluent). However, this same economic power can be applied for the good of society, when companies ensure that they offer fair payment and safe job opportunities, operate ethically and ensure the continuation of the business venture through continuous innovation and market orientation. They can ensure that their operations do not cause damage to the physical environment. In addition, they can support social development.

> **DEFINITION**
>
> Corporate social responsibility 'calls for companies to strive for balance between:
> 1. the economic responsibility to reward shareholders with profits,
> 2. the legal responsibility to comply with the laws of countries where it operates,
> 3. the ethical responsibility to abide by society's norms of what is moral and just, and
> 4. the discretionary philanthropic responsibility to contribute to the non-economic needs of society' (Gamble & Thompson, 2011:201).

Thus, it is the responsibility of the business owner and the top management team to balance the interests of all stakeholders – shareholders, employees, customers, suppliers, communities in which the business operates, and the society at large. From socially responsible actions, companies can earn trust and respect from all their stakeholders.

Typical corporate social responsibility programmes involve:

▸ Actions to prevent any damage to the environment as a result of the operations and business activities of the company, such as the toxic fumes spewed out of factory chimneys, polluting the air we breathe. As stewards of the environment, companies are expected not only to

comply with the minimum legal requirements but to do more than is legally
required to protect the environment.
▶ Actions to create a great place to work by
creating a work environment that aug-
ments the quality of life for employees.
Such actions could include a healthy and
safe work environment, flexible working
hours, exercise facilities, day-care centre
and equal gender pay.
▶ Actions to create an atmosphere of
inclusiveness for employees of all races,
religions, nationalities, interests and talents.
▶ Actions to improve the society in which
the business operates through community
engagement projects.

22.1.1.1 Corporate social responsibility and corporate citizenship

Some companies use the terms 'corporate citizenship' and 'corporate social responsibility'
interchangeably. What is corporate citizenship?

In 2002, a joint statement of a task force of
the World Economic Forum (WEF) CEOs
was developed in partnership with The Prince
of Wales International Business Leaders
Forum on global corporate citizenship (WEF,
2002). Known as the WEF Global Corporate
Citizenship Initiative, they developed the
global corporate citizenship framework for
action and identified the following four goals
(WEF, 2002:4):
1. **Provide leadership:** Set the strategic
   direction for corporate citizenship in your
   company and engage in the wider debate
   on globalisation and the role of business in
   development.
2. **Define what it means for your company:**
   Define the key issues, stakeholders and
   spheres of influence that are relevant for
   corporate citizenship in your company and
   industry.
3. **Make it happen:** Establish and implement appropriate policies and procedures
   and engage in dialogue and partnership
   with key stakeholders to embed corporate

citizenship into the company's strategy
and operations.
4. **Be transparent about it:** Build confidence
   by communicating consistently with
   different stakeholders about the company's
   principles, policies and practices in a
   transparent manner, within the bounds of
   commercial confidentiality.

The framework enlarges in detail upon each of
these four goals. With regard to the second goal,
to know what it means for your company, the
WEF global corporate citizenship statement
provides the following detail (WEF 2002:6):
▶ Good corporate governance and ethics
  – including compliance with the law,
  existing regulations and international
  standards, efforts to prevent bribery and
  corruption and other issues addressed
  through ethical conduct policies or
  statements of business principles.
▶ Responsibility for people – for example,
  product and employee safety programmes
  to ensure that consumers and people
  involved in the sourcing, production and
  distribution of products are not placed at
  risk; also human and labour rights that
  may include equal opportunities, non-
  discrimination, prevention of child labour,
  freedom of association and fair wages
  within the workforce and along supply
  chains, and in some cases, issues such as
  indigenous peoples' rights and the use of
  security forces in zones of conflict.
▶ Responsibility for environmental impacts
  – for example maintaining environmental
  quality, adopting clean and eco-efficient
  production processes, sharing environmental technologies and for some industries,
  engaging in global challenges such as
  climate change and biodiversity protection.
▶ Broader contribution to development
  – efforts to contribute to broader social and
  economic benefits in host countries and
  communities, for example: building local
  business linkages; spreading international
  business standards; increasing access to

essential products and services for poorer communities, such as credit, water, energy, medicines, education and information technology; and so on. These contributions to development may be part of a company's core business operations or part of its social investment, philanthropic or community relations activities, depending on the industry sector and company concerned.

Comparing the WEF statement on global corporate citizenship with the definition of corporate social responsibility in the previous section, it seems there is no difference between the two concepts. However, currently the term 'corporate social responsibility' seems to be preferred.

Some later definitions of corporate citizenship do not clarify the difference. For example, the term 'corporate citizen' is seen to be fraught with controversy, according to Du Toit, Erasmus and Strydom (2010:145) who link the definition of corporate citizenship to the fact that a corporation is a legal person with certain rights and responsibilities. The authors state that the controversy arises because of two assumptions, namely that property deserves rights, and that property interests are equal or even superior to human rights. Thus, good corporate citizenship would take human rights into consideration.

From a strategic management perspective, Gamble and Thompson (2011:202) differentiate corporate citizenship from corporate social responsibility by stipulating that good corporate citizenship is demonstrated by addressing unmet non-economic needs of society.

However, we will adhere to the definition of corporate citizenship as developed by the WEF.

22.1.1.2 Corporate social responsibility and corporate social investment

Corporate social investment (CSI) tends to be associated with corporate philanthropy and investment in community-based projects. In the WEF Global Corporate Citizenship statement (WEF 2002:7), under 'broader contribution to development', it states: 'These contributions to development may be part of a company's core business operations or part of its social investment, philanthropic or community relations activities, depending on the industry sector and company concerned'. It follows that corporate social investment is not from the company's core business activities, such as creating employment and training opportunities (Du Toit et al., 2010:145).

Corporate social investment is therefore a subsection of corporate social responsibility.

22.1.1.3 Corporate social responsibility and the UN Global Compact's ten principles

The United Nations (UN) Global Compact is a strategic policy initiative for businesses that are committed to aligning their operations and strategies with ten universally accepted principles in the areas of human rights, labour, environment and anti-corruption. These principles have universal consensus and ask companies to embrace, support and enact, within their sphere of influence, a set of core values in four areas, namely in the areas of human rights, labour standards, the environment and anti-corruption (UN, n.d.):

Human Rights
▶ Principle 1: Businesses should support and respect the protection of internationally proclaimed human rights; and
▶ Principle 2: Make sure that they are not complicit in human rights abuses.

Labour
▶ Principle 3: Businesses should uphold the freedom of association and the effective recognition of the right to collective bargaining;
▶ Principle 4: The elimination of all forms of forced and compulsory labour;
▶ Principle 5: The effective abolition of child labour; and

▸ Principle 6: The elimination of discrimination in respect of employment and occupation.

Environment

▸ Principle 7: Businesses should support a precautionary approach to environmental challenges;
▸ Principle 8: Undertake initiatives to promote greater environmental responsibility; and
▸ Principle 9: Encourage the development and diffusion of environmentally friendly technologies.

Anti-Corruption

▸ Principle 10: Businesses should work against corruption in all its forms, including extortion and bribery.

Comparing the UN Global Compact's ten principles with the WEF Global Corporate Citizenship Initiative, in essence the same corporate social responsibility issues are addressed.

22.1.2 Corporate governance

South Africa has been at the forefront of establishing corporate governance codes. The Institute of Directors in Southern Africa (IoDSA) established in July 1993 the King Committee on Corporate Governance. The King Committee produced the first *King Report on Corporate Governance* in 1994, followed by the King II report in 2002 and the King III report in 2009, amended in May 2012. The first King Report received international recognition as the most comprehensive publication on corporate governance, embracing the inclusive stakeholder approach to corporate governance.

King III states that good **corporate governance** is in essence about effective and responsible leadership regardless of size or structure because governance applies to any form of business (IoDSA, 2009). It follows that good corporate governance also applies to small and medium-sized businesses.

22.1.2.1 OECD principles of corporate governance

The Organisation for Economic Co-operation and Development (OECD) followed South Africa with their first release in May 1999, revised in 2004, of the *OECD Principles of Corporate Governance*. The six principles elucidated in the report are (OECD, 2004:7):

1. Ensuring the basis for an effective corporate governance framework
2. The rights of shareholders and key ownership functions
3. The equitable treatment of shareholders
4. The role of stakeholders in corporate governance
5. Disclosure and transparency
6. The responsibilities of the board.

These principles are not cast in stone. On the contrary, companies are advised that to ensure their competitiveness in a changing world, they should be innovative and adapt their corporate governance practices to avail themselves of new opportunities in the marketplace, taking into consideration significant changes in the environment. In 2010, the OECD published a set of recommendations for improvements in priority areas such as remuneration, risk management, board practices and the exercise of shareholder rights. However, these recommendations focused on the Asian market. If your company exports or imports from Asian countries you should study this document.

22.1.2.2 King III report on corporate governance

Whereas the King II report applied to only Johannesburg Securities Exchange (JSE) listed companies and state-owned entities, excluding many small and medium-sized enterprises, King III is inclusive, applying to all entities, adopting a stance of 'apply or explain' to

Table 22.1 *King Code of Corporate Governance* (2009): Key elements and features

KING III REPORT ELEMENT	SUMMARY OF THE KEY FEATURES OF THE ELEMENT
1. Ethical leadership and corporate citizenship	Those responsible for governance (the board according to King III) should provide effective leadership based on an ethical foundation, ensure integrity permeates all aspects of the company operations, effectively manage ethics, develop a code of conduct for ethical business and ensure the company is a responsible corporate citizen.
2. Boards and directors	The board and directors act as a focal point and custodians of corporate governance. Their responsibilities include: ▸ Balancing strategy, risk, performance and sustainability, ▸ Reporting on effectiveness of internal control systems, ▸ Ensuring integrity of the integrated report, ▸ Acting in company's best interest, ▸ Considering business rescue sooner when company shows financial distress, ▸ Appoint the CEO, ▸ Disclosing individual director and senior executives' remuneration, and have ▸ Shareholders approve the remuneration policy.
3. Audit committees	Appointed by the board and must be made up of skilled and experienced non-executives. Responsibilities are to: ▸ Ensure that integrated reporting, combined assurance model was applied, ▸ Be satisfied regarding finance function's expertise, resources and experience, ▸ Oversee internal audit function and risk management process, and ▸ Appoint or approve external auditors and process.
4. Governance of risk	The board's responsibility to determine level of risk tolerance; design, implement, monitor risk management plan and ensure complete, relevant and accessible risk disclosure to stakeholders.
5. Governance of information technology	To have an IT governance framework, the board to monitor and evaluate significant IT investments and expenditure and oversee management of IT governance risks.
6. Compliance with laws, rules, codes and standards	The board to ensure compliance with applicable laws and consider adherence to non-binding rules, codes and standards.
7. Internal audit	Establishment of effective risk-based internal audit (IA) function that follows a risk based audit plan, IA to provide a written assessment of effectiveness of company's internal control and risk management systems.
8. Governing stakeholder relationships	Striving for appropriate balance for stakeholder groupings in the best interest of the company, ensuring equitable treatment of shareholders and ensuring transparent and effective communication with stakeholders.
9. Integrated reporting and disclosure	Ensure reporting of both finances and sustainability. Integrate disclosures for sustainability with financial reporting. Should ensure independent assurance is obtained for sustainability disclosures.

Source: Shezi (2013:19).

reporting. King III focuses on integrated sustainability reporting, directorship appointments, shareholder approval of remuneration policies, board approval of executive directors' remunerations, combined assurance for internal audit function, information technology governance, risk management processes and business rescue (IoDSA, 2009). Selected items from the King II report, namely the duties, responsibilities and obligations of directors and prescribed offices; and the business rescue process were legally incorporated into the 2008 Companies Act, with effect from 1 May 2011.

To ascertain to what extent King III applies to small and medium-sized businesses, necessitates exploring the key elements in the report. The nine key elements are listed in Table 22.1 together with a summary of the key features of each element (Shezi, 2013:19).

22.1.2.3 King III relevance to SMEs

Brief comments follow on the applicability of each element to small and medium-sized enterprises (SME):

1. *Ethical leadership and corporate citizenship.* Where the SME has a board of directors this would apply to the board. In the absence of a board, the SME should consider the appointment of a board. However, if this is not feasible at this stage of the operation of the SME, the owner of the business would have to ensure compliance with ethical leadership and corporate citizenship.

2. *Boards and directors.* Obviously, this only applies where the SME has a board of directors. Medium-sized enterprises without a board of directors, should consider appointing a board of directors.

3. *Audit committees.* Closed corporations are not required to appoint auditors, merely an accountant. Companies are compelled by law to appoint an auditor. King refers to the board appointing an audit committee. Where an SME has a board, this element would apply. Nevertheless, even if an SME does not have a board of

directors, the business owner should take cognisance of the stipulations and ensure the auditor or accountant addresses the finance and risk related issues satisfactorily.

4. *Governance of risk.* It applies to SMEs with boards, but in the absence of a board, disclosure to all stakeholders would be at the discretion of the business owner.

5. *Governance of information technology.* It applies to SMEs with boards, but in the absence of a board, it is in the interest of the continued existence of the SME for the business owner to monitor significant IT investments and expenditure and to oversee management of IT governance risks.

6. *Compliance with laws, rules, codes and standards.* It applies to SMEs with boards but all SMEs have to comply with applicable laws and must consider adherence to non-binding rules, codes and standards.

7. *Internal audit.* This element applies to all SMEs registered as companies as they are compelled by law to appoint auditors. Nevertheless, SMEs without auditors should seriously consider having an assessment conducted of the effectiveness of the company's internal control and risk management systems.

8. *Governing stakeholder relationships.* Where an SME has shareholders, this element is of particular relevance. All SMEs have stakeholders such as suppliers, customers, employees and all SMEs should have effective communication with their stakeholders.

9. *Integrated reporting and disclosure.* Only SMEs registered as companies would have to comply with this element.

The financial and economic crisis in 2008 revealed severe shortcomings in corporate governance and the need for greater use of regulation over self-regulating codes and standards. Implementing the checks and balances that companies need in order to cultivate sound business practices would be to the benefit of the companies and contribute to their long-term sustainability.

IoDSA (2009) advocates that King III applies to all entities regardless of the manner and form of incorporation, whether in the public, private sector or non-profit sectors. It then suggests that all entities, including SMEs, should apply the principles in the Code, consider the best practice recommendations, and make disclosures about how the principles were, or were not, applied.

22.1.2.4 Corporate governance and corporate social responsibility

The focal point of the *King Code of Corporate Governance* is the chairman of the company and its board of directors who are responsible for monitoring risks and opportunities and engaging with stakeholders. They would also govern the corporate social responsibility programmes. The board should have a CSR subcommittee to establish the policy for CSR. Such a policy can adopt different approaches, such as (Du Toit et al., 2010:158):

▸ A values-based system: aligning the CSR policy with the company's vision, mission, values and code of conduct
▸ A stakeholder-engagement process: allowing stakeholders to decide on the issues to be addressed by the company
▸ A combination of both a values-based system and a stakeholder-engagement system: the policy evolves from the company defining its needs and then involving the stakeholders' needs and in so doing satisfying the needs of both the company and the stakeholders.

It can be concluded that corporate social responsibility should be an integral part of corporate governance.

22.2 Sustainable development

Sustainable development as defined by the Brutland Commission is 'development to ensure that it meets the needs of the present without compromising the ability of future generations to meet their own needs'; 'the concept of sustainable development does imply limits – not absolute limits but limitations imposed by the present state of technology and social organization on environmental resources and by the ability of the biosphere to absorb the effects of human activities' (UN, 1987:15). This definition has also been used by the Institute of Directors (IOD, n.d.). A key challenge of sustainable development is to operationalise the concept and to realise that it is a never-ending process.

When considering policies on sustainable development, the Brutland Commission 'focused its attention on the areas of population, food security, the loss of species and genetic resources, energy, industry, and human settlements – realizing that all of these are connected and cannot be treated in isolation one from another' (UN, 1987:16).

In the position paper on 'Implementing Sustainable Development as a Strategic Business Model' the Sustainable Business forum of the Institute of Directors Identified 11 deadline risk areas for business and suggested appropriate actions for some of the risk areas, listed in Table 22.2 (IOD, n.d.)

These risk areas for business are relevant to the sustainable development of SMEs.

22.3 Broad-based Black Economic Empowerment – new codes

In Chapter 17 the existing Codes of Good Practice (Codes) for Broad-based Black Economic Empowerment (B-BBEE) as per the Broad-Based Black Economic

SOUTH AFRICAN SUCCESS STORY

Aveng clams up on tender rigging
Business Day
3 November 2013

Aveng, one of South Africa's top five construction companies, said on Friday at its annual general meeting (AGM) that it would not approach any of its clients to disclose any collusion or tender rigging that may have taken place on their projects.

The company was involved in building some of the largest projects in the country, including building Soccer City where the 2010 World Cup final took place, building office blocks at the Coega industrial development zone near Port Elizabeth, and road projects for the South African National Roads Agency (Sanral).

At its AGM, shareholders grilled Aveng about the fact that while it was implicated in 57 'prohibited practices' under the competition law, such as collusion, it revealed details of only nine of them. This meant that 48 other clients (or projects) remained none the wiser about whether they were short changed by Aveng.

Chairman Angus Band said it would not be in Aveng's interests to disclose such practices to its clients. 'We have no embargo on talking to clients when they approach us, but in line with our legal advice, we will not be putting out a list or anything like that', he said.

Shareholder activist Theo Botha said after the AGM that he wasn't comfortable with this approach. 'Rather than sitting and waiting for clients to come to them, these construction companies should approach them', said Mr Botha.

This June, the Competition Commission fined the construction industry altogether R1.46bn for colluding on 300 projects (about R50bn in value), mainly during the construction timeline before the World Cup. Aveng alone was fined R307m for its role in the scandal.

Sanral CEO Nazir Ali recently told *Business Times* that the agency was considering laying criminal charges against construction companies that overcharged it, as well as civil action. While investors in construction companies believe the Competition fine would draw a line under this scandal, a spate of new civil actions from clients could hit their pockets hard.

However, identifying the people directly involved in the construction cartel and bringing them to book might prove more difficult. The hard-hat cartel took part in at least two major meetings including the Road Contractors Meeting and the 2010 Fifa World Cup Stadiums Agreement, and Aveng took part in both of them. With the stadiums, profits agreed on were as high as 17.5%. In total, these rigged stadiums cost more than R15bn, which makes the margin the companies were trying to achieve through the rigging just short of R3bn.

Mr Band said it would be very difficult to charge implicated individuals for damages, but pointed out that Aveng had taken action against a number of individuals that were personally involved in collusion. Aveng also suspended seven executive members, and eight resigned because the company withheld incentives. Eleven other implicated employees went without incentives. An executive director and senior executive who were implicated in Competition Act violations in other companies before joining Aveng also resigned. Another two people were demoted. The company's CEO, Roger Jardine, resigned in August after five years at the helm, saying the commission's investigation process had been personally very taxing.

Source: Prinsloo (2013:1).

Table 22.2 Deadline risk areas for business – and possible solutions

RISK AREA	POSSIBLE SOLUTIONS
Opportunities for work-life balance	Organisation strategy and policy takes into account stakeholder views
Training and advancement opportunities	Companies share their vision with stakeholders
Occupational health and safety are actively managed	Community health is not adversely impacted on by organisation activities and is preferably enhanced
Flexibility for self-determination within the organisation	Business contributes constructively within its sphere of influence to addressing matters of social injustice
Emotional intelligence and social intelligence are important measures of organisation success	Business operates in full partnership with government, civil society and labour to set and achieve its objectives, as well as contribute to the objectives of other parties
Creativity and entrepreneurship is encouraged and rewarded	Stakeholders actively participate in decisions that affect them or their environment
Employees actively participate in the development of organisation policy and strategic direction	Political risk is recognised, lobbying, and ongoing engagement is pursued with government on issues of concern
Human skill and innovation is maximised in organisation operations	
Employees actively participate in decisions affecting them	
Employees are encouraged to use their discretion at a level appropriate to their occupation	
Equitable remuneration policies are implemented	

Empowerment Act 53 of 2003 are discussed (see Section 17.7).

On Friday 11 October 2013, the final B-BBEE codes were gazetted. After a series of debates, the new codes include amendments to the codes which were released by the Minister of Trade and Industry (Minister) in October 2012 (Polity, 2013).

Under these final Codes, enterprises have been given a one-year transitional period starting 11 October 2013 to align their affairs with the Codes' requirements. This concession is welcomed. During this transitional period, enterprises may elect to be measured in terms of the generic scorecard under the final Codes or the historic generic scorecard under the old Codes. However, enterprises which are governed by sector-specific codes will continue to be measured in terms of those sector codes.

The compliance net has been widened by the final Codes. The following persons will be subject to measurement under the final Codes:
▸ All organs of state and public entities; and
▸ Natural or juristic persons who conduct a business, trade or profession in South Africa, that undertakes any economic activity with organs of state or public entities.

The generic scorecard in the Codes provides that all enterprises will be measured in terms of five B-BBEE elements, namely:
1. Ownership
2. Management control
3. Skills development
4. Enterprise and supplier development
5. Socio-economic development.

Sub-minimum targets apply for three priority elements, namely ownership, skills development, and enterprise and supplier development, according to the new Codes:

▶ 40% of net value points for ownership, net value being one of the measurements for ownership which evaluates the extent to which shares (held by black shareholders) are free from encumbrance;
▶ 40% of the total weighting points for skills development; and
▶ 40% for each of preferential procurement; enterprise development and supplier development.

While large entities must comply with all three priority elements, qualifying small enterprises (QSE) must comply with at least two of the three priority elements, one of which being the ownership priority element. Should the above-mentioned targets not be met, the Codes provide for the downgrading by one level of the B-BBEE status level of both large entities and QSEs. For large companies this ruling is an improvement on the draft Codes, which originally proposed that large entities be subject to a two level downgrade. Nevertheless, large companies will find that the more stringent targets in the final Codes are likely to have a negative impact on current B-BBEE ratings even without the additional one level downgrading that has been finally introduced.

A significant change in the final Codes is the increased threshold in points required to achieve a better B-BBEE status. For example, a company currently needs 65 points to achieve a level four B-BBEE status (and 100% recognition level). Under the final Codes, a company would need at least 80 points to achieve the same status.

The thresholds for enterprises to qualify as Exempted Micro Enterprises (EME), QSEs or large entities, are as follows:

▶ The threshold for EMEs increased from ZAR 5 million to ZAR 10 million
▶ The threshold for QSEs increased from ZAR 5–35 million to ZAR 10–50 million

▶ The threshold for large entities increased to ZAR 50 million and above.

22.3.1 Eligibility as an Exempted Micro Enterprise

As an SME these rulings may apply to you:

Item 4.1:	Any enterprise with an annual total revenue of R10 million or less qualifies as an Exempted micro enterprise (EME)
Item 4.2:	An EME is deemed to have a B-BBEE status of 'Level Four Contributor' having a B-BBEE recognition level of 100% under paragraph 8.2.
Item 4.3:	Enhanced B-BBEE for an EME
Item 4.3.1:	Despite paragraph 4.2 an EME that is 100% black owned qualifies for elevation to 'Level One Contributor' having a B-BBEE recognition of 135%.
Item 4.3.2:	Despite paragraph 4.2 and 4.3.1 an EME which is at least 51% black owned qualifies for elevation to 'Level Two Contributor' having a B-BBEE recognition of 125%.
Item 4.4:	Despite paragraph 4.2 and 4.3 an EME is allowed to be measured according to the QSE scorecard should they wish to maximise their score points and move to a higher B-BBEE recognition level.

22.3.2 Eligibility as a Qualifying Small Enterprise (QSE)

As a small enterprise these rulings may apply to you:

Item 5.1:	A Measured Entity with an annual total revenue of R10 million and R50 million qualifies as a QSE

Item 5.2:   A QSE must comply with all the elements for B-BBEE for purposes of measurement.
Item 5.3: Enhanced B-BBEE for a QSE
Item 5.3.1:   A QSE which is 100% black owned qualifies for a level one B-BBEE recognition
Item 5.3.2:   A QSE that is at least 51% black owned qualifies for Level Two B-BBEE recognition.

22.1.5.3 Start-up enterprises

As a start-up enterprise these rulings may apply to you:

Item 6.1:   Start-up enterprises must be measured as an EME under this statement for the first year following their formation or incorporation. This provision applies regardless of the total revenue of the enterprise.
Item 6.2:   A start-up enterprise is deemed to have the qualifying B-BBEE status in accordance with the principles to paragraph 4 of this statement.
Item 6.3:   In order to qualify as a start-up enterprise, the enterprise must provide an independent confirmation of its status in accordance with paragraph 4.5.
Item 6.4:   Despite paragraph 6.1 and 6.2 a start-up enterprise must submit a QSE scorecard when tendering for any contract or seeking any other economic activity covered by section 10 of the Act, with a value higher than R10 million or less than R50 milllion. For contracts of R50 million or more they should submit the generic scorecard. The preparation of such scorecards must use annualised data.

Source: Government Gazette 580, number 36928 published 11 October 2013 (dti, 2013).

ENTREPRENEURIAL DILEMMA

To obtain B-BBEE scorecard or not

Jack started a business in 2006 and through hard work and long hours has grown the business to a turnover of R9 million. He is planning to tender for a lucrative contract at a company but they insist that he must submit his B-BBEE scorecard to be included on their procurement list. He has been on their procurement list for a number of years without the B-BBEE scorecard but the company now insists. He does not have a black partner and is wondering whether he should appoint a black partner. It seems he would have to give the black partner at least 51% ownership in his business. It would mean the black partner would have a controlling share in his company that he had spent blood, sweat and tears building up. On the other hand, if he does not appoint a black partner, he may not be granted any further contracts from the supplier. What would you advise Jack to do?

CONCLUSION

In this chapter we explored the concept of corporate social responsibility as well as other related concepts such as corporate citizenship, corporate social investment, corporate governance, sustainable development and broad-based black economic empowerment. Each of these concepts was clearly defined and further detail provided to gain a fuller understanding of the concepts. The most recent B-BBEE codes were detailed in particular as they are relevant to EMEs, QSEs and start-up businesses and these could be relevant to SMEs. This chapter explores each of these concepts in greater depth.

SELF-ASSESSMENT QUESTIONS

Multiple-choice questions

1. Corporate social responsibility calls for companies to strive for balance between the economic, legal, ethical and _____ responsibility.
   a. labour
   b. physical
   c. philanthropic
   d. populace
2. Corporate citizenship incorporates _____.
   a. responsibility for government corruption
   b. responsibility for environmental impacts
   c. responsibility for failure of other companies
   d. responsibility for natural disasters
3. The UN Global Impact Principles asks companies to embrace, support and enact, within their sphere of influence, a set of core values in four areas, namely in the areas of human rights, labour standards, the environment and _____.
   a. anti-corruption
   b. anti-animal cruelty
   c. anti-global warming
   d. anti-whaling
4. The King III report on corporate governance focuses primarily on _____.
   a. guidelines for small businesses
   b. guidelines for the medical profession
   c. guidelines for operational staff
   d. guidelines for boards of directors
5. The new codes for B-BBEE have stipulated the following:
   a. The threshold for EMEs increased from ZAR 10 million to ZAR 15 million
   b. The threshold for QSEs increased from ZAR 5–35 million to ZAR 10–50 million
   c. The threshold for large entities increased to ZAR 100 million and above
   d. There are no changes in thresholds

DISCUSSION QUESTIONS

1. Discuss corporate social responsibility.
2. Differentiate between corporate social responsibility and corporate social investment.
3. Explain the nine elements of the King III report on corporate governance.
4. Apply the nine elements of sustainable development to your business.
5. Explain the new B-BBEE codes.

EXPERIENTIAL EXERCISE

1. 'I'm 35 years old and have been running this business (Squeeky Clean) since 2006 and only formalised it in 2012, but I'm not sure if I'm well-equipped in terms of running a business', said Mina. What do you think she means with 'formalised'? Is she being a good corporate citizen?
2. A fruit and vegetables retailer, Sipho, said: 'I experienced this issue of mixing my personal money with business money when I started this business three years ago. It resulted in serious problems, and put me in and out of business'. What are the implications of Sipho not taking responsibility for the financial management of his business, in particular the cash-flow management? Which of his stakeholders suffered as a result of his actions?
3. You own a smallholding on which you successfully grow vegetables. You have decided to expand and grow more vegetables, but you would need more water. The water from the borehole would not be sufficient. You could build a weir in the stream that flows through your property, dam up the water and irrigate from the dam. However, if you dam up the water, the people living further down would not have access to water from the stream. What should you do? Would it be socially responsible to dam up the water?
4. Work through the deadline areas for business risk and work out strategies to ensure that your business will be sustainable.

5. Even though your company's turnover is below the required limit for obtaining a B-BBEE scoring, your customer, a large retailer, insists that you obtain a B-BBEE score to remain on their procurement list. What should you do?

MAKING MORE BEER USING LESS WATER

In South Africa, water is high on the public agenda. Commentators have made serious predictions of imminent systems collapse and water shortages. According to the National Water Resource Strategy, South Africa will face a supply-demand deficit of -17% by 2030 under current efficiency levels.

As a leading corporation South African Breweries (SAB) is increasingly developing strategies for identifying water risks. Investors are also becoming more interested in understanding water risks and implications for the future competitiveness of companies.

By its nature, brewing is a water-intensive process. SAB is one of the first to undertake a comprehensive water foot-printing exercise, which revealed that more than 90% of the water footprint of a bottle of beer is found in the agricultural supply chain.

SAB's water strategy is based on 4 Rs – pRotect, Reduce, Reuse, Recycle in the value chain. The strategy focuses on four key areas:

1. In the brewery – using less water to make more beer and manage effluent standards. On average SAB uses 3.9 litres of water to produce

Source: S.A. Breweries, (2011:1).

one litre of beer, an improvement of 8% over the past two years. As part of the SABMiller group, we are committed to reducing our water consumption in the brewing environment by 25% to 3.5 litres per litre of beer by 2015.

2. In the supply chain – working with suppliers and farmers to identify water risks and options to reduce water use across the supply chain.
3. In communities – identifying community projects that will help provide safe and sustainable drinking water to communities.
4. Water governance – keeping water on SAB's strategic and risk agenda, mobilising employees to save water, engaging with government on policy issues and delivering on the Water Futures Partnership. The company is also one of the pioneering partners in the Strategic Water Partners Network (SWPN), a joint effort by the public and private sector.

Long-term water assessments of all its breweries have been undertaken and SAB has a comprehensive understanding of the risks it faces over the next ten years.

1. From a corporate governance perspective, has SAB taken into consideration their various stakeholders in trying to reduce their water footprint?
2. In which other areas of their operations could SAB exhibit characteristics of good corporate social responsibility?
3. Could they reduce their energy and carbon footprint?
4. Could they start paper recycling?
5. SAB is committed to football development. Would you classify their donations to football development as corporate social investment?

SUGGESTED WEBSITE LINKS

King III in a nutshell: http://www.cliffedekkerhofmeyr.
com/export/sites/cdh/en/legal/sectors/downloads/
Cliffe-Dekker-Hofmeyr-King-III-in-a-Nutshell.

B-BBEE Verification Agencies: Sanas <http://www.
sanas.co.za/af-directory/bbbee_list.php>

The B-BBEE Verification Manual: https://www.google.
co.za/url?sa=t&rct=j&q=&esrc=s&source=web&cd=
1&ved=0CE8QFjAA&url=http%3A%2F%2Fwww.
thedti.gov.za%2Feconomic_empowerment%2Fbee_
veri_manual.jsp&ei=BYJWU772K8OQ7AagnYG4
Ag&usg=AFQjCNFX_jZH9h4iL9LRO3H3kYm
ET7AQBA&sig2=RbBw4W_d02s4Vnxt
OM2Z3w> : www.thedti.gov.za/economic_
empowerment/bee_veri_manual.jsp

Corporate social responsibility: Sappi <http://www.
sappi.com/regions/sa/Supportandsponsorships/
CSR/Pages/default.aspx>

Corporate Social Responsibility and Corporate Social
Investment: <http://www.csisolutions.co.za/
why-csi.php>

REFERENCE LIST

Department of Trade and Industry. 2013. *B-BBEE Codes of Good Practice*: Gazette No.36928. [Online]. Available: http://www.thedti.gov.za/economic_empowerment/bee_codes.jsp [3 November 2013].

Du Toit, GS, Erasmus, BJ. & Strydom, JW. 2010. *Introduction to Business Management*. 8th ed. Cape Town: Oxford.

Gamble, JE. & Thompson, AA. 2011. *Essentials of Strategic Management: the Quest for Competitive Advantage*. 2nd ed. New York, NY: McGraw-Hill.

IOD. n.d. Implementing Sustainable Development as a Strategic Business Model: Sustainable Business forum. Position Paper 1. Johannesburg: IOD. [Online]. Available:http://www.iodsa.co.za/?page=ForumSDF [3 November 2013].

IoDSA. 2009. *King Code of Governance for South Africa*. Johannesburg: Institute of Directors Southern Africa. [Online]. Available: www.iodsa.co.za. [3 November 2013].

OECD. 2004. *OECD Principles of Corporate Governance*. Paris, France: OECD.

Polity. 2013: Final revised B-BBEE Codes of Good Practice. Webber Wentzel. Published 2013-10-14. [Online]. Available http://www.polity.org.za/article/final-revised-bbbee-codes-of-good-practice-2013-10-14. [3 November 2013].

Prinsloo, l. Day. 2013. Aveng clams up on tender rigging. *Business Day*, 2 November 2013. [Online]. Available: http://www.bdlive.co.za/business/industrials/2013/11/03/aveng-clams-up-on-tender-rigging. [3 November 2013].

S.A. Breweries. 2013. Sustainable development: Water - Making more beer using less water. [Online]. Available: http://www.sab.co.za/sablimited/content/en/sustainable-development-listing?cat_id=107 [3 November 2013].

Shezi, M. 2013. SMEs' corporate governance systems: Status and effect on continuity. MCom dissertation. Gordon Institute of Business Science, University of Pretoria: Pretoria.

UN – United Nations. Undated. United Nations Global Compact: The Ten Principles. Online. Available: http://www.unglobalcompact.org/abouttheGC/TheTenPrinciples/index.html [3 November 2013].

United Nations – Brutland Commission. 1987. Report of the World Commission on Environment and Development: Our common future. [Online]. Available: http://conspect.nl/pdf/Our_Common_Future-Brundtland_Report_1987.pdf

WEF – World Economic Forum. 2002. Global Corporate Citizenship: *The Leadership Challenge for CEOs and Boards*. Geneva: World Economic Forum. [Online]. Available: http://www.weforum.org/pdf/GCCI/GCC_CEOstatement.pdf [3 November 2013].

Bibliography

Adams, D. 2012. How To: Develop An Entrepreneurial Mindset. [Online]. Available: http://www.bitrebels. com/business-2/develop-an-entrepreneurial-mindset/ [14 August 2013].

Alleman, G. 2012. Data management and cleansing – not about the data. *iWeek*, 18 July 2012:17.

Allen, KR. 2010. *Launching New Ventures*. 5th ed. Boston: Houghton Mifflin.

Allinson, CW, Chell, E. & Hayes, J. 2000. Intuition and entrepreneurial behavior. *European Journal of Work and Organizational Psychology*, 9(1):31–43.

AMC Editorial Team. 2013. African Marketing Confederation *The coffee brand that's living the life of 'Vida'*. [Online]. Available: http://www.africanmc. org/index.php/knowledge-portal/item/84-the-coffee-brand-thats-living-the-life-of-vida [23 June 2014].

American Marketing Association (AMA). 2014. *Definition of marketing*. [Online]. Available: https:// www.ama.org/AboutAMA/Pages/Definition-of-Marketing.aspx [11 April 2014].

Andrews, C. 2014. *The 3 myths about creativity in business*. [Online]. Available: http://www.theguardian.com/ media-network/media-network-blog/2014/ jan/17/3-myths-creativity-in-business [4 March 2014].

APC Solutions SA. 2013. Case study: Pearl Valley Golf Estate. Press release 30 July 2013. [Online]. Available: http://www.itweb.co.za/index. php?option=com_content&view=article&id=66111 #prcontacts [27 October 2013].

Amstrong, G. & Kotler. P. 2013. *Marketing: An Introduction*. Global edition.11th ed. Upper Saddle River, N.J: Pearson.

Arkebauer, JB. 1993. *Ultrapreneuring: Taking a venture from start-up to harvest in three years or less*. New York: McGraw-Hill.

ASEN, n.d. *Social enterprise feature – Iyeza Express*. [Online]. Available: http://asenetwork. org/2013/08/15/social-enterprise-feature-iyeza-express/ [2 March 2014].

Attio, E. 2007. *Global Entrepreneurship Monitor: 2007 Global Report On High-Growth Entrepreneurship*. Babson College, London: Business School and Global Entrepreneurship Monitor (GERA).

Badal, S., 2012. Building corporate entrepreneurship is hard work. *Gallup Business Journal*, 25 September.

Bangs, DH. 2005. *Business Plans Made Easy*. Portsmouth: Entrepreneur Press.

Bannock, G, Baxter, RE. & Davis, E. 2003. *The Penguin Dictionary of Economics*. London: Penguin.

Baron, RA. 1998. Cognitive mechanisms in entrepreneurship: Why and when entrepreneurs think differently than other people. *Journal of Business Venturing*, 13(4):275–294.

Baron, RA. 2004. Opportunity recognition: A cognitive perspective. Academy of Management Best Conference Paper 2004ENT: A1–A6. [Online]. Available: http://faculty.insead.edu/andersonp/ VOBM_MAYJUN2005/Anderson%20VOBM%20 readings/Session%202%20 How%20venture%20 opportunities%20are%20screened/Baron,%202004. pdf [1 August 2011].

Baumgartner, JP. 2005. Ten creative myths. [Online]. Available: http://www.jpb.com/creative/article_ creative_myths.php [1 August 2011].

Benade, ML, Henning, JL, Delport, PA, Du Plessis, JJ, De Koker, L. & Pretorious, JT. 2003. *Entrepreneurial Law*. 3rd ed. Butterworths: Durban.

Bezuidenhout, S, Cloete, M, Joynt, C, Nortjé-Rossouw, D. & Van Pletsen, L. 2013. *Accounting and Basic Financial Literacy*. 3rd ed. Pretoria: Salt and Pepper Publishing.

Bienkowski, S. 2013. *Quiz: Do you have the entrepreneurial mindset?* [Online]. Available: http:// www.success.com/article/quiz-do-you-have-the-entrepreneurial-mindset [3 September 2013].

Bishop, K. 2005. Creativity Myths, 17 March 2005. [Online]. Available: http://enzinearticles. com/?Creativity-Myths&id=21178 [1 August 2011].

Bishop, K. & Nixon, RD. 2006. Venture opportunity evaluations: Comparisons between venture capitalist and inexperienced pre-nascent entrepreneurs. *Journal of Developmental Entrepreneurship*, 11(1):19–33.

BizConnect. 2012. Standard Bank BizConnect. *How to tell when the price is right. Accurately evaluating franchise costs*. [Online]. Available: http:// bizconnect.standardbank.co.za/sector-news/ franchising/how-to-tell-when-the-price-is-right. aspx [6 June 2014].

BizConnect. 2012a. Standard Bank BizConnect. *Franchising in SA: A home-grown success story*. [Online]. Available: http://bizconnect. standardbank.co.za/sector-news/franchising/ franchising-in-sa-a-home-grown-success-story.aspx [12 June 2014].

BizConnect. 2014. Standard Bank BizConnect. *Huizemark: Changing with the times.* [Online]. Available: http://bizconnect.standardbank.co.za/sector-news/franchising/huizemark-changing-with-the-times.aspx [23 June 2014].

Blank, S. 2012. Deadliest start-up sins. [Online]. Available: http://steveblank.com/202/05/14/9-deadliest-start-up-sins/ [29 January 2014].

Bolton, T. 2014. Social media is fast becoming a valuable tool for retailers. *Wholesale business,* 1.

Bonkowski, F. 2008. Breaking barriers to creativity: Five strategies for third agers. [Online]. Available: http://www.selfgrowth.com/articles/Breaking_Barriers_to_Creativity_5_Strategies_for_Third_Agers.html [10 December 2010].

Boucher, C. 2012. Exactexh: Antonio Pooe. *Entrepreneur Magazine.* [Online]. Available: www.entrepreneurmag.co.za [5 January 2014].

Bounds, GM, Dobbins, H. & Fowler, OS. 1995. *Management: A Total Quality Perspective.* Cincinnati: South-Western Publishing Co.

Bradt, G. 2012. *Corporate Culture: The only truly sustainable competitive advantage.* [Online]. Available: http://www.forbes.com/sites/georgebradt/2012/02/08/corporate-culture-the-only-truly-sustainable-competitive-advantage/ [October 2013].

Brand-Jonker, N. 2014. Werkneste open vir Entrepreneurs. Hier broei koel idees uit. *Die Burger,* 5 Februarie 2014. [Online]. Available: http://www.dieburger.com/sake/2014-02-05-hier-broei-koel-idees-uit [15 February 2014].

Brand Finance. 2013. South Africa Top 50. The annual report on South Africa's 50 Most Valuable Brands. August 2013, Johannesburg: Brand Finance plc, in partnership with Brand South Africa and Brand Africa.

Brands and Branding in South Africa. 2013. *20th Anniversary Edition.* Johannesburg; Affinity Advertising & Publishing.

Breen, B. 2004. The six myths of creativity. [Online]. Available: http://www.fastcompany.com/magazine/89/creativity.html [5 January 2011].

Bridge, S. & Hegarty, C. 2013. *Beyond the Business Plan.* Hampshire, UK. Palgrave Macmillan Publishers.

Bruwer, P. & Plaatjies, D. 1999. *Entrepreneurship and Business Management.* Revised ed. Observatory: Future Management (Pty) Ltd.

Burkhardt, V. 2009. Creative Myths: Interview with Keith Sawyer, author of *Explaining creativity: The science of human innovation,* 29 March 2009. [Online]. Available: http://www.ideaconnection.com/open-innovationarticles/00106-Creativity-Myths.html [5 January 2011].

Burkus, D. 2014. *The Myths of Creativity: The Truth About How Innovative Companies and People Generate Great Ideas.* San Francisco, CA: Jossey-Bass.

Busenitz, LW. & Barney, JB. 1997. Differences between entrepreneurs and managers in large organizations: Biases and heuristics in strategic decision-making. *Journal of Business Venturing,* 12(1):9–30.

BSSA. n.d *Young entrepreneur now helping others.* [Online]. Available: http://www.bssa.co.za/success-stories/young-entrepreneur-now-helping-others [October 2013].

Bush, G. 2011. Don't tell me … 'It's NOT my job'! *Supermarket & Retailer,* February, 32.

BusinessDictionary.com. 2014a. BusinessDictionary.com. *Business format franchising.* [Online]. Available: http://www.businessdictionary.com/definition/business-format-franchising.html [16 June 2014].

BusinessDictionary.com. 2014b. BusinessDictionary.com. *Product franchise.* [Online]. Available: http://www.businessdictionary.com/definition/product-franchising.html [18 June 2014].

Business Directory. 2014a. *Business Directory.com/Definitions/Operations strategy.* [Online]. Available: http://www.businessdictionary.com/definition/operations-strategy.html#ixzz35jXQ6JGZ [26 June 2014].

Business Directory. 2014b. *Business Directory/Definitions/Operating plan.* [Online]. Available: http://www.businessdictionary.com/definition/operating-plan.html [26 June 2014].

Bygrave, W. & Zacharakis, A. 2011. *Entrepreneurship.* 2nd ed. Hoboken, NJ: John Willey & Sons, Inc.

Byrd, MJ. & Megginson, LC. 2009. *Small Business Management, an Entrepreneur's Guidebook.* New York: McGraw-Hill/Irwin.

Byrd, MJ. & Megginson, LC. 2013. *Small Business Management: An Entrepreneur's Guidebook.* 7th ed. New York: McGraw-Hill.

Calitz, G. 2005. Promotion of Access to Information Act: Section 14 Manual. 29 April 2005. The dti: Sunnyside, Pretoria. Reference Number: 7/4/1/1.

Cameron, N. 2013. *Does your business comply with the Consumer Protection Act?* [Online]. Available: http://businessnews.howzit.msn.com/does-your-business-comply-with-the-consumer-protection-act [November 2013].

Cascio. W. 2013. *Managing Human Resources: Productivity, Quality of Work life, Profits.* 9th ed. New York: The McGraw-Hill Companies, Inc.

Cassim, A. 2013. *Slimline ATM Innovation – An African First for FNB!.* [Online]. Available: https://blog.fnb.co.za/2013/08/slimline-atm-innovation-an-african-first-for-fnb/ [23 March 2014].

Chase, F. & Jacobs FR. 2010. *Operations and Supply Chain Management.* 13th ed. New York: McGraw-Hill/Irwin.

CIPRO. 2008. Close Corporations transitional arrangements in new Companies Bill. Issued by Legal and Regulatory Services, 11 July 2008. [Online]. Available: http://www.cipro.co.za/notices/notice_cctransitionbill.htm [11 January 2011].

CIPRO. 2011. Patents. [Online]. Available: http://www.cipro.gov.za/products_services/patents.asp [1 August 2011].

Collins, CJ. & Porras, JI. 2000. *Built to Last: Successful Habits of Visionary Companies.* 3rd ed. London: Random House Business Books.

Cooper, AC, Woo, CY. & Dunkelberg, WC. 1988. Entrepreneurs' perceived chance of success. *Journal of Business Venturing,* 3(1):97–108.

Crankshaw, P. 2013. How to buy a franchise. *Small Business Connect* (4):8.

Cronje, GJ de J, Du Toit, GS. & Marais, A de K. 2004. *Introduction to Business Management.* 6th ed. Cape Town: Oxford University Press Southern Africa.

Cronje, GJ de J, Du Toit, GS, Mol, AJ, Neuland, EW. & Motlatla, MDC. (Eds). 1997. *Introduction to Business Management.* Johannesburg: International Thomson Publishing.

D'Amico, M. 2011. D'Amico Incorporated Attorneys. *Franchisors beware – update your franchise agreement!* [Online]. Available: http://www.damico.co.za/legal_article_details.asp?ARTICLE_ID=8 [12 June 2014].

Daniel, A. 2013. *The Kraal Gallery Entrepreneurship Award August 2013,* Gordons Bay: The Kraal Gallery.

Das, TK. & Teng, BS. 1997. Time and entrepreneurial risk behavior. *Entrepreneurship Theory and Practice,* 22(2):69–88.

David, FR. 1995. *Concepts of Strategic Management.* Englewood Cliffs, N.J.: Prentice-Hall.

Davies, A. 2013. *6 Myths about creativity.* [Online]. Available: http://www.huffingtonpost.com/2013/11/29/be-more-creative-creativity-myths_n_4343699.html. [4 March 2014].

Day, J. 1993. *Small Business in Tough Times: How to Survive and Prosper.* Amsterdam: Pfeiffer.

De Kock, A. 2012. *Working Paper 1 – October 2012. WEF GCI 2012/13 Report: Analysing performance and implications for South Africa,* Johannesburg: Brand South Africa.

De Beers Group. 2013. *As diamonds are a miracle of nature, so synthetics are a triumph of science.* [Online]. Available: http://www.debeersgroup.com/en/Operations/Element-Six/ [25 March 2014].

Department of Justice and Constitutional Development. 2014. [Online]. Available: http://www.justice.gov.za/scc/scc.htm [21 July 2014].

Department of Trade and Industry. 2005. *Integrated Strategy for the Promotion of Entrepreneurship and Small Enterprises,* Pretoria: The Department of Trade and Industry.

Department of Trade and Industry. 2007a. *Broad-based Black Economic Empowerment Act (53/2003): Codes of Good Conduct on Black Economic Empowerment.* Pretoria: Government Printers.

Department of Trade and Industry. 2007b. *Interpretative Guide to the Codes of Good Practice.* Pretoria: Department of Trade and Industry.

Department of Trade and Industry. 2010a. Department of Trade and Industry Press Release. The new consumer protection act and companies act to come into force on 1 April 2011.Issued by Communication and Marketing, the dti. 28 September 2010. [Online]. Available: http://www.cipro.co.za/notices/2010_10_01_Update_on_implementation_of_the_new_Companies_Act,2008.pdf [11 January 2011].

Department of Trade and Industry. 2010b. The Companies Act, No. 71 of 2008. An explanatory guide. Pretoria: the dti.

Department of Trade and Industry. 2013. *B-BBEE Codes of Good Practice:* Gazette No.36928. [Online]. Available: http://www.thedti.gov.za/economic_empowerment/bee_codes.jsp [3 November 2013].

Dingle, S. 2011. Battle with the big guys. *Finweek,* 3 March, 18–19.

Dlamini, P. 2012. *Soweto jewellery bound for London.* [Online]. Available: http://www.sowetanlive.co.za/news/business/2012/05/14/soweto-jewellery-bound-for-london [10 March 2014].

Donnelly, B. 2008. The CEO's entrepreneurial dilemma. [Online]. Available: http://www.paramuschamber.com/documents/TheCEOsEntrepreneurial Dilemma.pdf [28 February 2011].

Dorfling, C. 2007. Instant Button: Monique Robinson. *Entrepreneur Magazine,* June. [Online]. Available: http://www.entrepreneurmag.co.za/article/h/?a=1698&z=166&title=Instant+Button%3a+Monique+Robinson [15 March 2011].

Douglas, K. 2013. *Coffee shop brand, vida e caffé, says their next stop is Ghana.* How we made it in Africa. [Online]. Available: http://www.howwemadeitinafrica.com/coffee-shop-brand-vida-e-caffe-says-their-next-stop-is-ghana/27495/?fullpost=1 [23 June 2014].

Duffy, S. 2012. *12 Characteristics of a Highly Successful Entrepreneurial Mindset.* [Online]. Available: http://www.greatmindsinspire.com/archives/67 [20 August 2013].

Duncan, C. 2010. How to be creative and productive in every stage of a project. *Productive Flourishing: Strategies for Thriving in Life and Business.* 23 August 2010. [Online]. Available: http://www. productiveflourishing.com/how-to-be-creative-and-productive-in-everystage-of-a-project/ [20 December 2010].

Du Toit, GS, Erasmus, BJ. & Strydom, JW. 2010. *Introduction to Business Management.* 8th ed. Cape Town: Oxford.

Durham, L. 2011. Jwayelani - Centralisation leads to ultimate efficiency. *Supermarket & Retailer,* February, 33-35.

Element Six. 2013. *Our innovation capability.* [Online]. Available: http://www.e6.com/wps/wcm/connect/ E6_Content_EN/Home/Innovation/ Our+innovation+capability/ [25 March 2014].

E-Myth. 2010. Seven signs that your business is in trouble. 1 September 2010. [Online]. Available: http://www.e-myth.com/cs/user/print/post/7-signs-that yourbusiness-is-in-trouble [17 March 2011].

Entrepreneur. 2010. Building a multi-million rand online brand. *Entrepreneur Magazine,* April 2010.

Entrepreneur. 2012. *The Consumer Protection Act.* [Online]. Available: http://www.entrepreneurmag. co.za/advice/starting-a-business/start-up-guide/ the-consumer-protection-act/ [November 2013].

Entrepreneur of the Year. 2012. Eastern Cape female farmer named as Job Creator of the Year 2012. [Online]. Available: http://www.eoy.co.za/posts/ from-new-ground-springs-new-growth-628 [7 May 2014].

EOY – Envirodeck. 2013. *Envirodeck. Company profile.* [Online]. Available: http://www.envirodeck.co.za/ about-envirodeck-composite-decking/composite-decks-profile [21 March 2014].

Evans, JR. 1993. Creativity in MS/OR: Overcoming barriers to creativity. *Interface,* 23(6):101–106.

Fal, M, Sefolo, T, Williams, A, Herringtong, M, Goldberg, J. & Klaasen, M. (Eds). 2009. *The Entrepreneurial Dialogues: State of entrepreneurship in South Africa.* [Online]. Available: http://www. sabkickstart.net/index.php/forum/thought-leadership/108-dialogues.html [3 March 2014].

Faltin, G. 2001. Creating a culture of entrepreneurship. *Journal of International Business and Economy,* 2(1):123–140.

Fayerman, I. n.d *Highschool. South Africa Part 1. The Kraal Gallery.* [Online]. Available: http://projectexplorer. org/hs/za/kraal.php [October 2013].

FASA. 1998. *Franchising.* Johannesburg: Franchise Association of Southern Africa (FASA).

FASA. 2006. *FASA's 2007 Franchise Directory.* Bruma: Franchise Association of Southern Africa (FASA).

FASA. 2010a. *FASA's 2010 Franchise Directory.* Bruma: Franchise Association of Southern Africa (FASA).

FASA. 2010b. 'Keep the dream alive' advises Ben Fimalter of Mugg & Bean fame. *FASA Newsletter,* 17. [Online]. Available: http://www.fasa.co.za/ news/2010/newsletter17/newsletter-page3.html [1 August 2011].

Ferrell, OC. & Hartline, MD. 2014. *Marketing strategies: Text and Cases.* 6th ed. USA: South-Western Cengage Learning.

Finnemore, M. 1998. *Introduction to Labour Relations in South Africa.* Durban: Butterworths.

Finweek. 2011. Bringing in experience: Systems lead to success. 3 March 2011:49.

Finweek. 2012. *Overcoming entrepreneurial challenges.* [Online]. Available: http://finweek. com/2012/11/30/overcoming-entrepreneurial-challenges/ [21 March 2014].

Fisk, RP, Grove, SJ. & John, J. 2014. *Services Marketing – An Interactive Approach.* 4th ed. USA: South-Western Cengage Learning.

Florida, R. 2002. *The Rise of The Creative Class: And How it's Transforming Work, Leisure, Community and Everyday Life.* New York: Basic Books.

Forlani, D. & Mullins, JW. 2000. Perceived risks and choices in entrepreneurs' new venture decisions. *Journal of Business Venturing,* 15(3):305–322.

Franchise Finder. n.d. *The Consumer Protection Act - Part III: The CPA and Franchising.* Franchise Finder Online Directory of Franchises and Business Opportunities in South Africa. [Online]. Available:http://www.franchisefinder.co.za/ Article%20Archive/consumer-protection-act-part-three.shtml [8 June 2014].

Franchize Directions. 2013. *Franchising weathers the economic storm.* Bizmag.co.za [Online]. Available: http://www.bizmag.co.za/franchising-weathers-economic-storm/ [17 June 2014].

Franken, RE. 2007. *Human Motivation.* 6th ed. Independence, KY: Cengage Learning.

Friedman, TI. 2006. *The World is Flat: The Globalized World in the Twenty-First Century.* Updated and expanded ed. Rosebank, South Africa: Penguin Books.

Gamble, JE. & Thompson, AA. 2011. *Essentials of Strategic Management: The Quest for Competitive Advantage.* 2nd ed. New York, NY: McGraw-Hill.

GEM. 2012. [Online]. Available: http://www. gemconsortium.org/docs/2645/gem-2012-global-report [4 July 2014].

GEM. 2013. *Group profile.* [Online]. Available: http:// www.gemgroup.co.za/index.php/group-profile?id=5 [26 June 2014].

Gilkey, C. 2008. Demystifying the creative process. *Productive Flourishing: Strategies for Thriving in Life and Business.* 29 September 2008. [Online]. Available: http://www.productiveflourishing.com/demystifying-thecreative-process/ [5 January 2011].

Gitman, LJ. 1998. *Principles of Managerial Finance.* Brief edition. Boston: Addison-Wesley.

Gitman, LJ. 2007. *Principles of Managerial Finance.* Boston: Addison-Wesley.

Gitman, LJ. & Joehnk, MD. 2004. *Personal Financial Planning.* 10th ed. Mason: Thomson South-Western.

Gordon, B. 2006. *The Standard Bank Franchise Factor®.* September 2006. Franchise Directions.

Gordon, B. 2008. *The Standard Bank Franchise Factor®.* September 2008. Franchise Directions.

Greiner, LE. 1972. Evolution and revolution as organizations grow. *Harvard Business Review,* July–August 1972.

Grobler, PA, Wärnich, S, Carrell, MR, Elbert, NF & Hatfield, RD. 2011. *Human resource management in South Africa.* 4th ed. Hampshire, UK: South-Western Cengage Learning.

Grosse, RE. & Kujawa, D. 1995. *International Business: Theory and Managerial Applications.* Chicago: Irwin.

Gruble, C. 2010. The challenge that is the business cycle, 8 February 2010. [Online]. Available: http://www.articlesbase.com/business-articles/the-challenge-that-isthe-business-cycle-1832682.html [4 August 2011].

Hartman, D. 2014. *Operations strategy for product expansion.* [Online]. Available: http://smallbusiness.chron.com/operations-strategy-product-expansion-25609.html [26 June 2014].

Helmreich, C. 2009. *Social Entrepreneurship in South Africa: The Kraal Gallery – A Development Project and its impact on women's lives,* Wörth: Bachelor thesis for the obtainment of the academic degree Bachelor of Arts in International Management at the University of Applied Sciences Deggendorf.

Henderson, J.C. & Venkatraman, N. 1993. Strategic alignment: Leveraging information technology for transforming organisations. *IBM Systems Journal,* 32(1):472–484.

Herrington, M, Kew, J. & Kew, P. 2009. *Global Entrepreneurship Monitor: 2008 South African Report.* Cape Town: Graduate School of Business, University of Cape Town.

Hewitt, M. 2002. Confirming influencing factors on small medium enterprise (SME) activity. [Online]. Available: http://johannesburg.academia.edu/MagdaHewitt/Papers/696094 [24 February 2011].

Hewitt, M. 2010. Management and Generation-Y: A theoretical model perspective. [Online]. Available: http://johannesburg.academia.edu/MagdaHewitt/Papers/119608 [24 February 2011].

Hewlett-Packard. 2013. HP thin clients help transform customer experience, boost sales. [Online]. Available: http://www8.hp.com/ca/en/campaigns/thin-client-solutions/why-thin-clients.html [13 October 2013].

Hickerson, M. 2012. Will Blu-Ray be obsolete in four years? *Slice of Scifi,* June 14: 1. [Online]. Available: http://www.sliceofscifi.com/2012/06/14/will-blu-ray-be-obsolete-in-four-years/ [27 October 2013].

Hisrich, RD. & Peters, PM. 2002. *Entrepreneurship.* 5th ed. New York: McGraw-Hill.

Hisrich, RD, Peters, MP, & Shepherd, DA. *Entrepreneurship.* 6th ed. New York: McGraw-Hill Irwin. [Online]. Available: http://sbaer.uca.edu/publications/entrepreneurship/pdf/01.pdf [28 October 2013].

Hisrich, RD, Peters, MP. & Shepherd, DA. 2010. *Entrepreneurship.* 8th ed. New York: McGraw-Hill.

Hoyk, R. & Hersey, P. 2008. *The Ethical Executive: Avoiding the Traps of the Unethical Workplace.* London: Standford Business Books.

Human, SH, Clark, T, Baucus MS. & Eustis, AC. 2004. Idea or prime opportunity? A framework for evaluating business ideas. *Journal of Small Business Strategy,* 15(1):61–79.

Huizemark. 2014. *About Huizemark.* Huizemark.com. [Online]. Available: http://www.huizemark.com/about-us [23 June 2014].

ifix. 2013. *iCare Charity Project: Keeping it close to home.* [Online]. Available: http://ifix.co.za/keeping-it-close-to-home/ [29 May 2014].

ifix. 2014. *About us.* [Online]. Available: http://ifix.co.za/about-us/ [29 May 2014].

Illetschko, K. 1997a. *How to Franchise Your Business.* Johannesburg: Franchise Association of Southern Africa (FASA).

Illetschko, K. (Ed.). 1997b. *Let 18 Experts Tell You How to Franchise Your Business and Unleash its True Potential.* 2nd ed. Johannesburg: Franchise Association of Southern Africa (FASA).

Illetschko, K. 2000. *How to Franchise Your Business.* 3rd ed. Johannesburg: Franchise Association of Southern Africa (FASA).

Illetschko, K. 2002. *How to Evaluate a Franchise.* 2nd ed. Johannesburg: Franchise Association of Southern Africa (FASA).

Illetschko, K. 2005. *How to Franchise Your Business.* 4th ed. Johannesburg: Franchise Association of Southern Africa (FASA).

Illetschko, K. 2012. *How to Franchise Your Business.* 6th ed. Johannesburg: Franchise Association of Southern Africa (FASA).

IOD. n.d. Implementing Sustainable Development as a Strategic Business Model: Sustainable Business forum. Position Paper 1. Johannesburg: IOD. [Online]. Available:http://www.iodsa.co.za/?page=ForumSDF [3 November 2013].

IoDSA. 2009. *King Code of Governance for South Africa*. Johannesburg: Institute of Directors Southern Africa. [Online]. Available: www.iodsa.co.za. [3 November 2013].

Isaksen, SG. & Trefflinger, DJ. 1985. *Creative Problem Solving: The Basic Course*. Buffalo, NY: Bearly Publishing.

James, A. 2013. BDlive. *Cadet programme a boost for economy, job creation*. [Online]. Available: http://www.bdlive.co.za/Feeds/BusinessDay/2013/08/15/cadet-programme-a-boost-for-economy-job-creation [13 June 2014],

Jones, G. *Financial Mail*. 27 June 2013. [Online]. Available: http://www.financialmail.co.za/business/2013/06/27/issue-of-labour-brokers-a-work-in-progress [10 December 2013].

JurisPedia. 2011. Introduction to the law of contract (ZA). March 2011. [Online]. Available: http://en.jurispedia.org/index.php/Introduction_to_the_law_of_contract_(za) [14 March 2011].

Kaplan, RS. & Norton, DP. 1992. The balanced scorecard: Measures that drive performance. *Harvard Business Review*, January–February: 71–79.

Katz, JA. & Green, RP. 2011. *Entrepreneurial Small Business*. 3rd ed. New York: McGraw-Hill.

Kerin, RA, Hartley, SW. & Rudelius, W. 2013. *Marketing*. 11th ed. New York: McGraw-Hill.

King, ME. (Chair). 2009. *King III Report on Governance for South Africa*, 1 September 2009. [Online]. Available: http://african.ipapercms.dk/IOD/KINGIII/kingiiireport/ [1 August 2011].

Kriel, Z. 2011. IT head Honchos: Rapelang Rabana. *Leadership*, 314, April:50.

Kuratko, DF. & Hornsby, JS. 2009. *New Venture Management: The Entrepreneur's Roadmap*. New Jersey: Pearson Education.

Kruger, D, Ramphal, R. & Maritz, M. 2013. *Operations Management*. 3rd ed. Cape Town, South Africa: Oxford University Press Southern Africa (Pty) Ltd.

LC Solutions. 2011. *Consumer Protection Act: Impacts on Franchising*. Legal & Commercial Solutions. [Online]. Available: http://www.lcsolutions.co.za/2011/03/24/consumer-protection-act-impacts-on-franchising/ [5 August 2013].

Leibbrandt, M, Woolard, I, Finn, A & Argent, J. 2010. *Trends in South African Income Distribution and Poverty since the Fall of Apartheid*. s.l.:OECD Publishing.

Le Roux, I. 2005. Entrepreneurial cognition and the decision to exploit a venture opportunity. PhD. University of Pretoria, South Africa.

Levinthal, DA. 1991. Random walks and organisation mortality. *Administrative Science Quarterly*, 36:397–420.

Ligthelm, AA. 2005. *Measuring the Size of the Informal Sector in South Africa*. Pretoria: UNISA.

Longenecker, JG, Moore, CW, Petty, WJ. & Palich, LE. 2008. *Small Business Management: An Entrepreneurial Emphasis*. International ed. Mason: Thomson Publishers.

Longenecker, JG, Petty, JW, Palich, EP. & Moore, CW. 2010. *Small Business Management: Launching and Growing Entrepreneurial Ventures*. 15th ed. Mason: South-Western Cengage Learning.

Lussier, RN. & Halabi, CE. 2010. A Three-Country Comparison of the Business Success versus Failure Prediction Model. *Journal of Small Business Management*, 48(3):360–377.

Maake, M. 2014. *SA makes strong showing on Forbes list of promising young entrepreneurs*. [Online]. Available: http://www.citypress.co.za/business/sa-forbes-list-promising-young-entrepreneurs/ [29 May 2014].

Martins, AT. n.d. *Sources of Business Ideas*. [Online]. Available: http://www.mytopbusinessideas.com/sources-of-business-ideas/. [25 March 2014].

Marx, FW. & Churr, EG. 1985. *Fundamentals of Business Economics*. Pretoria: HAUM Educational.

Marx, S, Van Rooyen, DC, Bosch, JK. & Reynders, HJJ. 1998. *Business Management*. Pretoria: Van Schaik.

Maslow, AH. 1943. A theory of human motivation. *Psychology Review*, July:370–396.

Matshotyana, Z. 2011. *Franchise opportunities*. Smart Cape Business [Online]. Available: http://www.smartcape.org.za/business/business-advisory/franchise-opportunities.html [23 June 2014].

Mauzy, J. & Harriman, R. 2003. *Creativity,Inc. Building an Inventive Organization*. Boston: Harvard Business School Press.

Mayo, CM. & (revised by) Hausler, D. 2014. New Product Development. [Online]. Available: http://www.referenceforbusiness.com/management/Mar-No/New-Product-Development.htm. [3 March 2014].

McLeod, D. 2010. Trouble at Neotel as retrenchments looms. *Mail&Guardian Online*. December 2010. [Online]. Available: http://www.mg.co.za/article/2010-12-22-trouble-at-neotel-as-retrenchments-loom [15 March 2011].

Medical Diagnostech (Pty) Ltd. n.d. *Medical Diagnostech: About Us*. [Online]. Available: http://www.medi-tech.co.za/ [4 February 2014].

Megginson, LC, Scott, CR, Trueblood, LR. & Megginson, WL. 1998. *Successful Small Business Management*. Plano: Business Publications.

Meredith, GG, Nelson, RE. & Neck, PA. 1982. *The Practice of Entrepreneurship*. Geneva: Geneva International Labour Office.

Meyer, T. *The Wits Business School Journal.* 2012. Issue 28:20–21.

Miller, D. & Friesen, PH. 1982. Structural change and performance: Quantum versus piecemeal-incremental approaches. *Academy of Management Journal,* 25(4):867–892.

Miller, C. 2014. *Types of entrepreneurs.* [Online]. Available: http://resourcefulentrepreneur.com/types-of-entrepreneurs/ [2 March 2014].

Mitchell, R. et al. 2004. The Distinctive and Inclusive Domain of Entrepreneurial Cognition Research.. *Entrepreneursip: Theory and Practice,* 28(6):505-518.

Moore, CW, Petty, JW, Palich, LE. & Longenecker, JG. 2010. *Managing small business: An entrepreneurial emphasis.* 15th ed. Mason: South-Western Cengage Learning.

Morris, MH, Kuratko, DF. & Covin, JG. 2008. *Corporate Entrepreneurship and Innovation.* 2nd ed. Mason: Thompson.

Myburgh, J, Fouché, J. & Cloete, M. 2013. *Accounting an introduction.* 11th ed. Pretoria. LexisNexis.

MWeb. 2014. *Homegrown entrepreneur: Lebo Gungulusa, founder of the GEM Group.* [Online]. Available: http://www.mweb.co.za/Entrepreneur/ViewArticle/tabid/3162/Article/12968/Homegrown-Entrepreneur-Lebo-Gunguluza-founder-of-the-GEM-Group.aspx [26 June 2014].

Naiman, L. 2014. *What is creativity?.* [Online]. Available: http://www.creativityatwork.com/2014/02/17/what-is-creativity/ [26 March 2014].

National Small Business Chamber. 2013. *The CPA and small businesses.* [Online]. Available: http://www.fin24.com/Entrepreneurs/Resources/The-CPA-and-small-businesses-20130314 [November 2014].

Nel, PS, Swanepoel, BJ, Kirsten, M, Erasmus, BJ. & Tsabadi, MJ. 2005. *South African Employment Relations. Theory and Practice.* Pretoria: Van Schaik.

Nel, PS, Van Dyk, PS, Haasbroek, GD, Schultz, HB, Sono, T. & Werner, A. 2006. *Human Resources Management.* 6th ed. Cape Town: Oxford University Press.

Nel, PS, Werner, A, Poisot, P, Sono, T, Du Plessis, A. & Ngalo, O. 2011. *Human Resources Management.* 8th ed. Cape Town: Oxford University Press Southern Africa.

Nerdworks (Pty) Ltd. 2013. Dial a Nerd History. [Online]. Available: http://www.dialanerd.co.za/history.php [6 Jan 2014].

New Product Development. [Online]. Available: http://www.referenceforbusiness.com/management/Mar-No/New-Product-Development.html [7 November 2013].

Ngewu, A. 2013. *He's a diamond in the rough.* [Online]. Available: http://www.citypress.co.za/business/hes-a-diamond-in-the-rough/ [11 March 2014].

Nieman, G. & Bennett, A. (Eds). 2006. *Business Management: A Value Chain Approach.* 2nd ed. Pretoria: Van Schaik.

Nieman, G, Hough, J. & Nieuwenhuizen, C. 2003. *Entrepreneurship: A South African Perspective.* Pretoria: Van Schaik.

Nieman, G. & Nieuwenhuizen, C. 2009. *Entrepreneurship. A South African Perspective.* 2nd ed. Pretoria: Van Schaik.

Nieman, G & Nieuwenhuizen, C. 2014. *Entrepreneurship - A South African perspective.* 3rd ed. Pretoria: Van Schaik.

NOMU. [Online]. Available: http://www.nomu.co.za/about/story-so-far and http://www.nomu.co.za/about/why-nomu

Nsehe, M. 2014. *30 Most Promising Young Entrepreneurs In Africa 2014.* [Online]. Available: http://www.forbes.com/sites/mfonobongnsehe/2014/02/04/30-most-promising-young-entrepreneurs-in-africa-2014/ [29 May 2014].

Nussbaum, B. & Scheiffer, A. 2005. Dr Taddy Blecher: A South African social entrepreneur turns a new economic vision into practice. Merchants of Vision. *World Business Academy,* 19(1). 23 June 2005. [Online]. Available: http://www.c-cell.com/PDF/Schieffer_SouthAfricanSocialEntrepreneur.pdf [15 June 2011].

NYDA. 2014. *Beneficiary Stories.* [Online]. Available: http://www.nyda.gov.za/media-centre/beneficiary-stories/Pages/NYDA-supports-Soweto%E2%80%99s-first-black-owned-jewellery-manufacturing-business.aspx [11 April 2014].

OECD. 2004. *OECD Principles of Corporate Governance.* Paris, France: OECD.

Osborn, A. 1953. *Applied Imagination.* New York: Charles Scribner.

Parasuraman, A, Berry, LL. & Zeithaml, VA. 1988. SERVQUAL: A Multi-item Scale for Measuring Consumer Perceptions of Service Quality, *Journal of Retailing,* 64 (Spring):12–37.

Parker, E. & Illetschko, K. 2007. *Franchising in South Africa: The Real Story.* Northcliff, South Africa: Frontrunner Publishing.

Parnes, SJ. 1992. *Sourcebook for Creative Problem Solving.* Buffalo, NY: Creative Education Foundation Press.

Parsons, R. 2013. *The National Development Plan - getting down to business?* Potchefstroom (Gauteng): AHI.

Paul Spurgeon. 2013. *Cornerstone.* [Online]. Available: http://www.paulspurgeondesign.co.uk/page/cornerstone [11 April 2014].

Pearce, JA. & Robbins, K. 1993. Toward improved theory and research on business turnaround. *Journal of Management,* 19(3):613–636.

Perrault, WD, Cannon, JP. & McCarthy, EJ. 2014. *Basic Marketing: A Marketing Strategy Planning Approach.* 19th ed. New York: McGraw-Hill.

Pettit, J. 2009. *The entrepreneurial mindset.* [Online]. Available: http://www.smallbusiness-bigresults. com/entrepreneurial-mindset.htm [March 2014].

Phitidis, P. 2013. *Seven types of entrepreneurs.* [Online]. Available: http://www.aurik.co.za/business-accelerator/blog/seven-types-entrepreneurs/#sthash. DKDLISg3.dpuf [2 March 2014].

Pithey, M. 1993. Begin Jou Eie Onderneming: 'n Kleinsakegids vir Suid-Afrika. Dieprivier: Chameleon.

Pitman, J. 2013. Tim Tebeila on taking a gap. *Entrepreneur Magazine.* [Online]. Available: www. entrepreneurmag.co.za [5 January 2014].

Polity. 2013: Final revised BBBEE Codes of Good Practice. Webber Wentzel. Published 2013-10-14. [Online]. Available: http://www.polity.org.za/ article/final-revised-bbbee-codes-of-good-practice-2013-10-14. [3 November 2013].

Porter, ME. 1980. *Competitive Strategy: Techniques for analyzing industries and competitors.* New York: Free Press.

Porter, ME. 1990. *Competitive Advantage of Nations.* New York: Free Press.

Porter, ME. & Kramer, MR. 2006. Strategy and Society: The Link Between Competitive Advantage and Corporate Social Responsibility. *Harvard Business Review,* December, 84(12):78–92.

Potgieter, F. 1997a. The franchise agreement. In FASA (Ed.). *The 1998 Franchise Book on Franchising (Incorporating the Franchise Opportunities Handbook 1998).* Johannesburg: Franchise Association of Southern Africa (FASA).

Potgieter, F. 1997b. The franchise agreement. In Illetschko, K. (Ed.). *Let 18 Experts Tell You How to Franchise Your Business and Unleash its True Potential.* 2nd ed. Johannesburg: Franchise Association of Southern Africa (FASA).

Pretorius, M. 2009. Defining business decline, failure and turnaround: A content analysis. *Southern African Journal of Entrepreneurship and Small Business Management,* 2(1):1–16.

Pretorius, M. 2010. Drivers and moderators. *Acta commerci,* 222.

Prinsloo, l. Day. 2013. Aveng clams up on tender rigging. *Business Day,* 2 November 2013. [Online]. Available: http://www.bdlive.co.za/business/ industrials/2013/11/03/aveng-clams-up-on-tender-rigging. [3 November 2013].

ProductivitySA. 2010a. Lenong Road Maintenance. [Online]. Available: http://www. turnaroundsolutions.co.za/pebble.asp?relid=218 [1 August 2011].

ProductivitySA. 2010b. *Turnaround Solutions 2009/2010.* Midrand, South Africa: Productivity SA.

Raiz, A. 2013. Dangers small construction companies should look for. *Small Business Connect,* September:5.

Reuer, JJ, Ariño, A. & Olk, PM. 2011. *Entrepreneurial Alliances.* Upper Saddle River, New Jersey Prentice Hall.

Rhoodie, L., & Scriba, B. 2011. *Franchise agreements and the Consumer Protection Act.* DLA Cliffe Dekker Hofmeyer. [Online]. Available: http://www. cliffedekkerhofmeyr.com/en/news/press-releases/2011/franchise-agreements-and-consumer-protection-act.html [8 June 2014].

Riley, J. 2012. *Starting a business – sources of business ideas.* [Online]. Available: http://www.tutor2u.net/ business/gcse/enterprise_sources_business_ideas. html [25 March 2014].

Robbins, SP. & Coulter, M. 2009. *Management.* 10th ed. New Jersey: Pearson Education.

Rochford, L. 1991. Generating and screening new product ideas. *Industrial Marketing Management,* 20:287–296.

Rodkin, B. 1996. *The Franchisor's Handbook. A Practical Guide to Franchising in South Africa.* Johannesburg: Icessel & Feinstein Consulting in association with NED Enterprise.

Rogers, EM. & Shoemaker, F. 1971. *Communication of Innovation.* New York: The Free Press.

Rom, F. 2014. *Lubu Gunguluza: Self-made media millionaire.* [Online]. Available: http://www. emergingstars.com/success-stories/lebo-gunguluza-self-made-media-millionaire [26 June 2014].

Ropega, J. 2011. The Reasons and Symptoms of Failure in SME. *International Atlantic Economic Society* 17:476–483, DOI 10.1007/s11294-011-9316-1.

Rossman, J. 1931. *The Psychology of the Inventor.* Washington DC: Inventor's Publishing.

Rossouw, D. & Van Vuuren, L. 2006. *Business Ethics.* 3rd ed. Cape Town: Oxford University Press Southern Africa.

Russell, R. & Russell, C. 1992. An examination of the effects of organizational norms, organizational structure and environmental uncertainty on entrepreneurial strategy. *Journal of Management,* 18(4):639–657.

Russo, JE. & Schoemaker, PJH. 1992. Managing overconfidence. *Sloan Management Review,* 33(2):7–17.

Ryan, B. 2002. In the right place at the right time. *Financial Mail.* 27 September 2002.

Ryan, PMA. 2003. Zero to one million: How to build a company to one million dollars in sales. [Online]. Available: www.zeromillion.com [1 August 2007].

S.A. Breweries. 2013. Sustainable development: Water – Making more beer using less water. [Online]. Available: http://www.sab.co.za/sablimited/content/ en/sustainable-development-listing?cat_id=107 [3 November 2013].

SAinfo. 2013. *Cashless ATM extends banking's reach.* [Online]. Available: http://www.southafrica.info/business/trends/innovations/atm-20913.html. Uy2874XIl0E#ixzz2wi7LTeSa [22 March 2014].

SARS. 2013. *Taxation in South Africa 2012/13.* Pretoria: South African Revenue Service.

SARS. 2014a. *Small Business.* [Online]. Available: http://www.sars.gov.za/ClientSegments/Businesses/SmallBusinesses/Pages/default.aspx. [9 April 2014].

SARS. 2014b. *Registering for employees' tax pay-as-you-earn (PAYE).* [Online]. Available: http://www.sars.gov.za/ClientSegments/Individuals/Taxpayer/Pages/Register-for-PAYE.aspx. [9 April 2014].

SARS. 2014c. *Skills Development Levy (SDL).* [Online]. Available: http://www.sars.gov.za/TaxTypes/SDL/Pages/default.aspx. [9 April 2014].

Salamouris, IS. 2013. How overconfidence influences entrepreneurship. *Journal of Innovation and Entrepreneurship,* Volume 2:8.

Sánchez, JC, TC. & Gutiérrez, A. 2011 . The entrepreneur from a cognitive approach. *Psicothema,* 23(3): 433–438.

Scarborough, NM, Wilson, DL. & Zimmerer, TW. 2009. *Effective Small Business Management: An Entrepreneurial Approach.* 9th ed. New Jersey: Pearson Prentice Hall.

Schiebe, L. 2010. The changing world of work. *Succeed,* September 44–45.

Schumpeter, J. 1934. *The Theory of Economic Development.* Cambridge, MA: Harvard University Press.

Scilly, M. n.d. *Examples of cost leadership & strategy marketing.* [Online]. Available: http://smallbusiness.chron.com/examples-cost-leadership-strategy-marketing-12259.html [October 2013].

Shezi, M. 2013. SMEs' corporate governance systems: Status and effect on continuity. MCom dissertation. Gordon Institute of Business Science, University of Pretoria: Pretoria.

Simon, M. & Houghton, SM. 2002. The relationship among biases, misperceptions and introducing pioneering products: Examining differences in venture decision contexts. *Entrepreneurship: Theory and Practice.* 27(2):105–124.

Simon, M, Houghton, SM. & Aquino, K. 2000. Cognitive biases, risk perception and venture formation: How individuals decide to start companies. *Journal of Business Venturing,* 15(2):113–134.

Singer, S, Alpeza, M. & Balkić, M. 2009. *Corporate Entrepreneurship: Is Entrepreneurial Behaviour Possible in a Large Company?.* Maribor, IRP - Institute for Entrepreneurship Research.

Singh, S. 2014. *The Consumer Protection Act poses significant challenges to weaker franchises.* Durban Chamber of Commerce and Industry. [Online]. Available: http://durbanchamber.com/profiles/blogs/the-consumer-protection-act-poses-significant-challenges-to [12 June 2014].

Spinelli, S. & Adams, R. 2012. *New venture creation: Entrepreneurship for the 21st century.* 9th ed. New York: McGraw-Hill.

Sitkin, SB. & Weingart, L. 1995. Determinants of risky decision-making behaviour: A test of the mediating role of risk perceptions and propensity. *Academy of Management Journal,* 37(6):1873–1592.

Small Business Connect. 2013. Watch out for unscrupulous franchisors. *Small Business Connect* (3):10.

Smart, C. & Vertinsky, I. 1984. Strategy and the environment: A study of corporate responses to crises. *Strategic Management Journal,* 5(3):199–213.

SME Toolkit South Africa. 1993. How to finance your business. [Online]. Available: http://southafrica.smetoolkit.org/sa/en/content/en/478/How-to-Finance-Your-Business [1 August 2011].

SME Toolkit South Africa. 2011. Balance sheet template. [Online]. Available: http://southafrica.smetoolkit.org/sa/en/content/en/685/Balance-Sheet-Template [1 August 2011].

SME Toolkit South Africa. 2011. Cash flow budget worksheet. [Online]. Available: http://southafrica.smetoolkit.org/sa/en/content/en/2889/Cash-Flow-Budget-Worksheet [1 August 2011].

SME Toolkit South Africa. 2011. Income statement template. [Online]. Available: http://southafrica.smetoolkit.org/sa/en/content/en/317/Income-Statement- Template [1 August 2011].

Smit, PC, et al. 1996. *Economics – A South African Perspective.* Kenwyn: Juta & Co, Ltd.

Smith, D. 2010. *Exploring innovation.* McGraw Hill: Berkshire.

Sonfield, M, Lussier, R, Corman, J. & McKinney, M. 2001. Gender comparisons in strategic decision-making: An empirical analysis of the entrepreneurial strategy matrix. *Journal of Small Business Management,* 39(2):166.

South Africa. 1996. Small Business Act, No. 102, 1996. Pretoria: Government Printer. [Laws].

South Africa. 1998. Employment Equity Act, No. 55 of 1998. Pretoria: Government Printer. [Laws].

South Africa. 2003. National Small Business Amendment Act, No. 26, 2003. Pretoria: Government Printer. [Laws].

South Africa. 2009. Companies Act, No. 71, 2008. Pretoria: Government Printer. [Laws].

South Africa. 29 April 2009. Act No. 68 of 2008: Consumer Protection Act, 2008. No 32186 ed. Cape Town: Government Gazette.

South African Department of Labour. 2014. *Basic guide to UIF contributions.* [Online]. Available: http://www.labour.gov.za/DOL/legislation/acts/basic-guides/basic-guide-to-uif-contributions. [9 April 2014].

South African Reserve Bank. 2014. Research/statistics database. [Online]. Available: www.resbank.co.za.

Speeter, L. 2009. Checklist: What's your level of corporate social responsibility? *The Altruistic Marketer: Fostering Corporate Excellence for the Greater Good*. [Online]. Available: http://altruisticmarketer.wordpress.com/2009/0/26/checklist-what%E2%0%99s-your-levelof-corporate-social-responsibility/ [24 February 2011].

Spratt, J. 2012. Your idea is worth nothing. *Entrepreneur Magazine*. [Online]. Available: www.entrepreneurmag.co.za [5 January 2014].

Statistics South Africa. 1993. Standard industrial classification of all economic activities (SIC). [Online]. Available: http://www.statssa.gov.za/additional_services/sic/sic.htm [1 August 2011].

Statistics South Africa. 2010. Gross Domestic Product. Statistical release P0441. Pretoria: Statistics South Africa.

Statistics South Africa. 2013. Liquidations and insolvencies August 2013. Statistical release P0043. [Online]. Available: http://www.statssa.gov.za/publications/P0043/P0043September2013.pdf [27 October 2013].

Statistics South Africa. 2013. *Quarterly financial statistics: December 2012 and Quarterly financial statistics online database*. Pretoria: Statistics South Africa.

Statistics South Africa. 2014. *Quarterly financial statistics: September 2013 and Quarterly financial statistics online database*. Pretoria: Statistics South Africa.

Stats SA. 2014. *Statistical release P0211: Quarterly Labour Force Survey, Quarter 1, 2014*, Pretoria: Statistics South Africa.

Strachan, D. 2013. *Small business and the CPA*. [Online]. Available: http://www.fin24.com/Entrepreneurs/Opinions-and-Analysis/Small-businesses-and-the-CPA-20130221 [November 2013].

Sugars, B. 2009. Cut your HR, marketing and operation costs. *Entrepreneur Magazine*. [Online]. Available: http://www.entrepreneurmag.co.za/article/h/?a=585&z=31&title=Cut+Your+HR%2c+Marketing+%26+Operation+Costs+ [14 February 2011].

Swanepoel, BJ. (Ed.), Erasmus, BJ. & Schenk, HW. 2008. *South African Human Resource Management, Theory and Practice*. 4th ed. Cape Town: Juta & Co.

Tague, NR. 2004. *The QualityToolbox*. 2nd ed. Milwaukee: ASQ Quality Press.

Tams, E. 2002. Creating division: creativity, entrepreneurship and gendered inequality. A Sheffield case study. *City*, 6(3):393–405.

Tan, G. 1998. Managing creativity in organizations: A total systems approach. *Creativity and Innovation Management*, 7(1):23–31.

Tat Keh, H, Der Foo, M. & Chong Lim, B. 2002. Opportunity evaluation under risky conditions: The cognitive processes of entrepreneurs. *Entrepreneurship Theory and Practice*, 27(2):125–148.

Telkom. 2013. Telkom business: all products and services. [Online]. Available: http://business.telkom.co.za/enterprise/all-products/ [27 October 2013].

Terblance, B. 2009. From unemployed to top dog. *Mail&Guardian Online*. 21 October 2009. [Online]. Available: http://www.mg.co.za/article/2009-10-21-from-unemployed-to-top-dog [1 August 2011].

The Economist. 2007. The transcendental crusader. *The Economist*. 30 August 2007. [Online]. Available: http://www.economist.com/node/9723263 [17 January 2011].

The Kraal Gallery. n.d. *The Kraal Gallery. Our Story*. [Online]. Available: http://www.thekraalgallery.com/hand_woven_tapestries/about-us/our-story.php [October 2013].

The Times 100. 2014. *Marketing Theory - Needs and wants*. [Online]. Available: http://businesscasestudies.co.uk/business-theory/marketing/needs-and-wants.html#axzz2xBKGmwzg [27 March 2014].

The Wits Business School Journal. 2013. Issue 34:78–79.

The World Bank. 2013. *Insight Report. The Africa Competitiveness Report 2013*, Geneva: World Economic Forum.

Timmons, JA. 1994. *New Venture Creation: Entrepreneurship for the 21st Century*. Burr Ridge: Irwin.

Timmons, JA. & Spinelli, S. 2009. *New Venture Creation: Entrepreneurship for the 21st Century*. 8th ed. New York: McGraw-Hill/Irwin.Timm, S. 2012. *Science innovation passes business test*. [Online]. Available: http://www.bdlive.co.za/business/management/2012/12/10/science-innovation-passes-business-test [11 March 2014].

Timm, S. 2013. Glimpses of hope during the downturn. *Small Business Connect*, September, Issue 1:4.

Top 10 South African entrepreneurs. [Online]. Available: http://www.mweb.co.za/Entrepreneur/ViewArticle/tabid/3162/Article/7017/Top-10-South-African-entrepreneurs.aspx [7 November 2013].

Todd, N. 2012. Silulo Ulutho Technologies: Luvuyo Rani. *Entrepreneur Magazine*. [Online]. Available: www.entrepreneurmag.co.za [5 January 2014].

Trautmann, M. 2011. *25 Creativity quotes*. [Online]. Available: http://celestra.ca/25-creativity-quotes/. [26 March 2014].

Tshikwatamba, NE. 2003. The challenge of managing diversity in South Africa: A long-time observer and researcher shares his views on new opportunities the human resources community has to transform itself and shift to more inclusive personnel policies and approaches. *The Public Manager*, 32(3):36–39.

Turton, N. & Herrington, M. 2012. *Global Entrepreneurship Monitor 2012 South Africa*. Cape Town: UCT Centre for Innovation and Entrepreneurship. [Online]. Available: http://www.gsb.uct.ac.za/files/2012GEMSouthAfricaReport.pdf [19 August 2013].

Tutelman CJ. & Hause LD. 2008. *The Balance Point: New Ways Business Owners Can Use Boards*. Edina:Famille Press.

United Nations - Brutland Commission. 1987. Report of the World Commission on Environment and Development: Our common future. [Online]. Available: http://conspect.nl/pdf/Our_Common_Future-Brundtland_Report_1987.pdf

United Nations. n.d. United Nations Global Compact: The Ten Principles. [Online]. Available: http://www.unglobalcompact.org/abouttheGC/TheTenPrinciples/index.html [3 November 2013].

Usmani, F. 2013. *Lead time and lag time in project scheduling network diagram*. [Online]. Available: http://pmstudycircle.com/2013/02/lead-time-and-lag-time-in-project-scheduling-network-diagram/ [21 March 2014].

Van Aardt, CJ. & Schacht, A. 2003. *Demographic and Statistical Overview, 1994–2004*. Research Report. March. South Africa: Department of Social Development.

Vaughn, CL. 1979. *Franchising: Its Nature, Scope, Advantages and Development*. Lexington: Lexington Books.

von Oetinger, B. 2005. Nurturing the new: Patterns for innovation. *Journal of Business Strategy*, 26:29–36.

Wade, B. 2011a. The Consumer Protection Act – What to do? [Online]. Available: http://www.ei.co.za/entrepreneur-incubator-blog/the-consumer-protection-act-what-to-do- [November 2013].

Wade, B. 2011b. The CPA: Learner's Guide. [Online]. Available: http://www.ideate.co.za/2011/04/11/the-cpa-learner%E2%80%99s-guide/ [November 2013].

Wallas, G. 1926. *The Art of Thought*. New York: Harcourt Brace.

Wasu, S. 2010. Myths about creativity. 25 March 2010. [Online]. Available: http://tickledbylife.com/index.php/ myths-about-creativity/ [5 January 2011].

Weldon, R. 2014. *Soweto jeweller is a symbol of hope for South Africa*. [Online]. Available: http://www.gia.edu/research-news-soweto-jeweler-symbol-hope-south-africa [9 March 2014].

WEF – World Economic Forum. 2002. Global Corporate Citizenship: *The Leadership Challenge for CEOs and Boards*. Geneva: World Economic Forum. [Online]. Available: http://www.weforum.org/pdf/GCCI/GCC_CEOstatement.pdf [3 November 2013].

Westhead, P, Wright, M. & McElwee, G. 2011. *Entrepreneurship - perspectives and cases*. Essex: Financial Times Prentice Hall.

Whichfranchise. 2014a. *What is a franchise?* Whichfranchise.co.za. [Online]. Available: http://www.whichfranchise.co.za/what-is-a-franchise/ [17 June 2014].

White & Partners Ltd. 2010. *Step 6: Measuring and sustaining innovation*. [Online]. Available: http://www.corporateinnovationonline.com/innovative-ideas/tools/step-6-measuring-and-sustaining-innovation/ [08 June 2014].

Wholesale Business. 2014. Back to basics: Growing pains! Moving beyond close family store management for independents. 1, 25–27.

Wickham, PA. 2001. *Strategic Entrepreneurship: A Decision-Making Approach to New Venture Creation and Managment*. Harlow: Prentice Hall.

Woker, T. 2006. Understanding the relationship between franchising and the Competition Law. *FASA's 2007 Franchise Directory*. Bruma: Franchise Association of Southern Africa (FASA).

Wright, C. 1995. *Successful Small Business Management in South Africa*. 6th ed. Sandton: Struik.

Xavier, SR, Kelley, D, Herrington, M. & Vorderwulbecke, A. 2012. *Global Entrepreneurship Monitor. 2012 Global Report*, Massachusets:Global Entrepreneurship Research Association.

Youssry, A. 2007. *Social Entrepreneurs and Enterprise Development*. August 2007. Alexandria, Egypt: Sustainable Development Association.

Zhoa, F. 2005. Exploring the synergy between entrepreneurship and innovation. *International Journal of Entrepreneurial Behavior & Research*, 11(1):25–41.

Index

U

Unemployment Insurance Fund
(UIF) 178, 356, 359–360
United Nations (UN) Global
Compact 448, 449
core values 448–449

V

value-added tax (VAT) 113, 240,
354–355
definition 354
values 191–192, *191–192*

venture

venture
establishment of 129, 131, 136,
152, 153, 287, 349–352
legal aspects 366
operations management 314–315
operations strategy 315
screening guide 77–79, *78*
virtual hosting 95
dedicated 95
shared 95
'virtualising' business 89

W

Wage Act 5 of 1957 361
WEF Global Corporate Citizenship
Initiative 447–448, 449
goals 447
World Economic Forum
(WEF) 104, 447